Policy Sectors in Comparative Policy Analysis Studies

Volume Four

Volume Four of the *Classics of Comparative Policy Analysis,* "Policy Sectors in Comparative Policy Analysis Studies", contains chapters concerned with comparison within disciplinary policy sectors. The volume contains detailed analyses of policies within six major policy sectors, and illustrates the important differences that exist across policies healthcare, environment, education, social welfare, immigration, and science and technology.

The reader will find some common aspects and dimensions – theoretical or methodological – across all policy domains, as well as differences dictated by the characteristics of the discipline or the locus in which the policy point at issue takes place. Indeed, some scholars have argued that the differences and similarities that exist across and within policy sectors can transcend the differences or similarities across political systems.

"Policy Sectors in Comparative Policy Analysis Studies" will be of great interest to scholars and learners of public policy and social sciences, as well as to practitioners considering what can be reliably contextualized, learned, facilitated or avoided through lesson-drawing.

The chapters were originally published as articles in the *Journal of Comparative Policy Analysis* which in the last two decades has pioneered the development of comparative public policy. The volume is part of a four-volume series, *the Classics of Comparative Policy Analysis* including Theories and Methods, Institutions and Governance, Regional Comparisons, and Policy Sectors.

Each volume showcases a different new chapter comparing domains of study interrelated with comparative public policy: political science, public administration, governance and policy design, authored by the JCPA authored by the JCPA co-editors Giliberto Capano, Michael Howlett, Leslie A. Pal and B. Guy Peters.

Iris Geva-May has been recognized by Thomson Reuters for having pioneered the field of comparative policy analysis since 1998, when she founded the now high indexed *Journal of Comparative Policy Analysis*. She serves as its Founding Editor and the Founding President of the Scholarly Society for International Comparative Policy Analysis (ICPA-Forum). She has published among others *The Logic and Methodology of Policy Analysis, An Operational Approach to Policy Analysis (with Wildavsky), International Library of Policy Analysis Series, Routledge Handbook of Comparative Policy Analysis,* and *Policy Analysis as a Clinical Profession.* She is Professor Emerita at Simon Fraser University, Vancouver, Canada and currently an Honorary Visiting Professor at SPPA, Carleton University, Ottawa, Canada, and the Wagner School NYU, USA.

B. Guy Peters is Maurice Falk Professor of Government at the University of Pittsburgh, USA, and an Honorary Editor of the *Journal of Comparative Policy Analysis*. He is also the Founding President of the *International Public Policy Association* and Editor of the *International Review of Public Policy*. Among his seminal publications are as follows: *Comparative Politics Theory and Methods, Institutional Theory in Political Science, The Politics of Bureaucracy: A Comparative Perspective, An Advanced Introduction to Public Policy*, and *The Next Public Administration*.

Joselyn Muhleisen serves as the Awards Coordinator for the International Comparative Policy Analysis Forum and the *Journal of Comparative Policy Analysis*. She is a Doctoral Lecturer at the Marxe School of Public and International Affairs, Baruch College, City University of New York (CUNY), USA. She earned her doctorate in political science from The Graduate Center, CUNY, USA. She is the former Assistant Director of the European Union Studies Center, CUNY, USA. She has published work about the development of comparative policy analysis and its relationship to international studies.

Policy Sectors in Comparative Policy Analysis Studies
Volume Four

Edited by
Iris Geva-May, B. Guy Peters and Joselyn Muhleisen

With

Foreword by Laurence E. Lynn, JCPA Founding Co-Editor
Introduction to the Series, Iris Geva-May, JCPA Founding Editor, B. Guy Peters Co-Editor, Joselyn Muhleisen Co-Editor

And

Part 2, New Contribution: The Contribution of Comparative Policy Analysis to Policy Design Studies, Michael Howlett, JCPA Co-editor

Sponsored by

LONDON AND NEW YORK

First published 2020
by Routledge
2 Park Square, Milton Park, Abingdon, Oxon, OX14 4RN

and by Routledge
52 Vanderbilt Avenue, New York, NY 10017

Routledge is an imprint of the Taylor & Francis Group, an informa business

© 2020 The Editor, Journal of Comparative Policy Analysis: Research and Practice

All rights reserved. No part of this book may be reprinted or reproduced or utilised in any form or by any electronic, mechanical, or other means, now known or hereafter invented, including photocopying and recording, or in any information storage or retrieval system, without permission in writing from the publishers.

Trademark notice: Product or corporate names may be trademarks or registered trademarks, and are used only for identification and explanation without intent to infringe.

British Library Cataloguing-in-Publication Data
A catalogue record for this book is available from the British Library

ISBN13: 978-1-138-33272-0

Typeset in Times
by codeMantra

Publisher's Note
The publisher accepts responsibility for any inconsistencies that may have arisen during the conversion of this book from journal articles to book chapters, namely the inclusion of journal terminology.

Disclaimer
Every effort has been made to contact copyright holders for their permission to reprint material in this book. The publishers would be grateful to hear from any copyright holder who is not here acknowledged and will undertake to rectify any errors or omissions in future editions of this book.

 Printed in the United Kingdom
by Henry Ling Limited

Contents

Citation Information	viii
Notes on Contributors	xii
Foreword to the Book Series: *The Classics of*	
Comparative Policy Analysis	xvi
Laurence E. Lynn, Jr.	

PART 1
An Introduction to the Classics of Comparative Policy Analysis Book Series — 1

Why the Classics of Comparative Policy Analysis Studies? — 3
Iris Geva-May, B. Guy Peters and Joselyn Muhleisen

PART 2
Lesson Drawing Relationships: Comparing Associated Disciplines and Comparative Policy Analysis — 11

The Contribution of Comparative Policy Analysis to Policy Design Studies — 13
Michael Howlett

PART 3
The Classics: Policy Sectors in Comparative Policy Analysis Studies — 23

Healthcare

1 Translating Monetary Inputs into Health Care Provision: A Comparative Analysis of the Impact of Different Modes of Public Policy — 25
 Claus Wendt and Jürgen Kohl

2 Comparing Health Policy: An Assessment of Typologies of Health Systems — 46
 Viola Burau and Robert H. Blank

3 Six Countries, Six Health Reform Models? Health Care Reform in Chile, Israel, Singapore, Switzerland, Taiwan and The Netherlands — 60
 Kieke G. H. Okma, Tsung-Mei Cheng, David Chinitz, Luca Crivelli, Meng-Kin Lim, Hans Maarse and Maria Eliana Labra

4 Bottom–Up Policy Convergence: A Sociology of the Reception of Policy Transfer in Public Health Policies in Europe 99
Carole Clavier

5 How do Governments Steer Health Policy? A Comparison of Canadian and New Zealand Approaches to Cost Control and Primary Health Care Reform 115
Tim Tenbensel

6 National Values, Institutions and Health Policies: What do they Imply for Medicare Reform? 132
Theodore R. Marmor, Kieke G. H. Okma and Stephen R. Latham

Welfare

7 A Comparative Analysis of Paid Leave for the Health Needs of Workers and their Families around the World 150
Alison Earle and Jody Heymann

8 Three Worlds of Welfare Chauvinism? How Welfare Regimes Affect Support for Distributing Welfare to Immigrants in Europe 167
Jeroen Van Der Waal, Willem De Koster & Wim Van Oorschot

9 Public Funding, Private Delivery: States, Markets, and Early Childhood Education and Care in Liberal Welfare States – A Comparison of Australia, the UK, Quebec, and New Zealand 185
Linda A. White & Martha Friendly

10 Reconciliation Policies and the Effects of Motherhood on Employment, Earnings and Poverty 204
Joya Misra, Michelle J. Budig and Stephanie Moller

11 Less Bad than its Reputation: Social Spending as a Proxy for Welfare Effort in Cross-national Studies 225
Carsten Jensen

12 The Regulation of Working Time as Work-Family Reconciliation Policy: Comparing Europe, Japan, and the United States 239
Janet C. Gornick and Alexandra Heron

13 Social Citizenship of Young People in Europe: A Comparative Institutional Analysis 257
Tom Chevalier

Education

14 Comparative Analysis of Higher Education Quality Assurance in Colombia and Ecuador: How is Political Ideology Reflected in Policy Design and Discourse? 277
Nadia Rubaii & Mariana Lima Bandeira

CONTENTS

15 Federal Dynamics of Changing Governance Arrangements in Education: A Comparative Perspective on Australia, Canada and Germany 295
    Giliberto Capano

16 Importing Private Higher Education: International Branch Campuses 315
    Jason E. Lane

17 Private Higher Education and Public Policy: A Global View 330
    Daniel C. Levy and William Zumeta

Migration

18 Policy Analysis and Europeanization: An Analysis of EU Migrant Integration Policymaking 335
    Andrew Geddes & Peter Scholten

19 The Interplay of Knowledge Production and Policymaking: A Comparative Analysis of Research and Policymaking on Migrant Integration in Germany and the Netherlands 354
    Han Entzinger & Peter Scholten

20 Fiscal Federalism and the Politics of Immigration: Centralized and Decentralized Immigration Policies in Canada and the United States 369
    Graeme Boushey and Adam Luedtke

21 Bureaucratic Control and Policy Change: A Comparative Venue Shopping Approach to Skilled Immigration Policies in Australia and Canada 387
    Anna Boucher

22 Setting the Immigrant Policy Agenda: Expertise and Politics in the Netherlands, France and the United Kingdom 406
    Peter Scholten and Arco Timmermans

Biotechnology

23 Democracy, Colonial Legacy, and the Openness of Cabinet-Level Websites in Developing Countries 424
    Ivan Katchanovski and Todd La Porte

24 Federalism and the Regulation of Agricultural Biotechnology in the United States and European Union 444
    Adam D. Sheingate

25 Direct Legislation in North America and Europe: Promoting or Restricting Biotechnology? 465
    Christine Rothmayr Allison and Frédéric Varone

Index 491

Citation Information

The chapters in this book were originally published in the *Journal of Comparative Policy Analysis*. When citing this material, please use the original page numbering for each article, as follows:

Chapter 1
Translating Monetary Inputs into Health Care Provision: A Comparative Analysis of the Impact of Different Modes of Public Policy
Claus Wendt, Jürgen Kohl
Journal of Comparative Policy Analysis, volume 12, issues 1–2 (February–April 2010) pp. 11–31

Chapter 2
Comparing health policy: An assessment of typologies of health systems
Viola Burau, Robert H. Blank
Journal of Comparative Policy Analysis, volume 8, issue 1 (March 2006) pp. 63–76

Chapter 3
Six Countries, Six Health Reform Models? Health Care Reform in Chile, Israel, Singapore, Switzerland, Taiwan and The Netherlands
Kieke G. H. Okma, Tsung-Mei Cheng, David Chinitz, Luca Crivelli, Meng-Kin Lim, Hans Maarse, Maria Eliana Labra
Journal of Comparative Policy Analysis, volume 12, issues 1–2 (February–April 2010) pp. 75–113

Chapter 4
Bottom–Up Policy Convergence: A Sociology of the Reception of Policy Transfer in Public Health Policies in Europe
Carole Clavier
Journal of Comparative Policy Analysis, volume 12, issue 5 (November 2010) pp. 451–466

Chapter 5
How do Governments Steer Health Policy? A Comparison of Canadian and New Zealand Approaches to Cost Control and Primary Health Care Reform
Tim Tenbensel
Journal of Comparative Policy Analysis, volume 10, issue 4 (December 2008) pp. 347–363

Chapter 6
National Values, Institutions and Health Policies: What do they Imply for Medicare Reform?
Theodore R. Marmor, Kieke G. H. Okma, Stephen R. Latham
Journal of Comparative Policy Analysis, volume 12, issues 1–2 (February–April 2010) pp. 179–196

Chapter 7
A comparative analysis of paid leave for the health needs of workers and their families around the world
Alison Earle, Jody Heymann
Journal of Comparative Policy Analysis, volume 8, issue 3 (September 2006) pp. 241–257

Chapter 8
Three Worlds of Welfare Chauvinism? How Welfare Regimes Affect Support for Distributing Welfare to Immigrants in Europe
Jeroen Van Der Waal, Willem De Koster, Wim Van Oorschot
Journal of Comparative Policy Analysis, volume 15, issue 2 (2013) pp. 164–181

Chapter 9
Public Funding, Private Delivery: States, Markets, and Early Childhood Education and Care in Liberal Welfare States – A Comparison of Australia, the UK, Quebec, and New Zealand
Linda A. White, Martha Friendly
Journal of Comparative Policy Analysis, volume 14, issue 4 (August 2012) pp. 292–310

Chapter 10
Reconciliation policies and the effects of motherhood on employment, earnings and poverty
Joya Misra, Michelle J. Budig, Stephanie Moller
Journal of Comparative Policy Analysis, volume 9, issue 2 (June 2007) pp. 135–155

Chapter 11
Less Bad than its Reputation: Social Spending as a Proxy for Welfare Effort in Cross-national Studies
Carsten Jensen
Journal of Comparative Policy Analysis, volume 13, issue 3 (June 2011) pp. 327–340

Chapter 12
The regulation of working time as work-family reconciliation policy: Comparing Europe, Japan, and the United States
Janet C. Gornick, Alexandra Heron
Journal of Comparative Policy Analysis, volume 8, issue 2 (June 2006) pp. 149–166

Chapter 13
Social Citizenship of Young People in Europe: A Comparative Institutional Analysis
Tom Chevalier
Journal of Comparative Policy Analysis, volume 20, issue 3 (2018) pp. 304–323

Chapter 14
Comparative Analysis of Higher Education Quality Assurance in Colombia and Ecuador: How is Political Ideology Reflected in Policy Design and Discourse?
Nadia Rubaii, Mariana Lima Bandeira
Journal of Comparative Policy Analysis, volume 20, issue 2 (2018) pp. 158–175

Chapter 15
Federal Dynamics of Changing Governance Arrangements in Education: A Comparative Perspective on Australia, Canada and Germany
Giliberto Capano
Journal of Comparative Policy Analysis, volume 17, issue 4 (2015) pp. 322–341

Chapter 16
Importing Private Higher Education: International Branch Campuses
Jason E. Lane
Journal of Comparative Policy Analysis, volume 13, issue 4 (August 2011) pp. 367–381

Chapter 17
Private Higher Education and Public Policy: A Global View
Daniel C. Levy, William Zumeta
Journal of Comparative Policy Analysis, volume 13, issue 4 (August 2011) pp. 345–349

Chapter 18
Policy Analysis and Europeanization: An Analysis of EU Migrant Integration Policymaking
Andrew Geddes, Peter Scholten
Journal of Comparative Policy Analysis, volume 17, issue 1 (2015) pp. 41–59

Chapter 19
The Interplay of Knowledge Production and Policymaking: A Comparative Analysis of Research and Policymaking on Migrant Integration in Germany and the Netherlands
Han Entzinger, Peter Scholten
Journal of Comparative Policy Analysis, volume 17, issue 1 (2015) pp. 60–74

Chapter 20
Fiscal federalism and the politics of immigration: Centralized and decentralized immigration policies in Canada and the United States
Graeme Boushey, Adam Luedtke
Journal of Comparative Policy Analysis, volume 8, issue 3 (September 2006) pp. 207–224

Chapter 21
Bureaucratic Control and Policy Change: A Comparative Venue Shopping Approach to Skilled Immigration Policies in Australia and Canada
Anna Boucher
Journal of Comparative Policy Analysis, volume 15, issue 4 (2013) pp. 349–367

Chapter 22
Setting the Immigrant Policy Agenda: Expertise and Politics in the Netherlands, France and the United Kingdom
Peter Scholten, Arco Timmermans
Journal of Comparative Policy Analysis, volume 12, issue 5 (November 2010) pp. 527–544

Chapter 23
Democracy, Colonial Legacy, and the Openness of Cabinet-Level Websites in Developing Countries
Ivan Katchanovski, Todd La Porte
Journal of Comparative Policy Analysis, volume 11, issue 2 (June 2009) pp. 213–232

Chapter 24
Federalism and the Regulation of Agricultural Biotechnology in the United States and European Union
Adam D. Sheingate
Journal of Comparative Policy Analysis, volume 11, issue 4 (December 2009) pp. 477–497

Chapter 25
Direct Legislation in North America and Europe: Promoting or Restricting Biotechnology?
Christine Rothmayr Allison, Frédéric Varone
Journal of Comparative Policy Analysis, volume 11, issue 4 (December 2009) pp. 425–449

For any permission-related enquiries please visit:
http://www.tandfonline.com/page/help/permissions

Contributors

Christine Rothmayr Allison is a member of the Research Centre on Public Policy and Social Development (CPDS) and the Director of the Master in Political Science program of the University of Montreal.

Mariana Lima Bandeira is a Professor in the Department of Management Studies at Universidad Andina Simón Bolívar, Ecuador.

Robert H. Blank is an Adjunct Professor of Political Science at the University of Canterbury, Christchurch, New Zealand.

Anna Boucher is an Associate Professor in the Department of Government and International Relations at the University of Sydney, Australia.

Graeme Boushey is an Associate Professor in the Department of Political Science at the University of California, Irvine, USA.

Michelle J. Budig is the Vice-Provost for Faculty Development and a Professor of Sociology at the University of Massachusetts-Amherst, USA.

Viola Burau is an Associate Professor in the Department of Public Health at Aarhus University, Denmark.

Giliberto Capano serves as co-Editor of the *Journal of Comparative Policy Analysis*. He is a Professor of Political Science and Public Policy at the University of Bologna, Italy. His most recent books are *Making Policies Work* (Edward Elgar 2019), *Designing for policy effectiveness* (Cambridge 2018), and *Changing Governance in Universities* (Palgrave 2016).

Tsung-Mei Cheng is Health Policy Research Analyst at the Woodrow Wilson School of Public and International Affairs at Princeton University, USA.

Tom Chevalier is a Postdoctoral Research Fellow in the Department of Politics and International Relations at the University of Oxford, UK.

David Chinitz is a Professor of Health Policy and Management in the Department of Health Policy, Management and Economics of the School of Public Health at the Hebrew University of Jerusalem, Israel.

Carole Clavier is a Professor in the Department of Political Science at the University of Montreal, Canada.

Luca Crivelli is the Head of department and a Professor at the University of Applied Sciences and Arts of Southern Switzerland, a Titular Professor at the Università della Svizzera italiana and the Deputy Director of the Swiss School of Public Health.

CONTRIBUTORS

Willem de Koster is an Associate Professor of Sociology in the Department of Public Administration and Sociology at Erasmus University Rotterdam, the Netherlands.

Alison Earle is a Senior Research Associate in the UCLA Fielding School of Public Health at UCLA, USA.

Han Entzinger is a Professor of Migration and Integration Studies in the Department of Public Administration and Sociology at Erasmus University Rotterdam, the Netherlands.

Martha Friendly is the Founder and Executive Director of the Childcare Resource and Research Unit, Canada.

Andrew Geddes is a Professor of Politics at the University of Sheffield, UK.

Iris Geva-May has been recognized by Thomson Reuters for having pioneered the field of comparative policy analysis since 1998, when she founded the now high indexed *Journal of Comparative Policy Analysis*. She serves as its Founding Editor and the Founding President of the Scholarly Society for International Comparative Policy Analysis (ICPA-Forum). She has published among others *The Logic and Methodology of Policy Analysis, An Operational Approach to Policy Analysis (with Wildavsky), International Library of Policy Analysis Series, Routledge Handbook of Comparative Policy Analysis*, and *Policy Analysis as a Clinical Profession*. She is Professor Emerita at Simon Fraser University, Vancouver, Canada and currently an Honorary Visiting Professor at SPPA, Carleton University, Ottawa, Canada, and the Wagner School NYU, USA.

Janet C. Gornick is a Professor of Political Science and Sociology and the Director of the Stone Center on Socio-Economic Inequality at The Graduate Centre at the City University of New York, New York City, USA.

Alexandra Heron is an Independent Consultant and has worked on labor law issues for trade unions and in government in Britain and Australia, as well as international comparisons of discrimination law and working time.

Jody Heymann is the Director of the WORLD Policy Analysis Center as well as Distinguished Professor in the Fielding School of Public Health, the Luskin School of Public Affairs, and David Geffen School of Medicine at UCLA, USA.

Carsten Jensen is a Professor of political science at Aarhus University, Denmark.

Ivan Katchanovski is a Professor in the School of Political Studies and the Department of Communication at the University of Ottawa, Canada.

Jürgen Kohl is a Professor of Sociology at the Institute of Sociology at the University of Heidelberg, Germany.

Maria Eliana Labra is a Senior Professor at the National School of Public Health at Oswaldo Cruz Foundation in Rio de Janeiro, Brazil.

Jason E. Lane is Interim School of Education (SOE) Dean and Associate Professor, as well as Chair of the Department of Educational Policy and Leadership at the University at Albany, SUNY, USA.

Stephen R. Latham is the Director of the Yale Interdisciplinary Center for Bioethics, Senior Political Science Research Scientist, Adjunct Professor in Management, and Lecturer in Law at Yale University, New Haven, USA.

Daniel C. Levy is a Distinguished Professor in the Department of Educational Administration and Policy Studies at the University at Albany, SUNY, USA.

Meng-Kin Lim was an Associate Professor of Health Policy and Management at the Yong Loo Lin School of Medicine at National University of Singapore.

Adam Luedtke is an Assistant Professor of Political Science at Queensborough Community College (CUNY), New York City, USA.

Laurence E. Lynn, Jr. is the Founding Co-editor of the *Journal of Comparative Policy Analysis*. He is the Sydney Stein, Jr. Professor of Public Management Emeritus at the University of Chicago, USA. He chaired the Masters in Public Policy Program at Harvard's Kennedy School of Government. He has been a Fellow of the National Academy of Public Administration and of the Council on Foreign Relations, as well as APPAM President. He has been honored by Lifetime Academic Achievement Awards by the American Political Science Association, American Society for Public Administration, and the Public Management Research Association. He published, among others, *Public Management as Art, Science, and Profession* from the Academy of Management, *Oxford Handbook of Public Management*, and (with Hill) *Public Management: Thinking and Acting in Three Dimensions*.

Hans Maarse is Emeritus Professor of Health Policy Science at the University of Maastricht, The Netherlands.

Theodore R. Marmor is Professor Emeritus of Management in the Yale School of Management at Yale University, New Haven, USA.

Joya Misra is a Professor of Sociology and Public Policy at the University of Massachusetts, USA.

Stephanie Moller is a Professor of Sociology at the University of North Carolina at Charlotte, USA.

Joselyn Muhleisen serves as the Awards Coordinator for the International Comparative Policy Analysis Forum and the *Journal of Comparative Policy Analysis*. She is a Doctoral Lecturer at the Marxe School of Public and International Affairs, Baruch College, City University of New York (CUNY), USA. She earned her doctorate in political science from The Graduate Center, CUNY, USA. She is the former Assistant Director of the European Union Studies Center, CUNY, USA. She has published work about the development of comparative policy analysis and its relationship to international studies.

Kieke G. H. Okma is an international health consultant and Associate Professor at the Wagner School of Public Services at New York University, USA, and a Visiting Professor at McGill University, Montreal, Canada.

Wim van Oorschot is a Full Professor in the Centre for Sociological Research at KU Leuven, Belgium.

B. Guy Peters is Maurice Falk Professor of Government at the University of Pittsburgh, USA, and an Honorary Editor of the *Journal of Comparative Policy Analysis*. He is also the Founding President of the *International Public Policy Association* and Editor of the *International Review of Public Policy*. Among his seminal publications are as follows: *Comparative Politics Theory and Methods, Institutional Theory in Political Science,*

The Politics of Bureaucracy: A Comparative Perspective, An Advanced Introduction to Public Policy, and *The Next Public Administration.*

Todd La Porte is an Associate Professor in the Schar School of Policy and Government at George Mason University, USA.

Nadia Rubaii is a Professor and Chair of Public Administration and the Co-Director of the Institute for Genocide and Mass Atrocity Prevention at Binghamton University, State University of New York, USA.

Peter Scholten is a Full Professor of Migration and Diversity Policy in the Department of Public Administration and Sociology at Erasmus University Rotterdam, the Netherlands.

Adam D. Sheingate is a Professor and Chair of Political Science at Johns Hopkins University, Baltimore, USA.

Tim Tenbensel is an Associate Professor in Health Systems in the School of Population Health at University of Auckland, New Zealand.

Arco Timmermans is a Professor by Special Appointment in the Institute of Public Administration at the University of Leiden, the Netherlands.

Frédéric Varone is both a Professor and Director of the Department of Political Science and International Relations of the University of Geneva.

Jeroen van der Waal is a Full Professor of Sociology in the Department of Public Administration and Sociology at Erasmus University Rotterdam, the Netherlands.

Claus Wendt is a Professor of Sociology of Health and Healthcare Systems at Siegen University, Germany.

Linda A. White is RBC Chair in Economic and Public Policy and a Professor of Political Science and the Munk School of Global Affairs and Public Policy at the University of Toronto, Canada.

William Zumeta is a Professor in the Evans School of Public Policy and Governance at the University of Washington, Seattle, USA.

Foreword to the Book Series: The Classics of Comparative Policy Analysis

LAURENCE E. LYNN, JR.
Founding co-Editor, *Journal of Comparative Policy Analysis*
Sydney Stein, Jr. Professor of Pubic Management Emeritus
The University of Chicago, USA

The Classics of Comparative Policy Analysis Series is both a record of and a milestone in the development of the theories and methods not only of comparative public policy analysis but, as well, of comparative studies in public affairs-related disciplines and professions, which the *Journal of Comparative Policy Analysis (JCPA)* has advanced. Having been present at the founding of the field of public policy analysis in the 1960s and of comparative policy analysis studies through the *JCPA* in 1998, and having been contributed to a field of research, public governance, which is heavily influenced by comparative perspectives, I am pleased that this series calls attention to the extent to which public affairs research has been influenced by the intellectual ambitions of the kinds of scholarship represented in the four volumes of this series.

Publication of this series of research papers that appeared in volume 20:1 of the *JCPA*, 2018, marks and celebrates the twentieth anniversary of the journal. Selections of classic papers provide not only models for scholars, they are of immense value to teachers in creating reading lists and study assignments. As well, they reinforce awareness of the dimensions and content of a vital field of public affairs research.

Especially welcome are new chapters in each volume authored by the *JCPA* co-editors, highlighting the emerging symbiotic relationships between established disciplines and professions and comparative policy studies. These developments advance the fulfillment of an early intention of the policy analysis movement: promoting the integration of the social sciences in public affairs research. Also important in this regard is the attention in the *Classics of Comparative Policy Analysis* to recent development in research fields, such as policy design and governance, harkening back to the emergence in the original policy analysis movement of implementation studies and program evaluation, with their comparative bent. These newer research studies now appear not only in *JCPA* but in a patulous number of public affairs-oriented academic journals and conference agendas.

It is noteworthy that the *Classics of Comparative Policy Analysis Series* appears in unsettled and unsettling times in national and international affairs. The intellectual developments celebrated in this series have been taking place in a relatively stable and liberal global order. Beginning in the aftermath of World War II, various forms of international cooperation gradually took shape, including regional and the United Nations-sponsored governance and shared sovereignty institutions. This order is now challenged by the seemingly ascendant emergence of nationalism and authoritarianism in many of the world's largest and oldest nations and democracies. These developments threaten the rule of law and the rule of reason, both of which have largely come to be taken for granted in the teaching and research of public affairs-oriented disciplines and professions. Activism and tribalism are competing with analysis and democratic deliberation in the shaping of public policy, and it appears at the expense of fairness and social justice and institutional stability.

But the current political context could also provide opportunities for comparative policy studies. Its scholars have perspectives, models, and methods, as well as the disposition, to study the dynamics of instability, changing institutional and organizational environments and their consequences for policymaking and public administration. For example, researchers on federalism, already informed by comparative studies at subnational levels of governance and international institutions, have the tools to address new questions posed by evolving patterns of governance.

As depicted by Geva-May, Peters, and Muhleisen in their introduction to the series and evident throughout the four volumes, the comparative perspective is producing the kinds of intellectual capital that may be of unique value in policy formulation and design. Lesson drawing is increasingly appropriate in an era of worldwide reinventing of governance. Through the publication of this series, and through papers accepted for publication in future volumes of the *JCPA*, the journal will continue to be a pilot light for imaginative and pathbreaking research that sustains the momentum of the development of comparative policy studies.

Part 1

An Introduction to the Classics of Comparative Policy Analysis Book Series

Why the Classics of Comparative Policy Analysis Studies?

IRIS GEVA-MAY, B. GUY PETERS AND JOSELYN MUHLEISEN

The Classics of Comparative Policy Analysis is a collection of the most representative articles in the *Journal of Comparative Policy Analysis (JCPA)* on its twentieth anniversary. The *JCPA* has "pioneered the domain of comparative policy analysis" studies since 1998[1] and is still the only journal explicitly devoted to promoting comparative policy studies. The articles published in the *JCPA* have become classics in the field of comparative policy analytic studies, and have established it as a distinctive field of study since (Thomson Reuters 2008; Radin 2013; Geva-May, Hoffman and Muhleisen 2018). The papers published over the last two decades in *JCPA* are explicitly comparative and could be viewed as cornerstones of comparative public policy analysis theory, methodology, policy inter-disciplinarity, and inter-regional scholarship. Contributors include founders of the field of policy analysis, comparative politics, and comparative public administration and management from which comparative policy analysis (CPA) has derived: Peter deLeon, Duncan McRae, Laurence E. Lynn, B. Guy Peters, Beryl Radin, David Weimer, Frans Van Nispen, Yukio Adachi, as well as second- and third-generation policy analysis scholars who have set high scholarship bars in advancing the field.

The term "comparative" has normatively been associated with descriptive accounts of national similarities or dissimilarities with respect to content or to features of the public policy process requiring information sharing. At the research level, it has traditionally been concerned with cross-national generalizations or explanations of differences among policies. As the founding editors of the *JCPA* declare in the first volume, "JCPA seeks to go beyond these confines and offer an intellectual arena for analyzing comparative explanatory frameworks and research methods, testing models across spatial structures … and comparing different instruments for achieving similar ends".[2]

The collections of articles included in the volumes of this series support the aim and scope of the *JCPA* to establish points of reference for aspects of comparative policy analytic studies. The four volumes compile, respectively, those foundation articles which contribute to the four main aspects of CPA scholarship advanced by the *JCPA*: (a) Apply or develop comparative methodologies and theories; (b) Investigate valid and reliable means of performing inter-regional or inter-social units comparisons; (c) Investigate the connection among public policy, institutions, and governance factors that can explicate similarities or differences in policymaking; (d) Finally, they focus on the application or utilization of comparative public policy analysis in a variety of policy sectors such as immigration, technology, healthcare, welfare, education, economics, and many others.

Although the chapters included in each volume are classified according to a specific overarching topic, we do find overlaps between, for instance, regional comparisons and methodology or theories, or linkages to institutions as independent variables and policy sectors as dependent variables – thus transcending the single focus of the research presented in each of the volumes.

There is one more aspect that has been explicitly covered neither in the *JCPA* (except for its anniversary Vol 20:1) nor as a separate volume in the present series: the linkages among comparative public policy and the more established fields of comparative politics (political science) and public administration, as well as the newly emerging (or diverging) domains such as governance – from public administration and policy design – from public policy. To open a window to further comparisons among inter-related public domains we introduce a new chapter in Part II of each volume. Authored by the *JCPA* co-editors, the four chapters embrace the notion that the established political science and comparative politics, as well as public administration and comparative public administration, have much to offer to policy studies and to the developing field of CPA studies. It is also noteworthy that the comparative policy analytic studies domain is seen as a source of lesson drawing for the increasing interest in policy design and in governance. The cross-fertilization between these domains can range anywhere between theoretical, conceptual, methodological, and empirical. Identifying points of similarity or difference in enhancing lesson drawing, adaptation, transfer and borrowing, or missed opportunity thereof.

These fundamentals common to all domains of study are addressed by Guy Peters and Geva-May who note down the prospective gift of (comparative) political science to CPA and reciprocal missed opportunities in Volume One; Capano contributes a new chapter on governance, regimes, and comparative public policy in Volume Two; Leslie Pal writes about comparative public administration and comparative public policy in Volume Three; while Howlett addresses the newly emerging branch of policy design and what can be derived from comparative public policy in Volume Four.

In today's politics and policymaking, the reality of global policy convergence, economic competition, and political fads, the cross-national sources of information have proliferated to the extent that any policy analyst, public policy scholar, or policy decision-maker in any given country is bound to be aware of developments that happen in a different "social unit" as Ragin and Zaret (1983) label units of social analysis. Comparisons between social units may be nations or institutions, or points of reference such as policy goals, actor interference, market failures, or intervention in public policy issues of concern. The main reason is lesson drawing in order to maximize utility of policy solutions, avoid failure, or utilize information to seek advantage. Comparative cross-national policy analysis can extend insights, perspectives, or explanations that otherwise would be difficult or impossible to obtain. Lesson drawing (Rose 1991; Geva-May 2004), transfer, borrowing, adoption or adaptations, or sheer inspiration (DeLeon 1998; Geva-May 2002a) increases effectiveness and efficiency, and avoids fallacies. Notwithstanding this stipulation, there is a word of warning: CPA done badly has an immediate effect on the public, and can be financially wasteful or dangerous to the social units and populum immediately involved. Furthermore, it can be detrimental to the credibility of policymaking, as well as to policy analysis as a practical and scholarly domain.

One more contention is that in the *Classics of Comparative Policy Analysis Studies* the terms policy analysis, policy studies, and policy analytic studies are often used by authors interchangeably for a number of reasons: Foremost, because these domains are often similar in their possible points of linkage to the comparative aspects that they cover. Additionally, in today's third generation of policy analysis studies, the borderlines between policy studies, policy design, and policy analysis have frequently blurred and the terminology used has often been transposable. The terms used contain a wider perception of public policy within which domains and sub-domains complement one another despite their very distinct roles. Except for those actually studying or working in these sub-fields, the scholarly work refers to them frequently interchangeably.

We selected the articles in the series not only by thematic relevance and excellence, but also based on how they serve the aim and scope of the *JCPA* (Geva-May and Lynn 1998) which set clear intellectual avenues towards the development of the field beyond the mere prevalent perception of "comparative" as the comparison of two objects – whether institutions or regions. Proven valid enough to have served as scholarly cornerstones in the development of comparative policy studies for two decades, each respective *JCPA* aim drives the focus of each respective volume in the series. **Volume One** presents selections focused on **comparative theory and methodology** development, and comparative **theory testing**: two central aims of the *JCPA*. **Volume Two** addresses **institutions and questions about modes and types of governance** which speaks about the aim of examining the inter-relations between institutions and policy analysis either as dependent or independent variables. **Volume Three** builds on comparative empirical research, as well as lesson drawing and extrapolation, and evaluates comparative research methods through articles on regional policy differences or similarities. **Volume Four** touches on almost all the aims of *JCPA* through studies of specific policy sectors – healthcare, immigration, education, economics, welfare, technology, etc., – particularly allowing for lesson drawing, extrapolation, and possible avoidance of failures within sectors.

Volume One: Theory and Methodology

CPA depends upon the various theoretical and methodological approaches to public policy. The same theoretical perspectives such as the advocacy-coalition framework, multiple-streams models, and agenda-setting are important for understanding national and international policymaking and public policy comparatively. These are applied through lesson drawing and policy transfer, for instance, among others, by Pal (2014), and Wolf and Baehler (2018).

Of particular interest are the linkages of policy theories with various academic disciplines, including economics, political science, sociology, and law, all of which bring their own theoretical perspectives to bear on public policy. Each of the articles included in the first volume demonstrates the need to make difficult theoretical and methodological choices in the study of CPA.

Perhaps the most important aspect of these articles is that the researcher had to make a conscious choice about theory and method, and had to justify those choices. The articles also indicate how they frame policy problems and how they overcome methodological challenges in CPA (Ira Sherkansky 1998; Hoppe 2002; Green-Pedersen 2004; Peters 2005; Saurugger 2005; Stiller and van Kersbergen 2008; Capano 2009; Howlett and Cashore 2009; Greer et al. 2015; among others). In doing so, many address another aim of the *JCPA*: the evaluation of comparative research methods. One way to both evaluate the aptness of research methods and to test theory is to conduct empirical studies. For example, Green-Pedersen contends with the dependent variable problem in the context of social welfare research (Green-Pedersen 2004).

Volume Two: Comparative Policy Analysis and Institutions

"Evidence-based policymaking" is more difficult than sometimes assumed, depending, as it does, on understanding both the dynamics of public policy and the institutional contexts. Despite this difficulty, there has been a surge of interest in policy designed on the basis of "scientifically" demonstrated effectiveness and the ability to identify those successful policies within various structures.

Drawing on the larger institutionalism and governance literatures, many selections in the second volume are concerned with distinct forms of governance and types of political institutions. Governance and institutions are treated both as independent and dependent variables (Weimer and Vining 1998; Ng 2007; Radaelli 2008). The latter make an important distinction between first-order and second-order instruments. The first are those known to policy analysts, the second less transparent depend on features of institutions that "facilitate or constrain" the adoption of first-order policies. The authors contend that in order to make meaningful comparisons, it is important to analyze the usefulness of policy analysis against the analysis of the institutional features that condition policy choice. While public policy scholars and politicians have given increasing attention to new, innovative governance apparatuses, empirical work basically intends to document whether these instruments are effective in specific jurisdictions and institutional contexts and what can be extrapolated from one milieu to another.

One of the chief institutional explanations of policy variation is the nature of political and bureaucratic institutions within which the policies are developed or implemented. CPA has also considered the influence of particular governance arrangements, for example, public-private partnerships on policy outcomes (Vining and Boardamn 2018). But governance structures and institutions are also reflective of the societies, cultures, and polities that constitute them (Hoppe 2002; Geva-May 2002b). Other studies focus on the determinants of certain governance mechanisms, such as privatization (Breen and Doyle 2013), and the impact of the participation of certain societal groups in the policymaking process (Heidbreder 2015). Thus, public policy, institutions, and society are in complex and reciprocal relationships that require a great deal of care to properly disentangle and analyze.

Major themes that underscore several contributions in the volume on institutions and governance will be unsurprising to policy scholars; many selections are especially concerned with effectiveness, efficiency, and mechanisms of compliance (Lee and Whitford 2009; Ross and Yan 2015).

Volume Three: Comparative Inter-regional Policy Analysis Studies

The selections included in this volume make policy comparisons within and across regions. In fact, CPA studies are mostly regarded as comparisons across political systems, whether they are countries, provinces, cities, or another jurisdiction. Likewise, much of the policy analytic research focuses on how policies have fared in specific jurisdictions (Laguna 2011; Saetren 2015) and which factors that contribute to a policy's success can potentially be applied in other contexts.

This mode of analysis brings CPA closer to comparative politics and sociology, and focuses on many of the variables used in the other social sciences to explain observed similarities or differences in the policy choices made by different political systems. The policy choices of federalist systems, for example, are compared by Radin and Boase (2000); Boushey and Luedtke (2006); Sheingate (2009); and Capano (2015). The latter, for instance, compare the Canadian and US federal systems in order to identify similarities and differences between them that explicate the divergence in their social and economic policies. The argument is based on two typologies – Lowi's typology refers to different types of policies, and Deil Wright's typology refers to different models of intergovernmental systems. Here, we also glance at how other theories and related typologies can be applied to CPA across units of comparative analysis.

Focusing on regional comparisons can offer a solid methodological basis for comparative studies by eliminating sources of variation and allowing scholars to isolate more clearly the influence of independent variable(s). To the extent that countries in a region share culture, language, history, or institutional design, inter-regional studies can also target alternate explanations for policy differences. Alternatively, where there is a high degree of policy similarity in very different countries, the existence of a regional power or institution may explain policy convergence. Several studies included in this volume take this approach when considering the phenomenon of Europeanization, for instance, which considers both regional and institutional policy determinants (Mendez et al. 2008; Raedelli 2008; Sarugger 2005). Many contributions compare the policies or policymaking process in a domain across jurisdictions (Ng 2007; Smith and Williams 2007). Other scholars rather focus on tendencies towards regional agglomeration (May et al. 2005) or policy convergence (Clavier 2010).

The *JCPA* has contributed substantially to the body of inter-regional comparative public policy literature and has devoted a number of Special Issues to the topic. This is reflected in the diversity of regions addressed by this volume's selections: Latin America, North America, East Asia, Southeast Asia, Southern Africa, the Baltic states, the Nordic states, Western Europe, Central Europe, Eastern Europe, and Europe as a whole. Dedicated to CPA, the wide range of cases published in the *JCPA*, and the attempt to understand policy and policymaking in many contexts, has served as a major object of interest among authors, readers, and researchers of comparative inter-regional studies.

Volume Four: Comparing Policy Sectors

Our volume on comparative policy sectors focuses on the major areas of strength in the *JCPA*: markets, money and economy, healthcare, welfare, education, migration, and biotechnology policy. These articles explicitly compare policies within policy sectors. The reader can readily identify the marked differences between more technical domains such as technology (Allison and Varone 2009), and more politicized domains such as immigration (Scholten and Timmermans 2010; Geddes and Scholten 2015), healthcare (Marmor et al. 2010), and higher education (Levy and Zumeta 2011).

Many of the articles in this volume deal with comparisons of differences and similarities in various policy disciplines and sectors within and among political systems. For example, Gornick and Heron (2006) compare working time policies across eight European countries, the US, and Japan. Sheingate (2009), on the other hand, compares biotechnology policy decision-making in the European Union and the US, which are treated in his analysis as different styles of federalist regimes.

The absence of papers that explicitly compare *across* policy sectors is noteworthy in the *JCPA*. This is why the *JCPA* anniversary Special Issue Vol. 20:1 and Part One of each volume in this series have been devoted to the comparison of policy, politics, and administration studies. Yet, we still do not find comparative papers between healthcare and immigration, or policy analysis and psychology, or medicine, or law (Geva-May 2005).

To some extent, this phenomenon represents the difficulties of scholars to master the details of any other policy domain, much less several that might be appropriate for comparison. This does not come as a surprise. To cite Gary Freeman (1985), indeed, the differences across domains within a single country would, on average, be greater than differences between the same domain across countries. That was a rather bold claim, but there are some reasons to expect policy domains to be significantly different, and therefore more difficult to compare. For example, some policy domains – such as defense or taxation – tend to be dominated by the government itself, while others – education, social policy – tend to have significant direct influence by citizens. Still other policy domains such as health and technology will be dominated by expert professionals who can reduce some of the role of government in policy. We could add to this list of variables, but the fundamental point remains that the nature of the policy does influence the ways in which policy is made and implemented. That said, differences across political systems do continue to show up in these domains, and it remains crucial for the student and the researcher of CPA to be sensitive to several sources of variation in process and outcomes.

In sum, the four volumes in the *Classics of Policy Analysis Studies* seek to present scholars the most salient work that the *JCPA* has covered in the last two decades and illustrate the multiple levels of study on which we can pursue the intellectual dialogue on comparative public policy. First, the series offers a centralized resource of work that furthers the aims of the new discipline of CPA and the inter-related fields of political science, sociology, and economics. Second, it contributes to the database of knowledge by investigating, applying, or developing theories and methodologies that ensure the validity and reliability of the comparative policy studies. Third, it extends case studies that enrich the ongoing discussions about what can be learned through comparative policy analytic studies to increase efficiency, effectiveness, transparency, and equity in public policy.

We wish the readers of the *Classics of Comparative Policy Analysis Studies* an interesting journey, from which they can adopt, adapt, borrow, transfer, extrapolate, or be inspired for their comparative studies.

Notes

1. Thomson Reuters. (2008). *Whos Who*.
2. Geva-May, I., & Lynn, E. L, Jr. (1998). Comparative policy analysis: Introduction to a new journal. *JCPA, 1*(1), 1.

References

Allison, C. R., & Varone, F. (2009). Direct legislation in North America and Europe: Promoting or restricting biotechnology? *Journal of Comparative Policy Analysis, 11*(4), 425–449.
Boushey, G., & Luedtke, A. (2006). Fiscal federalism and the politics of immigration: Centralized and decentralized immigration policies in Canada and the United States. *Journal of Comparative Policy Analysis, 8*(3), 207–224.
Breen, M., & Doyle, D. (2013). The determinants of privatization: A comparative analysis of developing countries. *Journal of Comparative Policy Analysis: Research and Practice, 15*(1), 1–20.

Boardman, A. E., Greenberg, D.H., Vining, A.R. & Weimer, D.L. *Cost-Benefit Analysis: Concepts & Practices*, 2018, Cambridge University Press: Cambridge, UK.

Capano, G. (2009). Understanding policy change as an epistemological and theoretical problem. *Journal of Comparative Policy Analysis*, 11(1), 7–31.

Capano, G., Howlett, M., & Ramesh, M. (2015). Bringing governments back in: Governance and governing in comparative policy analysis. *Journal of Comparative Policy Analysis: Research and Practice*, 17(4), 311–321.

Clavier, C. (2010). Bottom–up policy convergence: A sociology of the reception of policy transfer in public health policies in Europe. *Journal of Comparative Policy Analysis*, 12(5), 451–466.

DeLeon, P., & Resnick-Terry, P. (1998). Comparative policy analysis: Déjà vu all over again?, *Journal of Comparative Policy Analysis: Research and Practice*, 1:1, 9–22.

Dunn, W. N. (2008, 2015). *Public Policy Analysis: An Introduction* (4 ed.). Upper Saddle River, NJ: Pearson Prentice Hall.

Freeman, G. P. (1985). National styles and policy sectors: Explaining structured variation. *Journal of Public Policy*, 5(4), 467–496.

Geddes, A., & Scholten, P. (2015). Policy analysis and Europeanization: An analysis of EU migrant integration policymaking. *Journal of Comparative Policy Analysis: Research and Practice*, 17(1), 41–59.

Geva-May, I. (Ed.) (2005). *Thinking Like a Policy Analyst: Policy Analysis as a Clinical Profession*. New York: Palgrave Macmillan.

Geva-May, I. (2002a). Comparative studies in public administration and public policy. *Public Management Review*, 4(3), 275–290.

Geva-May, I. (2002b). From theory to practice: Policy analysis, cultural bias and organizational arrangements. *Public Management Review*, 4(4), 581–591.

Geva-May, I. with Wildavsky, A. (1997, 2001, 2011). *An Operational Approach to Policy Analysis: The Craft: Prescriptions for Better Analysis*. Kluwer Academic Publishers.

Geva-May, I., & Lynn, L. E. Jr. (1998). Comparative Policy Analysis: Introduction to a New Journal. *Journal of Comparative Policy Analysis*, 1(1).

Geva-May, I., Hoffman, D. C., & Muhleisen, J. (2018). Twenty years of comparative policy analysis: A survey of the field and a discussion of topics and methods. *Journal of Comparative Policy Analysis: Research and Practice*, 20(1), 18–35.

Green-Pedersen, C. (2004). The dependent variable problem within the study of welfare state retrenchment: Defining the problem and looking for solutions. *Journal of Comparative Policy Analysis: Research and Practice*, 6(1), 3–14.

Greer, S., Elliott, H., & Oliver, R. (2015). Differences that matter: Overcoming methodological nationalism in comparative social policy research. *Journal of Comparative Policy Analysis: Research and Practice*, 17(4), 408–429.

Heidbreder, E. G. (2015). Governance in the European Union: A policy analysis of the attempts to raise legitimacy through civil society participation. *Journal of Comparative Policy Analysis: Research and Practice*, 17(4), 359–377.

Hoppe, R. (2002). Cultures of public policy problems. *Journal of Comparative Policy Analysis: Research and Practice*, 4(3), 305–326.

Howlett, M., & Cashore, B. (2009). The dependent variable problem in the study of policy change: Understanding policy change as a methodological problem. *Journal of Comparative Policy Analysis*, 11(1), 33–46.

Laguna, M. I. (2011). The challenges of implementing merit-based personnel policies in Latin America: Mexico's civil service reform experience. *Journal of Comparative Policy Analysis*, 13(1), 51–73.

Lee, S. Y., & Whitford, A. B. (2009). Government effectiveness in comparative perspective. *Journal of Comparative Policy Analysis*, 11(2), 249–281.

Leslie A. Pal (2014). Introduction: The OECD and policy transfer: Comparative case studies. *Journal of Comparative Policy Analysis: Research and Practice*, 16(3), 195–200.

Levy, D. C., & Zumeta, W. (2011). Private higher education and public policy: A global view. *Journal of Comparative Policy Analysis: Research and Practice*, 13(4), 345–349.

Marmor, T. R. (2010). Introduction: Varieties of comparative analysis in the world of medical care policy. *Journal of Comparative Policy Analysis*, 12(1–2), 5–10.

May, Peter, Jones B. D., Beem, B. E., Neff-Sharum, E. A. & Poague, M. K. (2005). Regional Policy Agglomeration: Arctic Policy in Canada and the United States, *Journal of Comparative Policy Analysis: Research and Practice*, 7(2), 121–136.

Mendez, C., Wishlade, F., & Yuill, D. (2008). Made to measure? Europeanization, goodness of fit and adaptation pressures in EU competition policy and regional aid. *Journal of Comparative Policy Analysis*, *10*(3), 279–298.

Ng, M. K. (2007). Sustainable development and governance in East Asian world cities. *Journal of Comparative Policy Analysis*, *9*(4), 321–335.

Peters, G. B. (2005). The problem of policy problems. *Journal of Comparative Policy Analysis*, *7*(4), 349–370.

Radaelli, C. M. (2008). Europeanization, policy learning, and new modes of governance. *Journal of Comparative Policy Analysis*, *10*(3), 239–254.

Radin, B. A. (2013). *Beyond Machiavelli: Policy Analysis Reaches Midlife*. Georgetown University Press.

Radin, B., & Boase, A. (2000). Federalism, political structure, and public policy in the United States and Canada, *Journal of Comparative Policy Analysis: Research and Practice*, *2*(1), 65–89.

Ragin, C. C. (1994). Introduction to qualitative comparative analysis. *The Comparative Political Economy of the Welfare State*, *299*, 300–309.

Ragin, C. and Zaret, D. (1983) Theory and Method in Comparative Research: Two Strategies. *Social Forces*, *61* (3), 731–754.

Rose, R. (1991). What is lesson-drawing? *Journal of Public Policy*, *11*(1), 3–30.

Ross, T. W., & Yan, J. (2015). Comparing public–private partnerships and traditional public procurement: Efficiency vs. flexibility. *Journal of Comparative Policy Analysis: Research and Practice*, *17*(5), 448–466.

Rothmayr Allison, C., & Varone, F. (2009). Direct legislation in North America and Europe: Promoting or restricting biotechnology?. *Journal of Comparative Policy Analysis*, *11*(4), 425–449.

Saurugger, S. (2005). Europeanization as a methodological challenge: The case of interest groups. *Journal of Comparative Policy Analysis*, *7*(4), 291–312.

Scholten, P., & Timmermans, A. (2010). Setting the immigrant policy agenda: Expertise and politics in the Netherlands, France and the United Kingdom. *Journal of Comparative Policy Analysis*, *12*(5), 527–544.

Sheingate, A. D. (2009). Federalism and the regulation of agricultural biotechnology in the United States and European Union. *Journal of Comparative Policy Analysis*, *11*(4), 477–497.

Smith, A. J., & Williams, D. R. (2007). Father-friendly legislation and paternal time across Western Europe. *Journal of Comparative Policy Analysis*, *9*(2), 175–192.

Stiller, S., & van Kersbergen, K. (2008). The matching problem within comparative welfare state research: How to bridge abstract theory and specific hypotheses. *Journal of Comparative Policy Analysis: Research and Practice*, *10*(2), 133–149.

Thomson Reuters (2008). Iris Geva-May, *Who's Who*.

Vining, A. R., & Weimer, D. L. (1998). Informing institutional design: Strategies for comparative cumulation. *Journal of Comparative Policy Analysis*, *1*(1), 39–60.

Wolf, A., & Baehler, K. J. (2018). Learning transferable lessons from single cases in comparative policy analysis. *Journal of Comparative Policy Analysis: Research and Practice*, *20*(4), 420–434.

Part 2

Lesson Drawing Relationships: Comparing Associated Disciplines and Comparative Policy Analysis

The Contribution of Comparative Policy Analysis to Policy Design Studies

MICHAEL HOWLETT

Introduction: Defining and Studying Effectiveness in Policy Design

The essence of policy design can be found in the development of the products of policy analyses, the policy options expected to meet government goals (Howlett 2019). Not all policies are as well or as carefully formulated as they could be, of course, and policy studies – and especially comparative ones across different nations, sectors, and times – have been instrumental in aiding understanding of why some policies are well designed, while others not, and why some designs work effectively, while others do not.

Comparative studies of policy analysis have addressed questions around these topics such as why some policy alternatives are developed, while others are not; why these are developed at the specific time they are; why some are successfully adopted, while others are not; and how some policies emerge from carefully crafted formulation processes, while others are more heavily influenced by processes such as political or legislative bargaining or partisan and electoral maneuvering (Howlett and Mukherjee 2014).

The Contribution of Comparative Policy Analytical Studies to the Study of Policy Formulation and Policy Design

Although aspects of policymaking such as implementation and evaluation contribute greatly to policy success and effectiveness, studies of policy "design" in general treat it as a specific kind of formulation process. These, in general, are thought to fall on a spectrum of types ranging from legislative and electoral bargaining to detailed evidence-based analysis (Howlett and Mukherjee 2017). Policy design, in this sense, is thought to fall on the more purposive and instrumental end of the spectrum (Colebatch 2017; Howlett and Mukherjee 2017).

That is, design is commonly seen to entail the deliberate endeavor of authoritative policymakers to link policy tools with clearly articulated policy goals (Majone 1976; Linder and Peters 1984; May 2003; Bobrow 2006; Colebatch 2017). This involves a systematic effort to analyze the impacts of policy instruments on policy targets, as well as the application of this knowledge to the creation and realization of policies that can reasonably be expected to attain anticipated policy outcomes (Weaver 2009a, 2009b; Bobrow and Dryzek 1987; Sidney 2007; Gilabert and Lawford-Smith 2012).

Such activities, however, assume that it is feasible to generate realizable alternatives through formulation and design processes, that policymakers are well-intentioned in so doing, and that such alternatives will emerge triumphant in deliberations and conflicts involved in policymaking activities, all conditions that may be very difficult to reach in practice and whose pre-conditions, practical modalities, and procedural variations, therefore, require serious analysis and study (Turnbull 2017).

To date the research emphasis on policy design unfortunately has often seen design processes less as problematic, conflict-laden, processes of policy formulation requiring careful empirical analysis than as ones in which it is simply assumed that "first best" conditions prevail. Many studies in fields such as economics and environmental or health policymaking, for example, thus focus on important questions such as those exploring the trade-offs and interactions between the various tools of governance used in policy "toolkits" and the need to manage their inherent complementarities as well as contradictions and overlaps (Gunningham et al. 1998; Howlett 2014; Howlett et al. 2014) but without examining the conditions and circumstances which make such activities problematic. Similarly, many studies have focused on the articulation of different kinds of policy analytical activities – from rational analysis of quantitative data to politicized public participation exercises – which can contribute to realization of optimal designs. But this has often been done without giving due consideration to the obstacles and barriers which may prevent such designs from even being articulated, let alone approved and implemented in "pure" form (Mayer et al. 2004).

Studies of comparative policy analysis have been instrumental in overcoming these gaps in knowledge and establishing when such conditions arise and when they do not, and when policymaking is likely to involve "design" activities rather than "non-design" ones (Howlett and Mukherjee 2014). Comparative studies, for example, have emphasized factors such as the different processes and patterns through which policy toolkits are developed as well as the impact of timing and sequencing as many such designs have emerged over time – primarily through their layering on top of past policy elements (Thelen 2004; Howlett and Rayner 2013; van der Heijden 2013). In a needed development, these and other works have begun to pay more attention to the "design vs non-design" character of many policy processes and outcomes.

The Contribution of Comparative Policy Analytical Studies to the Study of Policy Effectiveness

One area which has received a great deal of attention is the study of *policy effectiveness*. In the context of policy design studies this needs to be understood at three levels of analysis. The first entails a specific focus on what accounts for and constitutes the effectiveness of particular types of policy tools. The second is at the level of better understanding what entails an effective formulation environment – or "design space" – that is conducive to effective design. The third and related issue concerns how policy tool portfolios or mixes can be constructed to effectively address complex policy goals within these specific design and non-design contexts. Each of these is addressed in turn below.

The Effectiveness of Specific Policy Tools

The discussion of effective design environments and that of complementary or integrated instrument mixes have developed in parallel over the last two decades. Comparative literature that consolidates lessons regarding the specifics of effective individual tool design is an older one, however, which began at the national and sub-national level but has been updated by more recent cross-sectoral comparative policy studies and incorporated into the design literature.

Comparisons of differences or similarities, effectiveness or lack thereof in policy arrangements, are the bedrock foundation for any work on policy designs. In the early 1980s scholars focused on more precisely categorizing policy instruments and better analyzing the reasons for their use (Salamon 1981). Careful examination of instruments and instrument choices, it was argued, would allow practitioners and researchers to more readily draw lessons from the experiences of others with the use of particular techniques in specific circumstances, leading to more effective designs (Linder and Peters 1984; Woodside 1986; Bobrow and Dryzek 1987; Dryzek and Ripley 1988).

Among the most significant findings made in this literature were not only that the plethora of possible tools can be grouped into four relatively small categories ("carrots", "sticks", "sermons", and "organizations") (Balch 1980; Bemelmans-Videc 1998), but that each of these categories relied on a particular kind of governing resource being available and wielded competently for that tool to be able to operate effectively (Hood 1986; Wu et al. 2015). Further comparative studies across both time and countries revealed the significance of factors such as standard operating procedures and historical and institutional legacies in affecting choices to employ particular kinds of tools (Kagan 1989, 1991, 1997; Knill 1998, 1999; Knill and Lenschow 1998).

These are all subjects needed in order to move forward beyond abstract theorizing and tool taxonomies towards better comprehending the reasons why policy mixes formed and how to design or reform new ones.

Effective Design Environments

By the late 1990s, comparative studies had moved on from the study of single instrument uses to those involving more complex mixes of policy tools (Grabosky 1994; Gunningham et al. 1998; Howlett 2004). This era also saw a substantial shift in scholarly attention towards more "meta" level studies of policy formulation and design, sparked by the emergence of globalization and its preference for market-based tools as well as the start of "governance" studies in Europe and elsewhere which emphasized the role of non-state actors – especially networks – in policymaking (Howlett and Lejano 2013).

These studies were useful in helping to link policy design studies to other comparative work on the impact of these kinds of institutional and other arrangements which transcended individual policy sectors (Hood 2007, Hood and Margetts 2007). Moreover, this work raised questions about how formulation processes were able to link activity at this "meta" level to the more specific level of policy tools. This led to a new area of comparative policy research into the understanding and demarcation of the kinds of design spaces which allow deliberations and debates around effectiveness to occur and "better" designs to be adopted (Howlett 2011).

As early as 1991, Linder and Peters (1991) had suggested that policy design could be thought of as an area of study oriented towards the understanding of such spaces. That is, they noted that design was "a systematic activity composed of a series of choices ... design solutions, (which) will correspond to a set of possible locations in a design space" and that "this construction emphasizes not only the potential for generating new mixtures of conventional solutions, but also the importance of giving careful attention to tradeoffs among design criteria when considering instrument choices" (Linder and Peters 1991).

The policymaking milieu within which designs unfold, thus, presents a distinct set of conditions affecting policy effectiveness. For example, Ansell and Gash (2008) highlighted several governance-related variables that are critical for effectiveness of modes of collaborative governance, including reconciling the "prior history of conflict or cooperation, the incentives for stakeholders to participate, power and resource imbalances, leadership and institutional design" (p. 543).

The idea that policy design processes are embedded within, and their effectiveness linked to their congruence with prevailing modes of governance is a powerful one and has many implications for considerations about effective designs and design activities. The idea is that design spaces are delimited and characterized by on-the-ground political realities which shape overall public and elite preferences for certain kinds of tools and mixes over others. This relates to preferences for market-based portfolios over state-based ones, for example, but also those related to electoral and ideological concerns of political parties, the nature and character of government leaders, and the like. This is an important insight with respect to the nature of effective designs (Howlett 2019). It means, for example, that policy designers need to be cognizant about the internal mechanisms of their polity and constituent policy sectors which can boost or undermine their ability to think systematically about policy and develop effective policies (Braathen and Croci 2005; Braathen 2007; Grant 2010; Skodvin, Gullberg and Aakre 2010). It also suggests that although design spaces are often given, they themselves can also be "designed". And, further, it suggests that constructing an inventory of potential public capabilities and resources that might be pertinent in any problem-solving situation is a critical step in any formulation situation (Anderson 1975).

Determining exactly what intellectual, organizational, and governing capacities are required in order to develop the design spaces needed to carry out complex design processes in a more or less formal, analytical fashion is currently a subject of much interest in the field today. This is especially apparent around the idea of attaining an "evidence-based" policy process (Considine 2012; Wu et al. 2015; Head 2016), and the possibility of this occuring can be determined through underlying comparisons of instances of policy formulation in different countries and sectors. The vast existing policy analysis literature emphasizing the mapping of the context of a policy situation lends itself to lesson drawing for superior policy formulation and design.

Effective Instrument Mixes

Contemporary design studies have placed a greater emphasis on a third element of effectiveness and comparative policy studies have also contributed in this area: better understanding tool portfolios themselves and upon the processes that create complex policy tool bundles (Hood 2007; Howlett 2011; Howlett and del Rio 2015; Rogge and Reichardt 2016). Such portfolios are combinations of policy instruments that are expected to achieve specific policy objectives and are much more common than single instrument efforts (Gunningham, Grabosky and Sinclair 1998).

The components of such mixes include various elements of policies which are combined in the design process including both general goals and means (Cashore and Howlett 2007; Howlett 2009; Kern and Howlett 2009). These in turn are linked to tools and to the settings or calibrations of those tools. Design and instrument selection in these contexts "are all about constrained efforts to match goals and expectations both within and across categories of policy elements", and effective policy design requires a detailed knowledge of the interactions of tools within mixes (Howlett 2009, 74).

In this regard, comparative policy studies have been engaged in a lengthy and useful scholarly discussion as to how to more effectively integrate policy mixes (Gunningham et al. 1998; Doremus 2003; Briassoulis 2005; Peters et al. 2005; Howlett 2011; Jordan et al. 2011, 2012; Yi and Feiock 2012). In this work it is recognized that some instruments work well with others – in fact, often better in combination, as is the case with "self-regulation" set within a regulatory compliance framework, for example (Grabosky 1994; Trebilcock Tuohy and Wolfson 1979; Gibson 1999) – while other combinations may not interact at all or in a less positive fashion.

Comparative works on "smart regulation" inspired by the pioneering efforts of Gunningham, Grabosky, and Sinclair (1998) in Australia, for example, led scholars to focus on how instruments within a policy mix or "portfolio" could effectively complement each other or conversely, lead to conflicts, resulting in guidelines for the formulation of more sophisticated policy designs in which complementarities were maximized and conflicts avoided (Blonz, Vajjhala and Safirova 2008; Barnett and Shore 2009; Buckman and Diesendorf 2010; del Rio et al. 2010; Roch, Pitts and Navarro 2010). This is latter situation the case, notably, with independently developed subsidies and regulation if they work at cross-purposes to simultaneously reward and constrain the same kinds or types of activities or behaviors – such as buying SUVs and attempting to restrain gasoline consumption and improve fuel standards. Comparative policy studies have shown that achieving effectiveness in such policy portfolios relies upon ensuring policy mechanisms, calibrations, objectives, and settings display "coherence", "consistency", and "congruence" with each other (Howlett and Rayner 2007).

Conclusion

Policy design studies is a relatively new field, albeit one with strong roots in traditional policy studies. Throughout its history it has drawn extensively from many fields, such as economics, political science, history, geography, law, and many others. As a subset of policy formulation, design studies have also benefitted greatly from works in the policy sciences focused on this topic, especially those studies of comparative policy analysis, which have helped explicate the complexities of policy analysis and its role, and limits, in informing and driving policy formulation and, hence, policy design.

The emphasis, in more recent comparative policy studies, on the complexity of policy mixes, layering, and temporality, for example, distinguishes current design literature from earlier approaches. Those earlier works typically examined aspects of policymaking and especially policy tool selection by concentrating only upon simple policy contexts and the selection of singular tools within the context of an ideal design environment (Salamon 1989; Linder and Peters 1990; del Rio and Howlett 2013; Goodspeed et al. 2016; Mintrom and Luetjens 2016; Rogge and Reichardt 2016). A newer focus on more complex issues and choices has added important new dimensions to the study of issues around "who designs what, when and how" as policy formulation processes unfold (Howlett 2010; Howlett and Lejano 2013; Howlett 2014; Howlett et al. 2015).

In particular, these newer approaches have given rise to a more precise and sophisticated notion of the merits and feasibility of particular kinds of designs in specific design contexts (Howlett and Rayner 2013; Chindarkar et al. 2017) which has added a measure of realism to studies claiming to have identified "best practices" in formal policy designs. That is, these studies, through comparisons, have underlined how understanding and making public policy must integrate a solid understanding of policy processes along with a deep understanding of the characteristics of policy tools and how they operate both – singly and in tandem with others – in order to understand what is feasible in a given context and why (Meltsner 1972; Gilabert and Lawford-Smith 2012).

References

Anderson, J. E. *Public Policymaking*. New York: Praeger, 1975.

Ansell, C., & Gash, A. Collaborative governance in theory and practice. *Journal of Public Administration Research and Theory*, 18, no. 4 (2008), 543–571.

Balch, G. I. The stick, the carrot, and other strategies: A theoretical analysis of governmental intervention. *Law and Policy Quarterly*, 2, no. 1 (1980), 35–60.

Barnett, C. K., & Shore, B. Reinventing program design: Challenges in leading sustainable institutional change. *Leadership & Organization*, 30, no. 1, 16–35.

Bemelmans-Videc, M. L., Rist, R. C., & Vedung, E. eds. *Carrots, Sticks and Sermons: Policy Instruments and Their Evaluation*. New Brunswick: Transaction Publishers, 1998.

Blonz, J. A., Vajjhala, S. P., & Safirova, E. *Growing Complexities: A Cross-sector Review of US Biofuels Policies and their Interactions*. RFF Discussion Paper. Washington, DC, Washington DC: RFF Discussion Paper, 2008.

Bobrow, D. B., & J. S. Dryzek. *Policy Analysis by Design*. Pittsburgh: University of Pittsburgh Press, 1987.

Bobrow, D. Policy design: Ubiquitous, necessary and difficult. In *Handbook of Public Policy*, edited by B. Guy Peters and J. Pierre, 75–96. Beverly Hills: Beverly Hills: SAGE, 2006.

Braathen, N. A., & Croci, E. Environmental agreements used in combination with other policy instruments. *The Handbook of Environmental Voluntary Agreements*, 43 (2005), 335–364. Dordrecht: Springer.

Braathen, N. A. Instrument mixes for environmental policy: How many stones should be used to kill a bird? *International Review of Environmental and Resource Economics*, 1, no. 2 (May 16, 2007): 185–235.

Briassoulis, H. *Policy Integration for Complex Environmental Problems*. Aldershot: Ashgate Publishing, Ltd, 2005.

Buckman, G., & Diesendorf, M. *Design Limitations in Australian Renewable Electricity Policies. Energy Policy*, 38, no. 7 (2010), 3365–3376.

Cashore, B., & Howlett, M. Punctuating what equilibrium? Institutional rigidities and thermostatic properties in Pacific Northwest forest policy dynamics. *American Journal of Political Science*, 51, no. 3 (2007), 532–551.

Chindarkar, N., Howlett, M., & Ramesh, M. Introduction to the special issue: 'Conceptualizing effective social policy design: Design spaces and capacity challenges.' *Public Administration and Development*, 37, no. 1 (February 1, 2017), 3–14. doi:10.1002/pad.1789.

Colebatch, H. K. The idea of policy design: Intention, process, outcome, meaning and validity. *Public Policy and Administration*, May 18, 2017. doi:10.1177/0952076717709525.

Considine, M. Thinking outside the box? Applying design theory to public policy. *Politics & Policy*, 40, no. 4 (2012), 704–724.

Del Rio, P., & Howlett, M. P. *Beyond the "Tinbergen Rule" in Policy Design: Matching Tools and Goals in Policy Portfolios*. SSRN Scholarly Paper. Rochester, NY: Social Science Research Network, April 8, 2013.

Del Río, P. Analysing the interactions between renewable energy promotion and energy efficiency support schemes: The impact of different instruments and design elements. *Energy Policy*, 38, no. 9 (September 2010), 4978–4989.

Doremus, H. A policy portfolio approach to biodiversity protection on private lands. *Environmental Science & Policy*, 6 (2003), 217–232.

Dryzek, J. S., & Ripley, B. The ambitions of policy Design. *Policy Studies Review*, 7, no. 4 (1988), 705–719.

Geva-May, I., & Lynn, E. L., Jr. Introduction to the launching of the journal of comparative policy analysis. *Journal of Comparative Policy Analysis: Research and Practice*, 1, no. 1 (1998), 5–8.

Gilabert, P., & Lawford-Smith, H. Political feasibility: A conceptual exploration. *Political Studies*, 60, no. 4 (2012): 809–825. doi:10.1111/j.1467-9248.2011.00936.x.

Goodspeed, R., Riseng, C., Wehrly, K., Yin, W., Mason, L., & Schoenfeldt, B. Applying design thinking methods to ecosystem management tools: Creating the great lakes aquatic habitat explorer. *Marine Policy*, 69 (July 2016): 134–145. doi:10.1016/j.marpol.2016.04.017.

Grabosky, P. N. Green markets: Environmental regulation by the private sector. *Law and Policy*, 16 no. 4 (1994), 419–448.

Grant, W. Policy instruments in the common agricultural policy. *West European Politics*, 33, no. 1 (2010), 22–38.

Gunningham, N., Grabosky, P., & Sinclair, N. *Smart Regulation: Designing Environmental Policy.* Oxford: Oxford University Press, 1988.

Head, B. W. Toward more 'evidence-informed' policy making? *Public Administration Review*, 76, no. 3 (May 1, 2016), 472–484.

Hood, C. Intellectual obsolescence and intellectual makeovers: Reflections on the tools of government after two decades. *Governance*, 20, no. 1 (2007), 127–144.

Hood, C. *The Blame Game: Spin, Bureaucracy, and Self-Preservation in Government.* Princeton: Princeton University Press, 2010.

Hood, C., & Margetts, H. Z. *The Tools of Government in the Digital Age.* Basingstoke: Palgrave Macmillan, 2007.

Hood, C. *The Tools of Government.* Chatham: Chatham House Publishers, 1986.

Howlett, M. *Designing Public Policies: Principles and Instruments.* Second Edition. New York: Routledge, 2019.

Howlett, M. From the 'old' to the 'new 'policy design: design thinking beyond markets and collaborative governance. *Policy Sciences*, 47, no. 3 (2014), 187–207.

Howlett, M., Mukherjee, I., & Woo, J. J. From tools to toolkits in policy design studies: The new design orientation towards policy formulation research. *Policy & Politics*, 43, no. 2 (2015), 292–311.

Howlett, M., & Mukherjee, I. Policy design and non-design: Towards a spectrum of policy formulation types. *Politics and Governance*, 2, no. 2 (November 13, 2014), 57–71.

Howlett, M. Beyond good and evil in policy implementation: Instrument mixes, implementation styles and second generation theories of policy instrument choice. *Policy & Society*, 23, no. 2 (2004), 1–17.

Howlett, M. Governance modes, policy regimes and operational plans: A multi-level nested model of policy instrument choice and policy design. *Policy Sciences*, 42 (2009), 73–89.

Howlett, M. P., & Mukherjee, I. Policy design and non-design: Towards a spectrum of policy formulation types. *Lee Kuan Yew School of Public Policy Research Paper*, (2014), 14–11.

Howlett, M., & Rayner, J. Patching Vs packaging in policy formulation: Assessing policy portfolio design. *Politics and Governance*, 1, no. 2 (2013): 170–182.

Howlett, M., & Lejano, R. Tales from the crypt: The rise and fall (and Re-Birth?) of policy design studies. *Administration & Society*, 45, no. 3 (2013): 356–380.

Howlett, M. Policy design: What, who, how and why? In *L'instrumentation et Ses Effets*, edited by Charlotte Halpern, Lascoumes, Pierre, and Patrick Le Gales. Paris: Presses de Sciences Po, 2014.

Howlett, M., & Mukherjee, I. *Handbook of Policy Formulation.* Cheltenham: Edward Elgar, 2017.

Howlett, M., & Mukherjee, I. The contribution of comparative policy analysis to policy design: Articulating principles of effectiveness and clarifying design spaces. *Journal of Comparative Policy Analysis: Research and Practice* 20, no. 1 (January 1, 2018): 72–87.

Howlett, M. *The Policy Design Primer: Choosing the Right Tools for the Job.* New York: Routledge, 2019.

Jordan, A., Benson, D., Zito, A., & Wurzel, R. Environmental policy: Governing by multiple policy instruments? In *Constructing a Policy State? Policy Dynamics in the EU*, edited by J. J. Richardson, 104–124. Oxford: Oxford University Press, 2012.

Jordan, A., Benson, D., Wurzel, R., & Zito, A. Policy instruments in practice. In *Oxford Handbook of Climate Change and Society*, edited by J. S. Dryzek, R. B. Norgaard, & D. Schlosberg, 536–549. Oxford: Oxford University Press, 2011.

Kagan, R. A. Adversarial legalism and American government. *Journal of Policy Analysis and Management*, 10, no. 3 (1991): 369–406.

Kagan, R. A. Editor's introduction: Understanding regulatory enforcement. *Law and Policy*, 11, no. 2 (1989): 89–119.

Kagan, R. A., Axelrad, L., Adversarial legalism: An international perspective. In *Comparative Disadvantages? Social Regulations and the Global Economy*, edited by P. S. Nivola, 146–202. Washington, DC: Brookings Institution Press, 1997.

Kern, F., & Howlett, M. Implementing transition management as policy reforms: A case study of the dutch energy sector. *Policy Science*, 42, no. 4 (2009), 391–408, 95–306.

Klijn, E.-H., Koppenjan, J. Governance network theory: Past, present and future. *Policy & Politics*, 40, no. 4 (2012), 587–606.

Knill, C. European policies: The impact of national administrative traditions. *Journal of Public Policy*, 18, no. 1 (1998), 1–28.

Knill, C. Explaining cross-national variance in administrative reform: Autonomous versus instrumental bureaucracies. *Journal of Public Policy*, 19, no. 2 (1999): 113–139.

Knill, C., & Lenschow, A. Change as 'appropriate adaptation': Administrative adjustment to european environmental policy in Britain and Germany. *European Integration Online Papers*, 2, no. 1 (1998). http://eiop.or.at/eiop/texte/1998-001.htm.

Linder, S. H., & Peters, B. G. (1984). From social theory to policy design. *Journal of Public Policy*, 4, no. 3 (1984), 237–259.

Linder, S. H., & Peters, B. G. Policy formulation and the challenge of conscious design. *Evaluation and Program Planning*, 13 (1990), 303–311.

Linder, S., & Peters, B. The logic of public policy design: Linking policy actors and plausible instruments. *Knowledge, Technology & Policy*, 4, no. 1 (March 1, 1991), 125–151.

Majone, G. On the notion of political feasibility. *European Journal of Political Research*, 3, no. 2 (1975), 259–274.

May, P. Policy design and implementation. In B. Guy Peters and J. Pierre (Eds.), *Handbook of Public Administration*, 223–233. Beverly Hills: Sage Publications, 2003.

Mayer, I., Bots, P., & van Daalen, E. Perspectives on policy analysis: A framework for understanding and design. *International Journal of Technology, Policy and Management*, 4, no. 1 (2004): 169–191.

Meltsner, A. J. Political feasibility and policy analysis. *Public Administration Review*, 32 (1972), 859–867.

Mintrom, M., & Luetjens, J. Design thinking in policymaking processes: Opportunities and challenges. *Australian Journal of Public Administration*, 75, no. 3 (September 1, 2016), 391–402. doi:10.1111/1467-8500.12211.

Peters, B. G. Conclusion: The future of instruments research. In P. Eliadis, M. Hill, & M. Howlett (Eds.). *Designing Government: From Instruments to Governance*, 353–363. Montreal: McGill-Queen's University Press, 2005.

Peters, B. G., & Pierre, J. Governance without government? Rethinking public administration. *Journal of Public Administration Research and Theory*, 8, no. 2 (1998): 223–244.

Roch, C., Pitts, D., & Navarro, I. Representative bureaucracy and policy tools: Ethnicity, student discipline, and representation in public schools. *Administration & Society*, 42, no. 1 (2010), 38–65.

Rogge, K. S., & Reichardt, K. Policy mixes for sustainability transitions: An extended concept and framework for analysis. *Research Policy*, 45, no. 8 (October 2016): 1620–1635. doi:10.1016/j.respol.2016.04.004.

Salamon, L. Rethinking public management: Third party government and the changing forms of government action. *Public Policy*, 29, no. 3 (1981): 255–275.

Salamon, L. M. The tools approach: Basic analytics. In L. S. Salamon & M. S. Lund (Eds.). *Beyond Privatization: The Tools of Government Action*, 23–50. Washington, DC: Urban Institute, 1989.

Sidney, M. S. Policy formulation: Design and tools. In *Handbook of Public Policy Analysis: Theory, Politics and Methods*, edited by F. Fischer, G. J. Miller, & M. S. Sidney, 79–87. New Brunswick, NJ: CRC Taylor & Francis, 2007.

Skodvin, T., Gullberg, A. T., & Aakre, S. Target-group influence and political feasibility: The case of climate policy design in Europe. *Journal of European Public Policy*, 17, no. 6 (2010), 854. doi:10.1080/13501763.2010.486991.

Thelen, K. *How Institutions Evolve: The Political Economy of Skills in Germany, Britain, the United States and Japan*. Cambridge: Cambridge University Press, 2004.

Trebilcock, M. J., Tuohy, C. J., & Wolfson, A. D. *Professional Regulation: A Staff Study of Accountancy, Architecture, Engineering, and Law in Ontario Prepared for the Professional Organizations Committee*. Ontario Ministry of the Attorney General, 1979.

Turnbull, N. Policy design: Its enduring appeal in a complex world and how to think it differently. *Public Policy and Administration*, (May 31, 2017). doi:10.1177/0952076717709522.

Van der Heijden, J. Institutional layering: A review of the use of the concept. *Politics*, 31, no. 1 (January 10, 2011): 9–18. doi:10.1111/j.1467-9256.2010.01397.x.

Weaver, K. *If You Build It, Will They Come? Overcoming Unforeseen Obstacles to Program Effectiveness*. The Tansley Lecture – University of Saskatchewan, 2009a.

Weaver, K. *Target Compliance: The Final Frontier of Policy Implementation.* Washington, DC: Brookings Institution, 2009b.

Woodside, K. Policy instruments and the study of public policy. *Canadian Journal of Political Science,* 19, no. 4(1986), 775–793.

Wu, X., Ramesh, M., & Howlett, M. Policy capacity: A conceptual framework for understanding policy competences and capabilities. *Policy and Society,* Special Issue on The Dynamics of Policy Capacity, 34, no. 3–4 (September 2015): 165–171. doi:10.1016/j.polsoc.2015.09.001.

Yi, H., & Feiock, R. C. Policy tool interactions and the adoption of state renewable portfolio standards. *Review of Policy Research,* 29, no. 2 (March 1, 2012): 193–206.

Part 3
The Classics: Policy Sectors in Comparative Policy Analysis Studies

Translating Monetary Inputs into Health Care Provision: A Comparative Analysis of the Impact of Different Modes of Public Policy

CLAUS WENDT and JÜRGEN KOHL

ABSTRACT *This article investigates different modes of public policy in health care and their impact on health care financing and health service provision. In order to investigate the relationship between health expenditure and health service provision, we construct an "index of health care providers". The empirical analysis of expenditure and this index demonstrates that there is only a weak correspondence between the level of total health expenditure and the number of health service providers in OECD countries. Different modes of health policy can help to explain why some countries are more successful in translating monetary inputs into health care personnel than other countries. Our results indicate that policies which favor self-regulation by non-governmental actors (as in Germany) lead in general to high levels of health care providers at above OECD average health expenditure. Policies which favor direct state control (as in the United Kingdom), on the other hand, are characterized by lower levels of health care providers and below average health expenditure. Policies which favor market elements are more difficult to categorize. However, it is noteworthy that especially countries that give market mechanisms higher priority than other countries (as the United States) offer below average numbers of health care providers at comparatively high total health care costs.*

Introduction

Health care systems in advanced welfare states are facing major challenges. The most notable pressures are related to the processes of economic globalization, socio-demographic change, and persistent unemployment. More specifically, due to medical-technical innovations the scope for medical treatment has been expanding continuously while the financial resources have reached their limits to grow in most OECD countries. Reforms aiming at retrenchment or recalibration in health care systems have been widespread in recent years (Marmor et al. 2005).

In this paper, we analyze the impact of public policies on the level and structure of health care financing and service provision in OECD countries. While there are numerous cross-national studies of financing and expenditure (e.g. Culyer 1990, Schieber and Poullier 1990, Evans 1996, Jönsson and Musgrove 1997, Chinitz et al. 1998, Kanavos and McKee 1998), and of health service provision (e.g. McPherson 1990, Hsiao 1995, Freeman 2000, Figueras et al. 2004, Wendt and Thompson 2004), the comparative analysis of public policies is a more recent topic in health care system research.

Tuohy (2003), for instance, differentiates between "agency", "contract", and "networks" as modes of governance in the health care arena, and Rico et al. (2003) draw a distinction between "market", "hierarchy", and "networks". Based on these and further concepts (see Marmor and Okma 1998, Moran 1999, 2000, Bambra 2005, Rothgang et al. 2005, Burau and Blank 2006), we suggest three (ideal) types of public policies with regard to health care:

- policies that favor direct public control of health care financing and service provision;
- policies that favor self-regulation by non-governmental actors;
- and policies that favor market mechanisms.

These policies have been discussed in a similar way by Giaimo and Manow (1999), who distinguish between a "state-led", a "corporatist-governed", and a "market-driven" health care system. There are also similarities to the components of the "institutional mix" (hierarchy, market and collegiality) in health care systems as defined by Tuohy (2009). The main difference between the three modes of public policy and Tuohy's concept is our focus on self-regulation by non-governmental actors (including doctors) while Tuohy concentrates on collegiality between doctors and pays less attention to other non-governmental influences.

In line with Tuohy, however, we are aware that these types never exist in pure form, but that existing health care systems typically represent mixes of direct public control, self-regulation, and market elements. Grouping countries under the same category, therefore, only means that the respective mode of public policy is given higher priority than the two alternative ones. The more specific question of this paper is how the financing of health care systems and the provision of health care services is affected by the (dominant) mode of public policy.

The paper analyzes health expenditure and service provision in 25 OECD countries.[1] Within the limits of this paper, however, it is not possible to provide detailed information on public policies in the "health care arena" (Tuohy 2003) for such a large number of countries. We therefore select three countries for closer scrutiny, each representing one of the three types of public policy. While the United Kingdom is still a good example of state hierarchy and Germany contains strong self-regulatory elements, cases that represent the mode of public policy that favors market mechanisms are more ambiguous. However, a wide range of authors agree that the US health care system is dominated by consumer choice and market competition to a higher degree than other OECD countries (Marmor et al. 1992, Hsiao 1995, Giaimo and Manow 1999, Hacker 2002, 2004, Tuohy 2003, Rothgang et al. 2005). Following their arguments, we take the US case not as an example for a pure "private market model" but for a mode of public policy that favors market solutions in the health care arena to a greater extent than alternative public policies. This "embedded design" offers us the opportunity to combine a quantitative analysis of health care financing and service provision in a larger number of countries with a more qualitative analysis of health reform processes in some "paradigmatic" cases: the UK, Germany, and the US.

After discussing recent policy developments in these three countries, we examine the financing of health care services in section three. Discussing both the respective mode of public policy and the method of financing, we explore how these factors may influence the development of total health expenditures. In section four, we investigate how the respective mode of public policy may influence the number of health care providers. Is the level of health employment related to the level and structure (the public/private mix) of health care financing? And which mode of public policy is more successful in translating monetary inputs into health care services? To analyze these questions, we construct an "index of health care providers" which provides us with more comprehensive information on the "input side" of health care systems than, for instance, the number of total health employment or the number of doctors.

Keeping in mind that health systems always incorporate a mix of public policy elements and that we only focus on the predominant one, our analysis is guided by the following hypotheses:

H1: Public policies that favor direct public control of health expenditure and service provision are in general more successful in keeping health care costs under control, a success, however, that might be achieved at the expense of the quality and quantity of health care services.

H2: Self-regulation, on the other hand, is likely to promote high volume and high quality health care – due to the direct involvement of service providers. In such a system, the state is responsible for the legislative framework, but has only limited direct means for stabilizing health expenditure.

H3: Market mechanisms also set incentives for suppliers to offer high-quality health care services. However, since the access to these services – at least partly – depends on the ability to pay for them, the health care services actually provided (and thus the number of providers) may be lower than in self-regulated systems. The capacity of the state to control health care costs, moreover, is particularly low.

Modes of Public Policy in the Health Care Arena

The process of producing health care services can be conceptualized in the following way (see Figure 1): "Monetary inputs" (health expenditure) are transformed into "real inputs" (health care personnel, facilities), and these, in turn, are used to generate "real outputs" (number of doctor/patient contacts, medical treatments of various kinds). The variety of health services is then evaluated by the population which results in certain levels of subjective satisfaction. In the context of this paper, we concentrate on the question how "monetary inputs" are translated into "real inputs" (health service providers) as well as the potential impact of health policies on this process. Questions regarding the output side and the evaluation of the output (or other indicators for the quality of health care services) will not be dealt with in this essay.[2] While indicators of health care provision like the ones we use are sometimes considered as objective indicators of health care quality, we would like to insist upon the difference between "real inputs" and "real outputs". In our view, the number of doctors and other medical personnel and the number of medical facilities are the "production factors" which may be combined in various ways to produce services which meet the needs and demands of the citizens.

In the following we discuss health policy measures by taking the examples of the US, the UK, and Germany where different modes of public policy are predominant. Thus, our country sample includes a hierarchical, a self-regulated, and a market-oriented health care system, even if we admit that our "ideal-typical" approach does not fit the empirical reality of these countries in all respects.

The British National Health Service (NHS) can be taken as an example of a mode of public policy where direct control over the health care system has for many years been concentrated at the national level. The central cost control system was even strengthened by the introduction of cash limits in 1980. From the early 1990s onwards, however, the establishment of "internal markets" reduced direct state control and increased competition between service providers for contracts with purchasers (Powell 2003). The purchaser/provider split and the set-up of GP (general practitioner) fundholding schemes, Hospital Trusts and, later, Primary Care Trusts (PCTs) (Ham 2004) strengthened not only the autonomy of smaller NHS units with regard to the allocation of resources but also their competencies in further areas of the British health care system. The central government, for instance, still controls the number and location of GPs, but state restrictions were eased by the introduction of

Figure 1. The "production process" of health care services

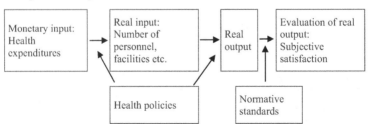

Source: Kohl and Wendt 2004: 326.

fundholding models and Primary Care Trusts. Within PCTs, today not only GPs but also specialists and further health personnel can be employed on a salary basis (Grimmeisen 2009). Responsibilities regarding the access of service providers to the "health care market" and the method of remuneration have therefore partly shifted from the central government level to local units. As Freeman and Moran (2000) argue, these and further changes accumulated to a process of devolution where Primary Care Trusts, Hospital Trusts and further units have been given a higher degree of responsibility and autonomy. PCTs, established in 2001, gained control over 75% of the NHS budget and, initially serving at average a population of about 200,000, are responsible for the full range of health care services for the respective population (Ham 2004, Grimmeisen 2009). Within these units co-operation between service providers is of major importance so that the utilization of market-style elements has lost ground. To put it in the words of Freeman and Moran (2000: 55):

> Competition... perhaps the signal term in the international discourse of reform, may well turn out to have been one of the more transient. In the UK, where it was promoted most vigorously, and in Sweden, competition has turned relatively quickly into collaboration between larger units with more clearly defined functions of planning and providing care.

Processes of devolution have also taken place in other NHS systems as, for instance, in Denmark, Finland, Sweden or Spain. The reduction of direct control by national governments and the strengthening of responsibilities at the regional or local level seem to represent a more general trend in NHS systems.

Social Health Insurance (SHI) systems, on the other hand, can be characterized by a high level of self-regulation. In Germany, sickness funds and doctors' associations traditionally negotiate on the budget and conditions for health care provision. These and further actors sought to be powerful veto players, what has been a major reason why structural reforms could successfully be blocked in Germany for many years (Wendt 2006). From the early 1990s onwards the self-regulatory core came under pressure from two sides, bringing a remarkably stable development (Tuohy 2009) to an end. The state has improved its capacity for direct intervention, and at the same time market mechanisms have been introduced, as some commentators argue, to bypass established veto positions (Giaimo and Manow 1999, Tuohy 1999, Giaimo 2002, Wendt 2006). These market elements were different from those implemented in NHS systems since in SHI systems a separation between purchasers and providers exists almost by definition (Freeman 2000). In contrast to NHS systems, this process also included the funding side, and in some SHI systems (e.g. Germany, Netherlands) competition between sickness funds has been extended in the belief that this would increase both efficiency and quality (Busse *et al.* 2004).

While in Germany for many years the overall budget was set by negotiations between associations of sickness funds and associations of panel doctors, sectoral budgets (for out-patient, in-patient, and pharmaceutical health care) have been introduced by the federal government in 1993. In 1997, free choice of sickness funds has been extended to almost the whole insured population. The launch of competition between sickness funds and the introduction of a corresponding risk-adjustment mechanism for the first time introduced competition as a co-ordinating mechanism in its own right (Wendt et al. 2005). In this way, stronger state intervention has been complemented by a greater importance of market mechanisms. In other SHI systems, as for instance in Austria, direct state intervention is even stronger since social insurance contribution rates are set by the government and not, as in Germany, by the self-administration of sickness funds. Further examples for an increase of state intervention in the German SHI scheme are the introduction of a flat-rate component for the remuneration of GPs (traditionally paid on a fee-for-service basis), a tightening of the conditions for panel doctors to enter the health care market, and a strengthening of GPs' "gatekeeping role" by financial incentives. Other SHI schemes experienced similar changes. The French social health insurance, for instance, which is traditionally characterized by a high degree of centralization, experienced a further strengthening of the role of the state, especially with regard to the setting of global budgets (Hassenteufel and Palier 2007). Germany not only sought to increase macro-economic control over costs, but also improved possibilities to negotiate individual contracts between purchasers and providers and thereby increased competition between sickness funds. Until now, however, health units that are comparable to the British PCTs, e.g. local health clinics or doctors' networks, have not been established in great numbers in SHI schemes.

The US health care system gives more scope to markets than other OECD health care systems. However, far from being a pure "private market model" it combines social insurance elements (Medicare), means-tested programs (Medicaid), private insurance, and direct private out-of-pocket payments. Private health insurance, which is (often in the form of a company-based plan) for most Americans the first line of protection against the risk of medical costs and today provides collective coverage for about 70% of the US population is heavily regulated by the state. However, since the 1960s public programs such as Medicare and Medicaid have become increasingly important and today cover about 25% of the population. Since private insurance, too, is heavily tax subsidized, about half of total health expenditure is financed out of public funds (Moran 2000, Cacace 2009). Especially private out-of-pocket financing has been reduced from 48.5% of total health expenditure in 1960 to 13.2% in 2005 (OECD Health Data 2006). At the same time more than 17% of the US population below the age of 65 are today without coverage by private insurance or by public schemes in the case of sickness (White 2007).[3] Thus, public policies with strong emphasis on private solutions leave room for the exclusion of larger groups of the society from access to health care (Hacker 2004), even if health care services are primarily financed out of the public purse.

While NHS and SHI systems introduced market elements, the US health care system experienced a stronger emphasis of hierarchical co-ordination within "managed care" plans, and particularly in Health Maintenance Organizations (HMOs). From the late 1980s and early 1990s onwards, the federal government has been actively encouraging Medicare beneficiaries to receive their health care through managed care organizations, and the states also started to shift Medicaid recipients into managed care plans (Patel and Rushefsky 1999). As a result of this process, physicians, traditionally paid on a fee-for-service basis, were confronted with new models of remuneration. Depending on the respective managed care scheme, primary care physicians and specialists may now either be paid on a salary basis, a capitation fee, or a (discounted) fee-for-service. Also, patients' choices of service providers have been restricted in various ways. In managed care, the choice is generally limited to a pre-selected network of service providers. While in HMOs, enrolees have no choice of provider and receive access to specialists only through the primary care provider, in preferred provider organizations (PPOs), members may choose to opt out of the network of providers but at the cost of higher private co-payments. In case of point-of-service (POS) plans there is a primary care provider as gatekeeper, and members have also the freedom to opt out when choosing higher co-payments (Newbrander and Eichler 2001).

Since the late 1980s conventional indemnity coverage nearly disappeared from the field of private insurance. While in the beginning the more restrictive and hierarchical HMOs gained the largest market share, from the mid-1990s onwards the more flexible and less hierarchical PPOs grew more quickly. By 2005, about 61% of all privately insured persons were enrolled in PPO plans and only 21% in HMO plans (White 2007). Market forces thus generated not only "an explosive growth of complex contracting arrangements" (Tuohy 2009), but within this system less hierarchical managed care plans (PPOs) with fewer constraints on doctors and patients have gained greater market shares than more tightly regulated managed care plans (HMOs) (White 2007).

These examples from the three selected countries suggest that health policies are increasingly oriented towards adopting "best practices" even when the respective solutions are beyond the traditional paths of reform. Other comparative studies (Moran 1999, Freeman 2000, Giaimo 2002, Rico et al. 2003, Kangas 2004, Wendt et al. 2005) have also indicated a convergence of the way in which different health care systems are regulated. Despite these changes the three types have demonstrated remarkable stability, and health policy measures that have been adopted from other types of health care systems have been attenuated and adjusted to the overall institutional and structural characteristics of the "receiving" system (Tuohy 2009). Even if modes of public policy have become more similar in recent years, the UK, Germany, and the US therefore still represent three distinct types of health care systems. In the following sections, we analyze whether these modes of public policy are mirrored in levels of expenditure and service provision. By including further OECD countries we try to detect whether countries following similar public policies show similar patterns with regard to health expenditure and health care provision.

Health Expenditure and Health Care Financing

The control of health care expenditures seems to be a perennial problem in all types of health care systems (Jönsson and Musgrove 1997, Chinitz et al. 1998, Kanavos and McKee 1998, Marmor et al. 2005). There are both demand-side and supply-side reasons why health care expenditures are accounting for an ever growing share of GDP. On the demand side, these reasons include new diseases as HIV/AIDS (Steffen 2005), population aging (with more expensive health needs), and a growing demand for health services in affluent societies in general ("health" as a "superior good"). On the supply side, reasons include the labor-intensive character of health services which are not easily amenable to productivity gains, and medical and technological progress which leads to cost-intensive treatment of ever more diseases. However, while these factors are general trends affecting more or less all advanced health care systems alike, it is an important policy question whether some health systems are better able to control health expenditure development than others.

In Figure 2, we see an average increase of total health expenditures in OECD countries from 5.3% of GDP in 1970 to 9.6% of GDP in 2005. That is, the share of health care expenditures in GDP has risen by more than 80% of its initial level during that period, thereby crowding out other expenditure items. This analysis shows that the British NHS has been the most successful in controlling health care costs. The German SHI scheme also managed to stabilize total health expenditure (in percentage of GDP) in the period after the oil price shocks of the 1970s. Following German unification in 1990, however, total health expenditure reached its highest level so far. Compared to the mainly publicly financed types, the market-oriented US health care system experienced a virtual explosion of health care costs – in contrast to the claim often made that market mechanisms would contribute to more competition among service providers and thereby exert more control on costs. Until 2005, total health financing has risen to more than 15% of GDP and thereby doubled its initial level in 1970. As a result of the much more pronounced expenditure increase in the US, a growing divergence between the three health care systems with regard to total expenditure development becomes apparent.

According to Alber (1988), in periods of welfare state expansion health expenditures increase in all types of health care systems. In periods of cost containment, however, NHS systems with higher interventionist power of the state

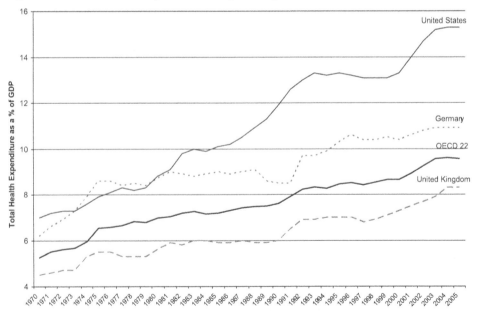

Figure 2. Total health care expenditure as a percentage of GDP, 1970–2005

Notes: Germany: data until 1990 are for West Germany and from 1992 onwards for United Germany. CEE countries have been excluded since data are only available from 1990 onwards.
Source: OECD 2006.

are in general more effective in controlling the increase of health care costs than either SHI systems or market-based systems.

The hypothesis that publicly financed systems have a greater potential for cost containment is supported when we correlate the share of public health financing[4] with total health expenditure (in percentage of GDP) (see Table 1, Figures 3 and 4). While in 1970 there is almost no correlation, in 2003 we find a strong negative

Table 1. Correlations of public health expenditure (PHE) and total health expenditure (THE)

	Pearson's R	N
Public Health Expenditure (in % of THE) and Total Health Expenditure (in % of GDP), 1970	−0.15	18
Public Health Expenditure (in % of THE) and Total Health Expenditure (in % of GDP), 2003	−0.67**	25
Public Health Expenditure (in % of THE) and Total Health Expenditure (in % of GDP), 2003 (only countries included for which 1970 data are available)	−0.66**	18

Notes: **$p < 0.05$, *$p < 0.1$.
Source: OECD 2006; own calculation.

Figure 3. Total health care expenditure as a percentage of GDP and public share of total health expenditure, 1970

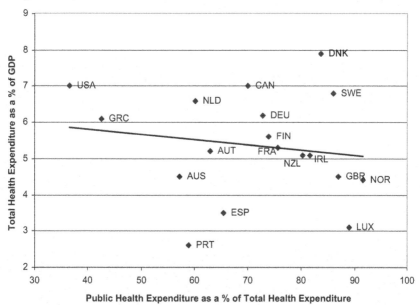

Notes: Abbreviations are as follows: AUS: Australia, AUT: Austria; BEL: Belgium; CAN: Canada; DNK: Denmark; FIN: Finland; FRA: France; DEU: Germany; GRC: Greece; IRL: Ireland; ITA: Italy; LUX: Luxembourg; NLD: Netherlands; NZL: New Zealand; NOR: Norway; PRT: Portugal; ESP: Spain; SWE: Sweden; CHE: Switzerland; GBR: United Kingdom; USA: United States. Data for Belgium, Italy, and Switzerland are missing.
Source: OECD 2006.

Figure 4. Total health expenditure as a percentage of GDP and public share of total health expenditure, 2003

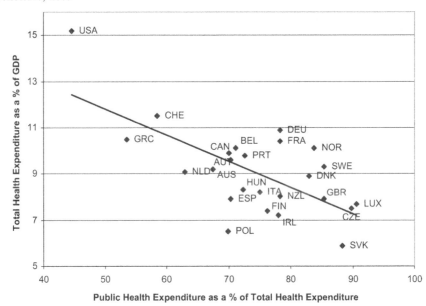

Notes: For 2003, data for CEE countries have been included (abbreviations are: CZE: Czech Republic; HUN: Hungary; POL: Poland; SVK: Slovak Republic); the correlation (r = –0.66) is at a similar level when excluding CEE countries (see Table 1).
Source: OECD 2006.

correlation of r = −0.67 (even when excluding the US case, the correlation is at r = −0.48) (see as well Tuohy et al. 2004).

Therefore, the more a health care system is financed out of private sources, the higher is the *level* of total health care expenditure (in percentage of GDP) and also the *increase* in total health care spending (Rothgang et al. 2005). This indicates that public agencies – by regulation and/or as purchasers of health care services – can control health care costs more effectively than market forces. However, while state regulation may be able to slow down the increase of health expenditures, examples for a reduction of an already achieved level of health care costs are very rare (Wendt and Thompson 2004; Tuohy 2009).

Even if no clear country groups can be identified, "mature" NHS systems (Finland, New Zealand, UK, Denmark, and Sweden) are in general more successful in keeping health care costs under control than later developed NHS schemes (Greece, Portugal). Early developed social insurance systems (Germany, France, Belgium, and Austria), on the other hand, allow a higher share of private funding and consume in general a higher share of the GDP than NHS systems. The new social insurance systems in CEE countries are currently characterized by higher shares of public funding and lower levels of total health expenditure. Those health care systems where a large part of the health care budget is funded out of private sources (Switzerland and the US) also consume the largest share of GDP.

The brief discussion of health policies in the UK, Germany, and the US provides some first arguments for the different potential in keeping total health care costs under control. In the UK, for the whole period under consideration, total health expenditure as a share of GDP remained below the OECD average, a fact that can be considered to be highly related to the centralized planning and control system of the British NHS. With the introduction of internal markets into the British NHS, total health expenditure increased at a *higher* rate than in previous years. In the German SHI system, total health care costs are well above the OECD mean. In spite of the large number of cost control measures by the German government since the late 1970s, total health care expenditure (as a share of GDP) today is the third highest in the OECD world. The system of negotiations between sickness funds and service providers seems not to be able to establish effective cost control mechanisms, a deficit that became obvious in the years following German unification when health care costs increased from 8.5% of GDP in 1990 to 10.6% of GDP in 1996. In the 1990s, the federal government intervened directly in the corporatist self-regulating structure by introducing, among other things, a (partly) flat-rate payment system for family doctors and fixed budgets for drug prescriptions (Health Care Structure Act 1993). Furthermore, the ability of sickness funds to determine contribution rates autonomously was restricted by the same act and by further acts in 1997 and 2003. In the late 1990s, total health care financing remained more or less at the same level, indicating that direct state intervention has been (partly) effective. Other examples point in a similar direction. In the Austrian SHI system, for instance, contribution rates are set by state agencies (not by sickness funds as was the case in Germany until 2009!), leading to a level of total health expenditure below the OECD average.

The high level of total health expenditure in the US (more than 15% of GDP, nearly 6 percentage points above OECD average) provides strong arguments that a high share of private financing – in combination with a low level of state intervention – opens the door for disproportionate cost increases. In line with this proposition, we find the third highest share of private funding in Switzerland where health care expenditure ranks second in the OECD world. In the US system, the process of cost increase has only leveled off during the 1990s. In this period, managed care settings which allow for a higher degree of control towards providers (with respect to remuneration systems), such as HMOs, have become more and more important. However, this seems to have had only a temporary effect, for since 2000 total health expenditure is again surging. One possible reason for this development is that coverage by HMOs decreased while the market share of managed care plans with less restrictive cost control mechanisms (such as PPOs) increased. According to White (2007: 418), for a short period "managed care" has been successful in driving down prices by selective contracting but "failed when the providers developed sufficient market power to resist".

Health Service Provision

While in most countries cost containment of health *expenditure* is the main focus of reforms, the production side of health *services* is often neglected in the health policy debate. Focusing exclusively on health expenditures, however, misses the point of what health policy is all about. Neither maximizing nor minimizing health expenditures is a reasonable policy goal in itself. High levels of health expenditure only make sense under the assumption that these monetary inputs are efficiently converted into real inputs (such as medical facilities and personnel) and finally into real outputs. Likewise, containing or reducing health expenditure would not make much sense if it were tied to cuts in real resources and/or in the quality of services. It only makes sense under the opposite assumption that it is *not* accompanied by a proportionate reduction in the quantity and/or quality of services. The real challenge of health policy is, therefore, to make effective use of (monetary and real) resources in order to provide medical and social services meeting the needs and demands of citizens.

The neglect of service provision in comparative studies is probably related to the difficulties of measuring the level and/or quality of health services. Alber (1988), for example, used as indicators for the "quality of health care" the density of medical doctors and hospital beds in OECD countries. Compared with these input indicators, the "quality of health service index" developed by Kangas (1994), is more complex and takes into account the earnings replacement ratio of sickness benefits, the coverage rates of health care systems, the number of waiting days, and the length of the contribution period required for the access to benefits. However, while this index covers essential "social rights" elements of health (insurance) systems, it does not directly measure the availability and quality of health services. For a comparison of the *level* of health care provision further or, more precisely, different health care indicators have to be included.

In order to investigate the relationship between health care expenditure and health service provision, we constructed an "index of health care providers" (for an earlier version see Kohl and Wendt 2004: 323ff.).[5] By using factor analysis (see note to Table 2) we selected two indicators for specialist health care (specialists and hospital nurses), one indicator for primary health care (general practitioners), and one indicator for pharmaceutical health care (pharmacists). We aggregated these indicators into an index of health care providers in the following way: first, the raw values for the various indicators, expressed per 1,000 of population, were standardized and recalculated as percentages of the OECD 25 average (=100). Our index was then calculated as the average value for all four health provider indicators. All indicators are weighted equally, thus giving in-patient health care (specialists and nurses) and out-patient health care (GPs and pharmacists) the same importance.

Comparing the index of health care providers with the level of health expenditure (in percent of GDP), we find only a weak correlation ($r = 0.26$) with a wide dispersion (see Table 3 and Figure 5). Some countries, such as, for instance, Finland or Luxembourg are able to provide an above average level of health service providers with below average health care spending while in other countries, such as the US or Switzerland, the coverage by health service providers is only about the OECD average, despite high levels of health care spending.

Inasmuch as our index is an adequate measure of "real inputs" to the health care system, the former group of countries can be said to have more effectively transformed their monetary inputs into "real inputs" and thus to have achieved a superior policy path compared to the latter group of countries. Notably the US with by far the highest level of health expenditure barely reaches an average level with regard to our index of health care providers. Austria, on the other hand, only spends

Table 2. Indicators of health care providers (per 1,000 population), 2003

	Practicing specialists	Practicing nurses	General practitioners	Practicing pharmacists	Index of health care providers
Australia	1.2	10.4	1.4	0.8	117.0
Austria	2.0	9.4	1.4	0.6	118.7
Belgium	1.9	5.8	2.1	1.2	148.8
Canada	1.1	9.8	1.0	0.7	98.1
Czech Republic	2.8	8.0	0.7	0.5	100.9
Denmark	1.3	7.0	0.7	0.6	80.3
Finland	1.4	7.3	0.7	1.5	113.0
France	1.7	7.3	1.6	1.1	131.4
Germany	2.3	9.7	1.0	0.6	111.4
Greece	3.3	3.8	0.3	0.8	93.7
Hungary	2.0	8.6	0.7	0.5	91.4
Ireland	0.6	14.8	0.5	0.9	96.7
Italy	2.4	5.4	0.9	1.2	117.6
Luxembourg	1.8	12.3	0.9	0.8	115.5
Netherlands	0.9	13.9	0.5	0.2	74.7
New Zealand	0.7	9.1	0.7	0.8	84.6
Norway	1.9	14.4	0.7	0.4	103.2
Poland	2.1	4.9	0.1	0.7	70.4
Portugal	1.9	4.2	0.5	0.9	84.7
Slovak Republic	2.3	6.5	0.4	0.5	80.3
Spain	1.5	7.5	0.7	0.9	94.7
Sweden	1.8	10.3	0.6	0.7	97.1
Switzerland	2.5	10.7	0.5	0.5	98.3
United Kingdom	1.5	9.1	0.7	0.5	85.8
United States	1.4	7.9	1.0	0.7	96.9
OECD 25 Mean	**1.77**	**8.72**	**0.81**	**0.74**	**100.0**

Notes: In a first step we included all available OECD data on health care personnel in our analysis (specialists, nurses, GPs, dentists, pharmacists). The result of an unrotated principal component factor analysis was that two factors accounted for 64% of the variance of the included variables. However, the uniqueness of dentists turned out to be comparatively high. Therefore, we calculated a second model without dentists. In this model, two factors accounted for 75% of the variance. The first factor captures in-patient health care with a negative correlation between specialists and nurses. The second factor accounts for out-patient health care with a positive correlation between GPs and pharmacists. Based on the factor analysis we decided to use specialists, nurses, GPs, and pharmacists for the creation of the "Index of Health Service Providers".
Sources: OECD 2006; own calculation.

about the OECD average for health care (i.e. 5% of GDP less than the US), but is able to achieve a higher ranking with regard to health care provision.

Our analysis of the financing dimension has shown that the level of total health care spending is negatively correlated with the share of public financing: the higher the share of public financing, the lower the level of total health expenditure. In the service dimension, however, no such relationship can be detected. The index of health care providers shows no correlation with the public share of health care financing (see Figure 6). We find, for instance, countries with a high public share of the health care budget that maintain a below average supply of health care providers

Table 3. Correlations between health expenditure and health service providers, 2003

	Pearson's R	N
Total health expenditure (as a % of GDP) and index of health care providers	0.26	25
Total health expenditure (in US$ per capita) and index of health care providers	0.39*	25
Public share of total health expenditure and index of health care providers	0.04	25
Total health expenditure (as a % of GDP) and GPs per 1,000 population	0.35*	25
Total health expenditure (in US$ per capita) and GPs per 1,000 population	0.40**	25
Public share of total health expenditure and GPs per 1,000 population	−0.03	25

Notes: **p < 0.05, *p < 0.1.
Since GPs are in general the first point of contact for patients and often decide on medical treatments provided by further health care providers we additionally calculated the effect of the level and structure (the public–private mix) of health care financing on the number of GPs. The correlation between total health expenditure and the number of GPs is slightly higher than with regard to the "index of health care providers". However, the factor analysis has shown that GPs (together with pharmacists) are loading on another factor than specialists and nurses (see annotation in Table 2). This indicates that the number of GPs is not a sufficient predictor for the "real input" in health care systems and that, therefore, information on inpatient/specialist health care have to be added.
Sources: OECD 2006; own calculation.

Figure 5. Total health expenditure as a percentage of GDP and index of health care providers, 2003

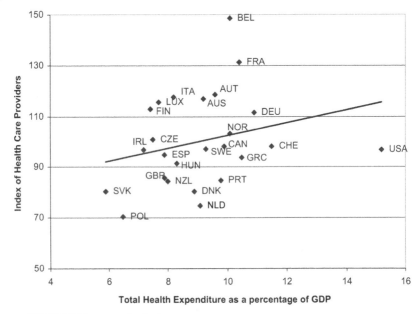

Sources: OECD 2006; own calculation.

(like the UK, Ireland, or New Zealand) and also cases with above average numbers of health care providers (Luxembourg, Germany, or France). Some countries with a lower share of public financing are able to provide a health care package well above

Figure 6. Public share of total health expenditure and index of health care providers, 2003

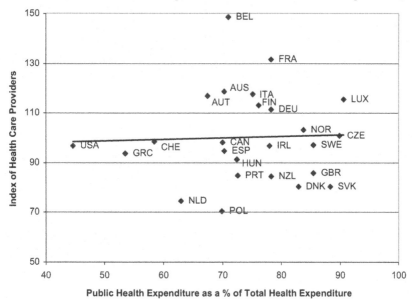

Sources: OECD 2006; own calculation.

the OECD 25 mean (such as Belgium or Austria) while others offer a below average level of health care providers (Netherlands, Switzerland, Greece, United States).

This seemingly inconsistent pattern may be explained in the following way: total health expenditure is apparently more important in determining the level of health service providers than is the public share of health care financing. Since countries with a high public share of financing are better able to control overall health care spending (negative correlation), one would expect that lower expenditure levels in these countries might lead to lower employment in the health care sector. This, however, is not the case. Despite lower expenditure levels, a high share of public financing enables them to maintain numbers of health service providers which are, on average, similar to the level in countries with a low share of public financing (and a higher level of total expenditures).

When grouping OECD health care systems according to their level of total health expenditure and their level of health care providers (see Table 4) we find some support for our hypotheses H1–H3 introduced in the first section. The combination of both high levels of total health expenditure and health care providers is characteristic of SHI schemes. However, the NHS systems of Norway (with a level of health care providers close to the OECD average) and Australia (with health expenditure near the OECD average) are also placed in this field. The German case demonstrates that even if direct state intervention has increased and at the same time market mechanisms have been given greater emphasis (Giaimo and Manow 1999, Tuohy 1999, Giaimo 2002, Wendt 2006) the actors of the traditional self-regulatory system seem still to be able to assert a high level of health care providers at comparatively high costs.

Table 4. Relative level of health expenditures and index of health care providers, 2003

Relative level of health expenditures (in % of GDP)	Index of health care providers					
	Above average (>100)			Below average (<100)		
Above average (>9.08%)	Germany	10.9	111.4	United States	15.2	96.9
	France	10.4	131.4	Switzerland	11.5	98.3
	Belgium	10.1	148.8	Greece	10.5	93.7
	Norway	10.1	103.2	Canada	9.9	98.1
	Austria	9.6	118.7	Portugal	9.8	84.7
	Australia	9.2	117.0	Sweden	9.3	97.1
				Netherlands	9.1	74.7
Below average (<9.08%)	Italy	8.2	117.6	Denmark	8.9	80.3
	Luxembourg	7.7	115.5	Hungary	8.3	91.4
	Czech Republic	7.5	100.9	New Zealand	8.0	84.6
	Finland	7.4	113.0	Spain	7.9	94.7
				United Kingdom	**7.9**	**85.8**
				Ireland	7.2	96.7
				Poland	6.5	70.4
				Slovak Republic	5.9	80.3

Sources: OECD 2006; own calculation.

A lower level of health care providers at below average costs is, in line with our hypothesis H1, typical for NHS systems. Although market mechanisms have been introduced and health expenditure increased from the early 1990s onwards, neither the costs nor the level of health care providers in the United Kingdom have exceeded the OECD average. Not only NHS type countries but also SHI type countries of Central and Eastern Europe are represented in this cluster.

The unfavourable combination of high costs and low levels of service providers is shared by private health insurance schemes, some SHI schemes, and some NHS systems alike. It has to be emphasized, however, that especially countries with a high share of private health financing are characterized by this pattern. The Netherlands, Switzerland, and especially the United States rely to a large extent on private funding which in general restricts access to health care services. In particular patients in Greece and Portugal are charged a relatively high amount of private out-of-pocket payments, and therefore access to health care is more difficult for lower income groups or people with a poor health status in these countries. However, this does not apply for all countries of this group. Canada, for instance, has relatively low private co-payments and therefore the above average level of total health expenditure associated with the below average level of the health care provider index (which might be related to weaker self-regulatory capacities) needs some further investigation.

Above average health care costs with a comparatively low level of health employment may be partly explained by the price of health services or, more specifically, to the remuneration of health professionals. According to White (2007: 401), especially market oriented health care systems "should impose fewer institutional constraints on income maximization and also create fewer social obstacles (such as norms of restraint) to that behavior". In line with this argument, the United States and the Netherlands are characterized by high income levels of (self-employed) general practitioners and specialists (OECD 2005). The favorable income position of health professionals in these countries indicates that health care systems where private health insurance is of great financial and structural importance also tend to support the market power of suppliers (Moran 2000, White 2007). High remuneration levels of service providers contribute to high health care costs but do not necessarily result in superior levels of health care providers. But cases like the Swedish one that exhibits a below average level of health service providers despite restricted income chances for doctors show that we need further information to fully understand the "production process" in health care systems and especially how high levels of health care providers can be achieved without dramatic cost increases in health care systems.

Finally, it should be emphasized that high levels of health care providers do not necessarily result in good quality health care nor in high levels of citizens' satisfaction with the health care system. There is a fair chance, however, that better health care services can be provided with a sufficient number of qualified health care personnel, and that better health care services will be reflected in higher levels of citizens' satisfaction (Kohl and Wendt 2004, Marmor *et al.* 2006, Tuohy 2009).

Discussion

As our empirical analysis has demonstrated, the mode of public policy matters above all with regard to health expenditure development. There can be no doubt that the market-oriented US system shows the highest level and the most dramatic increases of total health expenditures. The self-regulated German SHI scheme also faces major problems in stabilizing health care costs. The example of the Austrian health care system, however, demonstrates that a SHI system with a higher level of state intervention can also implement effective cost control mechanisms. Finally, the British NHS system proved to be most successful in keeping relative health expenditures (in percentage of GDP) in check. Overall, there is a fairly strong negative correlation between the public share of health care financing and total health expenditure in 2003 which can be taken as evidence that the stronger interventionist and regulatory powers of the state are more effective in controlling health care costs than competitive market mechanisms. As the US example demonstrates, cost control requires effective limits on prices and therefore on income chances. In this regard, selective contracting by multiple purchasers has turned out not to be effective (White 2007).

The main focus of this article, however, is not on cost control in general but on the relation between monetary inputs and levels of health care services. In order to measure the input of real resources to health care systems more accurately, we constructed an "index of health care providers". The correlation between relative health expenditure levels (in percentage of GDP) and the index of health care providers in 2003 turned out to be very low. This seemingly negative finding can be interpreted as evidence that high expenditures for health care do not necessarily translate into a better provision of services, but are mediated by public policies. The more general observation is that the "high cost/high provider index" combination is typical for social health insurance schemes, including the German case. The "low cost/low provider index" combination is more prevalent in NHS, including the UK case. SHI systems of CEE countries are also grouped in this cluster which is possibly related not only to severe budgetary restrictions, but also to the still existing strength of the state and the weakness of the collective actors of the self-regulatory system in these countries. The unfavorable "high cost/low provider index" combination, finally, is represented especially by countries with high shares of private funding, including in particular the US case.

A closer analysis of changes in three countries representing the three modes of public policy (UK, Germany, and the US) leads to the conclusion that such distinctions become increasingly blurred when certain ideas and policy instruments are adopted from alternative health care systems. For instance, internal markets and thus competitive mechanisms have been implemented in the British NHS, and in the US health care system, market forces have been reduced by strengthening hierarchical control within managed care settings. In the German SHI system, besides direct state intervention (e.g. setting of sectoral budgets) competitive mechanisms were introduced by offering all members of sickness insurance funds the freedom of choice between different funds.

The quantitative empirical analysis, however, has shown that despite these policy changes, the US, Germany, and the UK still fall into different clusters with regard to health care financing and health service provision. Although the monetary resources for the British NHS have been increased at a high rate in recent years, both the level of monetary inputs and of health care providers are still below the OECD average. In Germany, the weakened position of actors within the self-regulatory system (especially of doctors' associations) did not result in a reduction of health service providers or of health expenditure. It remains to be seen whether SHI systems of CEE countries will approximate the SHI schemes of Western Europe or whether they remain – with regard to expenditure and provider levels – closer to the group of NHS schemes. The example of the US health care system demonstrates that a large share of private funding paves the way for cost increases. The comparatively low level of service providers might be related to the fact that private (out-of-pocket) expenses make access to health care more difficult for lower income groups and people with a poor health status so that the demand for service providers by these groups is reduced.

Although more detailed studies are necessary to show how public policies influence health expenditure and numbers of health service providers in a given country, our comparative analysis demonstrates that changes in health policy have until now not resulted in a substantial convergence process with regard to health expenditure and health employment. The shift to collaboration in the British "internal market" (Freeman and Moran 2000) or the "triumph" of less hierarchical managed care plans in the US (White 2007) demonstrate that policy measures that are adopted from other types of health care systems have to be adapted to the overall institutional characteristics of the "receiving" system (Tuohy 2009). This lends support to the proposition derived from institutional theory that types of health care systems (see Freeman and Frisina in this issue) maintain their formative power even when certain characteristic elements are modified.

Acknowledgements

The authors gratefully acknowledge the helpful comments and criticism by Ted Marmor and the other members of the Yale workshop on comparative health policy analysis in 2007 as well as by Carolyn Tuohy, David Wilsford, Bernhard Ebbinghaus, Bruno Palier, and Olli Kangas. The research reported here has received financial support from the German Research Foundation (DFG). Claus Wendt would also like to thank Harvard's Minda de Gunzburg Center for European Studies for the time and intellectual community provided to him when working on the final draft of this article as a John F. Kennedy Memorial Fellow.

Notes

1. Due to lack of data, Japan, Korea, Mexico, and Turkey are not included in the analysis. Iceland with a population of about 289,000 has also been excluded. Hence, our study covers 25 of the currently 30 OECD countries (OECD 25). However, reliable data are not provided by the OECD for all time points, thus the analysis is partly based on less than 25 countries.
2. For the debate on the perception of health care systems see Mossialos 1997, Gelissen 2002, Kohl and Wendt 2004, Marmor et al. 2006.
3. Due to double counting the figures on coverage by private insurance, Medicaid, Medicare, and on those without coverage do not add up to 100%.
4. "Public health financing" here comprises financing by general tax revenues as well as by social security contributions.
5. Alternatively one could analyze the effect of different modes of public policy and/or of health care financing on the numbers of each health care provider type available in OECD Health Data. In this case, however, it would be difficult to estimate the relation between health expenditure and the overall level of health employment.

References

Alber, Jens, 1988, Die Gesundheitssysteme der OECD-Länder im Vergleich, in: Manfred G. Schmidt (Ed) *Staatstätigkeit. International und historisch vergleichende Analysen* (Opladen: Westdeutscher Verlag), pp. 116–150.

Bambra, Clare, 2005, Cash versus services: 'worlds of welfare' and the decommodification of cash benefits and health care services. *Journal of Social Policy*, **34**(2), 195–213.

Burau, Viola and Blank, Robert H., 2006, Comparing health policy: an assessment of typologies of health systems. *Journal of Comparative Policy Analysis*, **8**(1), 63–76.

Busse, Reinhard, Saltman, Richard B. and Dubois, Hans F.W., 2004, Organization and financing of social health insurance: current status and recent policy development, in: Richard B. Saltman, Reinhard Busse and Josep Figueras (Eds) *Social Health Insurance Systems in Western Europe* (Maidenhead: Open University Press), pp. 33–80.

Cacace, Mirella, 2009, United States: the coexistence of market and hierarchy in the US healthcare system, in: Heinz Rothgang, Mirella Cacace, Simone Grimmeisen, Uwe Helmert and Claus Wendt (Eds) *The Changing Role of the State in OECD Health Care Systems* (London: Palgrave), forthcoming.

Chinitz, David, Preker, Alex and Wasem, Jürgen, 1998, Balancing competition and solidarity in health care financing, in: Richard B. Saltman, Josep Figueras and Constantino Sakellarides (Eds) *Critical Challenges for Health Care Reform in Europe* (Buckingham: Open University Press), pp. 55–77.

Culyer, Anthony J., 1990, Cost containment in Europe, in: OECD (Ed) *Health Care Systems in Transition. The Search for Efficiency* (Paris: OECD), pp. 29–40.

Evans, Robert G., 1996, Marketing markets, regulating regulators: who gains? Who loses? What hopes? What scope?, in: OECD (Ed) *Health Care Reform. The Will to Change* (Paris: OECD), pp. 9–114.

Figueras, Josep, Saltman, Richard B., Busse, Reinhard and Dubois, Hans F.W., 2004, Patterns and performance in social health insurance systems, in: Richard B. Saltman, Reinhard Busse and Josep Figueras (Eds) *Social Health Insurance Systems in Western Europe* (New York: Open University Press), pp. 81–140.

Freeman, Richard, 2000, *The Politics of Health in Europe* (Manchester: Manchester University Press).
Freeman, Richard and Moran, Michael, 2000, Reforming health care in Europe. *West European Politics*, **23**(2), 35–59.
Gelissen, John, 2002, *Worlds of Welfare, Worlds of Consent? Public Opinion on the Welfare State* (Leiden: Brill).
Giaimo, Susan, 2002, *Markets and Medicine. The Politics of Health Care Reform in Britain, Germany, and the United States* (Ann Arbor: University of Michigan Press).
Giaimo, Susan and Manow, Philip, 1999, Adapting the welfare state – the case of health care reform in Britain, Germany, and the United States. *Comparative Political Studies*, **32**(8), 967–1000.
Grimmeisen, Simone, 2009, The role of the state in the British health care system – between marketisation and statism, in: Heinz Rothgang, Mirella Cacace, Simone Grimmeisen, Uwe Helmert and Claus Wendt (Eds) *The Changing Role of the State in OECD Health Care Systems* (London: Palgrave), forthcoming.
Hacker, Jacob S., 2002, *The Divided Welfare State: The Battle over Public and Private Social Benefits in the United States* (Cambridge: Cambridge University Press).
Hacker, Jacob S., 2004, Privatizing risk without privatizing the welfare state: the hidden politics of social policy retrenchment in the United States. *American Political Science Review*, **98**(2), 243–260.
Ham, Christopher, 2004, *Health Policy in Britain: The Politics of Organisation of the National Health Service* (London: Palgrave).
Hassenteufel, Patrick and Palier, Bruno, 2007, Towards neo-Bismarckian health care states? Comparing health insurance reforms in Bismarckian welfare systems. *Social Policy and Administration*, **41**(6), 574–596.
Hsiao, William C., 1995, A framework for assessing health financing strategies and the role of health insurance, in: David W. Dunlop and Jo M. Martins (Eds) *An International Assessment of Health Care Financing. Lessons for Developing Countries* (Washington DC: The World Bank), pp. 15–30.
Jönsson, Bengt and Musgrove, Philip, 1997, *Government Financing of Health Care* (Washington DC: The World Bank).
Kanavos, Panos and McKee, Martin, 1998, Macroeconomic constraints and health challenges facing European health systems, in: Richard B. Saltman, Josep Figueras and Constantino Sakellarides (Eds) *Critical Challenges for Health Care Reform in Europe* (Buckingham: Open University Press), pp. 23–52.
Kangas, Olli, 1994, The politics of social security: on regressions, qualitative comparisons, and cluster analysis, in: Thomas Janoski and Alexander M. Hicks (Eds) *The Comparative Political Economy of the Welfare State* (Cambridge: Cambridge University Press), pp. 346–364.
Kangas, Olli, 2004, Institutional development of sickness cash-benefit programmes in 18 OECD countries. *Social Policy & Administration*, **38**(2), 190–203.
Kohl, Jürgen and Wendt, Claus, 2004, Satisfaction with health care systems. A comparison of EU countries, in: Wolfgang Glatzer, Susanne von Below and Mathias Stoffregen (Eds) *Challenges for Quality of Life in the Contemporary World* (Dordrecht: Kluwer Academic Publishers), pp. 311–331.
Marmor, Theodore R. and Okma, Kieke G. H., 1998, Cautionary lessons from the west: what (not) to learn from other countries' experience in the financing and delivery of health care, in: Peter Flora, Philip de Jong, Julian Le Grand and Jun-Young Kim (Eds) *The State of Social Welfare, 1997. International Studies on Social Insurance and Retirement, Employment, Family Policy and Health Care* (Aldershot: Ashgate), pp. 327–350.
Marmor, Theodore R., Mashaw, Jerry L. and Harvey, Philip L., 1992, *America's Misunderstood Welfare State. Persistent Myths, Enduring Realities* (New York: Basic Books).
Marmor, Theodore R., Freeman, Richard and Okma, Kieke, 2005, Comparative perspectives and policy learning in the world of health care. *Journal of Comparative Policy Analysis*, **7**(4), 331–348.
Marmor, Theodore R., Okma, Kieke G. H. and Latham, Stephen R., 2006, Values, institutions and health politics. Comparative perspectives, in: Claus Wendt and Christof Wolf (Eds) *Soziologie der Gesundheit* (Wiesbaden: VS Verlag), pp. 383–405.
McPherson, Klim, 1990, International differences in medical care practices, in: OECD (Eds) *Health Care Systems in Transition. The Search for Efficiency* (Paris: OECD), pp. 17–28.
Moran, Michael, 1999, *Governing the Health Care State. A Comparative Study of the United Kingdom, the United States and Germany* (Manchester: Manchester University Press).
Moran, Michael, 2000, Understanding the welfare state: the case of health care. *British Journal of Politics and International Relations*, **2**(2), 135–160.

Mossialos, Elias, 1997, Citizens' views on health care systems in the 15 member states of the European Union. *Health Economics*, **6**, 109–116.

Newbrander, W. and Eichler, R., 2001, Managed care in the United States: its history, forms, and future, in: Aviva Ron and Xenia Scheil-Adlung (Eds) *Recent Health Policy Innovations in Social Security* (New Brunswick: Transaction Publishers), pp. 83–106.

OECD, 2005, *Health at a Glance. OECD Indicators 2005* (Paris: OECD Publishing).

OECD, 2006, *OECD Health Data 2006. A Comparative Analysis of 30 Countries* (Paris: OECD Publishing).

Patel, Kant and Rushefsky, Mark E., 1999, *Health Care Politics and Policy in America* (Armonk, NY: M.E. Sharpe).

Powell, Martin, 2003, Quasi-markets in British health policy: a longue durée perspective. *Social Policy & Administration*, **37**(7), 725–741.

Rico, Ana, Saltman, Richard B. and Boerma, Wienke G.W., 2003, Organizational restructuring in European health systems: the role of primary care. *Social Policy & Administration*, **37**(6), 592–608.

Rothgang, Heinz, Cacace, Mirella, Grimmeisen, Simone and Wendt, Claus, 2005, The changing role of the state in health care systems. *European Review*, **13**, Supp. No. 1, 187–212.

Schieber, George J. and Poullier, Jean-Pierre, 1990, Overview of international comparisons of health care expenditure, in: OECD (Ed) *Health Care Systems in Transition. The Search for Efficiency* (Paris: OECD), pp. 9–15.

Steffen, Monika, 2005, Comparing complex policies: lessons from a public health case. *Journal of Comparative Policy Analysis*, **7**(4), 267–290.

Tuohy, Carolyn Hughes, 1999, *Accidental Logics. The Dynamics of Change in the Health Care System in the United States, Britain, and Canada* (New York: Oxford University Press).

Tuohy, Carolyn Hughes, 2003, Agency, contract, and governance: shifting shapes of accountability in the health care arena. *Journal of Health Politics, Policy and Law*, **28**(2–3), 195–215.

Tuohy, Carolyn Hughes, 2009, Health care reform, health care policy: Canada in comparative perspective, in: Theodore R. Marmor, Richard Freeman and Kieke G.H. Okma (Eds) *Comparative Studies and the Politics of Modern Medical Care* (Yale: Yale University Press), 61–87.

Tuohy, Carolyn Hughes, Flood, Colleen M. and Stabile, Mark, 2004, How does private finance affect public health care systems? Marshalling the evidence from OECD nations. *Journal of Health Politics, Policy and Law*, **29**(3), 359–396.

Wendt, Claus, 2006, Der Gesundheitssystemvergleich: Konzepte und Perspektiven, in: Claus Wendt and Christof Wolf (Eds) *Soziologie der Gesundheit. Sonderheft 46 der Kölner Zeitschrift für Soziologie und Sozialpsychologie* (Wiesbaden: VS-Verlag), pp. 270–297.

Wendt, Claus, Grimmeisen, Simone and Rothgang, Heinz, 2005, Convergence or divergence in OECD health care systems?, in: Bea Cantillon and Ive Marx (Eds) *International Cooperation in Social Security. How to Cope with Globalisation* (Antwerpen: Intersentia), pp. 15–14.

Wendt, Claus and Thompson, Theresa, 2004, Social austerity versus structural reform in European health systems: a four-country comparison of health reforms. *International Journal of Health Services*, **34**(3), 415–433.

White, Joseph, 2007, Markets and medical care: the United States, 1993–2005. *The Milbank Quarterly*, **85**(3), 395–448.

Comparing Health Policy: An Assessment of Typologies of Health Systems

VIOLA BURAU and ROBERT H. BLANK

ABSTRACT *Typologies have been central to the comparative turn in public policy and this paper contributes to the debate by assessing the capacity of typologies of health systems to capture the institutional context of health care and to contribute to explaining health policies across countries. Using a recent comparative study of health policy and focusing on the concept of the health care state the paper suggests three things. First, the concept of the health care state holds as a set of ideal types. Second, as such the concept of the health care state provides a useful springboard for analyzing health policy, but one which needs to be complemented by more specific institutional explanations. Third, the concept of the health care state is less applicable to increasingly important, non-medical areas of health policy. Instead, different aspects of institutional context come into play and they can be combined as part of a looser "organizing framework".*

Comparative policy analysis has become a "growth industry". Advances in information technology have expanded the availability and dissemination of data across many countries, while at the same time many policy fields have become increasingly internationally oriented. The greater interest in information about policies in other countries has also been fostered by the perception of shared policy challenges arising from economic and welfare state crises. Deleon and Resnick-Terry (1999) refer to this development as the "comparative renaissance". The comparative perspective is now widely used in both the academic field of public policy analysis and in more applied policy studies (see for example Castles 1999, Heidenheimer *et al.* 1992). Parallel to discussions about the insights generated by comparative analyses is a debate about the methodologies of cross-country comparison (for comparative politics see for example Lane and Errson 1994, Peters 1998; for comparative social policy, see for example Clasen 1999, Hantrais and Mangen 1996).

The use of typologies has been central to the comparative turn in policy analysis and they have been used to conceptualize the (institutional) context in which policies are embedded. Prominent examples include: Castles' (1993) notion of "families of nations", which describes different clusters of cultural, historical and geographical features of nations; Esping-Andersen's (1990) welfare state regimes, which identify distinct welfare state logics; and Lijphart's (1999) and Blondel's (1990) typologies of democratic and state regimes respectively. Cross-country comparison generates an abundance of information and ordering this information through typologies is central to using comparison to build, review and revise explanations about policy emergence, policy making and policy cycles.

This paper contributes to the debate in comparative policy analysis by analyzing the uses and limitations of typologies of health systems in the comparative study of health policy. This is an area of comparative analysis that has grown significantly over the last 20 years (for an overview of the literature see Marmor *et al.* forthcoming), but it has featured less prominently in the mainstream literature on comparative policy analysis and social policy analysis.

Using a recent comparative study of health policy the paper assesses the use of typologies of health systems and their capacity to capture the institutional context of health care and thereby to contribute to explaining health policies across countries. More specifically, based on Moran's (1999, 2000) typology of health care states the paper suggests three things. First, modeled on paradigmatic cases the concept of the health care state holds as an ideal type. Second, as such the health care state provides a useful springboard for the analysis of health policy, but one which needs to be complemented by more specific institutional explanations. Third, the concept of the health care state is less applicable to increasingly important, non-medical areas of health policy. Instead, different aspects of institutional context come into play and they can be combined as part of a looser "organizing framework".

The paper begins by reviewing the comparative literature on health policy and suggests that while the OECD typology of health system has been influential, studies have more or less explicitly adapted the definition of the health system. A prominent example is the concept of the health care state developed by Moran (1999, 2000). The following two sections apply the typology to a recent comparative study of health policy that included a wide range of countries and areas of health policy. From this, the concluding discussion summarizes the uses and limitations of typologies of health systems.

Typologies of Health Systems in Comparative Health Policy

The comparative analysis of health policy often uses typologies of *health systems* to help capture the institutional context of health care and contribute to explaining health policies across different countries. In this regard, the typology developed by a series of OECD studies has been particularly influential (see Figure 1). The typology defines the health system as an ideal typical set of macro-institutional characteristics based on variations in the funding of health care and corresponding differences in the organization of health care provision. This reflects the fact that the public funding of

Figure 1. Types of health care systems by provision and funding

health care (or lack of it) is often seen as the defining characteristic of the degree of public involvement in health care (Freeman 1999).

The first of these studies was especially influential (OECD 1987: 24) and classified the health system on the basis of a dichotomy between patient sovereignty (and the predominance of incentives) and social equity (and the predominance of control), and introduced three basic models of the health system. The national health service (or Beveridge) model is characterized by universal coverage, funding out of general taxation and public ownership and/or control of health care delivery. Although this model is most identified with the UK, New Zealand created the first national health service in its 1938 Social Security Act that promised all citizens open-ended access to all health care services they needed free at the point of use. Sweden is another example of the national health service model, although all three countries, to varying degrees, have moved away from this pure model.

In contrast, in the social insurance (or Bismarck) model compulsory, universal coverage is as part of a system of social security. Health care is financed by employer and employee contributions, through non-profit insurance funds, and the provision of health care is in public or private ownership. Germany, Japan, and the Netherlands are often viewed as examples of this type. Singapore, with its compulsory Medisave system is a variation on the theme of social insurance, although in terms of the sources of funding, private insurance dominates.

Finally, in the private insurance (or consumer sovereignty model), employer based or individual purchase of private health insurance is key. Health care is funded by individual and/or employer contributions and health delivery is predominantly in private ownership. This type is most clearly represented by the US and until recently by Australia, but many systems contain some elements of this type.

The initial typology developed by the OECD is a descriptive categorization of how health care is organized in different countries and reflects its specific origins in applied policy analysis. As Freeman (2000) observes, the typology emerged from a search, dominated by economists, for better solutions to common problems. This corresponds to a focus on the internal workings of health care rather than on its political and social embeddedness. However, this situation has changed with the wide use of the basic typology in the comparative analysis of health policy (see for example Freeman 2000, Ham 1997, Raffel 1997, Scott 2001, Wall 1996). Together with the increasing interest in neo-institutionalism, the typology has been a facilitator for critical analyses of the health system as the institutional framework in which health policies are embedded and how the institutions of health care (among others) shape health policies (and politics). Scott (2001), for example, uses the typology as part of her framework to analyze public and private roles and interfaces in health care across different countries. In contrast, Ham (1997) in his cross-country comparative analysis focuses more explicitly on health reform. The same applies to Freeman (2000), who specifically looks at the politics of health in relation to a range of areas of health policy.

However, these analyses also have in common their consideration of other aspects of the institutional context of health care in addition to the typology of health systems. Freeman (2000), for example, explicitly includes in his analysis the mechanisms by which health care is co-ordinated ("health care governance"). This inclusion clearly demonstrates that applying the typology of health systems to a wider range of cases has also led to its adaptation. As Collier and Levitsky (1997; similarly Collier and Mahon 1993) note, such a process is characterized by a tension between increasing analytical differentiation in order to capture the diverse forms of the phenomenon at hand, while avoiding the pitfalls of conceptual stretching and applying the concept to cases that do not fit. The literature on comparative health policy has addressed this tension by adding, although more or less explicitly, new attributes to the definition of the health system.

Moran's work (1999, 2000) is particularly interesting here as he explicitly sets out both to better account for the institutional embeddedness of health care and to revise the typology of health systems. He starts with the observation that health policy is about more than health care and that modern health care systems are about more than delivering a personal service: "Health care facilities in modern industrial societies are great concentrations of economic resources – and because of this they are also the subject of political struggle" (Moran 1999: 1). This means shifting the focus of the analysis from the organization to the governance of health care. Moran goes on to argue that with its emphasis on the access to health care the OECD typology only captures one aspect of the governance of consumption and also misses out on other important dimensions of governing health care. On that basis, he introduces the concept of the health care state that consists of the institutions related to governing the consumption, provision and production of health care.

The institutions of governing the consumption of health care are concerned with the mechanisms by which individual patients have access to services (such as social citizenship and earned insurance entitlements) and the mechanisms that decide on the total volume of resources allocated to the financing of health care (such as governing through public management and setting regulatory frameworks). In contrast, the institutions of governing the provision of health care include the mechanisms for regulating hospitals (such as the amount of public regulation and the mix of differently owned hospitals) and the regulation of doctors (especially different forms of private interest government). This reflects the centrality of hospitals and doctors for the provision of health care. Finally, the institutions of governing the production of health care focus on the mechanisms regulating medical innovations. The three sets of institutions vary in terms of the relative degree of public control and on that basis Moran constructs four different types of health care states.

The remainder of the paper applies the typology of health care states to a recent cross-country comparative study of health policy. The analysis uses examples from a recent comparative study of health policy (Blank and Burau 2004) that is distinct because it covers both a diverse range of countries and multiple areas of policy. With its emphasis on complexity and inclusiveness, the study is well suited to offer new insights into the uses and limitations of typologies of health systems and, specifically, the concept of the health care state. The study includes nine countries (Australia, Britain, Germany, Japan, New Zealand, the Netherlands, Singapore and the US) that differ not only in relation to the key dimensions of the health care state, but also on other factors that impact on health policy such as type of political system and the wider cultural, economic and societal context. In addition, the study incorporates a wider range of areas of health policies than often studied, including home and community based public health policies. Although both have traditionally been marginal, they have become increasingly central to health policies. This shift reflects demographic changes, especially the ageing of population, and the increasing focus on the responsibilities of the individual for his or her own health.

The next section applies the concept of the health care state to the nine countries included in our study and discusses the importance of institutional embeddedness beyond the health care state. The subsequent section assesses the use of the concept of the health care state in relation to non-medical health policies and explores an alternative "organizing framework". The key question here is if the concept of the health care state also captures the new cases presented in the study. Or, to paraphrase Harrop (1992: 3; similarly Arts and Glissen 2002), does the concept of the health care state help to discover how countries vary (or are similar) in the health policies they adopt and to gain insights into why these differences (or similarities) exist.

Health Care States and Institutional Embeddedness

Based on the distinction between institutions related to the governance of consumption, provision and production, Moran (1999, 2000) constructs different types of health care states, three of which are especially relevant for our set of countries. In entrenched command and control health care states, the governance of consumption consists of extensive public access based on citizenship and extensive control of resource allocation through administrative mechanisms. This gives the state a central role in governing the collective consumption of health care. The same applies to the governance of provision with hospitals in public ownership and subject to extensive public control, and with the private interest government of doctors closely circumscribed. There are also moderate constraints on medical innovation, which is at the heart of the governance of production.

In contrast, in the corporatist health care state funding through social insurance contributions makes for de facto public access to health care and gives public law bodies (such as statutory, non-profit insurance funds) an important role. This limits the public control over health care costs. The same is true for the governance of provision, where private hospitals are often prominent and where there are only some constraints on the private interest government of doctors, who therefore play a potentially influential role in the governance of provision. Not surprisingly, there are only some constraints on medical innovation.

The role of providers is even more extensive in the supply health care state, where funding through private insurance limits public access to health care as well as the public control of costs. Similarly, private hospitals not only dominate, but also remain relatively unchecked. The same applies to doctors, and private interest government is strong. There are also de facto no constraints on medical innovation. Table 1 maps out our countries using the typology of health care states developed by Moran.

Looking at the health care states in our countries across the different types and respective dimensions of governing health care several findings stand out. Only four out of the nine countries included in the study fully fit one of the three types of health care state. In contrast, the remaining countries are more or less close approximations of the individual ideal types. This highlights the fact that the institutional contexts of governing of health care are more complex than suggested by the definition of the health care state. Instead, institutional contexts are often highly specific in terms of how individual aspects combine themselves in individual countries. Such specificities also point to additional aspects of institutional context. Consequently, within a country the two sets of institutions associated with the governance of consumption may actually fit different types of health care states thus making categorization problematic. The same problem might also apply to the governance of provision and production.

According to the typology, public control of the total resources allocated to health care can be expected to be highest in entrenched command and control health care states with access to health care based on social citizenship and lowest in supply health care states where access to health care is based on private insurance, with public control in corporatist health care states lying in between. This is true for four of our countries, but the picture is more complex in the remaining five countries, pointing to the importance of country-specific institutional contexts. In Australia, for example, federalism combined with the legacy of the private insurance systems weakens government authority over funding (Palmer and Short 2000). In contrast, the unitary political system in Japan helps to concentrate authority in the hands of central government (Campbell and Ikegami 1998). Despite significant decentralization of health services and insurance plans, for example, all billing and payment in Japan is centralized through the payment fund of the National Health Insurance.

The Netherlands and Singapore are particularly interesting examples of how country-specific institutional contexts shape the public control of health care costs, thus making differences between countries particularly pertinent. In the Netherlands, the high public control of funding reflects the unusual combination of a social insurance with strong universalist elements (for an overview see Exter *et al.* 2004, Maarse 1997). Health funding combines a considerable diversity of sources, including private insurance for acute medical risks for those earning above a certain ceiling, and compulsory social insurance contributions in case of exceptional medical risks. This reflects the historical legacy of a society segmented into different groupings and the gradual weakening of this legacy in the Netherlands. The semi-federal political system also helps to concentrate authority in the hands of the central government, and, in contrast to Germany, corporatism is confined to the national level.

In Singapore, country-specific institutional contexts are such that public control is strong not only in relation to health care costs but also other key aspects of health care (for an overview see Barr 2001, Ham 2001). Strong government control of funding co-exists with health care funding that is predominantly based on individual responsibility and limited familial risk pooling. Health care is funded by individual

Table 1. Health care states across nine countries

	Governance of consumption • extent of public access to health care • extent of public control of total health care costs	*Governance of provision* • extent of public control of hospitals* • extent of constraints on private interest government of doctors**	*Governance of production* • extent of public constraints on medical innovation
Entrenched command & control health care state • extensive public access, high public control of costs • high public control of hospitals, highly constrained private interest government • moderate constraints on medical innovation	BRITAIN SWEDEN Australia (access) New Zealand (access) Netherlands (cost control) Singapore (cost control) Australia (cost control)	BRITAIN SWEDEN New Zealand	BRITAIN SWEDEN Netherlands New Zealand
Corporatist health care state • de facto public access, moderate public control of costs • moderate public control of hospitals, some constraints on private interest government • some constraints on medical innovation	GERMANY Japan (access) Netherlands (access) New Zealand (cost control)	GERMANY Australia Japan Netherlands Singapore	GERMANY Australia Japan
Supply health care state • limited public access, low public control of costs • little public control of hospitals, few constraints on private interest government • de facto no constraints on medical innovation	US Singapore (access)	US	US Singapore

*share of hospitals in public ownership together with the degree of public regulation used as proxy for extent of public control of hospitals.
**share of publicly employed (hospital) doctors together with the degree of professional self-regulation used as proxy for extent of constraints on self-government of doctors.

savings accounts, which are compulsory. The government also caps contribution rates, while out-of-pocket payments are high. As such, Singapore defies the dictum that private funding is unlikely to make for public control. The strength of government control reflects not only the spatial concentration of political power typical of city-states, but also a strongly centralized approach to health policy. Government education programs are aimed at lowering the demand for health care and also emphasize the importance of primary health care and prevention over hospital care. Not surprisingly, public health policies are strong, and the government heavily subsidizes health promotion and disease prevention programs that emphasize the responsibility of the individual to look after his or her own health.

The importance of country-specific institutional contexts also applies, though to a lesser extent, to the governance of provision and production. In the Netherlands and Singapore the respective institutions fit different types of health care states and together with the institutional specificity of the governance of consumption, the two countries emerge as hybrids. As noted earlier, in relation to the governance of consumption the Netherlands combine access based on social insurance contributions with extensive public control of health costs. This ambivalence extends to the other dimensions of governance. The governance of provision is closest to the logic of the corporatist health care state. Private, non-profit hospitals dominate, but are subject to extensive public control through centralized hospital planning. The same is true for doctors and, for example, while many hospital specialists are independent entrepreneurs they work under a public contract. In contrast, the governance of production resembles the logic of entrenched command-and-control health care states, where central regulation together with hospital planning put moderate constraints on medical innovation.

Singapore, for its part and as mentioned above, has a highly controlled health system but one based on individual savings accounts that give the impression of minimal government control over consumption. Thus, it crosses the line between a corporatist and supply health care state. Furthermore, Singapore gives those persons with sufficient Medisave account balances considerable freedom of choice as to public and private doctors and hospitals as well as allowing them to purchase private insurance with their account should they so desire. While provision and especially production appear to best fit a supply health care state, a large proportion of health care is provided in publicly-owned hospitals by government-set salaried doctors. Despite this, there are few controls on medical intervention in Singapore because in the end individuals have the choice of what services to use with their compulsory but private accounts.

What does the analysis presented so far say about the concept of the health care state and its capacity to capture the institutional arrangements across our countries and contribute to explaining health policies? The analysis suggests two things. First, the concept of the health care state holds as an approximation of "real" health care states. It is therefore a classical ideal type that is useful as a heuristic device that simplifies the complex real world of governing health care (following Weber 1949). Thereby, the concept of the health care state helps to move the analysis beyond the specificity of individual cases and towards more generalized observations, overcoming a salient tension inherent in comparative enquiry (Goodin and Smitsman

2000). The health care state as an ideal type, therefore, does not need to fit the real types completely in order to be useful.

Second, it is important to remember, however, that it is primarily through the comparison and contrast with real types that explanations can be advanced (see Arts and Glissen 2002). The central question, then, is how to explain the extent to which "real" health care states do or do not fit the ideal types of health care states. The different degrees of "misfits" among these nine countries and the types of health care states presented in the analysis raises many such "why" questions. In turn, this underlines the fact that the concept of the health care state indeed only provides a starting point for a comparative analysis and must be complemented by additional, more specific institutional explanations. The importance of a detailed study of institutional contexts is well recognized in the comparative study of health policy (see for example Döhler 1991, Immergut 1992, Wilsford 1994). Nevertheless, this point is particularly significant in the present context, because the concept of the health care state specifically aims to better account for the institutional embeddedness of health care. In this respect, Moran (1999, 2000) emphasizes that understanding health policy requires examining the ways in which health care is embedded in the broader contexts of market economies and democratic competitive politics.

Significantly, then, there is institutional embeddedness beyond the health care state. As the analysis of our countries suggests, governing health care is embedded in institutional contexts that are broader than those institutions making up the health care state, and institutional contexts that are often also highly specific to individual countries. As the literature emphasizes (see for example, Campbell and Ikegami 1998, Feldman 2000, Ham 2001, Klein 2001, Raffel 1997) such contexts can encompass a wide range of aspects, including social values and cultural factors, as well as the legal and political systems together with social structures. Our analysis, for example, points to the importance of the specific characteristics of political systems (such as federalism in Australia), social structures (such as the legacy of societal pillars in the Netherlands) and social values (such as the high degree of individual self-reliance in Singapore). The governing of health care reflects specific configurations of these different aspects of institutional context, all of which are changeable over time. Therefore, more often than not, health policies follow trajectories that are highly complex and specific.

Health Care States and Non-medical Health Policies

The analysis presented in the previous section suggests that the institutional context of governing health care itself is highly complex. This echoes Freeman's (2000: 7) observation that the organization of health care is actually not very systematic. The complex historical emergence of policies of health care often defies the order implied by the notion of a *system*. As a result, the health system perspective may be looking for order where there is little. Instead, the institutional context of governing health care is highly differentiated, to the extent that such contexts are often somewhat specific to individual countries. Importantly, there is also specificity in relation to subsectors of health care and policy. This is particularly apparent in relation to those subsectors that have traditionally been at the margins of the "health system", but that are increasingly central to health policy. Focusing on home and community based health care as an example, the present section assesses the use of the concept of the health care state for capturing the institutions central to non-medical health care and for explaining such "new" health policies across countries.

Debates about ageing populations and their implications for health care costs and services have put home and community based health care on the health policy agenda. At international level it is indicative, for example, that long-term care for elderly people was one of the components of the recent OECD Health Project (OECD 2005). More specifically, the project reviewed policy developments across countries as well as the organization of long-term care in terms of financing, expenditure and care recipients. The OECD Health Project echoes developments across the countries included in our study in which there are many examples of major policy initiatives relating to home and community based health care (Glenndinning 1998, Jacobzone 1999, Jenson and Jacobzone 2000). Such policies often aim at the expansion of existing services to support informal care givers by integrating home and community based health care into the regular organization of health care. The expansion of the social insurance in Germany and Japan is an indicative example. Starting in the late 1980s, the government in Japan introduced a publicly funded scheme, the so-called Gold Plan, to expand care services for older people. The scheme was extended in the late 1990s and in effect became a separate branch of the social insurance, funded by a mixture of social insurance premiums and taxes. Considering the traditional strength of family responsibility for care of the elderly, this is a significant policy development (Furuse 1996).

This emergence of non-medical based health care raises the question of how policies related to home and community based health care fit into the concept of the health care state. The concept focuses on institutions and policies related to medical care. This is apparent in Moran's (1999, 2000) definition of the governance of provision, which is concerned with the institutions related to the regulation of doctors (as the key providers of health care) and hospitals (as the key settings for the provision of medical care). In contrast, home and community based health care is located on two sets of interfaces: between formal and informal care, and between health and social care. In relation to the first aspect, it is indicative that few older people receive home nursing care and even when they do it only accounts for a small share of their care. Instead, home care predominantly means unpaid (informal) care by women and often also includes social care, such as help with domestic tasks. This reflects not only the inadequacy of existing home nursing services, but also the fact many of the health care needs of older people are often not principally medically related.

This puts a number of limitations on using the concept of the health care state for capturing the institutions governing home and community based health care and for explaining corresponding health policies. The institutions related to the governance of consumption are relevant to the extent that home and community based health care is part of the organization of medical health care. Traditionally, parts of home and community based health care have by default been funded by the same scheme as medical health care. At the same time, parallel funding schemes relating to social care have existed. In Germany, for example, before the introduction of the long-term care insurance, funding for home and community based health care came from both the health insurance and locally funded social assistance schemes. In many cases this organizational division continues and also applies to the newly established schemes.

This is also the case in Japan whereas in Australia, New Zealand, the Netherlands and Sweden funding of home and community based health care is integrated. Further, there tend to be formal or de facto limits to the scope of collective consumption. Instead private consumption in the form of private payments for formal services and informal care paid by lost income are important complementary aspects of consumption. The last aspect even applies to countries like Sweden, where the level of publicly funded services is relatively high. A study in the mid-1980s for example found that informal care accounted for 64 per cent of the total care time (OECD 1996: 166). There are even more extensive limitations in relation to applying the definitions of the governance of provision and production. Medical technology is of little importance for home and community based home care. The same applies to hospitals as settings of care provision and doctors as providers of care. Instead, care workers such as community nurses, care assistants and social workers together with informal carers, all working in home and community based settings, are central to the provision of this type of health care. Taken together this suggests that shared values and beliefs (and corresponding practices) are important for understanding non-medical health policies. Freeman and Ruskin (1999) refer to this as "cultural embeddedness" and thereby point to diversity beyond the macro level and, notably, a type of diversity that is shaped by organizational bases that are ethnic, gendered, local and personal, rather than national and public.

Where does this leave capturing institutional arrangements as they apply to home and community based health care and explaining corresponding non-medical health policies across our countries? The concept of the health care state is of some use, notably to the extent to which home and community based health care is part of the organization of medical health care. However, beyond that, using the concept of the health care state has clear limits, as some institutions do not have the same importance, whereas others not included in the definition are central for understanding non-medical health policies. Considering the extent of such limitations adding new attributes to the concept of the health care state is not necessarily an option. Instead, different aspects of institutional context need to be taken into consideration. This requires two things: first, redefining the institutions related to the governing of consumption and provision so as to reflect the specific characteristics of home and community based health care (and, where applicable, across the health and social care divide); and second, to include gender as a set of social and cultural institutions. In this respect Pfau-Effinger's (2004) concept of "gender arrangements" is particularly useful. The concept consists of two components. Gender order describes existing structures of gender relations not least as reflected in gendered divisions of labor. Gender culture for its part refers to deeply embedded beliefs and ideas about the relations between the generations in the family and the obligations associated with such relations.

Against this background one way forward would be to combine the different yet complementary aspects of institutional context discussed above as part of an "organizing framework". In the context of their study of multilevel governance Bache and Flinders (2004: 94) define this as an analytical framework that provides a map of how things relate and that leads to a set of research questions. The value of such an approach is that it helps to explore complex issues and identifies interesting areas for further research.

Putting Typologies of Health Systems in Perspective

The present paper set out to assess the use of typologies of health systems in the comparative analysis of health policy. Here, the central question is to what extent typologies help to capture institutions central to health care and thereby contribute to explaining health policies across different countries.

The review of the literature demonstrates that the early typology of health systems developed by the OECD has provided a springboard for many comparative analyses of health policies that examine how sector-specific institutional contexts shape health policies. The definition of the health systems, though, has changed in the course of this process with new attributes being added, thus reaffirming the complexity of the institutional context of health care. Moran's concept of the health care state systematically engages with both institutional embeddedness and typology building, and as such provides a suitable basis for assessing the use of typologies of health systems. Based on a recent study that included a diverse range of countries and areas of health policies the analysis suggests three things.

First, modeled upon paradigmatic cases the concept of the health care state holds as an ideal type and as a heuristic device to help capture theoretically relevant aspects of the institutional context of health policy. Second, despite this contribution, as with all typologies the concept of the health care state is historically and culturally contingent. Not surprisingly, in our analysis only few countries fully match the ideal types and some even emerge as hybrids. At the same time, it is also clear that cross-country comparisons cannot do without a common framework. As Marmor and Okma (2003: 749) observe, in comparative health policy analyses there is a need for a framework that is applicable across different countries and that helps to describe and understand the anatomy and the physiology of the organization of health care. So what are the options? If the institutional context of health care is more diverse and complex than the concept of the health care state, it needs to be treated first and foremost as a starting point for more detailed analyses of the country-specific institutions of health care. Such a complementary analysis has to take account of the country-specific trajectories as well as the broader institutional contexts of health care. It is, therefore, through analyzing the relative degree an individual country matches the respective ideal type that a more detailed understanding of the country-specific institutions emerges.

Third, complementing the concept of the health care state with more specific analyses of the institutional context is particularly appropriate in the case of medical health policies, whereas this is not necessarily possible in relation to the increasingly important non-medical health policies. Here, it is more appropriate to work with a looser organizing framework that brings together the very different and diverse aspects of institutional contexts of non-medical health policies, such as those related to home and community based health care. However, no matter how inclusive, such a looser framework has its own limitations. As Mabbett and Bolderson (1999) argue, the deconstruction of single broad-brush categorizations (and typologies) makes all encompassing cross-country comparisons and contrasts more difficult. In relation to non-medical health policies, however, limitations of this kind may be outweighed by the advantage of being able to include a new set of policies in the comparative analysis of health policy. Although this more complex approach might lack the comfort that comes with the orderliness of typologies it more accurately reflects the real world of health policy.

References

Arts, Will and Glissen, John, 2002, Three worlds of welfare capitalism or more? A state-of-the-art report. *Journal of European Social Policy*, 12, 137–148.
Bache, Ian and Flinders, Matthew, 2004, Multi-level governance and British politics, in: Ian Bache and Matthew Flinders (Eds) *Multi-level Governance* (Oxford: Oxford University Press).
Barr, Michael D., 2001, Medical savings accounts in Singapore: a critical inquiry. *Journal of Health Politics, Policy and Law*, 26, 709–726.
Blank, Robert and Burau, Viola, 2004, *Comparative Health Policy* (Basingstoke: Palgrave).
Blondel, Jean, 1990, *Comparative Government: An Introduction* (Hemel Hempstead: Philip Allan).
Campbell, John C. and Ikegami, Naoki, 1998, *The Art of Balance in Health Policy: Maintaining Japan's Low-Cost, Egalitarian System* (Cambridge: Cambridge University Press).
Castles, Francis G., 1993, *Families of Nations: Patterns of Public Policy in Western Democracies* (Aldershot: Dartmouth).
Castles, Francis G., 1999, *Comparative Public Policy. Patterns of Post-war Transformation* (Cheltenham: Edward Elgar).
Clasen, Jochen (Ed.), 1999, *Comparative Social Policy* (Oxford: Blackwell).
Collier, David and Mahon, James E. Jr., 1993, Conceptual "stretching" revisited: adapting categories in comparative analysis. *American Political Science Review*, 87, 845–855.
Collier, David and Levitsky, Steven, 1997, Democracy with adjectives: conceptual innovation in comparative research. *World Politics*, 49, 430–451.
Deleon, Peter and Resnick-Terry, Phyllis, 1999, Comparative policy analysis: déjà vu all over again? *Comparative Policy Analysis*, 1, 9–22.
Döhler, Marian, 1991, Policy networks, opportunity structures and neo-conservative reform strategies in health policy, in: Bernd Marin and Renate Mayntz (Eds) *Policy Networks: Empirical Evidence and Theoretical Considerations* (Boulder, CO: Westview Press).
Esping-Andersen, Gøsta, 1990, *The Three Worlds of Welfare Capitalism* (Oxford: Polity Press).
Exter, André van den, Hermans, Herbert, Dosljak, Milena and Busse, Reinhard, 2004, *Health Care Systems in Transition: Netherlands* (Copenhagen: WHO Regional Office for Europe).
Feldman, Eric, 2000, *The Ritual of Rights in Japan: Law, Society, and Health Policy* (Cambridge: Cambridge University Press).
Freeman, Richard and Ruskin, Michael, 1999, Introduction: welfare, culture and Europe, in: Prue Chamberlayne et al. (Eds) *Welfare and Culture in Europe: Towards a New Paradigm in Social Policy* (London: Jessica Kingsley).
Freeman, Richard, 1999, Institutions, states and cultures: health policy and politics in Europe, in: Jochen Clasen (Ed) *Comparative Social Policy* (Oxford: Blackwell).
Freeman, Richard, 2000, *The Politics of Health in Europe* (Manchester: Manchester University Press).
Furuse, Tohru, 1996, Changing the balance of care: Japan, in: OECD (Ed.) *Caring for Frail Elderly People* (Paris: OECD).
Glenndinning, Caroline (Ed.), 1998, *Rights and Realities. Comparing New Developments in Long-term Care for Older People* (Bristol: Policy Press).
Goodin, Robert E. and Smitsman, Anneloes, 2000, Placing welfare states: the Netherlands as a crucial test. *Journal of Comparative Public Policy*, 2, 39–64.
Ham, Chris (Ed), 1997, *Health Reform: Learning from International Experience* (Buckingham: Open University Press).
Ham, Chris, 2001, Values and health policy: the case of Singapore. *Journal of Health Politics, Policy and Law*, 26, 739–745.
Hantrais, Linda and Mangen, Steen (Eds), 1996, *Cross-national Research Methods in the Social Sciences* (London: Pinter).
Harrop, Martin, 1992, *Power and Policy in Liberal Democracies* (Cambridge: Cambridge University Press).
Heidenheimer, Arnold J., Heclo, Hugh and Adams, Caroline Teich, 1992, *Comparative Public Policy: The Politics of Social Choice in America, Europe and Japan* (New York: St. Martin's Press).

Immergut, Ellen, 1992, *Health Politics: Interests and Institutions in Western Europe* (Cambridge: Cambridge University Press).
Jacobzone, Stephane, 1999, *Ageing and Care for Frail Elderly Persons: An Overview of International Perspectives*. Labour Market and Social Policy Occasional Papers #38 (Paris: OECD).
Jenson, Jane and Jacobzone, Stephane, 2000, *Care Allowances for the Frail Elderly and Their Impact on Women Care-givers*. Labour Market and Social Policy Occasional Papers #41 (Paris: OECD).
Klein, Rudolf, 2001, *The New Politics of the NHS*. 4th edition (Harlow: Prentice Hall).
Lane, Jan-Erik and Errson, Svante, 1994, *Comparative Politics: An Introduction and New Approach* (Cambridge: Polity Press).
Lijphart, Arend, 1999, *Patterns of Democracy: Government Forms and Performance in Thirty-Six Countries* (New Haven, CT: Yale University Press).
Maarse, J. A. M., 1997, Netherlands, in: Marshall W. Raffel (Ed) *Health Care and Reform in Industrialized Countries* (University Park, PA: Pennsylvania State University Press).
Mabbett, Deborah and Bolderson, Helen, 1999, Theories and methods in comparative social policy, in: Jochen Clasen (Ed) *Comparative Social Policy* (Oxford: Blackwell).
Marmor, Theodore R., Freeman, Richard and Okma, Kieke, forthcoming, Health policy, comparison and learning, in: Theodore R. Marmor, Richard Freeman and Kieke Okma (Eds) *Learning from Comparison in Health Policy* (New Haven, CT: Yale University Press).
Marmor, Theodore and Okma, Kieke G. H., 2003, Review essay. Health care systems in transition. Copenhagen: World Health Organisation Regional Office Europe, 1996. *Journal of Health Politics, Policy and Law*, **28**, 747–754.
Moran, Michael, 1999, *Governing the Health Care State: A Comparative Study of the United Kingdom, the United States and Germany* (Manchester: Manchester University Press).
Moran, Michael, 2000, Understanding the welfare state: the case of health care. *British Journal of Politics and International Relations*, **2**, 135–160.
OECD, 1987, *Financing and Delivering Health Care: A Comparative Analysis of OECD Countries* (Paris: OECD).
OECD, 1996, *Caring for Frail Elderly People. Policies in Evolution* (Paris: OECD).
OECD, 2005, *OECD Health Project*, available at: http://www.oecd.org/document/28/0,2340,en_2649_37407_2536540_1_1_1_37407,00.html.
Palmer, George R. and Short, Stephanie D., 2000, *Health Care and Public Policy: An Australian Analysis*. 3rd edition (Melbourne: Macmillan).
Peters, B. Guy, 1998, *Comparative Politics: Theory and Methods* (Basingstoke: Macmillan).
Pfau-Effinger, Birgit, 2004, *Development of Culture, Welfare State and Women's Employment in Europe* (Aldershot: Ashgate).
Raffel, Marshall W. (Ed.), 1997, *Health Care and Reform in Industrialized Countries* (University Park, PA: Pennsylvania State University Press).
Scott, Claudia, 2001, *Public and Private Roles in Health Care Systems* (Buckingham: Open University Press).
Wall, Ann, 1996, *Health Care Systems in Liberal Democracies* (London: Routledge).
Weber, Max, 1949, *The Methodology of the Social Sciences* (New York: Free Press).
Wilsford, David, 1994, Path dependency, or why history makes it difficult but not impossible to reform health care systems in the big way. *Journal of Public Policy*, **14**, 251–283.

Six Countries, Six Health Reform Models? Health Care Reform in Chile, Israel, Singapore, Switzerland, Taiwan and The Netherlands

KIEKE G. H. OKMA, TSUNG-MEI CHENG, DAVID CHINITZ, LUCA CRIVELLI, MENG-KIN LIM, HANS MAARSE and MARIA ELIANA LABRA

ABSTRACT *This research contribution presents a diagnosis of the health reform experience of six small and mid-sized industrial democracies: Chile, Israel, Singapore, Switzerland, Taiwan and The Netherlands during the last decades of the twentieth century. It addresses the following questions: why have these six countries, facing similar pressures to reform their health care systems, with similar options for government action, chosen very different pathways to restructure their health care? What did they do? And what happened after the implementation of those reforms? The article describes the current arrangements for funding, contracting and payment, ownership and administration (or "governance") of health care at the beginning of the twenty-first century, the origins of the health care reforms, the discussion and choice of policy options, processes of implementation and "after reform adjustments". The article looks at factors that help explain the variety in reform paths, such as national politics, dominant cultural orientations and the positions of major stakeholders.*

Introduction

This research contribution presents a diagnosis of the health reform experience of six small and mid-sized industrial democracies – Chile, Israel, Singapore, Switzerland, Taiwan and The Netherlands – during the last decades of the twentieth century. The countries span the globe, hailing from Asia and the Middle East to Latin America and Europe. The study is a truly international collaborative undertaking. The authors have all lived and worked in one or more of those countries, combining varied academic and administrative backgrounds with personal experiences. They have brought together a unique degree of in-depth knowledge of all six countries that has allowed for more detailed findings than studies solely based on aggregate data of the OECD or similar international sources. This has greatly improved our understanding of similarities and differences between the national experiences.

Recent decades have seen a rapid proliferation of cross-national studies of social policy, in particular in the field of health care (Klein 1995). The majority of those studies, however, consist of collections of descriptive case studies. They often lack a common vocabulary and suffer from poorly defined terms (Marmor and Okma 2003). For example, the term "health reform" is regularly used but rarely defined in any operational way. Another common problem is the assumption that policy as formally stated in policy documents or law is the same as policy actually implemented (and adjusted later on). As we will show, for a variety of reasons the ultimate outcome of reform often differs greatly from the original policy intentions. This study seeks to contribute to cross-national policy learning by structured multi-country research. It looks at the health reform experience of six quite different countries. In that sense, it represents a selection of dissimilar systems that may bring explanatory insight or lesson drawing (Klein and Marmor 2006).

In this contribution, we take "health reform" as major shifts in both decision-making power over the allocation of resources as well as financial risks in health care funding, contracting and ownership.[1] Shifts in decision-making include, among others, the abolishment (or reinstatement) of selective contracting with providers, changes in the authority over capital investments, expansion or contraction of entitlements of public health insurance, or (new) restrictions on medical decisions imposed by practice guidelines and other rules. Further, decision-making and financial risk can shift from national to regional and local governments (or in the other direction), or from government control to individual insurers and individual patients and insured.

Changes in the distribution of the financial risk of medical treatment across the system also affect the organization of health care. As an example, the market-oriented change in The Netherlands in the early 1990s widened the power of health insurers to selectively contract health services. Anticipating this change, providers developed strategic alliances and sometimes regional monopoly positions to safeguard their positions (Okma and De Roo, 2009). As another example, in 1996 the Swiss health insurance shifted decision-making power from the cantons to the federal level, but left financial risks for public health expenditure at the canton level. The individual mandate to take health insurance increased the role of private health insurers. As the insurers still have to contract all health providers, however, the latter faced few financial risks and thus did not change their positions as much as their Dutch counterparts.

This contribution addresses the following questions: why have these six countries, facing similar pressures to reform their health care systems, with similar options for government action, chosen very different pathways to restructure their health care? What did they do? And what happened after the implementation of those reforms?

The second section addresses the issues of categorizing countries, health systems and health policies. The study combines analytical categories from economic theory with concepts from political science in order to better understand the policy experience of the six countries of this study. The economic terms describe the basic constituent elements of health care: funding, contracting and provision of health services. The terms borrowed from political science to analyze the "working" of the system refer to governance models, government regulation and underlying social values (or "*dominant cultural orientations*").[2]

The following sections analyze the health reform experiences of Chile, Israel, Singapore, Switzerland, Taiwan and The Netherlands, describing the current arrangements for funding, contracting and payment, ownership and administration (or "governance") of health care at the beginning of the twenty-first century. They also address the origins of the health care reforms, the selection of policy options, processes of implementation and "after reform adjustments", looking at factors that help explain the variety in reform paths, such as national politics and the positions of major stakeholders. The Tables in the Appendix contain some core data on the six countries of this contribution and their health care systems.

The final section contains general conclusions about comparative methodology and empirical findings. The main conclusion is that, indeed – and not surprising for scholars of public policy – national values (or dominant cultural orientations), institutions and politics all play an important role in the shaping and outcomes of health policy. The combination of fiscal and budgetary pressure and ideological change led to reassessments of existing arrangements everywhere (Ranade 1998, Timmins 1995). Only a few countries systematically studied experiences abroad in their search for new policy directions. The cases reveal a remarkable variety in reform activity, ranging from the implementation of a uniform nationwide social health insurance (Taiwan) to quasi-privatized schemes in Singapore and The Netherlands, regulated private insurance within a regionally decentralized health system in Switzerland, to the continuation of the basic sick fund model in Israel with new procedures to establish uniform entitlements, and adjustments of the public/private mix of health insurance in Chile.

At first sight, the cases we have selected do not have much in common. The countries are located in different continents and show great variety in size, population, ethnicity and historical backgrounds (the tables in the appendix present data on size, population, income levels, economic growth and health care in the six countries). The countries also differ in "dominant cultural orientations" (see below) and economic circumstances, with very different traditions and styles of social policy-making.

However, they also have some common features. They all are small to mid-size industrialized democracies with open economies.[3] They share the general policy goal of providing universal access to good quality health care, and all six have sought to broaden insurance coverage while restraining public expenditure. Over time, they have faced similar fiscal strains, growing (and changing) demand for medical services and health insurance and changing views of the role of the state in society. Moreover, all have discussed a similar range of reform options, and all have sought to enlarge access to health care services by expanding (public and private) health insurance and tax-based funding. Another common feature that sets the group apart is that – illustrating the need to make a careful distinction between policy as *intention* or plans and policy as *actually implemented* change – all six countries actually undertook major reforms (as defined above) in the last two decades, rather than just discussing reform intentions. Public discontent, political willingness to act and the availability of policy options combined to create "windows of opportunity" (Kingdon 1984) for such change. Finally, and perhaps most importantly, the countries selected are "under the radar screen": they are usually not included in international comparative studies.

The seemingly common experience in reform goals and means can easily lead to generalized conclusions of (global) convergence. However, the health politics of the six countries in this study have not converged into one common direction. Each country has implemented change within the restraints of existing national institutions and political boundaries. While the goals and range of options considered were strikingly similar, the six countries diverged widely in the actual reform models and process of implementation. Ideas, interests and political institutions played important roles. The differences reflect country-specific cultural values (for example, solidarity versus individual consumer choice), ideological views of the role of state and citizens, institutions (for example centralized versus decentralized political power) and interests (stakeholders that encourage, thwart or slow down reforms).

The timing and speed of change varied as well. In some countries, governments were able to rapidly implement major change. Others, facing strong opposition by organized stakeholders, had to adjust or even abandon their reform efforts. In several cases, the introduction of market competition went hand-in-hand with increased government control, leading to increased "hybridization" of health care systems. The current reality of growing diversity and hybridization (or perhaps, rather, "*complexification*") of health care arrangements illustrate that systems do not fit easily within common categorizations.

At the level of specific programmes and policies rather than at the national country level, however, we see more similarity in experience. For example, in several cases the efforts to change payment modes and methods for medical care took more time than originally envisioned. In most if not all countries, governments softened the effects of market competition by imposing restrictions on both health insurers and providers of care (for example, by mandating entitlements of private health insurance, forcing private insurance to accept everyone seeking insurance, imposing national fees and tariffs and quality norms for both publicly and privately funded health care and providing subsidies for low-income groups). In all cases, faced with popular opposition, governments moderated the effects of patient co-payments by exempting certain groups.

The conclusions confirm the need to collaborate across countries and disciplines. No individual researcher can do a systematic study of change and non-change in, say, more than three or four countries at this depth of understanding and detail. Second, the study confirms the need to pay more attention to small and medium countries. The vast majority of comparative research in the field focuses on the big countries, with the US, Canada, the UK, and sometimes France, Germany and Australia as the usual suspects. There is little research focusing on the experience of smaller and mid-sized countries while, in fact, the vast majority of the world's nations fall into those categories. To fill this gap, many more studies are needed. This research aims to take a step in that direction. Small nations, unite – in our comparative research!

Categorizing Countries and Health Care Systems

According to reports of the Organization for Economic Co-operation and Development (OECD) it is possible to describe any given health care system in terms of a country-specific mix of public and private funding, contracting and modes of providing medical services (OECD 1992, 1994). There are five main sources of funding and three dominant contracting models. In industrial countries, the major funding sources are general taxation (general revenue, earmarked taxes and tax expenditure), public and private insurance, direct patient payments (co-payments, co-insurance, deductibles and uninsured services) and voluntary contributions. There are three basic contracting models. The first is the "integrated model", with funding and ownership of services under the same (public or private) responsibility. The best-known example of this model is the original British National Health Service (NHS). Examples of integrated private model are some of the "Health Maintenance Organizations" (HMOs) in the US – that, in fact, closely resemble the nineteenth century German sickness funds that owned clinics and employed physicians. The second model is the "contracting model", where governments or other third payers negotiate long-term contracts with health care providers. The third model, common in private insurance, is that of reimbursement where the patient first pays his provider and then seeks reimbursement from his insurance agency.

On the provision side, the ownership and management of health services can be public, private (both for profit and not for profit), or – common in most countries – a mix of those. Moreover, there are country-specific mixes of formal and informal care, traditional and modern medicine, and medical and related social services. In this contribution, the emphasis is on medical care, but borderlines with other services are not always clear, and national health policies express divergent cultural views about such borderlines.

The combination of those three core elements: funding, contracting (including the payment modes) and ownership largely determines the allocation of financial risks and decision-making power over the main players in health care. For example, tax funding and government ownership make for strong government influence whereas private funding (insurance and direct patient payments) combined with legally independent providers restricts the role of the state (as in Switzerland or The Netherlands), even while governments often can – and do – impose rules to protect patients or safeguard the quality of health care.

OECD countries have developed a variety of health governance models and institutions (Immergut 1992, Okma 2002, Hirschman 1970). Those institutions offer organized interests the opportunity to slow down or thwart or block policy efforts and force policy makers to adjust their plans. In the political arena, such veto powers create important barriers to change. Douglas and Wildavsky (1982) identify three "dominant cultural orientations" in welfare states: "competitive individualism", "hierarchical collectivism" and "sectarianism". The majority of the social democratic states of North Western Europe base their fiscal and social policy on principles of solidarity and equality. They have strong collectivist traditions, with modest individualism and weak sectarianism. They also have strong bureaucratic traditions. In some countries, in particular Germany and The Netherlands, those bureaucracies engage in semi-permanent consultation with the organized stakeholders in the "neo-corporatist" style of governance (even while in The Netherlands that practice has declined in the last two decades). The United States, in contrast, is a more liberal welfare state, with weak collectivism and an outspoken streak of sectarianism. Market competition and individual liberty are guiding principles in much of its social policy. Another categorization of social policy takes the underlying welfare principles as a starting point, distinguishing *income protection, behaviorist, residualist* and *populist redistributive* principles to characterize social policy (Marmor et al. 1990). Those general orientations and principles translate into certain styles of policy making in health care (Okma 2002).

It would be an error, however, to take such general orientations as representations of particular countries. Models do not cover countries on a one-to-one basis. Different styles of governance can exist side by side, and over time there may be shifts from one style to another. For example, Dutch health policies shifted from a solidarity-based model towards elements of market competition, with a rise of behaviorist principles and a more residualist role of the state in unemployment and disability policies. Taiwan, as we will show, went in the opposite direction by transforming its existing health insurance schemes into a population-wide national insurance. The Swiss, Israel and Dutch health policy arenas all reveal features of neo-corporatist policy making where governments share the responsibility over social policy with organized interests. Of the six countries of this study, Singapore appears least bounded by ideology or labels, preferring a pragmatic approach. In fact, as we will see, the above typologies of welfare state arrangements serve more to characterize certain categories of policies than entire countries or health care systems.

Health Care Reform in Chile

Chile is a mid-sized industrial country in southeastern Latin America located between Argentina and the Pacific Ocean, with a population of about 16 million in 2004. Over 90 per cent live in urban areas. Chile has long been one of the leaders in social policy change in Latin America, sometimes called the "regional benchmark for structural reforms" (OECD 2003). In 1924, Chile was one of the first countries in Latin America with public pensions and health insurance (De Viado and Flores 1944, Barrientos 2002). Three factors combined to open a "window of opportunity" (Kingdon 1984) for introducing social insurance at that time, not only in Chile, but also in other countries in Latin America. First, European countries, in particular Germany, provided the model of employment-based social insurance to protect the family incomes of industrial workers in case of disability, illness and old age. Second, there was growing awareness of the need for government action to address the poor health of the working population, poverty and labor unrest after World War I. Third, there was political willingness (and ability) to act.

The social health insurance of 1924 only covered urban manual workers. It explicitly excluded rural and domestic workers and the self-employed. There were separate schemes for employees and civil servants. The entitlements included sickness and medical benefits, maternity benefits, health services for infants up to two years old, and benefits in case of invalidity, old age and death. In 1942, the above schemes for white-collar workers merged into the Servicio Médico Nacional de Empleados (SERMENA). SERMENA was based on individual capitalization funds and preferred provider arrangements with independent providers (Labra 1995). In 1952 Chile began to implement the Sistema Nacional de Salud (SNS), resembling the British National Health Service. Public health was seen as a universal citizen's right. Both membership and range of entitlements of the social health insurance gradually expanded. "Indigents" without formal income received a "certificate of poverty" that provided access to the SNS.

In September 1973, the Pinochet military regime overthrew socialist President Allende who had been elected three years before. Heavily influenced by the neoliberal ideology of the University of Chicago School of Economics, the regime favored a reduced role of the state and a shift towards privatization and consumer choice as driving forces in healthcare (Jost 1999). It drastically reduced social spending and public health services.

Since the early 1980s, insured under the public scheme FONASA can opt out and seek coverage from the private insurance scheme, Institución de Salud Previsional (ISAPRE). The expectation was that the exodus from the social insurance scheme would strengthen private insurance and reduce the public sector to a minimum. In fact, predictably – and similar to the experience of other countries – the "opting out option" led to a spiraling process of risk selection as the young and healthy went private, but the sick and elderly had to remain in (or return to) the public scheme as they faced serious access barriers in the private market.

The return to democracy in March 1990 brought social policy based on a mix of market orientation, social solidarity and strong public responsibility. The new government announced massive additional investment to improve the quality of public services and reduce waiting times. It did not do away with the dual health insurance system, however, but imposed extensive regulation on health providers and insurers. The share of private insured has since dropped from 25 per cent in 1996 (Jost 1999) to 23 per cent in 1999 (Sapelli 2004) and 16.3 per cent of the population in 2006 (FONASA 2007). In 2006, almost 80 per cent of the population had coverage under the public scheme, and 5 per cent under other schemes (armed forces and private liberal medicine). General taxation provided 49.9 per cent of health funding, public health insurance 42 per cent, patient co-payments 6.6 per cent and other sources 2.5 per cent (FONASA 2007). Patients under the public scheme face modest amounts of co-payments, but over 60 per cent of the population is exempt from paying those fees. The public health programs (including prevention) cover 100 per cent of the population. It is important to underline the centrality of the public health system: together with the decline in poverty in the 1990s (poverty rates dropped from 46 per cent to 13 per cent of the population), it has contributed to the great improvement of the health of Chile's population.

The private ISAPRE schemes mostly function as traditional for-profit insurers. They offer coverage for health care and pay for sick leave. Since 2005, they face extensive government regulation: a certain minimum coverage, uniform premium structure, and community-rated premiums. ISAPREs do not have to accept all applicants, but they must cover both insured and dependants. Families cannot split their coverage between the public and private insurance – if one spouse is in, the whole family must be under the same scheme. Most ISAPREs charge user fees, with co-payments between 30 and 50 per cent, subject to caps to mitigate the financial burden for lower income families. Some of the private insurers own health facilities, or have preferred provider arrangements with health care providers (Jost 1999). The largest one, CONSALUD, owns clinics and hospitals and is able to steer its insured towards those facilities. Another large one, Banmedica, has formed an integrated financing and delivery model with a large hospital in Santiago. It requires its members to choose a gatekeeper primary care physician (an internist or pediatrician) from a closed panel list.

Chile has a long tradition with free choice of provider (the SNS introduced free choice to its white-collar workers in 1968), and insurers are hesitant to impose too many restrictions on their insured (or face the wrath of the medical association). The introduction of "integrated forms of managed care" has been a slow process (Jost 1999). There are separate schemes for the police and armed forces. As in other countries, the dual insurance system with voluntary enlisting faces rising problems of risk selection and moral hazard (Sapelli 2004, Höfter 2006). The public system is plagued by a lack of funding and shortages of qualified personnel. There are frequent strikes by health professionals dissatisfied with low pay and poor working conditions.

In total, the system offers fairly broad access to public health services (including primary care, immunization and other preventive services, elderly care and mother and child care). For other health care services, however, there are two separate systems: the public one (for the FONASA insured) and the private one (for the ISAPRE insured). The latter tend to be concentrated in wealthy urban areas, especially in Santiago (FONASA 2007). The majority of hospitals as well as local clinics and municipal primary care centers are under public ownership and control. The SNSS/MS administers hospitals, specialized centers and emergency services as well as the primary health centers in Santiago. After the decentralization of the 1980s, local authorities became responsible for the primary health centers in the rest of the country, under regulation by the Health Ministry. Long-term contracts between FONASA and hospitals provide the base for paying for inpatient care. Hospitals receive prospective budgets (over 60 per cent is historically based) plus additional payments for specific activities. Private insurers provide about 15 per cent of the hospital income; they negotiate contracts and fees with (preferred) providers.

In the late 1990s, the government announced a shift towards capitation payment of primary care and case-based payments (or DRG-based payments) for hospital care (Jost 1999). But this turned out to be a complex process. In the mid-2000s, case-based payments contributed only about 10 per cent of hospital budgets. Facing much opposition to market-oriented change, the government reaffirmed its strong commitment to maintaining a public health system as a viable alternative to the private sector. As another example of this commitment, in 2002 it introduced the Garantías Explícitas Plan (Explicit Guarantees Plan), a compulsory coverage for both SNSS and Isapres for a basic "basket" of approximately 60 pathologies.

The Chilean experience illustrates that a change in political regime can create a "window of opportunity" for change. But dominant values as well as long-standing institutions constrain what governments can in fact implement. Even while the military regime shifted towards private health insurance, it did not do away with all public health services. Likewise, the restoration of democracy in 1991 did not do away with private health insurance. There have been efforts to regulate the private insurance, but private insured still face problems of risk selection and exclusion of pre-existing conditions from coverage.

Health Care Reform in Israel

Israel, a small country at the Eastern shore of the Mediterranean bordered by Lebanon, Jordan and Egypt with about 6 million inhabitants, is another country with a long tradition of public health insurance. In 1911, labor unions established the first mutual sick fund, followed by three other funds in the 1920s and 1930s (Rosen 2003). The health insurance started as an employment-based scheme modeled after the employment-based (Bismarckian) social health insurance of Germany, but gradually expanded to cover all but the entire population. In the late 1980s, 95 per cent of the population had voluntarily enrolled with one of the four (not-for-profit) funds. Despite this nearly universal coverage, the system was plagued by financial instability, public and provider dissatisfaction, hospital overcapacity and fragmentation of services. Finally – at least in the eyes of Israeli public and politicians – there were too many uninsured (as in The Netherlands, even a small share of uninsured can cause political pressure on government to take action, see below).

In 1995 Israel enacted the National Health Insurance Law (NHI) that mandates all residents to register with a sick fund. By extending the social insurance from employed persons to the entire population, it created a hybrid between the Bismarckian model and the National Health Insurance. The NHI is a population-wide social health insurance, administered by four major (competing) sick funds. The NHI was part of a three-pronged reform proposed by the 1990 Netanyahu Commission, a state commission of inquiry. Two other planks of the reform – changing government hospitals to public trusts and the reorganization of the Ministry of Health – never materialized because of too much resistance from hospital labor unions. From a rational planning point of view, the partiality of the reform is a recipe for frustration. Nonetheless, from a policy-learning point of view (Helderman et al. 2005), NHI's enactment set in motion a chain of events worth examining. The NHI led to one radical change that in itself did not depend on the full implementation of the envisioned reform: a legally defined universal standard basket of services. Previously, each fund could determine its own entitlements, and was not required to provide any particular service. While other countries like the Netherlands (Berg and Van der Grinten 2004) and New Zealand (Chinitz 1999) abandoned the idea of (explicitly) defining a core basket of health services, Israel went quite clearly, if not always resolutely, down this road.

The major funding sources for health care in Israel are social insurance contributions, tax subsidy and modest amounts of patient co-payments. In recent years, co-payments for hospital stay and prescription drugs have gone up, but there are many exemptions and caps on the total amount that families pay each year, with lower caps for the elderly. As the mandatory social health insurance offers a wide range of entitlements, supplemental health insurance plays an insignificant (but growing) role. This covers the costs of private physicians, treatment in private clinics and complementary medicine (Highlight on Israel 2003).

Israelis can choose the fund they want to register with, and can change twice per year. In 1995, the first year they had this option, about 4 per cent of the population actually switched, but after that, the rate of change went down to about 1 per cent. The largest fund, Chalit, covers 60 per cent of the population, the other three about 36 per cent. The NHI explicitly lists its entitlements in an appendix. It not only specifies procedures and pharmaceuticals, but also provides guidelines for applications. If a physician prescribes an "off indication" or "outside of the guideline" use of a particular drug, the sick fund is within its legal rights to refuse reimbursement.[4] Parliament can add (or de-list) entitlements within the available public budget to cover the anticipated costs (the Ministry of Finance agreed to expand the annual budget by about 1 per cent for this expansion). In 1998 the government set up a Public Committee to assess the addition of new services (Gross *et al.* 1998). The Committee meets several times a year and the media regularly cover its activities. It ranks potential new services, based on health technology assessment by the Ministry of Health (MoH). In a typical neo-corporatist mode, the Committee is made up of 24 physicians, experts of the MoH and sick funds, and public representatives. It bases its deliberation on ethical, economic and social criteria in order to decide which services will be included. Not surprisingly, the list of services seeking entrance into the basket, mainly pharmaceuticals, usually exceeds the available funding, and there is much pressure from patients and lobby groups.

Insured can seek supplementary insurance offered both by sick funds and private health insurance (one-quarter of the population choose the latter). In the early 2000s, some funds expanded their supplemental coverage with drugs and some other services not covered under the basic insurance. Ironically, the Ministry of Finance opposed this move, as it would increase national health expenditure and create a two-tiered system.

Health care providers include hospitals owned by government and sick funds, clinics owned by sick funds, self-employed physicians who have contracts with funds, and private for-profit hospitals, laboratories and institutes. Mother-and-child care, mental health care and nursing care are not included in the NHI and are subject to different arrangements (Bentur *et al.* 1998). All insured can select a primary care physician who works in a nearby clinic of their health fund, or a self-employed physician with a contract with their fund. Access to non-emergency care generally requires a referral from the health fund physician or pre-approved from the fund. While Israelis can, and do, exercise choice of hospital, referrals generally include direction to a specific provider. Hospitals receive capped budgets, though the funds typically reimburse 50 per cent of budget overruns. Emergency care and outpatient clinics are paid on a fee for service basis. Physicians in hospitals usually receive salaries, while independent general practitioners receive capitation payment for each individual on their patient list. Independent physicians receive a capitation payment for those patients making a visit. The capitation payments are generally a form of capped fee for service, and do not involve risk bearing on the part of the physician. The MoH sets the per diem rates and fee schedules for the entire country.

National professional associations of hospital physicians, nurses and other providers negotiate salaries on behalf of their members. In Jerusalem, physicians are permitted private work in hospital under strict regulation. Elsewhere, ad hoc arrangements allowed physicians to do private work in hospital, but these were halted by order of the State Attorney General and the issue has not been resolved. Many physicians based in public hospitals have after-hours private practices and perform procedures at private hospitals.

The sick funds are legally independent entities, but the MoH has overall responsibility. It sets the rules, defines benefits, is involved in planning and allocation of budgets, sets hospital budgets and imposes limits on public spending as well as numbers of physicians. The National Health Insurance Institute administers the funding of the NHI. It collects contributions via the tax system and allocates those over the funds. The collective bargaining and active participation of the main organized stakeholders resembles the neo-corporatist style of social policy making of Western Europe. In general, this gives providers of care a strong veto position.

Private insurers can set their own premiums, and membership is subject to underwriting. The National Health Insurance Regulator, a branch of the Ministry of Finance, regulates private health insurance. Recently, the Insurance Regulator intervened and overturned the refusal of private insurers to pay for pharmaceuticals for which a substitute existed in the national standard basket of services. Traditionally the MoH has monitored both the basic insurance and supplemental coverage. The ministry has the reputation of an ineffective regulator. It owns two-thirds of general hospital beds. This has created a conflict of interest and sometimes inability to turn its attention from the day-to-day management of hospitals towards planning and regulation. In recent years, the MoH has turned out to be a better at financial regulation than at quality assurance. Through control over hospital reimbursement rates, it has been able to stabilize hospital expenditure. As of 2006, the health funds were, by and large, working within balanced budgets for the standard basket of services. The Ministry has been less adept at regulating quality of care. Lacking resources, and confronting less than complete co-operation from physicians' associations, it has not been able to create a framework for ongoing quality assurance in provision and insurance. Physicians' associations and health funds participate in benchmarking and other quality assurance efforts, but they do not agree on public disclosure of measured results. The MoH is a frequent target of critical media coverage of medical error and malfeasance, and has set up investigative and disciplinary committees to deal with these concerns.

Israeli health policy-making thus provides an interesting example of a combination of strong government involvement on one hand and political timidity to enact radical change. The strong veto position of organized interests evidently contributes to the government's incapacity to implement change rapidly. The Israeli experience also illustrates another possible interpretation: namely, that partially implemented reforms may offer a more realistic and interesting comparative experience than "perfect" policy reform that is not implemented.

Health Care Reform in Singapore

Singapore is a tiny island city-state with a population of 4.5 million, one of the most densely populated countries in the world. It is a parliamentary democracy that gained self-rule from the British in 1959, and independence from Malaysia in 1965. The ruling People's Action Party has been in power since 1959 – hence it has the rare advantage of being able to pursue its reform agenda without much opposition or undue interruption. In 2005, Singapore spent about S$7.6 billion or 3.8 per cent of its gross domestic product (GDP) on health care. Of this, the government expended only about S$1.8 billion or 0.9 per cent of GDP. The main funding sources for health care are employer benefits (35 per cent), government subsidies (25 per cent) and out-of-pocket payment (25 per cent). In addition, there are three schemes to help families pay their medical bills: Medisave, Medishield and Medifund. Medisave accounts for 8 per cent of total health care expenditure, while Medishield and Medifund together account for about 2 per cent. Private insurance covers about 5 per cent of all costs.

The Singaporean health care reforms date back to 1960. Barely six months into office, the newly elected government introduced user fees for the first time. It charged 50 cents (US$1 = S$1.48 in 2007) per visit to a government outpatient clinic. Further, it decentralized primary care from the overcrowded General Hospital (which registered 2400 out-patients a day) to a network of 26 satellite outpatient dispensaries and 46 maternal and child health clinics – a process that would take four years to complete. These steps were, in hindsight, a harbinger of things to come.

Before 1960, health care was mainly funded from government revenues, but standards in the decrepit and poorly equipped hospitals were not high. Fewer than 50 doctors were in possession of higher qualifications. The Minister of Health declared in 1967 that "health would rank, at most, fifth in order of priority" for funds – after national security, job creation, housing and education, in that order (Yong 1967). It was not until the 1970s that medical specialization began in earnest, and not until the 1980s that the government responded to the rising aspirations that accompanied growing affluence. In 1983, it unveiled a National Health Plan that included an ambitious hospital construction and expansion program to replace the old buildings inherited from the British colonial times, and an innovative health funding model to propel Singapore medicine into the modern, high-tech era. The philosophy behind the reform – that nothing comes free – was very unorthodox for a government elected on a democratic socialism platform. The emphasis was on individual responsibility, with the state as payer of last resort.

In the early 1960s, the political leadership had taken an abrupt right turn ideologically (leading to its eventual withdrawal or perhaps expulsion from the Socialist International in 1976). It trumped the political left (from which it had openly split) in the battle for the hearts and minds of the hard-working Singaporeans. Since then Singapore has eschewed, at least rhetorically, egalitarian welfarism in favor of market mechanisms to allocate finite resources. In practice, this meant using pricing to curb demand but at the same time softening the consequences to protect lower income groups. Pragmatism, not ideology, would guide social policies in the decades that followed. The government and the people focused single-mindedly on expanding the size of the economic pie. The government encouraged citizens to assume personal responsibility for their own welfare, while it pledged to continue subsidizing vital areas like housing, health and education to make them affordable for all.

Singapore introduced Medisave in 1984 as an extension of the existing national superannuation scheme, the Central Provident Fund (CPF). The CPF is a compulsory, tax-exempt, interest-yielding pension savings scheme. It started in 1955 (it was already implemented elsewhere in Britain's colonies including British Malaysia and some African countries to ensure that the social security needs would not drain British public funds). Medisave represents 6–8 per cent of wages (depending on age) sequestered from the individual's CPF account. The account holders can use Medisave to pay for hospitalization and acute medical care (including hospice care, certain expensive outpatient treatments like day surgery, radiotherapy, chemotherapy, renal dialysis, in vitro fertilization and hepatitis B vaccination). Account holders can also use the fund to pay for hospitalization of their spouses, children, siblings or parents and any unspent balance passes on to their beneficiaries after their death (Lim 2004a).

Medishield, the voluntary, low cost catastrophic illness insurance scheme complements Medisave. Medisave funds can be used to pay for the Medishield premiums. The third "M" – Medifund – is the state-funded safety net that takes care of those without the means to pay, including people not covered by Medisave or Medishield, or those who have run out of their quota in these schemes. Medifund was set up as an endowment fund. Its interest is distributed to the public hospitals to cover costs of patients genuinely unable to pay their hospital bills. The government periodically tops up (from budget surpluses) the various schemes in such way as to preferentially benefit low-income families and the elderly. In addition, in 2000, it set up an "Eldercare Fund" to provide subsidies to voluntary welfare organizations that offer care to the elderly. This fund is expected to reach S$2.5 billion by 2010. Eldercare was followed in 2002 by Eldershield, an insurance scheme for severely disabled elderly Singaporeans, with premiums payable out of their Medisave accounts. The combined Medisave accounts of all Singaporeans now amount to S$36 billion (or US$24.3 billion). That is a not insignificant sum considering that the annual total healthcare expenditure in Singapore is almost S$7 billion. A further redistributional element is embedded in the graded hospital wards, ranging from single rooms to open dormitories with eight or more beds. Patients in class A beds pay full costs, while those in Class C enjoy 80 per cent subsidy. The MoH estimates that more than 96 per cent of B and almost 98 per cent of C patients should be able to pay fully for their bills from their Medisave account. Access to necessary medical care for the poor is guaranteed by a government promise that "no Singaporean will ever be denied needed health care because of inability to pay" (Lim 1998).

Singapore's hospital restructuring process started in 1985 and took 20 years to roll out. The backdrop of this was the economic recession of the mid-1980s when the government sought to transfer the engine of economic growth from the public to the private sector. A 1986 Report of the Economic Committee mentioned healthcare as a prime candidate for deregulation and privatization. The government considered various models to reduce or eliminate control by the Ministry of Health and to grant hospitals autonomy, ranging from a statutory board to manage public hospitals to wholesale privatization to increase efficiency. At first, the government chose the latter. Widespread public unhappiness over the planned privatization, however, led to months of intense debate in public forums, media and parliament. In a rare instance of retreat in the face of negative public opinion, the government modified its original privatization plan. It opted instead for "corporatization" of the public hospitals and specialty centers (Phua 1991, Preker and Harding 2003). Thus, one by one, these institutions gained autonomy in fiduciary and operational matters as independent entities within the meaning of Singapore's Companies Act. The government created a monolithic government company, the Health Corporation of Singapore (HCS) Private Limited in 1987 to own and manage all corporatized hospitals and specialty centers. The independent hospitals, although "private" in name, each under its own board of directors, were actually public since they were owned 100 per cent by the HCS, which in turn was 100 per cent government-owned.

By the year 2000, every public hospital and specialist medical center had become corporatized. Hospitals were free to set their own direction and to compete with each other. As market mechanisms and structures replaced old bureaucratic ones, efficiency and service levels improved. As each hospital increasingly focused on its own survival, however, competition became counter-productive. Dysfunctional aspects surfaced such as the poaching of staff from other hospitals by offering higher salaries. Non-cooperation between institutions resulted in missed opportunities for exploiting economies of scale such as central drug purchasing or developing a common information technology (IT) platform for electronic medical records. Each hospital Chief Executive Officer (CEO) vied to increase its market share through high-tech acquisitions and other means, confident that HCS or the MoH would eventually bail them out if they ran up deficits. Hospital expenditures rose sharply, contributing to health care cost inflation.

The government intervened in 2000. Believing the competition would work better with a smaller number of competitors, it arbitrarily regrouped the corporatized institutions into two competing "clusters" – the National Healthcare Group and the Singapore Health Services. These quasi-independent clusters would still report to the MOH as the Ministry appointed its boards. Simultaneously, the two clusters took control over all the government polyclinics for primary care. Thus, in one fell swoop government achieved horizontal and vertical integration of all public sector health care providers at the primary, secondary and tertiary levels. Shortly after, it introduced DRG-based payments, followed by global budgeting, both aimed at curbing supply-side moral hazard.

The reforms resulted in raised standards of care and levels of service that are a far cry from the overcrowded wards and unresponsive outpatient clinics of yesteryear. Average waiting time for elective surgery nowadays is a mere two weeks while a recent survey showed overall patient satisfaction at 80 per cent (Lim 2004b). Mandatory hospital quality committees and voluntary Joint Commission International (JCI) accreditation ensure clinical quality and patient safety. In fact, one-third of Asia's JCI-accredited health care facilities are now found in Singapore (Newsweek 2007). The city-state's vibrant biosciences research and development environment also enhances its reputation as a center of medical excellence. In 2005, more than 374,000 foreign patients sought treatment in Singapore, four out of five in private clinics and hospitals. Growth in the number of foreign patients has been averaging 20 per cent in the last few years, thanks to the stepped-up efforts by Singapore Medicine, a government/industry partnership established in 2003 to turn Singapore into a leading medical hub.

Patients have complete freedom of choice of providers, which include 29 well-equipped hospitals and specialty centers with 12,000 beds (or 3.7 beds per 1000 population). A thriving private sector accounts for about 21 per cent of inpatient beds and 80 per cent of outpatient attendance (Ministry of Health 2007). The government has signaled it would like to see the private share of hospital beds increase to 30 per cent. Four of the for-profit chains are currently listed on the Singapore Stock Exchange. The government actively encourages competition and publishes hospital bill sizes and selected quality indicators on its website to encourage consumer choice.

The health care system of Singapore thus reflects a mix of strong market orientation and individualism, with a high acceptance of government intervention.

The absence of a tradition of well-organized stakeholders and opposition groups has contributed to the rapid adoption of top-down policies. The combination of individual savings accounts with employer subsidies and public (means-tested) subsidies targeted at low-income families make for a quasi-private system under tight government control. Another unique feature of Singapore is its extraordinary high savings rate that combined with high economic growth rates (averaging 8 per cent per annum over the last 20 years) makes for a comfortable starting point for public policy. Patients are accustomed to cost sharing rather than depending on state largesse. The cost-sharing formula has to some extent countered the "moral hazard" generally associated with fee-for-service, third-party reimbursement. Singapore has deliberately avoided the more costly "leveling down" option of universal access regardless of ability to pay, in which the "undeserving rich" enjoy the same benefits as the poor. Compared to OECD countries, Singapore has been very successful in containing the level of health care spending to below 5 per cent of GDP (see Table 2). It remains to be seen, however, whether it will be able to maintain that low level of spending. As Singapore's economy matures, economic growth will inevitably slow down, lessening the masking effect of the expanding GDP denominator. Moreover, Singapore has a very young population. The elderly now constitute only 8 per cent of the population, but are projected to increase to 25 per cent in 2030. Hence, rising healthcare expenditure is likely to create sharper trade-offs between efficiency, quality and equity and may also accentuate disparities between the different socio-economic classes (Lim 2005).

Paradoxically, just when governments elsewhere are mulling over cutbacks in health spending, Singapore's health care planners are busy laying the groundwork for the *expansion* and upgrading of its health facilities over the next 10 years, costing billions of dollars. There are two reasons for this. First, in order to generate the human capital needed to sustain Singapore's dynamic economy, the population needs to grow by another 2 million (largely through immigration), stabilizing at 6.5 million persons. Second, Singapore Medicine is targeting 1 million foreign patients by 2012 and it reckons this will generate S$3 billion in revenues and create 13,000 new jobs (Choo 2002). Hence demand for quality health care services, on both domestic and foreign fronts, cannot but rise. For the pragmatic government with a knack for turning necessity into virtue, that is not necessarily a bad thing.

Health Care Reform in Switzerland: From Social Insurance to Federalist Arrangements

Switzerland is a small landlocked country in Central Europe between Germany, Austria, Italy and France (it shares three of its four formal languages with its neighboring countries). It is a federal state composed of 26 smaller states (cantons), with a population of 7.2 million. Three particular characteristics of the political and institutional context provide a high degree of voice, choice and exit opportunities (Hirschman 1970) to Swiss citizens: a decentralized political system with institutions of direct democracy, a long tradition of social security and a liberal economic culture. Swiss health care has its historical base on the two institutional pillars of direct democracy and federalism.[5] Swiss citizens can intervene directly in the political decisional process by referendum to approve or reject reform proposals. Historically, this has slowed down major change. Federalism, expressed in the autonomy of the cantons, allows for distinct regional models. Combined, those two factors have resulted in large regional variations and seemingly insurmountable barriers to nationwide (and pro-poor) reform (Crivelli *et al.* 2007).

Health Insurance

Having been given the mandate to legislate on sickness and accident insurance in 1890, the federal government passed the first Swiss health insurance law in 1911 (Civitas 2002). This law established a statutory package of benefits. In contrast to the social insurance in France and Germany, it stated that individuals, not employers are to contract insurance. By 1990, nearly 98 per cent of the population had purchased (voluntary) insurance.[6] The sick funds faced financial difficulties throughout the middle of the twentieth century. Moreover, the left-wing parties made several attempts to improve the equity of health insurance by making the premiums dependent on income. However, only three of the ten reforms proposed by Parliament of civil society between 1974 and 2003 passed via popular vote, two of those based on federal decrees and focusing on minor aspects.

The third proposal accepted via popular vote, however, was a major reform – the Revised Health Insurance Law of 1994. It came into effect in January 1996. The three main objectives of the reform were to strengthen solidarity, to improve cost control and to promote fair competition between health insurers. The law strengthened the role of the federal state, and ushered in the ability for sick funds to offer innovative insurance plans organized along "managed care" lines. It mandated all citizens to take health insurance and safeguards access to standard benefits that include inpatient and outpatient treatment and care for the elderly and handicapped, with unlimited stays in nursing homes and hospitals. In 1999, alternative and complementary medicine benefits became part of the basic coverage, but they were dropped again in 2005. Within the framework of federal and cantonal regulation, about 90 insurers (that have to be not-for-profit for the mandatory basic coverage, but can be both for-profit or not-for-profit when offering supplemental coverage) offer today a wide array of plans with varying conditions and costs.

The insurance companies were originally federal, regional, religious, or occupationally based (Civitas 2002). Due to frequent mergers, their number has dropped since the mid-twentieth century from 1100 local insurers to about 90 in the early 2000s. Most are operating on a national scale. Membership varies greatly, ranging from 102 to 1.3 million insured in 2006. They have lost their original identity as social insurer and now act as regular commercial insurers. Insurers group together in the national association, Santesuisse, to negotiate fees with providers.

The Swiss Constitution confers full sovereignty upon the cantons for administering health insurance (as it does for all other matters not specifically in the domain of the federal government, the Confederation). For health insurance programs, the Constitution sets three basic requirements: universal access to a benefit basket defined by the Confederation, the right of insured to change health insurer yearly, and uniform insurance contracts. Within those legal limits, independent and competing health insurers negotiate contracts with providers, and offer the basic insurance coverage under a wide array of insurance plans. Insurers must register with the Federal Office of Public Health. This agency also monitors the insurance market. The cantons administer and regulate any insurance programs that meet the standards.

Swiss consumers (and not employers or government) select health insurance plans, the size of deductibles and other conditions according to their own needs and preferences. They can change insurer every year (and insurers have to accept them). The 1994 law made insurance compulsory for all, expanded the guaranteed benefit package and reduced inequities by an extended (and complicated) system of cross-subsidization. It also allowed citizens to switch between insurers more easily than in the past. Each adult citizen signs an individual insurance contract.

Government regulation plays a significant role, for example in mandating that all citizens take insurance, defining the basic coverage and minimum deductible, co-payments, open enrollment and mandated contracting of all providers by all health plans. It is interesting to note that with the exception of the mandatory contracting, quite a few of those rules are similar to the current Dutch laws (see below). Health insurers have to offer community-rated premiums for all who live within a given area, independent of income, wealth or individual health risk of the insured person. Insurers receive extra funds to compensate for over-representation of high-risk groups such as the elderly or chronically ill in their portfolio (Beck *et al.* 2003). Community rating was seen as one of the core elements of the reform to safeguard coverage for the high-risk poor. Insurers can offer discounts to young adults (age 19–25) and have to offer lower premiums for children (up to age 18). To alleviate the impact of this regressive financing, the state gives subsidies to low-income households. In 2004 the subsidies amounted to 20 per cent of total premium revenues. It is worth noting, however, that subsidies have failed to grow apace with premiums, and low and middle-income families now pay a higher share of their means than better off.

Managed Care and Consumer Choice

There is no limit in choice of provider, unless the insured opt for an alternative plan that restricts choice in exchange for lower premiums. The current health insurance is based on a notion of "managed competition" that shifts competition mechanisms from the patient/physician relation to both the health insurer/insured and health insurer/provider relationships (Bolgani *et al.* 2006). Those are similar to the family of US health maintenance organizations (HMO), "preferred provider organizations" (PPO), or "independent practice associations" (IPA) that include networks of family doctors. Those plans entail practices of selective contracting, gatekeeping, and financial bonus-malus incentives for providers to adhere to guidelines (Lehman and Zweifel 2004). Insured can switch insurer or opt for another plan each year. "Managed care" plans offer premium discounts in exchange for a restricted freedom in choosing a doctor. A second set of discounted plans offers lower premiums but higher deductibles. As in other countries, such plans tend to attract younger, healthier, better-informed and more mobile people.

In 1996 and 1997, the first years after the introduction of the new insurance, membership in managed care plans quadrupled. In the early 2000s, after a period of stagnation, policyholders seemed to be migrating again to managed care contracts to escape rising premium levels. Still, in 2005, only about 10 per cent of insured had chosen one of those models. Limited financial benefits (there are legal restrictions to the maximum deductibles insurers can offer) as well as cultural factors (in the French and Italian speaking cantons, only a small minority of the population has chosen for those plans) explain the limited growth in managed care. Some insurers offer supplementary coverage in addition to the obligatory basic federal plan.[7] Insurers have latitude in all matters beyond the coverage of the federal benefit basket, combined with the effects of federalism that leaves much regulation to the canton level. This has resulted in a wide variation of plans. As cantons also differ significantly in their public spending strategy, per capita health spending, supply of hospital and ambulatory care and consumption levels greatly vary across cantons. This has resulted in large differences of financial burdens to the insured between and within cantons, perpetuated by a lack of consumer mobility across plans. For example, in 2004 a family of two parents and two small children with an income of US$42,000 paid 4.7 per cent of their disposable income in the canton Obwalden but 16 per cent in Neuchatel (Baltasar et al. 2005).

Despite those differences, citizens did not exit from either their canton or health insurance on a large scale (Colombo 2001, Frank and Lamiraud 2007). Obviously, most Swiss do not want to switch and remain faithful to their fund even if premiums are (much) higher than elsewhere. Less than 3 per cent of the policyholders switched insurer in 2006. Empirical evidence shows – similar to the experience of other countries where insured can choose their plan – that people who do change mostly represent "good risks": the young, healthy and higher educated (Strombom et al. 2002, Beck et al. 2003). The alternative is "partial exit", a change to another policy with the same insurer. Here, the evidence shows that most change occurs in the high band of deductibles (more than 1200 francs per year). The death rate of those who had selected the minimum deductible is twice as high as that of the insured who had selected the average amount (Geoffard et al. 2006). Without doubt, a process of self-selection lies behind this pattern of preferences in deductibles.

The mandatory nature of the statutory package means that insurers cannot compete on the basis of the benefits or quality of care. They must contract with all hospitals and self-employed practitioners in the canton of the insured person's residence. In case of an emergency, they also have to reimburse treatment in other cantons. They can only differentiate with the level of the basic premium and the quality of administrative services, or with alternative plans that restrict choice of provider in exchange for lower premiums. Self-employed health professionals receive fees for service payments, while hospital budgets are based on a mix of direct government subsidy, DRG-based payment and other fees.

Health Care Provision in Switzerland

Swiss citizens receive their medical treatment in a wide range of settings in hospitals, clinics and ambulatory care facilities. Switzerland has over 400 hospitals, around 270 of which are public or publicly subsidized. There are 5.6 beds per 1000 people, and hospital stays are relatively long. Perhaps due to these factors, hospital expenditure is the highest in Europe. Medical specialists practice privately and in hospitals, though most patients are referred to hospitals for specialized procedures.

The basic insurance covers one-third of prescription drugs, subject to a 10 per cent co-payment. Patients pay for all other drugs directly, or seek supplementary coverage. This means that the Swiss pay heavily for pharmaceuticals and there is generally a desire to increase the use of generic drugs.

The Swiss health care system is based on a liberal conception of health and medicine. The patient-consumer plays a central role, with freedom to choose a health plan as well as a provider. Proponents of "consumer-driven" health care (Herzlinger and Parsi 2004) argue that this model of competing health plans promises to combine universal coverage with effective cost control. However, critics point to the fact that extensive government regulation, not competition or high out-of-pocket payments, has been the driving force to keep costs down (Reinhardt 2004). The underlying regressivity in the design of premiums and the failure of fiscal subsidies to match the rates of increase in insurance cost (and premiums) has become a source of discontent for much of the lower and middle classes (Bolgiani et al. 2006). The federal government has repeatedly tried to reduce the inequity of premium levels across the cantons, but has made little progress so far.

Decentralized Decision-making and Cost Control

Empirical evidence shows that the Swiss model has not been very successful in controlling health spending. The decentralized decision making has led to wide regional variety in regulatory settings, roles of public and private actors, capacity, use and spending levels (Crivelli et al. 2006). In fact, there is not one system but 26 cantonal subsystems, connected by the Federal Health Insurance Law since 1996. This decentralized system offers little room for regional cross-subsidization. In spite of the decentralized nature of the Swiss health insurance, the system has kept some neo-corporatist elements in the bargaining over fees and tariffs. The associations of providers represent their members in collective bargaining at the federal and canton level, and insurers still have to contract with all providers.

One of the problems in assessing the working of the Swiss system is that most experts limit their comparison to Switzerland and the US, often ignoring the particular political and social context of both countries. It is not possible to understand the Swiss health system without paying attention to the crucial role of direct democracy and federalism on the one hand, and the economic and social traditions on the other. The Swiss can exercise their "sovereignty" as citizen-voter, insured and patient. The system provides radical forms of vote in the institutions of federalism and direct democracy that effectively provide veto points to any system change. Insured can switch health insurer each year. In principle, they could also move from one canton to another, but in general the mobility of Swiss citizens is very low; linguistic barriers explain part of that low mobility. Rather than "voting by feet" (Tiebout 1956), citizens can induce change by the instruments of direct democracy: referendums and popular initiatives. The referendum is similar to a veto and has the effect of delaying or freezing the political process; the popular initiative can lead to constitutional amendment. Both mechanisms reduce the power of federal and cantonal government, and make decision making complex and often slow.

The fact that Swiss citizens can choose between exit, choice and voice has caused strong tensions, and resulted in weak governance of the health care system.

The competitive model assumes that consumers are willing and able to use their options based on full information about price and quality. That assumption is particularly questionable in a system characterized by a chronic lack of information and transparency. There is no systematic information available about performance indicators like clinical quality, efficacy and effectiveness of individual providers, prerequisites for consumer choice and exit. Another problem is that the proliferation of plans does not combine well with cantonal responsibility for the availability of health care. By law, cantons have to safeguard sufficient health care capacity and this has led to the creation of regional monopolies and fragmentation of the hospital system (Crivelli 2007).

Health Care Reform in Taiwan

Taiwan consists of one major and several smaller islands, with a total land size of 36,000 square kilometers. It has one of the highest population densities in the world. Of the population of 22.8 million, the majority lives in urban areas and less than 2 per cent live in the mountainous areas and offshore islands.

Taiwan's total national health spending was 6.2 per cent of GDP in 2005. National Health Insurance (NHI) accounted for 57 per cent, out-of-pocket spending 34 per cent, tax subsidies almost 6 per cent and other (private) sources about 4 per cent (DoH data). The NHI is financed on a pay-as-you-go basis with the income-based contributions typical of social insurance. Insured, employers, and government all pay a share of premiums (Cheng 2003). In 2005, 35 per cent of the NHI revenue came from employers, 38 per cent from insured, and 27 per cent from government (Bureau of National Health Insurance – BHNI). The contributions are levied on a per capita basis up to a maximum of three dependants per insured. Any additional dependants enjoy the NHI coverage for free. The government subsidizes 100 per cent of the contributions for the poor and unemployed veterans.

For over 50 years (1949–2000), Taiwan was under the one-party rule by the Nationalist government (Kuomintang, or KMT) that retreated to the island after defeat by the Chinese communists in 1949. From the 1960s to the 1990s, Taiwan's economy enjoyed high growth rates, propelling Taiwan into the ranks of the "Asian Tigers", the groups of four Asian economies –Taiwan, South Korea, Singapore and Hong Kong – that impressed the world by their robust and sustained economic growth and development.

Health Insurance

As Taiwan's economy prospered, the government turned its attention to social policy. By the late 1980s, there were 10 different health insurance schemes, each covering a particular subset of the population, for example Labor Insurance (1950), Government Employees Insurance (1958), Farmers Insurance (1985) and Low Income Household Insurance (1990). Altogether, the schemes only covered about 59 per cent of the population, leaving 41 per cent or 8.6 million of the then population of 21.4 million people uninsured. The uninsured were mostly children under 14 and adults over 65 – vulnerable populations with the greatest health care needs. Private health insurance such as that in the US did not exist (Cheng 2003).

The surprising wholesale move to universal coverage in 1995 built on these schemes, and was made possible by a window of opportunity created by the confluence of several factors: the abolition in 1987 of the martial law that had ruled Taiwan since 1949 in favor of a democratic government, rising popular demand for universal coverage, a political challenge of Taiwan's Nationalist government from the opposition party, the Democratic Progressive Party (DPP), and last but not least, the strong, personal leadership on the issue by Taiwan's then President Lee Teng-Hui (Cheng 2003). That leadership played a critically important role in establishing Taiwan's National Health Insurance in 1995.

To prepare for the introduction of the NHI, government bureaucrats and scholars conducted extensive studies of health systems abroad in the 1980s. The planning took seven years, from 1986 to 1993. The planners drew heavily on foreign experience. The end product of this planning process – the NHI – was described as "a car that has been domestically designed and produced, but with many component parts imported from over ten countries" (Cheng 2003). Next, Taiwan's Parliament deliberated over the NHI bill for over 18 months and passed the bill in July 1994. On March 1, 1995 the NHI was implemented by presidential decree, an amazing five years ahead of schedule (Cheng 2003). Virtually overnight the hitherto uninsured (41 per cent of Taiwan's population) gained equal access to health care. Within a year, their health care utilization approached the same level as those who had health insurance prior to 1995 (Cheng 2003).

The action of an impatient President to push the implementation of the NHI so far ahead of schedule led to a period of confusion and chaos not unlike that which accompanied the introduction of the Medicare program for America's elderly in 1965 (Cheng 2003). Critics and skeptics alike expected that the NHI would fail before it could take off because of inadequate preparation. In retrospect, however, the hasty implementation of the NHI may have been a blessing in disguise. In 1997, a financial crisis struck Asia. Even though it affected Taiwan less than Thailand, Malaysia, Indonesia and South Korea, Taiwan's economic growth nevertheless slowed after 1998. Growth rates dropped to just over 4 per cent in 2000 and to minus 1.7 per cent in 2001 (compared to the high average growth rate of 10.7 per cent from 1992 to 1995, the period before the NHI). In such an economic climate, the government might have raised more concerns about the affordability and sustainability of the ambitious NHI (Cheng 2003, DoH 2006).

The public warmed to the program quickly. In nationwide surveys of satisfaction, for most of the time after its inception, over 70 per cent of the respondents declared themselves satisfied with the NHI, a ratio much higher than in many other countries (Cheng 2003). Only in 2006, after budgetary strains caused increases in out-of-pocket spending, public satisfaction fell to 64 per cent (BNHI 2006). Significantly, the satisfaction rate of the residents in remote mountainous areas and offshore islands reached 89 per cent in 2005. Those populations were particularly happy with their improved access to health care through the government program of Integrated Delivery Service (IDS) designed specifically to improve access for those groups.

In brief, the NHI is a mandatory single payer health insurance. The BHNI administers the NHI under the Department of Health. The administrative costs of the BHNI were a mere of 1.5 per cent of NHI's total budget in 2007 (Cheng 2007).

This low administrative cost is largely due to the efficiency of the nationwide modern and uniform administration supported by a powerful information system, absence of costs of litigation, absence of marketing and advertising expenses and price controls by government.[8] In 2002, Taiwan's Supreme Court ruled that no one in Taiwan may be denied care because of lack of ability to pay (Cheng 2003). Clearly, Taiwan's society considers access to health care as a fundamental right for all.

The NHI benefits are comprehensive. They include inpatient care, ambulatory care, laboratory tests, diagnostic imagining, prescription drugs and dental care (except orthodontics and prosthodontics), traditional Chinese medicine, day care for the mentally ill, limited home care, and certain preventive services (pediatric immunizations, well-child check-ups, adult health checks including prenatal care and pap smears). Moreover, the NHI covers vision care, kidney dialysis, and DoH-approved orphan drugs to treat rare disorders (Cheng 2003).

Health care services in Taiwan are delivered through a predominantly private delivery system. Patients enjoy free choice of provider and of therapy. Providers receive their revenues from three sources: predominantly fee-for-service payments by the BNHI, direct payments by patients (user fees and co-payments), and sales of goods and services not covered by the NHI (Cheng 2003).

Like most if not all health systems around the globe, Taiwan's NHI has been plagued by financial woes since 1998, three years after the NHI was implemented. On the one hand, the public enjoys free choice of providers and there is relatively high utilization of health services. On the other hand, policy pundits and the media have convinced the public that there is "waste, fraud and abuse" in the system, which the government should eliminate before raising charges to households and employers (Cheng 2003, 2005).

It has become fashionable in the debate on health policy – not only in the US but also in many other countries – to equate the word "choice" with "choice among private health insurers and health insurance products". It is doubtful, however, that this is the choice ordinary people have in mind when they speak of "choices in health care". More likely, they have in mind unrestrained choice of provider and therapy. The most important lesson to be drawn from Taiwan's experience is that a single payer system – without choice among private insurers or wide variety in insurance products – can easily and relatively cheaply provide consumer choice of health care providers and therapies. Taiwan's experience also illustrates the need for policy adjustments after reform. In fact, it confirms the general finding that health reform does not mean the once and for all fixing of problems. The "after reform maintenance" requires permanent monitoring and adjustment.

Health Care Reform in The Netherlands

The Netherlands is a small, densely populated country (population of 16 million in 2006) located between Germany in the east, Belgium in the south, and the North Sea in the north and west. The country is a mid-size open European economy with a strong international trade position. It has a stable democracy, and a long tradition of consensual, "neo-corporatist" policy making, where governments share the responsibility for social policy making with organized groups in society (Lijphart 1968, De Swaan 1988).

In 2007, total health spending exceeded €50 billion (US$70 billion), or about €3100 (US$4340; in 2006 €1 equaled about US$1.4) per person per year. Of this total, about 47 per cent came out of the new basic health insurance (introduced in 2006, see below), 42 per cent from contributions for the long-term care insurance Algemene Wet Bijzondere Ziektekosten (AWBZ), about 7 per cent from patient co-payments and about 5 per cent from tax subsidies (MoH 2006). All legal residents have to sign up with one of the 40 or so health insurers to obtain coverage for the basic insurance, and most Dutch citizens have done so. They pay, on average, about €1200 (US$1440) per person per year as flat rate premiums directly to their insurer (they also pay about €1000 for the AWBZ scheme). The government pays for the premiums of children up to 18 years old. The insurers receive the other half of their incomes from earmarked taxes that employers pay into a central fund administered by the Tax Department.

The Netherlands health reform debate started in the early 1970s with efforts to centralize funding and administration, and regionalized health care planning (Okma 1997a). In the early 1980s, the combination of the economic shock of the oil crises (with economic stagnation and high unemployment), the fear of an aging population and the erosion of faith in government planning led to a change in direction of Dutch welfare policies. Successive governments implemented cuts in levels and duration of welfare support, unemployment and disability benefits and (only partly successfully) tried to reduce unemployment rolls and numbers of disability beneficiaries (Visser and Hemereijk 1997). Next, the attention shifted to health care (Okma 1997). In 1987, an expert committee proposed to reduce the role in government and strengthen competition and consumer choice (Commissie Dekker 1987, Schut 1997, Okma 1997). At first, the proposals met with strong resistance from health providers and many other stakeholders. Parliament only hesitantly supported the bill (all major parties were internally divided). Government decided to gradually implement the plans and the first "health reform bill" passed in 1989 (MoH 1988). After a few years, however, opposition resurfaced, political support eroded and the reform process effectively came to a halt (Okma 1997). The 1994 "Purple Coalition' of Labor, Liberal Conservatives and Liberal Democrat parties shelved the reforms, and announced piecemeal improvement of the current system instead (Okma and De Roo, 2009). Interestingly, it did not reverse the reform steps of its predecessors. In the early 2000s, health reform made its comeback on the political agenda (De Roo 2002, Strategisch Akkoord 2002). The 2003 governing coalition of Liberal Conservatives and Christian Democrats decided to take up the basic ingredients of the earlier Dekker proposals, with an even stronger orientation on market competition (Hoofdlijnenakkoord 2003). As the coalition had a comfortable majority, the reform bill passed Parliament in a surprisingly quick and uncontested way in 2005. The return of the Labor, Party Partij van de Arbeid (PvdA), in 2007 to the coalition government did not affect the introduction of the insurance (Regeerakkoord 2007). The main players in the field, in particular health insurers and some large providers, had already anticipated the introduction of the new scheme, and expressed far less opposition than during earlier reform debates.

In January 2006, a new "basic health insurance" (or rather mandate to take out private insurance, somewhat similar to the Swiss health insurance mandate) replaced the former mix of public and private health insurance (Bartolomee and Maarse

2007).[9] The funding of the new scheme consists of a mix of direct contributions, earmarked taxes and government subsidy. The scheme combines elements of both the former private and former social insurance.[10] All residents can choose their insurance for the basic coverage and can take out supplemental coverage. The term "basic" is actually somewhat misleading as the entitlements include a wide range of preventive services, inpatient and ambulatory medical care, prescription drugs and medical aids. The coverage more or less equals that of the former sick fund scheme. Efforts in the last 10 years to scale down this range of entitlements by de-listing items from the social health insurance in the past have not been very successful; in fact, they read as a "catalogue of failure" (Maarse and Okma 2005).

Health insurers receive about 50 per cent of their revenue from flat rate premiums directly from their insured, and about 50 per cent from a central fund that channels the earmarked contributions withheld by employers via the tax system. Low-income families can apply for fiscal subsidy.[11] Patients face modest amounts of co-payment for inpatient and outpatient care. By law, premiums for the basic coverage are community-based, but insurers set their own premiums. Insurers cannot turn down applicants. They attract new customers (or try to retain their clients) by offering low flat-rate premiums and good services; providers are competing for contracts with the insurers by offering low rates and good services. In that way, at least on paper, all Dutch citizens will get good quality and not too expensive health care.

In 2006, about one-fifth of the population changed their insurer and coverage at the introduction of the new scheme, mostly via collective contracts. That number was higher than expected, and prompted some to declare the victory of the competition model (Laske-Aldershof *et al.* 2004). In the second year of the new insurance, however, less than 5 per cent of Dutch insured changed fund, over 80 per cent of those as part of a collective employment-based contract (Smit and Mookveld 2007). Thus, in fact, only about 1 per cent of the change of health plan was "consumer-driven". In a way, the new scheme has strengthened the employment base of the health insurance even while its basic underlying notion is that of individual choice. A new phenomenon in the Dutch insurance market is the rise of collective contracting by certain groups of patients (at least for groups that insurers are willing to accept).

In 2007, the number of uninsured was rising as families had difficulty in paying the monthly flat rate premiums (that before were withheld by employers as part of earmarked taxation or by welfare offices). Even while compared to the US the number of uninsured is still very low, less than 3 per cent of the population, it poses a political problem for the government. First, the government proposed that if uninsured ended up in hospital, they would face the costs of hospitalization themselves and would not only have to take out insurance on the spot but pay a fine as well. Then, as a study showed that (young) immigrants, single parents and welfare recipients were over-represented in the delinquent population, it realized that model would be hard to enforce (CBS 2007). The government next proposed to abolish the direct payment of flat rate premiums for welfare recipients altogether and have the local welfare offices administer those charges (a solution already proposed by the welfare offices of Amsterdam and Rotterdam in 2005). The MoH also took over the costs of debt collection from the insurers as long as they would keep the delinquents on their roll (MoH 2007).

Thus far, the new competition has not been successful in driving down premiums or health expenditure (Kreis 2005). In 2007, average premiums went up by about 10 per cent and most experts expect a further hike as several health insurers have spent excessive amounts on marketing and advertising to keep or extend their market share (Smit and Mookveld 2007). As the new competitive model went into effect in January 2006, it is too early to assess to what extent competition has improved the quality and efficiency or patient-friendliness of the system.

Dutch hospitals and other health facilities have a centuries-long tradition of private, not-for-profit ownership and governance by self-appointed boards (De Swaan 1988, Okma 1997a). The last two decades have seen the rise of new specialty investor-owned for-profit clinics (mostly for elective surgery on an outpatient basis). Still, that has hardly affected the dominant not-for-profit pattern. And many hospital managers do not feel at ease with the new demands of market competition (Rosenberg 2006, 2007). There has been a rapid process of mergers and takeovers that led to smaller numbers of bigger hospitals as well as vertical and horizontal integration of health services (Boot 1998, RVZ 2003). This market concentration has raised concerns of the national competition authority (NMa). In some cases, NMa denied approval of mergers when they might lead to regional monopolies or exclude competition altogether.

One of the side effects of the increased emphasis on competition has been the erosion of the traditional corporatist bargaining model in The Netherlands (Okma 2002). For many decades, associations of hospitals, medical professionals and other providers met with representatives of the public and private health insurers to negotiate contracts and discuss policy developments. As the NMa has ruled that such collective bargaining, in fact, implied undue market protection and exclusion of newcomers, they had to abandon this practice. Hospitals, general practitioners, dentists and others now have to seek contracts with the health insurers on an individual basis. This has greatly added to the administrative complexity (and costs) of the system.

The majority of general practitioners and dentists work in solo or small group practices. Other health professionals, for example physical therapists, dieticians or speech therapists, work in hospitals or nursing homes, and a minority work as self-employed practitioners. Within the overall framework of government regulation, insurers negotiate with hospitals, self-employed health practitioners and other health care providers.[12] The incomes of family physicians consist of a mix of payments. They receive a fixed amount ("capitated payment") for each patient, fees for certain activities and special subsidies (e.g. for buying computers). The largest share of hospital budgets is (still) based on historical costs, but the system is slowly shifting to case-based payments. At first, the government encouraged medical specialists and hospitals to develop case-based tariffs themselves, but this decentralized process led to over 40,000 tariffs (only covering about 10 per cent of all hospital activity) and turned out too complicated to administer. The implementation of the "home-grown" and very complicated DRG-based hospital payment model has slowed down, and in 2007, government announced a drastic simplification.

While the policy rhetoric in The Netherlands emphasizes market efficiency, less government and more consumer choice,[13] the state has not reduced its presence. In fact, it has extended its role in different ways. Under the responsibility of the

Ministry of Health and the Ministry of Finance, a new health competition authority *Zorgauthoriteit*, monitors the functioning of insurance and health care markets. The MoH itself has become active in sponsoring the development of new payment models and other cost control mechanisms.

In 2002, it announced that the responsibility for long-term care AWBZ would shift to local authorities (and not, as in former reform plans that failed, to the health insurers). That would also have meant the imposition of stricter means testing to restrain access to those services. However, in 2007, government announced a moratorium on changes in the long-term care insurance AWBZ. Thus far, there has been not much debate on the question whether the area of long-term care should be open to more competition and consumer choice (Okma 1997b). In the past, certain patient groups in this field (in particular groups of psychiatric patients and relatives of mentally retarded persons) have been effective in pushing for improvement. Also, the AWBZ scheme offers vouchers or cash benefits to chronically ill patients who then can contract services of their own choice. Within a few years, this cash benefit scheme became very popular and in 2005 over 50,000 patients received on average over €20,000 per year. The total budget for those vouchers now exceeds €1 billion, while the total budget for home care, serving over 600,000 patients per year, is about €2 billion. Clearly, those developments in long-term care are examples of direct consumer voice and consumer exit (Hirschman 1970). It is less clear whether patients are keen to develop such a role in the area of acute medical care (Okma and Ooijens 2005).

Is important to note that the 2006 health insurance reforms have not (fully) replaced earlier models of government planning and control. Reflecting strong support for solidarity in social policy, Dutch governments have regularly taken steps to mitigate the financial effects of privatization, for example by exempting certain services or population groups from user fees. Some experts argue that the different modes of governance complement each other (Helderman 2007). In fact, the current Dutch health care system shows an intricate layering and overlap of competing and sometimes conflicting governance models. Traditional models of social insurance, notions of regionalized governance, and new elements of market competition combine with increased central government control. The current health governance in The Netherlands reflects efforts to decentralize into a territorial direction (from central government to regional and local authorities) and to decentralize in a "functional" sense (from state to markets and individuals). At the same time, faced with budget pressures (or perceived budget pressures, or perceived potential future budget pressures), central government has not given up its role (MoH 2001, Scheerder 2005), nor has it reduced the size of central administration. It has actually expanded its role in monitoring and supervision of health care and health insurance. The system is less market-oriented than some experts claim (Schut and Van de Ven 2005, Enthoven and Van de Ven 2007), or some foreign observers who see the Dutch model as an example for the US seem to hope (Harris 2007, Naik 2007).

The Dutch experience also confirms the need for post-reform maintenance. For example, in 2007 the government abandoned the no-claim restitution (only implemented one year before) and replaced it with a modest mandatory deductible for the basic insurance after critics claimed the no-claim bonus was unfair to insured with higher levels of health expenditure. In several cases, the government reinstated entitlements it had de-listed only a few years before (e.g. dental care) because of widespread opposition (Maarse and Okma 2005). Likewise, the rise in numbers of uninsured in 2007 prompted government to take action.

Conclusions: Debates, Reforms and Policy Adjustments

This section summarizes our findings on the origins and the fate of the health reform debates in Chile, Israel, Singapore, Switzerland, Taiwan and The Netherlands. Why (and when) did those countries embark on the health reform trail in the 1980s and 1990s? What were the major policy goals and reform options discussed? Was there explicit reference to other countries' reform experience? Who were the main stakeholders and what were their positions? What option became reality? And finally, what were the (intended and unintended, expected and unexpected) outcomes, and what happened during implementation?

In the 1980s and 1990s, all six countries undertook systematic reviews of their health care. Both endogenous and exogenous factors added to the pressure to change. The oil crises of the mid-1970s, the end of the post-war baby boom and changing ideological views of the role of state and citizens combined to trigger extensive debate about the future of the welfare state. Thus budgetary and fiscal restraints, changing ideology and changing economic conditions played a role in reshaping social policy. The Asian countries faced a unique situation created by long periods of high economic growth. The new prosperity increased the expectations of the populations that government would not only initiate income-protection schemes for old age and illness, but also provide the fiscal means for making sure the entire populations could benefit. In the 1970s and 1980s, periods of phenomenal economic growth, two of the "Asian tigers", Singapore and Taiwan, saw the need for a systematic buildup of the income protection schemes that had started in Western Europe after the industrial revolution. Both countries realized universal coverage for health insurance. In both countries, expansion, rather than contraction of the welfare state was the main point, though in strikingly different ways.

The goals of the reforms in all six countries were similar: improved access to health services (through expanding public or private health insurance), improved quality and efficiency of services (through a mix of market-oriented and regulatory measures) and greater consumer and patient choice (freedom to switch to another insurer, or to a different plan with different financial conditions, but also freedom of choice of provider).[14] All countries except Chile realized universal or near-universal health insurance coverage, but their success with other goals, in particular consumer choice, has been more modest. Insured now have a larger choice of health plans in Switzerland, the Netherlands and Israel. In Chile, they can opt out from the public scheme to take out private coverage. At the same time, there is decreased choice of providers because of selective contracting in Chile, Switzerland and The Netherlands. In those countries, insurers gained decision-making power in contracting with providers. In Chile and Singapore, governments strengthened their role in contracting services by imposing new rules and in Taiwan government itself became the sole health insurer. The expansion of private insurance led to increased risk selection in Chile, Switzerland and The Netherlands. Shifts toward decentralized private governance also increased the administrative complexity and overhead costs in those countries. The goal of cost containment, it seems, has been most successful in the most centralized systems; low overhead costs because of uniform administration and the imposition of country-wide fees and tariffs played an important role (e.g. in Taiwan). The complexity of the Swiss model is reflected in its rising costs. Within a few years, Switzerland reached the world top of health expenditure after the US.

At the two extremes of the range of options considered are full privatization of health insurance and provision (considered by Chile, Singapore, Switzerland and The Netherlands) and nationalization (considered by Chile). In the end, no country has fully privatized or fully nationalized its entire health care system. After considering alternatives, Israel extended its Bismarckian model of employment-based insurance to cover the entire population, but left responsibility for administering the scheme in the hands of the existing sick funds. It also introduced choice of fund for the insured. Singapore, despite 140 years of British rule and influence, never went Beveridgean but instead emphasized individual over state responsibility and encouraged private sector participation. Taiwan nationalized its health insurance but the provision of health care services remained predominantly private. During the military regime of 1974–1991, Chile shifted towards private health insurance. After the restoration of democracy, it strengthened the public sector and sought to impose strict rules on the private sector to counteract the problems of risk selection. Over four decades, The Netherlands reform debate shifted from considering a fully nationalized health insurance with state controlled health care provision (based on regional planning) towards market-oriented options. In 2006, it implemented a new insurance model that, like the Swiss one, combines public and private elements. Switzerland took the lead in experimenting with a new health insurance model that combines public rules with private insurance administration (somewhat similar to the Dutch scheme of 2006). The model offers basic coverage to all, with the possibility to opt out to alternative schemes with different financial conditions. It kept the existing mix of public, and both not-for-profit and for-profit providers.

Not only the direction, but also the speed of implementation of reforms varied widely. In the mid-1990s, after carefully considering alternatives, Taiwan opted for a nationwide public health insurance scheme, by far the simplest model for universal coverage and uniform administration (and thus, as experience has shown, with low administrative costs). It implemented the model in a very short time span. With similar speed, Singapore put a complicated mix of private (but mandatory) savings schemes and public safety net funding in place. It successfully implemented an ingenious financing mechanism that, combined with public subsidies for primary care and hospitals, ensures that everyone has reasonable access to basic medical services. Singapore first wanted to privatize all of its hospitals, but, faced with public dissatisfaction, the government reversed its course within a few months. It retained the hospitals and other health facilities under government control and integrated hospital and outpatient services under broader governance structures. The quality of care improved, but it came at higher costs. Singapore is an example of a country where a strong central government can design and implement (and rapidly adjust) major policy change without much opposition from organized interests. Taiwan has seen a rise in political opposition and citizen empowerment in recent years. Governments of countries with "older" models in place, like Chile, Israel or The

Netherlands, have had a much harder time changing the system in the face of opposing stakeholders. In fact, both Israel and The Netherlands (and to a lesser degree, Switzerland as well) have neo-corporatist policy traditions, the model that assumes that government shares the responsibility for social policy with other organized stakeholders in society. That tradition also provides ample veto power to stakeholders who feel that proposed change will negatively affect their positions. In none of the countries of this study did organized citizens or patients play a dominant role in the reform process even while governments often quoted expanding consumer and patient choice as one of the main reasons for change. In several cases, broad popular support for existing social policy severely restrained governments' possibilities to shift costs to patients, or forced policy makers to adjust their course.

All countries have shifted, or are in the process of shifting, payment for hospital care from overall global budgets or per diem payments to some form of diagnosis-related groups (DRG) or case-based payment. The DRG model rarely covers all expenses as hospitals often receive separate funding for their capital investment and certain very expensive treatments. In all countries, self-employed health professionals receive fees for their services, often combined with additional payments for specific activities. Thus instead of a shift from one payment model to another, all countries have shifted to mixed methods.

Some countries studied the experience abroad before deciding on their reform course. Chile looked to the US for inspiration of its earlier reforms. Both Singapore and Taiwan did explicitly "shop around" for health reform models and considered the experience abroad as possible options before finally implementing two entirely different models. In The Netherlands, the 1987 "Dekker Committee" report has no references to other countries' experience. The 2006 insurance in Holland resembles the Swiss model (but without the restraints of devolved administration). In fact, in the early 2000s Dutch policymakers and politicians had visited Switzerland and were clearly impressed with what they saw (or wanted to see).

One common experience is that the labels used in the international reform debate do not always reflect reality. For example, Singapore is often quoted as the country that successfully introduced individual savings accounts to pay for medical care. In fact, those accounts only count for a modest share of total health care funding as government subsidy and employers' mandatory contributions are more important. Moreover, there are several forms of cross-subsidies to safeguard access to health care for lower income groups. The Dutch health insurance of 2006 was initially labeled as "private" but for various reasons it ended as "public".

What are the lessons we can draw from this experience? First, major change is rare. The cases in this study contain clear examples of "windows of opportunity" for change (Kingdon 1984). For example, the confluence of political willingness to change, popular perceptions of the need to reform and the availability of reform options that fit the national context created fertile ground for success in Taiwan and Singapore to implement major reforms. Israel shares some of the neo-corporatist features of the social policy arena with Germany, Switzerland and The Netherlands. This model traditionally provided organized interests with veto power to thwart or slow down change proposed by government. In The Netherlands, the erosion of some of the institutions that traditionally dominated social policy making (and offered ample opportunity for organized stakeholders to block change) combined with the strong position of the new governing coalition dominated by the Christian Democratic Party allowed for a surprisingly rapid passage of reform law in 2006.

Second, values matter. Over time, dominant cultural orientations or values in society have shaped political and other institutions that serve to channel interests, but conversely, such institutions themselves shape values as well (Marmor et al. 2006). For example, the Canada Health Act of 1984 (CHA) expresses general support for universal access to health care for all Canadians. Over time, the CHA itself has become a symbol of national unity, adding to the sense of common values in Canada. In many countries, there is strong popular support for old age pension schemes and health care (perhaps even more than for unemployment and disability benefits). Everywhere, strong popular support for government-sponsored (not necessarily government-provided) arrangements that safeguard universal access to health care has limited options for governments to shift too much of the financial burden to families.[15] In a way, Singapore is an exception: an entitlement culture has not taken root. Government has successfully coaxed the highly disciplined rags-to-riches immigrant population to assume greater responsibility for its own health care. Mitigated by government subsidies, health care financing has shifted to private pockets without much fuss. Singapore's Medisave scheme appealed to traditional Asian values by identifying the family rather than the state as the basic unit of solidarity and risk pooling.

Third, institutions matter. In a narrow sense, political institutions as defined as the political decision-making structure are crucial for enabling not only reform, but also the speed of change, for example in Singapore and Taiwan. In contrast, the particular institutional configuration of the Swiss federalist tradition has limited the range of options available for policymakers. In a wider sense, including more organizations in society (and generally accepted practices), institutions have been important in explaining slow policy change in Israel and The Netherlands, with powerful stakeholders thwarting or slowing down reform efforts. Certain policies, once in place, can create their own constituencies (Pierson 1994). For example, old age pension schemes and social health insurance have become popular in many countries. The experience in The Netherlands shows that beneficiaries (in the case of health care, patients and their families and providers) will resist shifts in financial burdens by increasing patient cost-sharing or delisting entitlements.

Fourth, reforming health care systems is not a one-shot effort. Most countries have adjusted their reform pathways when outcomes did not meet expectations. In all cases, there was a need for "after reform maintenance". Facing unexpected and unwanted side-effects, public dissatisfaction and strong opposition by organized stakeholders, governments had to adjust policy, and in some cases reversed their policy course or abandoned policies altogether. In fact, "after reform maintenance" seems to be a more or less permanent feature everywhere (Palmer and Short 1989). Both endogenous and exogenous factors contribute to this process of permanent change. The main actors in the health system anticipate strategically and adjust to new realities. Innovation in medical technology has improved the quality of care and expanded treatment options, but it also has driven up costs. New managerial ideas and information technology affect the organization and governance of hospitals and health facilities. Unexpected and undesired outcomes may force governments to adjust their course or reverse earlier steps. External fiscal strains and budgetary pressures restrain the availability of public funding.

Sixth, country categorizations do not fit easily. It is hard if not impossible to design or apply any meaningful categorization of countries or entire health care systems. Countries face similar challenges and options, but differ greatly in the direction and speed of implementing social policy change because of country-specific contextual factors. This study shows common problems and policy options, common system elements and a common range of policy instruments and measures considered, but there is no clear pattern of the constellation of those system elements before or after the health reforms. It thus may be more important to focus on system elements than on entire countries or "health care systems". It is easier to categorize (or characterize) programs and policies than an entire country's health arrangements. Moreover, the level of programs and policy measures offers a realistic laboratory of policy change rather than (announced) health system reform at the national level. For example, the slow implementation of the DRG-based payment of hospitals in Israel and The Netherlands contrasts with the rapid speed of introducing similar change in Singapore (where DRG payments took only one year to roll out). Israel's successful experience with defining the entitlements of the social health insurance (or "explicit rationing") stands out as a policy experience not shared by other countries.

And finally, despite the rhetoric of retrenchment, consumer choice and market competition, there has been more rather than less government action almost everywhere. Nowhere did governments give up their regulatory authority over health care, even in cases where they strongly supported markets and consumer choice as instruments to allocate resources. Some countries developed new instruments for monitoring markets and informing consumers, but kept the old ones for controlling public (and sometimes private) expenditure, for example by delisting of entitlements from social insurance, imposing budgets, user fees and changes in the mix of payment methods.

Acknowledgements

This study has its roots in a meeting of the German Bertelsmann Foundation in Helsinki in 2006, attended by four of the authors of this article. Over dinner, they agreed to join forces in an effort to describe and analyze the health reform experience of their countries in a separate publication. The authors are grateful to the Bertelsmann foundation for the opportunity to meet and discuss their project.

This contribution is the result of an international collaborative effort. The authors share the introduction and general conclusions, but the country experts wrote the country pictures. Thus Kieke Okma and Hans Maarse wrote the section on Dutch health reform, Tsung-Mei Cheng on Taiwan, David Chinitz on Israel, Luca Crivelli on Switzerland, Meng-Kin Lim on Singapore and Maria Eliana Labra on Chile.

Notes

1. One important methodological issue is the need to carefully define terms and concepts. That seems to be a superfluous and self-evident remark, but many policy debates (and studies) are clouded by fuzzy terms. For example, in the last decades the term "health care reform" has appeared in numerous

articles, journals, papers, books, conferences and academic meetings. However, few if any clearly define the term "reform" (Okma 1999, Marmor and Okma 2003). Many comparative studies aim to analyze processes of health reform across the globe, but few pay attention to what it is, conceptually, they seek to explain.

2. "Governance", another example of a conceptually fuzzy term, is a rising star in the terminology of today. Basically, the term refers to the administration of health insurance and health care. Interestingly, it has traveled from government to the corporate sector and back again to the public sector (Okma 2002: notes 14 and 18). During this journey, it also shed its neutral meaning and took on a normative connotation under the label of "good governance". In this contribution, we take "governance" in a neutral sense: administration (both public and private) of health services and health insurance. We characterize governance styles by looking at the "dominant cultural orientation" and dominant welfare orientations that affect the style of social policy making in each country.

3. One question we have not addressed extensively in this paper is what counts as a "small" or "medium" country. Most international comparative studies take one or more of the world's large countries as the main comparator: the US, the UK, Canada, Germany, France and sometimes other large OECD member states. We use the term "small and medium sized" to indicate countries that clearly do not belong that group. In the introduction to his grand oeuvre *Rich Democracies*, Harold Wilensky addresses the issue of the size of countries. He argues that rather than actual size in terms of population or geography, it is the complexity of administration that matters (Wilensky 2002).

4. Qualitative research by Chinitz (1999) indicates that Israeli physicians spend up to 10 per cent of their time engaged in quarrels with sick fund managers over these points. The physicians often win the argument, but the organizational consequences in terms of efficiency and morale are significant.

5. For an updated general presentation of the Swiss health care system see OECD (2006).

6. It is important to note that until the Revised Health Insurance Law of 1996, health insurance was optional at the federal level. Before 1994, four cantons had made affiliation to a health plan mandatory for the entire population, and eight cantons for special population groups like low-income families or foreigners.

7. As they are private (and governed by private law), the supplemental insurances face less government control than the basic coverage. Insurers can impose more restrictions. In practice, however, most people do not clearly distinguish between the two and the supplemental coverage may influence the choice of basic plan.

8. Those low overhead costs compare to other programs run by government, for example the Medicare or Veterans' health Services in the US. Those expenses are generally much higher for private health administration – some studies even suggest that those overheads cause 24 per cent of total health spending in the US (Woolhandler *et al.* 2003).

9. Until 2006, eligibility for social health insurance was limited to about 60 per cent of the Dutch population; almost all of the remaining 40 per cent of population insured with either work-related group insurance or individual health insurance.

10. There is some dispute over the question whether it should be labeled public or private – that question has not yet been tested by the European Court of Justice, the only authority that can decide on the matter.

11. Interestingly, for this purpose, over 40 per cent of the Dutch population qualifies as "low income". In 2005, the Tax Department hired over 600 extra staff to administer the subsidies, including a monthly income check of all applicants. In 2007, the Health Ministry announced plans to simplify that administration.

12. Since national competition law based on European law prohibits market collusion, Dutch health care providers have had to abandon their long tradition of collective bargaining between national associations of insurers and providers over fees and tariffs (in Germany, that traditional neo-corporatist model is still in place). Nowadays, hospitals, general practitioners and other independent providers have to sit down and negotiate individually with all the health insurance they seek contracts with; and health insurers no longer have to contract with every provider.

13. Actually, it is more correct to say that the reforms increased choice of health insurer and decreased choice of provider; selective contracting means that not all providers will get contracts, and some patients thus face a restricted choice.

14. Paradoxically, the introduction of market competition has in some cases actually reduced patients' choice of provider. For example, after the abolition of mandatory contracting in the Dutch sick

fund system in 1991, the funds no longer had to contract all independent health professionals. Thus, while the Dutch citizens have more choice of health insurer, their choice of provider may be curtailed because of selective contracting by their health insurer.
15. As we have observed elsewhere, values can direct policy making in a certain direction, or exclude certain options, but they do not tell policymakers exactly what to do (Marmor et al. 2006).

References

General references

Enthoven, A.C. and Van de Ven, W.P.M.M., 2007, Going Dutch – managed competition health insurance in The Netherlands, *New England Journal of Medicine*, **357**(24), 2421–2423.
Douglas, M. and Wildavsky, A., 1982, *Risk and Culture* (Berkeley, CA: University of California Press).
Hirschman, A.O., 1970, *Exit, Voice and Loyalty* (Cambridge, MA: Harvard University Press).
Immergut, Ellen M., 1992, *Health Politics: Interests and Institutions in Western Europe* (Cambridge: University Press).
Kingdon, John W., 1984, *Agendas, Alternatives, and Public Policies* (Boston: Little, Brown and Company).
Klein, Rudolf, 1995, *Learning from Others: Shall the Last be the First Markets? Report of the Four Country Conference on Health Care Reforms and Health Care Policies in the US, Canada, Germany and The Netherlands, Amsterdam, February 23–25* (The Hague: Ministry of Health, Welfare and Sport).
Klein, R. and Marmor, T.R., 2006, Reflections on policy analysis: putting it together again, in: M. Moran, M. Rein and R.E. Goodin (Eds) *The Oxford Handbook of Public Policy* (Oxford: Oxford University Press), 892–912.
Marmor, T.R., Mashaw, J.L. and Harvey, P.L. (Eds), 1990, *America's Misunderstood Welfare State, Persisting Myths, Enduring Realities* (New York: Basic Books).
Marmor, T.R., 1998, Hype and hyperbole: the rhetoric and realities of managerial reform in health care. *Journal of Health Services Research and Policy*, **3**(1), 62–64.
Marmor, Theodore R. and Okma, Kieke G.H., 2003, Health care systems in transition, by the World Health Organization (book review essay), *Journal of Health Politics, Policy and Law*, **28**(4), 747–755.
Marmor, T.R., Freeman, R. and Okma, K.G.H., 2005, Comparative perspectives and policy learning in the world of health care. *Journal of Comparative Policy Analysis*, **7**(4), 331–348.
Marmor, Theodore R., Okma, Kieke G.H. and Lathan, Stephen R., 2006, Values, institutions and health politics. Comparative perspectives, in: Claus Wendt and Cristof Wolf (Eds) *Soziologie der Gesundheit. Kolner Zeitschrift fur Soziologie und Sozialpsychologie*, Sonderheft 46, 383–405.
OECD, 1992, *The Reform of Health Care, A Comparative Analysis of Seven OECD Countries. Health Reform Studies No. 2* (Paris: Organization for Economic Cooperation and Development).
OECD, 1994, *The Reform of Health Care, A Review of Seventeen OECD Countries, Health Reform Studies No. 5* (Paris: Organization for Economic Cooperation and Development).
OECD, 2003, *Economic Survey of Chile* (Paris: Organization for Economic Cooperation and Development).
OECD, 2005, *Health at a Glance* (Paris: Organization for Economic Cooperation and Development).
Okma, K.G.H., 1999, Review of European Health Care Reform: Analysis of Current Strategies, by Richard B. Saltman and Josep Figueras (book review essay). *Journal of Health Politics, Policy and Law*, **24**(4), 835–840.
Okma, K.G.H., 2002, What is the best public/private model for Canadian health care? Research Paper, *Policy Matters*, 3, 6 (Montreal: Canadian Institute for Research on Public Policy, Montreal).
Palmer, G.R. and Short, S.D., 1989, *Health Care and Public Policy – An Australian Analysis* (Sydney: The Macmillan Company of Australia Pty Ltd).
Pierson, P., 1994, *Dismantling the Welfare State? Reagan, Thatcher and the Politics of Retrenchment* (Cambridge: Cambridge University Press).
Ranade, W. (Ed.), 1998, *Markets and Health Care: A Comparative Analysis* (New York: Addison Wesley Longman).
Timmins, N., 1995, *The Five Giants, A Biography of the Welfare State* (London: Fontana Press).
Wilensky, H.L., 2002, *Rich Democracies, Political Economy, Public Policy, and Performance* (Berkeley: University of California Press).

Woolhander, S., Campbell, T. and Himmelstein, D.U., 2003, Costs of health care administration in the United States and Canada. *New England Journal of Medicine*, **349**, 768–775.

World Bank, 2006, *World Development Indicators* (Washington: The World Bank).

Chile

Barrientos, A., 2002, Health policy in Chile: the return of the public sector. *Bulletin of Latin American Research*, **21**(3), 442–459.

De Viado, M. and Flores, A., 1944, Health insurance in Chile. *Canadian Medical Association Journal*, **52**(6), 564–570.

FONASA (Fondo Nacional de Salud), 2007, *Boletin Estadistico 2005–2006* (Santiago de Chile: FONASA).

Höfter, R.H., 2006, Private health insurance and utilization of health services in Chile, *Applied Economics*, **38**(4), 423–439.

Jost, T.S., 1999, Managed care regulation: can we learn from others? The Chilean experience. *Michigan Journal of Law Reform*, **32**, 863–898.

Kingdon, J., 1995, *Agendas, Alternatives and Public Policies*, 2nd edition (New York: Longman).

Labra, M.E., 1995, As políticas de saúde no Chile: entre a razão e a força, in: P. Buss and M.E. Labra (Eds) *Sistemas de saúde: continuidades e mudanças (Argentina, Brasil, Chile, Espanha, Estados Unidos, México, Québec)* (São Paulo: Hucitec; Rio de Janeiro: Editora Fiocruz), pp. 103–152.

Labra, M.E., 2002, La reinvención neoliberal de la inequidad en Chile. El caso de la salud. *Cadernos de Saúde Pública, Rio de Janeiro*, **18**, (4), 1041–1052.

Labra, M.E., 2007, Notas críticas sobre estatificación socioeconómica, copagos y acceso en los servicios públicos de salud de Chile. *Revista Española de Economía de la Salud, Barcelona*, **6**(1), 46–50.

Sapelli, C., 2004, Risk segmentation and equity in the Chilean mandatory health insurance system. *Social Science and Medicine*, **58**(2), 259–265.

Israel

Bentur, N., Berg, A. and Chinitz, D., 1998, Health system reform and the elderly: the case of Israel. *Journal of Aging and Social Policy*, **10**(2), 85–104.

Chinitz, D., 1999, The basic basket of health services under national health insurance. *Health Policy in Israel, Social Security*, 54, 53–68 (Hebrew).

Chinitz, D., Shalev, C., Galai, N. and Israeli, A., 1998, Israel's basic basket of services: the importance of being explicit. *British Medical Journal*, **317**, 1005–1007.

Gross, R., Rosen, B. and Chinitz, D., 1998, Evaluating the Israeli health care reform: strategies, challenges and lessons. *Health Policy*, **45**, 99–117.

Highlight on Israel, 2003, Organizational structure of the health system (Copenhagen: European Observatory on Health Care Systems, World Health Organization).

Rosen, B., 2003, *HiT Israel* (Copenhagen: European Observatory on Health Care Systems, World Health Organization).

Singapore

Choo, V., 2002, Southeast Asian countries vie with each other to woo foreign patients, *The Lancet*, **360**(9338), 1004.

Lim, M.K., 1998, Health care systems in transition II. Singapore, Part I. An overview of the health care system in Singapore. *Journal of Public Health*, **20**, 16–22.

Lim, M.K., 2004(a), Shifting the burden of health care finance: a case study of public-private partnership in Singapore. *Health Policy*, **69**(1), 83–92.

Lim, M.K., 2004(b), Quest for quality care and patient safety: the case of Singapore. *Quality and Safety in Health Care*, **13**, 71–75.

Lim, M.K., 2005, Transforming Singapore health care: public/private partnership. *Annals of the Academy of Medicine of Singapore*, **34**(7), 461–467.

Ministry of Health website, at http://www.moh.gov.sg/

Newsweek, 2007, Singapore medicine, Singapore - a global affair, October 5.
Phua, K.H., 1991, *Privatization and Restructuring of Health Services in Singapore*, Institute of Policy Studies, Occasional Paper no. 5 (Singapore: Time Academic Press).
Preker, A.S. and Harding, A., 2003, *Innovations in Health Service Delivery: The Corporatization of Public Hospitals* (Washington: World Bank).
Yong, Y.L., 1967, Speech by the Minister of Health at the opening of the WHO Seminar on Health Planning in Urban Development, Singapore, November 21.

Switzerland

Balthasar, A., 2001, *Monitoring 2000, Die Sozialpolitische Wirksamkeit der Prämienverbilligung in den Kantonen* [The Social–Political Effects of Lowering Health Insurance Premiums in the Cantons] (Berne: Office Fédéral des Assurances Sociales).
Balthasar, A., et al., 2005, *Monitoring 2004, Die sozialpolitische Wirksamkeit der Prämienverbilligung in den Kantonen* (Berne: Office Fédéral des Assurances Sociales).
Beck, K., Spycher, S., Holly, A. and Gardiol, L., 2003, Risk adjustment in Switzerland. *Health Policy*, **65**(1), 63–74.
Bolgiani, I., Crivelli, L. and Domenighetti, G., 2006, The role of health insurance in regulating the Swiss health care system. *Revue française des affaires sociales*, **60**(2–3), 227–249.
Civitas, 2002, *The Swiss Healthcare System* (London: CIVITAS), http://www.civitas.org.uk/pdf/Switzerland.pdf
Colombo, F., 2001, *Towards more choice in social protection? Individual choice of insurer in basic mandatory health insurance in basic mandatory health insurance in Switzerland*, Occasional papers no. 53 (Paris: Organization for Economic Cooperation and Development).
Crivelli, L., 2007, Current problems and future challenges in the Swiss healthcare system, in: A. Greco and M.C. Vichi (Eds) *Patient Pathways. The Canton of Ticino Experience* (Milano: McGraw-Hill), pp. 3–19.
Crivelli L., Filippini, M. and Mosca, I., 2006, Federalism and regional health care expenditures: an empirical analysis for the Swiss cantons, *Health Economics*, **15**(5), 535–541.
Crivelli, L., Domenighetti, G. and Filippini, M., 2007, Federalism versus social citizenship: Investigating the preference for equity in health care, in: P.L. Porta and L. Bruni (Eds) *Handbook on the Economics of Happiness* (Cheltenham: Edward Elgar), pp. 487–511.
Frank, R.G. and Lamiraud, K., 2008, *Choice, Price Competition and Complexity in Markets for Health Insurance*, NBER Working Papers.
Geoffard, P.Y., Gardiol, L. and Grandchamp, C., 2006, Separating selection and incentive effects: an econometric study of Swiss health insurance claims data, in: P.-A. Chiappori and C. Gollier (Eds) *Competitive Failures in Insurance Markets* (Cambridge, MA: MIT Press), pp. 81–96.
Herzlinger, Regina E. and Parsa-Parsi, R., 2004, Consumer-driven health care: lessons from Switzerland. *Journal of the American Medical Association*, **292**, 1213–1220.
Hirschman, A., 1970, *Exit, Voice and Loyalty. Responses to Decline in Firms, Organizations, and States* (Cambridge, MA: Harvard University Press).
Lehman, H.J. and Zweifel, P., 2004, Innovation and RISK SELECTION in regulated social health insurance. *Journal of Health Economics*, **23**, 997–1012.
OECD, 2006, *OECD Reviews of Health Systems: Switzerland* (Paris: Organization for Economic Cooperation and Development).
Reinhardt, U.E., 2004, The Swiss health system: regulated competition without managed care. *Journal of the American Medical Association*, **292**, 1227–1231.
Strombom, B.A., Buchmueller, T.C. and Feldstein, P.J., 2002, Switching costs, price sensitivity and health plan choice. *Journal of Health Economics*, **21**(1), 89–116.
Tiebout, C., 1956, A pure theory of local expenditures, *Journal of Political Economy*, **64**(5), 416–424.

Taiwan

Bureau of National Health Insurance (BNHI), 2006, National Health Insurance in Taiwan, Profile, Bureau of National Health Insurance, Department of Health, Taipei, Taiwan, Republic of China, May.

Cheng, Tsung-Mei, 2003, Taiwan's new national health insurance program: genesis and experience so far. *Health Affairs*, **22**(3), 61–76.
Cheng, Tsung-Mei, 2005, Quality of Health Care in Taiwan in the 21st Century: Challenges and Opportunities, Proceedings of the International Symposium on Achievements and Challenges of National Health Systems in celebration of the 10th anniversary of Taiwan's National Health Insurance, Bureau of National Health Insurance, Department of Health, Taipei, Taiwan, Republic of China, March.
Cheng, Tsung-Mei, 2007, Interview of officials of the Planning Division, Bureau of National Health Insurance, Department of Health, Taipei, Taiwan, Republic of China, April.
Department of Health, 2007, *Health Statistical Trends 2006* (Taipei, Taiwan, Republic of China: Department of Health).

The Netherlands

Bartolomee, Y. and Maarse, H., 2007, Health insurance reform in the Netherlands. *Eurohealth*, **12**(2), 7–9.
Berg, M. and Klazinga, N., 2004, Technology assessment, priority setting and appropriate care in Dutch health care. *International Journal of Technology Assessment in Health Care*, **20**(2), 35–43.
Boot, J.M., 1998, Schaalvergroting en concentratie in het Nederlandse ziekenhuiswezen [Concentration and increase in operational scale of Dutch hospitals]. *Bestuurskunde*, **7**(1), 28–37.
CBS, 2007, *Kenmerken van wanbetalers zorgverzekeringswet* [Characteristics of the Non-payers of Health Insurance] (Voorburg: Centraal Bureau voor de Statistiek).
Commissie Dekker, 1987, *Bereidheid tot Verandering* [Willingness to Change; Report of the Committee on Health Care Reform] ('s-Gravenhage: Distributiecentrum Overheidspublicaties).
De Roo, A. A., 2002, Naar een nieuw zorgstelsel? [Towards a new health care system?], Unpublished lecture, Tilburg University.
De Swaan, A., 1988, *In Care of the State. Health Care, Education and Welfare in Europe and the USA in the Modern Era* (Oxford: Polity Press).
Harris, G., 2007, Looking at Dutch and Swiss health systems. *NYT*, October 30.
Helderman, J.-K., 2007, Institutional complementarity in Dutch health care reforms. Going beyond the pre-occupation with choice (Paper), European Health Policy Group, Berlin, April.
Helderman, J.-K., Schut, F.T., van der Grinten, T.E.D. and Van de Ven, W.P.M., 2005, Market-oriented health care reforms and policy learning in the Netherlands. *Journal of Health Politics, Policy and Law*, **30**(1–2), 189.
Hirschman, A.O., 1970, *Exit, Voice and Loyalty* (Cambridge, MA: Harvard University Press).
Hoofdlijnenakkoord [Governing Manifesto], 2003, *Kamerstukken II. 2002–2003*, 28637, 19 ('s Gravenhage: SDU).
Klein, R., 1995, *Learning From Others: Shall the Last be the First Markets? Four Country Conference on Health Care Policies and Health Care Reforms in the United States, Canada, Germany and The Netherlands (Conference Report)* (Rijswijk: Ministerie van Volksgezondheid, Welzijn en Sport).
Kreis, R., 2005, Marktwerking maakt zorg niet beter of goedkoper [Market competition does not make care better or cheaper]. *De Volkskrant*, February 22.
Laske-Aldershof, T., Schut, E., Beck, K., Shmueli, A. and Van de Voorde, C., 2004, Consumer mobility in social health insurance markets: a five-country comparison. *Applied Health Economics and Health Policy*, **3**(4), 229–241.
Lijphart, A., 1968, Verzuiling, pacificatie en kentering in de Nederlandse politiek [Pillarization, Pacification and Changes in Dutch Policies] (Amsterdam: J.H. De Bussy).
Maarse, H. and Okma, K.G.H., 2004, The privatisation paradox in Dutch health care, in: H. Maarse (Ed) *Privatisation in European Health Care* (Maarssen: Elsevier Gezondheidszorg), pp. 97–116.
MoH, 1988, Verandering Verzekerd [Change assured]. *Kamerstukken II, 1987–1988*, 19945 ('s-Gravenhage: SDU).
MoH, 1994, Kostenbeheersing in de zorgsector [Controling health care expenditures]. *Kamerstukken II, 1994–1995*, 24124 ('s-Gravenhage: SDU).
MoH, 2001, *Vraag aan Bod* [Demand at the Centre] (The Hague: Ministry of Health).
MoH, 2006, *Rijksbegroting Volksgezondheid, Welzijn en Sport 2007* [Health Budget 2007] (Den Haag: Ministerie van Volksgezondheid, Welzijn, en Sport).

MoH, 2007, Brief aan TK over wanbetalers zorgverzekering [Letter to Parliament about delinquent payers of health insurance].
Naik, G., 2007, Dutch treatment: in Holland, some see model for U.S. health care system. *WSJ*, September 6.
Okma, K.G.H., 1997a, Studies in Dutch health politics, policies and law (PhD Thesis, University of Utrecht).
Okma, K.G.H., 1997b, Concurrentie, markten en marktwerking in de gezondheidszorg [Markets and market competition in health care]. *Tijdschrift voor Politieke Ekonomie*, **20**(2), 64–178.
Okma, K.G.H., 2001, Health care, health policies and health care reform in The Netherlands (brochure) (The Hague: Ministry of Health, Welfare and Sports).
Okma, K.G.H., 2002, Health care and the welfare state: two worlds of welfare drifting apart?, in: J. Berghman *et al.* (Eds) *Social Security in Transition* (Leiden: Kluwer Law International), pp. 229–238.
Okma, K.G.H. and Ooijens, M., 2005, De patient centraal. Zijn de Verenigde Saten ons voorland? *Tijdschrift voor de Sociale Sector*, Juni, 26–29.
Okma, K.G.H. and de Roo, A., 2009, The Netherlands: From Polder model to modern management, in: T.R. Marmor, R. Freeman and K.G.H. Okma (Eds) *Comparative Studies and the Politics of Modern Medical Care* (New Haven, CT: Yale University Press), pp. 120–152.
Regeerakkoord, 2007, http://www.regering.nl
Rosenberg, E., 2006, Ziekenhuizen moeten hard zijn [hospitals must be hard]. *NRC Handelsblad*, January 18.
Rosenberg, E., 2007, Concurrentie in de zorg blijft uit [competion in health care does not materialize], NRC Handelsblad, May 15.
RVZ, 2003, *Marktconcentratie in de Ziekenhuiszorg* [Market Concentration in Dutch Hospital Care] (Zoetermeer: Raad voor de Volksgezondheid & Zorg).
Scheerder, R., 2005, Kostenbeleid 2005. *Zorg & Financiering*, **193**(2), 8–28.
Schut, F.T., 1997, Competition in Dutch health care (PhD thesis, Erasmus University Rotterdam).
Schut, F.T. and Van de Ven, W.P.M.M., 2005, Rationing and competition in the Dutch health-care system. *Health Economics*, **14**, S59–S74.
Smit, M. and Mookveld, P., 2007, Verzekerdenmobiliteit en keuzegedrag [Mobility and choice in Dutch health insurance]. *Vektis*.
Strategisch Akkoord [Governing Manifesto], 2002, *Kamerstukken II, 2001–2002*, 28375, 5, ('s Gravenhage: SDU).
Visser, J. and Hemerijck, A., 1997, *A Dutch Miracle – Job Growth, Welfare Reform and Corporatism in The Netherlands* (Amsterdam: Amsterdam University Press).

Appendix: Tables

Table 1 shows that surface-wise, Chile is the largest country of the group and Singapore the smallest. Taiwan has the biggest population, Singapore the smallest. Population density is by far the highest in Singapore, followed by The Netherlands and Israel. Switzerland has the highest average income (and the highest mountains), with The Netherlands and Singapore second and third. In the early 2000s, Chile and Taiwan had the highest economic growth rates while the economies of The Netherlands and Switzerland were lagging behind. The large differences between the national income per person measured in current US dollars and in "purchasing power parity" illustrates that it is not easy to compare patterns of health spending across nations without taking real family incomes into account. The PPP amounts show much smaller income differences between the countries are than the plain dollar amounts. Similarly, the amounts of health spending per person usually shown in international statistics can underestimate (or overestimate) what those amounts can buy for a family.

Table 2 shows large variations in health care spending, inputs (as an example, the numbers of health professionals and hospital beds) and health outcomes (life expectancy and child mortality) across the six countries of this study. Switzerland has the highest GDP share of health expenditure as well as the highest amount per capita, followed by The Netherlands. The lowest is Singapore, followed by Chile and Taiwan. Thus Singapore is the "exception" of the close statistical relation that seems to exist in the OECD world between income level and health spending. There is not that much variation in life expectancy; clearly, as many other studies have shown, health spending does not explain variations in health outcomes. The data also illustrates that life expectancy or child mortality – commonly taken as measures of the quality of health care – are not closely related to spending levels or numbers of health professionals. All countries saw the average life expectancy of the population go up and child mortality go down in the 1990s. The share of public spending in total health expenditure ranges between 34 per cent (Singapore) and 70 per cent (Israel). But the terms "public" and "private" are sometimes misleading as government regulation severely restricts private actors in several countries.

Table 1. Size, population, income and economic growth in Chile, Israel, Singapore, Switzerland, Taiwan and The Netherlands, early 2000s

Statistic	Chile	Israel	Singapore	Switzerland	Taiwan	Netherlands
Size (1000 sq. km)	757	22	0.7	41	36	42
Population, 2005 (millions)	16.1	6.8	4.2	7.4	22.9	16.3
Population density, 2005 (people/sq. km)	21.8	319.9	6301.6	185.9	63.6	483.2
Share of population in urban area, 2005 (%)	87.6	91.6	100	75.2	63.2	80.2
Economic growth 1990–99 (%)	6.6	5.3	7.7	1	8.7	2.9
Economic growth 2000–04 (%)	3.7	0.8	2.9	0.6	3.5	0.5
GDP per capita, 2005 (US$)	6,040	18,580	26,620	55,320	15,036*	39,340
GDP per capita, 2005 (PPP)	10,610	23,770	27,370	35,660	28,552	29,500

Note: *2004.
Source: World Bank (2006), Central Intelligence Agency, *CIA World Factbook 2005*, https://www.cia.gov/library/publications/the-world-factbook/index.html, Department of Health, Republic of China, 2005 Taiwan Public Health Report, Department of Health, ROC (Taiwan), 2006, Department of Health, Republic of China, 2005, Health Care Statistical Trends, Department of Health, ROC (Taiwan), 2006.

Table 2. Health expenditure, health care professionals and health profile of Chile, Israel, Singapore, Switzerland, Taiwan and The Netherlands, 1980–2004

Statistic	Year	Chile	Israel	Singapore	Switzerland	Taiwan	Netherlands
Total health expenditure (% GDP)	2000	6.3	8.5	3.6	10.4	5.7	8.0
	2004	6.1	8.7	3.7	11.5	6.2	9.2
Health expenditure per capita (current US$)	2000	307	1,605	820	3,562	794	1,925
	2004	359	1,534	943	5,572	908	3,442
Public expenditure as share of total (%)*	2000	47.9	71.8	35.4	55.6	60.6	63.1
	2004	47.0	70.0	34.0	58.5	64.2	62.4
Physicians per 1,000 people**	2000–2003	1.1	3.8	1.4	3.6	1.4	3.1
Physicians, nurses and midwives per 1,000 people**	2000–2003	1.7	10.3	5.6	12.1	5.8	16.7
Life expectancy at birth (years)	1980	69.3	73.9	71.5	75.5	n.a.	76.7
	1990	73.7	76.6	74.3	77.2	74.5	76.9
	2000	76.9	79.0	78.1	79.7	75.6	78.0
	2005	78.2	79.7	79.7	81.2	77.6	79.3
Infant mortality rate (per 1000 births)	1980	35.0	16.1	11.7	9.1	n.a.	8.7
	1990	18.0	9.9	6.7	6.8	8.0	7.2
	2000	10.0	5.8	2.9	4.9	5.7	4.6
	2005	8.0	5.0	3.0	4.0	5.0	4.0

Notes: *Although financed by means of (income independent) community-rated premiums for private health insurance, in international comparisons mandatory health insurance expenditure is usually included for Switzerland and The Netherlands in the share of public expenditure.
**Most recent year available.
Sources: World Bank (2006); OECD (2005); Taiwan Department of Health, Office of Statistics, National Health Expenditures 2004, Taiwan, ROC: Department of Health, 2006; Department of Health of Republic of China, 2005 Taiwan Public Health Report, Department of Health, ROC (Taiwan) 2006; Department of Health of Republic of China, Health Care Statistical Trends, Department of Health, ROC (Taiwan), 2006; Cheng, 2003.

Recipient of the *JCPA* and ICPA-Forum Award for Best Comparative Paper, The International Francophone Political Science Conference, Grenoble, 2009

Bottom–Up Policy Convergence: A Sociology of the Reception of Policy Transfer in Public Health Policies in Europe

CAROLE CLAVIER

ABSTRACT *Policy convergence is generally studied from the point of view of the state and explained in terms of policy transfer. However, policy convergence also takes place between countries. The sociology of reception of policy transfer argues for the need to consider convergence from the point of view of the local actors involved in the transfer. Based on a case study of public health policy in France and Denmark, this paper shows that while the local embeddedness of public policy does indeed limit convergence, it also allows for policy transfer and therefore convergence.*

This paper is a case study of local policy convergence across national borders – that is, how local policies in different countries become more alike. For local public health policies in France and Denmark, convergence occurs primarily at the level of objectives and content, whereas instruments and policymaking processes remain specific (Bennett 1991). Objectives and content are both based on a conception of health as not simply the absence of disease, but rather "a state of total physical, mental and social well-being" (WHO 1948) and, therefore, influenced by factors such as income, nutrition and social relationships. The impact of these factors, known as the social determinants of health (SDOH), has been widely studied since the 1970s, and the results of this work disseminated through various academic and institutional channels, primarily by the World Health Organization (WHO) (Kickbusch 2003). But how has this knowledge influenced local public health policies like the ones studied in this case study? In the existing literature, the concept of transfer – that is, how institutions in a given time or place use ideas or policies developed by institutions in other times or places (Dolowitz and Marsh 1996) – is often used to explain convergence. In our case study, however, identifying voluntary or compulsory transfer is difficult because there is no direct contact between French and Danish local authorities, nor any constraining policies from central governments, the European Union or the WHO (Bennett 1991).

I have therefore opted for a bottom-up approach in my study of convergence and policy transfer. I examine the reception of policy transfer – that is, how external ideas are integrated into domestic policies and how these ideas circulate locally. Studying the reception of transfer focuses attention away from the initiation of policy transfer and toward the receiving end of transfer. Rather than analyzing how the WHO circulates public health practices based on SDOH, this approach looks at how local health policy actors discover and adopt public health concepts and related practices.

My approach departs significantly from classical policy studies, which place the emphasis on government initiatives. It embraces a political sociology approach to the policy process, considering public policy to be a collective construction that involves a plurality of public and private actors from all levels of government (Hassenteufel 2008). It means that when observing actors at the receiving end of transfer, not only are local policymaking elites (politicians and civil servants) considered, but also public health practitioners who have an input into the content of local public health policies. This paper therefore proposes a sociology of the reception of transfer, examining how new ideas based on SDOH are integrated into local public health policies and how local public health professionals contribute to the transfer and integration of these ideas.

I will first present my theoretical framework, which is based on a review of the literature on policy transfer and its reception. I then describe my empirical research method. The third and fourth sections present my results: how SDOH concepts were integrated into newly emerging policies in the four regions studied, and how the background and career paths of public health professionals contributed to the introduction of SDOH concepts into these policies. The conclusion discusses what this study adds to our understanding of policy transfer and convergence.

The Reception of Policy Transfer

In general, the study of policy transfer aims to understand how public action is inspired by policies from other jurisdictions or from policies adopted in the past. Transfer can explain convergence, although transfer does not necessarily result in convergence and, conversely, convergence can occur without transfer (Evans 2009). Distinguishing different types of transfer (voluntary versus compulsory) and the mechanisms that lead to policy transfer (for example, learning, imitation and diffusion) are major topics in policy transfer studies (Dolowitz and Marsh 1996,

Evans and Davies 1999, Stone 1999, Radaelli 2000, Holzinger and Knill 2005, Evans 2009). In such studies, the reception of policy transfer itself is rarely examined (Hassenteufel 2005); at best, it is seen as an aspect of the transfer process. Nevertheless, we can draw three conclusions from these studies that are useful to an analysis of the reception of policy transfer.

First, a growing body of research examines policy transfer through analyzing the career paths and relationships between policy transfer actors. Certain authors characterize the role of actors according to whether they initiate, facilitate or receive policy transfer (Wolman and Page 2002). Others map the circulation of ideas by collecting biographical data on the careers and networks of transfer actors; examples are studies of economic and policy reform actors in Latin America and studies of healthcare policy elites in France (Dezalay and Garth 2002, Genieys and Smyrl 2008). Studying the actors involved in transfer can also be a gateway to an analysis of the Europeanization process; an example is the influence of the French judicial model in Eastern Europe (Piana 2007). Examining policy actors' career paths is thus an indicator of how ideas circulate among different countries and/or policy sectors. Yet the most studied actors of transfer are the political and administrative elites of governments and international organizations who initiate transfer, along with the material resources and legitimacy they use to impose their opinions (True and Mintrom 2001, Greener 2002, Ogden et al. 2003, Nakano 2004, Stone 2004, Busch and Jörgens 2005, Bomberg 2007, Delpeuch 2008). In contrast, less attention has been paid to transfer between local actors and to the role of local actors in the reception of transfer initiated by national governments (Evans and Davies 1999, Wolman and Page 2002).

Second, proximity is a factor that facilitates policy transfer: ideas are more likely to be transferred if they fit with domestic institutions, representations of policy and political issues and if they provide (partial) solutions to these domestic issues. The importance of proximity has been demonstrated both at the macro level – for example, between a country's institutional, cultural and economic preferences (Lenschow et al. 2005) – and at the micro level – for example, between actors' preferences and the characteristics of the institutions in which these actors operate. This explains, for instance, why the UK and US have adopted the same model of scientific (evidence-based), bureaucratic (complying with rules set by external authorities) medicine. Proximity between the principles of the scientific-bureaucratic model of medicine, the financing systems for the healthcare system, and the preferences of actors in a position to influence health policy in each country has led to policy convergence in the UK and US (Harrison et al. 2002). Macro-level factors satisfactorily explain policy transfer between two countries that share institutional and cultural characteristics, but they do not explain policy transfer between countries like France and Denmark, which have different cultures and institutions. However, transfer between such different contexts may be explained by micro-level proximity between ideas, the preferences of policy actors and domestic institutions. In terms of the reception of policy transfer, it implies that local actors are more likely to take up (or transfer) an idea that corresponds to their preferences and fits with local policymakers' representations of the problem at hand and existing opportunities for intervention.

Finally, research has shown that the ideas and practices exchanged during transfer are selected and adapted to a particular context (Pedersen 2007, Delpeuch 2008, Massey 2009). Whether a country is compelled to import European standards or is inspired to do so of its own accord by foreign policy models, the transferred elements are transformed to blend with the new context, namely with local policy issues, embedded configurations of actors and institutions with their respective responsibilities and interests. This has implications for policy convergence: it is generally thought that these transformations limit convergence because they reinforce the specificities of the particular context into which the idea is transferred (Radaelli 2005). This would suggest that when comparing the reception of an idea in different policies and/or contexts, we would observe differences in how the idea is conceptualized in the different cases.

The literature suggests that policy actors are vectors for the circulation of ideas and that transfer is facilitated by the proximity of the ideas transferred to the context and local policymakers' representation of the issue. It is also known that the original policy or idea transforms during transfer. This means that when comparing the reception of ideas transferred to different policies, we need to focus on how the transfer is conceptualized, on how well the transfer corresponds to the context and policymakers' representations of policy issues, and on how particular policy actors contribute to its circulation. My hypothesis is that the reception of transfer is a cause of convergence because the integration of SDOH into local policies leads to convergence between these local policies. And because the literature suggests that proximity between SDOH and the context of reception facilitates transfer, I also examine whether the context of reception is a secondary cause of convergence, rather than simply a factor that leads to the transformation of transfer and hence a factor that limits policy convergence.

As mentioned above, studying the reception of transfer reveals how ideas being transferred are integrated into local policies and circulated locally. The first results section therefore examines the integration of SDOH into local public health policies; it focuses on the conceptualization of SDOH, on the arguments put forward to legitimize the development of public health policies based on SDOH, and on the actors who circulated SDOH concepts locally. The following section maps the circulation of SDOH concepts from public health spheres to local policies by retracing the career paths of some key public health actors who were in a position to influence the content of local policies.

Case Study and Method

I analyzed the process of transfer reception in local public health policies for two regions in France, Nord-Pas-de-Calais and Alsace, and for two counties in Denmark, North Jutland and Ringkjøbing. Comparison is central to this research as the study of convergence requires comparing the reception of policy transfer between regions/counties. The use of case studies and comparisons is particularly useful in understanding the processes of reception of transfer because it allows for the testing of research hypotheses (Sartori 1991). Whereas strong similarities between local public health policies indicate convergence, significant differences between health systems exclude the argument that convergence is solely the result of functional requirements or similar problems.

Denmark is a universal welfare state where responsibility for health policy, including the provision of healthcare services, is decentralized to counties (Vallgårda 2003).

Counties and towns sometimes also include prevention and health promotion in their four-year health policy programs. By contrast, France is a conservative welfare state in which the central government retains control over both healthcare and public health policies (Rochaix and Wilsford 2005). Local authorities (regions, departments or towns) sometimes develop their own public health policies and can contribute to the central government's policies for the region (called regional health programs).

In this context, the actual development of local public health policies in both countries depends largely on the involvement of local health policy actors and there is great variation between regions within the same country. As the objective was to examine the processes leading to convergence, the four regions were chosen based on the involvement of local authorities, local politicians and other stakeholders (medical professionals, non-profit associations and health insurers). This case study does not provide a representative overview of the development of local public health policies in the two countries and downplays resistance to such policy development, including resistance to the integration of SDOH. However, comparing territories with different levels of policy development would have shifted the focus to differences between the regional cases, whereas the objective was to analyze convergence through an examination of exemplary cases.

The study covers a 15-year time span, from the emergence of local policies in the early 1990s to 2005, when major reforms that had a significant impact on public health were being prepared or implemented.[1] I opted for a qualitative field survey in each of the four regions studied, including long visits to Denmark. I studied the gray literature (health programs) in order to characterize the public health policies and to identify policy transfer and the actors involved in public health policy. Data was collected on the reception of transfer though 49 semi-structured interviews with actors in charge of public health policy within regional and municipal authorities, with co-ordinators involved in the local implementation of these policies, and with heads of national public health organizations supporting local policies. I also established the local context and collected data on the integration of transfer into local policies through another series of interviews with the representatives of partner institutions and non-governmental organizations at the local, regional and national levels, as well as with local politicians.

The Integration of Policy Transfer within Local Public Health Policies

It has been fairly convincingly demonstrated in the public health literature that a population's health status is influenced not only by healthcare, but also by social, environmental and economic factors such as income, housing, transport, social support networks and physical activity (Marmot and Wilkinson 2006). Based on these SDOH, the "new public health" movement promotes policies that: a) emphasize the link between lifestyle and living conditions, and how these affect the population's health, and b) grant public policy a role in supporting lifestyle choices deemed to be healthy and in creating supportive environments for health (Petersen and Lupton 1996). In general, policies are based on two strategies: disease prevention (for example, screening or vaccination) and health promotion (creating supportive conditions for health, such as facilitating access to services, as outlined in the Ottawa Charter for Health Promotion, drawn up in 1986 under the auspices of the WHO). In this section, I recount the emergence of public health policies in the Danish and French regions, placing particular emphasis on the actors who brought knowledge on SDOH to the local level.

Denmark

The two counties studied both launched public health policies informed by SDOH in the early 1990s. The national context was very favorable at this point in time due to evidence that life expectancy was rising at a lower-than-expected rate and to economic and financial pressures on the healthcare system. These factors sparked the government's interest in public health and led to the drawing up of the country's first national public health program in 1989 (Kamper-Jørgensen 1998, Vallgårda 2003). The underlying rationale was that preventing disease and creating better living conditions could help improve not only the population's health but also the country's finances by curbing healthcare expenditure.

In North Jutland, the county had been subsidizing accident prevention programs in the workplace since 1985. But what really triggered the development of public health policy was a large public event in 1990 called the "Health Market". Two nurses obtained the county's support to organize this major three-day event, which advertised existing health promotion interventions, initiated new programs and opened a dialogue between professionals, decision makers and the population on issues like the environment, addiction, traffic accidents, nutrition and health in the workplace. The event resulted in 22 policy recommendations and the county hired the two nurses to integrate these recommendations into the institution's first health program. One of the county's councilors, who later became head of the Health Commission in the county's assembly, supported the policy starting in the early 1990s, seeing it as a political opportunity consistent with his socialist values – a means to tackle social inequalities in health. Consistent with the counties being responsible for healthcare service provision (70 per cent of their budget), the economic argument was also a powerful motivation. This aspect was mentioned in the county's program (Nordjyllands Amt 2000: 17–18) and confirmed by a nurse involved in the implementation of the program in the early days: "It was a very good motivation in the first place because [if you could] keep people out of hospital, it would be cheaper. So I think that's why they started this [policy] in the county" (Interview, 12 May 2004). In 2004, North Jutland county spent DKK 30 million in public health (one per cent of its healthcare budget), which was more than any other county.

The main achievement of the county's health program was a health contract with municipalities based on the Healthy Cities movement initiated by the WHO. This was actually a recommendation from the 1990 Health Market and is still a cornerstone of the county's policy 15 years later. The objective of this initiative was to make cities more supportive environments for health – for example, by improving public and active transportation, creating green spaces and improving access to public spaces for the elderly. Twenty municipalities formally signed contracts with the county to set up Healthy City offices in their municipality, and to co-finance a local health co-ordinator and health interventions within priority areas, thus increasing the number of small-scale health projects implemented across the region. These contracts reflected in spirit the concept of health as a state of well-being that is influenced by a wide range of social determinants. One of the nurses who helped organize the 1990 Health Market was the architect of these contracts, while other health professionals who worked as co-ordinators for the Healthy City offices contributed to their implementation. A nurse, the first co-ordinator of the Healthy City office in Brønderslev (1992–1994), explained how health promotion guided her practice:

> "Health for All by the Year 2000" was the main [strategy]. ... We wanted to make it at the local level, and we believed [that] the closer we were to the citizens, the more healthcare we could provide. ... Healthcare is more than no sickness: it is to make choices, to be strong, and many other things. That was the challenge. (Interview, 12 May 2004)

This nurse's successor, a dental hygienist, explained how the same philosophy still prevailed in 2004 (Interview, 3 May 2004). For instance, at the request of the population and/or professionals, she organized activities like Nordic Walking; a club for overweight boys to practice physical activity and gain confidence; and talks about topics such as nutrition for diabetics.

The county's policy was grounded in the SDOH and health promotion in that it aimed to create conditions that would enable people to improve their health. This is evident in the objectives of policies which addressed issues related to inequalities in health, children, smoking, nutrition and obesity. And in the actions taken, including the creation of bicycle paths, subsidizing a center for healthy workplaces that offers nutrition, physical activity and smoking cessation services, and making the main city's hospital smoke-free in 2007. As one of the nurses explained, the Health Market had been informed by the concepts of disease prevention and health promotion (Interview, 18 June 2004). A booklet describing the Health Market further underlined that health is created outside the healthcare system, through lifestyle and living conditions. It referred to the WHO's program *Health For All by the Year 2000* (Nordjyllands Amt 1990). This commitment was later "strengthen[ed]" (Interview, county health consultant, 15 April 2004) through formal references to the WHO's definition of health and to the WHO's *Health for All by the Year 2000* program in the county's third public health program (Nordjyllands Amt 2000), and with the county's joining the Danish Healthy City network. The latter network has structured and linked the health policies of different local authorities across the country since the early 1990s.

The policy of Ringkjøbing county was also a prevention and health promotion policy. Among its priorities were to improve the health of disadvantaged children, the elderly and people living with chronic diseases; to prevent cancer by supporting workers in their workplaces and hospital patients to change their smoking, nutrition and physical activity habits. Two nurses who worked as health promotion consultants for the county's health department explained that their practice was grounded in the Ottawa Charter on Health Promotion and on the work of Aaron Antonovsky, a sociologist who claimed that specific personal dispositions and appropriate social conditions contribute to create health (Antonovsky 1996). In his theory on the sense of coherence, health is to have a feeling that daily life is understandable, manageable and meaningful. In policy terms, this approach aims to develop individuals' coping strengths by examining what they want and how they experience life, and by creating supportive environments. Antonovsky's work was also explicitly cited by a health policy co-ordinator in Holstebro, a city in Ringkjøbing county, especially in relation to policies on improving the health of children from disadvantaged and/or ethnic backgrounds. It is also implicitly mentioned in North Jutland's third public health program (Nordjyllands Amt 2000: 17).

France

The incorporation of SDOH in France coincided with the emergence of local public health policies in the early 1990s. In France, local public health policies are the result of a double process: implementation of the state's regional health programs and implementation of the policies of local governments (regions, municipalities and departments).

A 1992 report from the High Committee on Public Health (a public body whose mandate is to reflect on and propose health policy) was the first policy document to introduce the idea that health is a social and mental process, not just the absence of disease (HCSP 1992). Two years later, the same institution published another report on the health of the population that featured a presentation of SDOH (HCSP 1994). These reports served as references for regional health policymakers in the following years. At around the same time, the subject of SDOH was raised during the regional healthcare services planning process in Alsace. A public health physician inspector, a medical doctor with special public health training and who works for the state's administration, took part in the planning process and had this to say:

> Talking about health care needs and hospital planning, we told them what determined a population's health and what made people ill. It was news for them [clinicians and hospital directors] when we said that 80% of what makes people ill is not related to healthcare. ... So we organized a regional health conference with over 1000 participants. People fought – like they had never done before – but that was really interesting. They resisted when we presented them with the [consultation process] because it was qualitative and sociological, not at all epidemiological. (Interview, 30 April 2003)

Following the first discussion, the same public health physician inspector followed the advice of a colleague at the Ministry of Health on how to formally introduce SDOH into regional health policy. At the time, this colleague was experimenting with both regional health programs (focusing on aspects other than healthcare) and with a method to determine regional health priorities. They teamed up and organized a meeting with various health and other professionals in the region in order to collect their perceptions on the health of the population. They then went on to organize a conference to present the results of this consultation as well as epidemiological data to regional health policymakers. This inspector noted that this consultative process led to a clash between different epistemic communities. Epidemiologists, clinicians and public health academics (medical doctors with a specialty in public health) were especially averse to this social conception of health because it opened up the field of public health to non-medical actors. Despite opposition, six priorities emerged from the process, including cancer, cardiovascular disease, nutrition and vulnerability, and these priorities gave rise to regional health programs.

And so the ideas of one public health physician inspector working at the Ministry of Health gave rise to programs based on broad regional consultations that led to priority-setting and a rigorous planning process to define objectives and intervention strategies. Integrated into the state's health reform in 1996 (which also aimed to curb health expenditure), the regional health programs were then implemented in every region under the responsibility of the state's administration and in partnership with the Health Insurance and, on a voluntary basis, local governments. Calls for proposals for projects targeting local institutions, professionals and non-profit organizations then allowed for the selection of actions to be funded by the programs.

Implementation of this policy contributed to the introduction of SDOH in the Nord-Pas-de-Calais region in two different ways. First, the consultation process involved a wide variety of actors with an interest in health, whether from a medical, social, judicial or educational perspective. The chosen priorities in the region testify to the broad range of determinants covered: cardiovascular disease, cancer, addiction, vulnerability and social exclusion, children and young people, health and the environment. Second, the planning of the different programs included non-medical actors in the policymaking process and further spread the concept of SDOH. For instance, the public health physician inspector responsible for the children and young people's health program brought together a team of medical doctors, social workers, psychologists and youth workers from several state administrative units (sports, education, justice), local governments and non-profit organizations. Together, they wrote a program that spanned many determinants of health and relied on a number of different inspirations:

> We couldn't follow the same planning process as for cancer or heart diseases, which are centered around illness, because young people are not ill. So we had to find a model that accounted for all the influences on health. ... As a group, we read the Ottawa Charter and different [ecological] models and made our own interpretation. (Interview, 22 April 2002)

Additionally, smaller-scale programs were created in order to complement the regional programs in this region and meet the specific health priorities of each district. More co-ordinators and professionals were therefore exposed to SDOH concepts.

Parallel to the state's programs, the regional government in Nord-Pas-de-Calais developed its own policy with a strong emphasis on SDOH. The region's concern for public health stems from its responsibility for local development and dates back to the 1980s, when crises in the traditional mining and textile industries brought attention to the prevalence of social problems with a health dimension, such as alcoholism. A regional politician encouraged initiatives to combat alcoholism, and these were progressively consolidated into a regional public health policy (Cépré 1999). Among the achievements of this policy were the creation of a Regional Office for Health Promotion, which supports professionals and organizations in the development of health interventions, and the creation of "health" mandates within the regional executive assembly, meaning that starting in the early 1980s, one politician was always specifically responsible for health policy. Later, the regional government also contributed to the state's regional health program; its contribution represented 21 per cent of the program's cost between 2000 and 2003.

Similarly, some cities developed their own public health policy. Local policymakers were often alerted to health as a political issue during a time of crisis (for example, an epidemic or the closing of an industry or hospital), or when epidemiological data for their region revealed a specific health problem in their population. As they did not have any formal responsibility for public health, many of these policymakers built on SDOH concepts to make health intervention part of policies for urban revitalization and social exclusion, as in Lille (Nord-Pas-de-Calais) or Mulhouse (Alsace) (Clavier 2009).

This account of the emergence and main features of county and regional health policies shows how the idea that health is influenced by social factors has shaped local health policies in France and Denmark. Consistent with the literature, it suggests that the reception of transfer is facilitated inasmuch as the ideas transferred provide a solution to local policy and political issues, such as pressures to contain healthcare costs and evidence of social and health problems. Finally, in terms of the reception of policy transfer, it appears that a number of health professionals in key co-ordinating positions, namely nurses in Denmark and public health physician inspectors in France, provided theoretical arguments to ground local health policies (for instance, the Ottawa Charter and data on the SDOH). The next section focuses on how these key actors discovered these sources during their training and professional careers.

Mapping the Circulation of Policy Transfer through Actors' Backgrounds

This section maps the circulation of SDOH concepts and their integration into local policies by key local public health professionals. In addition to the nurses and public health physician inspectors identified in the previous section, I broadened the scope to include co-ordinators of health programs at the regional, county, city and departmental levels, as well as co-ordinators of national networks supporting local policies who were in a position to influence the content of public health policies or spread its principles to other actors by co-ordinating their implementation. Analyzing the characteristics of the background of these individuals provides information about the reception of policy transfer because it shows how these individuals were socialized to different versions of SDOH concepts through their training and career paths. Table 1 summarizes the profiles of these actors in the two countries.

Table 1. Profiles of the actors receiving policy transfer in local public health policies in France and Denmark

	France	Denmark
Profession	Medical doctors	Nurses
	Other	Other
Position	Civil servants	Employees from county and city departments of health
	Local government employees (regions, departments, cities)	
Career	International and domestic careers	Domestic careers
	Community health training	Continuing education in public health or health promotion
Sources for SDOH principles	National reports on SDOH and on community health	Declarations and programs from the WHO

In Denmark, nurses accounted for one-third of the 21 respondents (Table 2),[2] or one in eight medical professionals interviewed. It is not atypical that nurses were key actors in the reception and integration of SDOH into local policies in Denmark as public health training is available to nurses through the public health nursing institution. Founded in the 1930s to help reduce infant mortality by providing assistance to the mothers, the institution filled the state's broader ambition to "introduce a comprehensive program of health promotion, e.g. breastfeeding, tranquility, order, cleanliness and regularity" (Buus 2001: 490). The institution has been the bedrock of health promotion in Denmark ever since, attracting nurses who want to re-orient their practice toward more comprehensive interventions that tackle the root causes of ill health and create environments more supportive of health. For instance, the chief public health nurse in Holstebro, a municipality in Ringkjøbing county, had previously worked as a hospital nurse. She had noticed the high return rates for patients with certain pathologies, which led her to question why patients were being sent home with no prevention advice. She wanted to help improve the situation and so trained to become a public health nurse. The same dissatisfaction motivated the nurse who co-ordinated health promotion at Aalborg hospital (North Jutland); although not a public health nurse, she had previously discovered the WHO *Health for All* program while in nursing school and decided to obtain a degree in education because health promotion places an emphasis on education and empowerment.

The ongoing public health training given in Danish universities and in the Nordic School of Public Health in Sweden has contributed to the circulation of knowledge on SDOH and, in particular, on the work of Antonovsky. The later research has received a large audience in the Scandinavian countries because Antonovsky was for a time professor at the Nordic School of Health Promotion. His works have also been taught in nursing courses (as mentioned by the Holstebro public health nurse) and disseminated through a practical book on health promotion based on a study of health promotion practices in Ringkjøbing county (Jensen and Johnsen 2000). One-third of the 18 interviewees whose careers I was able to analyze supplemented their initial training – either in nursing, anthropology, social work, administration, education or journalism – with public health nurse training or public health university degrees. The others discovered SDOH concepts through colleagues who had received public health training or through participating in existing public health interventions.

In Denmark, references to SDOH were grounded in WHO statements or programs: this is representative of the national context as WHO publications have traditionally influenced Danish health policy (Kamper-Jørgensen 1998). Despite cognitive and geographical proximity with WHO-Europe, whose head office is in Copenhagen, only one of the interviewees in this study had actually worked there during her career. A pharmacist who had developed a smoking cessation concept to

Table 2. Initial training of the public health program co-ordinators interviewed in France and Denmark

	Healthcare professionals	Other initial training	Unknown initial training	Total
France	11	14	3	28
Denmark	8	10	3	21

be implemented at pharmacies, she then worked for the WHO to broaden her concept. Afterwards, she obtained a master's degree in public health to "learn more about the theory behind health promotion and disease prevention" and became co-ordinator of the Health Promoting Hospitals network (similar to the Healthy Cities network) (Interview, 16 June 2004).

In France, public health physician inspectors have been influential actors in the reception of SDOH because they have been in a position to implement the regional health programs, which really introduced the idea that health is socially influenced into local health policies. As public health physician inspectors are public health experts within the state's administrations, they are often responsible for writing and implementing regional health programs in the regions – five of the seven co-ordinators of regional health programs in Nord Pas-de-Calais and Alsace that I interviewed were medical doctors with such a public health inspector position (Table 2). In addition, some of them had previously experienced public health practice during research visits to Quebec (a French-speaking province in Canada that is known for its strong public health policy) or through overseas co-operation or international voluntary work in former African colonies and other developing countries. The most striking example is the founder of the regional health programs: he practiced community health[3] as a medical doctor in Africa and, upon his return, became a public health physician inspector. Working in the civil service, he then discovered the principles of Planning, Programming, and Budgeting systems (Benamouzig 2005) and trained in health planning with public health academics who had learned the methods in Quebec. All of these influences then later shaped the regional health programs.

While other professionals such as nurses and social workers also had international careers, most of our respondents discovered SDOH during training organized as part of the implementation of the regional health programs or through contacts with public health mentors. This, for instance, is how one regional health program co-ordinator in Nord-Pas-de-Calais switched from having a clinical practice to being a public health physician inspector. Others experienced the influence of social factors on health while working for non-profit organizations devoted to tackling poverty and exclusion via programs not based on the traditional clinical care model, such as *Association Abbé Pierre* or *ATD-Quart Monde*. These organizations help people in their daily lives (for example, with domestic chores such as meal preparation or laundry), and in so doing provide advice on family planning and help people access healthcare services. One public health inspector interviewed, having worked with ATD, promoted an official policy involving ATD, the state and municipalities so as to take into account the specific issues of deprived populations in the design of clinical practice and access to healthcare.

Half of my respondents (14 out of 28) were non-medical professionals, with 11 being in charge of local, smaller-scale programs such as municipal public health programs or local development programs with a health section. Trained in project management and co-ordination of partnerships encompassing several levels of public action, they were not public health experts but contributed to the integration of SDOH within local policies by spreading the methods of public health tried out within the regional health programs. Indeed, the planning process was based on consultations between the local institutions and professionals from various policy sectors with an interest in health, including healthcare, social work, employment, justice and sports. The ability to listen to the various actors with an interest in health (local government, health professionals, education or cultural non-profit organizations) and balance their respective interests was a highly valued competency.

As key actors in the reception of policy transfer, local program co-ordinators discovered SDOH concepts in various public health practices or documents emanating from the WHO, academics or national reports. French medical doctors trained in Africa and Quebec introduced community health and strategic programming into their health policies, while Danish nurses contributed to the diffusion of health promotion discourses and practices. A comparison of the two countries therefore shows that the reception of transfer in each country is influenced by actors who are in a position to shape local public health policies. The data also confirm the importance of context for the reception of policy transfer as this shaped opportunities for public health training and the public health traditions influent in each country (community health versus WHO-based programs).

Conclusion

The convergence of local public health policies in France and Denmark proceeds from the integration of one idea, namely the social determinants of health (SDOH), in emerging health policies in the regions. By comparing the reception of transfer in each regional case, I was able to identify the processes and conditions that facilitate the reception of SDOH into emerging local public health policies, namely proximity of SDOH to local context and the contribution of local public health professionals in circulating knowledge on SDOH. This study adds to our understanding of policy transfer and convergence in two ways.

First, and contrary to what the term suggests, reception is an active part of transfer that requires the contribution of local public health professionals: due to their training, experience and the positions they hold, they stand at the interface between institutions receiving transfer (in this case, local authorities) and institutions initiating transfer, such as the WHO and public health academics. Retracing their career paths is therefore a way to map the circulation of transfer between the different social spheres involved, and thus study the transfer process in a backward direction. In this case study, public health nurses in Denmark and public health physician inspectors in France acquired knowledge of SDOH concepts and related prevention and health promotion practices through different experiences, including public health nursing and clinical practice in developing countries or with deprived populations. Being in a position to influence local policies, they could facilitate the circulation of SDOH concepts among local policymakers.

This comparison of the reception of transfer in the two countries underlines the influence of the local embeddedness of public health policies on policy transfer and convergence. In each country, proximity between policy transfer and the local context facilitated and shaped the reception of policy transfer. Indeed, public health training and employment opportunities influenced the background of local public health professionals and how they discovered SDOH. The reception of transfer was also facilitated because SDOH offered local authorities opportunities for intervention on policy issues that arose from local governments' other responsibilities, such as pressure towards healthcare cost containment or evidence of social exclusion and sanitary problems.

These results confirm a conclusion from the literature: that policy transfer is transformed by its integration into new institutions and new configurations of actors (Radaelli 2005). But these results also have implications for the understanding of convergence. Context, or the policies' embeddedness, becomes not only a factor that limits convergence, but also one that facilitates the reception of transfer and, hence, convergence.

To arrive at a complete view of the integration of policy transfer within local policies, however, also requires that the practices that local public health professionals deploy to interest policymakers and other local health policy actors in these new ideas be taken into account (Clavier 2007). Besides, other studies need to investigate whether the absence of one or both of the factors identified here (proximity between contextual policy issues and transfer, and actors circulating transfer locally) influence or even impede the reception of policy transfer and explain policy divergence (Holzinger and Knill 2005). Some of my interviewees encountered difficulties in promoting policies based on SDOH when local policymakers did not perceive health as a priority area, which seems to indicate that a lack of proximity was impeding the reception of transfer.

Such a political sociology approach to the reception of transfer clearly furthers our understanding of policy transfer and convergence. By retracing the processes of transfer that have led to convergence in a backward direction, this study brings attention to converging processes in unrelated cases, thus departing from studies questioning how one case converged with another. It also focuses attention on elements of the local context that facilitate the reception of transfer. In this respect, local context becomes a secondary cause of convergence. Convergence therefore is explained "from the bottom up" insofar as it stems as much from the circulation of an idea or public policy model, as from its appropriation by the actors involved in local health policy.

Acknowledgements

This article won best article at the Francophone Political Science Association, in Grenoble, 2009. The award was underwritten by the *Journal of Comparative Policy Analysis* (JCPA), the International Comparative Policy Analysis Forum (ICPA) and Routledge. The English translation of this paper was financed by the CNRS Research Unit "PACTE" (UMR 5194, Institute of Political Studies, University of Grenoble, France), the French Political Science Association (AFSP) and the JCPA. The funding was granted as an Award for the Best Young Scholar's Comparative Paper delivered at the 10th Congress of the AFSP in Grenoble, 7–9 September 2009. The initiative was organized in collaboration with the *Journal of Comparative Policy Analysis*. The author also wishes to thank the Research Centre for Political Action in Europe (CRAPE) (Rennes, France) and Centre Léa-Roback (University of Montreal) for their support and Susan Lempriere for final revisions.

Notes

1. The empirical research in Denmark was carried out before the implementation of territorial organization reforms on 1 January 2007. This reform transformed the existing municipalities and

counties into larger units and split responsibility for health – to the new regions for healthcare, and to municipalities for public health. Likewise, in France the fieldwork was carried out before state regional health policies were affected by the public health law passed in 2004.
2. These data are not exhaustive insofar as they concern only those actors that I interviewed in the four areas studied.
3. Community health is a neighborhood practice which aims to help people take charge of their health and local social development.

References

Antonovsky, Aaron, 1996, The salutogenic model as a theory to guide health promotion. *Health Promotion International*, **11**, 11–18.
Benamouzig, Daniel, 2005, *La santé au miroir de l'économie, une histoire de l'économie de la santé en France* (Paris: PUF).
Bennett, Colin J., 1991, What is policy convergence and what causes it? *British Journal of Political Science*, **21**, 215–233.
Bomberg, Elizabeth, 2007, Policy learning in an enlarged European Union: environmental NGOs and new policy instruments. *Journal of European Public Policy*, **14**, 248–268.
Busch, Per-Olof and Jörgens, Helge, 2005, The international sources of policy convergence: explaining the spread of environmental policy innovations. *Journal of European Public Policy*, **12**, 860–884.
Buus, Henriette, 2001, *Sundhedsplejerskeinsitutionens dannelse: en kulturteorisk og kulturhistorisk analyse af velfærdstatens embedsvaerk* [The Institutionalization of Public Health Nursing] (København: Museum Tusculanum).
Cépré, Ludovic, 1999, L'alcoolisme: un enjeu politique régional de santé publique. *Hérodote*, **92**, 144–160.
Clavier, Carole, 2007, Le politique et la santé publique. Une comparaison transnationale de la territorialisation des politiques de santé publique (France, Danemark). Doctoral dissertation, Université de Rennes 1, Rennes.
Clavier, Carole, 2009, Les élus locaux et la santé: des enjeux politiques territoriaux. *Sciences Sociales et Santé*, **27**, 47–74.
Delpeuch, Thierry, 2008, L'analyse des transferts internationaux de politique publique: un état de l'art.Questions de recherche/Research in question, Centre d'études et de recherches internationales, Sciences Po, Paris.
Dezalay, Yves and Garth, Briant, 2002, *The Internationalization of Palace Wars. Lawyers, Economists, and the Contest to Transform Latin American States* (Chicago: The University of Chicago Press).
Dolowitz, David and Marsh, David, 1996, Who learns what from whom? A review of the policy transfer literature. *Political Studies*, **44**, 343–357.
Evans, Mark, 2009, Policy transfer in critical perspective. *Policy Studies*, **30**, 243–268.
Evans, Mark and Davies, Jonathan, 1999, Understanding policy transfer: a multi-level, multi-disciplinary perspective. *Public Administration*, **77**, 361–385.
Genieys, Wiliam and Smyrl, Marc, 2008, Inside the Autonomous State: Programmatic Elites in the Reform of French Health Policy. *Governance*, **21**, 75–93.
Greener, Ian, 2002, Understanding NHS reform: the policy-transfer, social learning, and path-dependency perspectives. *Governance*, **15**, 161–183.
Harrison, Stephen, Moran, Michael and Wood, Bruce, 2002, Policy emergence and policy convergence: the case of "scientific-bureaucratic medicine" in the United States and United Kingdom. *British Journal of Politics and International Relations*, **4**, 1–24.
Hassenteufel, Patrick, 2005, De la comparaison internationale à la comparaison transnationale. Les déplacements de la construction d'objets comparatifs en matière de politiques publiques. *Revue Française de Science Politique*, **55**, 113–132.
Hassenteufel, Patrick, 2008, *Sociologie politique: l'action publique* (Paris: Armand Colin).
HCSP, 1992, *Stratégie pour une politique de santé* (Paris: La Documentation française).
HCSP, 1994, *La santé en France. Rapport général* (Paris: La Documentation française).
Holzinger, Katharina and Knill, Christoph, 2005, Causes and conditions of cross-national policy convergence. *Journal of European Public Policy*, **12**, 775–796.
Jensen, Torben K. and Johnsen, Tommy J., 2000, *Sundhedsfremme i teori og praksis. En lære-, debat- og brugsbog på grundlag af teori og praksisbeskrivelsen* [Health Promotion in Theory and Practice] (Ringkøbing: Forfatterne og Ringkjøbing Amt).

Kamper-Jørgensen, Finn, 1998, Det forebyggende sundhedsarbejde. Forebyggelsesbegreber [Health-related prevention. Concepts of prevention], in: Finn Kamper-Jørgensen and Gert Almind (Eds.) *Forebyggende sundhedsarbejde* (København: Munksgaard), pp. 17–35.

Kickbusch, Ilona, 2003, The contribution of the World Health Organization to a new public health and health promotion. *American Journal of Public Health*, **93**, 383–388.

Lenschow, Andrea, Liefferink, Duncan and Veenman, Sietske, 2005, When the birds sing. A framework for analysing domestic factors behind policy convergence. *Journal of European Public Policy*, **12**, 797–816.

Marmot, Michael and Wilkinson, Richard (Eds.), 2006, *Social Determinants of Health 2nd Edition* (Oxford: Oxford University Press).

Massey, Andrew, 2009, Policy mimesis in the context of global governance. *Policy Studies*, **30**, 383–395.

Nakano, Koichi, 2004, Cross-national transfer of policy ideas: agencification in Britain and Japan. *Governance*, **17**, 169–188.

Nordjyllands Amt, 1990, *Sundhedsmarked 1990* [The Health Market]. Aalborg: Nordjyllands Amt.

Nordjyllands Amt, 2000, *Det 3. sundhedspolitiske handlings program 2000–2008. En plan for forebyggelse og sundhedsfremme* [The Third Action Plan for Health Policy 2000–2008. A Plan for Prevention and Health Promotion] (Aalborg: Aalborg County Council).

Ogden, Jessica, Walt, Gill and Lush, Louisiana, 2003, The politics of "branding" in policy transfer: the case of DOTS for tuberculosis control. *Social Science and Medicine*, **57**, 179–188.

Pedersen, Lene Holm, 2007, Ideas are transformed as they transfer: a comparative study of eco-taxation in Scandinavia. *Journal of European Public Policy*, **14**, 59–77.

Petersen, Alan and Lupton, Deborah, 1996, *The New Public Health. Health and Self in the Age of Risk* (London: Sage).

Piana, Daniela, 2007, Unpacking policy transfer, discovering actors: the French model of judicial education between enlargement and judicial cooperation in the EU. *French Politics*, **5**, 33–65.

Radaelli, Claudio M., 2000, Policy transfer in the European Union: institutional isomorphism as a source of legitimacy. *Governance*, **13**, 25–43.

Radaelli, Claudio M., 2005, Diffusion without convergence: how political context shapes the adoption of regulatory impact assessment. *Journal of European Public Policy*, **12**, 924–943.

Rochaix, Lise and Wilsford, David, 2005, State autonomy, policy paralysis: paradoxes of institutions and culture in the French health care system. *Journal of Health Politics, Policy and Law*, **30**, 97–119.

Sartori, Giovanni, 1991, Comparing and miscomparing. *Journal of Theoretical Politics*, **3**, 243–257.

Stone, Diane, 1999, Learning lessons and transferring policy across time, space and disciplines. *Politics*, **19**, 51–59.

Stone, Diane, 2004, Transfer agents and global networks in the "transnationalization" of policy. *Journal of European Public Policy*, **11**, 545–566.

True, Jacqui and Mintrom, Michael, 2001, Transnational networks and policy diffusion: the case of gender mainstreaming. *International Studies Quarterly*, **45**, 27–57.

Vallgårda, Signild, 2003, *Folkesundhed som politik. Danmark og Sverige fra 1930 til i dag* [Public Health as Policy. Denmark and Sweden since 1930] (Århus: Århus Universitetsforlag).

WHO, 1948, *Preamble to the Constitution of the World Health Organization as adopted by the International Health Conference, New York, 19 June–22 July 1946; signed on 22 July 1946 by the representatives of 61 States (Official Records of the World Health Organization, no. 2, p. 100) and entered into force on 7 April 1948.*

Wolman, Harold and Page, Ed, 2002, Policy transfer among local governments: an information-theory approach. *Governance*, **15**, 477–501.

How do Governments Steer Health Policy? A Comparison of Canadian and New Zealand Approaches to Cost Control and Primary Health Care Reform

TIM TENBENSEL

ABSTRACT *This paper compares the ways in which governments in Canada and New Zealand have attempted to pursue reforms in two major health policy arenas – cost control and primary health care – in the period 1992–2005. The framework for comparison is drawn from the "modes of governance" literature that deals with hierarchies, markets, provider-based networks and communities as means of steering policy. Recent literature has argued that governments are increasingly mixing and matching different modes of governance. This comparison shows that governance versatility applies in New Zealand, but not Canada, and this is primarily attributable to the differences in health policy institutions.*

Introduction

Governments have become increasingly ready and willing, and occasionally able, to make major reforms to health systems over the past 15–25 years. Health policy is an area in which government capacity to steer is often heavily circumscribed due to structural features of the policy terrain. A distinctive feature of health policy governance is the power of providers of health and medical goods and services in general, and the medical profession in particular (Salter 2004). Many key policy developments in the health arena in higher income countries can be best interpreted through the framework of countervailing powers between the state and organized medicine (Light 1995).

As part of this dynamic, governments may attempt to take on the power of the medical profession as and when they attempt to pursue policy directions that have the potential to adversely affect medical interests. The grounds on which health policy battles take place vary significantly between countries as a consequence of specific institutional developments in each jurisdiction (Wilsford 1994), notwithstanding many common dimensions to issues and conflicts (Light 1995).

Canada and New Zealand are two countries that have attempted to steer in similar health policy directions since the late 1980s. Two broad issues that achieved agenda prominence at the same times in both countries since 1990 are cost control and primary health care reform. These are issues in which the countervailing powers between states and the medical profession are in the foreground. Taken together, analyses of these two broad health policy reform agendas can help to build a comprehensive picture of each country's preferred means of steering in policy directions that present significant challenges for governments.

Steering Mechanisms (Modes of Governance)

The capacity of governments to steer policy is now commonly conceptualized in terms of governance. Within this highly eclectic field there is now an extensive theoretical literature on multiple modes of governance (Rhodes 1997, Pierre and Peters 2000, Jessop 2003, Thompson 2003). This approach to governance draws from and develops the more longstanding social science interest in modes of co-ordination – markets, hierarchies and networks – and applies it to the analysis of policy. These frameworks have also become more prominent in analyses of health policy (Exworthy et al. 1999, Tuohy 1999). One great advantage of this approach is its ability to provide a bridge between actor-focused and structural approaches to the analysis of policy.

The number of governance modes identified in this literature is usually either three or four. On the basis of arguments developed elsewhere (Tenbensel 2005), I have adopted a four mode typology, namely hierarchies, markets, provider-based networks and communities which is consistent with typologies of co-ordination and governance adopted by Streeck and Schmitter (1991) and Pierre and Peters (2000).

Hierarchical governance refers to command and control mechanisms of legislation and regulation and the use of state power to redesign the publicly funded health sector's organizational landscape. The use of financial incentives and penalties by the state also fits this category. Governments may also attempt to move in desired policy directions through negotiation, bargaining and persuasion with provider interests, often in tight policy communities which may take on more formal, corporatist forms. In health policy, corporatist arrangements are typified by joint steering and network arrangements between professional associations and state agencies on issues such as the regulation of professions and the incorporation of clinical governance.

Together, hierarchy and provider-based networks can be considered the "traditional" modes of governance, particularly for steering health policy, but both have been subject to challenge on the grounds that they privilege insider policy expertise and limit the capacity of citizens and/or consumers to shape policy. Over the past three decades, two further mechanisms have come to prominence as alternative mechanisms available to government.

The first of these is the use of market and quasi-market mechanisms to achieve policy objectives. It should not be confused with a preference for private sector involvement in health, although this element is often closely associated with the use of market mechanisms. For the state, using markets as a mechanism of health policy governance can best be thought of as harnessing the power of consumers and purchasers to steer policy either directly through means such as user-pays, vouchers or health savings accounts, or indirectly through government agencies operating as purchasers. Governments almost invariably use these mechanisms to attempt to weaken the position of providers.

As a second alternative, governments may also attempt to harness community and public input into health decision-making. The range of mechanisms that can be used to elicit public input into policy includes broad public consultations, granting privileged access for advocacy-based interest groups to policy making, involving local communities in the governance of health services and using local community consultation to inform the design and priorities of local health services. Such mechanisms are typically used by government to provide some counterweight to provider influence over policy.

Each mode draws on quite specific forms of power and knowledge. Hierarchical governance utilizes formal legal authority and places a high value on objective knowledge (legal and scientific) while provider-based power draws from the experiential, task-related knowledge of providers and their labour market position. Market power is drawn from the judgements of consumers/purchasers regarding value for money, and community power from value commitment and the capacity to organize. Governments, as central players in the policy game, attempt to steer in contexts in which other players are also trying to steer, often in different directions using different modes based on different sources of power/knowledge.

Versatility and Modes of Governance

Since the late 1990s there has been widespread interest in questions such as "what happens when different types of steering mechanism are combined?" (Rhodes 1997, Exworthy et al. 1999). A number of prominent scholars have developed the argument that governments have developed a degree of *versatility* in their utilization of modes of governance (Rhodes 1997, Hood 1998, Tuohy 1999, Jessop 2003). Each of these authors argues that governments need to adopt multiple modes to minimize the risk of governance failure resulting from relying on a single mode. Jessop (2003: 111) uses the term "requisite variety" and contends that "a flexible, adaptable political regime should seek to maintain a repertoire of modes of policymaking". Hood (1998: 211) likens the skill of public management to that of a "step-dancer" who has "the ability to shift the balance among a set of ambitious positions no one of which can be sustained for long". Tuohy (1999: 254) refers to governments engaging in "shuffling" (i.e. mixing and matching) between hierarchical, market and collegial instruments of governance.

If we translate this common claim regarding the importance of versatility in governance to the metaphor of the card game, sophisticated governance can be likened to the skill of a card player in a game involving tricks and trumps, such as Bridge, Whist or Euchre (Tenbensel 2005). In such card games, if a player were to concentrate on a single suit they are less likely to be successful. Skilled card play depends on the ability to use multiple suits (spades, clubs, diamonds and hearts) flexibly during the course of the game. The selection of suits to play during the course of the game is also influenced by an awareness of the strengths and weaknesses of other players. Table 1 applies this metaphor to the four modes of governance.

In health policy contexts in which governments face the possibility of resistance from the medical profession, there are different approaches available, analogous to

Table 1. The four modes of governance

Symbol	Description
Spades ♠ (Heirarchy)	Steering through the application of rational-legal state authority, generally administered and managed by bureaucratic agencies
Clubs ♣ (Provider-based)	Steering based on the central policy position of providers and their interest group representatives
Diamonds ♦ (Market)	Steering through use of market instruments, in which providers of goods and services compete for the custom of purchasers and consumers.
Hearts ♥ (Community)	Steering based on the values and preferences of communities, which can be defined on geographical, ethnic or other bases

different strategies in cards. Clearly, the medical profession's preferred suit for policy development is clubs, based as it is on provider expertise. Knowing this, governments can choose between adopting one or more other modes of governance: hierarchies (spades); markets (diamonds); and communities (hearts), particularly when they wish to circumvent provider power. Alternatively, governments can use clubs, governance based on stakeholder negotiation and peak-level bargaining with professional associations, in combination with other modes.

The bulk of the literature that draws attention to the mixing and matching of modes has had a predominantly British basis. However, these arguments do not suggest that the *need* for versatility is culturally specific. The ideas and questions raised in this literature should be applied in a comparative context, given that policy reform ideas involving any of the four modes can easily be found in the policy discourse in all higher-income countries. A central question, therefore, that this paper addresses is the extent to which Canada and New Zealand engage in "versatile governance" in health policy.

This question can be addressed by investigating whether there are patterns *across* broad policy issues. It is necessary to define the unit of comparison broadly rather than narrowly. The historical and institutional specificity of different health systems makes it difficult to make meaningful comparisons at a more specific level (Marmor *et al.* 2005). Although each of these policy reform categories contains a wide range of specific initiatives in different times and places, general comparisons can still be made, even though policy in these areas is the responsibility of sub-national governments in one of the countries compared. Albeit using different conceptual tools, such an approach for comparative analysis has been usefully adopted in areas such as fiscal policy (Lee 2003) and anti-poverty measures (Beaumont 2003). On a wider scale, Tuohy (1999) has used a similar framework in an exemplary way as the basis for overall comparisons of health policy and health systems.

Comparing Cost Control and Primary Health Care Reform in Canada and New Zealand: Health Policy Contexts

Canada and New Zealand are both predominantly tax-funded health systems operating in Westminster political systems adapted to local circumstances.

The most important and obvious difference in design of political institutions is that Canada is federal state, whereas New Zealand is unitary. Canadian provinces are reliant on the federal level of government for much of their funding and are required to comply with the Canada Health Act. In common with most Canadian provinces, the structure of New Zealand's health system is relatively decentralized with the bulk of administrative responsibility located in regional or district boards.[1]

In the 1980s and 1990s, controlling the costs of publicly financed health care was dominant on health policy agendas in advanced industrial countries. In both Canada and New Zealand, cost control reached its zenith in the early to mid 1990s, receding in relative importance from about 1997. In both cases, the impetus for cost control was partly generated by the ascendance of neoliberal, public choice paradigms of public policy and management. New Zealand undertook some of the most ambitious and radical welfare state restructuring in the OECD (Boston 1999). In Canada, the neoliberal influence was patchier and varied in strength between provinces while at the federal level the impetus for restraining welfare state spending was driven primarily by the size of the federal government deficit in the early 1990s.

Primary health care reform (PHCR) is concerned with strengthening the role and co-ordination of primary health care in health systems. Primary health care includes care given by primary care medical professionals (referred to as family physicians in Canada, and as general practitioners in New Zealand), nurses, pharmacists and a substantial range of other health professionals (Decter 2004). Three broad components of primary health care reform that have been prominent in both Canadian and New Zealand health policy discourse include:

i) improving access to PHC by minimizing barriers such as affordability or limited opening hours;
ii) moving from PHC based on individual practitioners to team-based care;
iii) adopting different forms of payment for primary care doctors – moving away from fee-for-service to either salaried payment or "capitation" (where practitioners are paid a set amount determined by the characteristics of enrolled patients.

In both countries, to varying degrees, PHCR has grown in policy agenda prominence as cost control has receded. In the early 1990s, governmental reform agendas in both countries sought solutions that would address both policy issues, and policy makers hoped that institutional restructuring would facilitate progress towards more integrated primary care and cost control. Significant developments in primary health care did take place in both countries as a consequence of restructuring. However, it has been only since the late 1990s that some of the key planks of PHCR, such as changing the ways in which doctors are paid, have become more prominent. This is mostly due to the fact such policy initiatives require an up-front injection of funds. Governments in Canada and New Zealand have released the tourniquet restricting publicly funded health sector growth and have made substantial new investments (Tuohy 2002, CIHI 2004, New Zealand Ministry of Health 2004).

In New Zealand, a key contextual factor for both types of policy reform has been the institutional dominance of the hospital sector. Hospital spending accounted for nearly 60 per cent of total healthcare spending in New Zealand in 1990 whereas the OECD average at that time was around 43 per cent (Anderson *et al.* 2002). Hospital care is publicly financed, with a small, niche private hospital sector. However, primary health care has been funded on a predominantly user-pays basis. In the early 1940s government began to fund the bulk of GP services (Gauld 2001). However, from the 1950s onwards the level of public subsidization diminished significantly (Brown and Crampton 1997) because GPs had always retained the right to charge co-payments, and the increase in government subsidy lagged well behind inflation.

This context has given cost control and primary care reform agendas a distinctive Kiwi flavour. Cost control efforts have been directed predominantly at the hospital sector rather than the primary care sector in New Zealand. Historically, the New Zealand health system has been characterized by comparatively low levels of government involvement in primary health care.

Canada's historical legacy is quite different. Canada has had universal coverage of both primary and hospital care since the 1960s, and this has been enshrined in the Canada Health Act (1984) as universal entitlement to "medically necessary" health care (Tuohy 1999). As a consequence of universal entitlement, primary health care is also a significant driver of cost in provincial health budgets. Cost control reforms, therefore, targeted primary care as well as hospitals. The stipulation of medically necessary care as a universal entitlement under Canadian Medicare has meant that less medicalized health care services have a more tenuous status. This creates a significant barrier to the element of primary care reform that involves widening scopes of practice in primary health care.

A closely related institutional factor is that Canadian medical practitioners lost the ability to charge patients above the scheduled government subsidy as the result of a series of battles culminating in the early 1980s (Naylor 1999, Tuohy 1999). As a consequence, Canadian medical professionals have necessarily become politically well organized to protect their income levels (Tuohy 1999, Davidson 2004) and this significant victory has proved to be a double-edged sword for Canadian provinces. It has created a situation in which provincial governments regularly negotiate with provincial medical associations to set the level of physician reimbursement, and consequently other policy changes that affect medical professionals are litigated in this forum.

Given that most health policy in Canada is located at the provincial level, any comparison between Canada and New Zealand requires investigation at the provincial level. Three provinces – Alberta, Nova Scotia and Ontario – were selected for more detailed study. These provinces vary significantly in terms of geography, size and political characteristics. Each of these provinces was at the more aggressive end of the spectrum of cost control (CIHI 2004: 34–35), and each of them has made relatively significant efforts regarding primary health care reform in the Canadian context (Wilson *et al.* 2004). The description and analysis that follows is based upon secondary literature and policy documents.[2]

Cost Control

Canada

In response to increasing budget deficits, both federal and provincial governments sought to increase central control of expenditure in the early 1990s. The federal government scaled back its contribution to provincial social programmes including health (Naylor 1999, Tuohy 2002) while the cabinet and finance ministries of provincial governments developed new mechanisms with the objective of making considerable reductions in expenditure across all social programmes.

In each of the three provinces studied, cost control agendas were primarily driven by cabinet and central government agencies. In 1992–93, the Alberta government's projected spending in health amounted to a 27 per cent reduction in both public spending overall and health care spending per capita over the consequent four years (Plain 1997). Nova Scotia's 1993–94 budget stipulated across the board budget cuts of between 2 and 5 per cent, including health programme expenditures of 5 per cent (Clancy *et al.* 2000: 66–67). In Ontario in 1995, the incoming Progressive Conservative government cut the overall budget for hospitals by 5 per cent and 6 per cent in its first two years in office (Pink and Leatt 2003: 5). The same government passed omnibus legislation which allowed it to unilaterally terminate any existing agreements between the government and the Ontario Medical Association (Williams *et al.* 2001).

Across Canadian provinces, the most common device for reining in physician costs during the 1990s was global budget caps (Hurley *et al.* 1997). Formally, governments have the authority to impose such restrictions unilaterally. However, in practice the introduction and maintenance of funding caps has required some degree of negotiation with provincial medical associations (Hurley *et al.* 1997).

In both Nova Scotia and Alberta, global budget caps were introduced in April 1992, prior to the onset of centralized budgetary control in these provinces (Hurley *et al.* 1997). Ontario also began attempting to limit doctors' fees in 1992 and by 1995 had introduced hard global caps as well as income ceilings for individual physicians (Williams *et al.* 2001). The Ontario legislation allowed the Minister of Health to exert fine-grained control over general practitioner fees, location of GP services and practising rights (Williams *et al.* 2001).

The other key mechanism, which applied more to the hospital sector, was regionalization. Under regionalization, provinces created sub-provincial regions with responsibility for governing health services in their geographic regions (Lewis and Kouri 2004). The rationale for regionalization was wide-ranging. Original plans for regionalization indicated a willingness to democratize the governance of health services (Williamson *et al.* 2003) and to work towards the integration of health services. It was also seen as a device for achieving efficiencies and economies of scale, particularly in the hospital sector. In effect, regionalization gave provinces the ability to curtail health spending because the regions' funding envelopes were determined by provincial government. The responsibility for deciding how to live within more meagre means was devolved to the regional level.

Ontario was the only province not to institute regionalization. This province came up with a different arms-length strategy to curtail hospital expenditure by setting up the Hospital Services Restructuring Commission (HSRC) which was given the task of rationalizing Ontario's highly complex sector. The HSRC was authorized to close and merge hospitals in order to achieve savings of $1.3 billion (Bryant 2003: 198). The HSRC's recommendations were largely implemented, although some proposed mergers were successfully thwarted (Pink and Leatt 2003).

New Zealand

In New Zealand, cost control efforts were primarily directed at two fronts, hospitals and pharmaceuticals. General practitioners were not targeted because they were not a significant cost driver. New Zealand health reforms of the 1990s were explicitly driven by formal institutional design principles championed by central government agencies, the most important of which was Treasury. The health sector redesign was consistent with broad principles of new institutional economics (NIE) (Boston et al. 1996).

The way to achieve cost control was to discipline providers, particularly hospitals and drug companies, by separating and/or consolidating the role of purchasers. There were attempts to harness the market power of health consumers through the introduction of co-payments for hospital costs, but these were highly unpopular and quickly abandoned (Laugesen 2005). More significant was the establishment of four Regional Health Authorities (RHAs) whose role was to purchase health services from hospitals and other providers on a competitive basis.

The same logic of institutionalizing government purchasing power was applied to the pharmaceutical sector. Pharmac, established in 1993, was "owned" originally by the four RHAs. As over 70 per cent of New Zealand pharmaceutical expenditure is funded by government, Pharmac has been able to exert considerable monopsonic purchasing power in the pharmaceutical market. It has done this by introducing techniques such as reference pricing, generic substitution and using cost-effectiveness comparisons to assist decisions about whether or not to fund new products. The creation of Pharmac had a dramatic and sustained effect on pharmaceutical expenditure (Davis 2004).

These reforms generally meant that the day-to-day responsibility for cost control was devolved from central government agencies to purchasing authorities. The government budgeted for much smaller increases in health expenditure between 1993 and 1996 (Ashton 1999). Hospitals, renamed Crown Health Enterprises (CHEs) during this period, were subject to overarching public sector legislation that required them to make a surplus. However, the element of market discipline that punishes enterprises that continually fail to make a profit or even avoid making a loss could not be easily simulated in the publicly funded hospitals. The vast majority of CHEs failed to return the required surplus, and recorded higher deficits, and these shortfalls were subsequently funded by government (Ashton 1999). After the 1996 election, a chastened National Party, now flanked in coalition by a party that opposed the commercialization of the health sector, rescinded many of the market reforms, although the organizational split between purchasers and providers was maintained.

This restructuring was an enormous and sweeping redesign of the publicly funded health sector that required extensive legislation. While market rhetoric was prominent in the mid 1990s, hospitals (CHEs) were also subject to stringent top-down performance measurement by central agencies as a consequence of the reforms. CHEs were expected to deliver on contracts negotiated with regional purchasers, but were also closely monitored by central agencies (Gauld 2001). Contracts effectively became instruments of top-down control by the RHAs in the absence of meaningful competition between hospitals.

Most of these reforms were dismantled by the incoming Labour-led government in 2000 and 2001. The new government restructured the health sector yet again, returning to a more decentralized structure based around 21 District Health Boards (DHBs), of which 7 of the 11 members are elected. These boards are responsible for hospitals and other health services within defined geographical areas. As such, specific hospital boards ceased to exist. DHBs are required under legislation to implement government priorities and be responsive to local communities.

Modes of Governance and Cost Control

The preceding accounts of cost control have some important commonalities and some noteworthy differences. Both Canada and New Zealand mustered the specific governance capacity of the state to take control of health spending to an unprecedented degree. Cost control agendas in both countries were driven principally by central government agencies, and in both countries the state's power to reshape the organizational landscape of health through legislation was used extensively.

However, Canada and New Zealand differed substantially regarding which mode of governance was used alongside state power. The predominant combination in New Zealand during the 1990s was spades and diamonds. New Zealand invoked a combination of hierarchical and market mechanisms in the 1990s, and in doing so it effectively sidelined professional interest groups from the cost control process. Numerous market-type mechanisms were introduced across the health sector. Predominantly, these were new market relationships in which government agencies acted as purchaser. Market governance was adopted in conjunction with beefed-up hierarchical mechanisms. But hospitals were also hierarchically accountable for their performance to other government agencies. The whole thrust of the health reforms was to subvert provider capture, so clubs governance was overtly eschewed in the New Zealand context. Apart from a community consultation process regarding an (unsuccessful) attempt to define core services (CSC 1993) there was no significant attempt to utilize hearts governance in New Zealand to steer towards cost control. Rather, professional groups banded together with citizen advocacy groups to resist the government's cost control agenda (Easton 1997). As such, clubs and hearts were played against the state's spades and diamonds.

In Canada, by contrast, spades governance provided exogenous shocks to the health policy status quo as a consequence of regulatory and budgetary intervention by central agencies, but the predominant mode of governance reverted to clubs in the aftermath of these shocks. Corporatist strategies requiring negotiation and bargaining with peak provider interest groups remained significant as the means of mediating higher level governmental reforms through health policy communities in Canadian provinces.

Market mechanisms were not significant as a mode of governance with one notable exception which was long-term and community care in Ontario, where the constraints of the federal Medicare programme did not apply (Randall and Williams 2006). None of the provinces instituted quasi-market mechanisms as a means of governing the medicalized parts of the health sector. The possibility of the state using purchasing power over the pharmaceutical industry was ruled out by a combination of competitive federalism, the lower level of state funding of pharmaceuticals, and the greater manufacturing presence of the pharmaceutical industry in Canada. Hearts governance, as might be expected, was not widely used to achieve cost control. Provision for community control was also not significant, even though it was prominent in early provincial discussions on regionalization (Williamson et al. 2003). Most provinces did not incorporate community representation into regional health structures, and those that did often later revoked it (Lewis and Kouri 2004: 21).

Primary Health Care Reform

Canada

Since the mid 1970s there has been a very articulate and vocal constituency within the Canadian health policy community pushing for significant reform of the structures and practices of primary health care delivery. However, the general tenor of commentaries has been that progress towards more integrated and population-based models of primary care has been painfully slow (Hutchison 2004). More recently, however, primary care has been transformed from "Cinderella into the belle of the health reform ball" (Maioni 2004: 97).

As with cost control, there have been important developments at both federal and provincial levels since the late 1990s. At the federal level, two broad inquiries stressed the centrality of primary care to health systems. In 2003, the federal government injected $800m into the Primary Health Transition Fund with the aim of facilitating provincial reform.

At the provincial level, reform efforts have centred on the facilitating new organizational forms and the development of alternative payment mechanisms for general practitioners. The centrepiece of primary care reform in Alberta has been the Primary Care Initiative, which is part of an overarching formal agreement between the Ministry of Health and Wellness, the nine RHAs and the Alberta Medical Association (AMA) signed in 2003. This agreement established governance structures, including the Primary Care Initiative Committee to oversee the development and implementation of primary care reforms.[3]

Nova Scotia's organizational innovation has been the multidisciplinary Primary Health Centres (PHCs) which are funded by the District Health Authorities. All GPs in PHCs are funded through "alternate funding plans" (AFPs), which are bulk-funded contract payments offered as an alternative to fee-for-service. By 2005, these PHCs covered 10–15 per cent of the population and just over one-third of doctors (primary, secondary and tertiary) were signed up to AFPs (Marchildon 2006).[4]

Among family physicians, AFPs were more attractive to those based in rural areas. Nova Scotia's approach has been described as "incremental and voluntary", built on a process that has incorporated a wide range of stakeholder and community organizations (Wilson et al. 2004).

Ontario's primary care environment shows the legacy of successive reform waves and organizational experiments over the past 30 years (Suschnigg 2001, Hutchison et al. 2002). A number of schemes have been devised which were designed to induce physicians to move away from fee-for-service delivery of care. Each initiative was the product of peak-level negotiation between the health ministry and the Ontario Medical Association. A series of more comprehensive reform proposals developed by policy advisory committees, including the Health Services Restructuring Committee, were developed in the late 1990s, but each was effectively blocked by the OMA (Hutchison et al. 2002). Since 2004, with the election of a Liberal government, the latest primary care reform policy has centred on the organizational form of Family Health Teams (FHTs) with an emphasis on integrating a wider range of practitioners. Elements of this scheme have attracted criticism from physician interest groups (Urquhart 2005) and it remains to be seen how far the provincial government will be able to advance this agenda.

New Zealand

The centrepiece of primary health care reform in New Zealand since 2001 has been the Primary Health Care Strategy (PHCS) which has seen an additional amount of between $2 and $4 billion dollars spent on primary care over 5–8 years from 2001 (Hefford et al. 2005). Significant new funding for primary care is being channelled through Primary Health Organizations (PHOs). PHOs are non-government, not-for-profit organizations paid according to a capitation formula. Individual GPs are members of PHOs and receive an indirect government payment on the basis of their enrolled patient registers and retain the right to charge a co-payment. The greater the proportion of the population in the high-needs categories, the higher the level of government subsidy flows to the GP.

The first PHOs were established in 2002 and by 2005 well over 90 per cent of general practitioners were part of the PHO system, and around 95 per cent of New Zealanders were enrolled in PHOs (Cumming et al. 2005). Many larger PHOs have been formed out of existing associations of general practitioners. However, central government guidelines stipulate that PHOs cannot consist solely of general practitioners – other providers and representatives of the community must be involved at governance and operational levels (New Zealand Minister of Health 2001).

The processes of policy development and implementation were noteworthy because interest groups of medical professionals had minimal involvement in the formulation of the Primary Health Care Strategy (Mays and Cumming 2004). As the government wished to see a primary care delivery system which was more broad-based, general practitioner groups did not have much formal influence over many key aspects of the policy that had some potential to adversely affect their interests. These aspects included the move away from fee-for-service and the requirement that GPs share power with community representatives in the governance of PHOs. For many GPs, the requirement of community representation has been problematic because they regarded it as increasing their financial risk (Cumming *et al.* 2005, McAvoy and Coster 2005). However, the implementation of the PHCS has required substantial involvement from medical professional interest groups. Providers noted a significant policy gap in the Primary Health Care Strategy with regard to people with high needs and chronic conditions. At the initiative of the Independent Practitioners Association Council, a GP interest group, a scheme for funding primary care for this category of citizens was developed jointly by the Ministry of Health and IPAC (McAvoy and Coster 2005).

Modes of Governance and Primary Health Care Reform

In all three Canadian provinces, strategies based on negotiation, persuasion and peak-body corporatism (either formal or informal) have been paramount. To this point there has been little willingness to make the task of reform more difficult by introducing elements that could be seen as a head-on challenge, although recent developments in Ontario may signify a shift in that province. Clubs has been the dominant mode of governance, with spades as the main support suit. To the extent that hierarchical mechanisms have been used, these have generally been financial carrots. Although community participation is a central element of the PHCR movement more generally, the degree to which community participation and control has been built in to PHCR initiatives has been very limited. While some provinces have provided incentives for family physicians to take part in schemes in which the community is involved in governance of primary care organizations, these have not been on the same scale as those instituted in New Zealand.

Provincial governments are acutely aware that any proposed changes in primary health care that are seen by the medical profession as adversely affecting professional interests would be brought to the table when governments negotiate with medical associations over reimbursement and other policy issues. As a consequence, the buy-in of medical professionals is generally sought as part of any primary care reform process and change is cautious and incremental. The dominance of clubs governance makes it difficult for provincial governments to propose more far-reaching reforms.

In New Zealand, the government led by the Labour Party has actively mixed three modes of governance – spades, clubs and hearts. The government has used its hierarchical authority to define the parameters of PHO status in an attempt to create an environment in which alternative payment mechanisms for GPs would become the norm. Spades governance has also been evident through the use of significant financial incentives to induce doctors to sign up to PHOs.

Hearts steering mechanisms have been central to the Primary Health Care Strategy. The organizational model for PHOs was the pre-existing community, non-profit primary care providers. These were regarded as an appropriate model by the incoming Labour Party which had taken on board many of the tenets of the international primary health care reform agenda which has constantly stressed the role of community governance (Starfield 1998). The degree to which primary care providers are actually steered by the community varies significantly. The larger PHOs, by and large, are effectively controlled by medical practitioners, whereas the smaller ones tend to be more clearly community-based (Cumming *et al.* 2005).

The New Zealand government eschewed a corporatist approach to devising the Primary Health Care Strategy, knowing that its policy objectives would be watered down if professional groups were included in policy development. Nevertheless, clubs governance became significant when the government ran into some difficulty in the initial stages of PHC reform implementation.

Discussion

This brief comparison of approaches to cost control and primary care reform reveals a striking contrast between Canada and New Zealand. New Zealand governments have made substantial use of all four modes of governance at one time or other. In both case studies New Zealand attempted to use hierarchical authority combined with either market or community modes in an attempt to circumvent or dilute provider-based power at key moments in the policy process. Canada, by contrast, is noteworthy because the same pair of modes – spades and clubs – was used in both policy arenas.

Governance versatility is not strictly a British phenomenon – it clearly applies in New Zealand. This is not surprising since the incoming Labour government self-consciously adopted many Third Way governance ideas from Britain's Blair administration. Canada, in contrast, shows less evidence of versatility.

The reason for Canada's more restricted range of governance strategies is not due to the lack of governmental interest in market and community participation modes. In Canada, the Ontario government in particular was very interested in harnessing market mechanisms in health governance, but was only able to do this in the area of the health sector in which medical professionals had little direct interest. Community involvement has featured prominently in the rhetoric of Canadian health reform, but this rhetorical commitment has had few major policy consequences.

The different degrees of versatility in health policy is in large part attributable to institutional differences between Canada and New Zealand. The most important New Zealand institutional factor is the high level of concentrated executive power of central government (Goldfinch 2000). This enables it to engage in far more experimentation in both the ends and means of health policy, New Zealand governments have the capacity to sideline provider interest groups from policy formulation, and have used this capacity in their efforts to steer towards cost control and primary health care reform. Given that the use of market mechanisms tends to be more attractive to parties of the right, and community governance tends to be favoured more by parties of the left, changes of government have enabled New Zealand to experiment with the full range of governance modes over the 1992–2005 period.

The key institutional difference lies in the particular "accidental logics" (Tuohy 1999) that have driven Canadian health policy. The enshrinement of medically necessary care in the Canada Health Act, together with the fact that medical professionals are, in the main, totally dependent on the state for their income, has created powerful constraints on the capacity of Canadian governments to utilize modes of governance other than spades or clubs in their efforts to steer health policy. State-profession corporatism, which has been institutionally embedded due to the need to negotiate the income levels of doctors, has been progressively extended to cover broader health policy issues. This institutional legacy effectively crowds out the possibility of using diamonds and hearts governance mechanisms as ways of steering health policy if the use of these steering mechanisms by governments is viewed as threatening by provider interests.

This institutional inertia does offer some benefits including policy continuity and stability (Weaver and Rockman 1993). It has provided a bulwark against a number of provincial reform agendas that have had the potential to undermine the Canadian health policy settlement. These reform agendas, particularly those suggesting a greater role for private sector funding, have been driven by professional and private sector interests, and championed by some provincial governments such as Alberta, had made little headway until 2005. However, it remains to be seen whether or not the policy window opened by the Supreme Court decision with the Chaoulli case in 2005 (Marchildon 2006), and the election of a federal government more sympathetic to this reform agenda will result in significant departures from the established path.

The New Zealand experience with versatility thus far seems to indicate that diamonds and hearts, as newer tools for steering, are restricted to support roles to mechanisms based on hierarchical authority. Even in an institutional environment that is conducive to governance versatility, it appears that governments are unable or unwilling to place too much weight on them in steering policy reform. Steering through market mechanisms was only effective in challenging the pharmaceutical industry, and had little impact on the medical profession, although nursing and other health professionals suffered significant collateral damage in the 1990s. Community-based steering has so far had only a marginal impact on the direction of DHBs and PHOs. In addition, market and community-based mechanisms are generally more fragile and difficult to embed in policy processes because they tend to be more vulnerable to changes in governments.

Conclusion

From this comparison of New Zealand and Canada, the capacity to harness community and/or consumer power and knowledge for governing health policy is either blocked by institutional configurations or at a very early stage of development. What then of the claim that governments are increasingly required to be versatile in order to meet the challenges of steering policy in the twenty-first century? Governance theorists may well be right that continued reliance on traditional hierarchical and/or stakeholder modes may limit the effectiveness of governance. However, there is still some way to go before there is convincing evidence that the harnessing of community and/or purchasing power actually enhances the capacity of governments to steer health reform effectively, particularly where provider interests are concerned. In contexts in which the medical profession holds a strong clubs hand, a hand full of spades still appears to be more useful to governments than one based on diamonds or hearts.

Notes

1. With the exception of the period 1997–2000.
2. The author also conducted five interviews in each province to gather contextual information about provincial policy. Any details elicited in these interviews, where relevant, have been supported, where possible, by documentary sources.

3. Alberta Minister of Health and Wellness, Alberta Medical Association, Alberta Regional Health Authorities Primary Care Initiative Agreement, 1 April 2003.
4. Interview with official from Nova Scotia Department of Health.

References

Anderson, Gerard, Petrosyan, V. and Hussey, Peter, 2002, *Multinational Comparisons of Health Systems Data 2002* (New York: Commonwealth Fund).

Ashton, Toni, 1999, The health reforms: to market and back?, in: Jonathan Boston, Paul Dalziel and Susan St John (Eds) *Redesigning the Welfare State in New Zealand* (Melbourne: Oxford University Press).

Beaumont, Justin, 2003, Governance and popular involvement in local antipoverty strategies in the U.K. and the Netherlands, *Journal of Comparative Policy Analysis*, **5**, 189–207.

Boston, Jonathan, 1999, New Zealand's welfare state in transition, in: Jonathan Boston, Paul Dalziel and Susan St John (Eds) *Redesigning the Welfare State in New Zealand* (Melbourne: Oxford University Press), pp. 3–19.

Boston, Jonathan, Martin, John, Pallot, June and Walsh, Pat, 1996, *Public Management, the New Zealand Model* (Auckland: Oxford University Press).

Brown, M. C. and Crampton, Peter, 1997, New Zealand policy strategies concerning the funding of general practitioner care, *Health Policy*, **41**, 87–104.

Bryant, Toba, 2003, A critical examination of the hospital restructuring process in Ontario, Canada, *Health Policy*, **64**, 193–205.

CIHI (Canadian Institute for Health Information), 2004, *National Health Expenditure Trends 1975–2004* (Ottawa, Canadian Institute for Health Information).

Clancy, Peter, Bickerton, James, Haddow, Rodney and Stewart, Ian, 2000, *The Savage Years: The Perils of Reinventing Government in Nova Scotia* (Halifax: Formac).

CSC (National Advisory Committee on Core Health and Disability Support Services), 1993, *Seeking Consensus: A Discussion Document* (Wellington: CSC).

Cumming, Jacqueline, Raymont, Antony, Gribben, Barry, Horsburgh, Margaret, Kent, Bridie, McDonald, Janet, Mays, Nicholas and Smith, Judith, 2005, *Evaluation of the Implementation and Intermediate Outcomes of the Primary Health Care Strategy*, Victoria University of Wellington, Health Services Research Centre (Wellington: Health Services Research Centre, Victoria University of Wellington).

Davidson, Alan, 2004, Dynamics without change: continuity of Canadian health policy, *Canadian Public Administration*, **47**, 251–279.

Davis, Peter, 2004, "Tough but fair"? The active management of the New Zealand drug benefits scheme by an independent crown agency, *Australian Health Review*, **28**, 171–181.

Decter, Michael, 2004, Introduction: reflections on primary care in Canada, in: Ruth Wilson, S. E. D. Shortt and John Dorland (Eds) *Implementing Primary Care Reform: Barriers and Facilitators* (Montreal-Kingston: McGill-Queens University Press), pp. 1–10.

Easton, Brian, 1997, *The Commercialisation of New Zealand* (Auckland: Auckland University Press).

Exworthy, Mark, Powell, Martin and Mohan, J., 1999, The NHS: quasi-market, quasi-hierarchy and quasi-network?, *Public Money and Management*, **19**, 15–22.

Gauld, Robin, 2001, *Revolving Doors: New Zealand's Health Reforms* (Wellington: Victoria University of Wellington).

Goldfinch, Shaun, 2000, *Remaking Economic Policy* (Wellington: Victoria University Press).

Hefford, Martin, Crampton, Peter and Foley, Jon, 2005, Reducing health disparities through primary care reform: the New Zealand experiment, *Health Policy*, **72**, 9–23.

Hood, Christopher, 1998, *The Art of the State* (Oxford: Oxford University Press).

Hurley, Jeremiah, Lomas, Jonathan and Goldsmith, Laurie, 1997, Physician responses to global physician expenditure budgets in Canada: a common property perspective, *Milbank Quarterly*, **75**, 343–363.

Hutchison, Brian, 2004, Primary health care renewal in Canada: are we nearly there?, in: Ruth Wilson, S. E. D. Shortt and John Dorland (Eds) *Implementing Primary Care Reform* (Montreal/Kingston: McGill-Queens University Press), pp. 111–128.

Hutchison, Brian, Abelson, Julia, Woodward, Chris and Johnston, Riley, 2002, Environmental scan of primary health care in Ontario, Working Paper, Centre for Health Economics and Policy Analysis, McMaster University, Hamilton, Ontario.

Jessop, Bob, 2003, Governance and metagovernace: on reflexivity, requisite variety and requisite irony, in: Henrik P. Bang (Ed.) *Governance as Social and Political Communication* (Manchester: Manchester University Press), pp. 101–116.

Laugesen, Miriam, 2005, Why some market reforms lack legitimacy in health care, *Journal of Health Politics, Policy and Law*, **30**, 1065–1100.

Lee, Simon, 2003, The governance of fiscal policy in the United Kingdom and Canada, *Journal of Comparative Policy Analysis*, **5**, 167–187.

Lewis, Steven and Kouri, Denise, 2004, Regionalization: making sense of the Canadian Experience, *Healthcare Papers*, **5**, 12–33.

Light, Donald, 1995, Countervailing powers: a framework for professions in transition, in: Terry Johnson, Gerry Larkin and Mike Saks (Eds) *Health Professions and the State in Europe* (London: Routledge), pp. 7–24.

Maioni, Antonia, 2004, From Cinderella to belle of the ball: the politics of primary care reform in Canada, in: Ruth Wilson, S. E. D. Shortt and John Dorland (Eds) *Implementing Primary Care Reform* (Montreal/Kingston: McGill-Queens University Press), pp. 97–110.

Marchildon, Gregory P., 2006, *Health Systems in Transition, Canada* (Toronto: University of Toronto Press).

Marmor, Ted, Freeman, Richard and Okma, Kieke, 2005, Comparative perspectives and policy learning in the world of health care, *Journal of Comparative Policy Analysis*, **7**, 331–348.

Mays, Nicholas and Cumming, Jacqueline, 2004, Experience abroad II: implementing New Zealand's primary health care strategy, in: Ruth Wilson, S. E. D. Shortt and John Dorland (Eds) *Implementing Primary Care Reform: Barriers and Facilitators* (Montreal/Kingston: McGill-Queens University Press), pp. 49–72.

McAvoy, Brian and Coster, Gregor, 2005, General practice and the New Zealand health reforms – lessons for Australia?, *Australia and New Zealand Health Policy*, **2**, 26.

Naylor, C. David, 1999, Health care in Canada: incrementalism under fiscal duress, *Health Affairs*, **18**, 9–26.

New Zealand Minister of Health, 2001, *Minimum Requirements for Primary Health Organisations* (Wellington: Ministry of Health).

New Zealand Ministry of Health, 2004, *Health Expenditure Trends in New Zealand 1990–2002* (Wellington: Ministry of Health).

Pierre, Jon and Peters, B. Guy, 2000, *Governance, Politics, and the State* (New York: St. Martin's Press).

Pink, George H. and Leatt, Peggy, 2003, The use of "arms-length" organizations for health system change in Ontario, Canada: some observations by insiders, *Health Policy*, **63**, 1–15.

Plain, Richard H. M., 1997, The role of health care reform in the reinventing of government in Alberta, in: Christopher Bruce, Ronald Kneebone and Kenneth McKenzie (Eds) *A Government Reinvented: A Study of Alberta's Deficit Elimination Program* (Toronto: Oxford University Press), pp. 283–327.

Randall, Glen E. and Williams, Paul A., 2006, Exploring the limits to market-based reform: managed competition and rehabilitation home care services in Ontario, *Social Science and Medicine*, **62**, 1594–1604.

Rhodes, R. A. W., 1997, From marketisation to diplomacy: it's the mix that matters, *Australian Journal of Public Administration*, **56**, 40–53.

Salter, Brian, 2004, *The New Politics of Medicine* (Basingstoke: Palgrave Macmillan).

Starfield, Barbara, 1998, *Primary Care: Balancing Health Needs, Services and Technology* (New York: Oxford University Press).

Streeck, Wolfgang and Schmitter, Phillippe, 1991, Community, market, state and associations? The prospective contribution of interest governance to social order, in: Grahame Thompson, Jennifer Frances, Rosalind Levacic and Jeremy Mitchell (Eds) *Markets, Hierarchies and Networks: The Co-ordination of social life* (London: Sage), pp. 277–292.

Suschnigg, Carole, 2001, Reforming Ontario's primary care system: one step forward, two steps back? *International Journal of Health Services*, **31**, 91–103.

Tenbensel, Tim, 2005, Multiple modes of governance, *Public Management Review*, **7**, 267–288.

Thompson, Grahame, 2003, *Between Hierarchies and Markets* (Oxford: Oxford University Press).

Tuohy, Carolyn Hughes, 1999, *Accidental Logics: The Dynamics of Change in the Health Care Arena in the United States, Britain and Canada* (New York: Oxford University Press).

Tuohy, Carolyn Hughes, 2002, The costs of constraint and prospects for health care reform in Canada, *Health Affairs*, **21**, 32–46.

Urquhart, Ian, 2005, Family doctors balk at health-care reforms, *Toronto Star*, 29 October.

Weaver, R. Kent and Rockman, Bert (Eds), 1993, *Do Institutions Matter? Government Capabilities in the United States and Abroad* (Washington, DC: Brookings Institute).

Williams, Paul, Deber, Raisa, Baranek, Pat and Gildiner, Alina, 2001, From Medicare to home care: globalization, state retrenchment, and the profitization of Canada's health-care system, in: Pat Armstrong, Hugh Armstrong and David Coburn (Eds) *Unhealthy Times: Political Economy Perspectives on Health and Care* (Toronto: Oxford University Press), pp. 7–30.

Williamson, Deanna, Milligan, C. Dawne, Kwan, Brenda, Frankish, C. James and Ratner, Pamela, 2003, Implementation of provincial/territorial health goals in Canada, *Health Policy*, **64**, 173–191.

Wilsford, David, 1994, Path dependency, or why history makes it difficult but not impossible to reform health care systems in a big way, *Journal of Public Policy*, **14**, 251–283.

Wilson, Ruth, Shortt, S. E. D. and Dorland, John (Eds), 2004, *Implementing Primary Care Reform: Barriers and Facilitators* (Montreal-Kingston: McGill-Queens University Press).

National Values, Institutions and Health Policies: What do they Imply for Medicare Reform?

THEODORE R. MARMOR, KIEKE G. H. OKMA and STEPHEN R. LATHAM

ABSTRACT *This contribution explores the relation between national values and national health policy. The article emphasizes the difficulty in describing "national values" in nations with heterogeneous populations. Values, we characterize as general, and as conflicting with one another. And the article briefly describes the factors besides* ideas *(including values) that shape national policy:* interests *and social* institutions. *The article demonstrates substantial differences in the OECD countries' institutional arrangements – differences in the extent of health insurance coverage, in how organized interest groups bargain about the rules of health financing policy, and which policy instruments are adopted, maintained, or changed over time. At the same time the article provides evidence of widespread public support among the populations of industrialized democracies for the principle of universal access for health care, with the sharing of costs according to ability to pay. This evidence supports the argument that a wide variety of institutions are consistent with the same set of values.*

Introduction

The Medicare program, it is quite often asserted, is special for Canadians because the program is taken to embody something distinctive and superior about Canadian national values. For some Canadians, it follows that any effort to alter Medicare amounts to an attack on Canadian values and should be rejected. On the other hand, others have claimed that Canadian national values have undergone substantial changes, and that this shift in values may justify (or excuse) amendments and alterations to the Medicare program.

Both the anti- and pro-amendment positions assume a fairly tight connection between what are called "*Canadian national values*" and the particular structural features of Medicare. Is that assumption warranted? What role do "*national values*" play in the shaping (or reshaping) of health insurance programs in Canada, and more generally in the world of developed democracies?

Section two of this paper is first a methodological commentary on what is and can sensibly be meant by appeals to "national values". It then addresses the general theoretical concerns about how such values might be embodied in the institutions of different Western democracies. Section three briefly reviews the large number of reports that have recently called for a variety of different reforms to the Canadian health care system; rather than commenting on the substantive policy recommendations of those reports, it concentrates on the surprising extent to which these various "calls to reform" share – or claim to share – underlying value presumptions. Section four provides some comparative evidence showing how loose the connections really are between anything coherently termed "national values" and the concrete forms of social institutions. Many variables besides "values" are at work in shaping and reshaping particular institutions of social policy. And, conversely, many quite differently shaped social institutions may reasonably be said to embody the same set of values. Section five returns to the Canadian discussion of Medicare, and argues that a range of possible amendments would be perfectly consistent with – and therefore would not greatly threaten – Canadian national values. Choosing among those options requires a degree of prudence – an attention to the political realities of conflicting interests, and to the practical realities of resource management and information – at least as important as the values that prudence aims to advance. That a social welfare institution expresses the right values is a necessary, but is not a sufficient, basis for its adoption as a wise course of action. Section six concludes.

What are "National Values?" The Presumptions of the Inquiry

Social science has long been suspicious of the notion of "national values" (Schumpeter 1908). After all, values are held by persons, not by corporate entities that have neither minds nor desires. It is true that we may speak loosely of the "values of the common law", or the "values of the Catholic church". By such usage we mean to locate fundamental doctrines that emerge from the writings, or from the beliefs of the elite, within a certain tradition. But, in general, "values" refers to subjective views of individuals about what is worthy or important. In politics, these are views about the ends that social institutions ought to advance, and the virtues they ought to embody.

One's values are *general*; they do not dictate preferences for particular institutional structures at any level of detail (Rawls 1971). That one values privacy in health care need not lead one, for example, to endorse a particular set of detailed privacy rules (those contained in the new United States Health Insurance Portability and Accountability Act of 1996 [HIPAA] regulations, say). It leads one only to prefer institutional arrangements that protect privacy over those that do not, and arrangements that protect privacy more over those that protect it less. One's values also *compete with one another* (Berlin 1998). Efficiency, for example, may need to be sacrificed to favor participatory governance or vice versa. A strong commitment to equality may lead one to limit liberty to some extent. Multiple institutional arrangements may thus have equal claim to instantiating one's values, by giving prominence to them differentially. Precision in statements about "national values" is thus doubly imperiled: such statements are necessarily a summation across a broad population of varied individuals' – already general, and already potentially conflicting – values.

These cautionary observations should not, however, blind us to the important role that values may play in creating a political community and in guiding its actions. Statements of values may inspire, unite, even "constitute" a people: think of the Declaration of Independence and the Bill of Rights in the United States, or the Magna Carta in Britain. And public statements of shared values – even if the values come to be shared only after they are publicly stated – may serve as important guides to action. The fact that values are general and may compete with one another does not, after all, render them meaningless. Values are no policy straitjacket, but there are certain choices they rule out.

In the context of the Medicare debate, Canada's core national values have been well expressed by Michael Ignatieff (2000): "We [Canadians] think that public taxation should provide for health care and that it is wrong for decent medical care to depend on the size of our bank balances". The five criteria mentioned in the *Canada Health Act* – public administration, comprehensiveness, universality, portability and accessibility – are themselves values, though perhaps narrower, more "instrumental" values, which give shape to the broad but fundamental public and egalitarian values expressed by Ignatieff. Since their articulation in the Hall Commission Report of 1964 and the *Canada Health Act* of 1984, the five criteria have gained widespread public support. (It is no coincidence that nearly every contemporary report that calls for Medicare reform feels compelled to do so by alleging the consistency of their proposed reforms with the five criteria.) It seems plausible, however, that those five values, because they are general and may have to be traded off against one another, may be advanced by a number of different institutional arrangements. At the same time, it is equally plausible that there are certain proposed reforms that they rule out.

Before attempting to establish the truth of those plausible claims, however, it will be worthwhile to pause to distinguish values from a number of other important forces that shape public institutions. On the top of that list must be *interests*. Interests are states of affairs or courses of action that persons are motivated to pursue based on the powerful drive for self-aggrandizement (including self-aggrandizement's prerequisite, self-preservation) (Hirschman 1992, Mansfield 1995). Persons have multiple interests; these are calculable, predictable, objective, and – like values – can be traded off against one another (Mansfield 1995). Institutional arrangements that were created because they advanced shared values may survive because they further powerful interests. And institutions created from self-interested motives may well embody values, or serve to establish them in society over time (Immergut 1992).

Public opinion, too, can shape institutions.[1] Opinions are views, prudential or ethical, about states of affairs or courses of action. These are notoriously more subject to short-term amendment than either values (which, because they are general, are less subject to amendment in light of short-term factual changes) or interests (which one can, in principle, objectively calculate). General opinions grounded in values ("Access to health care should be universal") appear to be more "sticky" than opinions about particular states of affairs ("Medicare is working well") (Maioni and Martin 2001).

Social institutions are also to some degree the product of the governmental and policymaking systems that create them, and those systems are, to use a difficult expression, value-informed. Thus centralist governments will more likely create centralized social welfare institutions; corporatist governments will more frequently create corporate entities whose bargains will determine the particular means of implementing social values. Here is a path by which societal values, by influencing styles of policymaking, may influence public policy. So, for example, Douglas and Wildavsky (1982) distinguish three distinguishable policymaking styles: *competitive individualism*, *hierarchical collectivism*, and *sectarianism*.

The social democratic states of Northern Europe have, according to this line of argument, strong traditions of hierarchical collectivism, with moderate support of individualistic norms and weak embrace of sectarian modes of policy promotion (Okma 2002). The United States, by contrast, displays a weaker appeal to collectivism and an active streak of sectarian political mobilization. Market efficiency and individual liberty are, according to polling studies, leading American values. Yet, as Douglas and Wildavsky (1982) acknowledge, it is a mistake to assume a very close fit between value-informed modes of policymaking and actual policy. Even the United States, with its seemingly dominant competitive-individualist values in policymaking, managed to establish Medicare, Medicaid, the Veterans Administration health program, the Indian Health system, a law mandating emergency medical care regardless of patients' ability to pay, tax incentives to encourage the purchase of private insurance, tax incentives for the provision of private charity care, and publicly funded hospitals that give free or discounted care. No one could reason their way to this set of health care institutions and programs from a premise of "competitive individualism" in policymaking. And this is so even if one concedes the accuracy of the characterization of US values. The concrete details of health policy, in short, are not tightly linked even to styles of policymaking that reflect dominant value orientations.

Finally, social and political institutions, once created, develop lives of their own (Tuohy 1999). For example, the historically contingent fact that Britain's National Health Service (NHS) was created just after the Second World War made its centralized organization likely, and that has shaped much of its subsequent development (Klein 1995). In the United States, the postwar development of private health insurance markets (driven, partly, by employer tax benefits) has made it very difficult for government to assume as central a role in the delivery and financing of health care as it has in other developed countries. The constitutional model for Canada's Medicare required bargaining between provinces and the federal government. From the beginning, also, there was regular bargaining with medical associations. Those features have conditioned Canadian policymaking and further developments of Medicare have emerged to a large extent out of the institutional processes and rules of this Canadian "game" (Tuohy 1999).

The next section briefly characterizes the range of reform proposals that have marked the Canadian political scene in recent years. The purpose of this review is not to evaluate any of the policy proposals contained in these reports; that has been done adequately elsewhere. Rather, the aim is to set the Canadian context for the more concrete discussion of national values and health policy. Section four will consider some concrete evidence regarding the question whether and to what extent different countries may, on the basis of similar distributions of values, establish quite different national institutions of social welfare. The evidence collected there shows that many of the core structural differences in national health care arrangements are the product not of differences in fundamental social values but of differences in political superstructure, of differing accommodations of clashing interests, and of the historically contingent "accidental logics" of established social institutions. This substantiates this paper's first core contention, namely, that national values are not a policy straitjacket. Section five turns to the second core contention: that contemporary Canadian values neither require a major change in Medicare nor do most of the reforms proposed require a change in values to be justified.

Calls for Reform in Canadian Health Care: Context and Convictions

This is not a "crisis moment" for Canadian health care. Nonetheless, the call for reform is alarmist, and many Canadians believe the values Medicare embodies are at stake. It is important to understand the origin of this "crisis mentality". Canadian public expenditure on health care, as with most industrial democracies, has faced great pressures in recent years. Economic stagnation, high levels of unemployment and rapidly increasing fiscal deficits in the 1970s and 1980s fuelled debates about the sustainability of welfare states everywhere (OECD 1992, 1994). Throughout the Western industrial world, politicians and commentators raised questions about the proper role of the state and the private market in providing for and safeguarding the welfare of individual citizens. In Canada, efforts to rein in national government spending included a freeze of federal transfers that, over time, caused a considerable shift away from federal funding to the provincial and territorial level. In the last few years – with the coming, significantly, of improved economic times – participants at every level of the Medicare program have been vocal about the losses suffered during the long period of fiscal belt-tightening. The Canadian press has been filled with fearful anecdotes and talk about a "crisis" in Medicare (Marmor 2002). For all the crisis language, few if any reform proposals explicitly demand a radical transformation of Medicare on the basis of a clear rejection of the values it embodies. Indeed, the Canadian debate has thus far included little explicit discussion of radical alternatives to Medicare's basic funding model. This contrasts both with long-term debates in the United Kingdom and with proposals by the current coalition cabinet of the Netherlands, for example; in these and other cases a number of fundamental funding options have been extensively investigated (but thus far not chosen).

Canadian reform proposals have nonetheless received enormous attention. They range from the imposing of prospective budgets on providers of care to de-listing certain services from public health insurance. Some provinces promote the introduction of private funding, and many have celebrated improved management (Okma 2002). The 2001 Canadian Institute for Health Information (CIHI) report aptly concludes that the reform debates in fact call for "overlapping generations of reform" (CIHI 2001). As in other OECD countries, many of these proposals have met with strong resistance from various constituencies. And reform ideas have prompted counter-ideas. There are, for example, proposals to devolve authority and to further decentralize the governance of medical institutions. At the same time, there are demands to centralize and assume stronger government control – for example, in the monitoring of outcomes or the provision of information about health care services to the general public. But, as in other OECD countries and in spite of much discussion, the basic public contracting model of public funding and private provision of health care has not, it appears, been challenged explicitly (Ranade 1998, Tuohy 1999).

Do any of these proposals amount to a threat to Canadian national values? Is the adoption of any of them contingent upon Canadians' changing their core values? Do the different reform proposals reflect fundamentally different values regarding the social provision of health care to the sick or injured, or are they in fact simply the products of different views about management and governance in service of shared values? To these questions this paper now turns.

What follows is not a summary of the various reports. Rather, it is an attempt to locate them on a value spectrum in connection with the purposes of this inquiry. Among the many recent reports making reform recommendations for Medicare, it is possible to distinguish three basic types. One type, in the course of recommending incremental improvements, ardently affirms the values of Medicare as unchangingly valid. Thus the report of the Tommy Douglas Institute of February 2001 proclaims: "[O]pponents [of Medicare] have always exaggerated its weaknesses. They now allege that Medicare's principles of universality and public, not-for-profit care are 'tired' and no longer relevant. These claims are demonstrably false" (Rachlis et al. 2001: 3). At the other end of the spectrum, there are reports that propose changes in Medicare that, regardless of the report's professed attachment to Medicare's values, are in fact incompatible with the egalitarian values the program now embodies. An example of that category is the Mazankowski report of December 2001 (Mazankowski Commission 2001), which has been characterized as leaving "virtually no stone unturned in the quest to open Canada's public healthcare system to the private sector" (Marshall 2002) and as "adopt[ing] a thoroughly American neo-conservative political stance that declares government the worst of all possible actors, and taxation the worst of all possible financing mechanisms" (Lewis and Maxwell 2002).

Between these points on the spectrum are many reports which urge "reinterpretation" or "modernization", though not departure from, the core values of Medicare. They claim to propose reforms that are compatible with Medicare's fundamental values, but that interpret them in light of a variety of different issues of practicality, political acceptability or managerial feasibility. These range from the 1997 report of the National Forum on Health, which explicitly recommended the preservation of Medicare's public funding, "single payor" organization, and the five principles of the Canada Health Act (National Forum on Health 1997) to the 2000 commentary of the Institute for Research on Public Policies, which recommended a broader interpretation of the five principles as well as the addition of principles of quality and accountability (Decter et al. 2000). The Clair Commission in Quebec, for example, recommended many policy and managerial changes, none of which was thought to depend upon or imply changes in Canadian or Quebec values; instead, the Commission characterized its recommendations as a "modern interpretation" of the five Canada Health Act principles, which it characterized as "socially legitimate" and seriously challenged by "no one" (Clair Commission 2000). In Ontario, a restructuring commission struggled to implement substantial reforms in the structure of the province's hospitals and provision of medical services. But, as with Quebec, this commission embraced Medicare's value premises while promoting policy reforms (Ontario Health Services Restructuring Commission 2000).

The Saskatchewan Commission on Medicare proposed a major reorganization of provincial hospital and medical services. Again, its recommendations did not rest on either the claim that Canadian values had changed substantially or that changes in values were needed to support reform: "There is nothing wrong with the principles of Medicare (as a solid majority of Canadians continue to believe); one can make a strong case that they are essential in a humane and efficient society" (Fyke Commission 2001).

In 2000, Senator Kirby's committee began its own two-year review of health care. Its final report, issued in October 2002, was a virtual catalogue of the various reform proposals (Kirby Committee 2002). It did not call for comprehensive change in Medicare, but suggested that the "public administration" feature needed revisiting and piecemeal alteration.

In early 2001, the Romanow Commission began its effort "to examine the state of health care in Canada including the benefits and negatives of the current system". It had a substantial mandate, conducted extensive research and consultation, and prompted intense media interest. Both its interim report and its final report of November 2002 prompted considerable debate, an indication of just how much interest Medicare arouses in Canadian life (Romanow Commission 2002). The Romanow final report recommended a "new Canadian Health Covenant" be established "as a common declaration of Canadians' and their governments' commitment to a universally accessible, publicly funded health care system". It also reaffirmed the five principles of the Canada Health Act, though it recommended limiting "portability" to portability within Canada; recommended a more expansive view of "comprehensiveness" to include not just physician and hospital care, but also diagnostic services and home care; and recommended the addition of a sixth principle of "accountability" (Romanow Commission 2002).

Despite the rhetoric of crisis and the appeal to needed reforms, then, very few of the Canadian reform proposals actually challenge the fundamental values. Most reform proposals were cast as efforts to realize those values in a more modern way, with greater efficiency and accountability. This, itself, is an interesting and important feature of Medicare's place in Canada. The program is more than a vehicle for financing hospital and medical insurance. It is best understood as an icon. For this reason there is understandable political reluctance to directly challenge the program's premises. On the other hand, the iconic status of Medicare makes it perfectly clear why the media – and Medicare's advocates – are on the hunt for threats to this widely "valued" program.

And such threats do exist; not *every* proposal for reform is compatible with Medicare's values. Most proposals – calling for increased integration and improved co-ordination of services, greater oversight of costs, and so on – are efforts to improve

Medicare managerially and keep its outlays under reasonable control; they reflect different views about management and governance rather than fundamentally different values concerning the social provision of health care to the sick or injured. But as Lewis and Maxwell (2002) have pointed out, alone among the most prominent reform reports, the Mazankowski Commission's report (2002) – with its attacks on Medicare in Alberta as an inefficient "command and control" monopolistic system, and its recommendations for the introduction of more private-sector competition – constitutes a real (if veiled) effort to transform the values on which Medicare was founded.

Given that the reform reports, for all their policy differences, involve so few challenges to values and embody so little disagreement as to them, the question naturally arises: what relationship is there, if any, between national values and the details of national health policy? This question will be approached first through examination of evidence from other industrial democracies and then by addressing Canadian data more directly.

European Values and Medical Care: Similar Values, Divergent Arrangements

Public Attitudes Towards Government's Role in Health Care

Public attitudes towards "government provision" (or financing) of medical care in the European Union show, according to both recent and older research, "surprisingly constant patterns of popularity" (Ardigo 1995, Coughlin 1980, cited in Gevers et al. 2000). On the basis of data from seven European countries and the United States, Ardigo concluded that "citizens considered good medical care 'very important' and its provision an 'essential responsibility' of the government". Coughlin's earlier research had come to the same conclusion. On the surface, then, there are grounds for believing that the "Western European welfare state [can] be regarded as an organized system of solidarity" in the sense of redistribution from the healthy to the sick, from the young to the old, and from the employed to the unemployed (Gevers et al. 2000: 302). This is the standard interpretation of polling data from Western Europe and forms the background to more sophisticated investigations of variation in views and values among the European citizens.

Gevers et al. (2000) have produced detailed data on contemporary sentiments[2] in Western Europe towards the provision and financing of medical care. Table 1 shows evidence about the degree of agreement concerning the role of government in *assuring access* to medical care. It clearly reveals general disagreement with the idea that government should play only a minimal role.

> **Question 1** The government should provide everyone with only essential services such as care for serious diseases and encourage people to provide for themselves in other respects (1 = agree strongly, to 5 = disagree strongly). (Gevers et al. 2000)

But the proportion of those who "disagree completely" varies among the samples and provides some basis for the study's emphasis on a dispersion of values and beliefs among the nations of the European Union. In short, solidarity might generally describe the bedrock of Western European welfare state values, but there are understandably bases for making distinctions among them as well.

This same point emerges with reasonable clarity in the findings summarized in Table 2. The variations in respondents' answers to the three articulated views show that differences exist among the welfare states of the European Union. Though substantial majorities in every country chose the generally egalitarian alternative 1, Gevers et al. (2001) interpret the standard deviations and skewness to indicate clusters of countries with different attitudes toward the support of public health care.

These data establish two central points. First, they do indicate a broad similarity in the central, solidaristic conception of the role of medical care in the Western European welfare state. This general value orientation, however, exists side by side with substantial differences in the detailed administration, policies, and rules of European medical care arrangements. Second, the variation across Europe suggests that arrangements in more egalitarian (and homogeneous) societies like Sweden and

Table 1. Distribution measures for Question 1

Country	Percentage disagree completely	Mean	Standard deviation	Skewness
Austria	18.60	3.10	1.27	−0.10
Denmark	41.90	3.71	1.41	−0.70
Finland	23.30	3.28	1.38	−0.22
France	26.60	3.44	1.35	−0.45
Great Britain	44.90	3.98	1.21	−1.03
Greece	29.20	3.60	1.30	−0.67
Ireland	25.00	3.40	1.30	−0.32
Italy	41.90	3.44	1.54	−0.29
Netherlands	39.00	3.54	1.46	−0.44
Portugal	21.30	3.48	1.20	0.44
Spain	35.20	3.82	1.20	−0.84
Sweden	36.80	3.98	1.08	−1.06
West Germany	25.60	3.50	1.26	−0.47

Table 2. Distribution measures for Question 2

Country	Percentage choosing alternative 1	Mean	Standard deviation	Skewness
Denmark	86.50	2.86	0.38	2.52
West Germany	71.80	2.67	0.57	1.52
Greece	87.20	2.83	0.47	2.85
Italy	71.70	2.68	0.53	1.44
Spain	90.10	2.88	0.40	3.39
France	76.20	2.70	0.58	1.79
Ireland	58.90	2.55	0.58	0.84
Netherlands	77.70	2.75	0.50	1.84
Portugal	72.00	2.66	0.59	1.53
Great Britain	85.90	2.84	0.41	2.60
Finland	79.60	2.79	0.43	1.70
Sweden	94.80	2.94	0.27	4.87
Austria	65.00	2.59	0.61	1.18

Denmark reveal links between views about equal access to medical care and programmatic arrangements that minimize the role of income in access or financing.

> **Question 2** Here are three opinions. Please tell me which one comes closest to your own?
> The government has to ensure that health care is provided to all people residing legally here, irrespective of their income;
>
> The government has to ensure that health care is provided only to those people residing legally here, with low income;
> The government does not have to ensure that health care is provided to people residing legally here, not even those with low income. (Gevers *et al.* 2000)

The irony, from the standpoint of Canadian discussion, is that both Sweden and Denmark have in recent years experienced greater incremental policy changes than in Canada and have done so without dramatic shifts in values and attitudes, as opposed to fiscal conditions.

All the OECD countries, the data suggest, publicly express basic commitments to universal access to care and relatively equal treatment of similarly ill citizens. Their citizens embrace such attitudes at a very general level. There is expressed concern that any care given should be of high quality, even though there is little basis for believing that paying for care can ensure that care is appropriate. Leaders of these countries also voice concern about patient satisfaction; they call for some degree of choice of provider and typically acknowledge the importance of preserving physician autonomy in professional decisions (OECD 1992, 1994). (The operational definition of what would count as appropriate autonomy, satisfaction, or quality is far from settled, one must add, but the appeals to these values are real.) With public funds the largest single source of funding, cost control is a generally acknowledged goal as well. And, finally, there is implicit or explicit sponsorship in most of the OECD for health promotion and consumer safety. These are presented as worthy – or at least appealing – national policy goals. To what extent do these strikingly similar sets of expressed values result in similar social institutions for the delivery of health care?

Funding and Provision of Health Care in the OECD: Institutional Arrangements

The OECD provides a useful way to portray variations in arrangements for funding and contracting health care. In most if not all OECD countries, *public funding* sources (i.e., general taxation, earmarked taxation, social health insurance) are dominant compared to *out-of-pocket* expenditure or *private health insurance*. As to contracting, the OECD distinguishes three basic models. One is an *integrated system* in which – as is the case in Britain – the government handles both the funding and the provision of health care. The second is a *contracting model*, in which third-party payers negotiate agreements with independent providers. The third is a *reimbursement model*, in which patients pay their health care providers and then seek financial indemnification from their public or private insurers. According to the OECD, the *public contracting model* has been on the rise in recent decades, combining collective funding with independent providers of care. In the mid-1990s, the OECD summarized the systems as shown in Table 3.

What these portraits reveal is that, despite broad support for social solidarity in distributing and financing medical care, the OECD countries differ markedly in organizational features. They reflect a wide variety of legal forms of ownership and management, ranging from private for-profit firms and religious and charitable not-for-profit institutions to local or regional authorities providing community-based care. And some public financing arrangements cater to specific population groups, while others finance access to the entire population. How this developed over time is the subject of many studies. The following section reviews some of these historical developments in order to show how very similar baseline values have expressed themselves in very different social welfare institutions.

Germany was first to introduce compulsory health insurance for low-income industrial workers in 1883 (Okma 2002). Denmark followed within a decade. Over the course of many decades, other European countries followed these examples. They developed mandatory social insurance schemes covering the risks of disability, sickness, old age and death. Some, including France, Belgium, the Netherlands (as well as Japan and Korea), imported the "Bismarckian" model of employment-related health insurance from Germany. In this model, legally independent and semi-autonomous bodies ("sick funds") administer social health insurance and negotiate contracts with providers of care. Other countries expanded coverage beyond the working class and introduced population-wide schemes funded out of general taxation; this was the example set by the British NHS in 1948. In a few countries – for example, the United States, Germany and the Netherlands – access to social insurance is limited to specific population groups. In Germany, upper income people can opt out, and a group comprising about 10 per cent of the population has actually

Table 3. Funding and provision of health care in OECD countries

Country	Funding sources of health care	Provision of health care
Germany	Mix of public and private insurance	Mix of public and private providers
The Netherlands	Mix of public and private insurance	Mostly private providers
Denmark, Finland, Greece, Iceland, Ireland, Norway, Portugal, Spain and Sweden	Mainly financed out of taxation	Mostly public providers
Australia and New Zealand	Taxation and private health insurance (in Australia)	Mixed public and private providers
Canada	Mainly taxation (and supplemental voluntary private insurance)	Mainly private providers
Switzerland	Mainly voluntary private insurance	Mainly private providers
United States	Mix of private insurance and public schemes (Medicare, Medicaid, and Veterans Administration, Indian Health)	Mainly private providers

Source: OECD 1994.

done so. In the Netherlands, the compulsorily insured constitute 60 per cent of the population. The remaining 40 per cent has to take out private health insurance. In practice, 99 per cent of the Dutch population has health insurance (Okma 1997). The United States has separate schemes for the older and disabled under social insurance principles, categories of low-income Americans under Medicaid, programs for veterans and those on Native American reservations. In addition to universal Medicare, Canada has special arrangements for veterans and the armed forces, prison inmates, and First Nation populations. Belgium, France and Japan expanded the sickness fund model to include the entire population. By the late 1990s, the main funding sources for health care in Europe and North America were general (earmarked) taxation and health insurance premiums, both public and private (OECD 1992, 1994).

In the Scandinavian countries, local and regional authorities have primary responsibility for funding and providing health care and related social services to their populations. They bear the financial risk of acute medical and nursing care and have developed extensive social services, which include home care, support for adjusted housing for elderly or handicapped persons, and support for independent living. In the United Kingdom, there is a clear split between the administration of the NHS covering the costs of medical care and the social services provided by local authorities. The Netherlands (in 1988), Germany (in 1992) and Japan (in 1995) introduced separate population-wide social insurance covering the costs of long-term care and home care for their ageing populations. In those three countries, the long-term care insurance serves as a supplement to the existing schemes for acute medical care. The three countries accept a mix of public and private providers in this field, and all three are experimenting with cash benefits allowing consumers to directly contract providers of care instead of services in kind. Policy and institutional variation across the OECD world, then, is indisputable.

Styles of Policymaking

The variation extends to styles of policymaking as well. The centralist policy processes of the United Kingdom and France sharply contrast with the functionally decentralized models of Germany, Belgium and the Netherlands (Klein 1995). In the latter three countries, the label of *neo-corporatism* is broadly applicable, a decision-making model where governments and private actors (represented through their interest organizations) share responsibility for the shaping and outcome of social policies (Wilson 1990). This model implies that private actors are willing and able to take on public responsibilities in the form of active participation in the policy process as well as self-regulation. For example, the representative organizations or interest associations of the German and Dutch hospitals and physicians represent their members in regional or countrywide negotiations with the health insurance agencies over tariffs and volume of their services. Medical associations are empowered with public authority to regulate access to the medical profession, to set standards for medical education and for professional conduct, and to police the professional conduct of all medical professionals (members and non-members alike) with rules and sanctions. The main administrative bodies of social health insurance, the sickness funds, are legally independent actors, and their organizations have collective bargaining power to contract health services on behalf of their insured. In some Western European countries, a large share (and in the Netherlands, the largest share) of health facilities has always been under private, non-governmental ownership and management.

The German corporatist model limits the role of the state in social arenas like housing and health care. Moreover, its federal state has shifted much of administrative responsibilities for its social policies to the provinces or *Länder*. In this policymaking model, most if not all organized interests meet with government in the annual round of consultation, the Concerted Action or *Konzertierte Aktion*, to decide on spending levels and the broad allocation of public funding for health care. After establishing this financial framework, regional representatives of health insurers and providers negotiate contracts with detailed and binding agreements on the volumes and prices of health services.

Germany's neighbor Holland has copied many of the features of this model. Until the 1980s, Netherlands social policy process provided "a striking model of corporatist arrangements", with private agencies empowered with public authority (Freddi 1989). These institutions were not only set up along functional lines, but also based on religious denominations. After mounting criticism of this model in the 1970s and 1980s, successive Dutch governments took steps to reduce, and in some cases dismantle this model of "*consociational corporatism*" (Baakman *et al.* 1989, Okma 1997). While Germany and Belgium kept most of their corporatist structures intact, the Netherlands eliminated the direct representation of organized stakeholders in shaping social policies in an effort to streamline and speed up decision-making procedures. By the end of the 1990s, the main interest groups had lost their direct representation in the advisory and administrative bodies in social policies.

In contrast to such decentralized policy models, France and the United Kingdom largely maintained their tradition of central state dominance. Under the French *étatisme*, interest groups have not developed a strong role as participants in social policymaking. The medical associations are fragmented and show little inclination to collaborate with each other or with government. In contrast, the British Medical Association has had a significant (if now diminished) role in health policies. In the 1940s, it accepted the formation of the NHS, effectively nationalizing most hospitals, and in the 1990s the creation of primary care groups (effectively terminating the self-employed status of general practitioners). Yet British physicians have retained considerable professional autonomy and strong influence in the management of health care institutions (Klein 1995).

In habits of governance, then, developed democracies have developed very different public institutions on the basis of quite similar national values. A tradition of statism will promote values through institutions governed by a central authority. A tradition of neo-corporatism will promote similar values as the outcome of a more-or-less structured bargaining game played among organized stakeholders, of whom only one is the government. On the other hand, decisions about whether values are to be advanced by central authorities or by a contest among individuals or sectors – or primarily by the public or by the private purse – are obviously not neutral. The shape of social institutions – even when promoting very similar values – can nonetheless make particular values easier or harder to maintain or enhance.

Interest Bargaining

In addition to the ways in which different habits of governance affect the embodiment of values in public institutions, the play of interests among parties has considerable impact as well. In social policies, governments confront a large number of interested *stakeholders* (Alford 1974, Pross 1986, Sabatier et al. 1993). There are provincial, regional and local governments and semi-autonomous governmental agencies; labor unions and private business associations; consumer advocacy groups, public interest groups, and many others. In most industrialized countries, the funding and provision of public services like housing, education and health care are not a governmental matter alone. Governments depend on others to make public systems work. The health policy arena is crowded with many stakeholders and well-organized interests affecting the shaping and outcome of government policies (Okma 1997). Governments have to deal with such competing interests and stakeholders that often have strong veto powers. It is not easy to replace existing arrangements with new ones.

Canadian Values and Medical Care Arrangements

Section three of this paper noted that nearly all of the recent reports on Medicare support the five basic principles of the Canada Health Act (*universality, accessibility, comprehensiveness, portability,* and *public administration*), as well as Medicare's basic values of public funding and egalitarianism. Several polls conducted in the 1980s and 1990s also demonstrated strong public support of those principles, even as general confidence in government has declined. In the late 1980s, one poll reported a more general erosion of the public confidence in the state (Graves 1988). The Graves study concluded that public institutions in the industrialized world were facing a legitimacy crisis. Interestingly, Canadians did not share a categorical, negative judgment of government. But they expressed the wish to strengthen the public institutions. In explaining those results, the survey found evidence that the media played a role in fueling cynicism about all major public institutions.

Polling data from the 1980s and 1990s showed that Canadian support for the CHA's principles remained quite high (HayGroup 1999, *Hospital Quarterly* 2000, Maioni and Martin 2001). Though public support for "public administration" fell significantly during the 1990s, a commanding 59 per cent continued to regard that principle as "very important", with additional respondents regarding it as "important". Higher percentages rated "universality" (89), "accessibility" (81), "portability" (79) and "comprehensiveness" (80) as "very important". Despite concerns about the future of Medicare, Canadians express high satisfaction with the services they actually received (Picard 2000). (This finding, incidentally, is consistent with that in other industrial democracies.) About one-third of those Canadians polled feel that Medicare needs major reform. But over 44 per cent think that minor changes will do.

Some studies, however, emphasized problems, not principled support for Medicare. For example, the HayGroup study found widespread concern about waiting lists, lack of access to medical services and waste, and concluded that "Canadians are ready for reform" (Conference Board of Canada 2001). The

Conference Board reported declining confidence in Medicare. It concluded that Canadians believe their health care system has deteriorated even while they still are committed to the principles of the Canada Health Act and the values it embodies.

In short, there seems to be overwhelming, continuing support, both among policymakers and among Canadians at large, for the baseline values of the Medicare program. At the same time, concern about Medicare is widespread. And, beyond that, the various reform reports have drawn quite different portraits of what needs to be done. Some argue that because of the continuing popular support for Medicare's principles the program requires nothing but marginal adjustments. Others – like those of the Conference Board, the Mazankowski Commission, and the HayGroup – claim there is an urgent need for more fundamental changes in how Medicare operates.

Importantly, the appeal to general principles provides little guidance as to how to frame actual policy options or design concrete programs. For example, the above-mentioned HayGroup study reports widespread support for a national home care and pharmaceutical program but stops short of recommendations for the actual form of such programs. Nor do the reports pay much attention to the conditions that promote change or stability.

Yet even within Canada, as Carolyn Tuohy (1999) has shown, the play of historical contingency with political intrigue has yielded different social institutions and different approaches to health care reform. Quebec, with its French-influenced and comparatively "statist" political culture, is of course a special case. It came early to banning physician over-billing, and to placing global caps on medical bills. In Quebec also, negotiations between the medical profession and the province are more or less permanent and ongoing, marked by a concern for sharing and acting upon expert information. In British Columbia, in contrast, such negotiations are periodic and highly adversarial, marked by the use of confrontational tactics common in collective bargaining. Ontario physicians resisted the Canada Health Act's ban on extra billing even to the point of engaging in a strike during the 1980s; no comparable resistance arose elsewhere at that time. In contrast to British Columbia, Ontario, Alberta and Manitoba, the working relationships between the medical societies and the Atlantic provinces and Saskatchewan have been less formal and substantially less confrontational. In short, cross-province and cross-time evidence from Canada supports the proposition that the link between operational policies and underlying programmatic values is relatively loose, but not without constraints. That latter lesson Canadians learned in the struggle over extra-billing in the prelude to the Canada Health Act of 1984. The values expressed by the five operating principles of Medicare – presented in the 1960s and reasserted in the Canada Health Act of 1984 – have in large measure arisen from Medicare's performance, not its origins. None of the major studies of the origins of Medicare – whether the hospital insurance program of the late 1950s or the medical insurance program promoted by the Hall Commission – have concluded that the overwhelming support for the egalitarian values of the Medicare program preceded the passage of national health insurance legislation (Taylor 1987). Instead, the story is one of strengthened commitment to these values as Canadians discovered in disputes what was at stake. And, most important for comparative purposes, Medicare is more restrictive than any other

OECD country in restricting the role of private payment and private insurance in gaining differential access to care (Marmor et al. 1990).

Conclusion

Data from OECD countries, as well as evidence from Canadian debates about Medicare, support the claim that national values and program structure and practices in medical care are loosely associated. A substantial variety of institutional forms and policy practices have developed that have appeared consistent with broadly shared social values. Values may serve as the foundation for social programs but, as a review of the experience of Western European democracies shows, they do not supply those programs' architecture. Differences in social institutions are reflective not only of fundamentally different ideological positions, but of subtle historical (and contingent) differences in those programs' initial construction, and in the subsequent play of political and social interests.

It is not surprising that calls for Medicare reform arose in the 1990s, at a time of relative economic prosperity, when a long period of health care belt-tightening seemed to be coming to an end. It is to the political advantage of every interest group to attempt to secure a larger share of public financial resources by stressing the sacrifices it has made and the fiscal challenges it faces. "Crisis talk" – allegations to the effect that these times are extraordinary, and extraordinarily dangerous – is in fact a quite ordinary tool of interest-group politics. Canadian policymakers have thus far resisted the temptation to allow an unwarranted fear of collapse – or an unwarranted allegation of "abandonment of Canadian values" – to guide their deliberations. By every indication we reviewed, Canadian Medicare stands firm on its foundations of still-shared Canadian national values. The question for Medicare reformers, we suggest, is not whether to abandon or rethink those values. It is, instead, how best to embody those values in twenty-first century institutions. That question requires, for its answer, a prudent attention to the ground-level political and economic realities of Canada, and a prudent review of the health care managerial and financing arrangements that have been tried, for better or for worse, in other nations. That is not to claim that Medicare's values are consistent with just any prudential or managerial adjustment. The program's iconic status assures attention to the issue. And there is little doubt that some of the suggestions for "reforming" Medicare are actually threats to its continuation and do express values inconsistent with the values that Medicare's fundamental principles express. Most Canadians do not believe that access to medical care should depend on the size of their bank accounts. That is indeed a fundamental value, and there are some prominent Canadians who do not share it and yet will not explicitly say so. Clarity on this topic is, we suggest, hard to find and to maintain.

Acknowledgements

This paper was previously published for the Commission on the Future of Health Care in Canada, known as the Romanow Commission. Discussion paper no. 5, July 2002. It has been edited and revised for this *Journal of Comparative Policy Analysis*, Special Issue, **12**(1–2), February–April 2010.

Notes

1. Equally, institutions can shape opinions (Immergut 1992).
2. The terms "sentiments" and "attitudes" are used as synonyms in this section. Both can be based upon (the more fundamental) values, perhaps in combination with factual understanding and emotional commitment.

References

Alford, R., 1974, *Health Care Politics. Ideological and Group Barriers to Reform* (Chicago: The University of Chicago Press).
Ardigo, A., 1995, Public attitudes and changes in health care systems: a confrontation and a puzzle, in: O. Borre and E. Scarborough (Eds) *The Scope of Government* (Oxford: Oxford University Press), pp. 388–409.
Baakman, N., Van der Made, J. and Mur-Veeman, I., 1989, Controlling Dutch health care, in: G. Freddi and J.W. Björkman (Ed.) *Controlling Medical Professionals: The Comparative Politics of Health Governance* (London: Sage Publications).
Berlin, I., 1998, My intellectual path. *New York Review of Books*, May 14.
CIHI, 2001, *Health Care in Canada 2001. Annual Report* (Ottawa: Canadian Institute for Health Information).
Clair Commission, 2000, *Les solutions émergentes*. Commission d'étude sur les services de santé et les services sociaux, available at http://www.cessss.gouv.qc.ca/pdf/fr/00-109.pdf.
Conference Board of Canada, 2001, Universality, quality and efficiency – top values for health care. News release.
Coughlin, R., 1980, *Ideology, Public Opinion, and Welfare Policy: Attitudes Toward Taxes and Spending in Industrialized Societies* (Berkeley: University of California, Institute of International Studies).
Decter, M., et al., 2000, *IRPP Task Force on Health Policy: Recommendations to First Ministers* (Montreal: Institute for Research on Public Policy).
Douglas, M. and Wildavsky, A., 1982, *Risk and Culture* (Berkeley: University of California Press).
Freddi, G., 1989, Problems of organisational rationality in health systems: policy controls and policy options, in: G. Freddi and J.W. Björkman (Eds) *Controlling Medical Professionals: The Comparative Politics of Health Governance* (London: Sage Publications).
Fyke Commission, 2001, *Caring for Medicare. Sustaining a Quality System*. Regina, April.
Gevers, J. et al., 2000, Public health care in the balance: exploring popular support for health care systems in the European Union. *International Journal of Social Welfare*, 9, 301–321.
Graves, F., 1988, *Canadians and Their Public Institutions* (Ottawa: Ekos Research Associates and Paul Reed, Canadian Centre for Management Development).
HayGroup, 1999, Public behaviour, perceptions and priorities in the health care sector: an overview. Background document for the Health Services Restructuring Commission (Ontario).
Hirschman, A.O., 1992, The concept of interest: from euphemism to tautology, in: *Rival Views of Market Society* (Cambridge, MA: Harvard University Press).
Hospital Quarterly, 2000, Canadians and the Canada Health Act: renewed commitment to national principles. *Quarterly Index*, Fall, 80.
Ignatieff, M., 2000, Does history matter? in: R. Griffiths (Ed.) *Great Questions of Canada* (Toronto: Stoddart).
Immergut, E.M., 1992, *Health Politics. Interests and Institutions in Western Europe*, Cambridge Studies in Comparative Politics (New York: Cambridge University Press).
Kirby Committee (Standing Committee on Social Affairs, Science and Technology) 2002, *The Health of Canadian – The Federal Role. Final Report, Volume VI, Recommendations for Reform*. Available at http://www.parl.gc.ca/37/2/parlbus/commbus/senate/com-e/soci-e/rep-e/repoct02vol6-e.htm
Klein, R., 1995, *The New Politics of the National Health Service*, 3rd edition (Harlow, Essex: Longman).
Lewis, S., and Maxwell, C., 2002, Decoding Mazankowski: a symphony in three movements. *Healthcare Papers*, 2(4), Toronto: Longwoods, available at http://www.longwoods.com/hp/2-4Mazanowski/HP24SMarshall.html (accessed May 8, 2002).
Maioni, A. and Martin, P., 2001, *Is the Canadian Health Care Model Politically Viable? Some Evidence from Public Opinion* (Ottawa: Canadian Political Science Association).

Mansfield, H.C., 1995, Self-interest rightly understood. *Political Theory*, **23**(1), 48–66.
Marmor, T.R., 2002, Medicare: suspect messages. *The Globe and Mail and La Presse*, February 12.
Marmor, T.R., Mashaw, J.L. and Harvey, P.L. (Eds), 1990, *America's Misunderstood Welfare State. Persisting Myths, Enduring Realities* (New York: Basic Books).
Marshall, S., 2002, A healthcare "Trojan Horse": the Alberta Mazankowski Report. *Healthcare Papers*, **2**(4), Toronto: Longwoods, available at http://www.longwoods.com/hp/2-4Mazankowski (accessed May 8, 2002).
Mazankowkski Commission, 2001, *A Framework for Reform. Report of the Premier's Advisory Council on Health*, Edmonton.
National Forum on Health, 1997, *Canada Health Action: Building on the Legacy*, Final Report (Ottawa: Health Canada Communications).
OECD, 1994, *The Reform of Health Care. A Comparative Analysis of Seven OECD Countries*, Health Reform Studies No. 5 (Paris: Organization for Economic Cooperation and Development).
OECD, 1992, *The Reform of Health Care. A Comparative Analysis of Seven OECD Countries*, Health Reform Studies No. 2 (Paris: Organization for Economic Cooperation and Development).
Okma, K.G.H., 1997, Studies on Dutch health politics, policies and law (PhD Thesis, Utrecht University).
Okma, K.G.H., 2002, *What Is the Best Public – Private Model for Canadian Health Care?* (Montreal: Institute for Research of Public Policy).
Ontario Health Services Restructuring Commission, 2000, *1996–2000. Looking Back, Looking Forward. A Legacy Report* (Ottawa: Health Services Research Foundation).
Picard, A., 2000, Health care not so bad: survey. *The Globe and Mail*, November 27.
Pross, A.P., 1986, *Group Politics and Public Policy* (Toronto: Oxford University Press).
Rachlis, M. *et al.* 2001, *Revitalizing Medicare: Shared Problem, Public Solutions* (Vancouver: The Tommy Douglas Research Institute).
Ranade, W. (Ed.), 1998, *Markets and Health Care: A Comparative Analysis* (New York: Longman).
Rawls, J., 1971, *A Theory of Justice* (Cambridge, MA: Harvard University Press).
Romanow Commission, 2002, *Building on Values: The Future of Health Care in Canada*, Final Report (Saskatoon: Commission on the Future of Health Care in Canada).
Sabatier, R., Jenkins-Smith, P.A. and Jenkins-Smith, H.C. (Eds), 1993, *Policy Change and Learning* (Boulder, CO: Westview Press).
Schumpeter, J., 1908, On the concept of social value. *Quarterly Journal of Economics*, **23**, 213–232.
Taylor, M.G., 1987, *Health Insurance and Canadian Public Policy: The Seven Decisions that Created the Canadian Health Insurance System and their Outcomes* (Montreal: McGill-Queen's University Press).
Tuohy, C.H., 1999, *Accidental Logics: The Dynamics of Change in the Health Care Arena in the United States, Britain and Canada* (New York: Oxford University Press).
Wilson, G.K., 1990, *Interest Groups* (Oxford: Basil Blackwell).

A Comparative Analysis of Paid Leave for the Health Needs of Workers and their Families around the World

ALISON EARLE and JODY HEYMANN

ABSTRACT *The ability of workers to take time off work when they are ill, and when their children or adult family members are ill, is critical to the health of workers and their families. In this study, we examine labor codes and labor-related legislation for 178 countries available from the International Labor Organization, and 160 individual country reports in Social Security Programs Throughout the World to determine the availability of paid sick leave globally and explore whether there is a correlation with four measures of macro-economic status (unemployment, productivity, GDP, competitiveness). We find that 145 nations from around the globe provide paid sick leave for working adults, 33 for care of children and 16 for care of adult family members' needs, and find no evidence of a negative relationship between paid leave for personal or family health needs and macro-economic status.*

Introduction

The ability of workers to take time off work when they are ill, or when their children or adult family members are ill, is critical to the health of workers and their families. Taking leave from work can help provide working adults with the time required to care for their own health needs, to rest and recuperate (Gilleski 1998) and to avoid taking longer periods of time off in the future because their health worsens and minor conditions are exacerbated (Aronsson *et al.* 2000, Grinyer and Singleton 2000, Johannsson 2002). Having paid time off work may also reduce the cost of obtaining proper medical treatment when it is necessary (Cauley 1987, Gilleski 1998).

Having paid leave from work for family illness needs can also enable workers to be available to provide support to their family members, which has been shown to have important positive impacts on family members' health. Numerous studies have demonstrated that parental availability for curative care is critical to ensuring children's physical health (van der Schyff 1979, Taylor and O'Connor 1989, Palmer 1993, Kristensson-Hallstrom et al. 1997, Heymann 2000), particularly for children with chronic health and developmental conditions (Johnson 1994, Wolman et al. 1994, La Greca et al. 1995, Holden et al. 1997, Heymann 2000) as well as for children's mental health (Sainsbury et al. 1986, Waugh and Kjos 1992, McGraw 1994, Cleary et al. 1986). Studies have also shown that family support improves the health of adults. When they receive support from family members adults have better health outcomes from such conditions as coronary disease (Woloshin et al. 1997, Karner et al. 2004, Rantanen et al. 2004), myocardial infarction (Bennett 1993, Gorkin et al. 1993), and strokes (Tsouna-Hadjis et al. 2000). Studies also indicate that family support can improve longevity (Berkman 1995, Seeman 2000) and support from friends can improve mental health outcomes among the elderly (Salokangas 1997, Jubb and Shanley 2002, Stanhope 2002).

In working families, the ability to take time off work to care for a family member or to care for one's own health needs depends in part on the national and workplace policies and benefits available to the working adults in the family, specifically whether adults have paid leave to be at home during critical times.[1] For example, Heymann's study of urban working families in the US found that parents who have paid leave are significantly more likely to care for their sick children themselves. Parents with either paid sick or vacation leave were 5.2 times more likely to stay at home to care for their sick children than parents without these benefits (Heymann et al. 1999).

Despite the demonstrated importance of paid leave to meet the health needs of workers, their children and adult family members, a review of the comparative work/family policy literature cannot answer the question of how available this leave is or whether it is economically feasible to provide it due to two limitations. First, while the comparative work/family literature has gathered important information on the availability and characteristics of paid maternity and paternity leave and child care policies (Gornick et al. 1997, Kamerman and Kahn 1997, Waldfogel 2001, Gornick and Meyers 2003), other equally important forms of leave like short-term leave and sick leave have not yet been examined.[2] Second, this literature has focused almost entirely on wealthy countries (for example, Organization for Economic Cooperation and Development 1995). Not only is a global picture valuable in and of itself since it currently does not exist, but recent research shows that families in poor countries are struggling with parallel types of work/family issues to those in the developed countries (Heymann 2002, 2003a,b, 2004, 2006, Heymann et al. 2003).

The marked rise in globalization during the twentieth century, however, makes more broad global comparisons both compelling and necessary. Characterized by an increasing flow of jobs across borders with companies readily moving their jobs to the nation with the lowest labor costs, the globalized economy is increasingly interdependent and the interaction between developed and developing nations is on the rise. The dramatic increase in the speed of international communication and transportation and declining costs, along with the emergence of free trade zones and agreements and the consequent dropping of tax and tariff barriers, have meant that companies now readily move jobs in search of cheaper labor and establish factories on foreign soil. Rich nations therefore now need to be aware of the work conditions in countries in which they do business and with which they compete.

Wealthy countries can also learn from a global comparison particularly about what is truly economically feasible. If poor nations or the vast majority of nations from around the globe can provide short-term leave then it would be hard to argue that resource-rich nations like the United States are unable to. The United States' exceptional position relative to other rich nations is now well established with the US opposing many basic work/family policies on the grounds they are not economically feasible. However, the global position – with the exception of maternity leave – is not well documented and would provide further evidence on the question of the economic feasibility of paid leave for health needs.

Regardless of how widely available paid sick leave is and the implications of that for economic feasibility, there remains an argument suggesting the provision of paid leave is not economically sound. The theory posits that negative macro-economic consequences, such as increases in unemployment, lower productivity and lower Gross Domestic Product (GDP), will arise from instituting policies that raise labor costs thus lowering demand for labor. The theory suggests that in a global market where the widespread movement of labor and competition for jobs provides an incentive for companies and nations to keep labor costs low, nations that provide paid short-term leave for health needs would be at a competitive disadvantage. These arguments have been put forth and countered both in academic circles (for example, Blank and Freeman 1994, Nickell 1997, Siebert 1997, Blanchard and Wolfers 1999, Lindert 2005, Mishel *et al.* 2005) as well as in the mainly US popular press (for example, Ackerman 1999) and the policy arena (for example, Employment Policy Foundation 2000).

Evidence regarding the macro-economic impact of social welfare policies and programs including work/family policies was first based on the observation that during the 1980s and the early part of the 1990s European countries had much higher unemployment rates relative to the United States which experienced an almost unparalleled period of economic growth in the 1990s. Recent economic experience – that many European nations recovered economically in the 1990s while fundamentally maintaining their public policies and spending on family-friendly labor policies – as well as a series of reviews of the evidence suggests that the social policies in place in Europe are not primarily responsible for the divergent experiences (see Gornick and Meyers 2003, 2004, Gornick 2005). In a comprehensive review of the empirical evidence regarding the relationship between social protection and macro-economic performance, Blank and Freeman (1994) concluded that there was little support for the claim of a substantial trade-off. A study by Nickell (1997) examining the relationship between the provision of social protection and the unemployment rate found that in general the typical package of welfare state protection and labor market policies were not provided disproportionately in either high or low unemployment nations. Yet further evidence questioning the case against work/family policies are longitudinal empirical studies of national-level data from the 1990s and earlier. In an examination of long-term historical economic and policy data, Peter Lindert (2004) concludes that social spending has not hindered growth but instead has enhanced it. Mishel, Bernstein and Allegretto (2005) examine a range of recent economic indicators, provision of paid parental leave and social expenditure from 19 rich, industrialized countries and similarly conclude that social welfare protection often has positive macro-economic consequences. Analysis of the relationship between global policy data and global economic indicators available to us would make a unique and necessary contribution to this debate.

This paper contributes to the existing comparative work/family literature by addressing a form of paid leave – paid sick leave – that to date has been left out of the comparative literature; by broadening the scope of nations compared to be global; and adding further exploratory analyses of the relationship between economic competitiveness and the provision of paid sick leave. We examine national labor policies using global data, described in the next section, to assess how many countries guarantee their workers paid sick leave, how many countries have a specific paid leave policy for children or adult family members' health needs, and assess the economic feasibility of providing these forms of leave.

Methods

Data Sources

As part of the Work, Family and Democracy Initiative and with the support of the Ford Foundation, we developed a Work, Family, and Equity Index (WFEI), the first venture to systematically define and measure public policies for working families globally. A wide range of publicly available data were gathered and analyzed to assess progress in provision of work/family policies, including paid sick leave. The scope of this data collection was truly global and included data from nations with a wide range of political, social, economic and cultural characteristics. We collected data on a set of core features of sick leave policies including the duration of benefits, wage rate and existence of a waiting period. We searched for and reviewed both primary and secondary sources of data for information on sick leave policies.[3]

Sick leave rights are provided through a variety of mechanisms including national paid leave law, national labor codes, social security systems, employer regulations and collective bargaining, and are funded through a variety of arrangements ranging from payment through a national social security system (for example, Mexico) to a fundamentally employer-based payment and administration model (for example, Sweden), as well as a mix of these approaches such that social security benefits either supplement employer benefits or begin when employer-sponsored benefits run out (for example, Canada and Iceland). Because of the range of ways sick leave guarantees are made, we examined both labor codes and other labor-related legislation, as well as the foremost social security law database. In total, data sources covering paid leave laws and policies were reviewed for 178 countries. See Table 1 for description of sources.

In the data collection process, data sources were continuously checked and updates obtained as they became available. When multiple sources were available, they were cross-checked. When discrepancies were identified, primary sources and the most current sources were given priority.

The availability of paid sick leave or characteristics of it were coded as "yes" when we located sufficient evidence to verify that a policy or aspect of a policy exists, as "no" when in our comprehensive search we found no relevant legislation in existence, and "indeterminate" when we located some potentially relevant legislation which was limited in a fundamental way, preventing accurate coding. For example,

Table 1. Description of sources reviewed

Labor-related legislation and labor codes	Social security legislation	Regional sources or sources covering a range of countries
– NATLEX, an online global database of labor, social security and human rights-related legislation maintained by the International Labor Organization (ILO). – The ILO's on-site library at their headquarters in Geneva, Switzerland. – The Harvard University Law Library. – Official websites of various governments made available by ministries of labor and analogous bodies.	– Social Security Programs Throughout the World (SSPTW): a series of reports produced jointly by the US Social Security Administration and the International Social Security Association (SSA and ISSA 2002, 2003a, 2003b, 2004). – The most comprehensive source of global data on social security policies. – Database consists of a series of individual country reports describing the major features of the social security system of 174 countries and territories, 160 of which are classified as nations by the two major international statistical data repositories, the UN and the World Bank.* – Data are from the Annual Survey on Developments and Trends conducted by ISSA, as well as other supplemental sources including, among others, official publications, periodicals received from individual country institutions, non-governmental and inter-governmental organizations, foreign and US social security experts. – Country data are grouped according to regions (The Americas, Africa, Asia and the Pacific, Europe) and updates are published periodically.	– Bratislava International Centre for Family Studies, "Reflections of Recent Demographic Conditions on Family and Social Policies in Central and Eastern European Countries: Final Report, Part II" (2001) – The Clearinghouse on International Developments in Child, Youth and Family Policies at Columbia University (2003). – Six documents available on government websites (New Zealand Department of Labour, United States Department of Labor, United Kingdom Department of Trade and Industry 2000, International Labor Organization (ILO) 2002, Finland Ministry of Labor 2003, Canadian Department of Social Development 2004).

*Territories of other nations and states which are not independent were excluded.

Ghana was coded as indeterminate for paid leave for personal health needs because we found no sick leave legislation although annual leave legislation included text specifying that sick leave taken during regular annual leave would not be counted as annual leave. Five countries were coded as indeterminate for paid sick leave for personal health needs, eight for paid sick leave for children's health, and nine for paid leave for adult health needs.

Analyses

To assess the availability of paid sick leave, frequencies and percentages were calculated using national-level, categorical data in the WFEI database. First, we examined global availability of paid sick leave for workers. We next examined the availability of sick leave that can be used to care for children, defined as biological or adopted children aged 0–17, or adult family members, typically defined as family members over the age of 18. We further examined the characteristics of these policies including the wage replacement rate, the duration of the leave, and length of the waiting period.

To explore whether there is a strong relationship between the provision of paid sick leave and macro-economic criteria, we calculated the percentage of countries that had a national policy for each separate form of paid sick leave (for care of children, adults and for self) within each of four quartiles of four publicly available macro-economic measures that were collected globally in a comparable ways (see Table 2).

Results

Paid Leave for Children's Health

Thirty-three countries have policies guaranteeing employees some type of paid leave specifically to care for their children when they are ill. Of the countries for which duration data were available, 52 per cent mandate that employers guarantee one to ten days of paid leave, while 48 per cent guaranteed 11 days or more of paid leave for children's health needs. Three countries mandate paid leave of 31 days or more and the highest number of days allowed for children's health needs is 60.

Twenty-five nations offered paid sick leave at a fixed wage replacement rate. Wage replacement rates varied within other countries according to years of employment, the length of the leave, the severity of the illness, or age of child. Amongst those countries with fixed wage replacement rates, the modal rate of replacement was 100 per cent of wages.

Paid Leave for Adult Family Members' Health

Sixteen countries provide workers with paid leave to care for adult family members. The duration of paid leave ranges from two days to four months per year. Some provide leave of a set duration per case and others have a maximum number of days per month that can be taken. Amongst countries that provide paid leave, the wage replacement rate varies from 50 per cent to 100 per cent.

Table 2. Macroeconomic indicators and sources

Indicator	Description	Source
GDP	Per capita gross domestic product (GDP) in 172 countries	United Nations Development Program (UNDP), 2004
Competitiveness	Growth Competitiveness Index (GCI) is produced by the World Economic Forum and is intended to measure the capacity of an economy to achieve sustained economic growth. The GCI is constructed from three indexes: a technology index, a public institutions index, and a macroeconomic environment index. Data is available for 102 countries.	World Economic Forum. http://www.weforum.org/pdf/Gcr/Growth_Competitiveness_Index_2003_Comparisons, viewed on January 18, 2005.
Unemployment rate	Total unemployment as a percentage of the total labor force where unemployment refers to the share of the labor force that is without work but available for and seeking employment. Data are five year average of any points between 1998 and 2002. Data are available for 105 of 180 countries.*	World Development Indicators Online, Unemployment, total (% total labor force). http://devdata.worldbank.org.ezpz.harvard.edu/dataonline, viewed on December 14, 2004. The original source of data for some countries is ILO's Key Indicators of the Labor Market.
Productivity	Real GDP per hour worked in 1990 $US using "Geary-Khamis" purchasing power parity conversion constructed from the Groningen Growth and Development Center's GDP, Employment, and Annual Working Hours data series. Data on 43 countries for 2002.	Groningen Growth and Development Center (GGDC) – http://www.ggdc.net/dseries/gdph.shtml, 2002.

*A five year average was used in order to minimize annual fluctuation due to changing economic conditions.

Many of the laws have limitations. Countries sometimes specify that employees are only eligible to take leave to care for family members in certain family relationships, or limit leave to cases where family members are seriously ill or require a waiting period before payment of benefits begins.

Paid Leave for Employees' Health

One hundred and forty-five countries around the world provide paid sick leave to employees. Of these, 128 countries provide paid sickness benefits for at least one week. Ninety-five countries have paid sick leave for one month or more. Seventy-six countries provide paid sickness benefits for at least 26 weeks or until recovery.[4]

Wage replacement rate for paid sick leave varies between and even within countries. Of the 145 countries with paid sick leave, data about the rate at which that leave is paid were available for 135 countries. Of these countries, 53 paid their workers a fixed rate of 100 per cent of their wages. The majority of the remaining countries, 76, paid their workers a minimum rate that was between 50 and 90 per cent of their normal wages. Six countries paid a flat rate benefit to employees on sick leave.

Relationship to Macro-economic Criteria

To explore the hypothesis that guaranteeing paid sick leave has negative macro-economic effects, we compared the availability of all three forms of paid sick leave using a key, commonly used measure of economic status, per capita GDP. Across the three types of paid sick leave, there is a slight trend between provision of leave and GDP per capita quartile with higher GDP nations being more likely to guarantee paid sick leave (see Figure 1). With respect to paid sick leave for employees' health needs, nations in the top two income quartiles are slightly more likely to provide paid sick leave for employees' health than nations in the bottom two, but there is no strong, linear relationship between economic status and provision of this form of paid sick leave. There is, however, a stepwise income gradient in the provision of paid leave for children's health. Nations with the highest GDP per capita are most likely to provide paid leave for children's health, with those with GDP in the middle of the spectrum less likely but still more likely than those with the lowest GDP per capita. For paid leave for adult family members' health, the first quartile or nations with the highest GDP per capita were substantially more likely to provide paid leave than nations in the remaining three quartiles.

The slight trend with GDP could have multiple interpretations: wealthy countries are able to afford to provide paid sick leave or any form of paid leave has positive effects on national income. We thus next examined the association between sick leave provisions and international competitiveness. We find a clear, strong stepwise relationship between global measures of competitiveness and all three forms of paid sick leave (see Figure 2). With all three forms of paid leave, the nations with highest growth competitive index rankings were most likely to provide paid leave, those nations in the middle quartiles just less likely, and the nations in the bottom quartile the least likely.

Figure 1. Relationship between national paid sick leave and a country's GDP per capita

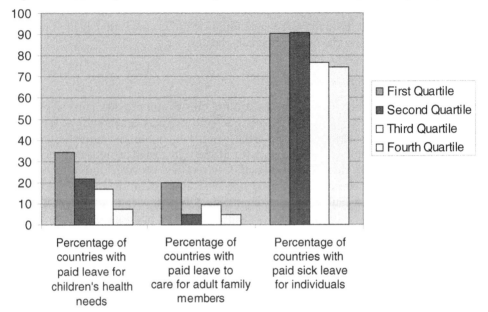

Note: The first quartile contains data for countries with the highest GDP per capita.
Source: UNDP Human Development Report 2004, http://hdr.undp.org/reports/global/2004/pdf/hdr04_HDI.pdf, viewed on September 13, 2004. Data on GDP per capita were available for 172 countries.

We next compared the availability of all three forms of paid sick leave using a five year average of unemployment rates, a frequently cited outcome impacted by provision of social welfare policies. We find no strong, linear relationship between unemployment rate and provision of any of these forms of paid sick leave (see Figure 3).

Productivity measures were not available on as widespread a scale as other economic indicators (N = 43 nations). However, we found similar trends even when using a measure for a smaller number of nations. Nations in the top two quartiles in terms of productivity were more likely than the nations in the third quartile to guarantee paid sick leave, and those in the third quartile more likely than nations in the bottom quartile to provide paid leave to care for children's and adult's health needs. There is no strong trend for paid leave for personal sickness.

Discussion

This study provides the first global comparison of an underexplored aspect of work/family policy: short-term leave for health needs. Findings from our examination of the availability and economic feasibility of guaranteed paid sick leave were striking in a number of dimensions, not least of which is the exceptional position that the United States finds itself in – an outlier among both wealthy and poor nations alike

Figure 2. Relationship between national paid sick leave and a country's economic competitiveness

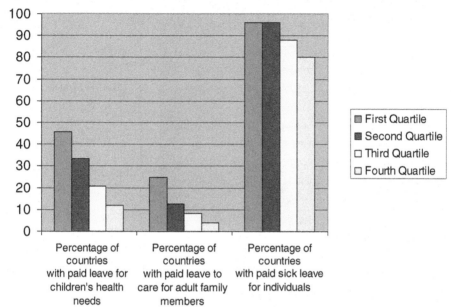

Note: The first quartile contains countries with the highest GCI scores.
Source: World Economic Forum, Growth Competitiveness Index, http://www.weforum.org/pdf/Gcr/Growth_Competitiveness_Index_2003_Comparisons, viewed on September 13, 2004. Data on 102 nations were available.

in not guaranteeing paid sick leave for employees or their families. Our findings clearly demonstrate the virtually global consensus that exists on the need for and economic feasibility of guaranteeing paid leave for personal health needs. At least 145 nations from around the globe provide paid sick leave for working adults, and most of these nations provide paid sickness benefits for at least one week. Equally striking was our finding that there was a significant minority of countries that mandate further guarantees of leave to care for family members' health needs: 33 providing paid leave for children's health needs and 16 for adult family members' health. These findings demonstrate that while movement is being made from coverage of only employees' health needs to those of their families, there is a substantially greater distance for the global community to cover in this area. However, the provision of paid sick leave was not associated with negative macro-economic measures as has been claimed by some. Instead we found a trend with nations that provide sick leave being more likely to demonstrate high productivity and be highly competitive. Moreover, there was no relationship between any form of paid sick leave and national unemployment rate. Together these provide suggestive evidence of the economic feasibility of expanding the global nature of paid leave for children's and adult family members' health needs. In addition, our findings are consistent with and illustrative of what economists have found with historical and longitudinal data regarding the affordability of guaranteeing these basic protections to workers.

Figure 3. Relationship between national paid sick leave and a country's unemployment rate

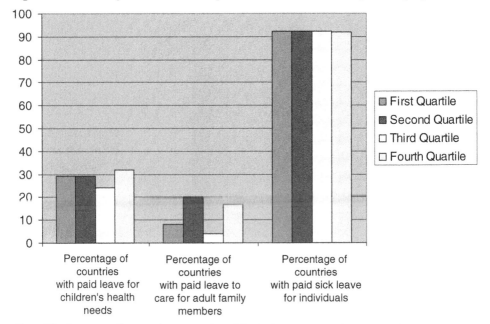

Note: The first quartile contains countries with the lowest unemployment rates.
Source: World Development Indicators Online, viewed on September 13, 2004. Data were available for 105 countries.

The importance of paid leave to working caregivers' ability to be involved in the care of their families' health needs and to their families' health status is clear. Commitment to paid sick leave *in jure*, while a critical first step, is not sufficient to guarantee that working adults can provide this essential support. Studies in the United States have illustrated the important role that flexibility and informal policies play in enabling workers to take advantage of what sick leave currently exists (Heymann 2000, Bond 2002). That workers sometimes face unsupportive supervisors, fear or experience penalties for using their leave in terms of promotion, wages, and job retention, highlights the need for addressing implementation of policies to achieve full and equal access to paid sick leave. Data on the extent of enforcement, on workplace culture, and perceived access to paid sick leave are not available on a global scale. However, these data are unlikely to change the several trends reported here as higher GDP countries have more resources available for enforcement.

The truly global availability of paid sick leave for employees and the lack of an association with negative macro-economic conditions demonstrate its feasibility in a wide range of countries. Theoretical concerns have been raised that providing social protection will ultimately hurt low-wage workers and low-income nations as a result of the trade-off between wages and benefits that employers face. The theory assumes that employers face a maximum total amount to spend on compensation that can be split between wages and benefits. Moreover, the theory does not take into account the economic benefits of providing paid sick leave, ranging from a decrease in illness spread in the workplace to increased productivity and retention. Even were there no benefits, the approximate cost of providing a week of paid sick leave with 100 per cent wage replacement is only 2 per cent of average wages whether in a low- or high-income country. Finally, the cost of providing paid sick leave is automatically adjusted to local wages. Because wages in low-income countries are lower than in high-income countries, this same 2 per cent will be less in absolute international dollars than the value of 2 per cent of average wages in a high-income country. The relatively low and self-scaling cost of providing these benefits further contribute to their feasibility.

Enhancing working adults' ability to care for their children is an important and increasingly critical need at this point in time. Recent increases in urbanization and paid labor force participation in most of the world's regions have meant that parents are increasingly working away from their homes and any children they are caring for. When children are separated from their caregivers, and parents' work hours and schedules are dictated by the employers, paid sick leave to care for family members becomes critical. Without paid sick leave, caregivers may have little choice but to send sick children to day care or school, have young children stay home alone or miss needed meetings with doctors with potentially serious health consequences (Loda et al. 1972, Doyle 1976, Strangert 1976, Sullivan et al. 1984, Haskins and Kotch 1986, Hillis et al. 1992, Mottonen and Uhari 1992, Heymann 2000). Without paid leave policies, working families are placed at risk economically as well, experiencing wage or job loss if they take time off work to provide care (Murphy et al. 1997), or losing earnings if they reduce working hours, quit their jobs, or engage in part-time or informal work with more flexible hours in order to accommodate caregiving demands (Fadayomi 1991, Psacharopoulos and Tzannatos 1992, Joshi et al. 1999, Davies et al. 2000, NAC and AARP 2004, Heymann 2006).

While the need to move forward on ensuring parents' ability to care for children's health is critical, enabling family care of the elderly is a growing issue. The population of individuals aged 60 and older is estimated to grow three-fold by 2050, and the population of the oldest-old, those 80 and older is projected to rise even more rapidly to 379 million by 2050 or more than five times its present number (United Nations Population Division 2001). At the same time, the number and availability of full-time caregivers is likely to fall as a result of urbanization and movement away from extended family in developing nations (Jamuna 1997, Chattopadhyay and Marsh 1999, Chow 1999), and the global increase in labor force participation among women, who still are most likely to be care providers for elderly and disabled family members (Doress-Worters 1994, Restrepo and Rozental 1994, Davis et al. 1995, Ineichen 1998, Medjuck et al. 1998, Rawlins 1999, Hashizume 2000, Long and Harris 2000). The proportion of adults having to meet the needs of elderly and disabled adult family members while working is growing and will continue to do so as the world's population ages. Increasing the number of nations with policies to address this issue is critical.

The ultimate effect of global demographic, labor and residence transformations on child and adult health will be critically influenced by whether workers are able to take time off work when they are ill and when their children or adult members of their family are sick and in need of care. A key issue in the debate around whether policies to guarantee this time off are feasible is the degree to which short-term paid leave hampers or helps national economic progress. Our global exploratory analyses of the relationship between macro-economic status and the provision of paid sick leave make a critical contribution to this debate. The absence of an association with negative economic consequences suggests that economic infeasibility should not hold nations back from trying to achieve the goal of ensuring the health of all their working families. No worker should be left to choose between the income they need and meeting the health needs of their family.

Notes

1. While some family care and support is needed and can take place outside work hours, some certainly cannot. Illnesses are as likely to occur during the day as at night, and serious health conditions often require either round-the-clock care and assistance with activities of daily living that occur at all times of the day and night, or require interaction with agencies, services or care providers that can be accessed only during regular work hours. The ability of workers to take time off work with pay is thus a necessary condition for family members to be involved in their children's and adult family members' care.
2. This may be due in part to the initial focus among researchers of the European experience on cash transfers which has since evolved over the last 10 years to what has been termed "work/family reconciliation policies" which consist of a new package of policies that go beyond the cash policies and include child care, paid leave, flexibility and part-time work protection.
3. We do not consider the voluntarily offered paid sick leave due to the focus of the Index on government progress in guaranteeing that the needs of working families are met.
4. The unpaid waiting period to qualify for state sickness benefits was not counted in the calculation of the duration of paid leave; however, the main source for data on waiting periods, the SSPTW is unclear as to whether the employee receives wage payment during this time, i.e. the source does not specify if the employee is paid during this period by the employer or whether the employee is paid retroactively for the unpaid waiting period upon qualifying for state sickness benefits, so the paid duration estimates may be underestimates.

References

Ackerman, S., 1999, Supply-side journalism: an all-American prescription for German unemployment. *Harpers Magazine* (October), 66–67.

Aronsson, G., Gustafsson, K. and Dallner, M., 2000, Sick but yet at work. An empirical study of sickness presenteeism. *Journal of Epidemiology and Community Health*, **54**, 502–509.

Bennett, S. J., 1993, Relationships among selected antecedent variables and coping effectiveness in postmyocardial infarction patients. *Research in Nursing and Health*, **16**, 131–139.

Berkman, L. F., 1995, The role of social relations in health promotion. *Psychosomatic Medicine*, **57**, 245–254.

Blanchard, O. and Wolfers, J., 1999, The role of shocks and institutions in the rise of European unemployment: the aggregate evidence, available at: http://econ-www.mit.edu/faculty/index.htm?prof_id=blanchar&type=paper (accessed September 13, 2005).

Blank, R. and Freeman, R. B., 1994, Evaluating the connection between social protection and economic flexibility, in: Rebecca Blank (Ed) *Social Protection and Economic Flexibility: Is There a Trade-Off?* (Chicago, IL: The University of Chicago Press).

Bond, J. T., 2002, *Highlights of the National Study of the Changing Workforce* (New York: Families and Work Institute).

Bratislava International Centre for Family Studies, 2001, *Reflections of Recent Demographic Conditions on Family and Social Policies In CEE (Central and Eastern European Countries) Final Report: Part II* (Bratislava: Bratislava International Centre for Family Studies).

Canadian Department of Social Development, 2004, *Employment Insurance (EI) Compassionate Care Benefits*, available at: http://www.sdc.gc.ca/asp/gateway.asp?hr=en/ei/types/compassionate_care.shtml&hs=tyt (accessed May 3, 2004).

Cauley, S. D., 1987, The time price of medical care. *The Review of Economics and Statistics*, **69**, 59–66.
Chattopadhyay, A. and Marsh, R., 1999, Changes in living arrangement and familial support for the elderly in Taiwan: 1963–1991. *Journal of Comparative Family Studies*, **30**, 523–537.
Chow, N. W. S., 1999, Aging in China. *Journal of Sociology and Social Welfare*, **26**, 25–49.
Clearinghouse on International Developments in Child, Youth and Family Policies at Columbia University, 2003, *Country Profiles*, available at: http://www.childpolicyintl.org/ (accessed March 18, 2004).
Cleary, J., Gray, O. P., Hall, D. J., Rowlandson, P. H., Sainsbury, C. P. and Davies, M. M., 1986, Parental involvement in the lives of children in hospital. *Archives of Disease in Childhood*, **61**, 779–787.
Davies, H., Joshi, H. and Peronaci, R., 2000, Forgone income and motherhood: what do recent British data tell us? *Population Studies*, **54**, 293–305.
Davis, A. J., Martinson, I., Gan, L. C., Jin, Q., Liang, Y. H., Davis, D. B. and Lin, J. Y., 1995, Home care for the urban chronically ill elderly in the People's Republic of China. *International Journal of Aging and Human Development*, **41**, 345–358.
Doress-Worters, P. B., 1994, Adding elder care to women's multiple roles: a critical review of the caregiver stress and multiple roles literatures. *Sex Roles*, **31**, 597–616.
Doyle, A. B., 1976, Incidence of illness in early group and family day-care. *Pediatrics*, **58**, 607–613.
Employment Policy Foundation, 2000, News Release: Should the U.S. follow Europe's work-family policies? Paid family leave mandates will be costly in U.S., book finds, available at: http://www.epf.org/media/newsreleases/2000/nr20000424.pdf (accessed September 13, 2005).
Fadayomi, T., 1991, The Nigerian working mother and her pre-school age children: the incipience of role incompatibility and its resolutions. *International Journal of Sociology*, **21**, 229–242.
Finland Ministry of Labor, 2003, Family leaves – a matter for both parents, available at: http://www.mol.fi/english/working/familyleaves2003.html (accessed September 15, 2005).
Gilleski, D. B., 1998, A dynamic stochastic model of medical care use and work absence. *Econometrica*, **66**, 1–45.
Gorkin, L., Schron, E. B., Brooks, M. M., Wiklund, I., Kellen, J., Verter, J., Schoenberger, J. A., Pawitan, Y., Morris, M. and Shumaker, S., 1993, Psychosocial predictors of mortality in the Cardiac Arrhythmia Suppression Trial-1 (CAST-1). *American Journal of Cardiology*, **71**, 263–267.
Gornick, J. C., 2005, Overworked, time poor, and abandoned by Uncle Sam. *Dissent* (Summer), 65–69.
Gornick J. C. and Meyers, M. K., 2003, *Families That Work: Policies for Reconciling Parenthood and Employment* (New York: Russell Sage Foundation).
Gornick, J. C. and Meyers, M. K., 2004, More alike than different: revisiting the long-term prospects for developing "European-style" work/family policies in the United States. *Journal of Comparative Policy Analysis*, **6**(3), 251–273.
Gornick, J. C., Meyers, M. K. and Ross, K. E., 1997, Supporting the employment of mothers: policy variation across fourteen welfare states. *Journal of European Social Policy*, **7**, 45–70.
Grinyer, A. and Singleton, V., 2000, Sickness absence as risk-taking behaviour: a study of organizational and cultural factors in the public sector. *Health, Risk, and Society*, **2**, 7–21.
Hashizume, Y., 2000, Gender issues and Japanese family-centered caregiving for frail elderly parents or parents-in-law in modern Japan: from the sociocultural and historical perspectives. *Public Health Nursing*, **17**, 25–31.
Haskins, R. and Kotch, J., 1986, Day care and illness: evidence, cost, and public policy. *Pediatrics*, **77**, 951–982.
Heymann, S. J., 2000, *The Widening Gap: Why Working Families Are in Jeopardy and What Can Be Done About It* (New York: Basic Books).
Heymann, S. J., 2002, Social transformations and their implications for the global demand for ECCE. *UNESCO Policy Brief* (November–December).
Heymann, S. J., 2003a, School children in families with young children: educational opportunities at risk. *UNESCO Policy Brief* (February).
Heymann, S. J., 2003b, The impact of AIDS on early childhood care and education. *UNESCO Policy Brief* (June).
Heymann, S. J., 2004, The role of early childhood care and education in ensuring equal opportunity. *UNESCO Policy Brief* (January).
Heymann, J., 2006, *Forgotten Families: Ending the Growing Crisis Confronting Children and Working Parents in a Global Economy* (New York: Oxford University Press).

Heymann, J., Fischer, A. and Engelman, M., 2003, Labor conditions and the health of children, elderly and disabled family members, in: J. Heymann (Ed) *Global Inequalities at Work: Work's Impact on the Health of Individuals, Families, and Societies* (New York: Oxford University Press), pp. 75–104.

Heymann, S. J., Toomey, S. and Furstenberg, F., 1999, Working parents: what factors are involved in their ability to take time off from work when their children are sick? *Archives of Pediatrics and Adolescent Medicine*, **153**, 870–874.

Hillis, S. D., Miranda, C. M., McCann, M., Bender, D. and Weigle, K., 1992, Day care center attendance and diarrheal morbidity in Colombia. *Pediatrics*, **90**, 582–588.

Holden, E. W., Chmielewski, D., Nelson, C. C., Kager, V. A. and Foltz, L., 1997, Controlling for general and disease-specific effects in child and family adjustment to chronic childhood illness. *Journal of Pediatric Psychology*, **22**, 15–27.

Ineichen, B., 1998, Influences on the care of demented elderly people in the People's Republic of China. *International Journal of Geriatric Psychiatry*, **13**, 122–126.

International Labor Organization (ILO), 2002, Child-care and family-care leave law – Japan, available at: http://www.ilo.org/public/english/employment/gems/eeo/law/japan/care.htm (accessed September 15, 2005).

Jamuna, D., 1997, Stress dimensions among caregivers of the elderly. *Indian Journal of Medical Research*, **106**, 381–388.

Johannsson, G., 2002, Work-life balance: the case of Sweden in the 1990s. *Social Science Information*, **41**, 303–317.

Johnson, K., 1994, Children with special health needs: ensuring appropriate coverage and care under health care reform. *Health Policy and Child Health*, **1**, 1–5.

Joshi, H., Paci, P. and Waldfogel, J., 1999, The wages of motherhood: better or worse? *Cambridge Journal of Economics*, **23**, 543–564.

Jubb, M. and Shanley, E., 2002, Family involvement: the key to opening locked wards and closed minds. *International Journal of Mental Health Nursing*, **11**, 47–53.

Kamerman, S. B. and Kahn, A. J., 1997, *Family Change and Family Policies in Great Britain, Canada, New Zealand, and the United States* (Oxford and New York: Clarendon Press).

Karner, A. M., Dahlgren, M. A. and Bergdahl, B., 2004, Rehabilitation after coronary heart disease: spouses' views of support. *Journal of Advanced Nursing*, **46**, 204–211.

Kristensson-Hallstrom, I., Elander, G. and Malmfors, G., 1997, Increased parental participation in a paediatric surgical day-care unit. *Journal of Clinical Nursing*, **6**, 297–302.

La Greca, A. M., Auslander, W. F., Greco, P., Spetter, D., Fisher, E. B., Jr. and Santiago, J. V., 1995, I get by with a little help from my family and friends: adolescents' support for diabetes care. *Journal of Pediatric Psychology*, **20**, 449–476.

Lindert, P., 2004, *Growing Public: Social Spending and Economic Growth since the Eighteenth Century* (New York: Cambridge University Press).

Loda, F. A., Glezen, W. P. and Clyde, W. A., Jr., 1972, Respiratory disease in group day care. *Pediatrics*, **49**, 428–437.

Long, S. O. and Harris, P. B., 2000, Gender and elder care: social change and the role of the caregiver in Japan. *Social Science Japan Journal*, **3**, 21–36.

McGraw, T., 1994, Preparing children for the operating room: psychological issues. *Canadian Journal of Anaesthesia*, **41**, 1094–1103.

Medjuck, S., Keefe, J. M. and Fancey, P. J., 1998, Available but not accessible: an examination of the use of workplace policies for caregivers of elderly kin. *Journal of Family Issues*, **19**, 274–299.

Mishel, L., Bernstein, J. and Allegretto, S., 2005, *The State of Working America: 2004–2005* (Ithaca, NY: Cornell University Press).

Mottonen, M. and Uhari, M., 1992, Absences for sickness among children in day care. *Acta Paediatrica*, **81**, 929–932.

Murphy, B., Schofield, H., Nankervis, J., Bloch, S., Herrman, H. and Singh, B., 1997, Women with multiple roles: the emotional impact of caring for ageing parents. *Ageing and Society*, **17**, 277–291.

National Alliance for Caregiving (NAC) and American Association of Retired People (AARP), 2004, Caregiving in the U.S., available at: http://www.caregiving.org/data/04finalreport.pdf (accessed September 15, 2005).

New Zealand Department of Labour, no date, Your rights to holidays and other leave, available at: http://www.ers.dol.govt.nz/publications/pdfs/holidays.pdf (accessed September 15, 2005).

Nickell, Stephen, 1997, Unemployment and labor market rigidities: Europe versus North America. *Journal of Economic Perspectives*, **11**(3), 55–74.

Organization for Economic Cooperation and Development (OECD), 1995, Long-term leave for parents in OECD countries, in: *Employment Outlook* (Paris: OECD), pp. 171–230.

Palmer, S. J., 1993, Care of sick children by parents: a meaningful role. *Journal of Advanced Nursing*, **18**, 185–191.

Psacharopoulos, G. and Tzannatos, Z. (Eds), 1992, *Case Studies on Women's Employment and Pay in Latin America* (Washington, DC: World Bank).

Rantanen, A., Kaunonen, M., Astedt-Kurki, P. and Tarkka, M. T., 2004, Coronary artery bypass grafting: social support for patients and their significant others. *Journal of Clinical Nursing*, **13**, 158–166.

Rawlins, J. M., 1999, Confronting ageing as a Caribbean reality. *Journal of Sociology and Social Welfare*, **26**, 143–153.

Restrepo, H. E. and Rozental, M., 1994, The social impact of aging populations: some major issues. *Social Science and Medicine*, **39**, 1323–1338.

Sainsbury, C. P., Gray, O. P., Cleary, J., Davies, M. M. and Rowlandson, P. H., 1986, Care by parents of their children in hospital. *Archives of Disease in Childhood*, **61**, 612–615.

Salokangas, R. K., 1997, Living situation, social network and outcome in schizophrenia: a five-year prospective follow-up study. *Acta Psychiatrica Scandinavica*, **96**, 459–468.

Seeman, T. E., 2000, Health promoting effects of friends and family on health outcomes in older adults. *American Journal of Health Promotion*, **14**, 362–370.

Siebert, H., 1997, Labor market rigidities: at the root of unemployment in Europe. *Journal of Economic Perspectives*, **11**(3), 37–55.

Social Security Administration (SSA) and International Social Security Administration (ISSA), 2002, Social security programs throughout the world: Europe, 2002, available at: http://www.ssa.gov/policy/docs/progdesc/ssptw/2002-2003/europe/index.html (accessed September 15, 2005).

Social Security Administration (SSA) and International Social Security Administration (ISSA), 2003a, Social security programs throughout the world: Africa, 2003, available at: http://www.ssa.gov/policy/docs/progdesc/ssptw/2002-2003/africa/index.html (accessed September 15, 2005).

Social Security Administration (SSA) and International Social Security Administration (ISSA), 2003b, Social security programs throughout the world: Asia and the Pacific, 2002, available at: http://www.ssa.gov/policy/docs/progdesc/ssptw/2002-2003/asia/index.html (accessed September 15, 2005).

Social Security Administration (SSA) and International Social Security Administration (ISSA), 2004, Social security programs throughout the world: The Americas, 2003, available at: http://www.ssa.gov/policy/docs/progdesc/ssptw/2002-2003/americas/index.html (accessed September 15, 2005).

Stanhope, V., 2002, Culture, control, and family involvement: a comparison of psychosocial rehabilitation in India and the United States. *Psychiatric Rehabilitation Journal*, **25**, 273–280.

Strangert, K., 1976, Respiratory illness in preschool children with different forms of day care. *Pediatrics*, **57**, 191–196.

Sullivan, P., Woodward, W. E., Pickering, L. K. and DuPont, H. L., 1984, Longitudinal study of occurrence of diarrheal disease in day care centers. *American Journal of Public Health*, **74**, 987–991.

Taylor, M. R. and O'Connor, P., 1989, Resident parents and shorter hospital stay. *Archives of Disease in Childhood*, **64**, 274–276.

Tsouna-Hadjis, E., Vemmos, K. N., Zakopoulos, N. and Stamatelopoulos, S., 2000, First-stroke recovery process: the role of family social support. *Archives of Physical Medicine and Rehabilitation*, **81**, 881–887.

United Kingdom Department of Trade and Industry, 2000, Frequently asked questions about time off for dependants, available at: http://www.dti.gov.uk/er/faqs.htm (accessed September 15, 2005).

United Nations Development Program (UNDP), 2004, *Human Development Report 2004: Cultural Liberty in Today's Diverse World* (Oxford: Oxford University Press), available at: http://hdr.undp.org/reports/global/2004/ (accessed September 15, 2005).

United Nations Population Division (UNPD), 2001, *World Population Prospects: The 2000 Revision Highlights* (New York: Department of Economic and Social Affairs, UN).

United States Department of Labor, no date, Compliance assistance – Family and Medical Leave Act (FMLA), available at: http://www.dol.gov/esa/whd/fmla (accessed September 15, 2005).

Van der Schyff, G., 1979, The role of parents during their child's hospitalisation. *Australian Nurses' Journal*, **8**, 57–58, 61.

Waldfogel, J., 2001, What Other nations do: international policies toward parental leave and child care. *The Future of Children*, **11**(4), 99–111.

Waugh, T. A. and Kjos, D. L., 1992, Parental involvement and the effectiveness of an adolescent day treatment program. *Journal of Youth and Adolescence*, **21**, 487–497.

Wolman, C., Resnick, M. D., Harris, L. J. and Blum, R. W., 1994, Emotional well-being among adolescents with and without chronic conditions. *Journal of Adolescent Health*, **15**, 199–204.

Woloshin, S., Schwartz, L. M., Tosteson, A. N., Chang, C. H., Wright, B., Plohman, J. and Fisher, E. S., 1997, Perceived adequacy of tangible social support and health outcomes in patients with coronary artery disease. *Journal of General Internal Medicine*, **12**, 613–618.

Three Worlds of Welfare Chauvinism? How Welfare Regimes Affect Support for Distributing Welfare to Immigrants in Europe

JEROEN VAN DER WAAL, WILLEM DE KOSTER
& WIM VAN OORSCHOT

ABSTRACT *Analyzing the 2008 wave of the European Social Survey, this study assesses whether an elaborate institutional theory is able to explain why levels of welfare chauvinism differ among welfare regimes. As expected, native populations in liberal and conservative welfare regimes prove more reluctant to distributing welfare services to immigrants than those in social-democratic ones. Adding country-level data, it is demonstrated that neither differences in the selectivity nor differences in employment protection and unemployment levels can explain these varying levels of welfare chauvinism. Instead, regime differences in welfare chauvinism can be fully attributed to their differences in income inequality.*

Introduction

A common idea among scholars of politics and policy is that extensive and universal welfare regimes result in a stronger sense of solidarity and more tolerance towards outgroups among majority populations than do residual ones. Such assertions can already be found in classical readings on the welfare state by Marshall (1950) and Titmuss (1968), and several studies have empirically tested these arguments by comparing the opinions of people living in welfare regimes that differ in the level of generosity and the extent of decommodification. Most of these comparisons are based on Esping-Andersen's well-known typology of welfare regimes

(1990). These by and large expect that social-democratic welfare states result in the highest levels of solidarity and tolerance among their majority populations, followed by conservative and liberal ones respectively (cf. Dallinger 2010). Although research along these lines has produced scattered findings (for overviews, see Jaeger 2006, 2009), a clear pattern is found in studies focusing on opinions about welfare policies in the "narrow sense" (cf. Larsen 2006, 2008): majority populations in liberal welfare regimes are on average less supportive of policies directed at the poor and the unemployed than those in conservative regimes, and especially less than those in social-democratic ones (see e.g. Jaeger 2009).

Such studies seem to fit in an institutional approach to politics, which is informed by the idea that political preferences and attitudes are shaped by political institutions, whose endogenous nature is emphasized (March and Olsen 1996). This has been recognized by Christian Albrekt Larsen (2006, 2008), who concluded that commonly used theories – "power resource theory", "new politics theory", and "culture theory" – proved to be remarkably impotent for explaining why people in liberal welfare states are least supportive of welfare directed at the poor and the unemployed. He has therefore formulated and tested a different, "institutional line of reasoning", which combines insights from welfare regime theory as formulated by Marshall (1950) and Titmuss (1968, 1974; cf. Myles and Quadagno 2002), with theorizing on deservingness criteria (cf. Van Oorschot 2000). The overall idea is that "the institutional structure of the different welfare regimes influences or – using another terminology – frames the way the public perceives the poor and the unemployed" (Larsen 2008: 148). More specifically, Larsen has demonstrated that the institutional structure of three different welfare regimes affects the extent to which the public perceives the poor and unemployed as (1) deviant, (2) in need of welfare, and (3) in control of their own situation. These three "deservingness criteria" in turn influence whether or not the poor and unemployed are considered to be entitled to welfare.

While this specific branch of institutional theory has already proven its merits when it comes to explaining views on the poor and the unemployed, it also seems promising when it comes to opinions on the deservingness of another group holding a minority position, immigrants. A salient discussion in the literature focuses on immigrants' entitlements to welfare arrangements. In all European countries, although to a varying degree, the public at large considers immigrants less entitled to welfare benefits and services than the native population (Van Oorschot 2006). Various studies have assessed the antecedents of this sentiment, which has been aptly summarized by Andersen and Bjørklund as the idea that "welfare services should be restricted to 'our own'" (1990: 212). Their label, "welfare chauvinism", has become the standard term for the opinion that immigrants are less entitled to welfare benefits and services than the native population (cf. Van der Waal et al. 2010; Mewes and Mau 2012; Reeskens and Van Oorschot 2012; De Koster et al. 2013).[1]

In the light of Larsen's formulation of institutional theory, this raises the question of whether three worlds of welfare chauvinism can be distinguished: are the native populations of liberal welfare states most reluctant to distribute welfare benefits and services to immigrants, followed by natives living in conservative welfare states, while those living under social-democratic regimes are most willing to do so? And, if so, can this pattern be explained in accordance with the mechanisms addressed in Larsen's theory? Before we turn to our empirical analyses, we must first discuss this theory in more detail.

An Institutional Theory of Welfare Chauvinism

By and large, the specific branch of institutional theory formulated by Larsen (2006) ranks liberal, conservative and social-democratic welfare regimes on three dimensions. The first one is the "selectivity dimension", which indicates the extent to which a welfare regime is universal. The second dimension indicates the extent to which a welfare regime reduces market-driven inequalities between "the rich" and "the poor". While Larsen refers to this dimension as the "generosity dimension", we will denote it as the "inequality dimension" in order to avoid conceptual confusion that could arise from the generosity label, which is often employed with a different meaning in the literature on welfare arrangements (e.g. referring to the share of the population that is covered by these, see Scruggs 2004). The third dimension, "labor-market trajectory", addresses the extent to which a welfare regime creates labor-market opportunities for the least skilled. These three dimensions are thought to affect the three deservingness criteria – deviance, need and control – that guide the opinions of the majority population concerning whether or not (potential) welfare recipients are entitled to welfare. First we discuss the selectivity and inequality dimensions, and later we consider the labor-market trajectory dimension.

Before we do so, it should be noted that Larsen's model is a simplified representation of a complex reality, just as any theory is. It is, after all, plausible that welfare regimes do not unidirectionally shape public opinions: public opinions most likely also affect welfare arrangements. Nevertheless, strong theoretical arguments have been made in favor of the causal direction implied by Larsen's model (see Rothstein and Stolle 2008), and recent research (Raven et al. 2011) demonstrates that the direction of the relationship differs between policy domains. Public opinion only informs public policies if these are new and not yet institutionalized, whereas the relationship is reversed in the case of highly institutionalized welfare arrangements. The latter do affect public opinions, which supports the assumption underlying the theoretical model under scrutiny.

The Impact of the Selectivity and Inequality Dimensions on the Deviance Criterion

The selectively and inequality dimensions rank welfare regimes in a way that resembles the classic ideas of Marshall (1950) and Titmuss (1968). On the basis of the selectivity dimension, welfare regimes are ordered by the extent to which they are characterized by selective – "means tested" – programmatic structures of benefits and services instead of universal ones. The inequality dimension ranks welfare regimes by the level of inequality that results from their programmatic structures. These two dimensions result in the following order: liberal (most selective; most unequal), conservative (medium selective; medium unequal), and social-democratic welfare regimes (least selective; least unequal). Liberal regimes merely provide welfare for the most needy which leads to the highest levels of inequality between the rich and poor. Social-democratic ones include benefits and services for large parts of the population and are characterized by the lowest levels of inequality between the rich and poor. Conservative regimes rank in-between on both dimensions (Rothstein 1998; Larsen 2006).

The selectivity and inequality dimensions are theorized to influence opinions on the deservingness of (potential) welfare recipients, because both affect the extent to which majority populations consider them to be deviant. The underlying mechanisms are, however, different. In the case of the *selectivity* dimension, it is important to note that "the very act of separating out the needy almost always stamps them as socially inferior, as 'others' with other types of social characteristics and needs" (Rothstein 1998: 158). The framing implied by selective welfare services thus decreases the extent to which majority populations perceive welfare recipients as "one of us". Selective programmatic structures of benefits and services furthermore draw a sharper and more easily discernible line between those who benefit from the welfare state and those who do not. As a result, "the needy" and "the poor" are clearly separated from other citizens in public debates on welfare, aggravating the us-versus-them divide (cf. Larsen 2007: 87–88). The selectivity of welfare services consequently makes it harder for majority populations to identify with the poor and those in need – with "those people" (Rothstein 1998: 157) – and the former are consequently more likely to consider the latter a "public burden" (Titmuss 1968: 129), deviant, and therefore undeserving of welfare.

The *inequality* dimension is also assumed to affect the extent to which majority populations consider (potential) welfare recipients as deviant. The crucial difference with the selectivity dimension is, however, that the inequality dimension does not involve frames embedded in the institutional make-up of welfare regimes. Instead, the explanation lies in the different outcomes brought about by different welfare regimes. The underlying idea is that some welfare states mitigate income inequality more strongly than others, while "reduced differences in economic resources between 'the majority' and 'the bottom' of society generate more similar living styles, as a consequence making it easier for 'the bottom' to fulfill the identity criterion" (Larsen 2006: 57). Put differently, welfare states that diminish market-driven inequalities least are most likely to result in strongly articulated social divisions between the rich and poor – resulting in "two nations", instead of one (cf. Titmuss 1968: 122). In such welfare states, the rich hardly identify themselves with the poor, and they are, therefore, more likely to consider the latter deviant, and thus less entitled to welfare.

Whereas these ideas about the selectivity and the inequality dimensions have originally been developed with the poor and the unemployed in mind, several research findings suggest that both dimensions might also be relevant for explaining different levels of welfare chauvinism. In the first place, studies of opinions related to the rather general question of whether immigrants should get the same rights as natives or citizens (Mau and Burkhardt 2009) and of views pertaining to the question of whether immigrants take away jobs and are a burden for the welfare state (Crepaz and Damron 2009) find similar patterns to those addressing views on the poor and the unemployed. Even though these studies do not focus on welfare chauvinism,[2] and although Mau and Burkhardt (2009) use a typology that differs from Esping-Andersen's, their results suggest that native populations in social-democratic welfare regimes take a more inclusive stance towards immigrants and are less concerned about "negative" labor-market and welfare effects of immigration than those in liberal ones.

In the second place, the identity criterion that intermediates the impact of the selectivity and inequality of welfare regimes on the perceived deservingness of the poor and unemployed – that of deviance – seems to be applicable to immigrants, too (cf. Larsen 2006: 49). Universal welfare regimes are likely to obstruct the marking out of immigrants in discussions on welfare, and welfare regimes producing low levels of income inequality are likely to hamper identifying immigrants as deviant due to poor living conditions.

The above gives rise to two hypotheses. First, we expect that differences in the extent to which majority populations living under liberal, conservative and social-democratic welfare regimes consider immigrants to be entitled to welfare services can be explained by differences in the selectivity of these regimes (*hypothesis 1*). Second, we expect that such differences in welfare chauvinism can be explained by differences in inequality among the populations of these welfare states (*hypothesis 2*).

The Impact of the Labor-Market Trajectory on the Need and Control Criteria

The labor-market trajectory is the third dimension of welfare regimes that affects the opinion of the majority about the poor and the unemployed (Larsen 2006) and possibly about immigrants as well. It is theorized that this dimension relates to the deservingness criteria of "need" and "control". More specifically, it influences the extent to which the poor and the unemployed are thought to be in need of welfare benefits and services and the extent to which majority populations perceive them to be in control of their own situation.

When it comes to the "need" criterion, it is important that the institutional make-up of liberal, conservative and social-democratic welfare regimes results in differences in job opportunities at the bottom of their labor markets (Esping-Andersen 1990). The deregulated liberal welfare regimes have low wage levels and consequently yield high labor demand for low-skilled service workers in the private sector. Social-democratic welfare regimes are also characterized by high labor demand for low-skilled service workers, albeit in the public, instead of the private, sector. Conservative regimes, on the other hand, do not yield high demand for service workers –in the private or the public sector – as these are directed at protecting sole-wage-earner families. Referring to Esping-Andersen, Larsen explains this as follows: "conservative regimes followed a labour reduction route. It did not boost employment in the service sector, but instead protected the male insider against the risk of unemployment through strict job protection and early retirement schemes" (2006: 59). Clearly, then, as compared to conservative welfare regimes, liberal and social-democratic ones are characterized by more job opportunities at the bottom of the labor market that enable people to be self-supportive instead of dependent on welfare benefits and services (see for findings corroborating this suggestion: Raveaud 2007). Therefore, majority populations in liberal and social-democratic regimes most likely perceive the unemployed as less in *need* of welfare services, and consequently as less entitled to welfare, than majority populations in conservative welfare regimes do.

The second mechanism is not about need, but about the extent to which (potential) welfare recipients are considered to be in *control* of their own situation. The basic argument here is that employment regulation, which substantially decreases the extent to which jobseekers are likely to be successful, is most strict in social-democratic and conservative welfare regimes (cf. Lindbeck and Snower 1988). First, working conditions in social-democratic and conservative welfare regimes are hardly open to negotiation. Liberal ones, in contrast, facilitate such negotiations and enable the unemployed to reduce their wage demands. The unemployed in liberal regimes are consequently more in control of their own situation than those in social-democratic and conservative ones. Second, the protection of "insiders" on the labor market – i.e. those who already have a steady job – is strongest in conservative regimes, followed by social-democratic and liberal ones. If insiders on the labor market are more protected, the unemployed face more difficulties in finding employment. Hence, the institutional make-up of liberal welfare regimes leaves the unemployed more in control over their own situation than those in social-democratic and conservative ones.

Figure 1. The institutional theory of welfare chauvinism

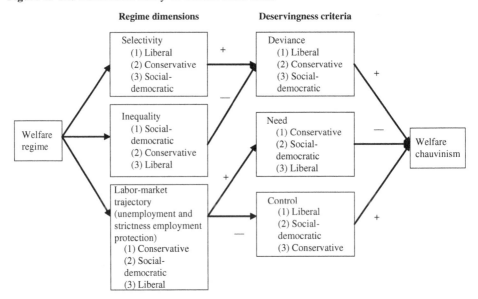

Extending these theoretical arguments to views on the welfare entitlements of immigrants, we can formulate two additional hypotheses. We expect that differences in the extent to which majority populations in liberal, conservative and social-democratic welfare regimes consider immigrants to be entitled to welfare services can be explained by differences in unemployment levels (*hypothesis 3*). In addition, we expect that such differences in welfare chauvinism can be explained by differences in the strictness of employment protection (*hypothesis 4*).

Figure 1 summarizes the institutional theory of welfare chauvinism outlined above. On the left-hand side, it shows that welfare regimes differ on three dimensions: (1) *selectivity*, ranging from residual or means-tested to universal; (2) *inequality*, indicating the level of income inequality; and (3) *labor-market trajectory*, indicating the extent to which regimes offer employment opportunities. For each of these dimensions, the expected rank order of the three welfare regimes is indicated. The next column displays rank orders on the three deservingness criteria: (1) *deviance*, indicating the extent to which majority populations consider immigrants to be deviant; (2) *need*, representing the extent to which majority populations perceive immigrants to be in need of welfare services; and (3) *control*, indicating the extent to which those populations perceive immigrants to be in control over their own employment situation.

Research Format, Data and Operationalization

Our hypotheses will be tested by means of multilevel modeling on a dataset that combines individual-level data of the *European Social Survey* (ESS 2008) with country-level data retrieved from various sources. To our knowledge the ESS 2008 is the only internationally comparative dataset containing a measure of welfare chauvinism. The country-level data needed for testing our hypotheses could not be retrieved for all countries in the ESS, but ten countries for which such data are available can be categorized according to Esping-Andersen's typology of welfare regimes. Our categorization is in accordance with that of Larsen (2006: 68) in formulating the institutional theory addressed in this article. In addition to five social-democratic regimes (Denmark, Finland, the Netherlands, Norway and Sweden) and three conservative ones (Belgium, France and Germany),[3] there are only two liberal welfare regimes in the dataset: Ireland and the United Kingdom. Note, however, that those are the only two liberal welfare regimes in Europe.

Since our study deals with majority populations' opinions concerning the welfare entitlements of immigrants, we focus on native respondents: respondents not born in their country of residence and respondents who have at least one parent who was not born in their country of birth and residence are excluded from the analyses.

Furthermore, due to lack of data suitable for measuring public opinions on the three deservingness criteria depicted in Figure 1, we are – just like Larsen (2006: 74–77) – compelled by necessity to test our hypotheses merely by means of data on the regime dimensions that according to the institutional theory on welfare attitudes inform opinions on deservingness.

Country-Level Variables

Selectivity is measured by means of the coverage of welfare services – i.e. the share of the population covered by these services – provided by Scruggs's (2004) well-known and widely used *Comparative Welfare Entitlement Dataset*. Its mean regime scores are as expected: liberal (25.90), conservative (28.53), social-democratic (35.48). Country scores have been inverted so that the variable indicates *selectivity* instead of universality.[4]

We measure *inequality* in two ways. For measuring *inequality I* we use the Gini coefficient of each country in the year 2007/2008 (United Nations Development Program 2007). A higher Gini coefficient indicates a wider income gap, and mean regime scores are ranked as expected: (1) liberal (35.95), (2) conservative (31.33), (3) social-democratic (26.66). *Inequality II* is measured by means of the 80/20 ratio, which indicates the ratio between the income share of the top 20 per cent and the bottom 20 per cent of the income distribution for each country (Eurostat s.d.a). Higher scores on this variable also indicate more inequality, and mean regime scores are also ranked in accordance to our expectations: (1) liberal (5.00), (2) conservative (4.40), (3) social-democratic (3.72).

Unemployment is used to indicate a general lack of job opportunities at the bottom of the labor market. It is measured as the unemployment level in each country in the year 2008 (Eurostat, s.d.b). Higher scores stand for higher unemployment levels, and thus fewer job opportunities at the bottom of the labor market, indicating that there are fewer possibilities for sustaining oneself instead of relying on welfare. As predicted by Larsen (2006), the highest level of unemployment can indeed be found in the conservative regimes (mean score 7.36), as unemployment levels in liberal (mean score 5.95) and social-democratic ones (mean score 4.24) are lower.

For each country, *strictness of employment protection* is measured as the degree of employment protection along

> 21 basic items which can be classified in three main areas: (I) protection of regular workers against individual dismissal; (II) regulation of temporary forms of

employment; and (III) specific requirements for collective dismissals. The information refers to employment protection provided through legislation and as a result of enforcement processes. (OECD, s.d.).[5]

A higher score indicates that employment protection is stricter, and average regime scores are in line with our expectations: (1) conservative (2.79), (2) social-democratic (1.82), (3) liberal (0.50).

To properly test the empirical validity of the institutional theory outlined above, there is need to control for the primary competing theory: that of ethnic heterogeneity (Alesina and Glaeser 2004). Roughly put, this theory holds that there is less support for economic redistribution in liberal welfare regimes because their more ethnically heterogeneous character undermines the social solidarity that underlies this support. Hence, we will control for the *share of non-western immigrants* in each country (Schneider 2008) in the analyses that follow (cf. Mau and Burkhardt 2009; Manevska and Achterberg 2011). The underlying idea is that this variable indicates the share of immigrants in the population that are (perceived to be) culturally different and (perceived to) have different values and are consequently (perceived to be) a cultural threat to the native population (cf. Schneider 2008: 58). The mean regime scores are, however, not ranked in accordance to what is generally expected, as liberal welfare regimes have the lowest, instead of highest, share of non-western immigrants: (1) conservative (6.72), (2) social-democratic (5.55), (3) liberal (4.23).

Ethnic diversity of immigrants is the second indicator that will be used in order to control for ethnic heterogeneity theory. It is constructed by calculating the Herfindahl index of immigrant respondents in all four waves of the European Social Survey since 2002. In each of these waves the respondents reported their country of birth, which made it possible to measure the diversity of the immigrant population within each country. *Ethnic diversity of immigrants* indicates the mean scores of the Herfindahl indices that were calculated for these countries for each ESS wave. It ranges from 0 (perfectly ethnically homogeneous immigrant population) through 1 (perfectly ethnically heterogeneous immigrant population). As such, higher scores indicate higher levels of ethnic diversity within the immigrant population of a country. The mean regime scores of this indicator for ethnic heterogeneity theory are ranked as expected: (1) liberal (0.17), (2) conservative (0.16), (3) social-democratic (0.13).[6]

Individual-Level Variables

The dependent variable *welfare chauvinism* is measured by means of the following question: "Thinking of people coming to live in [country] from other countries, when do you think they should obtain the same rights to social benefits and services as citizens already living here?" This is the best available measure for an international comparison of welfare chauvinism as conceptualized here. Unsurprisingly, the only other internationally comparative studies on welfare chauvinism we know of also utilize this question (Mewes and Mau 2012; Reeskens and Van Oorschot 2012). Its answer categories are (1) "Immediately on arrival", (2) "After living in [country] for a year, whether or not they have worked", (3) "Only after they have worked and paid taxes for at least a year", (4) "Once they have become a [country] citizen", (5) "They should never get the same rights". Please note that the wording of both the question and its answer categories indicates that this item does not focus on the desirability of welfare benefits and services in general. Instead, the item's "specific wording ... assesses Europeans' support for welfare chauvinism quite well" (Mewes and Mau 2012: 130).[7]

Unfortunately, higher scores do not validly indicate a stronger reluctance towards entitling immigrants to welfare services. There is no problem with answer categories 1, 2, 3 and 5: when placed in this specific order, higher scores stand for more welfare chauvinism. Category 4, however, does not fit into this pattern: it addresses the legal status of immigrants – citizens versus non-citizens – which is substantially different. Furthermore, the conditions that need to be met in order to gain citizenship vary widely among European countries, which severely hampers international comparability of this answer category (cf. Mewes and Mau 2012: 130–131). Therefore, we have left answer category 4 out of our measurement of welfare chauvinism: we have recoded categories 1 to 3 and 5 into 1 to 3 and 4 respectively. A higher score on this variable thus indicates a stronger resistance toward entitling immigrants to welfare.

To properly test our hypotheses, we need to control for compositional effects. Therefore, the analyses include the following individual-level indicators.

We control for level of education because it has been found numerous times that education affects attitudes towards ethnic minorities and immigrants (Emler and Frazer 1999). *Education* is measured as the minimum number of years of schooling needed to attain the highest level of education achieved by the respondent.

Income needs to be controlled for, too, because one's economic position affects one's attitudes towards economic redistribution (Van der Waal et al. 2007). The variable *income* indicates respondents' total household income, after tax and compulsory deductions. It is measured in deciles of the actual household income range in the country in which the respondents reside. A higher score indicates a higher income level.

As previous research demonstrates that the unemployed (Houtman et al. 2008) and those dependent on welfare (Van der Waal et al. 2010) tend to favor economic redistribution, the analyses that follow will also control for respondents' *unemployment* and *welfare dependency*. For *unemployment* we have coded respondents who were unemployed and looking for a job at the time of the interview as "2" and those who were not as "1". For *welfare dependency* we have coded respondents not dependent on welfare as "1" and those who are welfare dependent as "2".

Finally, we include the control variables *female* (male = 1; female = 2), because women are generally more inclined to support welfare arrangements than men are, and *age* (in years), as the elderly are more inclined to such support than the young (Koster 2010).

Results

Before assessing whether Larsen's (2006) branch of institutional theory can account for different levels of welfare chauvinism in different welfare regimes, we have first explored the differences in welfare chauvinism between welfare regimes by calculating the share of the native population stating that immigrants should never get the same rights. The results are in accordance with our expectations: the percentage is 11.7 in liberal regimes, 9.3 in conservative ones and 3.6 in social-democratic regimes.

Of course, this merely provides a first indication. For assessing and explaining welfare regime differences in welfare chauvinism, ordered-logit multilevel analyses are needed, the results of which are displayed in Table 1. Because we can use only a limited number of countries, we will not introduce the explanatory variables all at once when testing our

Table 1. Multilevel ordered logit regression analyses with dependent variable welfare chauvinism of 9,381 natives in 10 European countries in 2008 (method: maximum likelihood, entries are ordered log-odds regression coefficients, standard errors in parentheses)

	Null model	Model 1	Model 2	Model 3	Model 4	Model 5	Model 6	Model 7	Model 8	Model 9	Model 10	Model 11	Model 12
Individual-level variables													
Education		−0.090***	−0.090***	−0.090***	−0.090***	−0.090***	−0.090***	−0.090***	−0.090***	−0.090***	−0.090***	−0.089***	−0.090***
		(0.006)	(0.006)	(0.006)	(0.006)	(0.006)	(0.006)	(0.006)	(0.006)	(0.006)	(0.006)	(0.006)	(0.006)
Income		−0.003	−0.002	−0.002	−0.003	−0.002	−0.002	−0.003	−0.002	−0.003	−0.002	−0.003	−0.002
		(0.009)	(0.009)	(0.009)	(0.009)	(0.009)	(0.009)	(0.009)	(0.009)	(0.009)	(0.009)	(0.009)	(0.009)
Unemployed		0.052	0.050	0.049	0.052	0.052	0.052	0.050	0.053	0.052	0.050	0.049	0.041
		(0.133)	(0.133)	(0.133)	(0.133)	(0.133)	(0.133)	(0.133)	(0.133)	(0.133)	(0.133)	(0.133)	(0.133)
Welfare dependent		0.199	0.201	0.202	0.199	0.199	0.202	0.195	0.202	0.199	0.203*	0.197	0.204*
		(0.102)	(0.102)	(0.102)	(0.102)	(0.102)	(0.102)	(0.102)	(0.102)	(0.102)	(0.102)	(0.102)	(0.102)
Female		−0.045	−0.045	−0.045	−0.045	−0.045	−0.045	−0.047	−0.045	−0.045	−0.045	−0.046	−0.044
		(0.042)	(0.042)	(0.042)	(0.042)	(0.042)	(0.042)	(0.042)	(0.042)	(0.042)	(0.042)	(0.042)	(0.042)
Age		0.002	0.002	0.002	0.002	0.002	0.002	0.002	0.002	0.002	0.002	0.002	0.002
		(0.001)	(0.001)	(0.001)	(0.001)	(0.001)	(0.001)	(0.001)	(0.001)	(0.001)	(0.001)	(0.001)	(0.001)
Country-level variables													
Liberal (ref.)													
Conservative			−0.535										
			(0.271)										
Social-democratic			−1.221**	−0.899**							−0.571	−0.274	−0.421
			(0.250)	(0.222)							(0.316)	(0.260)	(0.277)
Share non-western immigrants					−0.082								
					(0.077)								
Ethnic diversity immigrants						2.379							
						(4.645)							
Selectivity							0.083**				0.041		

(continued)

Table 1. (Continued)

	Null model	Model 1	Model 2	Model 3	Model 4	Model 5	Model 6	Model 7	Model 8	Model 9	Model 10	Model 11	Model 12
Inequality I (Gini)							(0.022)	0.122*** (0.020)			(0.030)	0.096* (0.031)	
Inequality II (80/20 ratio)									0.782*** (0.165)				0.519 (0.228)
Unemployment										0.127 (0.088)			
Strictness employment protection										−0.127 (0.155)			
Variance country level	0.300	0.320	0.084	0.118	0.287	0.312	0.133	0.066	0.095	0.255	0.099	0.059	0.076

Notes: * $p < 0.05$; ** $p < 0.01$; *** $p < 0.001$

hypotheses: the relevance of each explanatory dimension will be tested separately – we first determine whether the effect of a certain dimension is statistically significant, and if this is the case, we test whether it is responsible for differences in welfare chauvinism among welfare regimes. It should, however, be noted that the limited number of countries does not rule out multilevel modeling. As Gelman and Hill (2007: 275) observe in their authoritative work on the subject:

> Advice is sometimes given that multilevel models can only be used if the number of groups is higher than some threshold ... Such advice is misguided ... When sample sizes are small (...) it should still work at least as well as classical regression.

The null model shows that there is a significant multilevel structure in the data, and model 1 introduces the individual-level control variables. Controlling for this composition effect, model 2 demonstrates that the differing levels of welfare chauvinism across welfare regimes that were found above are less salient if individual-level socio-economic background characteristics are taken into account: natives in social-democratic welfare regimes are less welfare chauvinistic than natives in liberal welfare regimes, but those in conservative ones are not. Hence, strictly speaking, there are two instead of three worlds of welfare chauvinism, as shown in our adjusted baseline model (model 3), in which liberal and conservative regimes are combined into a single reference category, so as to minimize the number of country-level variables.

Before testing our hypotheses, we assess whether differences in ethnic heterogeneity can explain differences in welfare chauvinism. Models 4 and 5 indicate that this is not the case: neither of the two variables used to measure ethnic heterogeneity (share of non-western immigrants and ethnic diversity of immigrants) has a significant effect on welfare chauvinism, even though the latter's regime scores are in line with ethnic heterogeneity theory. This indicates that in testing our hypotheses, we will not find spurious effects caused by regime differences in ethnic heterogeneity.

Model 6 addresses our first hypothesis, which holds that differences in welfare chauvinism can be explained by differences in the selectivity of welfare regimes. Selectivity does, indeed, have a significant effect in the expected direction: in countries with the most selective welfare regimes, the native population is most welfare chauvinistic.

Models 7 and 8 both address our second hypothesis, which relates to the inequality dimension and states that differences in welfare chauvinism can be explained by differences in income inequality among welfare regimes. The analyses show that in countries that display more income inequality, measured with either the Gini coefficient or the 80/20 ratio, natives consider immigrants to be less entitled to welfare than in countries characterized by lower levels of income inequality.

Having established this, we turn to the part of the institutional theory of welfare attitudes that deals with the labor-market trajectory. On the basis of this theory, we expect that differences in welfare chauvinism can be explained by differences in unemployment levels (*hypothesis 3*) and by differences in the strictness of employment protection (*hypothesis 4*). Model 9, however, indicates that neither of those hypotheses stands the test: the effects of unemployment and strictness of employment protection are not significant. In countries with low levels of unemployment or unregulated employment relations, the native population does not consider immigrants more or less entitled to welfare than in countries with high levels of unemployment or more regulated employment relations.

In order to determine whether selectivity and inequality not only have an effect on welfare chauvinism, but are also responsible for the observed differences in welfare chauvinism between the social-democratic welfare regimes on the one hand and the liberal and conservative ones on the other, we have to conduct two additional analyses. The first one is depicted in model 10, where the regime dummy for the social-democratic welfare regimes and selectivity are entered simultaneously. Although the coefficient of the regime dummy in this model is no longer significant, this cannot be attributed to the low level of selectivity in the social-democratic regimes, as the coefficient of selectivity is not significant either.

The low levels of inequality in those regimes can, however, explain their low levels of welfare chauvinism. This is shown in model 11, where the effect of wage inequality, as measured by the Gini coefficient, takes over the effect of the social-democratic regime dummy that was found in our baseline model. Strictly speaking, the other measure of wage inequality, the 80/20 ratio, does not yield the same result as its coefficient is not significant at the 5 per cent level (model 12). It needs to be emphasized, however, that it is close to being so ($p = 0.057$). All in all, the last three models indicate that the lower levels of welfare chauvinism in social-democratic regimes as compared to liberal and conservative ones can be attributed to the low levels of income inequality in the former ones.

Conclusion and Discussion

Drawing on literature demonstrating that three worlds of welfare capitalism have resulted in three worlds of public support for the poor and the unemployed (Larsen 2006, 2008), we expected to find three worlds of welfare chauvinism. Strictly speaking, however, our analyses indicate that there are two, instead of three, worlds of welfare chauvinism: the native populations of liberal and conservative welfare regimes are more reluctant to entitle immigrants to welfare than those living under social-democratic regimes. This pattern is in line with the institutional theorizing on welfare attitudes. We therefore formulated hypotheses for testing whether a specific branch of institutional theory, developed by Larsen by combining insights from previous theorizing on the welfare state (most notably by Marshall 1950; Titmuss 1968, 1974; Van Oorschot 2000; Myles and Quadagno 2002), can account for it.

Not all hypotheses derived from this theory have been corroborated. First, we hypothesized that welfare regimes that are most selective, that is, regimes in which welfare services are "means-tested", result in high levels of welfare chauvinism. Our findings indeed point in that direction: high levels of selectivity yield high levels of welfare chauvinism. Contrary to our expectations this cannot, however, account for the low levels of welfare chauvinism in social-democratic regimes. This needs to be interpreted with care, as our analysis uses a rather crude measure of selectivity (cf. Gilbert 2009). Therefore, if suitable and more fine-grained data become available for countries that can be categorized according to Esping-Andersen's typology of welfare regimes, these should be used in order to test the robustness of these results.

Second, the different labor-market trajectories brought about by the different welfare regimes do not affect the level of welfare chauvinism at all. Neither the unemployment level nor the strictness of employment regulation has any impact on the degree to which native populations consider immigrants to be entitled to welfare benefits and services. These results suggest that differences in welfare chauvinism are not related to differences in (perceptions of) the extent to which immigrants are considered to be in need of welfare or to the extent to which they are considered to be in control of their own labor-market situation.

Things are different, however, when it comes to the inequality brought about by welfare regimes. Our analyses indicate that higher levels of income inequality go hand in hand with higher levels of welfare chauvinism. This suggests that less diverging lifestyles between the rich and the poor lead to more understanding towards (potential) immigrant welfare recipients among majority populations. Put differently, in more unequal societies the rich are more likely to consider minority groups deviant, and therefore less entitled to welfare. Importantly, this relationship between income inequality and welfare chauvinism can account for the different levels of welfare chauvinism between welfare regimes: the native populations in social-democratic welfare regimes consider immigrants most entitled to welfare because of the low levels of income inequality. Thus, one of the three regime dimensions around which the institutional theory of welfare attitudes under scrutiny revolves can explain the existence of two worlds of welfare chauvinism.

In addition, it needs to be noted that it is very unlikely that two dominant *non*-institutional theories on welfare attitudes can account for the existence of two worlds of welfare chauvinism. First, we have included two measures to control for the theory of ethnic heterogeneity (Alesina and Glaeser 2004), neither of which had any effect. This indicates that the level of welfare chauvinism does not differ among welfare regimes because of differences in levels of solidarity brought about by differences in ethnic heterogeneity.

Second, our findings indicate that "ethnic competition theory" (Olzak, 1992) – which suggests that welfare chauvinism is inspired by a desire to exclude ethnic outgroups in a competition over scarce welfare entitlements – is also an unlikely candidate for explaining regime differences in welfare chauvinism. The high levels of welfare chauvinism in regimes characterized by a higher level of income inequality might, at first sight, also be interpreted in accordance with this theory, as interethnic struggle for welfare entitlements is fiercer if there is a more pronounced economic underclass. Yet, national-level unemployment, which is a more valid indicator for testing ethnic competition theory as it measures the need for welfare assistance more directly, does not have a significant positive effect on welfare chauvinism. This suggests that differences in ethnic competition are not responsible for different levels of welfare chauvinism in different welfare regimes. This suggestion is substantiated by our control variables at the individual level: neither unemployment nor welfare dependency has any effect whatsoever, indicating that welfare chauvinism is not inspired by ethnic competition over scare welfare resources (cf. Van der Waal et al. 2010). In short, neither a cultural nor an economic non-institutional theory of welfare chauvinism seems to be able to provide an alternative explanation for the existence of two worlds of welfare chauvinism.

In addition to our findings, the explanatory value of the institutional theory on welfare attitudes addressed warrants further scrutiny for three reasons. As these go far beyond the scope of the present study, future research needs to bring additional insights. First, the formulation of the commonly used dependent variable is rather broad: it deals with social benefits and services without further specification. In line with institutional reasoning, it can be expected that the extent to which immigrants are considered entitled depends on the nature of the services and benefits involved. Therefore, future research could benefit from more fine-grained measures addressing various types of welfare services and benefits. Second, other policies might also affect the perceived entitlement of immigrants among the public at large. The two most salient ones for the question at hand seem to be multiculturalism policies, which are discussed by Banting and Kymlicka (2006), and immigration regimes (cf. Sainsbury 2006). Both affect the extent to and the way in which immigrants are institutionally incorporated and might therefore affect the welfare chauvinism of the native population. Third, in light of institutional theory and our findings, remarkable differences have occurred across social-democratic welfare regimes in recent years. Denmark practically installed a two-tier welfare system, in which immigrants have less access to welfare benefits and services than the native population, while Sweden and Norway did not. As Bay and colleagues (2013) demonstrated – in accordance with our findings – this occurred while the level of welfare chauvinism among the public at large hardly differs among those countries. They indicate that electoral competition, as well as agenda setting and mobilization by right-wing populist parties in Denmark, are key to understanding these differences across social-democratic regimes (Bay et al. 2013). Future research on the impact of institutions on welfare opinions could gain from this insight: welfare institutions that foster high levels of solidarity can go hand in hand with exclusive policies due to political processes.

All that said, we would like to conclude with discussing the relevance of our findings in the policy domain. Although we are not the first to demonstrate that institutions affect the welfare opinions of the people, the insight that institutions matter in this respect is highly salient for those who consider the existence of exclusionary sentiments as worrying in itself. We have demonstrated that egalitarian policies and institutions can help in fighting such sentiments. Our results indicate that strengthening policies and institutions aimed at reducing income inequality can be utilized for that cause.

Furthermore, inspired by Alesina and Glaeser (2006), it is often assumed that the ethnic heterogeneity stemming from immigration in Europe in recent decades undermines the solidarity that is needed for extensive welfare states. A combination of high levels of ethnic heterogeneity and high levels of solidarity is therefore deemed impossible. Our findings, however, indicate that such a "progressive dilemma" (Banting 2010), is by no means inevitable: our heterogeneity measures had no effect on welfare chauvinism whatsoever. This is a salient finding, because one might expect that if ethnic heterogeneity indeed hampered solidarity, the most likely type of solidarity to be negatively affected would be solidarity towards ethnic others, such as immigrants. Our analyses, however, indicate that this is not the case. High levels of ethnic heterogeneity and solidarity can therefore go hand in hand, which is a vital insight for academics and policymakers alike.

Acknowledgments

The authors would like to thank the three anonymous reviewers for their helpful and constructive comments and suggestions. In addition, they are grateful to Miriam Miller for carefully editing the manuscript. Jeroen van der Waal's contribution to this research has been enabled by a *Rubicon* grant from the Netherlands Organization for Scientific Research (NWO), grant number 446-10-002.

Notes

1. The concept is sometimes used differently. Crepaz and Damron (2009), for instance, label concerns over the potential detrimental effects of immigration on the welfare state and employment opportunities of natives as "welfare chauvinism". Note that this is not how welfare chauvinism is conceptualized here. The sentiments assessed by Crepaz and Damron are commonly denoted as (perceived) ethnic threat, ethnocentrism, or anti-immigrant attitudes.
2. See note 1.

3. While the Netherlands is considered an ambiguous welfare regime (cf. Goodin and Smitsman 2000), it should be noted that "in terms of welfare *state* structures and the living conditions of potentially poor, the country holds the most in common with the social democratic regimes" (Larsen 2007: 84, italics in original). In response to a query made by an anonymous reviewer, we have, however, also performed the analyses with the Netherlands categorized as a conservative regime. This also leads to a rejection of hypotheses 1, 3 and 4, and a corroboration of hypothesis 2. The corroboration of hypothesis 2 is even somewhat more convincing, as both inequality indicators can account for regime differences in welfare chauvinism in these analyses (available upon request).
4. Because Scruggs's instrument is rather crude, we also performed analyses with the selectivity measure available through *Social Citizenship Indicator Program* (SCIP) (Korpi and Palme 2008). This has been recommended by Larsen (2006: 73), who conducted his research when this data source was not yet available. There is, however, hardly any variance on this measure, and the regime scores are not in accordance with Larsen's theory. It therefore does not surprise that it does not affect welfare chauvinism at all (analyses available upon request).
5. For details, see: http://www.oecd.org/employment/protection (accessed September 30, 2010).
6. We thank Ferry Koster for generously sharing his calculations.
7. An anonymous reviewer asked whether our analyses allow disentangling welfare chauvinism and a more general preference for fewer social benefits and services for citizens (that is, regardless of whether a citizen is an immigrant or not). In order to control for the degree to which one desires social benefits and services in general, we have replicated our analyses while controlling for economic egalitarianism. This does not lead to meaningfully different results: again, hypothesis 2 is corroborated and hypotheses 1, 3 and 4 are rejected (analyses available upon request).

References

Alesina, A. and Glaeser, E. L., 2004, *Fighting Poverty in the US and Europe. a World of Difference* (Oxford: Oxford University Press).
Andersen, J. G. and Bjørklund, T., 1990, Structural changes and new cleavages: The progress parties in Denmark and Norway. *Acta Sociologica*, **33**(1), pp. 195–217.
Banting, K. G., 2010, Is there a progressive dilemma in Canada? Immigration, multiculturalism and the welfare state. *Canadian Journal of Political Science*, **43**(4), pp. 797–820.
Banting, K. and Kymlicka, W. (Eds), 2006, *Multiculturalism and the Welfare State. Recognition and Redistribution in Contemporary Democracies* (Oxford: Oxford University Press).
Bay, A. -H., Finseraas, H. and Pedersen, A., 2013, Welfare dualism in two scandinavian welfare states: Public opinion and party politics. *West European Politics*, **36**(1), pp. 199–220.
Crepaz, M. M. L. and Damron, R., 2009, Constructing tolerance: How the welfare state shapes attitudes about immigrants. *Comparative Political Studies*, **42**(3), pp. 437–463.
Dallinger, U., 2010, Public support for redistribution: What explains cross-national differences. *Journal of European Social Policy*, **20**(4), pp. 333–349.
De Koster, W., Achterberg, P. and Van der Waal, J., 2013, The new right and the welfare state: On the electoral relevance of welfare chauvinism and welfare populism in the Netherlands. *International Political Science Review*, **34**(1), pp. 3–20.
Emler, N. and Frazer, E., 1999, Politics: The education effect. *Oxford Review of Education*, **25**(1–2), pp. 251–273.
Esping-Andersen, G., 1990, *The Three Worlds of Welfare Capitalism* (Cambridge: Polity Press).
Esping-Andersen, G., 1996, *Welfare States in Transition. National Adaptation in Global Economies* (London: Sage Publications).
European Social Survey, 2008, *European Social Survey Round 4 Data, 2008*, Data file edition 3.0 (Norwegian Social Science Data Services, Norway - Data Archive and distributor of ESS data).
Eurostat., s.d.a, Income quintile share ratio (S80/S20). http://epp.eurostat.ec.europa.eu/tgm/table.do?tab=table&-init=1&language=en&pcode=tessi180&plugin=1 (accessed 15 February 2011).
Eurostat., s.d.b, Unemployment rate, annual average. http://appsso.eurostat.ec.europa.eu/nui/show.do?dataset=une_rt_a&lang=en (accessed 15 February 2011).
Gelman, A., and Hill, J., 2007, *Data Analysis Using Regression and Multilevel/Hierarchical Models* (Cambridge: Cambridge University Press).
Gilbert, N., 2009, The least generous welfare state? A case of blind empiricism. *Journal of Comparative Policy Analysis: Research and Practice*, **11**(3), pp. 355–367.

Goodin, R. E. and Smitsman, A., 2000, Placing welfare states: The Netherlands as a crucial test case. *Journal of Comparative Policy Analysis: Research and Practice*, **2**(1), pp. 39–64.

Houtman, D., Achterberg, P. and Derks, A., 2008, *Farewell to the Leftist Working Class* (New Brunswick, N.J: Transaction).

Jaeger, M. M., 2006, Welfare regimes and attitudes towards redistribution: The regime hypothesis revisited. *European Sociological Review*, **22**(2), pp. 157–170.

Jaeger, M. M., 2009, United but divided: Welfare regimes and the level and variance in public support for redistribution. *European Sociological Review*, **25**(6), pp. 723–737.

Korpi, W. and Palme, J., 2008, *The Social Citizenship Indicator Program (SCIP)* (Swedish Institute for Social Research, Stockholm University).

Koster, F., 2010, Welfare state attitudes and economic integration in the EU, 1992–2002. A multilevel investigation across 24 countries. *Policy & Politics*, **38**(2), pp. 179–195.

Larsen, C. A., 2006, *The Institutional Logic of Welfare Attitudes: How Welfare Regimes Influence Public Support* (Aldershot: Ashgate).

Larsen, C. A., 2007, How welfare regimes generate and erode social capital: The impact of underclass phenomena. *Comparative Politics*, **40**(1), pp. 83–101.

Larsen, C. A., 2008, The institutional logic of welfare attitudes: How welfare regimes influence public support. *Comparative Political Studies*, **41**(2), pp. 145–169.

Lindbeck, A. and Snower, D., 1988, *The Insider-Outsider Theory of Unemployment* (Cambridge, MA: MIT Press).

Manevska, K. and Achterberg, P., 2011, Immigration and perceived ethnic threat: Cultural capital and economic explanations. *European Sociological Review*, doi:10.1093/esr/jcr085.

March, J. G. and Olsen, J. P., 1996, Institutional perspectives on political institutions. *Governance*, **9**(3), pp. 247–264.

Marshall, T. H., 1950, *Citizenship and Social Class and Other Essays* (Cambridge: Cambridge University Press).

Mau, S. and Burkhardt, C., 2009, Migration and Welfare State Solidarity in Western Europe. *Journal of European Social Policy*, **19**(3), pp. 213–229.

Mewes, J. and Mau, S., 2012, Unraveling working-class welfare chauvinism, in: S. Svallfors (Ed) *Contested Welfare States: Welfare Attitudes in Europe and Beyond* (Stanford: Stanford University Press), pp. 119–157.

Myles, J. and Quadagno, J., 2002, Political theories of the welfare state. *Social Service Review*, **76**(1), pp. 34–57.

OECD, s.d. Calculating Summary Indicators of Employment Protection Strictness. http://www.oecd.org/dataoecd/24/40/42740190.pdf (accessed 30 September 2010).

Olzak, S., 1992, *The Dynamics of Ethnic Competition and Conflict* (Stanford: Stanford University Press).

Raveaud, G., 2007, The European Employment strategy: Towards more and better jobs?. *Journal of Common Market Studies*, **45**(2), pp. 411–434.

Raven, J., Achterberg, P., Van der Veen, R. and Yerkes, M., 2011, An institutional embeddedness of welfare opinions? The link between public opinion and social policy in the Netherlands (1970–2004). *Journal of Social Policy*, **40**(2), pp. 369–386.

Reeskens, T. and Van Oorschot, W., 2012, Disentangling the 'new liberal dilemma': On the relation between general welfare redistribution preferences and welfare chauvinism. *International Journal of Comparative Sociology*, **53**(2), pp. 120–139.

Rothstein, B., 1998, *Just Institutions Matter: The Moral and Political Logic of the Universal Welfare State* (Cambridge: Cambridge University Press).

Rothstein, B. and Stolle, D., 2008, The state and social capital: An institutional theory of generalized trust. *Comparative Politics*, **40**(4), pp. 441–459.

Sainsbury, D., 2006, Immigrants' social rights in comparative perspective: Welfare regimes, forms in immigration and immigration policy regimes. *Journal of European Social Policy*, **16**(3), pp. 229–244.

Schneider, S. L., 2008, Anti-immigrant attitudes in Europe: Outgroup size and perceived ethnic threat. *European Sociological Review*, **24**(1), pp. 53–67.

Scruggs, L., 2004, *Welfare State Entitlements Data Set: A Comparative Institutional Analysis of Eighteen Welfare States*, Version 1.2.

Titmuss, R. M., 1968, *Commitment to Welfare* (London: Allen and Unwin).

Titmuss, R. M., 1974, *Social Policy: An Introduction* (London: Allen and Unwin).

United Nations Development Program, 2007, *Human Development Report 2007/2008. Fighting Climate Change: Human Solidarity in a Divided World* (New York: Palgrave Macmillan).

Van Oorschot, W., 2000, Who should get what, and why? On deservingness criteria and the conditionality of solidarity among the public. *Policy & Politics*, **28**(1), pp. 33–48.

Van Oorschot, W., 2006, Making the difference in social Europe: Deservingness perceptions among citizens of European welfare states. *Journal of European Social Policy*, **16**(1), pp. 23–42.

Van der Waal, J., Achterberg, P. and Houtman, D., 2007, Class is not dead – it has been buried alive. Class voting and cultural voting in postwar western societies (1956–1990). *Politics & Society*, **35**(3), pp. 403–426.

Van der Waal, J., Achterberg, P., Houtman, D., De Koster, W. and Manevska, K., 2010, "Some are more equal than others." Economic egalitarianism and welfare chauvinism in the netherlands. *Journal of European Social Policy*, **20**(4), pp. 350–363.

Public Funding, Private Delivery: States, Markets, and Early Childhood Education and Care in Liberal Welfare States – A Comparison of Australia, the UK, Quebec, and New Zealand

LINDA A. WHITE & MARTHA FRIENDLY

ABSTRACT *Early childhood education and care (ECEC) spending and enrollment levels have increased in a number of liberal welfare states over the past two decades as part of a social investment strategy aimed at delivering long term economic and human capital benefits. Comparative evidence from social investment experiences in Australia, the UK, Quebec, and New Zealand suggests, however, that governments have made choices about financing and delivery of services that do not match these human capital development goals. Generally high quality ECEC services that would yield those expected human capital benefits have not developed because of the kinds of investments that are being made - particularly government reliance on private providers without strong regulatory regimes capable of ensuring high quality services. The article demonstrates that public investment in ECEC programs requires much greater consideration of the relationship between public finance, public regulation or "governance", and program delivery mechanisms.*

Introduction

Governments in many countries have come to view early childhood education and care (ECEC) as a partial solution to multiple issues including school readiness, child poverty, income and gender inequality, women's labor market participation, and population decline (Michel and Mahon 2002; Scheiwe and Willekens 2009). In response, most Organisation for Economic Co-operation and Development (OECD) countries have expanded ECEC programs over the past two decades. Although public ECEC spending and enrollment levels have increased significantly in most OECD countries, there is considerable variation in the amount of financing, and whether funding has been directed to childcare, kindergarten, or more blended programs (OECD Family 2011, PF 10.1; PF 3.2.A). Although it is nowhere near the public spending levels of Nordic states or continental Europe, ECEC spending has increased in what are called liberal welfare states (Esping-Andersen 1990; O'Connor et al. 1999) – Australia, New Zealand, the UK, the USA, and Canada's province of Quebec, where public ECEC spending almost reaches the OECD average.

While rationales for ECEC programs in social democratic and continental European welfare regimes are shaped at least partly by considerations of children's rights, women's equality, and social inclusion, liberal welfare states' conceptions of "early learning" tend to treat it as social investment aimed at economic returns and human capital benefits (Prentice 2009). Justification for ECEC investment in these states frequently links ECEC to brain development and neuroscience (Lindsey 1998), social dimensions of child and family well-being (Keating and Hertzman 1999), and ultimately to economic cost–benefit analyses that demonstrate the positive economic impacts of investment in the early years on children and on parental employment (Baker et al. 2008; Carneiro and Heckman 2003; Lefebvre et al. 2009; Temple and Reynolds 2007). Liberal ECEC policy rationales tend to be shaped by expectations of long term gains based on results from (mainly) US studies such as the Perry Preschool Project (Schweinhart et al. 2005; Heckman et al. 2010) and mostly focused on vulnerable children (Karoly and Bigelow 2005). It is therefore worth exploring – after two decades of enhanced social investment – the results of this public spending. While it may be premature to determine definitively whether long term educational and anti-poverty goals can be realized, there is generally good agreement with Mitchell et al.'s (2008: 7) review of this research that

> Good quality ECE has greater benefits for children from low socioeconomic families, but children from middle and high socioeconomic families also gain... Most of the economic evaluations of ECE programs have shown that benefits of public spending exceed the costs. Gains are not realized or not as great if the ECE is of poor quality.

A key policy question about the social investments made in liberal welfare states becomes: are high quality ECEC services emerging in liberal welfare states? Based on evidence from Australia, the UK, Quebec, and New Zealand, this paper argues that the choices governments have made about financing and delivery of services are not yielding the intended results. From this perspective, it is worth scrutinizing the characteristics of the policy infrastructure put in place to achieve the desired goals.

Through comparative case analysis, we document that high quality ECEC services have generally not developed due to the nature of the policy choices being made, particularly government reliance on market models and private providers without regulatory regimes capable of ensuring high quality. We argue that public investment in ECEC requires much greater consideration of the relationship between public finance, public regulation and ownership or "governance", and program delivery mechanisms.

The article first discusses ECEC in mixed economies, that is, in market economies containing some elements of public financing and delivery and some regulatory oversight. Mixed economies largely rely on demand-side funding mechanisms and private delivery. The article reflects on the components of public investment strategies capable of ensuring achievement of policy goals, and then explores the Swedish model whereby a mixed public/private delivery system evolved into a predominantly public system through public management. The article goes on to explore the disjuncture between stated goals and ECEC program outcomes observed in Australia, the UK, Quebec, and New Zealand. The final section discusses alternative pathways to "becoming Sweden" in liberal welfare states.

Public Finance and Private Delivery in Twenty-First Century Welfare States

Delegating responsibility for delivery of public programs and services to non-state actors is an increasing trend in twenty-first century liberal welfare states, affecting programs from health care to prisons to military services (Campbell and Morgan 2011; Freeman and Minow 2009; Gingrich 2011). It is not surprising to see liberal welfare states choosing similar policy instruments for ECEC. However, as other policy areas' literature demonstrates, delegation of responsibility to non-state actors to achieve public policy goals raises fundamental questions about how well these delegated agents can deliver on public goals and values. If government's goal is high quality early education, how can it be ensured that programs are indeed educational? Who are appropriate delivery agents to ensure conveyance of democratic goals and values – Schools? For-profit operators? Home-based providers? Non-profits? If government is not the delivery agent, how can standards to ensure high quality be set and monitored?

Tracking shifts in *how much* public financing is thus only a first step in determining whether significant ECEC program shifts have occurred. Researchers must also consider other elements – how public funds are delivered, who delivers programs, and features of regulatory regimes, as these factors are associated with program quality (Sosinsky et al. 2007). If there are suboptimal policy outcomes, fundamental questions should be asked about how public dollars are being spent.

Some analysts in other policy areas argue that there are some advantages to using private delivery agents for public goods and services (Donahue and Zeckhauser 2011). In early childhood, some argue that markets introduce competition between government and private delivery agents, leading to "leveling up" service provision (Levin and Schwartz 2007). These proponents of market-based social service delivery also argue that markets deliver "freedom of choice" and "productive efficiency", although Levin and Schwartz (2007) concede that public funding is needed to ensure fairness in distribution of access to services, and regulation to ensure that private providers meet quality standards.

Research in early childhood has generally found that good and bad quality services can be found in all early childhood sectors (Helburn 1995) but that for-profit services are significantly more likely to be poorer quality, while public and not-for-profit services are more likely to be higher quality (e.g. Morris and Helburn 2000; for a review, see Cleveland and Krashinsky 2009). And indeed, much of the childcare found in largely market-based systems, such as in the United States, has been found to be of poor quality. Researchers (e.g. Morris, 1999; Sosinsky et al., 2007) argue that the dismal quality of childcare in the United States is a result of failure by these largely market-based providers to deliver high quality care.

The problem, as Deber (2002: v) points out in observing health care management and delivery, is that private providers can include a vast range of actors: "not-for-profit (NFP) or for-profit (FP); in turn, for-profit includes a range from small businesses... to corporate organizations which are expected to provide returns on investment to their shareholders". Deber argues that using a range of private agents could improve service delivery and benefit the system but "the desirability of encouraging FP delivery depends on how such firms make their profits". Deber notes that for-profit services could encourage economies of scale and better management but that "savings frequently arise from more contentious measures, including freedom from labour agreements (and different wage levels and skill mixes), evasion of cost controls placed on other providers, sacrifice of difficult-to-measure intangibles... [and] cream skimming" (Deber 2002: v).

The market can further fail to deliver on the promise of social service "products" because clustering services into certain neighborhoods means inefficient delivery. Government funding can fuel these inefficiencies because market agents do not need to compete to deliver the best quality services and parent fee increases can be paid for by increases in government funding. Thus, public funding without an adequate regulatory regime to contain fees and ensure standards can lead to poor program outcomes. Government regulation to promote quality within a market system can diminish the supply of services and add to costs (Gormley 1999; Rigby et al. 2007) and research also demonstrates that parents are poor judges of quality (Zellman et al. 2008). Furthermore, even if they do recognize the care is of poor quality, high fees and limited options often prevent them from accessing higher quality providers (Cleveland and Krashinsky 2009).

Thus, in the absence of public operation of services whereby governments are responsible for service delivery, human resources, and regulation of fees, good governance suggests the need for strong public management. At the least, this requires a strong regulatory regime that imposes conditions such as fees charged, determines whether services are delivered on a for-profit or not-for-profit basis, sets high quality standards including professional standards and decent wages for educators, and monitors to ensure compliance with standards. That has not been the experience in a number of countries, as will be explored below, but it has been the experience in Sweden.

The Swedish Approach to ECEC

Sweden and other social democratic welfare states have not been devoid of markets in ECEC. When Sweden first began to guarantee ECEC for children up to school age in the mid-1970s, municipalities were responsible for ensuring access but the national government was neutral with regard to ownership. The major expansion in the 1970s and 1980s occurred primarily through expansion of municipal centers, created using start-up and operating grants from the national government and financed through a special levy on employers (Martin Korpi 2007: 34). Initially, preschools were targeted to children in need of "special support", leaving many parents to rely on forms of unregulated childcare. Unregulated family daycare providers, however, disappeared as they became "employed by the municipality, got training, received salaries, [and] paid taxes"; that is, as the public system expanded, private arrangements shrank so that by 1970 "almost all pre-schooling – 96 per cent – was municipal" (Martin Korpi 2007: 44) (see also Lenz Taguchi and Munkammar 2003).

Significantly, preschool expansion was subject to planning. Martin Korpi (2007: 6) notes, "the question of where daycare centers should be located, at the workplace or in housing areas, was decided by the Commission on nursery provision". The expansion was supported by stable, expanding funding: the national government and municipalities each contributed about 45 per cent of operating costs, with parent fees covering the remaining 10 per cent. Funding was based on quality-related requirements: "pedagogically trained staff, nutritional food, area per child, maximum number of children in groups and opening hours" (Martin Korpi 2007: 37).

In the 1980s, private centers such as employer-provided programs reemerged but operated on a cooperative basis to be eligible for government grants. They also were subject to municipal plans, fees could not exceed those charged by municipalities, and they had to accept children from municipal waiting lists (Martin Korpi 2007: 44). A center-right government (1991) introduced legislation to allow government funding to profit-making providers but a social democratic government returned to power (1995) and revoked the legislation so while private provision is possible, it is subject to regulation, including fee ceilings (Martin Korpi 2007: 53). Municipalities retain control over planning and can refuse permits to private providers.

Despite these restrictions, non-government provision has increased. Naumann (2011: 8) reports that non-government facilities increased from 500 in 1988 to 3,112 in 2002. In 2009 19 per cent of children enrolled in preschools attended non-government preschools – 43 per cent operated by private companies and 25 per cent by parent cooperatives (Skolverket 2010: 10). But this has not meant the government has abandoned governance. Approximately 82 per cent of children aged one to five now attend some form of preschool childcare in Sweden (Skolverket 2010: 9). Legislation from 2002 entitled all children over the age of three to 525 hours per year of preschool free of charge. This legislation also set a voluntary cap on fees charged to parents by municipalities (a formula based on 3 per cent of gross income for one child), with grants provided to municipalities to compensate for lower fees from implementing the cap (Skolverket 2004). In this way, the national government ensures low fees to parents but not at the expense of program quality.

The governance of ECEC services has also become much more integrated in Sweden. In 1996, Sweden moved ECEC for all ages to the Ministry of Education and Science from the Ministry of Health and Social Affairs (Lenz Taguchi and Munkammar 2003: 9; Skolverket 2004: 6). As part of this consolidation, the national government passed the Schools Act that includes a mandatory preschool curriculum framework (binding for all service providers) and minimum requirements regarding class size, child–staff ratios, and staff training (Skolverket 2004: 6).

In sum, Swedish preschool services are planned and primarily publicly funded and delivered. While priority is given to families in "special circumstances", the expectation is that services will be available to all. Regulations encourage the expansion of public agents to deliver the services at low cost to parents while encouraging programs of very high quality, with well-trained, well-remunerated staff.

ECEC Quality and Investment Choices in Liberal Welfare States

The Swedish national government expressly declared that the 1998 reforms were designed to achieve the goal of improving lifelong learning for children (Skolverket 2004: 7). Although Swedish ideas about the meaning of lifelong learning are quite different from those in liberal welfare states (Bennett 2005), governments in liberal welfare states have also expressed a desire to implement programs that will improve "human capital" and child development outcomes. Regardless of a government's conception of lifelong learning, the early child development goals that are embedded in most ECEC policies suggest that given the research on the importance of quality – concern about quality should be paramount.

A UNICEF Innocenti Research Centre report (2008) developed ten quantifiable benchmarks of ECEC quality and accessibility. These include: one year parental leave at 50 per cent of salary and a period of time exclusively for fathers; a national ECEC plan with priority for disadvantaged children; funded and regulated childcare services for 25 per cent of children under the age of three; subsidized and accredited early education services for 80 per cent of four-year-olds; 80 per cent of all childcare staff to have ECE training; 50 per cent of staff in accredited early education services have relevant tertiary education; minimum staff–child ratios of 1:15 in early education; 1.0 per cent of GDP spent on ECEC services for children aged zero to five; a child poverty rate of less than 10 per cent; and near-universal outreach of essential child health services (UNICEF 2008: 2).

The liberal welfare states scored at the bottom of the 25 OECD countries included, save New Zealand and the UK, which scored in the middle range. The Nordic states and France scored highest, with Sweden meeting all 10 benchmarks (UNICEF 2008: 2). Thus, despite their human capital and child development goals, liberal welfare states perform poorly on these quality and access benchmarks.

The question is why liberal welfare states are poor or – at best – mediocre performers on these benchmarks. We argue that three critical factors affect the achievement of quality and accessibility: funding levels; funding approaches (i.e. supply or demand side); and program delivery agents. The next sections draw on the approaches of Australia, the UK, Quebec, and New Zealand to explore the relationship between funding and service delivery. In each case, we observe substantial increases in public financing, private delivery, and, at best, modest public oversight and limited public management (there is, of course, some variation). The cases provide preliminary evidence of the impact policy choices have on whether ECEC programs can achieve quality and access goals.

Australia

Australia has witnessed the most dramatic shift among liberal welfare states in ECEC service delivery agents over the past 20 years. Private for-profit and community-based childcare and philanthropic preschools existed for many decades prior to state and federal (Commonwealth) involvement in funding and provision (Brennan 1998). In the 1950s and 1960s, in response to increased maternal employment, childcare provision for working mothers expanded, with provision varying by state. By the late 1960s, the federal government became increasingly involved in areas of state responsibility, establishing a Commonwealth Department of Education in 1966 (Brennan 1998: 58). The Commonwealth government began to fund childcare services directly in the early 1970s with the 1972 passage of the Commonwealth Childcare Act. It accepted the advice of experts such as the Australian Pre-school Association that "good quality, developmentally appropriate care (as distinct from custodial child-minding) was best provided in childcare centres under the auspices of non-profit organizations" rather than by governments (Brennan 2007: 214). The Act permitted the Commonwealth government to enter into shared-cost arrangements with state and local governments to provide financial assistance to community-based non-profit childcare centers if they met standards (Baker and Tippin 1999; Brennan 2007).

By the late 1980s, however, the Labor Commonwealth government began to move away from a primarily non-profit provision model. To expand childcare supply, in 1988 the government agreed to offer tax deductions to private childcare (Baker and Tippin 1999) and in 1991 extended parent subsidies to for-profit centers (Press and Hayes 2000). Supporters of "marketization" argued that childcare would be delivered more "efficiently" and at lower cost, particularly if non-union labor was used. Providers would also have a financial incentive to expand supply (Brennan 2007). A competitive market in childcare services, they argued, would encourage diversity of provision if less planning were involved. Thus, the government did not subject for-profit providers to any kind of planning restrictions, simply requiring that services be licensed and registered with the relevant state or territorial authority and with the Commonwealth government's new accreditation system covering both for-profit and non-profit services (Brennan 2007).

Wincott (2011: 160) notes that public subsidization of private childcare led to a "budget blowout", with private centers springing up, disproportionately "in desirable retirement locations... not in the poor outer suburbs or other areas where demand was high". The increased domination of corporate for-profit operations, intended to increase "diversity of provision" and "choice", ironically led to a more restrictive situation with ever-escalating fees. The situation was exacerbated by new, linked corporate entities that developed and owned childcare facilities, leased to corporate providers at high prices (Sumsion 2006; Brennan 2007; Press and Woodrow 2009). The high prices created a gap between fees and parent subsidies, pressuring governments to increase subsidies. In 2000, in response to high fees, the Commonwealth government created the Childcare Benefit (CCB) to provide parent subsidies based on income, number of children, and type of care. The regular infusion of government funding made childcare a very lucrative business. In 2001, ABC Learning Centers became the largest provider of childcare in Australia, listed on the stock exchange. As they expanded operations, corporate providers bought up independent for-profit and non-profit operators as well as other corporate providers, reducing choice in childcare across Australia (Brennan 2007).

In response to the increasingly high fees, the Commonwealth government introduced a Childcare Tax Rebate (CCTR) program in 2004. The CCTR provided a tax offset of 30 per cent of out-of-pocket childcare expenses (minus the CCB) to a maximum of AU$4,354 (Brennan 2007: 222). The Labor government elected in 2007 increased the CCTR to 50 per cent of out-of-pocket expenses to a cap of AU$7,500 (Gillard 2008). Unlike the CCB, which delivers the biggest benefits to lower-income families, the CCTR provides the biggest tax benefits to parents who pay the most for childcare (Brennan 2007). The program does nothing to encourage reduction of fees; in fact, it dilutes parental concerns about high fees while allowing providers to continue charge them.

Australia's childcare standards have been considered to be quite low. American early childhood expert Ron Lally noted that "one day we will look back in horror at standards such as New South Wales (state) staff:child ratios of 1:5 for infants" (Horin 2007). Governments were under pressure from for-profit operators not to strengthen regulations or make quality improvements as this would create barriers to profits (Brennan 2007: 220). The OECD (2006: 272) concluded that "despite state regulation and national monitoring... the low pay, low status and training levels of ECEC staff undermine quality". Brennan (2007) notes that corporate childcare businesses actively resisted introduction of government-subsidized paid maternity and parental leave given that such programs would provide competition for children, who often are in childcare centers at a very young age in Australia.

Thus, while the Commonwealth government substantially increased funding for childcare, government support to for-profit childcare led to much more expensive childcare and pressure on government to increase funding to offset high fees. The dominant presence of powerful childcare corporations led to increased uniformity of provision, downward pressure on regulations, gaps in service delivery in particular geographic areas and service types, and limited knowledge about quality as corporate operators did not allow researchers to study their centers, claiming such knowledge as "proprietary business secrets" (Brennan 2007; see also Press and Woodrow 2009). Federal funding also did not lead to consistency of provision across states and territories (Australian Senate 2009: 8).

The national government's focus on childcare may also explain the lack of effort to develop more full-time preschool services for younger children. Preschools, or "kindys", largely the responsibility of state/territorial governments, operate mostly for a full school day (5–6 hours per day) during the school year one year before primary school, and part-day two years before primary school (Press and Hayes 2000). There is huge variation in the provision of these services across states/ territories. For example, they are provided free-of-charge in some parts of the country, and are publicly delivered either with direct funding of services or fee subsidies to families; in other parts of the country fees are charged, depending on the service provider (SCRGSP 2008). They are delivered in a variety of settings including schools, stand-alone programs, childcare centers, and so on (Press and Hayes 2000).

Preschool attendance is increasing in popularity. All jurisdictions save Victoria State allow selected children to begin preschool before age four (aboriginal, or English as a second language), although the rate of participation two years before primary school is much lower (17 per cent) than participation one year before primary school (84 per cent) (OECD 2006: 269; SCRGSP 2008: 3.7). In its 2007 election platform the Australian Labor Party (2007: 1) committed to "ensure every four year old child has access to fifteen hours a week and 40 weeks a year of high quality preschool delivered by a qualified early childhood teacher", a promise that state governments committed to as well in 2008 (Dowling and O'Malley, 2009). The high proportion of four-year-olds attending preschool and the universal attendance of five-year-olds in primary school, along with the commitment to fund 15 hours per week of early learning, will probably encourage the expansion of these services. However, the government's agnosticism regarding the site of service delivery – the 2007 Labor Party platform (p. 9) commits the government to funding delivery via preschools, kindergartens, and public, private, and community-based childcare providers – and continued willingness to provide tax rebates to both for-profit and not-for-profit services most likely means the market for lower quality for-profit services will continue to expand.

The United Kingdom

Societal attitudes toward public provision of childcare in the UK mimicked those in other liberal welfare states throughout the twentieth century, although support for preschool education was stronger, even amongst Conservative party members. That support culminated in the passage of a nursery voucher scheme under John Major in his party's final term of office (Wincott 2011: 161). Under the Labour Prime Minister Tony Blair, the UK arguably experienced the most dramatic increases in ECEC investment amongst liberal welfare states in recent decades (Moss 2006b). Beginning with the 1998 National Childcare Strategy, and expanded in *Choice for Parents, the Best Start for Children,* the government committed to developing universal childcare so "all families with children aged up to 14 who need it" can have access to "an affordable, flexible, high quality childcare place that meets their circumstances" (HM Treasury 2004: 1). They also committed to a universal part-day preschool entitlement for three- and four-year-olds; a national curriculum that applies to any organization delivering early years education; new national standards with national monitoring; a large-scale Sure Start program for disadvantaged children including development of integrated all-purpose children's centers in every locality; and expanded maternity/parental leave (Moss 2006a). The National Childcare Strategy had several components: first, it moved all early childhood services under education; second, it established the Childcare Tax Credit (later the Working Tax Credit); and third, it provided a grant system for ECEC services. That these multiple components emerged from different government departments did not lend itself to a coherent policy design (Wincott 2011). (Scotland and Wales have developed their own ECEC systems (Wincott 2005; see also Cohen et al. 2004) so the discussion that follows focuses on England alone.)

The changes were intended, as Ball and Vincent (2005) describe, to combat child and family poverty, encourage low-income and single parents into the workforce, and address poor educational performance nationally (Cohen et al. 2004; Penn, 2007). The New Labour government, however, encouraged the development of these services predominantly through the already private childcare market (Melhuish and Moss 1992). The 1998 National Childcare Strategy (DfEE 1998: para. 1.26) stated that the government's goal was to "ensure quality affordable childcare for children aged zero to fourteen years in every neighbourhood, including both formal childcare and support for informal arrangements".

The government tackled the problem of affordability through a subsidy to parents. It introduced a Childcare Tax Credit (CTC) for low- and middle-income working families to cover a portion of childcare costs (DfEE 1998: para. 3.4), and then replaced the CTC in 2003 with the childcare element of the Working Tax Credit (WTC) (Cohen et al. 2004: 59). The WTC provides a tax credit to low-income families working a minimum of 16 hours/week; the amount varies by household income, hours worked, and number of children (Vincent et al. 2008: 23). WTC-eligible families who use registered or approved childcare are entitled to government funding for up to 70 per cent of childcare costs to a maximum reimbursement of £122.50/week for one child, £210/week for two children (HM Treasury 2004: para. 3.4 and boxes 3.1, 3.2; Vincent et al. 2008: 23). It can be used for both for-profit and non-profit services so long as the provider is registered, works toward government's learning goals, and permits the Office of Standards in Education (Ofsted) to inspect them (OECD 2006: 420).

In 1998, the government set up the third component of the National Childcare Strategy, a grant system for all ECEC services (the Nursery Education Grant) (Lewis 2003: 224). This covered not just schools but also playgroups, childcare centers, and child-minding services (Cohen et al. 2004: 67). It covers part-time provision in programs (12 hours per week over three 11-week terms) that work towards the early learning goals outlined in the document *Curriculum Guidance for the Foundation Stage* (2000), which became statutory in 2002 (Cohen et al. 2004: 68; Moss 2006a: 77). The government also established the New Opportunities Fund consisting of lottery-generated money to develop before- and after-school care, and integrated ECEC programs (Cohen et al. 2004: 114). The National Childcare Strategy also required local Early Years Development and Childcare Partnerships, made up of a variety of public, private, and community-based agencies to scrutinize childcare needs and draw up plans (Randall 2004). The government has also engaged in "pump priming" spending to encourage businesses to start up childcare centers (Cohen et al. 2004).

The result of these two policy choices with regard to funding – parental subsidies for almost all varieties of care, and grants for multiple forms of ECEC programs – encouraged the development of a largely private, corporatized childcare market. The UK currently has the highest percentage of private for-profit providers in Europe, where 97 per cent of services for children under the age of three are through private providers, and 40 per cent of services to children ages three to five (Gaunt 2011). Further encouraging this childcare market growth was the Blair government's guarantee of a *universal* part-time early education program for four-year-olds in 1998 (DfEE 1998: para. ES 9, 12), with a commitment to expand entitlement to three-year-olds as well (para. 4.0). The government expanded this in 2004 and further guaranteed an out-of-school place for all children to age 14 by 2010 (HM Treasury 2004: 1; OECD 2006: 415, 418). Given the commitment to a guarantee of hours, it became crucial to expand services, so the government decided that early education programs could be delivered through a variety of settings, not just schools, but also through private non-profit and for-profit providers (HM Treasury 2004: para. 3.5). By 2005, "35 per cent of three and four-year-olds attending early years education were enrolled in other non-school settings such as playgroups in the private and voluntary sectors, either instead of, or in addition to, their school place"

(UK Office for National Statistics, 2007, figure 3.1; appendix 3). By 2011, despite near universal attendance of three- and four-year-olds in some kind of early education program, approximately 44 per cent attended programs provided by private and voluntary providers or independent schools (DfE 2011).

True, the national government regulates private early education services. In addition to a national curriculum, in 2001 the government established national standards of care for children under the age of eight, transferring regulatory authority from local authorities to the Office of Standards in Education (Ofsted) (HM Treasury 2004: para. 3.27) and moved children's services, including childcare and early childhood education, into the Department of Education and Employment (Moss 2006b: 165). However, researchers and government agencies tracking childcare quality have found variation in quality between private for-profit, voluntary, and public sector providers. Notwithstanding Ofsted's rating of almost all ECEC services as at least "satisfactory" (HM Treasury 2004: para. 3.29), "around 30 per cent of staff in day nurseries were unqualified and the staff turnover rate is around 20 per cent" (HM Treasury 2004: para. 3.34) in a sector dominated by for-profit centers. The 2008 Ofsted report of 90,000 inspection visits to 84,000 providers (childcare, out-of-school clubs, and child-minders) over the previous three-year period found that only 57 per cent of providers were rated as good and only 3 per cent as outstanding, with huge variation in quality across the country (Ofsted 2008: 7, 11) and between public and private providers. Penn (2007: 198) notes, though, that "none of the major surveys of childcare commissioned by the Government, or undertaken by independent organisations, has focused on the differences (if any) between for-profit and non-profit care" with the exception of one small qualitative study. Mathers et al. (2007) and Mathers and Sylva (2007) used different data sets to examine the quality of provision across all settings (private for-profit, private voluntary, and "maintained" by local education authorities (public). They concluded that "the maintained settings were providing the highest quality provision overall, particularly with regard to the 'learning' aspects of provision" but the voluntary providers had made significant improvements in quality of provision (Mathers et al. 2007: 6). Thus, while the UK government rhetoric emphasizes quality, cost, and accessibility in ECEC service delivery (DfEE 1998: ES6; HM Treasury 2004: introduction), the reality appears to fall short, at least in the for-profit sector.

Penn (2007: 199) documents the trend towards the growing corporate dominance of the UK's childcare market which has grown from a negligible share in service delivery in 1997 to the largest share in 2006: 41 per cent of providers in the £3.5 billion nursery market were private, for-profit companies, 37 per cent were private, for-profit sole traders or partnerships, 11 per cent private, not-for-profit providers, and only 11 per cent were public local authorities. Penn (2007) notes that while wages for staff are kept low as a means to cut delivery costs, fees in for-profit sector services are high. Although fees are higher in wealthier areas, lower-income families often cannot access services due to unaffordable fees, leaving centers not fully subscribed. In a market model, "A minimum of 80% occupancy rates is necessary for financial viability. As a result there has been considerable turnover of providers and abrupt closure of nurseries, often without adequate notice or compensation to staff (Penn 2007: 201). This market instability has led private providers to lobby for decreased regulation, less competition in service delivery with state and independent market providers, and more government subsidies (ibid.). Penn (2011) also reports that the global recession beginning in 2008 had an additional destabilizing effect on services, with fluctuation in ownership among some big corporations. Indeed, the UK's largest childcare corporation, Busy Bees (once owned by Australia's ABC Learning Centers) is now owned by US-based Knowledge Universe, the world's largest education business (Gaunt 2009). None of this bodes well for a stable, high quality ECEC market.

Quebec

Canada's province of Quebec is by some accounts an exception to liberal welfare state policies (Albanese 2011). It is – in some ways – an outlier amongst Canada's ten provinces and three territories in that it provides substantially more funding for childcare than the rest of Canada (Beach et al. 2009). In 1997, the Quebec government announced a number of family policy measures as part of the government's "fight against poverty, [and to support] equal opportunity, the development of the social market economy, transition from welfare to the workforce and increased support to working parents" (Premier Lucien Bouchard, 23 January 1997, quoted in Tougas 2002). A first step was to expand from part-day to full-day kindergarten for all five-year-olds (Beach et al. 2009) and, at the same time, to introduce substantial funding directly to childcare programs for children aged 0–4 years, and school-age programs for 5–12-year-olds. This was coupled with a flat parent fee of $5/day CAD in childcare centers and regulated family childcare (increased to $7/day in 2003 by the provincial Liberal government that followed) and capital funding to encourage expansion of non-profit *Centres de la petite enfance* (CPEs) (small local networks of center-based and family daycare) (ibid.).

The Quebec government's decision to fund full-day kindergarten only for children aged five and to provide fixed-fee childcare for all children up to the age of four (regardless of maternal labor force participation) went against the trend in most other liberal welfare states to fund early childhood education (kindergarten) rather than childcare. This choice was similar to the policy choices made in Australia, which also had clear labor market goals. Unlike Australia, however, the Quebec government from the beginning explicitly labeled its programs "educational childcare" (Ministère de la Famille et de l'Enfance 1997; Ministère de la Famille et des Aînés 2007) and it clearly had educational goals in the initial creation of its policy (Jenson 2009), whereas the Australian Commonwealth government began to emphasize educational childcare only after the election of the Labor government in 2007 (Australian Labor Party 2007). Lack of strong governance or regulation, however, has yielded childcare of mixed quality, as research by Japel et al. (2005) shows. Programs for 0–4-year-olds are privately delivered by a range of providers; the initial program expansion relied heavily on regulated family childcare, while in the last five years or so there has been substantial growth in for-profit centers, including chains, which were relatively unknown in Quebec before the expansion (Beach et al. 2009).

A number of studies of childcare quality have been conducted in Quebec since the 1997 policy change. The Quebec government commissioned its own quality study in 2003 (Drouin et al. 2004), which found the quality of care being delivered in for-profit childcare settings to be lower than in not-for-profit settings. Japel et al. (2005: 6) found in its detailed analysis that while the majority of settings "meet the basic criteria for quality – that is, they ensure the children's health and safety... their educational component is minimal. Almost one setting in eight fails to meet the minimum standards". Baker et al.'s (2008) cohort study also raises concerns about the impact of the quality of childcare settings in Quebec.

When the provincial Parti Quebecois (PQ) government initially introduced the $5-per-day childcare program, it intended to expand non-profit centers and family childcare homes, while phasing out for-profit providers. Push-back from for-profit operators, however, led to the PQ government lifting the moratorium on for-profit providers in 2002 to expand supply (Jenson 2009: 58). The Liberal government continued to allow, and then to encourage, the expansion of for-profits once elected in 2003. While the percentage of non-profit childcare in Quebec remains high compared to some other provinces/territories (86 per cent compared to the Canadian average of 75 per cent (Beach et al. 2009: 184)), for-profit childcare continues to grow disproportionately (ibid.).

New Zealand

New Zealand at first glance seems to provide a mixed economy model that strives to ensure delivery of high quality early years services in the absence of a commitment to an essentially public delivery model such as Sweden's. New Zealand became an early leader in integrating ECEC in 1986 when the government moved all early childhood services, including childcare, from the Ministries of Education, Social Welfare, and Maori Affairs into a single department – the Ministry of Education (Meade and Podmore 2002: 7). That move occurred more than ten years before countries such as Sweden and the UK made their changes (Cohen et al. 2004). Then, in 1988, the government introduced an early childhood training program in teachers' colleges for both kindergarten and childcare staff, portending a number of other changes that were outlined in the government's *Education to be More* (New Zealand Department of Education, 1988) and *Before Five* (Lange, 1988) reports. These documents advocated improving educational standards in childcare centers. In 1989 the government established a Teacher Registration Board for ECEC teachers and by 1994 head teachers and directors of nearly all early childhood services were required to have a teaching diploma in early childhood education (Meade 2000: 87, 89), with requirements continuing to increase.

The government implemented a number of other reforms to improve quality in ECEC services including an Early Childhood Development Unit (ECDU) to provide development, advice, and coordination; an Education Review Office to perform annual audits (Meade 2000: 86, 90); instituting "quality funding" incentives where "services with better than minimum standards with regard to staff qualifications and staff to child ratios... receive a higher per child grant" (Meade 2000: 87); and giving charter status – and higher levels of funding – to childcare centers that have to meet additional quality guidelines (Meade 2000: 89).

In 2002 the New Zealand Ministry of Education released its Ten-Year Strategic Plan, which outlined specific goals for early childhood education quality improvement, largely through increasing the number of registered teachers delivering ECEC services, improving child–staff ratios and group sizes, increasing parent involvement, and legislating a national curriculum for all ECE services. The government also instituted a review of ECEC regulations (New Zealand Ministry of Education 2004) and committed to increasing the number of qualified and registered early childhood education teachers. By 2012 all staff in teacher-led ECE services were to be registered ECE teachers or enrolled in approved education programs. In 1996, New Zealand was the first country to introduce a national curriculum for 0–5-year-olds, *Te Whariki* (Meade 2000: 91).

New Zealand has not followed the social democratic and continental European welfare regimes, however, in that services are predominantly privately, not publicly, delivered. According to Mitchell (2012), ECEC places almost trebled between 1992 and 2010, with privately owned services "burgeoning" from 41 per cent in 1992 to 64 per cent in 2010. A diverse array of programs exists: community-based and for-profit centers (which include some sessional, some full-day, and some flexible hours programs for children from infancy to school age) (Meade and Podmore 2002: 6); sessional free kindergarten programs for three- and four-year-olds (usually community rather than government-run); parent-supervised and managed parent and child play centers; home-based services; and Maori (*kohanga reo*) and Pacific Islander language, cultural immersion, and school readiness services (Mitchell 2012).

All of these receive some kind of government funding (Meade 2000: 83), although "each type of early childhood service receive[s] different levels of funding from the government, based on different formulae". As the government has continuously expanded the system, it has also continued to fund for-profit and community providers. Most significantly, in 2007 the government committed to provide up to 20 hours of free early childhood education per week for children aged three and four participating in all teacher-led ECE services and *kohanga reo* in addition to the hours for which subsidies were already provided (New Zealand Ministry of Education 2007). After protestations from private operators, the government agreed that these services could be delivered in a variety of settings, so long as the service is teacher-led (ibid.; Mitchell 2012). The government initially encouraged the growth of community-based services, though the discretionary grants funding scheme ended in favor of "more effective options... includ[ing] looking at how DGS can be used more effectively to increase participation in early childhood education" (New Zealand Ministry of Education 2009).

The report of a national community-convened inquiry into "strengthening community-based early childhood education provision" notes that the "QPECE group proposals require a move from a market approach, where services alone are responsible for the provision of early childhood education, to a partnership model where services work with the Government and community to build a coherent network of provision in every community" (May and Mitchell 2011: 5). The report further suggests that "the proposals will require a Governmental commitment to fully implement the 2002–2012 strategic plan, staffing policies, and with the sector to develop accountability systems and further strategies to improve quality" (ibid.).

The report of a 2011 government-appointed ECEC task force made 65 recommendations for substantial changes in ECEC but did not really address the issue of marketization (Harvey et al. 2011). Mitchell (2012: 7) notes that – as documented in the other cases – the NZ commitment to fund a mix of ECEC services has encouraged growth of private ownership resulting in "duplications and gaps in ECEC provision, inequities in access particularly for low income, ethnically diverse and rural families" and the expansion of corporate providers as well, including – until its collapse – the Australian giant, ABC Learning. Mitchell notes both similar trends to those in Australia and the UK, where for-profit providers target higher income communities for their services, and similar differences in quality, as for-profit providers employ fewer qualified teachers and provide fewer employment supports (see also Mitchell 2002). Mitchell's (2002: 7) conclusion is that the market approach is the "Achilles heel" in building a high quality ECEC system.

Summary of Trends

This survey of trends in Australia, the UK, Quebec and New Zealand reveals incongruence between policy goals and policy implementation on the following dimensions:

- public spending (while liberal welfare states are increasing their ECEC spending from traditional levels, none of the liberal welfare states are even average spenders in terms of GDP);
- how public funds are delivered (liberal welfare states tend to favor demand-side rather than supply side funding) which does not allow for a focus on service improvement;
- who delivers services (liberal welfare states tend rely on private providers including for-profits without stringent regulatory standards and monitoring);
- who receives services (some liberal welfare states tend to target programs to certain groups, rather than make services available to all) which means parts of the population do not benefit from increased investment.

Conclusion

The New Zealand case is very informative as it illustrates that even when a government attempts to develop standards regarding planning, delivery of services, staffing, and training, the choice of delivery agents can undermine those efforts. Thus, the scale of government funding of ECEC programming is not the end of the story but the beginning.

If governments wish to promote early child development goals, and to deliver "educational" childcare, one cannot simply label the services provided "educational". Real questions must be addressed: first, is it a system or a market? Second, who is best to deliver services: schools, municipalities, voluntary/non-profit organizations or parent groups, for-profit operators, or multinational corporations? Third, what should governments require? Should there be a standard curriculum? What staff standards should there be in terms of duration and kinds of training? Is there a professional credential? What are the wages and working conditions? How much should parents pay? What are the child/staff ratios, physical environment, and so on? And most importantly, what are the goals and objectives for children and families, and what are the right program components in place to ensure that these can be achieved? So long as these questions are inadequately addressed, governments may commit considerable public dollars to ECEC and yet fail to achieve the high quality programs needed to deliver "results" for children. Human capital and human rights are likely to remain elusive.

References

Albanese, Patrizia. 2011, "Addressing the Interlocking Complexity of Paid Work and Care: Lessons from Changing Family Policy in Quebec." In *A Life in Balance? Re-opening the Family-Work Debate.* Eds. Catherine Krull and Justyna Sempruch (Vancouver: UBC Press).
Australian Labor Party, 2007, *Labor's Plan for Early Childhood.* Election 2007 Policy Document. Available at http://parlinfo.aph.gov.au/parlInfo/download/library/partypol/U6YO6/upload_binary/u6yo63.pdf;fileType=application%2Fpdf. Accessed 10 July 2012.
Australian Senate, Standing Committee on Education, Employment, and Workplace Relations, 2009, *Provision of Childcare: Final Report* (Canberra: Commonwealth of Australia).
Baker, M. and Tippin, D., 1999, *Poverty, Social Assistance, and the Employability of Mothers: Restructuring Welfare States* (Toronto: University of Toronto Press).
Baker, M., Gruber, J. and Milligan, K., 2008, Universal child care, maternal labor supply, and family well-being. *Journal of Political Economy*, **116**(4), pp. 709–745.
Ball, S. J. and Vincent, C., 2005, The "childcare champion"? New Labour, social justice and the childcare market. *British Educational Research Journal*, **31**(5), pp. 557–570.
Beach, J., Friendly, M., Ferns, C., Prabhu, N. and Forer, B., 2009, *Early Childhood Education and Care in Canada 2008* (Toronto: CRRU).
Bennett, J., 2005, Curriculum issues in national policy-making. *European Early Childhood Education Research Journal*, **13**(2), pp. 5–23.
Brennan, D., 1998, *The Politics of Australian Child Care: Philanthropy to Feminism and Beyond* (Cambridge: Cambridge University Press).
Brennan, D., 2007, The ABC of childcare politics. *Australian Journal of Social Issues*, **42**(2), pp. 213–225.
Campbell, A. L. and Morgan, K., 2011, *The Delegated Welfare State: Medicare, Markets, and the Governance of Social Policy* (Oxford: Oxford University Press).
Carneiro, P. and Heckman, J. J., 2003, Human capital policy, in: J. Heckman and A. B. Kruger (Eds) *Inequality in America: What Role for Human Capital Policies* (Cambridge, MA: MIT Press), pp. 77–239.
Cleveland, G. and Krashinsky, M., 2009, The nonprofit advantage: producing quality in thick and thin childcare markets. *Journal of Policy Analysis and Management*, **28**(3), pp. 440–467.
Cohen, B., Moss, P., Petrie, P. and Wallace, J., 2004, *A New Deal for Children? Re-forming Education and Care in England, Scotland and Sweden* (Bristol: The Policy Press).
Deber, R. B., 2002, Delivering Health Care Services: Public, Not-For-Profit, or Private? *Commission on the Future of Health Care in Canada Discussion Paper No. 17* (Ottawa: The Commission).
DfE (Department for Education), 2011, *Provision for Children Under Five Years of Age in England: January 20110.* Statistical First Release. SFR 13/2011 (London: DfE).
DfEE (Department of Education and Employment, UK), 1998, *Meeting the Childcare Challenge* (London: The Stationery Office).
Donahue, J. D. and Zeckhauser, R. J., 2011, *Collaborative Governance: Private Roles for Public Goals in Turbulent Times* (Princeton, NJ: Princeton University Press).
Dowling, A. and O'Malley, K. 2009, "Preschool Education in Australia." (December). Online: http://research.acer.edu.au/cgi/viewcontent.cgi?article=1000&context=policy_briefs. Accessed 10 July 2012.
Drouin, C., Bigras, N., Fournier, C., Desrosiers, H. and Bernard, S., 2004, *Grandir en Qualité: Enquête québécoise sur la qualité des services de garde éducatifs* (Quebec: Institut de la Statistique de Québec).
Esping-Andersen, G., 1990, *The Three Worlds of Welfare Capitalism* (Princeton, NJ: Princeton University Press).
Freeman, J. and Minow, M. (Eds), 2009, *Government by Contract: Outsourcing and American Democracy* (Cambridge, MA: Harvard University Press).
Gaunt, C., 2009, Busy Bees founders buy back shares from ABC receivers. *Nursery World*, 24 June.
Gaunt, C., 2011, UK and Ireland top European table of for-profit care providers. *Nursery World*, 1 November.

Gillard, Hon J., 2008, Early childhood initiatives to benefit individuals, the community and the economy. Media release, 13 May, by Minister for Education. Minister for Employment and Workplace Relations. Minister for Social Inclusion. Deputy Prime Minister. Available at http://mediacentre.dewr.gov.au/mediacentre/Gillard/Releases/Earlychildhoodinitiativestobenefitindividualsthecommunityandtheeconomy.htm. Accessed 10 July 2012.

Gingrich, J., 2011. *Making Markets in the Welfare State: The Politics of Varying Market Reforms* (New York: Cambridge University Press).

Gormley, W., Jr., 1999, Regulating childcare quality. *The Annals of the American Academy of Political and Social Science*, **563**, pp. 116–129.

Harvey, T., Johnstone, C., Mintrom, M., Poulton, R., Reynolds, P., Smith, A., Tamati, A., Tafa, L. and Viviani, R., 2011, *Early Childhood Education Taskforce: Final Report* (Wellington: Government of New Zealand. Ministry of Education).

Heckman, J. J., Moon, S. H., Pinto, R., Savelyev, P. A. and Yavitz, A., 2010, The rate of return to the High Scope Perry preschool program. *Journal of Public Economics*, **94**, pp. 114–128.

Helburn, S. (Ed), 1995, *Cost, Quality and Child Outcomes in Childcare Centers* (Denver: University of Colorado, Department of Economics, Center for Research in Economic and Social Policy).

HM Treasury, UK, 2004, *Choice for Parents, the Best Start for Children: A Ten Year Strategy for Childcare* (London: Stationery Office).

Horin, A., 2007, Child-care laws horrific: US expert. *Sydney Morning Herald*, 27 September. Online: http://www.smh.com.au/news/national/childcare-laws-horrific-us-expert/2007/09/26/1190486395861.html. Accessed 9 July 2012.

Japel, C., Tremblay, R. E. and Côté, S., 2005, Quality counts! Assessing the quality of daycare services based on the Quebec longitudinal study of child development. *IRPP Choices*, **11**(5), pp. 1–42.

Jenson, J., 2009, Rolling out or backtracking on Quebec's childcare system? Ideology matters, in: M.G. Cohen and J. Pulkingham (Eds) *Public Policy for Women* (Toronto: University of Toronto Press), pp. 49–70.

Karoly, L. A. and Bigelow, J. H., 2005, *The Economics of Investing in Universal Preschool Education in California* (Santa Monica, CA: RAND Corporation).

Keating, D. P. and Hertzman, C. (Eds), 1999, *Developmental Health and the Wealth of Nations: Social, Biological, and Educational Dynamics* (New York: The Guilford Press).

Lange, D., 1988, *Before Five: Early childhood care and education in New Zealand* (Wellington: Department of Education).

LeFebvre, P., Merrigan, P. and Verstraete, M., 2009, dynamic labour supply effects of childcare subsidies: evidence from a Canadian Natural experiment on low-fee universal child care. *Labour Economics*, **16**(5), pp. 490–502.

Lenz Taguchi, H. and Munkammar, I., 2003, Consolidating governmental early childhood. *Education and Care Services Under the Ministry of Education and Science: A Swedish Case Study*. UNESCO Early Childhood and Family Policy Series No. 6 (Paris: UNESCO).

Levin, H. M. and Schwartz, H. L., 2007, Educational vouchers for universal pre-schools. *Economics of Education Review*, **26**, pp. 3–16.

Lewis, J., 2003, Developing early years childcare in England, 1997–2002: the choices for (working) mothers. *Social Policy and Administration*, **37**(3), pp. 219–238.

Lindsey, G., 1998, Brain research and implications for early childhood education. *Childhood Education*, **75**(2), pp. 97–104.

Martin Korpi, B., 2007, *The Politics of Pre-School: Intentions and Decisions Underlying the Emergence and Growth of the Swedish Pre-school* (Stockholm: The Ministry of Education and Research).

Mathers, S. and Sylva, K., 2007, *National Evaluation of the Neighbourhood Nurseries Initiative: The Relationship between Quality and Children's Behavioural Development* Research Report SSU/2007/FR/022 (London: Department for Education and Skills).

Mathers, S., Sylva, K. and Joshi, H., 2007, *Quality of Childcare Settings in the Millennium Cohort Study* Research Report SSU/2007/FR/025 (London: Department for Education and Skills).

May, H. and Mitchell, L., 2009, *Strengthening Community Based Early Childhood Education in Aotearoa-New Zealand* Report of the Quality Public Early Childhood Education Project (Wellington: NZEI Te Riu Roa).

Meade, A., 2000, The early childhood landscape in New Zealand, in: J. Hayden (Ed) *Landscapes in Early Childhood Education: Cross-National Perspectives on Empowerment – A Guide for the New Millenium* (New York: Peter Lang), pp. 83–93.

Meade, A. and Podmore, V., 2002, *Early Childhood Education Policy Co-ordination under the Auspices of the Department/Ministry of Education: A Case Study of New Zealand*. UNESCO Early Childhood and Family Policy Series No. 1 (Paris: UNESCO).

Melhuish, E. and Moss, P., 1992, Day care in the United Kingdom in historical perspective, in: M. E. Lamb, K. J. Sternberg, C.-P. Hwang and A. Broberg (Eds) *Childcare in Context* (Hillsdale, NJ: Lawrence Erlbaum and Associates), pp. 157–183.

Michel, S. and Mahon, R. (Eds), 2002, *Childcare Policy at the Crossroads: Gender and Welfare State Restructuring* (New York: Routledge).

Ministère de la Famille et de l'Enfance, 1997, *Educational Programs for Childcare Centres* (Québec: The Ministry).

Ministère de la Famille et des Aînés, Québec, 2007, *Meeting Early Childhood Needs: Québec's Educational Program for Childcare Services Update* (Québec: The Ministry).

Mitchell, L., 2002, *Differences Between Community Owned and Privately Owned Early Childhood Education and Care Centres: A Review of Evidence*. NZCER Occasional Paper 2002/2 (Wellington: New Zealand Council for Educational Research).

Mitchell, L., 2012, Markets and childcare provision in New Zealand: towards a fairer alternative, in: E. Lloyd and H. Penn (Eds) *Childcare Markets, Local and Global: Can They Deliver an Equitable Service?* (Bristol: Policy Press), pp. 97–113.

Mitchell, L., Wylie, C. and Carr, M., 2008, *Outcomes of Early Childhood Education: Literature Review* Report to the Ministry of Education of the Government of New Zealand (Wellington: Ministry of Education).

Morris, J. R., 1999, Market constraints on childcare quality. *The Annals of the American Academy of Political and Social Science*, **563**, pp. 130–145.

Morris, J. R. and Helburn, S. W., 2000, Childcare center quality differences: the role of profit status, client preferences, and trust. *Nonprofit and Voluntary Sector Quarterly*, **29**(3), pp. 377–399.

Moss, P., 2006a, Farewell to childcare? *National Institute Economic Review*, **195**, pp. 70–83.

Moss, P., 2006b, From a childcare to a pedagogical discourse – or putting care in its place, in: J. Lewis (Ed) *Children, Changing Families and Welfare States* (Cheltenham, UK: Edward Elgar), pp. 154–172.

Naumann, I., 2011, Towards the marketization of early childhood education and care? Recent developments in Sweden and the United Kingdom. *Nordic Journal of Social Research*, **2**, pp.1–17

New Zealand Department of Education, 1988, *Education to be more: Report of the Early ChildhoodCare and Education Working Group*. (Wellington: Department of Education).

New Zealand Ministry of Education, 2004, *Review of Regulation of Early Childhood Education: Implementing Pathways to the Future: Nga Huarahi Arataki*. Consultation Document (Wellington: Ministry of Education).

New Zealand Ministry of Education, 2007, *Free ECE: Information for Parents* (Wellington: Ministry of Education).

New Zealand Ministry of Education, 2009, Changes to the discretionary grant scheme. *New Zealand Education Gazette*, 24 August. Available at http://www.edgazette.govt.nz/articles/Article.aspx?ArticleId=7908. Accessed 10 July 2012.

O'Connor, J. S., Orloff, A. S. and Shaver, S., 1999, *States, Markets, Families: Gender, Liberalism and Social Policy in Australia, Canada, Great Britain and the United States* (New York: Cambridge University Press).

OECD (Organization for Economic Cooperation and Development), 2006, *Starting Strong II: Early Childhood Education and Care* (Paris: OECD).

OECD, 2011, *Family Database*. Available at http://www.oecd.org/els/social/family/database. Accessed 8 February 2012.

Ofsted (Office of Standards in Education), UK, 2008, *Early Years Leading to Excellence: A Review of Childcare and Early Education 2005–2008 with a Focus on Organisation, Leadership and Management* (reference no. 080044) (London: Ofsted).

Penn, H., 2007, Childcare market management: how the United Kingdom government has reshaped its role in developing early childhood education and care. *Contemporary Issues in Early Childhood*, **8**(3), pp. 192–207.

Penn, H., 2011, Gambling on the market: the role of for-profit provision in early childhood education and care. *Journal of Early Childhood Research*, **20**(10), pp. 1–12.

Prentice, S., 2009, High stakes: the 'investable' child and the economic reframing of childcare. *Signs: Journal of Women in Culture and Society*, **34**(3), pp. 687–710.

Press, F. and Hayes, A., 2000, *OECD Thematic Review of Early Childhood Education and Care Policy: Australian Background Report* (Canberra: Commonwealth Government of Australia).

Press, F. and Woodrow, C., 2009, The giant in the playground: investigating the reach and implications of the corporatisation of childcare provision, in: F. Press and C. Woodrow (Eds) *Paid Care in Australia: Politics, Profits, Practices* (Sydney: Sydney University Press), pp. 231–252.

Randall, V., 2004, The making of local child daycare regimes: past and future. *Policy and Politics*, **32**(1), pp. 3–20.

Rigby, E., Ryan, R. M. and Brooks-Gunn, J., 2007, Childcare quality in different state policy contexts. *Journal of Policy Analysis and Management*, **26**(4), pp. 887–907.

Scheiwe, K. and Willekens, H. (Eds), 2009, *Childcare and Preschool Development in Europe: Institutional Perspectives* (London: Palgrave Macmillan).

Schweinhart, L. J., Montie, J., Xiang, Z., Barnett, W. S., Belfield, C. R. and Nores, M., 2005, *Lifetime Effects: The HighScope Perry Preschool Study through Age 40*. Monographs of the HighScope Educational Research Foundation, 14 (Ypsilanti, MI: High Scope Press).

SCRGSP (Steering Committee for the Review of Government Service Provision), 2008, *Report on Government Services, 2008* (Canberra: Productivity Commission).

Skolverket (Swedish National Agency for Education), 2004, *Pre-school in Transition: A National Evaluation of the Swedish Pre-school. A Summary of Report 239* (Stockholm: the author).

Skolverket. 2010. *Facts and Figures About Pre-school Activities, School-age Childcare, Schools and Adult Education in Sweden 2010* (Stockholm: the author).

Sosinsky, L. S., Lord, H. and Zigler, E., 2007, For-profit/nonprofit differences in center-based childcare quality: results from the National Institute of Child Health and Human Development Study of Early Childcare and Youth Development. *Journal of Applied Developmental Psychology*, **28**, pp. 390–410.

Sumsion, J., 2006, The corporatization of Australian childcare: towards an ethical audit and research agenda. *Journal of Early Childhood Research*, **4**(2), pp. 99–120.

Temple, J. A. and Reynolds, A. J., 2007, Benefits and costs of investment in preschool education: evidence from the child-parent centers and related programs. *Economics of Education Review*, **26**, pp. 126–144.

Tougas, J., 2002, *Reforming Quebec's Early Childhood Care and Education: The First Five Years* (Toronto: Childcare Resource and Research Unit).

UK Office for National Statistics, 2007, *Social Trends* No. 37 (Houndmills, Basingstoke, Hampshire: Palgrave Macmillan).

UNICEF, Innocenti Research Center, 2008, *The Childcare Transition: A League Table of Early Childhood Education and Care in Economically Advanced Countries* Report Card 8 (Florence: The Center).

Vincent, C., Braun, A. and Ball, S.J., 2008, Childcare, choice and social class: caring for young children in the UK. *Critical Social Policy*, **28**(1), pp. 5–26.

Wincott, D., 2005, Reshaping public space? Devolution and policy change in British early childhood education and care. *Regional and Federal Studies* **15**(4), pp. 453–470.

Wincott, D., 2011, Ideas, policy change, and the welfare state, in: D. Béland and R. H. Cox (Eds) *Ideas and Politics in Social Science Research* (New York: Oxford University Press), pp. 143–166.

Zellman, G. L., Perlman, M., Le, V.-N. and Setodji, C. M., 2008, *Assessing the Validity of the Qualistar Early Learning Quality Rating and Improvement System as a Tool for Improving Child-Care Quality* (Santa Monica, CA: RAND).

Reconciliation Policies and the Effects of Motherhood on Employment, Earnings and Poverty

JOYA MISRA, MICHELLE J. BUDIG and STEPHANIE MOLLER

ABSTRACT *We examine the consequences of welfare state strategies on women's economic outcomes in ten countries. These strategies are 1) the primary caregiver strategy, focused on valuing women's care work; 2) the primary earner strategy, focused on encouraging women's employment; 3) the choice strategy, which provides support for women's employment or caregiving for young children; and 4) the earner-carer strategy, focused on helping men and women balance both care and employment. We analyze the effects of motherhood and marital status on employment rates, annual earnings, and poverty rates. Our study suggests that the strategy taken by the earner-carer strategy may be most effective at increasing equality for both married and single mothers.*

The impressive development of work-family reconciliation policies across Europe suggests a substantial shift in how women's roles – as caregivers and employed workers – are conceptualized. Indeed, most mothers have now entered the labor market. Yet women who are mothers continue to face substantial penalties in the workplace in terms of employment and earnings, and significant challenges in ensuring adequate care for their families. Mothers' poverty rates also vary dramatically cross-nationally.

We focus on welfare state strategies regarding work-family reconciliation policies. Reconciliation policies include parental and family leave, subsidized childcare, and flexible work-time policies (Gornick and Meyers 2003, Hantrais 2000). Theoretically, reconciliation policies should give parents greater economic opportunities, while also ensuring adequate care for families. However, these policies draw upon different assumptions about women's roles in society. For example, long family leaves may weaken mothers' employment continuity and earnings (Morgan and Zippel 2003). On the other hand, childcare policies or policies that create incentives for men to take leave may lead to greater equality (Gornick and Meyers 2003). Placing support for caregiving within the context of other policies – for example, whether high-quality childcare exists alongside family leave – can help make sense of how motherhood affects women's economic opportunities.

We consider how variations in welfare state reconciliation strategies have led to different outcomes regarding employment, earnings, and poverty for mothers relative to women without children in the home. We identify four distinct strategies of care and employment and use data for ten countries from the Luxembourg Income Study (LIS) to examine the associations between these strategies and our outcomes.

Welfare State Regimes, Employment, and Caregiving

Welfare state restructuring reflects not only a response to globalization, increased immigration, and the weakening of labor (Rothstein and Steinmo 2002, Castles 2004) – but also important changes in the "gender order" (Fraser 1994, Gornick and Meyers 2004). Historically, the dominant vision of the Western welfare state during the twentieth century was the "male breadwinner/female caregiver" or "family wage" strategy (Fraser 1994, Sainsbury 1999). Policies presumed families to include a man earning enough to support a family, a woman providing care within the home, and their children. The welfare state intervened to replace the male breadwinner's wage in case of death, unemployment, disability, sickness, or old age, and occasionally to support women's caregiving within the home (Fraser 1994). Yet currently most jobs could not support an entire family, and most women are now employed (Crompton 1999). As families diversify to include more single-parent or non-heterosexual forms, the male breadwinner strategy is inadequate.

What does the "new" welfare state look like? How do states support families with children where both parents are likely to be employed? Recent welfare state scholarship emphasizes how nations cluster in terms of policy creation and outcomes (Esping-Andersen 1990, 1999). Esping-Andersen's (1990) welfare state regime typology is the predominant approach, dividing countries between the market-oriented *Liberal* regime, the status- and family-oriented *Conservative* regimes, and the redistributive *Social Democratic* regime. However, this model neglects gendered modes of caregiving and employment (Lewis and Ostner 1991, Orloff 1993). For example, Orloff (1993) argues that models must attend to women's access to paid employment and capacity to form and maintain autonomous households. Reflecting these critiques, Esping-Andersen's (1999) recent work also examines where caring responsibilities for households are lessened by state or market provision of care and where policy encourages household responsibility for care, arguing that his regimes remain valid (with a few minor exceptions).[1]

Drawing on Nancy Fraser's (1994) conceptualization of welfare state support for care, as well as Esping-Andersen's regime approach, we identify four major strategies: the Conservative primary caregiver/secondary earner strategy (where women are treated primarily as carers, and secondarily as earners), the Liberal primary earner/secondary carer strategy (where women are treated primarily as earners, and secondarily as carers), the Conservative choice model (where women are treated as choosing whether they are primarily earners or caregivers), and the Social Democratic earner-carer strategy (where women are treated as equally involved in both earning and caring).

The *primary caregiver/secondary earner strategy* (henceforth, primary caregiver) remains closest to the family wage model. This strategy explicitly values and rewards women for providing care, recognizing gender differences in its provision (Sainsbury 1999). Rather than encouraging women's full-time employment, the primary caregiver strategy attempts to compensate women for the time and effort they spend on care. This strategy (exemplified here by Austria, Germany, Luxembourg, and the Netherlands) is characterized by fairly generous caregiver and family allowances, as well as policies that help women provide in-home care, such as parental leave. Part-time employment is viewed as an ideal strategy for women who wish to combine employment and care. This strategy emphasizes women's caregiving within the family as the primary site for the provision of care (Fraser 1994). For example, Germany provides very generous parental leave policies, but less state provision of childcare, particularly for children under three (Gornick and Meyers 2003). Germany also provides care allowances and subsidizes pension contributions for up to three years of care for young children (for part-time workers, for up to ten years of care for children) (Seeleib-Kaiser 2004). Such programs recognize the carework done by women without challenging traditional gender norms.

The *primary earner/secondary carer strategy* (henceforth, primary earner) views both men and women as invested in employment, but provides little support for care (Fraser 1994). State policies work to engage women in the paid labor force, without significant state provision of care. Policies include "employment equality policies and the tax-encouraged market provision of services" (Orloff 2002: 16). Primary earner nations (exemplified here by Canada, the United States, and the United Kingdom), rely heavily on marketized care in addition to women's unpaid care. While this strategy provides women with opportunities for full-time employment and higher earnings, the net benefit to mothers is questionable because it does not ameliorate the privatized and feminized costs of caring. For example, the United States has passed legislation that equalizes women's opportunities in full-time positions in the workplace; however, the state does little to support care, and primarily expects families to rely on market provision of care, such as family daycare or childcare centers, or private provision from neighbors, friends, or grandparents, or from parents who stagger their working shifts to cover childcare.

The *choice strategy* values and rewards women for providing care while encouraging women to engage in employment. Policies provide substantial support for women's full-time employment, such as high-quality childcare, while also providing aid for women's caregiving, for example, through generous parental leave and caregiver allowances, and support for part-time employment. The countries falling into this mixed regime (France and Belgium) have ambivalent approaches to gender and women's roles, not fully challenging women's traditional roles within the family (Morgan 2002). For example, in principle, French women are given the support to achieve a career and provide care within their families, with more emphasis on care when their children are small (Laufer 1998). In France, high-quality state-provided childcare is widely available, along with generous parental leave and homecare allowances that support parental care for two or more children. These policies encourage women's balancing of employment and caregiving, rather than promoting men's equal role in caring.

Finally, the *earner-carer* strategy suggests a vision in which both women and men balance carework and employment. States encourage men's participation in caregiving and women's participation in employment, and require social institutions to adjust to meet their needs. The earner-carer regime (exemplified here by Sweden) can be characterized by generous support for care both within and outside of the home and shorter working weeks. Both men and women are encouraged to take parental leave, and high-quality childcare outside of the home is available (Gornick and Meyers 2003). Income transfers help families to balance care and employment. The earner-carer strategy attempts to break down gendered norms of care and employment (Fraser 1994, Crompton 1999, Gornick and Meyers 2003). For example, Sweden encourages women's employment through substantial state-provided care support, while also encouraging men's caregiving through paternity leave that only men can take (Gornick and Meyers 2003). Despite these efforts, gendered differences remain (Ellingsaeter 1999, Sainsbury 1999). However, as Sainsbury (1999: 196) notes, "The lack of far-reaching change ... should not blind us to the merits of policy construction which integrates market employment and care work in the home and simultaneously grants equal entitlement to men and women."

Theoretical Expectations

There is substantial variation regarding employment rates, earnings, and poverty rates for mothers as compared to non-mothers cross-nationally, as well as variation in these outcomes by marital status. We examine how different welfare state strategies are related to outcomes for mothers, relative to non-mothers, regarding employment, earnings, and poverty for ten countries. These cross-national differences may result from multiple factors, including cultural differences, women's preferences for employment, or unemployment rates within nations. For example, women in Germany might – regardless of the policy context – have a lower preference for full-time employment than women in Canada. To minimize the effects of contextual variations, we focus on differences between mothers and women without children within each country. The patterns of women without children should indicate baseline preferences and opportunities for employment, and the degree to which mothers differ should capture the impact of institutions and policies on women's ability to balance employment and family responsibilities.

Research suggests that reconciliation policies have positive effects on women's employment overall (Gornick and Meyers 2003, Mandel and Semyonov 2003).

Pettit and Hook (2005) show that high levels of childcare have a positive effect on women's employment, but generous maternity leave (measured as weeks of leave squared) has a negative effect. This outcome suggests that lengthy paid leave reduces the labor force attachment of mothers, while shorter paid leave more effectively helps mothers maintain labor force attachment. Given the variation in the strategies, we expect to see variation in employment outcomes. We should find higher levels of part-time employment for mothers (relative to childless women), and lower levels of full-time employment in the primary caregiver countries. In the primary earner, choice and earner-carer strategies we should see higher levels of full-time employment for mothers, which may be reduced by the lack of employment support in the primary earner model and the emphasis on women's choice in the choice model, particularly for mothers of very young children. We expect the earner-carer regime to be most effective at equalizing differences in full-time employment rates between mothers and non-mothers, by providing the most direct support for employed parents.

Mothers' earnings relative to non-mothers' also vary substantially cross-nationally (Waldfogel 1997, 1998, Harkness and Waldfogel 2003; Sigle-Rushton and Waldfogel 2006), although much research examines differences in earnings by gender (Mandel and Semyonov 2003; Huber *et al.* 2004). Previous research has argued that family policies may shape mothers' earnings relative to non-mothers (Waldfogel 1997, 1998, Budig and England 2001), by increasing mothers' share of earnings (Gornick and Meyers 2003) and decreasing gender wage gaps (Mandel and Semyonov 2003). We expect that the primary caregiver strategy may be least successful at limiting the motherhood earnings penalty. Given generous parental leave options, mothers may spend more time out of the workforce, losing experience and seniority and thus incurring a higher wage penalty for motherhood. We expect the primary earner strategy will be more successful at limiting mothers' wage penalties. However, without adequate care provision, mothers – particularly single mothers – should continue to incur penalties. We expect the choice and earner-carer strategies, with their greater employment supports, to be most effective at equalizing differences in earnings between mothers and women without children.

Previous research also explores cross-national gender gaps in poverty (Casper *et al.* 1994, Huber *et al.* 2004), and differences between mothers and non-mothers (Christopher 2002, Misra and Moller 2004). Scholars show that transfers, employment and earnings play an important role in reducing poverty, particularly for single mothers. We expect poverty rates for mothers relative to non-mothers to be highest in the primary earner countries, since among these liberal countries, transfers to families with children are fairly low, while mothers receive inadequate employment support. We expect poverty rates of single mothers relative to non-mothers to be high in the primary caregiver countries. While these countries provide more generous transfers to families with children, the lack of a second income may hurt these families. Finally, we expect poverty to be relatively low in the choice and earner-carer countries. These nations provide effective tax and transfer programs for families with children, and effective employment support for mothers. However, we expect poverty rates for mothers relative to childless women to be somewhat higher in the choice regime, given lower levels of employment for mothers of young children.

Measuring Equality

We use the Luxembourg Income Study to develop our measures of employment, earnings and poverty rates. The LIS database provides the best cross-national data for comparing income across wealthy countries, harmonizing data from a number of national surveys to ensure comparability. We utilize data from Waves IV and V, which represent the mid-1990s and early 2000s. Given our interests and the data available, we confine our attention to Austria (1997), Belgium (1997), Canada (2000), France (1994), Germany (2000), Luxembourg (2000), the Netherlands (1999), Sweden (1995),[2] the United Kingdom (1999), and the United States (2000).

We confine our sample to working-age adults between 25 and 49 to limit the number of students, pensioners and empty-nesters in the sample. We further limit our sample to female heads of households and to female partners/wives of male heads of households. We do this because the LIS identifies children living in households in relationship to the head. In this way we link children to the woman most likely mothering them while excluding other adult women in households from the analysis. It is possible that some mothers are counted as childless simply because they no longer have children living in the home. This bias is likely to lead to our underestimating the effect of motherhood.

We calculate employment rates separately for full- and part-time employment, defining full-time as more than 30 hours of work per week. We calculate wage rates separately for full- and part-time workers by using annual earnings.[3] In all earnings analyses we top-code annual earnings at ten times the median and bottom code at 1 per cent of mean annual earnings. Like most comparative researchers, we measure poverty rates relatively to capture the extent that families fall below 50 per cent of their countries' median income (Casper et al. 1994, Moller et al. 2003). We examine only post-tax and transfer poverty rates, and measure them as the percentage of mothers and non-mothers in households with disposable incomes (market income, governmental transfers, taxes) below 50 per cent of median income for all households.[4]

Marital status and parenthood status should play crucial roles in explaining women's employment, earnings, and likelihood of poverty. We are interested in how reconciliation policies affect the experiences of mothers, relative to other women, and how the experiences of single and married mothers differ. We measure marital status as 1 = currently married or cohabiting, and 0 as all others (including single, divorced or never married). Similarly, we measure motherhood = 1 if the respondent has any children under 18 living in the home. We conducted sensitivity analyses for the effects of motherhood on all dependent variables using additional measures of motherhood: two dummy variables to measure motherhood for mothers of young children (less than 6) and mothers with older children (6–17); and a measure of the number of children in the household.[5] This allowed us to examine how the penalties vary by age of child and the number of children in the home. Our findings are robust across these different specifications of motherhood; thus we present findings for the most parsimonious measure of motherhood. To examine whether motherhood affects the outcomes differently for married and single women, we also include interactions between motherhood and marital status.

Models control for age, marital status, educational attainment, and part-time employment status. Age is measured in years. Educational attainment is measured with a set of categorical variables based on the international standard classification of education from UNESCO. LIS has harmonized this variable across countries to create three educational categories: low (no education through lower secondary education), medium (upper secondary education through vocational post-secondary education) and high (university/college education through post-doctoral education).[6] We use low education as the reference category and include dummies for medium and high education in all regression models.

Findings

Employment Rates

Table 1 presents the numbers of observations for each country, as well as the percentages of mothers and non-mothers in each country who are employed full-time, part-time, and not employed. In every nation, mothers are less likely to be employed full-time and more likely to be employed part-time than non-mothers. Part-time employment is a central strategy for mothers in a wide variety of countries, although least so in the United States.

In Figure 1 and Table 2, we look more closely at the effect of motherhood on the odds of women's employment, controlling for age, marital status and education. To predict the effect of motherhood on employment rates, we used multinomial logistic regression.[7] These models predict the likelihood of full-time employment and

Table 1. Women's employment rates, by presence of children at home

	Number of observations	Full-time employment		Part-time employment		Not employed	
		No minor children	1 + minor children	No minor children	1 + minor children	No minor children	1 + minor children
Primary caregiver							
Austria	1,204	68.6%	39.0%	14.0%	28.1%	17.4%	32.9%
Germany	4,822	70.3%	30.5%	15.1%	30.7%	14.6%	38.8%
Luxembourg	1,151	71.9%	30.6%	12.6%	28.7%	15.5%	40.7%
Netherlands	2,491	63.4%	17.1%	21.1%	52.9%	15.5%	30.0%
Primary earner							
Canada	12,745	62.6%	45.7%	11.0%	19.8%	26.4%	34.5%
UK	10,105	70.7%	31.2%	12.4%	33.4%	16.9%	35.4%
US	21,064	79.2%	61.5%	6.1%	14.3%	14.7%	24.2%
Choice							
Belgium	1,959	48.3%	38.1%	14.1%	26.7%	37.6%	35.2%
France	5,286	59.4%	46.1%	18.3%	20.8%	22.3%	33.1%
Earner-carer							
Sweden	5,924	47.9%	37.5%	35.6%	46.0%	16.5%	16.5%

Notes: Person-weights are used in all estimations.

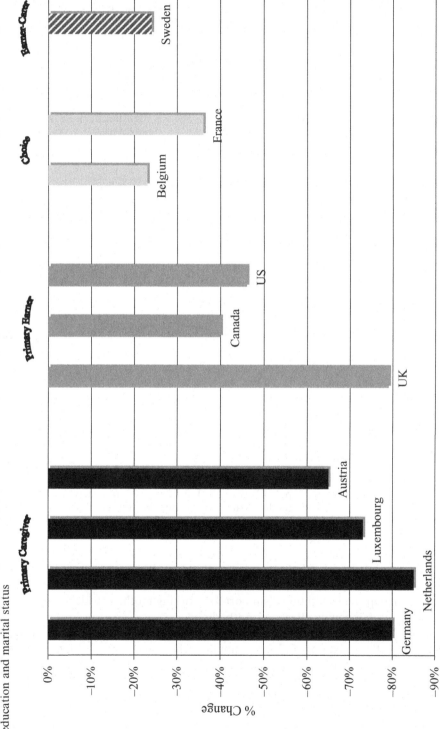

Figure 1. Effect of motherhood (in % change) on the odds of full-time employment relative to part-time and non-employment, controlling for age, education and marital status

Table 2. Relative risk ratios, robust standard errors, and percentage change in the odds of full-time employment from multinomial logistic regression models predicting the effect of motherhood on the odds of employment, by marital and part-time status

	Employed full-time			Employed part-time
	Main effect of motherhood Relative risk ratio (Std. Err.)	Effect of motherhood by marital status		Main effect of motherhood Relative risk ratio (Std. Err.)
		Single % change in odds of full-time employment	Married % change in odds of full-time employment	
Primary caregiver				
Germany	0.199 (0.022)***	−80.1%***	−80.1%***	0.841 (0.111)
Netherlands	0.148 (0.023)***	−85.2%***	−85.2%***	1.171 (0.175)
Luxembourg	0.273 (0.054)***	−72.7%***	−72.7%***	1.048 (0.244)
Austria	0.352 (0.066)***	−64.8%***	−64.8%***	1.140 (0.270)
Primary earner				
UK	0.209 (0.012)***	−83.0%***	−78.0%**	1.287 (0.095)***
Canada	0.604 (0.037)***	−39.6%***	−39.6%***	1.370 (0.120)***
US	0.540 (0.024)***	−27.2%***	−43%***	1.508 (0.110)***
Choice				
Belgium	0.770 (0.104)*	−23.0%*	−23.0%*	1.457 (0.255)**
France	0.639 (0.051)***	−36.1%***	−36.1%***	0.922 (0.108)
Earner-carer				
Sweden	0.757 (0.076)***	−24.3%***	−24.3%***	1.419 (0.169)***

***p < .001, two-tailed test; **p < .01, two-tailed test; *p < .05, two-tailed test.
Note: We test the impact of motherhood on employment. For full-time, we also add an interaction term between married and motherhood status. All models control for age, education, marital status, and work status and utilize sample weights.

part-time employment *relative to non-employment*. We expect motherhood would decrease the likelihood of employment in most countries.[8] However, the earner-carer strategy may provide additional support for working mothers, which might limit the employment-dampening effects of motherhood.

Table 2 presents the relative risk ratios, robust standard errors and percentage change in the odds of full-time employment from the multinomial logistic regressions, while Figure 1 summarizes the effects of motherhood (as percentages) on the odds of full-time employment, relative to non-employment.[9] As Figure 1 indicates, even with controls for age, education and marital status, mothers are less likely to be employed full-time in all countries. Motherhood reduces the odds of full-time employment by 24 per cent in Sweden as compared to 85 per cent in the

Netherlands – a very wide range. As we would expect, motherhood reduces the odds of full-time employment the most in the primary caregiver countries (and in the United Kingdom). As expected, Sweden is most effective in minimizing the negative impact of motherhood on full-time employment participation, although the "choice" model also appears to limit the effect of motherhood. Yet these effects compare the relative odds of full-time employment versus non-employment between mothers and women without children; all women – childless women as well as mothers – in the choice and earner-carer countries are less likely to be employed full-time than women in the primary earner countries, suggesting stronger norms for full-time employment for women in Canada and the United States.

Table 2 also presents the effects of motherhood on employment by marital status. We test for statistical interactions between marital/cohabiting status and motherhood. For ease of interpretation, we have transformed the coefficients for main effects and interactions into the percentage change in the odds of being employed full-time and present these results separately for single and married women. Where the interaction between single and married was not significant, the percentage change columns have the same results for single and married women. Results show that in most countries motherhood has similar effects on employment for single and married women. However, differences appear in two countries: the United States and the United Kingdom. In the United Kingdom, motherhood reduces the odds of employment for single mothers more than for married mothers, perhaps due to the presence of transfer payments directed at single mothers. In the United States, motherhood decreases the odds of full-time employment by 43 per cent, relative to non-employment, for married women, but only by 27 per cent for single women, reflecting the fact that welfare programs directed at single mothers in the United States encourage employment. In results not shown, we examined whether these effects of motherhood on full-time employment varied by the age of the youngest child in the home. In every country, the negative effect of children on women's full-time employment was largest when the youngest child was a preschooler.[10]

Table 2 also shows that motherhood increases the chance of part-time employment, relative to non-employment, particularly in the primary earner countries, but also in Belgium and Sweden. This counterintuitive result must be interpreted cautiously within the context of the model. As the results for full-time employment showed, motherhood pulls women away from full-time employment and thereby increases non-employment in all countries (see also Bardasi and Gornick 2000). Within this context, motherhood also increases the odds of working part-time in some countries: by 29 to 51 per cent in the primary earner countries and by 42 per cent in Sweden. In results not shown, we found that preschool children reduce the odds of part-time employment in France (relative to non-employment), while they increase the odds of part-time employment only in Canada and the US. In contrast, school-aged children increase the odds of part-time employment in the Netherlands, Canada, the UK, the US, Belgium, and Sweden.

Thus, while motherhood depresses employment participation generally, there is some variation across strategies. Given that the primary caregiver strategy does not emphasize women's full-time employment, we are not surprised that motherhood strongly decreases the odds of women's full-time employment in these nations. While the primary earner strategy does emphasize employment, it does not offer the services to support combining employment and caregiving. Mothers, relative to women without children, do best at full-time employment in the earner-carer and choice strategies, which encourage women's employment through substantial employment supports such as high-quality childcare.

Earnings

Table 3 presents the numbers of observations with valid earnings for each country, as well as a ratio of mothers' wage rates to childless women's wage rates. A value of 1 represents perfect equality, values less than 1 indicate relatively lower rates for mothers, and values greater than 1 indicate relatively higher rates for mothers. In every nation, mothers' full-time average earnings are lower than childless women's average earnings. These ratios are smallest among the choice countries, where wage differences, without controlling for other factors, appear to be fairly small. Possibly due to selectivity issues among women who work part-time, mothers appear to earn slightly more than women without children in Belgium, Canada, and the United States.

Table 4 presents the coefficient and standard errors for Heckman two-stage regressions, that show the partial effect of motherhood on annual earnings, first among all women, then separately by marital status.[11] We regress the natural log of annual earnings on motherhood status, marital status, age, educational attainment and part-time status.[12] Using logged earnings enables us to make comparisons across different currencies, minimize the effect of outliers and interpret coefficients in a straightforward manner: multiplying the coefficient by 100 gives us the percentage change in earnings, given a 1-unit increase in the independent variable. Figure 2 shows this transformation of motherhood coefficients on annual earnings from the main effects model. In showing the effects of motherhood separately by marital

Table 3. Ratio of mothers' annual earnings to annual earnings of women without a minor child at home

	# of observations w/valid earnings	Full-time	Part-time
Primary caregiver			
Germany	3,491	0.816	0.842
Netherlands	1,788	0.920	0.923
Luxembourg	748	0.805	0.774
Austria	648	0.841	0.782
Primary earner			
UK	6,641	0.870	0.943
Canada	10,074	0.902	1.014
US	16,701	0.839	1.174
Choice			
Belgium	1,107	0.981	1.029
France	3,682	0.966	0.959
Earner-carer			
Sweden	5,109	0.811	0.805

Notes: Person-weights are used in all estimations.

Table 4. Effect of motherhood on the natural log of annual earnings

	Main effect of motherhood	Effect of motherhood by marital status	
	All women Coefficient (Std. Error)	Single % change in earnings	Married % change in earnings
Primary caregiver			
Germany	−0.276 (0.033)***	n.s.	−25.3%***
Netherlands	−0.238 (0.047)***	−23.8%***	−23.8%***
Luxembourg	−0.188 (0.067)***	n.s.	−27.8%*
Austria	−0.150 (0.057)***	−15.0%***	−15.0%***
Primary earner			
UK	−0.146 (0.022)***	−26.2%***	−11.8%***
Canada	−0.178 (0.023)***	−27.2%***	−39.8%**
US	−0.112 (0.015)***	−24.7%***	−8.5%***
Choice			
Belgium	−0.122 (0.060)*	n.s.	−18.5%**
France	0.019 (0.031)	n.s.	n.s.
Earner-carer			
Sweden	−0.058 (0.077)	n.s.	n.s.

***p < .001, two-tailed test; **p < .01, two-tailed test; *p < .05, two-tailed test.
Note: We test the impact of motherhood on earnings; we then add an interaction term between married and motherhood status. All models control for age, education, marital status, and work status.

status, we make this transformation before presenting the numbers in the table. These models predict the wage penalty for all mothers by marital status, controlling for age, educational attainment and part-time status. We expect that the motherhood penalty should be lowest in the earner-carer and choice strategies, followed by the primary earner strategy.

As Figure 2 and Table 4 indicate, controlling for age, education and part-time employment status, motherhood decreases earnings in every country except France and Sweden. As expected, although there is overlap across strategies, motherhood decreases earnings most strongly in the primary caregiver countries. The negative effects of motherhood on earnings are minimized in the choice and earner-carer strategies, although motherhood negatively impacts married women's earnings in Belgium. In results not shown we examined whether the age of the youngest child affects the size of the motherhood pay penalty. When the youngest child is a preschooler, the wage penalty rises within Austria, Germany, Canada, the US, Belgium and Sweden. Interestingly, it is older children who increase pay penalties in Luxembourg, the Netherlands and the UK.

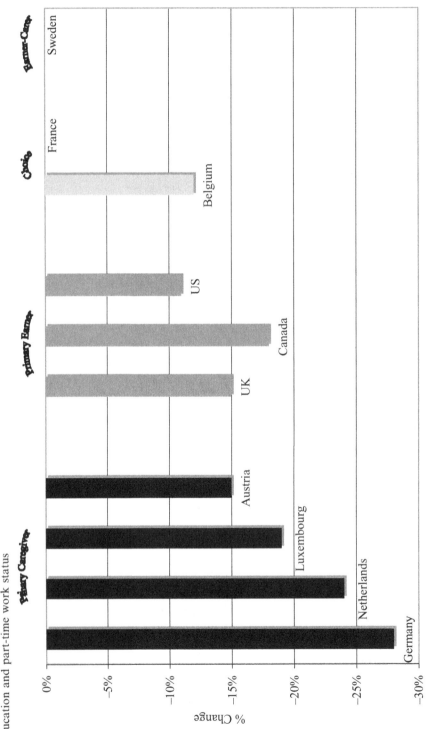

Figure 2. Effect of motherhood (in % change) on earnings from two-stage Heckman selection regression models, controlling for age, marital status, education and part-time work status

In several countries, the motherhood penalty varies by marital status. In the primary caregiver strategy, wage penalties are higher for married mothers than single mothers, except in Austria. Interestingly, single mothers' earnings are not significantly different from non-mothers' in Germany and Luxembourg, although married mothers suffer a significant penalty. However, in the primary earner strategy, the motherhood wage penalties are higher for single women in the US and the UK, indicating that the lack of work-family reconciliation policies hits single women the hardest. Finally, in the choice and earner-carer countries, we see few differences in earnings by motherhood or marital status, except that married mothers in Belgium pay an 18.5 per cent wage penalty, likely due to a history of employment targeted at single mothers. The care and employment supports provided by the choice and earner-carer strategy address some of the sources of the motherhood wage penalty, particularly for single mothers who particularly require support for their roles as both caregivers and earners.

Poverty

In addition to reconciliation policies, tax and transfer programs also play a major role in limiting poverty, and are highly correlated to the regimes we present. Welfare programs are most generous in the Social Democratic earner-carer countries, somewhat less generous in the Conservative choice and primary caregiver countries, and least generous in the Liberal primary earner countries. Therefore, we expect to see variation across these groups, not only due to the availability of reconciliation policies, but also due to the range of other welfare programs available for families in these nations.

We expect that the likelihood of poverty for mothers should be lowest in the earner-carer and choice strategies, where a combination of employment, support for care within the home, and tax-and-transfer policies should limit poverty for mothers. Poverty may be higher for mothers – particularly single mothers – in the primary caregiver strategy, where employment is a less effective way out of poverty for women, though additional support exists for caregivers and families. Finally, we expect that poverty rates will be particularly high in the primary earner strategy, where there are fewer transfer policies to help mediate the costs of children. Table 5 presents numbers of observations, and poverty rates for women, comparing married mothers, single mothers, married women without children, and single women without children. As Table 5 shows, in most nations mothers are more likely to fall into poverty than women without children. Indeed, married mothers in every nation are more likely to live in poverty than married non-mothers (although these differences are very small for France, Sweden, and the Netherlands), and single mothers in every nation except Sweden and Belgium are more likely to live in poverty than single non-mothers.

In Table 6 and Figure 3, we look more closely at the effect of motherhood on the likelihood of impoverishment among groups of women. Here, we use logistic regression; these models predict the odds of being in poverty for mothers and non-mothers, controlling for age, education and employment status (including two variables for part-time and full-time; not working is the excluded category).[13]

Table 5. Poverty rates by marital and motherhood status

	Number of Observations	Married with 1+ minor child	Single with 1+ minor child	Single with no minor child	Married with no minor child
Primary caregiver					
Germany	4,822	4.5%	26.2%	14.9%	1.7%
Netherlands	2,491	7.1%	26.6%	4.3%	5.7%
Luxembourg	1,042	6.1%	18.2%	5.4%	2.9%
Austria	976	6.6%	26.0%	5.6%	3.9%
Primary earner					
UK	9,029	8.3%	29.4%	9.2%	3.5%
Canada	11,353	9.1%	33.3%	18.2%	5.2%
US	19,316	12.0%	35.1%	15.8%	6.6%
Choice					
Belgium	1,723	5.1%	11.2%	16.5%	3.6%
France	5,286	4.6%	14.0%	8.5%	4.5%
Earner-carer					
Sweden	5,262	1.3%	5.9%	6.1%	1.2%

Notes: Person-weights are used in all estimations.

Table 6 presents the relative risk ratios, the standard errors and percentage change in odds of impoverishment from the logistic regressions.[14] The first column presents the effects of motherhood on the odds of impoverishment, controlling for marriage, age, education and employment status. Figure 3 summarizes these results. The next columns present the results separately by marital status. Here, we report the percentage change in odds of impoverishment for single and married mothers, controlling for age, education and employment status.

The impact of motherhood on poverty is as expected in the primary earner countries, with single mothers particularly hard hit (in the United States, for example, motherhood increases the odds of impoverishment by 111 per cent for single women and 39 per cent for married women). With lower levels of support for care, it is not surprising that motherhood increases the chance of poverty in these nations, particularly for single mothers. Similarly, the impact of motherhood on poverty is as expected in the choice and earner-carer countries. While motherhood does not affect the odds of impoverishment in France or Sweden, controlling for the other factors, it actually reduces these odds in Belgium. Given the generous transfers as well as employment support for single mothers in Belgium, this finding is consistent with our expectations. Clearly, the choice and earner-carer strategies have helped address the family gap in poverty.

However the primary caregiver model is more varied than expected. Motherhood does not have a statistically significant impact on poverty in Germany and Luxembourg (although poverty rates are generally higher in Germany than in Luxembourg; see Table 5). In the Netherlands, motherhood decreases the odds of poverty by 9 per cent for married women, while motherhood increases the odds of poverty 405 per cent for single women. On the other hand, in Austria, motherhood increases the odds of poverty by 463 per cent for single women and 25 per cent for married women. The policy packages in the primary caregiver countries are clearly

Table 6. Relative risk ratios, robust standard errors, and percentage change in the odds of impoverishment from logistic regression models predicting the effect of motherhood on impoverishment, by marital status

	Main effect of motherhood	Effect of motherhood by marital status	
	All women Coefficient (Std. Error)	Single women % change in odds of poverty	Married women % change in odds of poverty
Primary caregiver			
Germany	1.412		
	(0.261)	n.s.	n.s.
Netherlands	2.775		
	(0.306)**	405.3%***	−9.2%***
Luxembourg	1.944		
	(0.467)	n.s.	n.s.
Austria	2.792		
	(0.472)*	462.9%**	25.0%*
Primary earner			
UK	1.483		
	(0.112)***	80.6%***	19.6%*
Canada	1.556		
	(0.101)***	71.3%***	n.s.
US	1.772		
	(0.065)***	111.3%***	39.3%**
Choice			
Belgium	0.741		
	(0.251)	−57.4%*	n.s.
France	1.052		
	(0.152)	n.s.	n.s.
Earner-carer			
Sweden	0.900		
	(0.250)	n.s.	n.s.

***p < .001, two-tailed test; **p < .01, two-tailed test; *p < .05, two-tailed test.
Note: We test the impact of motherhood on impoverishment; we then add an interaction term between married and motherhood status. All models control for age, education, marital status, and work status, and utilize sample weights.

very varied. In Austria and the Netherlands, there may be contradictory impulses toward encouraging caregiving in traditional families, but lower levels of certainty in addressing the needs of single-parent families. However, this strategy appears too varied to make clear pronouncements about its effects on poverty.

These findings are clarified when considering alternative measures of motherhood (results not shown). We find that single mothers with older children are 87 per cent more likely to live in poverty than single non-mothers in Germany and 358 per cent more likely in Luxembourg. Indeed, we find that single mothers of older children are consistently the most disadvantaged group in the primary caregiver countries, even more so than single mothers of older children in the primary earner countries. Lower levels of attachment to the labor market may then have a continuing impact on poverty rates. Thus, when considering the age of children, the primary caregiver countries show greater homogeneity in terms of the effects of single motherhood on impoverishment. In the primary earner countries, the costs of motherhood are

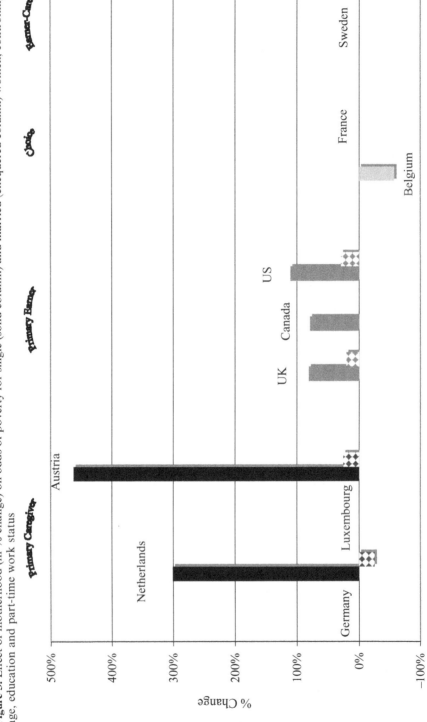

Figure 3. Effect of motherhood (in % change) on odds of poverty for single (solid column) and married (chequered column) women, controlling for age, education and part-time work status

greatest for mothers with preschool children. Motherhood remains non-significant in the choice and earner-carer countries, with the exception of France where mothers of older children have a 54 per cent greater odds of impoverishment.

Conclusions

What combination of welfare state policies and strategies are most likely to lead to equality among women? We began this paper considering strategies that emphasize equalizing women's opportunities in the labor force; strategies that emphasize supporting women's caregiving; strategies that emphasize giving woman a choice between employment and care; and a model meant to equalize women's employment opportunities through support for caring, while also equalizing men's engagement in caring. While our analyses in this paper cannot definitively make the causal link between particular policies and outcomes, they do provide some clues about the effectiveness of these different strategies.

The primary caregiver strategy is associated with the greatest gender inequality in employment, but it does not pretend to emphasize employment. For this reason, it is not surprising that this strategy is associated with larger employment and wage gaps by motherhood. As the results for poverty rates also show, however, this strategy has varied results. The high levels of poverty faced by single mothers in some of these nations suggest that this strategy remains problematic for mothers.

The primary earner strategy also appears to have mixed results. While full-time employment gaps and wage penalties faced by mothers are somewhat lower in these countries, negative effects remain fairly serious – particularly for single mothers. Poverty rates remain high for mothers, particularly so for single mothers. If policies are premised on women mimicking men's employment without increased support for care, married mothers struggle to find balance, while single mothers are simply left out of the equation.

While motherhood decreases the likelihood of full-time employment in the choice countries, earnings are more effectively supported through a variety of employment supports such as high-quality childcare. French mothers do not face wage penalties, and are no more likely to live in poverty. Belgian married mothers continue to face some wage penalty, but single mothers are actually less likely to live in poverty than single childless women. Clearly, in these countries, programs targeted to helping working families with children have helped equalize the situation for mothers.

Across the board, the earner-carer strategy (unfortunately, only represented here by Sweden) is most consistent with the highest levels of equality for all groups, including single mothers. Motherhood is associated with the least negative effects on employment and earnings, while poverty levels are quite low compared to other countries, including for single mothers. By providing substantial care support both outside and inside the home and approaches meant to encourage men's involvement in caregiving, Sweden's policies have begun to address many of the roots of the economic penalties paid by mothers.

Our analysis contributes to larger efforts to understand the effects of work-family policies. However, a range of other policies (tax policies, unemployment, family allowances, child support, single parent allowances, etc.) may be shaping the outcomes we find. Future research should attend to the effects of additional policies on these outcomes. At the same time, there is significant heterogeneity within each strategy. A more precise approach would more directly examine the effects of specific policies on these different outcomes and is a promising direction for future research.

However, our study suggests that certain policy strategies are more strongly associated with greater equality for mothers as compared to women without children in the home. While all of these strategies continue to be associated with certain inequalities due to motherhood, the earner-carer strategy appears to be most effective at increasing equality, particularly for single mothers. Our findings suggest that true equality among women requires policies that provide better support for both employment and care, and greater incentives for men's caregiving responsibilities.

Acknowledgements

This paper has been supported by the UMass Center for Research on Families, the UMass Center for Public Policy and Administration, and the UMass Social and Demographic Research Institute. Thanks to Kathryn Boggs and Karen Mason for their invaluable assistance, and to the reviewers and many colleagues who have provided comments, particularly Janet C. Gornick and Michael Ash.

Notes

1. Esping-Andersen (1999) finds differences between continental European countries and southern European countries, and notes that for measures focused on family support France and Belgium may "break ranks" with the other continental countries.
2. The 2000 Swedish data does not offer variables on part-time employment or hours worked.
3. Countries differ in whether gross (before employee tax/social insurance contributions are deducted) or net (post-tax) earnings are available. Both measures are post-employer tax/social insurance contributions, however. In our analyses Canada, Germany, the Netherlands, Sweden, the US and the UK have gross earnings, while Austria, Belgium, France and Luxembourg provide net earnings. If the relative difference in earnings is affected by taxation, comparing results based on net earnings to gross earnings may be problematic. Fortunately, we find our results are robust even when we limit our wage analyses to the six countries providing gross earnings.
4. Disposable income is adjusted for household size based on the square root of the number of persons in the household. In creating post-tax and transfer poverty rates, we excluded households with negative or no disposable income. We also dropped cases that did not report income.
5. The dichotomous measure may be the most accurate specification of motherhood given the available data since the other measures imply a false precision of motherhood. For example, the measure of number of children does include children 18 years or older at the time of the survey.
6. LIS has not harmonized this educational variable for Canada and the UK. We hand-coded educational attainment based on detailed measures available in the data.
7. We did not use an ordered probit model because we cannot assume that these are ordered states for mothers making employment decisions, and because it would not allow us to examine the varying effects of motherhood on full- versus part-time employment.
8. We assume that employment patterns of women without children indicate women's baseline employment preferences, which is feasible provided there is no differential selection into motherhood on factors other than age, education and marital status.
9. Relative risk ratios are calculated by exponentiating the logit coefficients. The percentage change in odds is calculated for models that include an interaction effect between marital status and parenthood. The percentage change for single mothers reflects the direct parenthood effect. It is calculated as $100(\exp(b_{parent})-1)$. The percentage change for married mothers reflects the sum of the direct and interactive effects. It is calculated as $100(\exp(b_{parent}+b_{interaction})-1)$. When the main effects of

motherhood are significant, but the interactions between motherhood and marital status are non-significant, we present the percentage change based on the main effects, illustrating no variation by marital status.
10. The negative effect increased by a minimum of 8 percentage points (Austria) to a maximum of a 21 percentage points (US). In contrast, where the youngest child in the home was school age or older, the negative effects of motherhood decreased in every country, and school-aged children had no effect on women's odds of full-time employment in Belgium and Sweden.
11. Differences in the motherhood penalty in earnings across countries could be due to differential selection of women into employment across countries. To control for this, we employ a two-stage Heckman sample selection correction estimation procedure where we include transfer income, other family income, and presence of a preschooler as selection criteria.
12. We also ran these analyses with a continuous measure of weekly hours; results did not vary.
13. Since poverty rates are based on household income and multiple women can reside in a single household, we adjust standard errors for the interdependence of individuals within households.
14. See the discussion of Table 2 for a detailed explanation of these statistics.

References

Bardasi, Elena and Gornick, Janet C., 2000, Women and part-time employment: worker's "choices" and wage penalties in five industrialized countries. Institute for Social and Economic Research Working Paper 2000–11.
Budig, Michelle J. and England, Paula, 2001, The wage penalty for motherhood. *American Sociological Review*, **66**, 204–225.
Casper, Lynne M., McLanahan, Sara S. and Garfinkel, Irwin, 1994, The gender-poverty gap: what we can learn from other countries. *American Sociological Review*, **59**, 594–605.
Castles, Francis G., 2004, *The Future of the Welfare State* (Oxford: Oxford University Press).
Christopher, Karen, 2002, Caregiving, welfare states, and mothers' poverty, in: D. Kurz, F. M. Cancian, A. S. London, R. Revier and M. Tuominen (Eds) *Child Care and Inequality* (New York: Routledge), pp. 113–128.
Crompton, Rosemary (Ed.), 1999, *Restructuring Gender Relations and Employment* (New York: Oxford University Press).
Ellingsaeter, AnneLise, 1999, Dual breadwinners between state and market, in: R. Crompton (Ed.) *Restructuring Gender Relations and Employment* (New York: Oxford University Press), pp. 40–59.
Esping-Andersen, Gosta, 1990, *The Three Worlds of Welfare Capitalism* (Cambridge: Polity).
Esping-Andersen, Gosta, 1999, *Social Foundations of Postindustrial Economies* (New York: Oxford).
Fraser, Nancy, 1994, After the family wage: gender equity and the welfare state. *Political Theory*, **22**, 591–618.
Gornick, Janet C. and Meyers, Marcia K., 2003, *Families That Work* (New York: Russell Sage).
Gornick, Janet C. and Meyers, Marcia K., 2004, Welfare regimes in relation to paid work and care, in: J. Giele (Ed.) *Changing Life Patterns in Western Industrial Societies* (Netherlands: Oxford Elsevier Press), pp. 45–67.
Hantrais, Linda, 2000, From equal pay to reconciliation of employment and family life, in: Linda Hantrais (Ed.) *Gendered Policies in Europe* (New York: St. Martin's Press), pp. 1–26.
Harkness, Susan and Waldfogel, Jane, 2003, The family gap in pay: evidence from seven industrialized countries. *Research in Labor Economics*, **22**, 369–414.
Huber, Evelyne, Stephens, John D., Bradley, David, Moller, Stephanie and Nielsen, François, 2004, The welfare state and gender equality. Luxembourg Income Study Working Paper No. 279, Luxembourg.
Laufer, Jacqueline, 1998, Equal opportunity between men and women: the case of France. *Feminist Economics*, **4**, 53–69.
Lewis, Jane and Ostner, Ilona, 1991, "Gender and the Evolution of European Social Policies." Center for European Studies Workshop "Emergent Supranational Social Policy: The EC's Social Dimension in Comparative Perspective," Cambridge, MA (November).
Mandel, Hadas and Semyonov, Moshe, 2003, The prevalence of welfare state policies and gender socioeconomic inequality: a comparative analysis. Luxembourg Income Study Working Paper No. 346, Luxembourg.

Misra, Joya and Moller, Stephanie, 2004, Familialism and welfare regimes: poverty, employment, and family policies. SADRI and CPPA, University of Massachusetts Working Paper Series.

Moller, Stephanie, Bradley, David, Huber, Evelyne, Nielsen, François and Stephens, John D., 2003, Determinants of relative poverty in advanced capitalist democracies. *American Sociological Review*, **68**, 22–51.

Morgan, Kimberly, 2002, Does anyone have a libre choix? Child care and the crisis of the welfare state in France, in: Sonya Michel and Rianne Mahon (Eds) *Child Care Policy at the Crossroads* (New York: Routledge).

Morgan, Kimberly and Zippel, Kathrin, 2003, Paid to care: the origins and effects of care leave policies in western Europe. *Social Politics*, **10**, 49–85.

Orloff, Ann Shola, 1993, Gender and the social rights of citizenship: the comparative analysis of gender relations and welfare states. *American Sociological Review*, **58**, 303–328.

Orloff, Ann Shola, 2002, Women's employment and welfare regimes: globalization, export orientation, and social policy in Europe and North America. United Nations Research Institute for Social Development, Programme Paper Number 12.

Pettit Becky and Hook, Jennifer, 2005, The structure of women's employment in comparative perspective. *Social Forces*, **84**(2): 779–801.

Rothstein, Bo and Steinmo, Sven (Eds), 2002, *Restructuring the Welfare State* (New York: Palgrave Macmillan).

Sainsbury, Diane, 1999, *Gender, Equality, and Welfare States* (New York: Cambridge).

Seeleib-Kaiser, Martin, 2004, Germany: still a conservative welfare state? Paper presented at the Annual Conference of Europeanists, Chicago, Illinois, available at http://www.europanet.org/conference2004/papers/J2_SeeleibKaiser.pdf (retrieved January 12, 2005).

Sigle-Rushton, Wendy and Waldfogel, Jane, 2006, Motherhood and women's earnings in Anglo-American, continental European, and Nordic countries. Luxembourg Income Study Working Paper No. 454, Luxembourg.

Waldfogel, Jane, 1997, The effect of children on women's earnings. *American Sociological Review*, **62**, 209–217.

Waldfogel, Jane, 1998, Understanding the "family gap" in pay for women with children. *Journal of Economic Perspectives*, **12**, 137–156.

Comparative Statistics

Editor: FRED THOMPSON

Less Bad than its Reputation: Social Spending as a Proxy for Welfare Effort in Cross-national Studies

CARSTEN JENSEN

ABSTRACT *The welfare state literature is characterized by a healthy methodological debate on how best to measure differences in welfare effort among advanced industrialized nations. Since Esping-Andersen noted that it is "difficult to imagine that anyone struggled for spending per se", a consensus has emerged in the methodological community that spending data is a poor proxy of cross-national differences in welfare effort. Social spending is arguably only able to capture one element of welfare effort, namely the size of the budget, whereas entitlement criteria and benefit type are not adequately captured. This paper brings some needed nuance to this consensus. It argues that the existing methodological literature, which almost exclusively studies old-age pensions, sickness insurance and unemployment protection, has inferred its conclusions to all welfare programs. This is misguided because welfare programs like health care and education exhibit much less cross-national variation in either entitlement criteria or benefit type. When studying cross-national differences in the willingness of decision-makers to promote these kinds of programs, social spending is in fact the most adequate measure.*

The large-N-based welfare state literature is characterized by a healthy methodological debate on how best to measure differences in welfare effort among advanced industrialized nations. Welfare effort has in large-N studies traditionally been measured as social spending and has been used in a large number of studies. Social spending data is readily available for a large number of countries and for many years, but has been argued not to capture some very important aspects of the concept of welfare effort (Esping-Andersen 1990, Korpi and Palme 1998, Green-Pedersen 2004, Clasen and Clegg 2007, Goul Andersen 2007, Kangas and Palme 2007, Kühner 2007, Siegel 2007).

Synthesizing Wilensky (1975) and Korpi and Palme (1998), welfare effort can be defined as political decisions concerning (1) entitlement criteria, (2) benefit type, and (3) budget size of individual welfare programs intended to temper dependence of individuals on the market or the family. There is general consensus that social spending is much better at capturing the size of the budget (when appropriate controls for social need are included) than the first two features. According to the critics of the social spending measure, this is critical because some of the most important cross-national differences relate to these features rather than to budget size (Esping-Andersen 1990). Moreover, as Clasen and Clegg (2007) note, cross-national studies relying on measures of entitlements and benefit type more often find changes than studies relying on social spending. It is therefore not trivial which measure of welfare effort is used when evaluating the merits of competing theories on the determinant of welfare effort.

That spending is a poor proxy for welfare effort has become conventional wisdom, often with the standard reference to Esping-Andersen (1990: 21) that it is "difficult to imagine that anyone struggled for spending *per se*" in the golden age of welfare state expansion. Importantly, the criticism of social spending is predominantly based on the evaluation of a few welfare programs, mainly old-age pensions, sickness insurance and unemployment protection (Esping-Andersen 1990, Korpi and Palme 1998, 2003, Allan and Scruggs 2004, Clasen and Clegg 2007, Kangas and Palme 2007, Kühner 2007, Scruggs 2007). I argue that this rather narrow focus has led to an overly pessimistic view of the merits of social spending as a proxy for welfare effort. The reason is simply that these three welfare programs are characterized by much greater cross-national variation when it comes to entitlement criteria and benefit type than most other welfare programs. Major welfare programs like health care and education are characterized by free access and equal treatment for all citizens in almost all Western countries. This entails that the primary determinant of cross-national variation in welfare effort for these types of programs becomes the size of the budget, i.e., social spending.

This paper, in sum, brings some needed nuance to the methodological debate in two ways. First, it argues that social spending under certain circumstances is an entirely valid measure of cross-national variation in welfare effort and not just the most conveniently available. Relatedly, it also shows that whether or not social spending or some other measure is the most appropriate depends on the individual welfare program. So far the criticism of social spending has, while based on studies of a few programs only, implicitly been inferred to all welfare programs. I argue that this is problematic and outline what programs are likely to be best captured by spending and what programs are better captured by other measures.

The first section presents the debate on how to conceptualize and measure welfare effort. Although the concept has fallen in and out of fashion, I argue that all of the major welfare state theories on how political actors allocate resources to generate economic redistribution (Stephens 1979, Korpi 1983; Bradley et al. 2003) or insurance against social risks (Esping-Andersen 1999, Iversen 2005, Bonoli and Armingeon 2006) de facto rely on the concept. Drawing on Wilensky (1975) and Korpi and Palme (1998), the following section presents an operationalization of welfare effort, which is used in the third section to distinguish between welfare programs where social spending is more or less valid as a measure of welfare effort. Given this conclusion, it becomes important to deal with another criticism against social spending, namely that it does not adequately capture political decisions on budget size, but is influenced by various unobserved factors (Green-Pedersen 2002, 2004, Siegel 2007, De Deken and Kittel 2007). I discuss these problems and conclude that although spending data should be used with great care, the problems do not disqualify social spending as such, and I also note that alternative measures appear to suffer from the same kind of problems.

Welfare Effort in the Literature

The concept of welfare effort was first introduced by Wilensky and Lebeaux (1958) and Wilensky (1975: 17) as "budget decisions of political elites" and highlights two separate elements: the budget and decision making by the political elite. The focus on both elements has been subject to criticism. The emphasis on decision making by political elites has been criticized for adopting an output focus, while being less concerned with outcome. That is, some authors have argued that the ultimate dependent variable for welfare state researchers should be the outcome of political decisions, e.g., the amount of actual economic redistribution, rather than the political decisions themselves (Bradley et al. 2003, Goul Andersen 2007). Since there is a long way from political decisions to the actual outcome it is evident that a focus on the former will often give a weak sense of the latter.

The outcome criticism seems to miss the mark, however. As noted by Green-Pedersen (2004), it is difficult to talk of *the* dependent variable in welfare state research: the choice must follow from the theories tested. This is important because some of the most dominant theories today are explicitly interested in decisions of political elites, the main difference between the theories being the assumed motivation of the elite. The power resource theory, to exemplify, focuses on how the labor movement fights to pass legislation that generates economic redistribution, which is seen as beneficial to their constituency (Stephens 1979, Korpi 1983, Huber and Stephens 2001; Bradley et al. 2003). The varieties of capitalism approach, as another example, argues that employers and employees in co-ordinated market economies develop identical preferences for insurance against social risks, which leads to the adoption of generous welfare provision, but less generous provision in liberal market economies (Estevez-Abe et al. 2001, Martin and Swank 2004, Iversen 2005). Precisely because of the difficulty of inferring from political decisions (whatever motivates them) to the outcome it is also pivotal not to test these arguments using outcome measures.

The focus on budgets has also met criticism because it is seen as entailing too narrow a focus on spending decisions. The criticism is valid in the sense that almost all of the early and a lot of the more recent work has relied heavily on social spending as the sole proxy of welfare effort. Esping-Andersen (1990) famously noted that spending as such cannot be what political actors are fighting for, although the alternative measures he introduced in fact rely heavily on social spending too (Siegel 2007). According to the critics, the core problem with social spending is that it fails to capture *how* the money is spent, which can have important consequences when evaluating cross-national differences in terms of how political elites try to redistribute or provide insurance against social risks.

Korpi and Palme (1998) elaborate the point and present the most well-known typology on the structure of welfare programs. They distinguish between the entitlements criteria governing a program and the benefit type of the program.[1] The entitlement criteria may be proven need, membership, occupational category, labor force participation, citizenship, or a combination. The type of benefits may either be minimum, flat-rate, earnings-related, or a combination. This basic typology has been used directly in a number of studies focusing on old-age pensions and sickness insurance (Korpi and Palme 1998, 2003, Korpi 2001, 2006, Kangas and Palme 2007) and seems indirectly to have inspired a lot of other studies as well (e.g., Allan and Scruggs 2004, 2006, Clasen and Clegg 2007).

The importance of taking the structure of welfare programs into account is frequently illustrated by comparing the Continental European welfare states with the Scandinavian welfare states, both of which allocate quite substantial fiscal resources to their welfare arrangements. The Continental European welfare states often rely on occupational category and labor force participation as the basis for entitlement, and benefits are earnings-related. In the Scandinavian welfare states the basis for entitlement is mostly citizenship, and benefits are both flat-rate and earnings-related. These differences, in turn, generate highly diverse outcomes whether measured as economic redistribution or social insurance. In the Continental European welfare states both redistribution and insurance take place within occupational categories generating limited redistribution and risk pooling across social groups. In the Scandinavian welfare states it takes place across the entire citizenry and thereby generates much more redistribution and risk pooling across social groups (Esping-Andersen 1990, 1999, Korpi and Palme 1998).

Korpi and Palme (1998), however, also underscore that the effect of the welfare program is a function not only of entitlement criteria and benefit type, but also of budget size. In a nutshell, the point is that unless we know how much money has been allocated to a given welfare program, we cannot say anything about the actual level of either redistribution or insurance. Welfare programs may, thus, be identical in terms of the entitlement criteria and benefit type, but still vary considerably if the level of payment that each recipient receives is dissimilar, leading to substantial differences in the overall resource allocation to the welfare program. As documented by Korpi and Palme (1998, see also Korpi 2001), countries like Denmark, the Netherlands, the United Kingdom and the United States share the same structure (the so-called basic security model), but the former two have allocated about twice as many fiscal resources to the programs as the latter two. In other words, looking at these countries, the main cross-national difference is not the structure of the program, but the budgets, which effectively is what distinguishes the social democratic/Christian democratic welfare states of Denmark/the Netherlands from the liberal welfare states of the United Kingdom and the United States.

The Concept of Welfare Effort across Different Welfare Programs

Following the above discussion it is possible to define welfare effort as a function of the entitlement criteria, benefit type and budget size. To understand cross-national variation in welfare effort, it is important to take all three elements into account. A lot of the welfare state literature has had excessive focus on the budget, presumably due to the easy availability. Yet a similar bias can also be observed in the methodological criticism, which has been overly focused on how poor a measure social spending is as it fails to take the structure of welfare programs into account.

The bias of the methodological literature appears to stem from its de facto focus on just a few core welfare programs: old-age pensions, sickness insurance and unemployment protection, which, as discussed above, are set up in very different ways in different countries (Esping-Andersen 1990, Korpi and Palme 1998, 2003, Hicks 1999, Korpi 2001, 2006, Allan and Scruggs 2004, 2006, Clasen and Clegg 2007, Kangas and Palme 2007, Kühner 2007, Scruggs 2007). It is evident that when welfare programs exhibit as much variation in terms of entitlement criteria and benefit type as these programs, it becomes problematic to rely on social spending as the only measure of welfare effort. It is therefore also problematic that some authors still do not even discuss alternative measures when studying transfer programs (e.g., Iversen 2005). Yet the focus on these three programs has probably led to a too pessimistic view of the merits of social spending, simply because there are few other welfare programs with that much variation in entitlement criteria and benefit types.

Old-age pensions, sickness insurance and unemployment effectively constitute around half of all welfare programs when measured as a share of the social budget. Other major welfare programs include health care and education, two cornerstone programs in all Western nations, but also elderly care and childcare. Compared to the three transfer programs that have been at the center of attention so far, these programs, and notably health care and education, are characterized by much less cross-national variation in entitlement criteria and benefit type. This implies that the main source of cross-national variation becomes the size of the budgets.

Health care, education, elderly care and childcare are all welfare services, so it is important to make sure that the entitlement criteria, benefit types and budget size make sense in this specific context. Essentially, however, all three elements are valid when it comes to welfare services as well. It is perfectly possible to imagine that access to a welfare service is dependent on proven need, membership contributions, occupational category, labor force participation, or citizenship. It is also possible to imagine that the benefit type can be both flat-rate, so that all citizens receive the same service, and earnings-related, so that those who provided most previously also benefit most, e.g., by getting access to services of higher quality. In short, whether or not these elements are used in real life is strictly an empirical question.

The size of the budget is evidently also important when evaluating welfare programs like health care and education. Yet both programs are characterized by the transformation of the budget allocations into specific benefits in kind like cancer treatments or more maths classes; a transformation that does not take place when it comes to cash benefits like old-age pensions or unemployment insurance. However, there are sound reasons why budget size nevertheless should remain the focal point. First, if we actually were to shift the focus from budget size to the amount of specific benefits in kind, it would in practice become impossible to compare the different programs. For example, are 40 hours of maths classes worth more or less than one knee surgery? Without the yardstick of money it is extremely difficult to assess the political willingness to allocate resources to different welfare programs, i.e., to prioritize them. What is more, it seems plausible that politicians actually use money as a yardstick when evaluating whether one program receives too little or too much attention. Statements by politicians about expanding provision of a welfare program without expanding the budget risk being perceived as merely symbolic. In sum, eligibility criteria, benefit type and budget size all seem suitable for the analysis of cross-national variation in welfare effort.

Cross-national Variations in Welfare Effort

Health care is one of the biggest welfare programs in almost all Western countries and has been expanded dramatically in the postwar decades. While the United States is often highlighted as a country where a large share of the population (around 15%) is without health insurance, this is in fact the exception that proves the rule.[2] All other Western countries are committed to "equal access to equal care to equal need" (OECD 2009: 31). Consequently, in all other Western countries, practically 100 per cent of the population is in fact covered (see Table 1), which means that access in reality is universal. Until 2005, high income groups in the Netherlands were not eligible for health care insurance and had to purchase private insurance until universal coverage was introduced in 2006. In Germany, a substantial share of the population is not covered by public health insurance, but again – and in direct contrast to the United States – those not covered are high income groups that have voluntarily opted out of the system (OECD 2008a). Thus, the fairly low level of public health insurance reported in Table 1 for the Netherlands and Germany overstates their uniqueness compared to other Western nations except the United States. The second column, which adds both public and private insurance, gives a much better impression of real access.

Table 1 also reports public spending as a percentage of GDP, while the bottom row reports the cross-national variation measured as the coefficient of variation.

Table 1. Health care statistics

Country	Insurance	Insurance incl. phi	Expenditure
Australia	100	100	6.4
Austria	98	98	7.7
Belgium	99	99	7.4
Canada	100	100	6.9
Denmark	100	100	7.7
Finland	100	100	5.9
France	99.9	99.9	8.9
Germany	89.6	99.8	8.2
Ireland	100	100	5.8
Italy	100	100	6.8
Japan	100	100	6.6
The Netherlands	62.1	97.9	5.7
New Zealand	100	100	7
Norway	100	100	7.6
Sweden	100	100	7.7
Switzerland	100	100	6.9
United Kingdom	100	100	7.2
United States	27.3	86.5	6.9
Coeff. of variation	0.20	0.03	0.12
Coeff. of variation w/o US	0.09	0.01	0.12

Notes: Insurance is measured as the share of the population covered by a public health insurance. Private health insurance (PHI) is measured as the share of the population that has private health insurance. Health expenditure is measured as percentage of the GDP.
Source: All data is taken from OECD (2007).

Even when the United States is included, the cross-national variation is four times smaller in terms of access than in terms of spending. If the United States is excluded from the sample, the variation is 12 times smaller than the variation for spending. Note also how the coefficient of variation is entirely unaffected by the exclusion of the United States in the bottom row calculation of the coefficient of variation for spending. This points to the fact that a large bulk of private health insurance in the United States in reality is heavily subsidized by the state, especially via tax breaks.

Education has become a much studied field in welfare state research over the past decade, not least because it constitutes a key link between public policy and the capitalist system in a country (Boix 1998, Castles 1998, Busemeyer 2007, 2009, Schmidt 2007, Iversen and Stephens 2008; Jensen 2011). Education is different from other welfare programs in the sense that it was introduced earlier than all other programs and that all Western nations, including the United States, have provided free access to primary and secondary schooling for all citizens for the past century. Like health care, public provision of education is best regarded as flat-rate because all citizens are entitled to similar benefits by the virtue of simply being a citizen. Of course, the quality in public provision may still vary across, e.g., sub-national regions, but not because of different social rights of citizens.

Given that access to primary and lower secondary schools is universal in all Western countries, the variation is by definition zero. But formal rights are one thing; actual usage something entirely different. How much does actual usage of primary and secondary education vary in modern welfare states? Table 2 provides an

Table 2. Education statistics

Country	Attainment	Expenditure
Australia	80	4.27
Austria	87	5.16
Belgium	82	5.78
Canada	91	4.68
Denmark	88	6.81
Finland	90	5.86
France	82	5.56
Germany	84	4.18
Ireland	82	4.29
Italy	67	4.26
Japan	N/A	3.38
Nethelands	81	4.63
New Zealand	78	5.24
Norway	83	5.67
Sweden	91	6.19
Switzerland	88	5.62
United Kingdom	76	5.00
United States	87	4.80
Coeff. of variation	0.07	0.16
Coeff. of variation w/o US	0.07	0.17

Notes: Attainment measured as 24–34-year-olds who have completed upper secondary education. Education spending measured as a percentage of GDP.
Source: Data taken from OECD (2008b).

impression by reporting how large a proportion of the population between age 24 and 34 has completed at least upper secondary education. I focus on this age group because we are interested in current-day welfare states rather than the welfare state of, say, the 1950s and 1960s when large cohorts of the older population attended school. Compare this measure with the spending measure reported in the final column and again a much larger cross-national variation emerges in the latter than in the former.

Moving on, we can contrast the pattern of health care and education with one of the programs most often studied, namely unemployment protection. Authors like Esping-Andersen (1990) and Korpi and Palme (1998) have, as mentioned, documented the great variation between nations in entitlement criteria and benefit types. Another way to assess the cross-national variation is to look at coverage and qualifying periods; both measures that have the important additional quality for the current purpose that they are measured on interval scales, meaning that I can compute statistics of variation and compare them with spending on unemployment protection.

As is evident from Table 3, a very different picture emerges compared with health care and education. Variation in coverage is two to four times greater here than in the other two programs, while variation in qualifying period is massively bigger, reaching a factor of 32 when compared with health care insurance including PHIs. Interestingly, the variation in expenditure is also bigger, a finding I return to in the

Table 3. Unemployment protection statistics

Country	Coverage	Qualifying period	Expenditure
Australia	1	0	1.1
Austria	0.66	156	1.7
Belgium	0.84	78	4.1
Canada	0.78	45	1.2
Denmark	0.82	52	5
Finland	0.73	43	2.9
France	0.58	61	2.8
Germany	0.69	104	3
Ireland	1	39	1.6
Italy	N/A	104	1.1
Japan	0.49	26	0.9
The Netherlands	0.88	208	2.9
New Zealand	1	0	1.3
Norway	0.93	4	1.3
Sweden	0.84	52	2.7
Switzerland	0.83	26	1.3
United Kingdom	0.85	10	0.7
United States	0.87	20	0.6
Coeff. of variation	0.17	0.96	0.60
Coeff. of variation w/o US	0.18	0.95	0.58

Notes and sources: Coverage measured as the share of the labor force insured for unemployment risk. Qualifying period measured as weeks of insurance needed to qualify for benefit. Both measures taken from Scruggs (2004). Expenditure measured as a percentage of the GDP. Data is taken from OECD (2009).

conclusion, yet what is most noteworthy right now is that the ratio between especially the qualifying period on the one side and expenditure on the other is very different from what we saw previously. The variation in qualifying period is greater than the variation in spending, which clearly sets this program apart from health care and education.

While evidently old-age pensions, unemployment protection, sickness insurance, health care and education constitute the main bulk of what conventionally is regarded as "the welfare state", a few other programs should be mentioned briefly because they take more intermediate positions. Elderly care and childcare are notable examples in this respect. Rauch (2007) documents that both elderly care and childcare are characterized by considerably cross-national variation in terms of entitlement criteria. Access may, in particular, vary depending on the applicants' familial and financial situation. In some countries access is only possible if the family is unable to provide care, or the individual cannot afford to purchase on the private market, whereas access is much more universal in other countries. Yet, while entitlement criteria vary considerably across countries, the public benefits received by those who are actually eligible are in general always flat-rate, i.e., independent of past earnings and payments.

Table 4 summarizes the discussion on cross-national variation in entitlement criteria and benefit type. It appears very stylized, but in fact it adds considerable nuance to the existing methodological debate in the sense that it highlights that the debate so far has been based on policy areas that exhibit very distinct characteristics. Compared to old-age pension, unemployment protection and sickness benefits, especially health care and education are characterized by much less cross-national variation in entitlement criteria and benefit type. Let me emphasize that it is a conclusion that relates to the concept of welfare effort specifically. Studying other aspects of the welfare state requires other measures, but given that some of the main welfare state theories actually focus explicitly on political decision making, this is in no way a marginal conclusion.

Does Social Spending Capture Political Decisions on the Size of the Budget?

So far the focus has been on the degree of cross-national variation in entitlement criteria, benefit type and budget size on different welfare programs. By and large I have simply assumed that political decisions on budget size are easy to capture using the standard spending measures provided chiefly by the OECD and other

Table 4. A typology of cross-national variation in entitlement criteria and benefit type

	Entitlement criteria	
Benefit type	Strong variation	Little variation
Strong variation	Old-age pensions Unemployment protection Sickness insurance	
Little variation	Elderly care Childcare	Health care Education

international organizations. Some authors have criticized this interpretation of secondary data, however. While I do not intend to defend this type of spending data uncritically, it is worth emphasizing how, as a minimum, the criticism does not appear to be isolated to spending measures. That is, there may be concrete problems associated with using spending data, but none that justify discarding spending on account of alternative measures of budget size, or more composite measures of social rights.

There are basically three points of criticism against secondary spending data as it is currently available. First, changes may not necessarily be due to new legislation, but may be caused by changing demographics or fiscal circumstances (Green-Pedersen 2002, 2004). Second, legislative changes in welfare programs may only gradually manifest themselves in spending levels (Green-Pedersen 2002, 2004). Third, the collection of spending data has been criticized as suffering from a lack of reliability (De Deken and Kittel 2007). The first point seems to miss the mark regarding cross-national variation in the sense that most statistical studies using spending data actually control for factors that automatically influence spending, including number of unemployed, proportion of the population aged 65 or older, etc. While such measures cannot perfectly capture developments in societal need, it is hard to identify a systematic cross-national bias in such imperfections, at least in large-N studies.

The second point appears more important and hints at some theoretically relevant aspects as well. As argued by Pierson (1994), politicians may have good reasons to enact legislation that is implemented some time after passage through parliament. Implementation delay can have important political benefits in terms of diminished electoral costs of reform. This is a highly valid point, but it does not seem to concern spending measures specifically. In fact, looking at the existing literature it appears that delayed implementation is just as often used when it comes to altering entitlement criteria and benefit type, as it is used to change the level of payment to the individual recipient (e.g., Pierson 1994, Green-Pedersen 2002). It is also worth noting that delayed implementation, while in principle a general strategy, seems to have particular appeal in reforms of old-age pension systems, i.e. a specific type of welfare program that is renowned for being slow moving (Myles and Pierson 2001). Finally, gradual manifestation of political decisions can to some extent be captured statistically with appropriate techniques (Plümper et al. 2005). Although rarely done, it is perfectly possible to model "gradual manifestation" of decisions using techniques like varying lag structure in a dynamic specification and error correction models.

The third problem concerns the reliability of secondary spending data. De Deken and Kittel (2007) have recently documented reliability problems in two often used datasets provided by the OECD and EU, at least in the data on the Netherlands and Germany. The problems highlighted by the authors are highly relevant because all conclusions inferred from spending data are premised on the accuracy of the data collection. Even though most empirical studies use tests of statistical significance, which may capture most of the noise in the data collection process,[3] reliability problems are of course always serious. Importantly, it seems quite clear that reliability problems are not confined to spending data, but pertain to other aggregated data sets as well. It has, thus, recently turned out that it is difficult to reproduce Esping-Andersen's (1990) findings using a new dataset intended to capture the same "social rights" (Allan and Scruggs 2006). The source of discrepancy is hard to locate, but illustrates how even these well-known alternatives to spending data also appear to suffer from reliability problems. Data on income replacement rates are also sensitive to developments in real wages of the average production worker (which is the baseline) both in absolute terms and relative to other income groups. If the average production worker experiences rising wages, as is normal, replacement rates will automatically decrease because they are measured as a percentage of wages even if no retrenchment has taken place. As it is, most studies using these kinds of data do not control for the development in wages. This is very interesting because it is the studies using these data that have found most retrenchment in the past few decades (Korpi and Palme 2003, Allan and Scruggs 2004).

Conclusion

Since the seminal work of Esping-Andersen (1990), a consensus seems to have formed in the methodological literature that social spending frequently does not capture what researchers are interested in. The most common justification for using spending data is simply the easy availability compared to all other alternatives. In this paper I have tried to nuance the discussion by arguing that spending in certain – non-trivial – situations is a highly valid measure of cross-national variation in welfare effort.

Given that this may be viewed as a controversial argument, it is also important to stress what I am *not* arguing. I am, first of all, not arguing that the substantial conclusions of the literature concerning old-age pensions, sickness benefits and unemployment protection are wrong. There does indeed seem to be so much cross-national variation on these programs in both entitlement criteria and benefit types that much information is lost when relying solely on social spending as a proxy for welfare effort. Yet I do contend that this conclusion has been inferred too uncritically to all other welfare programs. To researchers preoccupied with the large transfer programs this might seem irrelevant, but given the sheer size of programs like health care and education and the rising academic interest in these programs, it is pivotal to take these issues seriously.

I am, secondly, not arguing that the conclusions of the paper relate to any other aspect of the welfare state literature than welfare effort. As pointed out by Green-Pedersen (2004), different researchers mean different things when they talk about "the welfare state", which has caused great confusion. This paper has focused strictly on political decision making as understood by Wilensky (1975). Other well-established lines of research concern the outcome of political decisions, e.g., the actual economic redistribution (Bradley et al. 2003, Kenworthy 2004), and how existing institutions may de-couple from the macro-level and gradually self-transform (Streek and Thelen 2005). It is difficult to say to what extent social spending may work as a proxy in studies of these aspects, and this paper has made no attempt to infer its conclusions to encompass them.

Other scholars, and most notably Castles (2002, 2009), have also studied the qualities of spending measures. Castles shows that disaggregated spending measures in fact can capture welfare state characteristics rather well in the sense that a theoretically meaningful cross-national pattern emerges when looking at individual programs. Conversely, relying only on aggregated measures the patterns become murkier as a vast amount of information on spending priorities gets lost (for a similar conclusion, see Jensen 2008). Here I want to make two points. First, being interested in cross-national variation, the consistently most relevant variable is in fact spending. As can be gauged from Tables 1–3, the variation in spending is always fairly high, whereas the variation is the other measures fluctuates a lot more. This indicates that besides the fact that spending constitutes a common yardstick, spending is actually a rather attractive measure if we are seeking cross-program comparisons as for instance Castles has frequently done.

Second, there is considerable variation in the cross-national variation in all the various measures. Apparently, there is more room for variation when it comes to unemployment, childcare, and elderly care than when it comes to health care and education. As recently noted by Caramani (2010) and van Kersbergen (2010), the comparative politics literature at large seems to focus single-mindedly on variation over similarities. This certainly goes for the welfare state literature, as emphasized throughout this paper, where attention has been squarely on how to best measure variation between countries; the only exception being when authors try to explain similarities within welfare regimes, but here again, focus is really on the differences between regimes. Yet explaining *why* there is so limited variation in, e.g., access to health care would in many respects seem to be equally important to understanding variation, as the literature has done so far.

Notes

1. They call this the benefit level principle, but since this label may lead to the impression that the concept concerns the level of payments it has been changed for presentational purposes.
2. Only approximately 27% of the population is covered directly by public insurance, but given that private health care insurances are heavily subsidized via tax breaks, public involvement is in reality much greater.
3. Such control for measurement error is possible when spending is used as the dependent variable. If spending is also included among the explanatory variables it becomes much more problematic if nontrivial measurement problems exist. This is because it is a crucial assumption that "the explanatory variables are uncorrelated with the stochastic disturbance term. If this assumption is violated it can be shown that the OLS estimators are not only biased but also inconsistent, that is, they remain biased even if the sample size n increases indefinitely" (Gujarati 2003: 526).

References

Allan, J. P. and Scruggs, L., 2004, Political partisanship and welfare state reform in advanced industrial societies. *American Journal of Political Science*, **48**(3), 496–512.

Allan, J. P. and Scruggs, L., 2006, Welfare state decommodification in eighteen OECD countries: a replication and revision. *Journal of European Social Policy*, **16**(1), 55–72.

Boix, C., 1998, *Political Parties, Growth and Equality* (Cambridge: Cambridge University Press).

Bonoli, G. and Armingeon, K. (Eds.), 2006, *The Politics of Postindustrial Welfare States. Adapting Western Welfare States to the New Social Risks* (London: Routledge).

Bradley, D., Huber, E., Moller, S., Nielsen, F. and Stephens, J. D., 2003, Distribution and redistribution in postindustrial democracies. *World Politics*, **55** (January), 193–228.

Busemeyer, M. R., 2007, Determinants of public education spending in 21 OECD democracies, 1980–2001. *Journal of European Public Policy*, **14**(4), 582–610.

Busemeyer, M. R., 2009, Social democrats and the new partisan politics of public investment in education. *Journal of European Public Policy*, **16**(1), 107–126.

Caramani, D., 2010, Of differences and similarities: is the explanation of variation a limitation to (or of) comparative analysis, *European Political Science*, **9**(1), 34–48.

Castles, F. G., 1998, *Comparative Public Policy. Patterns of Post-war Transformations* (Cheltenham and Northampton, MA: Edward Elgar).

Castles, F. G., 2002, Developing new measures of welfare state change and reform. *European Journal of Political Research*, **41**(5), 613–641.

Castles, F. G., 2009, What welfare states do: a disaggregated expenditure approach. *Social Policy*, **38**(1), 45–62.

Clasen, J. and Clegg, D., 2007, Levels and levers of conditionality: measuring changing within welfare states, in: J. Clasen and N. A. Siegel (Eds) *Investigating Welfare State Change. The "Dependent Variable Problem" in Comparative Analysis* (Cheltenham and Northampton, MA: Edward Elgar), pp. 166–197.

De Deken, J. and Kittel, B., 2007, Social expenditure under scrutiny: the problems of using aggregated spending data for assessing welfare state dynamics, in: J. Clasen and N. A. Siegel (Eds.) *Investigating Welfare State Change. The "Dependent Variable Problem" in Comparative Analysis* (Cheltenham and Northampton, MA: Edward Elgar), pp. 72–104.

Esping-Andersen, G., 1990, *The Three Worlds of Welfare Capitalism* (Cambridge: Polity Press).

Esping-Andersen, G., 1999, *Social Foundations of Postindustrial Economies* (Oxford: Oxford University Press).

Estevez-Abe, M., Iversen, T. and Soskice, D., 2001, Social protection and the formation of skills: a reinterpretation of the welfare state, in: P. Hall and D. Soskice (Eds) *Varieties of Capitalism: The Institutional Foundations of Comparative Advantage* (London: Oxford University Press), pp. 145–183.

Goul Andersen, J., 2007, Conceptualizing welfare state change. The "dependent variable problem" writ large. CCWS Working Paper 51-2007, Aalborg.

Green-Pedersen, C., 2002, *The politics of justification. Party competition and welfare-state retrenchment in Denmark and the Netherlands from 1982 to 1998* (Amsterdam: Amsterdam University Press).

Green-Pedersen, C., 2004, The dependent variable problem within the study of welfare state retrenchment: defining the problem and looking for solutions. *Journal of Comparative Policy Analysis*, **6**(1), 3–14.

Gujarati, D. N., 2003, *Basic Econometrics*, 4th ed. (Boston: McGraw Hill).

Hicks, A., 1999, *Social Democracy and Welfare Capitalism. A Century of Income Security Politics* (Ithaca, NY and London: Cornell University Press).

Huber, E. and Stephens, J. D., 2001, *Development and Crisis of the Welfare State. Parties and Politics in Global Markets* (Chicago and London: University of Chicago Press).

Iversen, T., 2005, *Capitalism, Democracy, and Welfare* (Cambridge: Cambridge University Press).

Iversen, T. and Stephens, J. D., 2008, Partisan politics, the welfare state, and the three worlds of human capital formation. *Comparative Political Studies*, **41**(4/5), 600–637.

Jensen, C., 2008, Worlds of welfare services and transfers, *Journal of European Social Policy*, **18**(2), 151–162.

Jensen, C., 2011. Capitalist systems, de-industrialization, and the politics of education. *Comparative Political Studies*, **44**(4), 412–435.

Kangas, O. and Palme, J., 2007, Social rights, structural needs and social expenditure: a comparative study of 18 OECD countries 1960–2000, in: J. Clasen and N. A. Siegel (Eds) *Investigating Welfare State Change. The "Dependent Variable Problem" in Comparative Analysis* (Cheltenham and Northampton, MA: Edward Elgar), pp. 106–130.

Kenworthy, L., 2004, *Egalitarian Capitalism* (New York: Russell Sage Foundation).

Korpi, W., 1983, *The Democratic Class Struggle* (London: Routledge & Kegan Paul).

Korpi, W., 2001, Contentious institutions. An augmented rational-action analysis of the origins and path dependency of welfare state institutions in the Western countries. *Rationality and Society*, **13**(2), 235–283.

Korpi, W., 2006, Power resources and employer-centered approaches in explanations of welfare states and varieties of capitalism. *World Politics*, **58**(January), 167–206.

Korpi, W. and Palme, J., 1998, The paradox of redistribution and strategies of inequality: Welfare state institutions, and poverty in the Western countries. *American Sociological Review*, **63**(October), 661–687.

Korpi, W. and Palme, J., 2003, New politics and class politics in the context of austerity and globalization: welfare state regress in 18 countries, 1975–1995. *American Political Science Review*, **97**(3), 425–446.

Kühner, S., 2007, Country-level comparisons of welfare state change measures: another facet of the dependent variable problem within comparative analysis of the welfare state? *Journal of European Social Policy*, **17**(1), 5–18.

Martin, C. J. and Swank, D., 2004, Does the organization of capital matter? Employers and active labor market policies at the national and firm levels. *American Political Science Review*, **98**(4), 593–611.

Myles, J. and Pierson, P., 2001, The comparative political economy of pension reform, in: P. Pierson (Ed.) *The New Politics of the Welfare State* (Oxford: Oxford University Press).

OECD, 2007, *Health Data 2007* (Paris: OECD Publishing), available from: http://www.sourceoecd.org

OECD, 2008a, *Health at a Glance* (Paris: OECD Publishing), available from: http://www.sourceoecd.org

OECD, 2008b, *Education at a Glance* (Paris: OECD Publishing), available from: http://www.sourceoecd.org

OECD, 2009, *OECD.Stats* (Paris: OECD Publishing), available from: http://www.sourceoecd.org

Pierson, P., 1994, *Dismantling the Welfare State? Reagan, Thatcher, and the Politics of Retrenchment* (Cambridge: Cambridge University Press).

Plümper, T., Troeger, V. E. and Manow, P., 2005, Panel data analysis in comparative politics: linking method to theory. *European Journal of Political Research*, **44**(2), 337–354.

Rauch, D., 2007, Is there really a Scandinavian social service model? A comparison of childcare and elderlycare in six European countries. *Acta Sociologica*, **50**(3), 249–269.

Schmidt, M. G., 2007, Testing the retrenchment hypothesis: educational spending, 1960–2002, in: F. G. Castles (Ed.) *The Disappearing State. Retrenchment Realities in an Age of Globalisation* (Cheltenham and Northampton, MA: Edward Elgar), pp. 159–183.

Scruggs, L., 2004, *Welfare State Entitlements: A Comparative Institutional Analysis of Eighteen Welfare States*, available from: http://vm.uconn.edu/~scruggs/index.html

Scruggs, L., 2007, Welfare state generosity across space and time, in: J. Clasen and N. A. Siegel (Eds.) *Investigating Welfare State Change. The "Dependent Variable Problem" in Comparative Analysis* (Cheltenham and Northampton, MA: Edward Elgar), pp. 133–165.

Siegel, N. A., 2007, When (only) money matters: the pros and cons of expenditure analysis, in: J. Clasen and N.A. Siegel (Eds) *Investigating Welfare State Change. The "Dependent Variable Problem" in Comparative Analysis* (Cheltenham and Northampton, MA: Edward Elgar), pp. 42–72.

Streeck, W. and Thelen, K. (Eds), 2005, *Beyond Continuity. Institutional Change in Advanced Political Economies* (Oxford: Oxford University Press).

Stephens, J. D., 1979, *The Transition from Capitalism to Socialism* (Urbana and Chicago: University of Illinois Press).

Van Kersbergen, K., 2010, Comparative politics: some points for discussion. *European Political Science*, **9**(819), 49–61.

Wilensky, H. L., 1975, *The Welfare State and Equality* (Berkeley: University of California Press).

Wilensky, H. L. and Lebeaux, C. N., 1958, *Industrial Society and Social Welfare: The Impact of Industrialization on the Supply and Organization of Social Welfare in the United States* (New York: Russell Sage).

The Regulation of Working Time as Work-Family Reconciliation Policy: Comparing Europe, Japan, and the United States

JANET C. GORNICK and ALEXANDRA HERON

ABSTRACT *This article compares working time policies in eight European countries, Japan, and the US, specifically policies that embody three goals: (1) reducing the full-time working week to less than the traditional standard of 40 hours; (2) guaranteeing workers an adequate number of paid days, annually, away from the workplace; and (3) raising the quality and availability of voluntary part-time work. While working time policies can help to free up parental caregiving time, they also have some potentially problematic consequences – including an associated rise in nonstandard-hour scheduling and the possibility of negative effects on gender equality.*

Introduction: Working Time Regulation as Work-Family Reconciliation Policy

Across the industrialized countries, in the last two decades, researchers, policymakers, and advocates have increasingly called attention to the problem of "work-family conflict". This is hardly surprising given the dramatic rise, during the post-war era, in the employment rates of mothers, especially those with young children. Currently, in most OECD countries, the majority of couples with children have both parents in the labor force; single mothers' employment rates generally exceed those of married mothers. Throughout these countries, parents are struggling to balance the demands and rewards of employment with the needs of their families.

Although concerns about "work-family conflict" are prevalent everywhere, perceptions of "what's broke?" are, in fact, extraordinarily diverse – within and across countries – and often difficult to reconcile. Child development experts, for example, typically raise concerns about the consequences for children of insufficient time with their parents; in practice, this question is generally focused on children's time with their mothers. "Work-life" advocates, in contrast, often consider the problematic consequences of employment – not for children, but for parents, especially mothers. According to this perspective, working parents (mothers) are over-extended; their competing responsibilities lead to untenable levels of stress. Other critics of contemporary practices are troubled by persistent gender disparities in the labor market, disparities that are both cause and consequence of women's disproportionate assumption of caring work at home. Still others are alarmed by the financial implications for families of the high price of the non-parental care that is needed when parents are at the workplace – an especially serious concern in the US, and elsewhere, where public child care provisions are minimal.

Because perceptions of "what's broke" vary so widely, it is not surprising that there is a diversity of views as to what parents need to help them reconcile employment and family care. Some emphasize the need for more high-quality, affordable child care, and/or longer annual school hours, which would free up parents to devote more time to employment. Some focus, instead, on the need for paid leave, including leave to care for infants or sick children, or to attend to family-related emergencies. Others call for taxes or transfers that compensate mothers who stay home altogether. Still others advocate strengthening forms of employment – such as telecommuting, web-based work, and self-employment – that allow parents to work in closer proximity to their children.

In this article, we analyze yet another strategy that is crucial for helping parents reconcile the competing demands of parenthood and employment: *the regulation of working time*. We focus on a package of measures that embody three over-arching goals: first, to reduce the full-time working week to less than the traditional standard of 40 hours; second, to guarantee workers an adequate number of paid days, annually, away from the workplace; and third, to raise the quality and availability of voluntary part-time work.[1] Achieving the first two goals would, in effect, put a ceiling on annual hours worked, even among those with strong labor market ties. That would help to standardize the definition of full-time/full-year employment at a level that allows working parents to secure adequate time at home. Achieving the third goal would enable parents to choose part-time work, for short or long periods, without a disproportionate loss of compensation.

We analyze working time measures in comparative perspective, considering provisions in ten countries that span the leading economies of the world – eight European Union (EU) countries, Japan, and the United States. We focus on these countries because there is extensive variation among them in both working time policies and in working time outcomes – such as annual and weekly hours actually worked, and the availability and quality of part-time work.

In the EU, the regulation of working time has been prominent on policy agendas for decades, at both the supranational and national level. The EU enacted two Directives in the 1990s – the 1993 Directive on Working Time and the 1997 Directive on Part-Time Work. These were binding for EU member countries, requiring national-level policy implementation by 1996 and 2000, respectively. Working time reductions in Europe have been advocated for reasons that have varied both across countries and over time. In the 1980s, the emphasis was most often on combating unemployment by spreading available work, and the 1993 EU Directive on Working Time referred to health and safety reasons (European Communities 1993). But, more recently, public discourse in a number of countries has shifted more towards "work-family" – or "work-life" – balance (OECD 1998, OECD 2004a).[2] In several countries, the stated rationale for reducing work hours includes supporting a more even distribution of paid and unpaid work between men and women (see Fagnani and Letablier 2004).

Policy reforms aimed at reducing working time appear to have had an effect. In the last 20 years, average annual hours decreased in most EU countries and, in several countries, some portion of that decrease is attributed to declining full-timers' hours. In some countries, average hours also declined due to a rising percentage of workers (mostly women) employed part-time (Lehndorff 2000).

Japan and the US offer rich contrasting cases. In Japan, annual work hours also declined during the 1980s and 1990s (Lehndorff 2000), but to a level well above that seen in EU countries. In the 1990s, Japanese law gradually reduced the legal working week to 40 hours, with the goal of improving workers' quality of life and easing the longstanding culture of long work hours (Lee 2004). In 2001, working time reductions remained on the labor policy agenda in Japan, with the social partners considering further reductions, aimed in part at maintaining employment via work-sharing (Carley 2003).

In the US, in contrast to both the EU countries and Japan, average annual hours actually *increased* during the last two decades (Lehndorff 2000), overtaking the Japanese level (see Figure 1). The US is also distinct in other ways. Remarkably, the normal working week in the US, set by national legislation enacted in 1938, has not been reduced in over 60 years. In addition, efforts to reduce working time are virtually absent from contemporary US policy agendas. Messenger (2004: xviii) notes that "from an American perspective, until very recently working time never seemed to be more than an afterthought in discussions of labour issues and labour market policies. Even now, with changes to US overtime in the news, the focus is not on the *number of hours* that people work, but rather *how much they will be paid* for working those hours". As Messenger observes, Americans generally view long hours in a positive light – as evidence of Americans' industriousness and the cause of the US's comparatively high per capita GDP. Indeed, in US policy discourse, long work hours are often framed as worthy of replication. Perhaps more significant is that even "work-family" scholars and advocates in the US rarely address the length of the normal full-time working week, the definition of full-year work, or the quality of part-time work. American work-family advocates, instead, typically focus on the need for child care, paid family leave, and (employer-based) programs that permit flexibility in determining which – if not how many – hours workers will spend on the job (Gornick and Meyers 2003).

In the next section, we compare key working time regulations in ten countries, including measures that establish the normal full-time week, regulate minimum annual days of leave, and protect part-time workers. In the third section we assess actual working time in these countries, and consider the extent to which these outcomes are policy-sensitive.

Figure 1. Workers' average annual hours in paid work, 2000

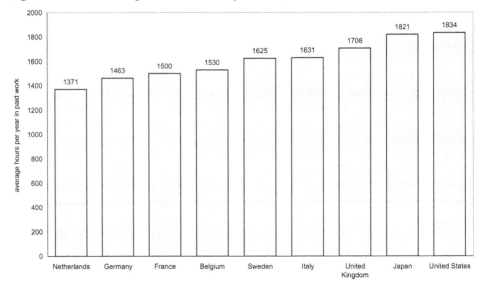

Source: OECD (data on Luxembourg not available).

In the final section, we reflect on two important concerns sparked by ongoing efforts to reduce working time. Each raises the possibility that shortening working time, in practice, may have some problematic consequences, especially for workers with family responsibilities. One concern is that the reduction in work hours, particularly in Europe, is being achieved at the cost of more nonstandard, and less controllable or predictable, work scheduling. A second is that strengthening reduced-hour work may exacerbate, rather than alleviate, gender inequalities in paid and unpaid work.

Policy Variation: Working Time Policies in Europe, Japan, and the US

Working time policies, and efforts to reform them, operate in diverse institutional frameworks. The institutional backdrops of our comparison countries – eight EU countries, Japan, and the US – are summarized in Table 1. As indicated, in six of these EU countries, working time is typically governed by a combination of labor law and collective agreements, while in France and Italy, labor law traditionally dominates. Coverage rates of collective bargaining in the continental European countries are 60 to 80 percent in Germany, Italy, Luxembourg, and the Netherlands – and 90 percent or higher in Belgium, France, and Sweden. The UK is set apart by the limited reach of collective bargaining; the coverage rate is about 30 percent, less than half that of most of the continental countries. In Europe, diversity in policy-setting mechanisms is supported at the supranational level. The EU Directives relating to working conditions allow member countries to implement required practices through legislation, formalized agreements among the social partners (groups representing employers and workers), or some combination of the two. In Japan and the US,

Table 1. Institutional framework, c. 2000

	Primary mechanism for regulation of working time	Employees covered by collective bargaining (as a percentage of the workforce)
	European Union	
Belgium	Combination of collective agreements and labour law.	90+%
France	Primarily labour law.	90+%
Germany	Combination of collective agreements and labour law.	68%
Italy	Primarily labour law.	80+%
Luxembourg	Combination of collective agreements and labour law.	60+%
Netherlands	Combination of collective agreements and labour law.	80+%
Sweden	Combination of collective agreements and labour law.	90+%
United Kingdom	Combination of collective agreements and labour law.	30+%
	Non-Europe	
Japan	Primarily labour law.	15+%
United States	Primarily national labour law, with some supplementation by state laws.	14%

Notes:
Collective bargaining coverage refers to the percentage of workers whose wages and working conditions are set, at least to some extent, by collective bargaining, regardless of whether they are union members.
Figures in column 3 with a + represent lower-bound estimates.
Sources: Carley 2003, Evans *et al.* 2001, Gornick and Meyers 2003, Jung 2000, Messenger 2004, OECD 2004b.

in contrast, only about one worker in seven is covered by a collective agreement. Not surprisingly, working time measures in these two countries are largely determined by labor law. And, clearly, individual agreements between employers and employees are also important for many workers – especially in the UK, Japan, and the US, where collective coverage is so far from universal.

One of the most powerful mechanisms for shaping working time is the establishment of a normal (or standard) full-time working week (see Table 2). Normal weekly hours generally refers to the threshold above which overtime becomes payable. Some EU countries establish normal weekly hours through legislation and collective agreement, while others regulate maximum hours (generally set at an average of 48) but leave the setting of normal hours exclusively to the bargaining table.[3] Currently, in the continental EU countries included here, the normal full-time working week, for at least a substantial majority of workers, is set by collective agreements below 40 hours – 35 in France and between 37 and 39 in the other countries. In the UK, an outlier among EU countries, there is no statutory normal working week[4] and, while collective agreements, on average, set the week at about 37 hours, only a third of the UK labor force is covered. Both Japan and the US set normal hours, via legislation, at 40 hours, above the standard typical in most EU countries – and a full five hours

Table 2. Normal weekly working hours, c. 2003

	By statute	By collective agreement (average collectively agreed weekly hours)
	European Union	
Belgium	38 with possible reduction through collective agreements.	38
France	35 with possible reduction through collective agreements.	35
Germany	Legislation sets maximum weekly hours (48) but not normal weekly hours.	37.7
Italy	40 with possible reduction through collective agreements.	38
Luxembourg	Legislation sets maximum weekly hours (48) but not normal weekly hours.	39
Netherlands	Legislation sets maximum weekly hours (48) but not normal weekly hours.	37
Sweden	40 with possible reduction through collective agreements.	38.8
United Kingdom	Legislation sets maximum weekly hours (48) but not normal weekly hours.	37.2
	Non-Europe	
Japan	40	Information on average award not available
United States	40	Information on average award not available

Notes:
Normal weekly hours (as distinct from maximum hours) generally refers to the threshold above which an overtime premium becomes payable.
The 1993 EU Directive on Working Time (WTD) – now Directive 2003/88/EC – was binding in all EU member countries with an implementation deadline of 1996. The WTD stipulates that maximum working hours must not exceed 48 weekly. National laws can permit this limit to be averaged over up to four months (six months for some workers) and up to 12 months by collective agreement. EU member countries also set normal weekly work hours and regulate averaging and overtime (within the WTD's parameters). Certain exceptions to the WTD are allowed if national laws permit, e.g., senior executives, or where an employer and employee agree to opt out of the working time limit (with the latter nearly exclusively used in the UK). Hours averaging can occur in the countries in this table, except in the US in relation to employees covered by the FLSA (see US note below). When hours are averaged, overtime payments may be calculated in ways that refer to hours worked during a longer reference period than a single week.
Belgium: The statutory working week (set by intersectoral agreement but effective as law) was cut from 39 to 38 in January 2003.
France: Since 1 January 2002, normal weekly hours must, by law, be set at 35 hours in all companies. The law calls on collective bargaining "to negotiate the practicalities of actual reduction of working hours". Enterprises with fewer than 20 employees have an exemption scheme relating to overtime.

(*continued*)

Table 2. (*Continued*)
Germany: Figures for hours set by collective agreement cover the whole of Germany. The figure for west Germany was 37.4 hours in both 2002 and 2003, and the figure for east Germany was 39.1 hours in 2002 and 39.0 in 2003.
Japan: Although there is no available information on average collective agreements, available data indicate that "average scheduled weekly working hours" equalled 39.2 in 2001. Note that Japan requires a worker-management agreement for overtime to be worked. Employers must then only "endeavor" to keep to a 15 hour weekly limit (with 45 monthly and 360 annually as overall limits).
Luxembourg: The collective agreements figure is an estimate.
Netherlands: The collective agreements figure is based on a sample of agreements.
United States: The Fair Labor Standards Act (FLSA), which regulates normal weekly hours (and requires a 50% premium for each hour worked over 40 in a week) excludes many workers (e.g. managers/supervisors and those over set earnings limits); approximately 27% of full-time workers are exempt. While no data are available on average collective agreements, survey data from 1999 indicate that, in medium and large establishments, 86% of full-time employees have weekly work schedules of 40 hours or more.
Sources: Carley 2004, 2003, Gornick and Meyers 2003.

per week above the French standard. In the US, any effects associated with the comparatively long standard week are compounded by the limited reach of the Fair Labor Standards Act (FLSA). The FLSA excludes many workers, including managers and supervisors and those over specified earnings limits, from its requirement that overtime is paid after 40 hours of weekly work; approximately 27 percent of full-time workers in the US are exempt.

In addition to setting weekly hours, countries effectively set the normal number of days worked per year – meaning that working time policies define the meaning of not just full-time work, but full-year work as well. The full year is defined, in practice, by the establishment of paid vacation and holiday entitlements (see Table 3). As with normal hours, vacation entitlements are embedded in diverse institutional frameworks. In these European countries, a statutory minimum exists and collective agreements typically raise that minimum for many covered workers (see columns 1 and 2). In Europe, some homogeneity is imposed by the EU Working Time Directive, which requires "that every worker is entitled to paid annual leave of at least four weeks in accordance with the conditions for entitlement to, and granting of, such leave laid down by national legislation and/or practice" (European Communities 1993). In practice, workers in these EU countries are typically entitled to between 25 and 33 days per year of paid vacation (or about five or six weeks) – meaning that full-year work corresponds to approximately 46 to 47 weeks a year.

Again, workers in Japan and, even more so, in the US work under substantially different rules. Japanese workers are entitled by law to 10 vacation days after 6 months of continuous service, increasing with length of service to a maximum of 20 days – thus workers with long tenures are entitled to vacation time nearing European levels. While no data are available on average collective agreements, Japanese workers are entitled, in practice, to about 18 days of paid vacation each year. In the US, national legislation is silent with respect to vacation days and collective bargaining reaches only a small share of workers. It is difficult to determine average vacation entitlements in the US. One survey found that American workers with 10 years of service in medium/large enterprises were entitled to, on average, about 17 vacation days per year (Carley 2003); workers with shorter tenures receive substantially fewer.[5]

Table 3. Annual paid vacation entitlement and public holidays, c. 2001–2003

	Annual paid vacation entitlement (number of days)		Statutory minimum annual vacation plus public holidays
	Statutory minimum	By collective agreement (average collectively agreed days)	
		European Union	
Belgium	20	Current information not available	30
France	25	25	36
Germany	20	29.1	29–32
Italy	20	27.5	32
Luxembourg	25	28	35
Netherlands	20	31.3	28
Sweden	25	32.5	36
United Kingdom	20	24.5	28
		Non-Europe	
Japan	10	Information on average award not available	25
United States	0	Information on average award not available	10

Notes:
The 1993 EU Directive on Working Time (see note to Table 2) stipulated not less than 4 weeks annual paid vacation.
Data given as weeks were converted to a number of days, assuming a 5-day working week.
Belgium: In 1993, the figure for average collective agreements was 25 days.
Germany: The collective agreement figure is for the whole country.
Italy: The collective agreements figure is calculated as 4 weeks' leave, plus the mid-range between 5 and 10 days awarded as a form of working time reduction.
Japan: Workers are entitled by statute to 10 days after 6 months' continuous service, increasing to a maximum of 20 days depending on length of service. While no data are available on average collective agreements, Japanese workers are entitled, on average, to 18 days of paid vacation.
Luxembourg: The collective agreement figure is an estimate.
Netherlands: The collective agreement figure represents 25.3 days of holiday, plus 6 days awarded in the context of reduction in working time.
Sweden: The collective agreement figure is calculated as the statutory 25 days, plus the mid-range between 5 and 10 days' additional leave awarded in most collective agreements.
United States: While no data are available on average annual vacation leave in collective agreements, survey data indicate that, in medium and large private sector establishments, average paid vacation days among full-time employees are: 9.6 days after 1 year, 11.5 days after 3 years, 13.8 days after 5 years, and 16.8 after 10 years.
Sources: Carley 2004, 2003, Jung 2000, OECD 2003.

The number of days that workers are permitted – and expected – to be away from work is also shaped by the establishment of public holidays.[6] While holidays also increase workers' time outside of work, sometimes substantially, they are generally less advantageous than vacation days, as workers typically have no control over when they can take them. When vacation and holiday entitlements are summed (see column 3), we see that workers in the EU countries are granted from 28 annual days off (in the Netherlands and the UK) to as many as 36 days (in France). Japanese workers' entitlement, at 25 days, is well above the US outcome (10 days), due to both the Japanese vacation statute and the larger number of public holidays.

A third set of working time measures complement those that directly influence work hours and days directly: policies that aim to raise the quality of part-time work and those that grant various rights to work part-time.[7] Measures intended to raise the quality of part-time work include, first, requiring pay and benefits parity between part-time and full-time workers, and, second, enabling workers to shift from full-time to part-time work without being forced to change jobs. The right-to-work-part-time measures are also intended to raise the availability of part-time work, for full-time workers who wish to reduce their hours and, depending on the law, for new labor market entrants who might otherwise refrain from employment. (Measures that raise the availability of shorter-hour employment could, in turn, affect labor force participation rates. Many women – mothers especially – choose non-employment because no high-quality reduced-hour work is available; see Clarkberg and Moen 2001).

Policies aimed at improving part-time work are widespread throughout Europe. A crucial force behind these measures is the 1997 EU Directive on Part-Time Work, whose official purpose was "to eliminate discrimination against part-time workers and to improve the quality of part-time work" (Europa 2004). All eight of the EU countries in this study have implemented the Directive via some mix of legislation and collective agreements. The Directive requires that member states enact measures prohibiting employers from treating part-time workers less favorably than "comparable full-time workers", unless they demonstrate that this is objectively justifiable. The national measures address various combinations of pay equity, social security and occupational benefits, training and promotion opportunities, and bargaining rights. In contrast, although Japan enacted a law aimed at the effective utilization of part-time workers' skills, Japanese law provides no pay and benefit parity protection. With the exception of coverage under the national minimum wage law, US labor law is entirely silent on part-time workers' remuneration.

The Part-Time Directive also urged, but did not require, member states to eliminate obstacles that limit opportunities for part-time work and instructed employers to "give consideration" to workers who request transfers between part-time and full-time work as their personal and family needs change (Europa 2004). Long before the Part-Time Directive, Sweden had already set the gold standard on the right to part-time work. Since 1978 Swedish parents have had the right to work six hours a day (at pro rata pay) until their children turn eight. After the Directive, other European countries added new protections. Germany now grants the right to work part-time to employees in enterprises with more than 15 workers; the Netherlands enacted a similar right in enterprises of 10 of more workers. Belgium grants employees the right to work 80 percent time for five years. In most cases, employers have a safety valve; they can refuse a change on business grounds but those grounds are often subject to official review. A recent UK law grants employees, in enterprises of any size, the legal right to request flexible working time – including part-time work – in order to care for a child under age six or a disabled child under age 18. The employer has seven different grounds on which to refuse an application and must give reasons for such a refusal. Italy and Luxembourg join Japan and the US in granting workers no particular legal rights to seek part-time work.

Does Policy Matter? Cross-National Variation in Hours Worked

How many hours per year do workers actually work in these ten countries? Figure 1 presents an OECD estimate of annual hours worked in 2000 in our comparison countries, except for Luxembourg (reported in Mishel *et al.* 2005). As the figure indicates, there is substantial variation within Europe. Annual hours are 1530 or fewer in Belgium, France, Germany, and the Netherlands, just over 1600 in Sweden and Italy, and substantially higher in the UK. Workers in Japan and the US work the longest hours, logging more than 1800 hours annually, nearly one-third more than the average Dutch worker and more than 10 percent more than Swedish and Italian workers.

Figure 2 shifts vantage points and considers actual hours worked per week – rather than annually – and specifically among parents. This figure reports average weekly hours worked jointly by dual-earner married/cohabiting couples with children.[8] Cross-national variation is again substantial, with American working couples averaging 16 more hours per week – or the equivalent of two full days – than Dutch parents. The figure also indicates that mothers' hours vary much more than fathers', ranging from 21 per week in the Netherlands to 36 in the US, although fathers' hours vary as well – from 38 in Sweden to a remarkable high of 48 in the UK.

Note that the cross-national rankings in the two figures are similar (correlation coefficient = .7) although some differences stand out. When the focus is on parents, Sweden and the UK both drop down in the country ranking – however, for different reasons. In Sweden both mothers and fathers work relatively reduced hours, whereas in the UK many mothers work reduced hours – with a large share working short part-time hours – while fathers log unusually long hours.[9] Finally, dual-earner couples in Italy are nearly as time-squeezed as their US counterparts, partly because part-time work in Italy remains relatively uncommon. Italian mothers who are in the labor market log hours as long as those of American mothers – although their employment rates are substantially lower.

Figure 2. Parents' average weekly hours in paid work, middle 1990s to 2000 (employed married/cohabiting parents)

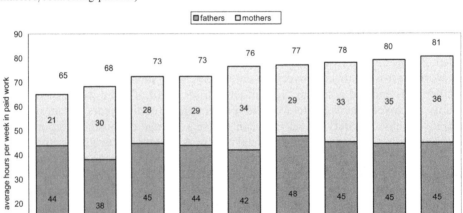

Source: Luxembourg Income Study (data on Japan not available).

Undoubtedly, work hours vary sharply across these countries. Is this variation demonstrably shaped by the policy variation presented in the previous section? Clearly, there is an association between the institutional frameworks and the policies, on the one hand, and actual hours worked on the other. That association is most evident when we contrast the continental European countries as a group with the UK, Japan, and the US. In the continental European countries, collective bargaining coverage is substantially higher than in the other three and policies go further in limiting weekly hours, capping annual days, and enabling and protecting part-time workers. Not surprisingly, then, workers in these countries work fewer hours than their British counterparts and even more so than their Japanese and American counterparts.

Yet, an association does not establish causality – obviously – and it is possible that other factors matter more than these policies. Some observers have argued that underlying preferences for working time vary across countries. Perhaps American and Japanese workers, including parents, simply want to work more hours than do most Europeans.[10] It is also possible that other structural factors are more important than these direct measures. Bell and Freeman (2001), for example, attribute Americans' relatively long hours to higher levels of wage dispersion such that an extra hour worked has a higher return in the US than elsewhere. Prescott (2004) argues similarly that lower taxation rates in the US motivate comparatively longer hours, as returns to additional hours are greater.

Research on working time indicates that the policies reported in the previous section in fact do matter – especially the regulation of normal and maximum hours. Several empirical studies assess the effects of normal-hour thresholds, and they all find evidence that lowering overtime pay thresholds reduce actual working time among employees (see OECD 1998 and Gornick and Meyers 2003 for reviews). A number of studies have estimated the magnitude of the effect of reducing regulated standard hours on actual hours worked. Estimates of the magnitude of the effect range from about 75 to nearly 100 percent of the change in standard work hours. Researchers have reported the effect on actual hours to be about 77 percent in the United Kingdom; 85 to 100 percent in Germany; and close to 100 percent in France (see Gornick and Meyers 2003 for a review of this research).[11] Although maximum hours have received less attention in empirical research, they too seem to have a strong effect on actual hours worked. Grubb and Wells (1993), for example, assessed the effects of restrictions on overtime hours. They found that, across Europe, maximum limits on annual overtime hours – which ranged from under 100 to over 500 hours per year – were a strong negative predictor of the observed frequency of overtime work.[12]

In addition, the limited evidence that exists also indicates that the generosity of vacation entitlements has a strong effect on the days per year actually worked – with the possible exception of Japan, where average vacation take-up is substantially less than that allotted (Carley 2003). Like European workers, American workers take up their rights at relatively high levels; one recent study found that about 70 percent of employed Americans take all of their allocated vacation days (Expedia 2004).

The effects of part-time legislation on part-time work rates and/or part-time workers' remuneration are not well known, in part because the EU Part-Time Directive and the national measures that followed were implemented only recently; several outcome evaluations are underway. There are correlational findings that link regulation to the availability or quality of part-time work; for example, more protective regulations are seen in countries with larger part-time labor markets and smaller pay penalties. One recent study, for example, finds that part-time/full-time wage differentials in Germany, the UK, and especially in Sweden are substantially smaller than those reported in the US, where part-time workers' compensation is not protected by law (Bardasi and Gornick 2002). However, virtually no research persuasively establishes a causal link.

Policy Conundrums: Reducing Work Hours – at What Cost?

Scholars, policymakers, analysts and advocates who are assessing and debating working time policies have raised the possibility that efforts to reduce working hours may have some worrisome consequences, especially for workers and their families. Most agree that shortening full-time workers' hours, and creating opportunities for high-quality part-time work, have the potential to free up parental time for caregiving. But at what cost?

Two concerns, both of them complex, frequently surface. First, a number of working time analysts have observed that, in many European settings, workers are gaining shorter hours but are being forced in return to accept more nonstandard schedules – often along with diminished control and predictability. Second, others argue that efforts to strengthen reduced-hour work inevitably create new forms of gender inequality, because it is women, overwhelmingly, who will reduce their hours or choose shorter-hour work. We close this article by reflecting on these two important policy conundrums.

First, in recent years, while several European countries have implemented reductions in total working hours, a number of these countries have ushered in new practices that increase employers' options to schedule workers "flexibly" – which, in practice, often means during nonstandard hours. These new practices are on the rise largely because an increasing number of European employers are operating under various "annualized hours" (AH) schemes. AH schemes allow employers to average workers' hours over periods of time ("reference periods") longer than a week – and, in some cases, up to a year (hence the terminology). AH schemes, of course, enable employers to fit workers' schedules to production or commercial needs, and the result is that more workers are scheduled during nonstandard hours – including during evenings, nights, and weekends – and/or assigned hours that rise and fall weekly, monthly, or seasonally. AH schemes also allow employers to pay less overtime, as overtime thresholds may be set not weekly but for the reference period as a whole.

Some of the momentum underlying AH schemes – which expanded in the 1990s – came from the EU itself. The 1993 Working Time Directive explicitly allows working hours up to the 48-hour weekly maximum to be calculated over a four-month period, which can be extended up to 12 months by collective agreement. Furthermore, the Directive implicitly allows member countries to establish reference periods of longer than a week for normal and/or overtime hours as well. In most countries, AH schemes are mainly designed at the bargaining table and they vary widely across and within countries. Although AH arrangements are usually favored by employers, employees' representatives typically agree to them – or even initiate them – in exchange for some compensatory benefit, most often, a reduction in total work hours (Kouzis and Kretsos 2003). Thus, in practice if not in principle, legions of European workers may have gained shorter hours at the cost of more nonstandard work scheduling and, in many cases, reduced control and predictability.[13]

For workers with family care responsibilities, even with reduced total hours, having a nonstandard, uncontrollable and/or unpredictable schedule can make reconciling work and family responsibilities difficult. In a groundbreaking study, Fagnani and Letablier (2004) report findings from a survey that queried French parents with young children about the impact of the 35-hour law on their ability to balance work and family. The French case is a significant one – with implications for other countries – because annualization schemes, set at the sectoral or company level, are widespread and reference periods of 12 months are not uncommon. Fully 58 percent of French parents report that the 35-hour law has made family care easier for them – a finding that underscores the importance of working time reductions for employed parents. However, that figure is substantially lower among workers who have nonstandard-hour schedules (that is, evenings, nights, weekends), those whose hours are imposed on them (rather than chosen by the worker or negotiated with the employer), and those whose employers do not respect notification periods in relation to working patterns (Fagnani and Letablier 2004). A recent OECD study concurs. OECD researchers used data from the Third European Working Conditions Survey, pooled across 19 countries, to assess factors that affect workers' ratings of their "degree of conflict between working life and family life". Not surprisingly, work-family conflict is higher among those with longer total work hours. However, controlling for total hours worked, conflict is also significantly higher when daily hours vary, work days per week vary, starting and finishing times vary, if schedules change with no notice or with only a day of notice, or if workers have little control over their working hours (OECD 2004a).[14] Fagnani and Letablier (2004: 568) sum up: "taking into account the extreme heterogeneity of workplaces, it is not sufficient to mechanically reduce working time for there to be an improvement in the daily lives of working parents". The scheduling of hours, and the processes governing that scheduling, matter a great deal.

Annualization schemes are widespread in several European countries and further extensions are proposed at the EU level and in a number of member countries as well. If annualization schemes gain strength in Europe, and elsewhere, the potential gains for parents of winning shorter hours are likely to be seriously compromised. Protective mechanisms for workers – such as enforceable minimum notification periods and/or time-bank agreements that divide control over scheduling between employers and workers – will be crucial or the advantages for parents of shorter work hours may be more than offset by increasingly problematic scheduling practices. Where consumers' or employers' demand for "24/7" operation is especially strong, it may be impossible to control the growth of nonstandard-hour work – in which case other policy responses may be needed to help working families cope. For example, although controversial on a number of grounds, primarily concerns about child well-being, it may become increasingly necessary to provide round-the-clock childcare options for parents whose working hours fall outside normal schedules.

Second, strengthening reduced-hour work also raises thorny questions about gender equality. If shorter full-time hours and more available part-time hours are taken up disproportionately by women, more parental caregiving time may become available, but gender equality in time spent in paid work will worsen. With respect to shorter-hour work (and parental leave as well), whether men will eventually take advantage of these options as often as women do remains an open question.[15] Part of the logic of improving the quality of part-time work, of course, is to draw more men into it. And, in fact, men's engagement in part-time work increased in the 1990s in a number of European countries, including Belgium, France, Germany, and the Netherlands (European Foundation 2004). Recent survey results indicate that the substantial majority of male part-time workers (like their female counterparts) are voluntarily working part-time, which suggests that the new rights-to-part-time-work may be a factor underlying this increase. Nevertheless, part-time work remains overwhelmingly feminized in most industrialized countries. A countervailing view argues that even if part-time work remains feminized, it still has some gender-equalizing potential in that establishing viable part-time work options also draws some women into paid work who would otherwise refrain from employment altogether. It is possible that improving the availability of quality part-time work may, in general, have the effect of reducing gender gaps in employment rates while increasing gender gaps in hours worked among the employed. In the end, this is an empirical question and one that calls for continuing study.

From a gender equality perspective, it seems likely that reducing full-time weekly hours is the more promising strategy. Mutari and Figart (2001: 40-41) make this argument persuasively: "The alternative to policies that accommodate work hours to the gendered division of labor are policies that change the male model of full-time employment. Reductions in the standard work week are a long-term solution for achieving gender equity in the labor market and the redistribution of domestic labor ... [A] shorter work week can enable both men and women to participate in the labor market on an equal basis." In fact, this view – that shortening the full-time week is a gender parity strategy – seems to be gaining ground in a number of European countries. Fagnani and Letablier (2004) observe that in France, where part-time work has always been viewed with skepticism, the French 35-hour law "had the [explicit] objective ... of improving equality between men and women". The effects of reducing normal weekly hours on gendered distributions of labor also call for further study.

In conclusion, reducing total employment hours, and raising the availability and quality of part-time work, are crucial components of work-family reconciliation policy in many countries. While most of the EU member countries are seriously pursuing working time reforms, working time is less prominent on policy agendas in Japan and especially in the US. While working time policies can help to free up parental caregiving time, there are hazards associated with cutting work hours and creating feasible part-time options. If working time is cut in exchange for increased employer flexibility in scheduling, workers in less accommodating enterprises may suffer. If shorter-hours options are taken overwhelmingly by women, gender equality may suffer. Throughout the industrialized countries, policy advocates, policymakers, and "work-family" researchers would do well to weigh these hazards while designing, implementing, and evaluating working time policy reforms.

Acknowledgements

This article originated when we were collaborating on a cross-national policy project under the auspices of the Organization for Economic Cooperation and Development. We are thankful to our colleagues at the OECD – especially Mark Pearson, Willem Adema and Paul Swaim – for their contributions. We are also grateful to Gary Burtless, Heather Boushey and three anonymous reviewers for their helpful comments on an earlier draft. Finally, we thank the Alfred P. Sloan Foundation for intellectual and financial support.

Notes

1. A note on terminology: We use the terms "the regulation of working time" and "working time policies" to refer broadly to national and local legislation, public labor market regulations, and collective agreements that affect a large share of the workforce. We use the term "reduced-hour work" to refer to paid work at less than 40 hours per week. We use the term "part-time work" to mean work that is not considered, by national standards, to be "full-time". Across our comparison countries, legal and statistical definitions of part-time work vary. In some, for example, the statistical definition of part-time work is less than 35 hours per week, in others, less than 30 hours per week; in the EU, the legal definition refers to someone whose normal hours of work are less than the normal hours of a comparable full-time worker. Finally, by the EU, we mean the EU-15 prior to the 2004 enlargement.
2. Fagnani and Letablier (2004) report that, in France, politicians arguing for work-time cuts adopted the slogan: *travailler moins pour vivre mieux* ("work less, live better").
3. The meaning of maximum hours varies. In most cases, maximum hour policies mean that workers may not work above the set ceiling, while in others workers may not exceed the ceiling unless they opt to do so (see notes to Table 2).
4. This is also the case in Germany, Luxembourg, and the Netherlands, but collective bargaining coverage is much greater in those countries.
5. Carley (2003) also reports that the percentage of US workers in medium/large enterprises with any paid vacation fell from 96 percent in 1988 to 89 percent in 1997.
6. Public holiday laws vary widely across countries and, in some cases, employers can limit workers' rights to take off holidays and/or to be paid for them. For example, EU citizens generally have a statutory right to public holidays. However, in some member states – including France, Sweden and especially the UK – some employers may require employees to work on these days or to take them as part of annual holiday entitlements (Mercer 2003). In the US, the federal government designates ten public holidays and, in addition, some employers observe state and local holidays. However, many employers reserve the right to schedule employees to work on holidays, although employers are required by law to allow workers to observe religious holidays consistent with their beliefs and practices (salary.com 2006).
7. A table with detailed information on country-specific part-time work policies is available from the first author.
8. Figure 2 reports results calculated by the authors, using the Luxembourg Income Study (LIS) datasets, from various years in the mid-1990s to 2000. Japan is not included in the LIS.
9. Other factors, in addition to direct working time regulations, contribute to British men's long work hours. One is that, traditionally, British wives have worked short hours, partly due to a history of state policies aimed at creating demand for female part-time labor.
10. Evans *et al.* (2001) report a revealing finding about cross-national variation in working time preferences. An international survey, in 1994, asked workers if they would prefer a reduction in working hours or an increase in pay. Americans were less likely than Europeans to choose a reduction in working hours. But when no reference was made to the trade-off with earnings, a somewhat higher percentage of US workers than European workers replied that they wished to reduce their hours of work. Americans' preferences for long hours appear to be bound up with concerns about economic security, at least more so than among many of their European counterparts.
11. Here, we are considering the question of the effects of overtime regulations on average actual hours worked. A distinct and also important literature addresses the question: what is the effect of reducing

workers' weekly hours on aggregate employment levels? This literature suggests that the impact is likely to depend on the mechanism used. If hours are subject to an absolute limit, new jobs may be created if employers hire new workers to supply the needed hours. If hours are limited by lowering the threshold above which overtime must be paid, or by raising overtime rates, employers might shed workers to compensate for the extra costs associated with paying the workers already employed. The empirical findings on this question are, in fact, mixed (see Hamermesh 2002 for a review). In addition, others have assessed the link between workers' actual hours and aggregate productivity. As with employment, the hours/productivity relationship is complex. Among the OECD countries, output-per-worker is highest in the US – largely due to Americans' long average hours. However, when output-per-worker-hour is compared, the US falls to eighth place among the OECD countries, falling below, for example, Belgium, France, Italy, Germany, and the Netherlands. Some conclude that the US's comparatively lower productivity per hour is the result of compositional differences – arguing that many lower-productivity workers in the US would be unemployed elsewhere – although Mishel et al. (2005) refute that explanation. An alternative interpretation is that Americans' long hours may be in the range of diminishing returns with respect to productivity.

12. The effect of maximum hours regulation also seems apparent when we consider our ten countries. Carley (2003) reports that the gap in actual hours between the EU countries, on the one hand, and Japan and the US, on the other, is caused not just by a gap in normal/scheduled hours but also in the overtime and additional hours worked (which are higher in the latter two cases). Japan limits maximum hours but in general allows longer hours than those set in most EU countries, and the US is the one case among these ten with no restrictions on maximum hours. For an overview of the effects of working time regulations, see Rubery, Smith and Fagan (1998: 75). Drawing on variation in statutory and bargained normal hours across Europe, they concluded that "national working time regulations can be seen to have a major impact on usual working time".
13. At the same time, the Directive includes a number of other components, many of which are clearly advantageous to workers. It requires minimum provisions related to daily rest, breaks, weekly rest periods and, as we have mentioned, annual leave.
14. These studies and others establish that parents perceive that shortening their working hours reduces their work-family conflict. Whether, and to what extent, parents spend those "freed-up" hours with their children is an empirical question that has received much less attention. One study that addresses this directly is also from the French case. According to a 2001 survey, among parents with children under age 12, 43 percent of French parents say that, since the enactment of the 35-hour week, they spend more time with their children (see Kamerman et al. 2003 for a review of research on the effects of the French law).
15. Whether women's working time preferences are different from men's – in some fundamental and enduring way – is a contested question. Catherine Hakim, for example, has long argued that while many women are career-oriented, substantial numbers are not – and it is their preferences, not constraints or institutional factors, that explain their relatively low working hours compared to men's (Hakim 1997). Others argue that women's intrinsic preferences cannot be identified until gendered expectations and institutional constraints erode (Gornick and Meyers 2003).

References

Bardasi, E. and Gornick, J. C., 2002, Explaining cross-national variation in part-time/full-time wage differentials among women. Paper presented at the workshop on Comparative Political Economy of Inequality. Cornell University, Ithaca, New York (April 5–7).

Bell, L., and Freeman, R. B., 2001, The incentive for working hard: explaining hours worked differences in the U.S. and Germany. *Labour Economics*, **8**(2), 181–202.

Carley, M., 2003, Industrial relations in the EU, Japan and USA, 2001. *European Industrial Relations Observatory* (EIRO). Downloaded on January 18, 2004 from http://www.eiro.eurofound.eu.int/2002/12/feature/tn0212101f.html

Carley, M., 2004, Working time developments, 2003. *European Industrial Relations Observatory* (EIRO). Downloaded on January 18, 2005 from http://www.eiro.eurofound.eu.int/2004/03/update/tn0403104u.html

Clarkberg, M. and Moen, P., 2001, Understanding the time squeeze: married couples preferred and actual work-hour strategies. *American Behavioral Scientist*, **44**, 1115–1136.

Clauwaert, S., 2002, *The Survey on the Implementation of the Part-time Work Directive/Agreement in the EU Member States and Selected Applicant Countries* (Brussels: European Trade Union Institute).

Europa, 2004, The part-time work directive. Downloaded on January 19, 2005 from http://europa.eu.int/scadplus/leg/en/cha/c10416.htm

European Commission, 2003a, The Implementation of Council Directive 96/34/EC of 3rd June 1996 on the Framework Agreement on Parental Leave concluded by UNICE, CEEP and the ETUC. Downloaded on April 8, 2004 from http://europa.eu.int/comm/employment_social/equ_opp/documents/com2003358_en.pdf

European Commission, 2003b, Bulletin on Legal Issues in Equality (number 2). Commission's network of legal experts on the application of Community law on equal treatment between women and men. Downloaded on April 8, 2004 from http://europa.eu.int/comm/employment_social/equ_opp/newsletter/bulletin2_2003_en.pdf

European Commission, 2003c, The Implementation of Council Directive 97/81/EC of 17 December 1997 Concerning the Framework Agreement on Part-Time Work concluded by UNICE, CEEP and the ETUC. Downloaded on January 20, 2005 from http://europa.eu.int/comm/employment_social/labour_law/docs/06_parttime_implreport_en.pdf

European Communities, 1993, Council Directive 93/104/EC, of 23 November, concerning certain aspects of the organisation of working time. Downloaded from http://europa.eu.int/smartapi/cgi/sga_doc?smartapi!celexplus!prod!DocNumber&lg=en&type_doc=Directive&an_doc=1993&nu_doc=104

European Foundation for the Improvement of Living and Working Conditions, 2004, Part-Time Work in Europe. Downloaded on December 14, 2004 from http://www.eurofound.eu.int/working/reports/ES0403TR01/ES0403TR01.pdf

Evans, J., Lippoldt, D. C. and Marianna, P., 2001, Labour market and social policy: trends in working hours in OECD countries. Occasional Paper Number 45 (Paris: Organization for Economic Cooperation and Development), pp. 17–59.

Expedia, 2004, Refill the commuter coffee mug: Expedia.com survey reveals Americans will forfeit 415 million vacation days this year. Downloaded on January 31, 2005 from http://www.expedia.com/daily/press/releases/2004-5-26Vacation_Deprivation.asp?CCheck=1&

Fagnani, J. and Letablier, M.-T., 2004, Work and family life balance: the impact of the 35-hour laws in France. *Work, Employment, and Society*, **10**(3), 551–572.

Flanders Foreign Investment Office, 2004, Business incentives in Belgium. Downloaded on January 19, 2005 from http://www.ffio.com/index_top.asp?fid=030204&did=index&sid=index&lid=en&publabel=&smID=&iPagenumber=1&iCatID

Gornick, J. C. and Meyers, M. K., 2003, *Families That Work: Policies for Reconciling Parenthood and Employment* (New York: Russell Sage Foundation).

Grubb, D. and Wells, W., 1993, Employment regulation and patterns of work in EC countries. *OECD Economic Studies*, **21** (Winter), 7–58.

Hakim, C., 1997, A sociological perspective on part-time work, in: H.-P. Blossfeld and C. Hakim (Eds) *Between Equalization and Marginalization: Women Working Part-Time in Europe and the United States of America* (Oxford: Oxford University Press), pp. 22–70.

Hamermesh, D., 2002, Overtime laws and the margins of work timing, Paper prepared for the Conference on Work Intensification, Paris, France, November 21–22.

Jung, L., 2000 (approx), ILO International Observatory of Labour Law: National Labour Law Profile (Japan: ILO). Downloaded on January 18, 2005 from http://www.ilo.org/public/english/dialogue/ifpdial/ll/observatory/profiles/jp.htm

Kamerman, S. B., Neuman, M. J., Waldfogel, J. and Brooks-Gunn, J., 2003, Social policies, family types, and child outcomes in selected OECD countries. OECD Social, Employment and Migration Working Papers No. 6 (Paris: Organization for Economic Cooperation and Development).

Kouzis, G. and Kretsos, L., 2003, Annualised hours in Europe. European Industrial Relations Observatory (EIRO). Downloaded on January 30, 2005 from http://www.eiro.eurofound.eu.int/2003/08/study/tn0308101s.html

Lee, S., 2004, Working-hour gaps: trends and issues, in: J. Messenger (Ed) *Working Time and Workers' Preferences in Industrialised Countries: Finding the Balance* (London: Routledge), pp. 29–59.

Lehndorff, S., 2000, Working time reduction in the European Union, in: L. Golden and D. M. Figart (Eds) *Working Time: International Trends, Theory, and Policy Perspectives* (New York: Routledge), pp. 38–55.

Mercer, 2003, Human resource consulting. Downloaded on January 15, 2006 from http://www.mercerhr.com/pressrelease/details.jhtml/dynamic/idContent/1104770

Messenger, J. (Ed.) 2004, *Working Time and Workers' Preferences in Industrialised Countries: Finding the Balance* (London: Routledge).
Mishel, L., Bernstein, J. and Allegretto, S., 2005, *The State of Working America: 2004–2005* (Washington, DC: Economic Policy Institute).
Mutari, E. and Figart, D. M., 2001, Europe at a crossroads: harmonization, liberalization, and the gender of work time. *Social Politics*, **8**(1), 36–64.
OECD, 1998, Working hours: latest trends and policy initiatives, Chapter 5 in *Employment Outlook* (Paris: Organization for Economic Cooperation and Development), pp. 154–188.
OECD, 2003, *Babies and Bosses: Reconciling Work and Family Life, Volume 2 (Austria, Ireland and Japan)* (Paris: Organization for Economic Cooperation and Development).
OECD, 2004a, Recent labour market developments and prospects. Special focus on clocking in (and out): several facets of working time, Chapter 1 in *Employment Outlook* (Paris: Organization for Economic Cooperation and Development), pp. 17–59.
OECD, 2004b, Wage-setting institutions and outcomes, Chapter 3 in *Employment Outlook* (Paris: Organization for Economic Cooperation and Development), pp. 127–181.
Prescott, E. C., 2004, Why do Americans work so much more than Europeans? NBER Working Paper 10316 (Massachusetts: National Bureau of Economic Research).
Rubery, J., Smith, M. and Fagan, C., 1998, National working-time regimes and equal opportunities. *Feminist Economics*, **4**(1), 71–101.
Salary.com, 2006, Time off. Downloaded on January 15, 2006 from http://www.salary.com/benefits/layoutscripts/bnfl_display.asp?tab=bnf&cat=nocat&ser=Ser27&part=Par65

Social Citizenship of Young People in Europe: A Comparative Institutional Analysis*

TOM CHEVALIER

ABSTRACT *This article explains the diversity of young people's access to social welfare by distinguishing between two models of social citizenship in a comparative analysis of 15 Western European countries. On the one hand, social citizenship can be familialized, when young people are considered as children and therefore do not receive state benefits in their own name. This form of citizenship is found in Bismarckian welfare states, based on the principle of subsidiarity. On the other hand, it can be individualized, in which case young people can be entitled to benefits in their own right, insofar as they are considered as adults. This form of social citizenship is found more in Beveridgean welfare states.*

Introduction

In the context of particularly high unemployment rates among 15–24-year-olds – peaking at an average of 22.7 per cent in 2013 in Western European countries (EU15) according to Eurostat – and the resulting risks of poverty, young people's access to social welfare is crucial. Yet this access to social welfare and to social citizenship more generally, understood as the possibility to claim social rights and benefits, as I will argue in the article, varies widely from one country to the next. In the case of income support, for example, age limits fluctuate considerably: 25 in France for the *Revenu de Solidarité Active* (RSA), 18 in the United Kingdom for the Jobseeker's Allowance (JSA), 15 in Germany for the *Arbeitslosengeld II* (ALG II), and no age limit in Sweden for the *Socialtjänstlagen*. The same goes for the rates of young people's access to social benefits; as shown in Figure 4, they ranged from 2.8 per cent in Italy to 48.1 per cent in Finland in 2011 – nearly a 45-point difference.

---

*This article is the winner of the joint award "Best Young Scholar's Comparative Paper" from the JCPA/ICPA-Forum and the AFSP.

How can we explain these differences and the diversity of forms of access to social citizenship among Europe's youth? In other words, what are the rationales underpinning this differentiated access and the public policies structuring it? In this study I demonstrate that two contrasting models of young people's social citizenship exist in Europe: a familialized model in Bismarckian welfare states, and an individualized one in Beveridgean welfare states. We will consider this in more detail in the next section. The distinction between the two models sheds light both on the rationales intrinsic to public support for young people and on the diversity of public policies in Western Europe.

Theorizing Young People's Social Citizenship in Europe

Literature Review: Young People and Social Welfare from a Comparative Perspective

In the comparative literature on social welfare, young people are taken into account only as a particularly vulnerable part of the population due to the transition to a post-industrial economy. In the literature on "new social risks", they are part of the social categories most exposed to these risks, along with women, low-skilled workers, immigrants and the dependent elderly (Taylor-Gooby 2004; Armingeon and Bonoli 2006; Bonoli and Natali 2012). Likewise, in recent work on the dualization of societies, young people are once again part of this "outsiders" category, along with women, immigrants and low-skilled workers (Emmenegger et al. 2012). This categorization stems from the fact that young people are considered as new entrants on the labour market: not only are they more exposed to unemployment, but they also benefit less often from unemployment benefits as they have not yet contributed sufficiently. To describe the diversity of access to social welfare among the youth, the classical distinction is sometimes made between citizenship-based social welfare in Beveridgean regimes on the one hand, and work-based social welfare in Bismarckian regimes on the other.

These studies suffer from two limitations however. First, they study the general category of "new social risk groups" or "outsiders", and can therefore lose sight of the particularities of each of the categories analysed, particularly young people. Second, insofar as unemployment is considered to be the main risk that young people can face, this research mainly focuses on unemployment benefits. This is why the distinction between citizenship and work can seem appropriate, since unemployment benefits, especially through unemployment insurance, are often contingent on a young person's presence on the labour market in the past, whereas social assistance is more citizenship-based. Yet the youth, and not just the unemployed youth, can also be eligible for other types of social benefits.

This is what the literature on young people highlights. The government support to which young people may be entitled is not just limited to unemployment benefits and social assistance: it also includes family allowances, particularly for students, housing benefits, and other student benefits such as grants and loans (Eurydice 1999). To understand these benefits, Eurydice (1999), Walther (2006) and Van de Velde (2008) have stressed the differing degrees of importance given to the family, although without systematically theorizing this aspect.

Social welfare, however, does not just vary significantly from one country to the next, depending on the role ascribed to the family, as Esping-Andersen's feminist critiques in particular have shown (Esping-Andersen 1990; Lewis 1992; Orloff 1993). It also plays an important role in structuring a person's life course in general (Mayer and Schoepflin 1989), be it institutionally (Kohli 1986) or normatively (Leisering 2003). Hence the value of situating this study in the framework of the life course, where youth is more generally understood as entry into adulthood, and therefore as access to independence, particularly financial independence (Jones 2003), in contrast with children's dependence on their family. The state can promote this independence in two ways: it can either facilitate young people's access to employment through education and employment policies, which relates to what we call young people's "economic citizenship", or else provide a public benefit directly, which relates to young people's "social citizenship" (Chevalier 2016). In his seminal definition of social citizenship, Marshall (1950) refers more generally to the state's responsibilities for granting "from the right to a modicum of economic welfare and security to the right to share to the full in the social heritage and to live the life of a civilized being according to the standards prevailing in the society". Hence, by looking at social citizenship we specifically address the issue of access to social rights, and specifically public aid and income transfers, in order to distinguish it from other kinds of policies included in economic citizenship. Unlike studies on new social risks and dualization, this approach to young people's social citizenship allows us to take into account all the public benefits to which young people may be entitled. According to the literature on student support (Eurydice 1999), the sociology of youth (Van de Velde 2008) and the literature on youth transitions and youth policies (Walther 2006), I have identified several aid policies of relevance to young people: family allowances, family tax relief, social assistance benefits, housing benefits, and student support (i.e. grants and loans).

The Two Figures of Young People's Social Citizenship

Young people have just left childhood, a period in which their family was responsible for looking after them. Public policy targeting children is familialized in the sense that it is geared towards families, which must then take care of their children. In the case of the youth, the familialization of their social citizenship depends on the conception that informs public policies regarding them: are they considered as children or adults?

Van de Velde (2008) has shown the extent to which public policy is familialized in France, yet without this resulting in excessive familialization of young people, particularly thanks to housing benefits which afford access to residential independence relatively early. In her comparative analysis, she shows how Spain stands out as the most advanced case of familialization of young people, while a familialization[1] of benefits is also present in France and in Germany.

Drawing on research on familialization and on the work of Gill Jones (2005) and Léa Lima (2008) on young people's access to social welfare, I first distinguish between two opposite ideal-typical figures of young people's social citizenship: the *familialization* of social citizenship in Bismarckian states, and the *individualization* of social citizenship in Beveridgean states. These figures depend on the representation of the period of youth within the life course. The familialization of social citizenship relates to an extension of the institutionalization of the age of childhood, whereas individualization relates to an institutionalization which has more to do with adulthood, and therefore with adult social citizenship. Thus, familialization implies a dependent-child status, which means that benefits are provided to the parents, and not directly to the young person. Young people's social rights in this kind of social citizenship are related to their status within the family. According to the "tripartition of the life course" (Kohli 1986), which distinguishes between childhood, adulthood and old age, childhood is closely related to compulsory schooling, and therefore being in education, whereas adulthood relates to work and the entry into the labour market. Young people still in education after compulsory schooling (or what is considered the basic level of education), i.e. those in higher education, are still considered as children. We therefore find a familialization of social rights that uses family policy[2] to support students, in addition to grants based on parental income, since parents are still expected to take care of their "dependent" children. This logic is reflected in the civil code, which requires parents to financially support their children even long after the completion of compulsory schooling and the age of civil majority.

On the other hand, when social rights are individualized, young people are considered as independent individuals who can claim those rights directly. As their parents are no longer supposed to take care of them, there are no maintenance obligations after civil majority. Likewise, since young people in higher education who have reached civil majority are no longer viewed as children, family policy does not provide support for them. It is entirely replaced by grants and/or loans that do not depend on parental income and are supposed to be available to all students irrespective of their income. Table 1 sums up these two figures by describing their institutional characteristics, which I will use as a comparative framework in the empirical part of this study.

Second, I show that the seminal distinction between the "Bismarckian" welfare state and the "Beveridgean" one (Bonoli 1997) is still appropriate to describe this differentiated access to social rights in Western Europe, but not for the reasons claimed in the literature. The distinction between work and citizenship as criteria of access to social welfare does not account for the diversity of forms of young people's access to citizenship. This diversity has more to do with the institutionalization of the principle of subsidiarity in Bismarckian states, stemming from its Catholic roots, insofar as it grants the family an important role in supporting vulnerable individuals. In other words, it leans towards the

Table 1. The two types of social citizenship of young people

	Familialization	Individualization
Representation of the youth	Childhood	Adulthood
Maintenance obligations towards young people of age (that is, having reached majority)	Yes	No
Status in social welfare	Dependent (dependent child)	Independent (recipient)
Age limits*	Late (often after 20, around 25)	Early (often before 20, around 18)
Student benefit	Yes	No
Family policy	Grants conditional on the parents' income	Universal grants and/or loans, independent of the parents' income
Student support		
Young people's social security cover	Low	High
Welfare regime	Bismarckian	Beveridgean

*These can be maximum age limits (a young person can receive a benefit until this age) or minimum age limits (the age from which it is possible to receive this benefit).

familialization of social rights. By contrast, the Protestant tradition in Beveridgean welfare states, be it Anglo-Saxon or Nordic, has led to both secularism and more individualized social rights (Rice 2013, p. 96). As a result, regarding young people in particular, a familialized social citizenship is more likely to be found in Bismarckian welfare states, whereas in Beveridgean welfare states young people's social citizenship will be more individualized.

Method

Based on this theoretical framework, I show the extent to which certain Western European countries (EU15) are closer to one or the other figure of young people's social citizenship. The aim is to situate and categorize European countries according to these two ideal-types. I therefore do not take temporality into account, or the evolution and dynamics of those two figures. Instead, I adopt a synchronic perspective with the primary aim of describing geographic and not time variation. I carry out a comparative institutional analysis in which I analyse each of the benefits mentioned for each of the countries, based on the theoretical framework that I have developed and drawing on the official literature, grey literature and secondary public policy analysis literature. At each step of the analysis I evaluate whether young people's social citizenship is indeed more familialized in Bismarckian countries, and more individualized in Beveridgean countries.

Comparative Institutional Analysis of Aid Policies for Young People

I systematically analyse each country's aid policies (family policy, student support, housing allowances and social assistance) in order to assess their situation in relation to the two figures of young people's social citizenship identified earlier (Table 1). These aid policies represent all the benefits that provide young people with an income during their period of transition before entering employment.

Family Policy

From our perspective, family policy is comprised of three distinct measures, which I analyse in turn: parents' maintenance obligations regarding their children of age, family allowances and tax relief for families. Young people therefore access these benefits as dependent children: hence the term "familialized" social rights.

The principle of subsidiarity means that responsibility for vulnerable individuals must primarily go to the family, and not the state, whenever possible. The state intervenes only when the family cannot fulfil this responsibility. As regards young adults, this principle was first institutionalized with the maintenance obligations found in continental countries' legal systems. Parents' maintenance obligation towards their children means that they are legally obliged to provide their children with support, which can be limited to maintenance support but can also go further, for example with accommodation, medical care and especially education costs. By institutionalizing the principle of subsidiarity, these obligations are at the origin of the familialization of state support for young people in Bismarckian states: they constitute the foundation of familialization, both as a principle and legally.

Table 2. Maintenance obligations in Western Europe

Country	Maximum age limit under common law to be considered a child	Conditions of payment for children of age		
		Age	To be in education	To be financially dependent
Belgium	18	No	Yes	No
Denmark*	18	24	Yes	No
Germany	None	No	Yes	Yes
Ireland	18	23	Yes	No
Greece	18	No	Yes	Yes
Spain	18	No	Yes	Yes
France	18	No	Yes	Yes
Italy	None	No	No	Yes
Luxemburg	18	No	Yes	Yes
Netherlands	18	21	Yes	No
Austria	None	No	No	Yes
Portugal	18	No	Yes	No
Finland***	18	20	Yes	No
Sweden	18	21	Yes	No
United Kingdom**	16	20	Yes	No

Sources: http://ec.europa.eu/civiljustice/maintenance_claim/maintenance_claim_gen_en.htm
*http://www.statsforvaltningen.dk/site.aspx?p=6404
**https://www.gov.uk/when-child-maintenance-payments-stop
***Hakovirta and Hiilamo (2012, p. 291).

Regarding maintenance obligations, there are several aspects to consider. First, we must see if an age limit exists for children, beyond which parents' obligation ceases, and if it does, at what age it is set. We then need to consider the extent to which this obligation continues beyond civil majority. Three conditions can justify this extension: a new age limit set later only for young people who have attained their majority and are in full-time education, irrespective of their age, or are financially dependent due to no access to paid employment. Table 2 sums up these different characteristics in Western European countries.

A first group of countries can be distinguished, combining an age limit for children at 18, in other words civil majority and the end of parental authority (except in the United Kingdom with a limit at 16, the age limit for compulsory education), with a second age limit a bit later for young people of age who are still in full-time education (Sosson 2001). In the United Kingdom, Sweden and Finland this covers the period of upper secondary education, which is considered the basic level of education, whereas in the Netherlands, Ireland and Denmark higher education is also covered. In the Netherlands parents are obliged to provide for medical care as well as education for children under 18, and for living expenses and training for young adults under 21, irrespective of their own income. These obligations stop at that age, even if the young person is still in education or still cannot support themselves. These are states with a "Beveridgean" and not a "Bismarckian" social welfare system. Bismarckian states are all part of continental

Europe, with the Netherlands being the only exception. Its essentially Beveridgean system reflects its "hybrid" nature already identified in the literature (Ferragina and Seeleib-Kaiser 2011, p. 588).

As regards the other states, there appear to be two subgroups. On the one hand, there are maintenance obligations for parents towards their children of age as long as the latter are not financially independent, with no age limit. The aim is to ensure that young people receive support in the general framework of family solidarity, irrespective of their age. This is the case of Italy and Austria, with Germany in an in-between position since a child's educational status can also be taken into account (Millar and Warman 1996). In Italy, parents have a maintenance obligation towards their children irrespective of their age, until the latter become financially independent. The same goes for Germany and Austria, where the living conditions of the child and the parents are taken into account to determine this financial autonomy.

On the other hand, there are maintenance obligations that stop at voting age, except for children of age who are either still in education or not yet financially independent. This is the case of Greece, Spain, France and Luxemburg. In the case of France there is a particularly strong maintenance obligation called *"obligation d'entretien"*, designed to ensure that the young person enjoys the conditions necessary for their development and education as long as they are in training, irrespective of their age (Rebourg 2001). When a young person of age is not or no longer in training, but is still not financially independent, the common maintenance obligation applies, and not the *"obligation d'entretien"*. In Luxemburg, the maintenance obligation can be conditional on the young person passing their exams if studying. Portugal and Belgium are in an intermediary position since the obligation only concerns young people of age in education, provided that the duration of their studies is considered to be reasonable. Here the family solidarity rationale focuses on young students in particular, insofar as they are still in education and are therefore still considered as *children*. These two subgroups encompass all continental Bismarckian countries (apart from the Netherlands), as "through the law or jurisprudence, [they] consecrate the right of the child of age to obtain a contribution from their parents towards their university or professional fees" (Meulders-Klein and Eeekelaar 1988, p. 115).

In geographical terms there is therefore a distinction between the north of Europe (Nordic and English-speaking countries) and continental countries:

> the respective roles of civil law and social law or of the administrative and judicial authorities' competences draw a demarcation line between Nordic countries which are more socialized and the others, especially Latin countries, which primarily prioritize family solidarity over national solidarity. (Labrousse-Riou 1986, p. 830)

In the first group of countries, parents' maintenance obligations towards their children of age stop relatively early, whereas in the second group they often extend until late, as long as the child is still in education, or more generally still economically dependent on their parents.

I continue my demonstration by analysing family allowances. There is a wide diversity of age limits for these benefits in Europe, as shown in Figure 1. Looking at the age limit for all children, there is hardly a marked difference between the different countries; the limit varies between 16 and 18. Only France stands out with an age limit

Figure 1. Age limits for family allowances

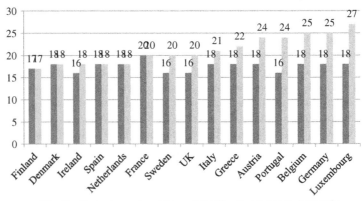

Source: MISSOC (2014).
Notes: *In Italy, the age limit applies to young people living in a household of at least six individuals (two parents and four children). This relates to the benefit called "*assegno al nucleo familiare*". There also exists a benefit called "*assegno familiare*", where the age limit for students is set at 26, irrespective of the composition of the household, and where a third age limit is set at 21 for apprentices and lower secondary school pupils (http://www.inps.it/portale/default.aspx?itemdir=5790).
**In Portugal, the age limit for students fluctuates between 18, 21 and 24, depending on the case.
In Germany (Bosch and Jansen 2010) and Austria (http://www.cleiss.fr/docs/regimes/regime_autriche-salaries.html#b) a third intermediary limit also exists, at 21, for unemployed young people. Moreover, in France family allowances are only available from the second child.

beyond civil majority, at 20. The difference is more striking between Beveridgean states and Bismarckian states with regard to the second type of age limit, i.e. those age limits for young people still in education. In Beveridgean states, either the two age limits are the same or the second one is set at the standard age to finish secondary education, excluding students in higher education. In most Bismarckian states this age limit is set much later, which creates a more marked difference between the two ages in question.

This illustrates the fact that, in Bismarckian states, family policy is used to support students, whereas this is not the case in Beveridgean states. With the familialization approach, if young people are still in education they are considered as children; and if they are children, their family must look after them. There is therefore a difference between Beveridgean states, in which age limits for family allowances are set relatively early (under 20) and where the difference between common law age limits and age limits for students is small or even non-existent, and Bismarckian states, where these age limits are set later (after 20), particularly for students.

The third type of support, in the framework of family policy, consists of family tax relief. In the same spirit as family benefits, tax relief is designed to compensate parents for children's maintenance and education costs. This involves a tax reduction rather than payment of an allowance (as with family allowances).

Table 3 shows the very clear distinction between Beveridgean countries and Bismarckian countries. In the first group, no tax relief is available for young adults:

Table 3. Tax relief for families in 2011 and 1997

	Type of tax relief	Maximum age limit	Main condition to be able to benefit from tax relief
Belgium	Tax exemption	–	Income
Denmark	–	–	–
Germany	Tax deduction	25 (27)	–
Ireland	–	–	–
Greece	Tax deduction	25	Education
Spain	– (Tax credit)	– (30)	– (income)
France	Tax credit Increase in the number of tax units	25	Education
Italy	Tax credit Tax deduction	– (26)	Education Income
Luxemburg	Tax rate reduction	27	Education
Netherlands	–	–	–
Austria	Tax credit	24 (26)	Education Income
Portugal	Tax credit (tax deduction)	– (25)	Income Education
Finland	–	–	–
Sweden	–	–	–
United Kingdom	–	–	–

Source: Eurydice (1999, 2011).
Note: the figures in brackets are the 1997 data where these have changed since.

this situation results from the financial autonomy granted to young people in these countries when they reach civil majority. Since this age generally coincides with entry into higher education, no tax measure exists de facto to support students in higher education. (Eurydice 1999, p. 75)

This confirms my hypothesis of the individualization of social rights for young people in these countries. Here again, the Netherlands corresponds to the Beveridgean model. By contrast, in Bismarckian states, the presence of tax relief, usually coupled with a late age limit and/or the condition that young adult dependants must be in education, supports the hypothesis of the familialization of social citizenship. Only Spain seemed no longer to offer tax relief in 2011, whereas a benefit was available in 1997.

Analysing family policy sheds light on the coherence of its frameworks with regard to the youth. This coherence is especially significant as it involves several legal spheres; the fact that familialization is at play in civil law (maintenance obligations), social law (family allowances) and tax law (family tax relief) demonstrates that a comprehensive approach is applied, cutting across the different forms of public benefits for young people.

Student Support

We will now look at student support, i.e. grants and loans for young people in higher education. I have posited that student benefits are provided mainly through family policy when young people's social citizenship is familialized, and through student support when they are individualized. Since young people are seen as children in Bismarckian states, family policy is mobilized. Direct student support can exist in these countries, but its underlying rationale is to assist families, which must be the primary carers of their children of age. Hence, student support (both access to it and the amount) depends on the parents' income, which has the effect of limiting the proportion of students receiving this type of benefit.

When young people's social citizenship is individualized, family policy to support them ends when they reach voting age, and concerns only compulsory education and in some cases upper secondary education, but not higher education. Beveridgean states therefore offer an individualized type of benefit exclusively for students: student benefits, comprised of grants and/or loans. This support is universal, in other words open to all students, independent of their parents' income, since these young people are considered to be financially autonomous, *even if they are in education.*

Figure 2 presents the distribution of European countries according to the proportion of undergraduate students who received student benefits for the academic year 2011–2012. We can see a clear distinction between Bismarckian and Beveridgean states, even though there is still intra-group variation. All continental countries present a low access rate, far below 50 per cent. Conversely, Beveridgean states have very high access rates, above 50 per cent and even 80 per cent for the most part. Surprisingly, on this graph Ireland seems closer to Bismarckian states with a rate of 43 per cent. Thus, all Bismarckian states offer grants to students who are dependent on their parents' income. The idea is to complement and not replace parental support when the family's income is too low to support their child in education. In Beveridgean states, on the other hand, the parents' income is not taken into account, which is why access to support is so broad. The fact that only students' individual income can potentially be taken into account illustrates that they are considered as financially autonomous (Eurydice 1999, p. 59).

In Beveridgean countries, student support combines both grants and loans, though in different proportions, unlike Bismarckian states which deliver grants almost exclusively,

Figure 2. Percentage of undergraduate students who received a grant and/or a loan in 2011–2012

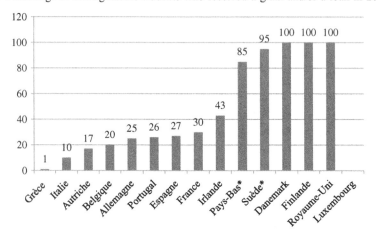

Source: Eurydice, 2011; OCDE, 2012 for the Netherlands and Sweden (*). Data not available for Luxemburg.

except in Germany where half of the BAföG allowance is comprised of grants and the other half of interest-free loans (Eurydice 1999, p. 54). The United Kingdom applies a universal system based on loans (student finance): all full-time undergraduate students can receive a tuition fee loan to pay for their tuition fees in full since higher education is not free and annual undergraduate fees can be as high as GBP 9,000. They may also be eligible for a maintenance loan combined (or not) with a maintenance grant to cover living expenses. These loans are "contingent on future income": if the student's income does not exceed a certain threshold when they enter the job market (GBP 21,000 per year in 2014), they do not need to repay their loan.

The three Scandinavian countries in our sample apply a universal system combining grants and loans available to all students, with an access rate of about 100 per cent (note also that higher education is completely free in these countries). The share of each component is fixed, and can be reduced if the student's personal income exceeds the maximum threshold. In Finland, since 1992, student grants have no longer been dependent on parents' income, in line with changes in family policy targeting students (Eurydice 1999, p. 229). The parents' income may nevertheless be taken into account in some cases, and the support amount can be reduced if this income exceeds a certain threshold. Since 1 August 2014, students have also been able to take out a state-guaranteed loan of up to EUR 400 a month. A housing benefit is furthermore included in this student support (see below).

In Sweden, students receive support consisting of a grant (one-third) and a loan (two-thirds). In 2012 the grant was SEK 3,063 a month and the loan SEK 6,712 a month (Eurydice 2013). Two-thirds of students choose to take out this loan, repayable over a period of 25 years with interest rates below market value but which increase over time, as does the grant. While this is officially a standard loan, it actually functions as a "loan contingent on future income in case of need", since borrowers encountering financial difficulty can ask to reduce repayments to a maximum of 4 per cent of their income (Charles 2012, p. 306). This benefit is contingent not on the parents' income, but on the student's personal income.

The proportions are reversed in Denmark, where one-third of student support consists of a loan and two-thirds a grant. Half of the students take out this loan, repayable over a period of 15 years. As in Finland, this benefit is not contingent on the parents' income, even though the amount can be reduced if the student still lives with them. In 2013 the grant for a student no longer living with their parents was DDK 5,753 a month, and the loan amount was increased to DDK 8,180 a month (Eurydice 2013).

The Netherlands is also part of this group of countries. The state provides a basic grant to all students, irrespective of their parents' income, which was set at EUR 269 a month in 2011. In addition to this universal grant, a complementary grant conditional on the parents' resources is also available (EUR 245 a month in 2011), along with a loan contingent not on the parents' income but on the amount of the additional grant (Eurydice 1999, p. 60) (up to a maximum EUR 289 a month in 2011). On the other hand, in contrast with Nordic countries, students must pay annual tuition fees, which can be as high as EUR 1,951 (2015).

Luxemburg's situation is particular: many young people study abroad because the local university offer is so limited. It therefore represents an original case insofar as access to student support in this country is virtually universal, but the distribution between grant and loan is determined by the parents' income: the higher the parents' income, the higher the share of the loan, at the expense of the grant (Eurydice 1999, p. 59).[3] Finally, as I have already pointed out, Ireland is also in an in-between position.

Certainly, its access rate does not match that of the other Beveridgean states since student support (student grants) depends on the parent's income. Yet that support proves to be quite generous as the access rate is still 10 percentage points higher than in France. As in the United Kingdom and the Netherlands, students must pay tuition fees (Eurydice 2013).

Thus, for young people in higher education in Bismarckian states, benefits are provided mainly through the family policy frameworks which we analysed earlier. Grants benefit only a small proportion of students because they are contingent on the parents' income. In Beveridgean states, on the other hand, student support was reformed to benefit a large majority of students, and family policy no longer had any role in student support. The fact that grants and loans are not contingent on the parents' income guarantees young adults' autonomy, even when they are in full-time education.

Housing Benefits

Several aspects need to be considered as regards the role of housing benefits in young people's social citizenship. First, do housing allowances exist at national level? Second, if they do, what is the minimum age limit to qualify? Third, are these housing allowances open to students? We have seen that students' status is telling of the underlying rationale since they can be considered as young people still in education and dependent on their parents, and therefore potentially as children. However, if students can receive a housing allowance in their own name, this implies that they have left the parental home, and consequently that there is more individualization.

Table 4 presents the different aspects of housing benefits in Western Europe in 2012. Unlike the benefits analysed until now, the separation between Bismarckian and Beveridgean states is less clear here. Certainly, Scandinavian countries and the Netherlands offer housing benefits for young people and particularly students, in keeping with the strong individualization of young people's social citizenship in these countries. Sweden and Finland, for example, have a specific housing benefit for young students, with the explicit aim of encouraging them to become independent of their family. But the United Kingdom and Ireland, despite a low minimum age to access housing benefits (18), restrict eligibility to these benefits to the poorest, provided they are not in (full-time) education.

Germany, Greece, Italy and France, however, offer frameworks open to students, although these are Bismarckian countries that are supposed to offer familialized citizenship. In most cases these benefits are limited. In Germany, beneficiaries of the BAföG student benefit cannot claim the housing benefit, unless the young student has a child or no longer lives with their parents. Greece offers a specific grant by the Ministry of Education, provided the young person is studying in a city other than where their parents reside, that they are renting a home which does not belong to their parents, and that they do not live in a university residence. In this familialization of student support approach, the parents' income is also taken into account. Moreover, the age limit to be considered as independent and therefore eligible for the basic housing allowance is set relatively high, at 21, and at 25 if the young adult is in higher education.

Italy does not strictly speaking provide a housing benefit, but instead tax relief for young people aged 20–30 with an income below a certain threshold. Students can also benefit from the tax relief even if they are still under their parents' care, provided they live in a different province to that of their parents, and that this residential mobility is for academic reasons. France's housing benefits seem to be the most widely accessible, since all students can claim the APL (*aide*

Table 4. Young people's access to housing allowances in Europe, 2012

	Housing allowance	Access criteria	Minimum age limits	Open to students
Belgium	–	–	–	–
Denmark	*Boligsikring*	Income, capital, rent, size of the apartment, and number of children		Yes
Germany	*Wohngeld*	Income, rent, size of the household		Yes (if the household has one person only, or with a child)
Ireland	*Rent supplement (as part of the Supplementary welfare allowance)*	Income	18	No
Greece	Two different frameworks exist	To be an undergraduate student, to live in a different city from one's parents, parents' income	21, and 25 for young people in education (to be considered as dependent)	For students only
Spain	–	–	–	–
France	*Aide personnalisée au logement, allocation de logement à caractère sociale*	Income	18	Yes
Italy	*Detrazione fiscale*	Income	For 20–30-year-olds	Yes, but with certain conditions
Luxemburg	–	To receive social welfare	25	No
Netherlands	*Huurtoeslag*	Income, rent level	18; but before 23, the maximum rent to be eligible for the benefit is lower	Yes
Austria	No national framework	–	–	–
Portugal	–	–	–	–
Finland	*Housing supplement*	To be a student without children	–	For students only

(*continued*)

Table 4. (Continued)

	Housing allowance	Access criteria	Minimum age limits	Open to students
Sweden	*Bostadsbidrag till unga utan barn*	Income, young adults without children	For 18–29-year-olds	Yes
United Kingdom	*Housing benefit*	Income, size of the home	18, but lower rate for under-25s*	No (with exceptions)

Sources:
Belgium, Greece, Spain, France, Luxemburg, Austria, Portugal, and the United Kingdom: see the OECD's *Tax-Benefits Systems* reports (2012);
Denmark: http://studyindenmark.dk/live-in-denmark/housing-1/how-to-find-housing;
Germany: https://www.international.hu-berlin.de/en/studierende/aus-dem-ausland/wegweiser/09/09_08;
Ireland: http://www.citizensinformation.ie/en/social_welfare/social_welfare_payments/supplementary_welfare_schemes/rent_supplement.html;
Italy: http://www.tasse-fisco.com/persone-fisiche/detrazione-sugli-affitti-per-i-fuori-sede-dedicata-ai-giovani-studenti-universitari/176/;
Netherlands: http://www.studyinholland.co.uk/accommodation.html;
Finland: http://www.kela.fi/web/en/financial-aid-for-students;
Sweden: Försäkringskassan 2008.
Notes: in Germany, the housing benefit is not available for ALG II beneficiaries, insofar as costs associated with housing are already taken into account in the calculation of this benefit.
*35 since 2012.

personnalisée au logement, personalized housing allowance) and ALS (*allocation de logement sociale*, social housing allowance), with the sole condition of not exceeding a certain income threshold. Finally, Belgium, Spain, Portugal, Austria and Luxemburg offer no housing benefits for students, which de facto prolongs the familialization of young people's social citizenship in these countries.

Housing benefits therefore once again reflect the distinction between the familialization and the individualization of young people's social citizenship. The classification of countries is however not as clear as for family policy or student benefits. The group of Bismarckian countries is more homogeneous than the Beveridgean ones, with only France standing out by offering housing benefits to students, which brings it closer to Scandinavian countries' approach, as Cécile Van de Velde (2008) has already pointed out.

Social Assistance

When only income is taken into account (unlike unemployment benefits, in particular), the minimum age limit is central to young people's access to benefits. If the welfare system were fully coherent, the age limit to be considered as a child for family allowances and tax relief would coincide with the age from which one could claim social assistance as an adult. These age limits for social assistance are presented in Figure 3, which on the surface of it hardly depicts our distinction between familialization and individualization. A more detailed analysis of these systems' functioning nevertheless highlights this distinction.

In Sweden there is no official age limit for the income support framework: social assistance is provided to the family as a whole as long as the parents have a maintenance obligation towards their children (Angelin et al. 2013). However, we saw earlier that this obligation stops

Figure 3. Age limits for social assistance, 2012

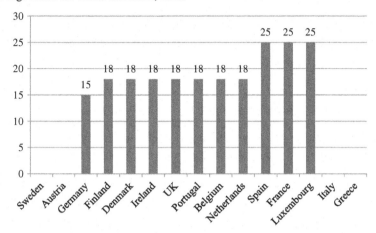

Source: MISSOC (2014).
Notes: The income support framework in Spain has been decentralized since 1995, but most of the autonomous communities in charge of it have kept this age limit. Sweden and Austria (to the left of the graph) have an income support framework but no official age limit, whereas in Italy and Greece (right), there is no national framework for income support.

relatively early (18), and as a result allows young people to claim income support from that age. In Denmark, social assistance is accessible from the age of 18 (Eardley et al. 1996), but for young people between 18 and 25 (now 30), access is conditional on doing training or an internship or having a job, in the framework of the "youth guarantees" (as in Sweden for young people under the age of 25, see Eurofound 2012). In Finland, young people of age living with their parents receive a reduced-rate benefit (Eardley et al. 1996, p. 130) as part of the *Toimeentulotuki*. Their benefit can also be reduced if they refuse a job or training offer (still in the framework of a youth guarantee).

In the Netherlands the minimum legal age to be eligible for income support is 18, but several conditions qualify this early access. First, between 18 and 21, parents' maintenance obligation continues, which means that this access to income support is limited and depends on the parents' situation. Second, a youth guarantee approach is also applied to young people until the age of 27 (Blommesteijn and Mallee 2009, p. 8).

In the United Kingdom, young adults can receive the JSA until the age of 18, but under-25s receive a reduced-rate benefit, irrespective of whether or not they live with their parents (Harris 2000). The same applies to Germany, with the ALG II. In both countries these reduced rates are combined with stricter conditions for under-25s, in terms of doing training and employment-related activities.[4] In Ireland (Eardley et al. 1996, p. 217), young people still in full-time education can be considered as dependent until the age of 21 and therefore qualify for the Jobseeker's Allowance. With the Supplementary Welfare Allowance, young people aged 18–25 receive a reduced-rate benefit based on their parents' income if they still live with them.[5]

The same goes for Belgium and Portugal until the age of 25. In Austria, with regard to eligibility for the *Sozialhilfe*, young people of any age can also be considered as dependent as long as they are not financially autonomous. This is in keeping with the maintenance obligations stipulated in the Civil Code (Eardley et al. 1996).

This prioritization of maintenance obligations over access to social benefits reflects the principle of subsidiarity. It also applies in Germany, where young people who can make maintenance claims cannot claim the ALG II welfare benefit as independent persons (Petzold 2013, p. 23). This benefit is open from the age of 15, but since 2006 young people under the age of 25 are automatically considered to be part of their family "community of need". To access the benefit in their own name they must prove that they have left the family home and need this benefit in order to seek employment (OECD 2009). This is also the approach followed by Austria.

This leaves a second group of countries where the age limit is higher: Spain, France and Luxemburg. The general rule is that young people under the age of 25 simply cannot claim income support in their own name, unless they have a dependent child. In Spain the income support framework is nevertheless strongly decentralized since there is no national legal framework to regulate it: each autonomous region has its own law. Although the age limit of eligibility for the benefit is usually 25, in some regions it has been reduced to 18 (OECD 2012). In France, young people under the age of 25 cannot usually receive the RSA. However, in 2010 a framework called the "*RSA jeune actif*" was introduced, allowing 18–24-year-olds to benefit from this income support provided they have worked for at least two years full-time over the last three years. Moreover, in keeping with the principle of subsidiarity, a young person must previously have claimed the maintenance for which their household is eligible.[6]

As for Greece and Italy, their "rudimentary assistance regime" no longer provides a social assistance or income support programme on a national scale (Gough 1996). This illustrates the extreme familialization of these Southern European welfare states, where it is primarily the family that must look after individuals in need (Ferrera 1996).

Thus, we have on the one hand Beveridgean countries with early age limits for social benefits, but often also with a "youth guarantee" approach, and on the other hand Bismarckian countries with very limited access to income support, due to the pervasiveness of the familialization approach. This may be implemented through high age limits or the principle of subsidiarity determining access to maintenance claims, or it may simply exist due to the absence of a national framework.

Young People's Social Security Cover

In this section I discuss the link between familialization and young people's social cover more generally; in other words their rate of access to social benefits in their own name. In the previous section I posited that the more young people's social citizenship is individualized, the greater this social cover will be, insofar as young people are adults who can claim benefits for themselves.

Figure 4 again reveals a distinction between Beveridgean and Bismarckian states, even though this distinction is not as clear as it was earlier. We have seen that the Scandinavian countries (Finland, Denmark and Sweden) and the United Kingdom offer a high level of social cover for young people aged 24–28, as opposed to Southern European countries (Italy, Greece, Portugal and Spain) and Luxemburg. In between, the trend is less clear, since the Netherlands is just above Southern European countries but below Bismarckian continental countries like Austria, France, Germany and Belgium. Likewise, Ireland is below the latter two countries.

Through a comparative institutional analysis of several public policies, I have thus been able to test my theoretical framework: on the one hand, Bismarckian countries offer a familialized social citizenship; on the other, Beveridgean countries follow an individualized social citizenship.

Figure 4. Social cover rate for young adults (18–24), 2011

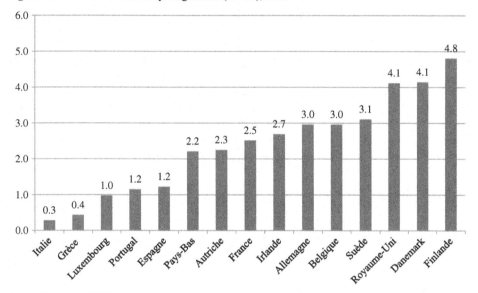

Source: Eurofound (2012); own calculations.

Conclusion

This article demonstrates how the diversity of access to social citizenship for young people in Western Europe can be accounted for. In continental countries with a Bismarckian tradition, where the principle of subsidiarity is institutionalized, this citizenship is familialized, whereas in the Nordic and English-speaking countries with a Beveridgean tradition, it is individualized. This result contributes to the comparative analysis of public policy in general, and to the literature on social welfare in particular, in two ways.

First, it fills a scientific gap in the comparative literature on social welfare, where young people had not yet been systematically analysed, by proposing an original theoretical framework to allow for this analysis. I have shown that in order to understand young people's social citizenship, the focus needs to be more on the role of the family in the social welfare system. The distinction between individualized social citizenship and familialized social citizenship informed by the principle of subsidiarity thus becomes crucial. Until now, familialization has not been conceptualized in opposition to individualization in a way that it would allow for systematic comparison of public policies. My theoretical framework, which relates familialization and individualization to the partition in a person's life course – childhood on the one hand and adulthood on the other – therefore makes a contribution to the literature. It has allowed us to list, analyse and categorize systematically for the first time a set of public policies targeting young people both from a comparative perspective, in 15 Western European countries, and across different sectors. I have thus been able to integrate the study of student benefits, until now largely overlooked in the literature on social welfare regimes, into the study of social welfare benefits. My comparative analysis has highlighted the coherence and complementarity between these benefits, based on my framework of analysis that distinguishes between familialization and individualization.

Second, although the categorization of countries may seem to reflect the usual distinctions, I have argued that this is not for the reasons put forward in the literature dealing with young people. Until now this literature has considered that young people are poorly covered by social security because they are new entrants on the job market, and consequently harder hit by unemployment while experiencing more difficulty in accessing unemployment benefits. It has therefore given central importance to the distinction between work-based social welfare and citizenship-based social welfare. The familialization/individualization distinction, by contrast, stems not from this distinction between work-based and citizenship-based social rights, but from the religious traditions of the welfare states, i.e. Catholicism and Protestantism. This result is therefore in line with the work underlying the role of religion in welfare development, for instance Manow and Van Kersbergen (2009), by bringing the concepts of familialization, Catholicism and Bismarckian welfare states closer on the one hand, and individualization, Protestantism and Beveridgean welfare states on the other.

Acknowledgements

I want to thank all those who gave me some feedback on this text, especially Bruno Palier, Olivier Giraud, Nathalie Morel, Monika Steffen, Jean-Claude Barbier, Philippe Zittoun, and anonymous reviewers.

Funding

This work was funded by the Ecole nationale Supérieure de Sécurité Sociale.

Notes

1. We must also distinguish this "familialization" of benefits for young people, based on the idea that benefits are supposed to help parents support their children, from the "familialization" of a social benefit, meaning that it is granted on the basis of the household's and not the individual's income.
2. The family policy can be here defined as the set of measures aimed at helping families to take care of their children. As Eurydice (1999) shows, there are three main measures potentially concerning young people in that respect: maintenance obligations for parents, family allowances and tax relief for families.
3. A reform changed this student benefit system in the summer of 2014. A basic grant now exists for all students, along with a mobility grant for students studying abroad, a means-tested grant based on the total income of the household in which the student lives, a family grant if the student has brothers and sisters also in higher education, and an optional state-guaranteed loan with a fixed 2 per cent interest rate. See http://www.guichet.public.lu/citoyens/fr/enseignement-formation/etudes-superieures/aides-logement/aide-financiere/index.html
4. In the United Kingdom and in Germany this is an unemployment benefit, but the characteristics are relatively similar, particularly regarding age limits for the Income Support and *Sozialhilfe* social security benefits.
5. http://www.citizensinformation.ie/en/social_welfare/social_welfare_payments/supplementary_welfare_schemes/supplementary_welfare_allow.html
6. See http://vosdroits.service-public.fr/particuliers/F286.xhtml. The new "youth guarantee" framework, however, rather supports individualization, even though this remains marginal in the system as a whole.

References

Angelin, A., Johansson, H., Koch, M., and Panican A., 2013, *Combating Poverty in Europe. National Report: Sweden* (Lund: Lund University).
Armingeon, K. and Bonoli, G., (Eds), 2006, *The Politics of Post-Industrial Welfare States: Adapting Post-War Social Policies to New Social Risks* (London: Routledge).
Blommesteijn, M. and Mallee, L., 2009, *The Netherlands. Minimum Income Scheme: Work and Social Assistance Act* (Bussels: European commission).
Bonoli, G., 1997, Classifying welfare states: A two-dimension approach. *Journal of Social Policy*, **26**(3), pp. 351–372. doi:10.1017/S0047279497005059
Bonoli, G. and Natali, D., (Eds), 2012, *The Politics of the New Welfare State* (Oxford: Oxford University Press).
Bosch, G. and Jansen, A., 2010, From the breadwinner model to 'bricolage': Germany in search for a new life course model, in: D. Anxo, G. Bosch and J. Rubery (Eds) *The Welfare State and Life Transition. A European Perspectives* (Cheltenham: Edward Elgar Publishing).
Charles, N., 2012, Les prêts à remboursement contingent au revenu: Un système de financement des études importable en France? *Revue Française De Sociologie*, **53**(2), pp. 293–333. doi:10.3917/rfs.532.0293
Chevalier, T., 2016, Varieties of youth welfare citizenship: towards a two-dimension typology. *Journal Of European Social Policy*, **26**(1), pp. 3–19. doi: 10.1093/0199247757.001.0001
Eardley, T., Bradshaw, J., Ditch, J., Gough, I., and Whiteford, P., 1996, *Social Assistance in OECD Countries* (London: Department of social security and OECD).
Emmenegger, P., Haüsermann, S., Palier, B. and Seeleib-Kaiser, M., (Eds), 2012, *The Age of Dualization: The Changing Face of Inequality in Deindustrializing Societies* (Oxford: Oxford University Press).
Esping-Andersen, G., 1990, *The Three Worlds of Welfare Capitalism* (Princeton: Princeton University Press).
Eurofound, 2012, *Neets. Young People Not in Employment, Education or Training: Characteristics, Costs and Policy Responses in Europe* (Luxemburg: Publications Office of the European Union).
Eurydice, 1999, *L'aide financière aux étudiants de l'enseignement supérieur en Europe* (Brussels: European Commission).
Eurydice, 2011, *National Student Fee and Support Systems* (Brussels: European commission).
Eurydice, 2013, *National Student Fee and Support Systems* (Brussels: European commission).
Ferragina, E. and Seeleib-Kaiser, M., 2011, Thematic review: Welfare regime debate: Past, present, futures? *Policy & Politics*, **39**(4), pp. 583–611. doi:10.1332/030557311X603592
Ferrera, M., 1996, The 'Southern Model' of welfare in social Europe. *Journal of European Social Policy*, **6**(1), pp. 17–37. doi:10.1177/095892879600600102
Gough, I., 1996, Social assistance in Southern Europe. *South European Society and Politics*, **1**(1), pp. 1–23. doi:10.1080/13608749608454714
Hakovirta, M. and Hiilamo, H., 2012, Children's rights and parents' responsibilities: Child maintenance policies in Finland. *European Journal of Social Security*, **14**(4), pp. 286–303. doi:10.1177/138826271201400405
Harris, N. S., 2000, *Social Security Law in Context* (Oxford: Oxford University Press).
Jones, G., 2005, Social protection policies for young people: A cross-national comparison, in: H. Bradley and J. Van Hoof (Eds) *Young People in Europe: Labour Markets and Citizenship* (Bristol: Policy Press).
Jones, G., 2003, Youth, dependence and the problem of support, in: S. Cunningham-Burley and L. Jamieson (Eds) *Families and the State: Changing Relationships* (London: Palgrave Macmillan), pp. 187–204.
Kohli, M., 1986, The world we forgot: A historical review of the life course, in: V.-W. Marshall (Eds) *Later Life: The Social Psychology of Ageing* (Beverly Hills: SAGE), pp. 271–303.
Labrusse-Riou, C., 1986, Sécurité d'existence et solidarité familiale en droit privé : Étude comparative du droit des pays européens continentaux. *Revue Internationale De Droit Comparé*, **38**(3), pp. 829–865. doi:10.3406/ridc.1986.2483
Leisering, L., 2003, Government and the life course, in: J.-T. Mortimer and M.-J. Shanahan (Eds) *Handbook of the Life Course* (New York: Kluwer Academic Publishers), pp. 205–225.
Lewis, J., 1992, Gender and the development of welfare regimes. *Journal of European Social Policy*, **2**(3), pp. 159–173. doi:10.1177/095892879200200301
Lima, L., 2008, Le temps de la prime insertion professionnelle : Un nouvel âge de la vie, in: A.-M. Guillemard (Ed.) *Où Va La Protection Sociale?* (Paris: PUF), pp. 49–67.
Manow, P. and Van Kersbergen, K., (eds.), 2009, *Religion, Class Coalition, and Welfare States* (Cambridge: Cambridge University Press).
Marshall, T-H., 1950, *Citizenship And Social Class* (Cambridge: Cambridge University Press).

Mayer, K. U. and Schoepflin, U., 1989, The state and the life course. *Annual Review of Sociology*, **15**, pp. 187–209. doi:10.1146/annurev.so.15.080189.001155

Meulders-Klein, M. T. and Eekelaar, J., (Eds), 1988, *Famille, Etat et sécurité économique d'existence* (Brussels: Story-Scientia).

Millar, J. and Warman, A., 1996, *Family Obligations in Europe* (London: Family Policy Studies Centre).

OECD, 2009, Germany, *Country specific information*. Available at: http://www.oecd.org/els/soc/benefits-and-wages-country-specific-information.htm

OECD, 2012, Spain, *Country specific information*. Available at http://www.oecd.org/els/soc/benefits-and-wages-country-specific-information.htm

Orloff, A. S., 1993, Gender and the social rights of citizenship: The comparative analysis of gender relations and welfare states. *American Sociological Review*, **58**(3), pp. 303–328. doi:10.2307/2095903

Petzold, N., 2013, *Combating Poverty in Europe*. (Germany: National Report).

Rebourg, M., 2001, Les prolongements de l'obligation alimentaire: Obligation d'entretien et obligation naturelle, in: I. Sayn and L. H. Choquet (Eds) *Obligation alimentaire et solidarités familiales. Entre droit civil, protection sociale et réalités familiales* (Paris: L.G.D.J), pp. 41–59.

Rice, D., 2013, Beyond welfare regimes: From empirical typology to conceptual ideal types. *Social Policy & Administration*, **47**(1), pp. 93–110. doi:10.1111/spol.2013.47.issue-1

Sosson, J., 2001, Analyse comparée des liens juridiques fondant la solidarité alimentaire légale dans les pays occidentaux, in: I. Sayn and L. H. Choquet (Eds) *Obligation Alimentaire Et Solidarités Familiales. Entre Droit Civil, Protection Sociale Et Réalités Familiales* (Paris: L.G.D.J), pp. 61–79.

Taylor-Gooby, P., 2004, *New Risks, New Welfare: The Transformation of the European Welfare State* (Oxford: Oxford University Press).

Van de Velde, C., 2008, *Devenir Adulte : Sociologie comparée de la jeunesse en Europe* (Paris: PUF).

Walther, A., 2006, Regimes of youth transitions: Choice, flexibility and security in young people's experiences across different European contexts. *Young*, **14**(2), pp. 119–139. doi:10.1177/1103308806062737

Comparative Analysis of Higher Education Quality Assurance in Colombia and Ecuador: How is Political Ideology Reflected in Policy Design and Discourse?

NADIA RUBAII & MARIANA LIMA BANDEIRA

ABSTRACT *Throughout Latin America there is evidence of policy change reflecting greater emphasis on quality assurance within higher education institutions and programs. Focusing principally on indicators such as adoption of laws and creation of regulatory agencies, prior studies have emphasized the similarities across countries. Given the stark contrasts in political ideologies among Latin American countries one might wonder if policy change in the realm of higher education quality assurance manifests differently in countries with different ideologies. Using discourse analysis, evidence is found to support theories which would predict differences between the neoliberal and externally focused orientation in Colombia and the more leftist and internally focused* Plan de Buen Vivir *in Ecuador. Our findings indicate the importance of examining more qualitative elements of policy discourse as one measure of policy change and not relying solely on concrete quantitative indicators.*

Introduction

Since the 1990s, Latin America has undergone dramatic changes in public policy, influenced by greater populist discourse, a wave of democratization, a changing international configuration, and new power arrangements. The public policies proposed, enacted,

---

An earlier version of this paper was presented at the 13th ICPA-Forum/JCPA Workshop on "Comparative Theory Testing and Theory Building: The Case of Policy Change in Latin America," Quito, Ecuador, August 24–25, 2015. The authors thank the discussants, participants, and workshop coordinators for their thoughtful feedback and suggestions.

and implemented in this complex environment reflect goals, problems, and solutions (Stone 2012) which need to be understood within their particular policy domains and country contexts (Perellon 2007). This paper examines public policies regarding higher education quality assurance (HEQA) in two countries in Latin America.

Accountability, Quality Assurance and Accreditation

Policy decisions within higher education encompass six fundamental choices (size, structure, location, admission, governance, and curricula), in combination with five fundamental values (excellence, equality, autonomy, accountability, and efficiency), with an increasing prioritization of accountability (Premfors 1992). "Accountability" has its roots in the notion of accounting or keeping the books, but it has evolved to more broadly refer to government being held accountable to citizens (Bovens 2007). Based on a meta-analysis of quantitative studies of accountability in public administration research, Brandsma and Schillemans (2013) developed an "accountability cube" to portray its three dimensions: extent of information, intensity of discussions, and severity of consequences.

Accountability is simultaneously "one of the cornerstones of democracy" (Brandsma and Schillemans 2013, p. 953) and one of "the least analyzed words in higher education" (Burke 2005, p. 1). The term accountability is even more problematic in Latin America where the word in Spanish *rendicion de cuentas* retains its original definition of rendering the accounts. In scholarship and practice in Latin America, accountability is largely absent from the discourse and the more widely used term is quality assurance.

Systems of HEQA can take various forms and serve different purposes. They may focus on institutions and/or programs; apply to public and/or private providers of higher education; be mandatory or voluntary; ensure basic (threshold) or high-level (excellence) quality; measure inputs, processes, and/or results; prioritize concerns about economic development, equity, accountability, public opinion, or market failures; be conducted only once or periodically; and be performed by governmental, quasi-governmental, or non-governmental actors (Billing 2004; Burke 2005; Blackmur 2007; Lemaitre 2011). An outcome of HEQA can be formal accreditation which certifies academic quality of a program or institution, its capacity to deliver on its promises, and its demonstrated record.

HEQA systems emerge in response to a variety of factors. Some factors are specific to higher education, including quantitative and qualitative growth of higher education or political concerns about the level of student achievement or the time to degree completion. Other domestic factors are broader than higher education, such as the general policy orientations or political ideology of a country. There are also international forces including pressures from international lending associations or activities of neighbors (Perellon 2007). In comparing systems of HEQA, key dimensions include the aims and objectives of the policy, who controls the process, the processes used, and how information is collected and used (Perellon 2007).

Higher Education QA in Latin America

Following the economic crises of the 1980s, most Latin American countries experienced pressures on their higher education systems which culminated in the development of quality assurance and accreditation systems. The first and most dramatic change was an increase in demand for higher education, followed by a proliferation of suppliers mostly from the private sector (Garcia Guadilla 2003; Martin and Stella 2007; De La Garza Aguilar 2008; Lopez Segrera 2010). The development of new forms of higher education institutions (HEIs) made the sector more diverse (Torres and Schugurensky 2002; De Wit et al. 2005; De La Garza Aguilar 2008).

These changes generated increased concerns about disparities in quality (Fernandez Lamarra 2003; Martin and Stella 2007). Latin America is home to public and private universities of great international prestige and strong research traditions. It is also home to institutions, largely private, that are referred to in the common vernacular as *universidades garajes* (garage universities), a derogatory term reflecting lack of academic rigor and sometimes without even the most basic physical infrastructure. Low quality education can limit the effectiveness of higher education as a tool for development (Garcia Guadilla 2003; Martin and Stella 2007; Lopez Segrera 2010), produce graduates unprepared to meet new labor-market demands related to a knowledge-based society (Orozco Silva 2010), inhibit student and professor mobility on an international scale (Garcia Guadilla 2003), and result in general inefficiencies in operations and finances (Leite et al. 2003). Multilateral lending organizations and other international bodies have pressured countries to implement QA and accreditation processes along with other reforms (Leite et al. 2003) and a trend in development of HEQA systems is evident beginning in the 1990s (Fernandez Lamarra 2003; Inga and Velásquez Silva 2005; De La Garza Aguilar 2008; Lemaitre 2011).

There is no shortage of research about the higher education changes in Latin America, the pressures for quality assurance and accreditation, and the policy responses of national governments. This research appears in the form of a small number of scholarly publications (Torres and Schugurensky 2002; Leite et al. 2003; Orozco Silva 2010; Villavicencio 2012) and a multitude of reports commissioned, published, and disseminated by international organizations such as the United Nations Educational, Scientific and Cultural Organization, the World Bank, and others. In what might appear to be a crowded field, this paper contributes to the body of knowledge in two key ways related to the scope and methodology of our research.

First, the scope of our study is a two-country comparison. Existing research primarily takes the form either of individual country case studies which do not provide the basis for systematic comparisons, or region-wide comparisons which lack attention to detail and individual circumstances. By focusing on two carefully selected countries, we reap the benefits of detailed case studies while also contributing to theory testing through systematic comparisons. Second, our research applies the methodology of discourse analysis to interpret and understand the motivations for and forms of policy change in the two countries. Earlier studies have relied almost exclusively on concrete quantitative indicators (such as number of new laws passed, agencies created, procedures established, or accreditations awarded) which have largely been interpreted as evidence of considerable similarity in the nature of policy changes across countries in the region despite notable differences in their political ideologies.

Two competing ideologies prevail in Latin America: neoliberalism and twenty-first century socialism. The policies associated with neoliberalism or the so-called "Washington Consensus" hallmark the values of transparency, results, anticorruption, privatization, trade liberalization, market economies, deregulation, and internationalization; this ideology is commonly associated with Chile, Colombia, Mexico, and Argentina

(Baer and Maloney 1997; Kurtz and Brooks 2008). In contrast, leftist, twenty-first century socialism or the so-called "pink tide" explicitly rejects market-oriented neoliberal policies and emphasizes increased state regulation and power to focus traditional institutions toward better serving the interests of the poor majority over the privileged few – Bolivia, Ecuador, and Venezuela are prime examples (Kennemore and Weeks 2011; Becker 2013). In the context of HEQA, neoliberal and leftist ideologies can be expected to manifest in differences in economic versus social justifications, market incentives versus government-control mechanisms, emphasis on attaining international standards versus meeting internal needs of marginalized populations, and conveying messages to international audiences versus providing information to reassure the domestic audience, respectively.

Our findings provide preliminary evidence of differences in policy change regarding HEQA linked to political ideology. Our research also suggests the value of discourse analysis as a means of measuring policy change, not only within this policy arena but also more generally. Finally, our analysis identifies potential challenges with planned collaborations across higher education systems in the region given the distinct motivations and methods reflected in their recent policy changes.

Methodology

Comparing Colombia and Ecuador

As neighboring countries in the Andean region of South America, Colombia and Ecuador share historical and geographic characteristics and both are classified by the Word Bank as "upper middle income". They have experienced similar rates of growth in their higher education sectors in terms of demand, and increases in the number and diversity of higher education suppliers. They have both responded by passing new laws, creating new agencies, and developing new policies and procedures.

Despite these similarities, Colombia and Ecuador represent settings in which distinctly different policy models and perspectives have been adopted in response to the pressures of globalization. Colombia is widely recognized as having adopted a neoliberal model, whereas Ecuador's *Plan Nacional de Buen Vivir* explicitly rejects many neoliberal principles in favor of a twenty-first century socialist framework. The two countries are thus guided by decidedly different philosophies of economic and social development, the role of the state and the market, and the relative importance of domestic and international actors. As such, we might expect to find differences in how they approach HEQA.

In December 2014, President Santos of Colombia and President Correa of Ecuador signed an agreement establishing a Binational Commission on Higher Education to study and present recommendations regarding mutual recognition. Thus, a comparative study in these two countries is timely and can contribute to practical as well as scholarly advances.

Examining Policy Change through Discourse Analysis

Studies of policy change within HEQA in Latin America have adopted what Fischer (2003, p. vii) labels as a "dominant neopositivist/empiricist approach" that effectively neglects the "basic value issues and social meanings inherent to their subject matter". At an aggregate level of regional comparisons, there is the appearance of similar changes occurring in almost all countries across Latin America as they enact new laws, create new organizations, and establish processes all in the name of "quality". These studies ignore the differences in policy change that may be reflected in the discourse and which may be reflective of the distinct contextual circumstances, not the least of which is the guiding political ideology of the country. Studies of policy change must focus on more than just the objective aspect of change, but also the subjective or discursive aspects (Zittoun 2009). Too often the complexities of policy change are downplayed and the implications of measurement decisions are not openly acknowledged (Capano 2009). Discourse analysis[1] can help avoid the errors of oversimplification and objectification by taking into account the way the problem is constituted and how policy is defined (Zittoun 2009). Our study is not the first application of discourse analysis to HEQA; Saarinen (2005) uses a similar approach to document the evolving usage and meaning of "quality" within and across countries in Europe as part of the Bologna Process.

While discourse analysis is often applied to public statements, Saarinen (2005, p. 189) notes that it can also be appropriately applied to policy texts as a means of not only "tracing policy changes and describing them, but also in explaining and understanding" them and "the (political) views which are embedded" within. Soler-Castillo (2011) also utilizes documents as the basis for her discourse analysis of higher education policies. Included in our analyses are the following source materials:

- national constitutions;
- national laws creating or defining the responsibilities of higher education quality assurance agencies enacted between the start of a quality assurance framework in each country through July 2015;
- historical and contemporary internal documents of those agencies articulating their standards and processes;
- data on websites of these agencies in summer 2015; and
- coverage in major newspapers in the most populous cities in each country for the entire period.

What differentiates our study from others is that, rather than count and quantify, our focus is on the language used and its significance in light of the particular sociopolitical and institutional contexts of each country. In utilizing varied source materials for our analysis, we intentionally blur the lines between potential units of analysis. In contrast to the post-positivist approaches which demand the identification of a single unit of analysis, we accept that individuals, groups, organizations, systems, etc. are not entirely distinct units of analysis (Jreisat 2011); all are socially constructed and influenced by their contexts. Similarly, we unavoidably and deliberately blur the lines between data collection and analysis (Meyer 2001). While the policy change literature calls for more precise operational definitions of the dependent variable of policy change (Howlett and Cashore 2009), discourse analysis applies a more holistic approach. Discourse analysis accepts that "texts not only describe the world, they also create and recreate it" (Saarinen 2005, p. 190). This holistic approach is not a weakness, but rather a reflection of the complexity and multifaceted nature of social constructs which may defy precision.

We seek to understand the extent and nature of policy change reflected in the discourse about the design and operation of quality assurance institutions and processes. This exploratory research is guided by two broad questions regarding HEQA in Colombia and Ecuador:

1. Do they define and discuss QA in higher education similarly or differently?
2. Do the contrasting philosophies of neoliberalism and *Buen Vivir* manifest themselves in similar or different policy changes and discourse regarding HEQA?

Capano and Howlett (2009) acknowledge that change can take many forms including cyclical, dialectic, linear, or teleological, and they warn of the danger of endorsing a particular model because it has implications for research and limits perspectives. Our goal is not to label the change so much as to describe and interpret it within its context. We want to determine if those policy changes can be better understood – separately and in relation to one another – in terms of distinct ideological models operating in the two countries.

Legal and Institutional Frameworks for Quality Assurance in Colombia and Ecuador

Before examining the discourse of HEQA, it is instructive to review the path of development and current status of QA systems in the two countries with particular attention to the legal and institutional elements. The organizations involved in each country represent a virtual alphabet soup; thus, for ease of reference, Table 1 provides a summary of acronyms, names in Spanish, and English translations.

Colombia

The current policy and regulatory framework for HEQA has its foundation in the 1991 Constitution, which refers to education as an "individual right and a public service that has a social function" and a means by which "individuals seek access to knowledge, science, technology, and the other benefits and values of culture" (Art. 67). It assigns "responsibility" to "the state to perform the final inspection and supervision of education in order to control its quality, to ensure that it fulfills its purposes" (Art. 69). Law 30 of 1992 creates a framework for putting these constitutional principles into practice. Article 53 of Law 30 created many related systems and organizations. Law 30 represents not only the first step, but also the continuing cornerstone, of Colombia's QA system. Refinements to the system have come in the form of decrees, accords, and resolutions, as well as procedures and informational documents from the agencies described below.

Colombia's higher education system is regulated by a network of governmental and quasi-governmental agencies, all linked in some way to the National Ministry of Education (MEN) and each other. The National Council of Higher Education (CESU) plans and coordinates policies regarding higher education and oversees the work of other organizations which comprise three distinct yet overlapping and interdependent systems for (1) development, (2) information, and (3) quality assurance. The QA component, labeled the System of Quality Assurance in Higher Education (SACES), consists of the National Commission for Quality Assurance in Higher Education (CONACES) and the National Accreditation Council (CNA).

Table 1. Abbreviations and acronyms

Acronym	Name in Spanish	English equivalent
Colombia		
CESU	*Consejo Nacional de Educación Superior*	National Council of Higher Education
CNA	*Consejo Nacional de Acreditación*	National Accreditation Council
CONACES	*Comisión Nacional Intersectorial para el Aseguramiento de la Calidad de la Educación Superior*	National Commission for Quality Assurance in Higher Education
DNP	*Departamento Nacional de Planeación*	National Planning Department
ICFES	*Instituto Colombiano para el Fomento de Educación Superior*	Colombian Institute for the Promotion of Higher Education
MEN	*Ministerio de Educación Nacional*	National Ministry of Education
SACES	*Sistema de Aseguramiento de la Calidad en Educación Superior*	System of Quality Assurance in Higher Education
SNA	*Sistema Nacional de Acreditación*	National System of Accreditation
Ecuador		
CEAACES	*Consejo de Evaluación, Acreditación y Aseguramiento de la Calidad de la Educación Superior*	Council of Higher Education Evaluation, Accreditation and Quality Assurance
CES	*Consejo de Educación Superior*	Higher Education Council
CONEA	*Consejo Nacional de Evaluación y Acreditación*	National Council of Evaluation and Accreditation
CONESUP	*Consejo Nacional de Educación Superior*	National Council of Higher Education
CONUEP	*Consejo Nacional de Universidades y Escuelas Politécnicas*	National Council of Universities and Polytechnic Schools
INEC	*Instituto Nacional de Estadística y Censos*	National Institute of Statistics and Census of Ecuador
SENESCYT	*Secretaría de Educación Superior, Ciencia, Tecnología e Innovación*	Secretary of Higher Education, Science, Technology and Innovation
SENPLADES	*Secretaría Nacional de Planificación y Desarrollo*	National Secretary of Planning and Development

Colombia's system of QA has two distinct levels: a mandatory review to ensure minimum quality overseen by CONACES and a voluntary accreditation process to recognize high quality coordinated by CNA. For institutions and most programs, the minimum quality process is referred to as the Qualified Registry (*Registro Calificado*). For programs with "wide social impact", minimum quality assurance is assessed *before* a program is authorized through a process called Prior Accreditation (*Acreditación Previa*).[2] The Qualified Registry process is temporary and must be renewed every seven years, whereas Prior Accreditation is a one-time recognition.

Accreditation of High Quality (*Acreditación de Alta Calidad*) is a voluntary process that seeks to publicly recognize programs and institutions for demonstrated excellence. CNA's mission is "to contribute to fostering high quality of higher education institutions and to guarantee to society that the institutions and programs that it accredits meet the highest levels of quality and they accomplish their purpose and objectives". CNA began accreditation of undergraduate programs in 1998, institutions in 2003, and graduate programs in 2011. As of

August 2015, CNA had accredited 1,049 undergraduate programs (690 have been reaccredited), 47 institutions (including 13 reaccreditations), and 62 graduate programs.

Ecuador

A policy and regulatory framework for higher education in Ecuador was slowly being built throughout the country's political history (Pacheco 2012), but only very recently has it focused explicitly and formally on evaluation, quality assurance, and accreditation. The Organic Law on Higher Education (LOES) of 2000 included provisions establishing guidelines for quality. The Act was modified in 2008 by Constitutional Mandate No. 14, which ordered the National Council of Evaluation and Accreditation (CONEA) and the National Council of Higher Education (CONESUP) to evaluate the quality of Ecuadorian universities. The CONEA evaluation established a baseline of information about higher education in Ecuador and led to a categorization scheme that has had a strong impact on the higher education system. Under this scheme, universities were assigned a category or grade from "A" (superior quality) to "E" (non-functioning). A CONEA report was published in 2009 and served as input for a new LOES issued in 2010.

The 2010 LOES marked the beginning of another regulatory logic. It created two new institutions – the Higher Education Council (CES) and the Council of Higher Education Evaluation, Accreditation and Quality Assurance (CEAACES) – to replace CONESUP and CONEA. CES produces rules to organize the Ecuadorian higher education system, and CEAACES is responsible for assuring quality through implementation of evaluation and accreditation processes. Additionally, the Secretary of Higher Education, Science, Technology and Innovation (SENESCYT) was assigned the task of facilitating integration within the Ecuadorian higher education system.

Since it was established in 2011, CEAACES has conducted evaluation processes and addressed questions of whether to continue using the "E" Category, how to evaluate satellite campuses, what processes to use for institutional evaluation and accreditation, how to evaluate undergraduate programs, and the role of national examinations for students in selected disciplines, beginning with medicine, with plans to expand to dentistry, law, nursing, administration, and education, over time. Among the most notable actions of CEAACES were the closing of 15 non-functioning universities and 44 satellite campuses judged to be in the "E" category.

The Discourse of Higher Education Quality Assurance in Colombia and Ecuador

Our analysis of the discourse within the Colombian and Ecuadorian systems is organized around four questions:

1. What story is being told about quality of higher education?
2. How is the story being presented?
3. To whom is the message being targeted and with what apparent purpose?
4. How can we understand and interpret this narrative within its context?

The Stories

The stories told in each country reflect how they define quality in higher education and what they say about the country's progress in achieving that quality. Neither country provides a single concise definition of quality, but the language used to discuss quality represents a working definition. In Colombia, CNA's Accreditation Guidelines identify core principles (capacity, relevance, responsibility, integrity, equity, coherence, universality, transparency, effectiveness, efficiency, sustainability, visibility, and sustainable development), factors for assessment of quality (mission and institutional plan, students, professors, academic processes, institutional well-being, social impact, administration and management, and physical and financial resources), and a series of indicators used to measure these factors. The indicators of quality for both institutions and programs include a mix of input, output, and outcome measures.

The story that Colombia tells about quality within its higher education system is that concerns about minimum quality have largely been addressed and the public and international community can be assured that all institutions and programs are fulfilling their constitutionally mandated social role. To the extent that concerns remain at a system level, it is not about quality, but rather about accessibility and equity. Higher education institutions and enrollments in Colombia continue to be concentrated in just four cities of Bogota, Cali, Medellin, and Barranquilla (Revelo Revelo and Hernandez 2003), and private institutions have high tuition fees, effectively excluding rural and less wealthy populations.

The Colombian story also projects pride in the excellence demonstrated by the programs and institutions that have been accredited. By emphasizing the reliance on international standards and processes and placing increasing emphasis on international collaborations and increased international mobility, the message is that Colombia is a global player in higher education. CNA portrays itself as a partner in the process more than a regulator, describing how the rules of the game are established through collaborative and open processes. The story is also one of an open and transparent system, both in terms of how programs and institutions conduct their business, and in how CNA shares information.

The story presented in Ecuador is noticeably different in its explicit links to the ideology of *Sumak Kawsay*, an indigenous term which translates in Spanish as *Buen Vivir* or in English as "good living" (Walsh 2010) or "harmonious or good life" (Misoczky 2011; Radcliffe 2012). This philosophy is based on the principles of tolerance of and respect for diversity, social inclusion, widespread equity, sovereign strength, and a notion of economic development grounded in the values of citizenship and sustainability (Cobey and Bandeira 2013). Quality in higher education is thus a right of citizens as part of a system of promoting collective well-being in which the government plays the role of protector.

Although quality is assessed across five areas – academics, research, organization, infrastructure, and efficiency – the institutional evaluation model adopted by CEAACES in 2013 relies almost exclusively on input measures (number of classrooms, number of publications, faculty–student ratio, class sizes, salaries, etc.). Similarly, the process of review through online data reporting, technical analysis of data by CEAACES, and an external visit is all about confirming the data reported and ensuring that the university has adequate resources. Quality is largely defined in terms of management capacity. Additionally, the story in Ecuador includes an element of competition because the rating scheme categorizes institutions based on a quantitative score relative to the average score of other HEIs.

All of the policy initiatives of CEAACES – including closure of low quality universities and satellite campuses, evaluation and accreditation, authorizing programs, direct intervention in some universities, development of national exams to assess students within their professions, and strict control of study abroad – are presented and justified in the context of the *Plan Nacional del Buen Vivir*. The imagery is thus of a powerful, caring state as the protector.

How the Story Is Conveyed

Stories are conveyed through a variety of mediums, including words, numbers, and images (Stone 2012). In Colombia, the central messages about achievement of basic levels of quality, the value of accreditation as a national and international symbol of excellence, and the centrality of collaboration and transparency are conveyed through public pronouncements and online information. Each time CNA recommends a program or institution for accreditation, the decision receives widespread, highly visible attention in the national media and on the websites of agencies that comprise the SNA. Notably absent from the public messages are negative decisions; these are instead communicated privately and confidentially to the institution's official representatives along with offers to work collaboratively to develop strategies for improvement.

Additionally, the websites of CONACES, CNA, and MEN make raw data, annual reports, statistical bulletins, analyses, guidelines, and other materials readily available to any interested party, and everything is published in English as well as Spanish. The impression provided by these sites is that the organizations which comprise the HEQA system in Colombia and the system as a whole have nothing to hide.

In Ecuador, the closure of universities and satellite campuses in 2011 was presented as a symbol not only of national strength and evidence of how the state would look after the interests of the population, but also using the narrative of cleansing and purifying. One of the images evoked by the discourse is that of environmental cleanup of entities that are contaminating the system, an image that is powerful and meaningful in the Ecuadorian context.

The categorization scheme used initially by CONEA and only slightly modified by CEAACES evokes a different kind of image. Using "A", "B", "C", "D", and "E" labels in a higher education context cannot help but be equated to grades; and evaluating institutions relative to the average performance suggests both competition among institutions and a moving target. Closure of the "E" category institutions in 2011 and then elimination of categories in 2013 was intended to convey a message that there were no longer any non-functioning universities in Ecuador. But it left those in the "D" category wondering about their fate. Although not closed, they are left with a clear stigma and in a kind of "limbo" in which they are closely monitored by CEAACES and required to prove themselves through another evaluation in order to be accredited and avoid closure. While universities in Ecuador have largely accepted the HEQA system, there are some strong criticisms about the lack of clearly defined concepts or criteria, the absence of reflection about the social consequences of these new "models", and lack of participation by key stakeholders (Salgado and Moran 2014).

In spite of all the data collected through these mandatory evaluation processes and a law that provides for the creation of a national information system accessible to the citizenry, there is practically no up-to-date publicly available official data about quality of HEIs in Ecuador. Rather than raw data, websites and press releases include graphs generated by the regulatory agencies themselves. These graphs tend to emphasize positive trends such as growing public investment in higher education or a decline in the percentage of people who do not attend higher education for financial reasons. They do not present data which suggest problems or continued weaknesses. When conflicting reports are released to the press, it is impossible to determine which is accurate given the inability to access raw data.

Targeted Audiences and Purposes

Stories do not exist in isolation; they are created for a purpose and with an intended audience in mind. In Colombia, the message itself and how it is conveyed suggest service to both internal and external stakeholders. CNA identifies five categories of stakeholders or users of its information and services: (1) participating HEIs, their students, teachers, researchers and administrative personnel; (2) the national government; (3) the private sector which depends upon the skills of graduates; (4) the general public; and (5) foreign individuals, HEIs and accreditation agencies. The story is packaged and presented in different ways and with different emphases for the various audiences.

In addressing the HEIs within Colombia, the message is one of the voluntary and collaborative nature of accreditation, the value of the process and the recognition, and the absence of risk to reputation should the decision be negative. The private sector is told that they have a role in helping to define what knowledge, skills, and abilities are required in their future employees and that they can trust the Colombian HEQA system to assess those competencies. And the message to international actors is that Colombian higher education is a peer that is worthy of research collaborations, faculty and student exchanges, mutual accreditation agreements, and financial investment.

In communicating a message about cleansing the system of its impurities and providing for the collective welfare, clearly the Ecuadorian discourse is targeted to the general population. The purpose of the message is to instill trust and confidence and reassure the public that the government will ensure that they have access to quality higher education. On the other hand, the manner in which data is shared (or, more accurately, not shared) suggests that the real audience for the information gathered through the evaluation and accreditation processes is the government itself, rather than the citizenry or the higher education system. The absence of clarity in the criteria used to assess quality makes it difficult for institutions to meet expectations and thus they clearly are not the priority audience.

Understanding the Story in Context

A central premise of discourse analysis is that narratives are socially constructed and must be understood in their context. Considered in light of the 50+-year violent conflict within Colombia along with contemporary peace negotiations, an international stigma as a major player in drug trafficking, and perceptions of widespread corruption, it should come as no surprise that Colombia is trying to leverage a positive message from its system of HEQA.

In an environment characterized by so much instability and conflict, conveying a message of stability, collaboration, legitimacy, and quality in higher education is important.

In speaking to domestic audiences, Colombia's message of transparency, stability, and collaboration provides a direct challenge to images of a corrupt system and a highly contentious political environment. The public attention on recognition of excellence provides a common reference for pride. As part of the recognized need for all social actors to contribute to a transition to peace should an agreement to end the violence be reached, in 2014 CNA updated its accreditation guidelines to make explicit the expectation that high quality institutions will promote social inclusion and peace in the country.

The messages targeted to international audiences, private sector employers, and investors can also be understood in the context of broader neoliberal policies. Since the adoption of a new Constitution in 1991, Colombia has been on a path toward neoliberal reforms through deregulation, market models, and internationalization (Kurtz and Brooks 2008), and higher education policies have not been immune to these reforms (Vanegas 2003). Colombia's initial emphasis on accrediting programs before institutions corresponds to the neoliberal model because it is at this level that we can define the specific knowledge, skills, abilities, and competencies needed by graduates in a particular field, and assess graduates' impact on the profession. The current hard push to promote graduate program accreditation reflects the desire for an even greater international image for research and innovation.

Ecuador's President Correa has explicitly rejected neoliberal policies and has offered a comprehensive socialist strategy or *Plan Nacional de Buen Vivir* (PNBV). Some of the discourse associated with quality assurance and accreditation in Ecuador can be linked to policy and philosophical elements of PNBV. In keeping with the twenty-first century socialist model, Ecuador's system of accreditation emphasizes equality of resources (inputs) into higher education institutions. In this way everyone, regardless of what university they attend, is assured of a comparable experience because the government has ensured minimum quality for its citizens. Ecuador's decision to begin by focusing on institutional accreditation also fits within this model; institutions are the means by which services are delivered and government must regulate them. As part of its regulatory and control function, government collects data on quality and uses it for its own purposes in determining the allocation of resources and the authority to operate; transparency is less important than meeting its requirement of assuring equality.

Interpreting the Findings

Having briefly summarized the discourses surrounding higher education quality assurance and accreditation policies in Colombia and Ecuador and placed them within their respective socio-political contexts, we can now engage in more systematic comparisons and reflections of our findings within the context of the literature. In contrast to prior studies which relied exclusively on quantitative measures of policy change and which asserted considerable similarities across Latin American countries, we find evidence of notable differences in both the design and the corresponding discourse surrounding HEQA policy changes in Colombia and Ecuador. On the surface there are similarities in the form of new laws, organizations, policies, and procedures, but when one examines how quality is discussed in key texts, there is considerable evidence of differences linked directly to the ideologies of the countries. These results are not surprising, yet they reflect a sharp departure from prior studies and thus provide some important lessons.

In examining and interpreting the discourse, we focused on the terms employed in the framing of a problem (Jones 1984) and how words and images are brought together to create social meaning, develop a storyline, and convey a message (Fairclough 1992, cited in Fischer 2003). Using Stone's (2012) notion of "stories" or narratives, we examined the discourse of Colombian and Ecuadorian policies as a form of "systematic discourse – more or less focused – between higher education and its environment" (Stensker and Harvey 2006, p. 66). Academics generally prioritize knowledge, employers want competencies, students are concerned about employability, society demands competent citizens, and the state has interests in social and human development, as well as efficiency. Quality may be limited to measures of efficiency, labor market competencies, and job placement which reflect neoliberal priorities, or it may prioritize social relevance and equity which may be more representative of socialism (De La Garza Aguilar 2008). The discourse surrounding quality may also vary in terms of the extent to which transparency is valued (Stensker and Harvey 2006), how and to whom information about results of accreditation or quality assessment decisions are released, and whether there are rewards or punishments based on the results (Inga and Velásquez Silva 2005).

Discourse analysis not only allows for a clearer understanding of how policy change differs in the two countries, but also allows us to appreciate the nuances – which often manifest in the form of policy paradoxes – in each country. Stone (2012) encourages policy analysts to embrace rather than resist the inherent paradoxes in public policy. The paradoxes provide evidence of Saarinen's (2005) assertion that discourse in text both reflects and shapes reality. One place where this is evident is with respect to the mandatory or voluntary nature of quality assessment and the extent to which the legal status and actual or perceived status may be at odds. In Colombia, the discourse on accreditation is designed to promote more widespread participation in the system of voluntary accreditation of high quality. While legally voluntary, the pressures and stakes are high, and institutions and programs competing for the top students and wanting to establish their international reputations feel compelled to undertake these processes. Colombia is thus allowing the market forces to drive participation. In Ecuador, the narrative is of the obligatory nature of institutional accreditation but this requirement is not as definitive as the policies would suggest. With the 2013 CEAACES evaluations, the lowest quality categorization no longer results in closure, but rather in being labeled as "working toward accreditation". As Ecuador moves toward program-level accreditation, there are also discussions within CEAACES about allowing unaccredited institutions to continue to operate if they offer accredited programs, representing another paradox within the policy of "mandatory" accreditation.

Additional paradoxes naturally arise because quality is a multifaceted concept. In Colombia there is a tension between the narratives espousing the values of access and equity in higher education which requires keeping costs down, and those encouraging more market-driven models in which institutions compete by virtue of their excellence and students "get what they pay for". Colombia has reconciled this tension by emphasizing equity and access in the qualified registry reviews, and allowing market forces to be more dominant within voluntary accreditation despite criticisms that this allows the most privileged strata to have access to "kind of a club of top-ranking public and private universities" (Lucio and Serrano 1993, p. 71). The CNA approach to Accreditation of Excellence is both praised for creating a culture of evaluation in Colombia (Revelo Revelo and Hernandez 2003) and criticized for being inefficient and costly, and for promoting the proliferation of programs by focusing on program-level accreditation (Gomez and Celis 2009).

In Ecuador, a paradox exists with respect to the widespread collection of data and the very limited availability of that data. On the one hand, the message is of a comprehensive and detailed system for gathering data which suggests governmental capacity, and which treats all institutions the same in terms of their reporting requirements. On the other hand, the limited data available to the public or to HEIs themselves, as well as the contradictions between what is said and what is done in relation to accountability, represent a lack of transparency.

Whether measured using empirical indicators counting the number of new laws or government agencies or through a careful analysis of the policy discourse, there is clear evidence of policy change in both Colombia and Ecuador regarding the growing importance of HEQA. The methodology and measures matter, however, if we are concerned not only about identifying *whether* change occurred, but also on understanding that change in its context and how it may differ from changes elsewhere. Despite the paradoxes identified which might seem to contradict ideological expectations, the discourse of each country overwhelmingly supports its respective ideological perspective.

The policies of both countries have been revolutionary (with the enactment of new laws and creation of new agencies), evolutionary (with minor revisions, refinements, and elaborations), and sense-making (with refined interpretations of policies within organizations and among actors). This third component – sense-making – is an often overlooked but important reflection of policy (Perellon 2007) which discourse analysis allows us to examine. Without the benefit of the discourse analysis, we might attribute observed differences in legal and institutional frameworks to other factors, such as maturity. Given that the Colombian system was initiated in the early 1990s and the Ecuadorian system almost two decades later, one might argue that the Colombian system has simply had more time to evolve to its current position and Ecuador could be expected to reach a similar position in 20 years. While maturity presents a reasonable counter-explanation, an examination of the discourse within Colombian higher quality assurance documents and agencies from their earlier periods suggests a generally consistent message over time.

The Colombian system settled into a common narrative and institutionalized legitimacy relatively quickly after its establishment, and the message has very much been one of stability. The organizations have clearly delineated division of responsibilities; the requirements and processes of accreditation are widely understood; and the system is generally respected and valued. Academic leaders have been and continue to be afforded multiple opportunities for input. Even in the absence of a succinct definition of quality, the concept has been operationalized and the system has developed a degree of legitimacy and institutionalization as a result.

In Ecuador, the instability and flux are occurring at policy- and sense-making levels, echoing back to the early history of higher education with its openings, closures, re-openings, etc. of universities. Ecuador's HEQA system remains a mystery to many in the higher education community. Some "rules of the game" are being constructed during the "game" and many rules are contradictory. Indeed, with so many agents linked to the quality assurance process, it becomes nearly impossible to reconcile and integrate their regulations in a single framework. Like Colombia, Ecuador has yet to develop a concise definition of quality; but in the case of Ecuador this has left universities uncertain of what is expected of them, frustrated with the frequency of regulatory changes, and nervous about the implications for their future. In this sense, the system has yet to be institutionalized and thus represents ongoing policy change, whereas the Colombian system reflects a degree of stability.

Conclusion

Our research reinforces concerns expressed by others about the dangers of aggregate-level comparisons which assert similarities based on superficial criteria (passage of new laws, creation of new agencies) but which do not examine in greater depth the language, socially constructed discourse, and context in which these policies are developed and implemented. When examined at a regional level, the adoption of new laws regarding higher education and the creation of new organizations suggests very similar policy changes across countries. When examined more closely, with attention to the discourse, the picture comes into focus. Our findings suggest the need for more widespread use of discourse analysis as a means of gauging and understanding policy change, not only within the realm of HEQA or in the Latin American region, but more broadly within comparative policy studies. Despite international pressures for and empirical evidence of global assimilation, nations still matter. Comparative policy studies of environmental policy, health policy, energy policy, and others could be enriched by discourse analysis. In the continuous effort to improve the quality of comparative analysis, our research reinforces the importance of augmenting quantitative large-n data analyses with qualitative methods and comparative case studies. Discourse analysis is not a substitute for or better than quantitative methods, but rather a tool by which comparative policy analysis can access the stories behind the numbers.

On a more practical policy level, our findings may have implications for Colombian and Ecuadorian officials who may be appointed to the Binational Commission on Higher Education established by the December 2014 agreements signed by Presidents Santos and Correa. In light of the extensive differences in the goals, problems, and solutions evident in the discourse of HEQA in these two countries, we might anticipate some serious challenges as they proceed with discussions on mutual recognition of accreditation within their higher education systems. A good starting point might be for the officials responsible for these negotiations to be cognizant of the discourse in their own and the other context.

Notes

1. A variety of labels exist including interpretive policy analysis (Yanow 1993), critical discourse analysis (Fairclough 1993), and political discourse analysis (Fairclough and Fairclough 2012) and the distinctions among them are debated (Finlayson 2013; Hay 2013). We adopt the broadest term: discourse analysis (Fischer 2003).
2. Programs with "wide social impact" include education and teacher training (Law 115 of 1994), medicine, dentistry, and nursing (Law 792 of 2001), and engineering (Law 917 of 2001).

References

Baer, W. and Maloney, W., 1997, Neoliberalism and income distribution in Latin America. *World Development*, **25**(3), pp. 311–327. doi:10.1016/S0305-750X(96)00116-7

Becker, M., 2013, The stormy relations between Rafael Correa and social movements in Ecuador. *Latin American Perspectives*, **40**(3), pp. 43–62. doi:10.1177/0094582X13479305

Billing, D., 2004, International comparisons and trends in external quality assurance of higher education: Commonality or diversity? *Higher Education*, **47**(1), pp. 113–137. doi:10.1023/B:HIGH.0000009804.31230.5e

Blackmur, D., 2007, The public regulation of higher education qualities: rationale, processes, and outcomes, in: D. F. Westerheijden et al. (Eds) *Quality Assurance in Higher Education* (Dordrecht: Springer), pp. 15–45.

Bovens, M., 2007, Analysing and assessing accountability: A conceptual framework. *European Law Journal*, **13**(4), pp. 447–468. doi:10.1111/eulj.2007.13.issue-4

Brandsma, G. J. and Schillemans, T., 2013, The accountability cube: Measuring accountability. *Journal of Public Administration Research and Theory*, **23**(4), pp. 953–975. doi:10.1093/jopart/mus034

Burke, J. C., 2005, *Achieving Accountability in Higher Education* (San Francisco: Jossey-Bass).

Capano, G., 2009, Understanding policy change as an epistemological and theoretical problem. *Journal of Comparative Policy Analysis: Research and Practice*, **11**(1), pp. 7–31. doi:10.1080/13876980802648284

Capano, G. and Howlett, M., 2009, Introduction: The determinants of policy change: Advancing the debate. *Journal of Comparative Policy Analysis: Research and Practice*, **11**(1), pp. 1–5. doi:10.1080/13876980802648227

Cobey, R. and Bandeira, M. L., 2013, Public policy and the indigenous influence in Ecuador: Wellbeing and pluri-nationality within a framework of 'Buen Vivir'. Presented at the 8th Iberoamerican Academy Conference, 2013, São Paulo, Brasil.

De La Garza Aguilar, J., 2008, Evaluación y acreditación de la educación superior en América Latina y el Caribe, en: C. Tunnermann Berhnheim (Ed) *La Educación Superior En América Latina Y El Caribe: Diez Años Después De La Conferencia Mundial De 1998* (Bogota: Pontificia Universidad Javeriana and IESALC/UNESCO).

De Wit, H., Jaramillo, C., Gacel-Ávila, J. and Knight, H. (Eds.), 2005, *Higher Education in Latin America: the International Dimension* (Washington, DC: International Bank for Reconstruction and Development).

Fairclough, I. and Fairclough, N., 2012, *Political Discourse Analysis: A Method for Advanced Students* (London: Routledge).

Fairclough, N., 1993, Critical discourse analysis and the marketization of public discourse: The universities. *Discourse & Society*, **4**(2), pp. 133–168. doi:10.1177/0957926593004002002

Fernandez Lamarra, N., 2003, Higher education, quality evaluation and accreditation in Latin America and MERCOSUR. *European Journal of Education*, **38**(3), pp. 253–269. doi:10.1111/ejed.2003.38.issue-3

Finlayson, A., 2013, Critique and political argumentation. *Political Studies Review*, **11**, pp. 313–320. doi:10.1111/psr.2013.11.issue-3

Fischer, F., 2003, *Reframing Public Policy: discursive Politics and Deliberative Practices* (Oxford: Oxford University Press).

Garcia Guadilla, C., 2003, Balance de la década de los 90 y reflexiones sobre las nuevas fuerzas de cambio en la educación superior. En Mollis, M. (Compiladora), in: *Las Universidades En América Latina: ¿Reformadas O Alteradas? La Cosmética Del Poder Financiero* (Buenos Aires: Consejo Latinoamericano de Ciencias Sociales, CLASCO).

Gomez, V. and Celis, J., 2009, Sistema de aseguramiento de la calidad de la educación superior: Consideraciones sobre la acreditación en Colombia. *Revista Colombiana De Sociología*, **32**(2), pp.87–110.

Hay, C., 2013, Political discourse analysis: The dangers of methodological absolutism. *Political Studies Review*, **11**, pp. 321–327. doi:10.1111/psr.2013.11.issue-3

Howlett, M. and Cashore, B., 2009, The dependent variable problem in the study of policy change: Understanding policy change as a methodological problem. *Journal of Comparative Policy Analysis: Research and Practice*, **11**(1), pp. 33–46. doi:10.1080/13876980802648144

Inga, M. G. and Velásquez Silva, D., 2005, *La Evaluación Y Acreditación De La Calidad En Las Nuevas Leyes De Educación Superior De América Latina* (Lima: Comisión de Coordinación de Reforma Universitaria UNMSM).

Jones, C. O., 1984, *An Introduction to the Study of Public Policy* (Monterey, CA: Brooks/Cole Publishing).

Jreisat, J., 2011, *Globalism and Comparative Public Administration* (Boca Raton: CRC Press).

Kennemore, A. and Weeks, G., 2011, Twenty-first century socialism? The elusive search for a post-neoliberal development model in Bolivia and Ecuador. *Bulletin of Latin American Research*, **30**, pp. 267–281. doi:10.1111/j.1470-9856.2010.00496.x

Kurtz, M. J. and Brooks, S. M., 2008, Embedding neoliberal reform in Latin America. *World Politics*, **60**(2), pp. 231–280. doi:10.1353/wp.0.0015

Leite, D., Contera, C. and Mollis, M., 2003, Evaluation and accreditation of higher education in Latin American countries: Argentina, Brazil, Chile, Colombia and Uruguay, in: *The Changing Worlds of Higher Education Policy: Portugal, Spain and Latin America* (Porto Alegre: Universidade Federal do Rio Grande do Sul). Available at. http://www.ufrgs.br/inov/docs/the-changing-worlds-of-higher-education-policy-portugal-spain-and-latin-america

Lemaitre, M.-J., 2011, Accountability in Latin America, in: B. Stensaker and L. Harvey (Eds) *Accountability in Higher Education: Global Perspectives on Trust and Power* (New York: Routledge), pp. 133–156.

Lopez Segrera, F., 2010, Trends and innovations in higher education reform: Worldwide, Latin America and in the Caribbean. *Center for Studies in Higher Education, Research and Occasional Paper Series* (University of California Berkeley).

Lucio, R. and Serrano, M., 1993, The state and higher education in Colombia. *Higher Education*, **25**, pp. 61–72. doi:10.1007/BF01384042

Martin, M. and Stella, A., 2007, *External Quality Assurance in Higher Education: making Choices* (Paris: UNESCO International Institute for Educational Planning).

Meyer, M., 2001, Between theory, method, and politics: Positioning of the approaches to CDA, in: R. Wodak and M. Meyer (Eds) *Methods of Critical Discourse Analysis* (London: Sage), pp. 14–31.

Misoczky, M. C., 2011, World visions in dispute in contemporary Latin America: Development x harmonic life. *Organization*, **18**(3), pp. 345–363. doi:10.1177/1350508411398730

Orozco Silva, L. E., 2010, Calidad académica y relevancia social de la educación superior en América Latina. *Revista Iberoamericana de Educación Superior*, **1**(1), pp.24–36.

Pacheco, 2012, *Historia de la Universidad en el Ecuador*. PUCE: Simposio Permanente sobre la Universidad. No. 3.

Perellon, J. F., 2007, Analysing quality assurance in higher education: Proposal for a conceptual framework and methodological implications, in: D. F. Westerheijden, B. Stensaker, and M. J. Rosa (Eds) *Quality Assurance in Higher Education* (Dordrecht: Springer), pp. 155–178.

Premfors, R., 1992, Policy analysis, in: B. Clark and G. Neave (Eds) *Encyclopedia of Higher Education* (Oxford: Pergamon), pp. 1907–1916.

Radcliffe, S. A., 2012, Development for a postneoliberal era? *Sumak kawsay*, living well and the limits to decolonisation in Ecuador. *Geoforum*, **43**, pp. 240–249. doi:10.1016/j.geoforum.2011.09.003

Revelo Revelo, J. and Hernandez, C. A., 2003., *The National Accreditation System in Colombia: experiences from the National Council of Accreditation (CNA)* (International Institute for Educational Planning). Available at http://www.unesco.org/iiep

Saarinen, T., 2005, 'Quality' in the bologna process: From 'competitive edge' to quality assurance techniques. *European Journal of Education*, **40**(2), pp. 189–204. doi:10.1111/ejed.2005.40.issue-2

Salgado, F. and Moran, E., 2014, ¿Universidad o uniformidad? Sumak Kawsay, diversidad e isomorfismo bajo la lupa. *Anales – Revista De La Universidad De Cuenca*, **56**(diciembre), pp.55–68.

Soler-Castillo, S., 2011, Analisis critico del discurso de documentos de política pública en educación. *Forma Y Función*, **23**(1), pp.75–105.

Stensaker, B. and Harvey, L., 2006. Old wine in new bottles? A comparison of public and private accreditation schemes in higher education. *Higher Education Policy*, **19**(1), pp. 65–85.

Stone, D., 2012, *Policy Paradox: the Art of Political Decision Making*. 3rd ed. (New York: W. W. Norton and Company).

Torres, C. A. and Schugurensky, D., 2002, The political economy of higher education in the era of neoliberal globalization: Latin America in comparative perspective. *Higher Education*, **43**, pp. 429–455. doi:10.1023/A:1015292413037

Vanegas, P., 2003, The northern influence and Colombian education reform of the 1990s, in: G. E. Fischman, S. Ball and S. Gvirtz (Eds) *Crisis and Hope: the Educational Hopscotch of Latin America* (NY: RoutledgeFalmer).

Villavicencio, A., 2012, *Evaluación Y Acreditación En Tiempos De Cambio: la Política Pública Universitaria En Cuestionamiento* (Quito, Ecuador: Instituto de Altos Estudios Nacionales, La Universidad de Posgrado del Estado).

Walsh, C., 2010, Development as *Buen Vivir*: Institutional arrangements and (de)colonial entanglements. *Development*, **53**(S1), pp. 15–21. doi:10.1057/dev.2009.93

Yanow, D., 1993, The communication of policy meanings: Implementation as interpretation and text. *Policy Sciences*, **26**, pp. 41–61. doi:10.1007/BF01006496

Zittoun, P., 2009, Understanding policy change as a discursive problem. *Journal of Comparative Policy Analysis: Research and Practice*, **11**(1), pp. 65–82. doi:10.1080/13876980802648235

Federal Dynamics of Changing Governance Arrangements in Education: A Comparative Perspective on Australia, Canada and Germany

GILIBERTO CAPANO

ABSTRACT *Education policy is a highly interesting field from the point of view of governance, given the substantial changes that have been made throughout the world to the governance of such policy over the last 30 years or so. Western governments in particular have made significant changes in the governance arrangements of their education policy in order to achieve two fundamental goals: increased efficiency and greater accountability. In this process, the role of governments has changed but not diminished. This paper explores such developments by comparing the trajectories of governance reforms in three federal countries (Australia, Canada and Germany). What emerges is that the role of governments is key to all governance mixes modelled by the reform processes in the three analysed countries, and that there is greater "national" coordination than before, but also significant differences in the strategies adopted and in the content of reform, due to the differing nature of such countries' federal dynamics.*

Introduction

Education (primary and secondary education) is a highly interesting policy field from the point of view of governance, given the important changes made to systems of education governance throughout the world over the past 30 years or so.

Such changes have been strongly pursued by governments faced with two intractable problems. Firstly, that of the universalization of education (with almost all school pupils now going on to take their high-school diplomas) has meant a significant increase in public expenditure. Thus the restructuring of welfare systems and public spending in all Western countries in recent years has focused, among other things, on the efficiency of educational policies. Secondly, governments have begun to perceive education as a strategic tool for, and the engine of, national socioeconomic growth, while society has reinforced its idea of education as a way of improving its own socioeconomic status, as well as the idea that families should have a greater choice of schools for their children.

In other words, the common problem shared by educational systems in recent years has been that of changing the governance arrangements towards strengthening the capacity for systemic coordination and steering. In this case, governments have been the real agents of change.

The present study explores the issue of governance reform in educational policy by focusing on empirical findings from three federal countries, to show how shifts in educational governance have developed in specific ways, and with specific policy content. The theoretical perspective adopted focuses on the features of federal dynamics (the interaction between formal constitutional dimensions and intergovernmental relations), which are hypothesized to significantly influence the way that governments have changed governance arrangements in education policy.

The second section presents the content of changes in governance modes in education policy. The third section covers the theoretical framework of this research, while the following three sections present the empirical evidence, by reconstructing developments in educational governance policy in the case of each country. The seventh section examines the study's empirical findings.

Governance Shifts in Educational Policies: Defining the Content of Change

Explaining why and how governance in education has changed implies considering governance modes not only as dependent variables, but also as specific dimensions of policy change. One question needs to be addressed here: a clear operationalization of the dependent variable is required.

So, by assuming that governance means the "way by which" public policies are steered (Benz 2004; Borzel 2006), at a higher level of abstraction, there are very few coordinating principles on the basis of which policies may be addressed and steered. Such principles concern the concepts of hierarchy, markets and networks. Each coordinating principle is assumed to bring together specific policy tools which are in keeping with the principle itself. So hierarchical governance is assumed to be a system in which command and control tools alone are actually at work; market governance is assumed to be implemented through inducements (incentives and sanctions); and network governance is assumed to function through the use of knowledge and capacity tools. However, the empirical evidence shows that these general policy-coordination principles very often coexist, and that hierarchy is always dominant, albeit in different forms – that is, through different combinations of policy tools (Capano 2011; Capano et al. 2012).

So, from this point of view any empirical analysis of governance changes in educational policy needs to focus also on changes in the adopted policy strategies, that is, on the policy tools used and their possible combinations. Due to the historical role of governments in educational policy, it is important to understand when and how governments have changed their ways of steering education, and the manner in which they have transformed inherited modes into new policy tools.

On the basis of the foregoing, then, any analysis of change in the governance modes of educational policy implies subdividing these changes into two types:

1. the change in the mix of coordination principles on which the existing governance mode is based;
2. changes in the nature of those policy strategies by which policies are formulated and implemented. Such changes may be marginal or radical, depending on the speed with which, and the degree to which, new policy tools are adopted. In order to grasp such changes, the following list of potential policy tools to be adopted in order to change governance strategies may be considered in analysing education policy (Whitty et al. 1998; Hannaway and Woodroffe 2003; Hudson 2007; Maroy 2009):

   – the centralization/decentralization of the curriculum;
   – the large-scale testing of students and the evaluation of individual schools;
   – the decentralization of management powers to individual schools;
   – school autonomy;
   – vouchers and charter schools;
   – teacher training and licensing;
   – transparent, well-established systems of information for the families of students.

As clearly stated in the introduction to this Special Issue, governments are thought to play a pivotal role in the redesigning of governance arrangements within a given policy field. Then it has to be assumed that there is no one exclusive way of governing, and governments do not necessarily have to be directly involved. Governments could prefer to steer at a distance (Kickert 1997). From this point of view, the hollowing out of the state (Rhodes 1994, 1997; Skelcher 2000) can be seen as the diversification of the ways in which governments act.

In accordance with the aforementioned basic underlying assumptions about the dependent variable, I am going to focus on governance shifts in education policies in federal states. This choice is due, among other things, to the fact that the re-modulation of the role of governments in governance shifts is more complex in those countries characterized by two levels of powerful government, as in the case of federal states. Furthermore, the case of federation is particularly significant in the field of education since such a policy field is, usually, constitutionally left in the hands of those states (or provinces) constituting the federation. This point of departure is extremely interesting in terms of the aims of the present study, where the fundamental assumption is that governments have not surrendered their own powers regarding the governance of public policies, but could in fact be deemed to have maintained such powers, although through different modes of governance. What needs to be understood here is the manner of development of the process of change; the kind of dynamics operating between the two levels of government; and the nature of changes that have occurred in terms of governance modes.

Governments as Agents of Change in Federal Countries: Theoretical Framework and Research Design

The redesigning of educational governance arrangements in federal states is particularly interesting when analysed by assuming that policy-making in federal systems is characterized not only by the formal constitutional framework, but also by the patterns of intergovernmental relations. This double focus (on the formal framework and on intergovernmental relations) can facilitate an understanding of how federal dynamics influence the actions of governments (at both levels) in redesigning public policy governance arrangements.

This perspective – which echoes the Elazar (1987) distinction between the structure and process of federal systems, Friedrich's (1962) emphasis on the processual nature of federalism, and those studies which have focused on the structural interdependence between the two levels of government in federal countries (Thorlakson 2003; Erk 2008; Erk and Koning 2010; Braun 2011; Bolleyer and Thorlakson 2012) – has been further developed recently by Colino (2010, 2013) in order to construct a typology of federal systems that helps frame the empirical analysis of governmental dynamics and interaction in policy-making. This typology is based on the dichotomization of the aforementioned two dimensions: the formal framework (which can be integrated or separated to a greater or lesser degree), and federal relations (which may be more or less centripetal or centrifugal).[1] The result is a four-fold typology based on four ideal types of federalism, or rather, federal dynamics (see Table 1). According to Colino (2013):

Table 1. Varieties of federalism according to formal framework and federal relations

Federal relations		Formal framework	
		Disintegrated	Integrated
	Centripetal	*Balanced*	*Unitary*
	Centrifugal	*Segmented*	*Accommodating*

Source: Colino (2013).

1. *Balanced federalism* derives from the aggregation of previously existing political communities or states. The constitutional pact guarantees the original powers of the founding members of the federation. The main value is thus the balance of powers. The constitutional design is normally interstate,[2] while the intergovernmental structure of decisions and resources is independent. The strategies of governmental actors tend to be self-assertive, with conflict lines and intergovernmental coalitions being more of a partisan type, although sometimes also territorially driven. The cases closest to this ideal type are those of the USA, Brazil, Australia and Switzerland (Watts 1996; Hueglin and Fenna 2006; Bellamy and Brown 2008; Erk 2008).
2. *Unitary federalism* usually originates from the decentralization of a previously centralist state, or from the renewal of a federal tradition abandoned in the past as a result of a phase of totalitarian or authoritarian rule. Since it originates in times of crisis, its value is that of guaranteeing agreement and cooperation among units. This is the type of federalism usually adopted by culturally homogeneous societies. The intergovernmental structure of decisions and resources is usually interdependent, based on shared competencies and aimed at guaranteeing similar conditions for the lives of all citizens. The intergovernmental rules of decision-making are usually of a hierarchical nature, dominated by federal initiatives but mitigated by certain mandatory joint decisions. Intergovernmental relations are normally based on a cooperative approach, and conflict lines and coalitions are partisan rather than territorial. Germany, South Africa, Austria and, to a certain degree, Spain are closer to this ideal type (Inman and Rubinfeld 2005; Erk 2008; Erk and Swenden 2010).
3. *Segmented federalism* is characteristic of those federations where two different cultural communities coexist, one being in the majority. The typical executive–legislative configuration of this subsystem is parliamentarianism. The constitutional design is

interstate, in which agreements between the leaders of the culturally diverse communities and intergovernmental institutions prevail. The intergovernmental structure of decisions and resources is highly independent, also because powers are mainly exclusive and separated. Intergovernmental decisional rules are usually negotiated between the two orders of government, and interaction tends to be of a competitive character, while the strategies of governmental actors tend to be self-assertive, with conflict lines and intergovernmental coalitions being predominantly of the territorial type. This ideal type is reflected in the fundamental evolution of federalism in both Canada and Belgium (Gagnon and Tully 2001; Huenglin and Fenna 2006).

4. *"Accommodating" federalism* originates in societies with a certain degree of cultural heterogeneity, through a process of devolution, or disaggregation, of a centralist state as a means of preserving a common state. Its values are usually the autonomy of the various units, and cultural affirmation, usually associated with asymmetric arrangements, designed to satisfy different self-government aspirations. The "accommodating"-type system usually has a constitutional design of an interstate nature, with weak second chambers and the devolutionary process controlled by the centre, which traditionally determines the pace and scope of devolution. The intergovernmental structure of decisions and resources is usually characterized by the interdependence of the levels, reflected clearly in the dependence of the units on central funding. Intergovernmental decisional rules are of the hierarchical type, and in practice interaction styles may be either cooperative or quite competitive, depending on the nature of the constituent units. Conflict lines and intergovernmental coalitions may be both territorial and partisan. This ideal type is reflected in the federal dynamics of India and, to a certain extent, of Spain (Burgess 2006; Sing and Rao 2006; Erk and Swenden 2010; Sala 2014).

This typology can help justify the choice of cases, and can also provide theoretical support to the hypotheses I shall be submitting here.

Regarding the selection of cases, this typological classification makes it possible to deal with cases as different as Canada and Australia, which very often are purported to boast the same type of federalism (which has been defined using a variety of different terms: executive federalism, dual federalism, competitive federalism, the commonwealth federations, etc.) and thus to develop similar federal dynamics. According to Colino's typology, they are characterized by rather different features, especially in terms of intergovernmental relations (and also in terms of certain small, albeit significant, differences in constitutional design, particularly with regard to the allocation of powers and responsibilities). Since Australia is characterized by a balanced federal dynamics, Canada by segmented federal dynamics, and Germany clearly belongs to the unitary type, the three national cases cover a broad spectrum of federal dynamics.[3] The aforementioned ideal types of federalism can help us identify certain potential effects on governance change. The features of the formal framework are of considerable importance in relation to the capacity of federal systems to be effective either in decision-making or in policy integration and coordination. From this point of view, balanced systems have a greater decision-making capacity but a smaller integrative capacity, while unitary systems have a greater integrative capacity and a smaller decision-making capacity (because the mandatory joint decision-making process very often leads to stalemate or to minimal changes being made). On the other hand, segmented systems are extremely weak from both points of view, while accommodating systems display weak centrifugal trends. It should also be pointed out that the four varieties of federalism include two with a clear incongruence between the features of the formal framework and those of intergovernmental relations, namely the balanced type (disintegrated framework but centripetal relations) and the accommodating type (integrated formal framework but centrifugal relations).

This theoretical framework leads us to assume that every ideal type of federalism ought to be characterized by a specific trajectory in terms of institutional and policy development and change. Thus, extending the theoretical proposals put forward by Falleti (2010) and Colino (2013) with regard to federal dynamics and focusing on the three types of federalism under scrutiny here, it is possible to outline the workings of federal dynamics when governments seek changes in policy-making:

1. Balanced federalism may suffer from policy disintegration and latent conflict (owing to the imbalance between the formal framework and the nature of federal relations), and thus the central level may tend to pursue the strong nationalization of policy coordination.
2. Unitary federalism may suffer from policy stalemate and blockage, and thus member states may advocate greater devolution, although its integrative nature structurally tends towards the intrastate negotiation and sharing of policy solutions.
3. Segmented federalism, owing to its low decisional and integrating capacity, will witness attempts (not only by central government but also by member states themselves) to construct common, voluntary measures (and thus the coordination effort will not affect the institutional equilibrium between the two levels of government. This cooperative approach, however, cannot guarantee any real common effectiveness in the implementation of the agreed guidelines).

This theoretical framework enables us to formulate certain guidelines for the purpose of empirical research. Since the empirical focus aims to explain how governance arrangements in education policy have changed in the three chosen countries, I would expect the following general trends, which I consider to constitute exploratory hypotheses:

H1. (Based on the assumption of the centrality of governments in governance redesign) the role of federal governments, or at least the degree of cooperation between member states, has been strengthened in terms of their increased efforts to implement a more "nationalized" policy, due to external pressures and challenges.

H2. The role of member states' governments has not really diminished (overall), although it may have changed concerning the steering of their respective education systems. Hence, increased systemic coordination also at state/provincial level is expected in response, albeit through different forms of governance.

H3. The policy strategies and instruments adopted have been mixed in different ways, according to the respective policy legacies and traditions in the field of education. However, the more disintegrated character of the Canadian and Australian frameworks increases the likelihood of a larger variety of experiences of reform in educational governance at the sub-national level.

From the methodological point of view, I am going to adopt a sequential perspective in the sense that I shall reconstruct policy dynamics in the three chosen cases by paying specific attention to:

- the timing of the process (through a sequential reconstruction in which the point of departure of the process and the critical juncture are highlighted for each country);
- the ideational context within which the changes have been formulated and implemented;
- the specific equilibrium of the political-institutional framework (which, in the case of federations, basically means the nature of relations between federal and individual state or province governments).

The empirical evidence corroborating my hypothesis and the instrumental content of the new governance modes is taken from the numerous studies of such topics, as well as from the available official documents, and has been supported by around 60 interviews of policy-makers both at federal and state/provincial levels.[4]

Australia

Point of Departures and Critical Junctures

Under Section 51 of the Australian Constitution education is a residual power, and thus rests with state governments. However, this exclusive responsibility changed radically in 1974 when, without any constitutional reform being implemented (but on the basis of a specific interpretation of Section 96 thereof,[5]) the Commonwealth (the federal government) started partially funding both public and private schools.[6] This "financial" involvement of the Commonwealth in education represented a means by which federal government could negotiate with the states from a strong position and, de facto, one that gave it the opportunity to steer the education system as a whole.[7]

Together with this financial watershed, the other most important dates with regard to education policy are 1972 (the Labour Party winning an election after years in opposition, and the establishment of the Karmel Commission); 1983 (the election of the Hawke Labour government; 1996 (the election of a Conservative government which continued with, and indeed radicalized, some of the previous Labour government's reforms); 2008 (the Labour Party winning the elections again). Basically, the various steps in the evolution of Australia's policy dynamics are linked to changes in the ruling party. What should be pointed out here is that the dynamics of education policy are characterized by the fact that all governments have put education policy high on their list of priorities.

However, this constant attention to educational policy does not mean that each stage in the dynamics of said policy corresponds to a critical juncture. From this point of view, two critical junctures may be identified at the national level and one at the state level. These critical junctures have consistently impacted on the inherited situation whereby prior to reform, education governance within Australia's states was highly centralized, with all power effectively lying with the states' departments of education, and very little institutional autonomy afforded to schools (Dudley and Vidovich 1995).

At the national level, the first critical juncture is represented by the period 1972–1975, when there was a significant shift in Australian educational policy and its governance modes. This shift centred around one fundamentally important event: the report issued in 1973 by a temporary committee appointed by the Australian Schools Commission (Karmel Report 1973) established guidelines which represented a substantial break from the prevailing education policy values at that time. In fact, the Karmel Report recommended the following forms of policy development: the devolution of power from central state departments to the country's schools, and the increased involvement of parents and communities in education; greater equality in educational opportunities; the institutional acceptance of the dual system (and thus the definitive legitimization of non-governmental schools) which was still a conflictual issue for Australians. Finally, it should be pointed out that the aforementioned federal policy, characterized by the direct involvement of federal government in funding schools, was introduced in 1974.

These general policy goals have constituted the core of all subsequent policy strategies pursued by the Commonwealth, and a kind of general objective accomplished by Australia's states, albeit at different moments in time. The second critical juncture is represented by the profound economic crisis that hit Australia at the beginning of the 1980s, which enabled Prime Minister Hawke to launch a wave of neo-liberal reforms, with the reform of education playing a prominent role. The ideological basis of this reform strategy (known as "corporate federalism") represented a significant shift towards a more general cooperative mood in Australian federalism, and a more substantial role for the Commonwealth in coordinating and steering primary and secondary education.

The critical juncture at the state level was the so-called Victoria reform (1992–1999), which represented the first full implementation of Hawke's vision for education.

Policy Developments

Australia's reform process got underway during a lengthy period of Labour government (1983–1996). Under the umbrella of so-called "corporate federalism", the then Prime Minister, Robert Hawke, launched a plan designed to revive the economic position of Australia (which was going through a period of substantial economic crisis), based on a neo-liberal policy in which education was considered key to the nation's interests (Lingard et al. 1993).

In 1987, this focus on education was put into practice through the following educational measures (DEET 1993):

- the reinforcing of the federal bureaucracy's role, through the establishment of a new Department of Employment, Education and Training;
- the launch of several recurrent performance-based grants to state education departments for school education under "resource agreements";
- a capital grants programme;
- various special grants for specific key issues (equity, gender, language);
- the reform of guidelines for the teaching profession, and the establishment of the Advanced Skills Teacher position.

In 1993, in an attempt to better coordinate Australia's new federal approach to education, the Ministerial Council of Education, Employment, Training, and Youth (MCEETYA) was set up. This body began work on the coordination of a number of important projects, including the establishment of a common school starting age, and a common measure of scholastic performance (Jones 2008), although clear difficulties were encountered in implementing shared strategies across Australia's various states.

Certain problems were encountered when it came to implementing these plans, due to the states' sole constitutional jurisdiction on educational matters; nevertheless, they represented the first clear sign of a radically different approach to steering and managing education in Australia. The federal plan was followed in a radical way by the State of Victoria, which introduced the "School of the Future" programme (1992–1999; under a Labour government). This state reform was very important not only for the positive effects it has had, but also because it has since become the benchmark for Australia's other states, and a template that all subsequent Australian governments have tried to adopt. The fundamental cornerstones of this reform programme were the attribution of greater autonomy to schools (more than 90 per cent of the state's education budget was directly allocated to schools, school heads were strongly empowered with regard to the recruitment and promotion of staff, and charter schools – schools publicly funded but with full operational autonomy – were set up) and the introduction of a centralized curriculum and of state-wide testing and reporting (Caldwell 1998). The example set by Victoria state has gradually been followed by Australia's other states as of 2008 (Hinz 2010).

Under the subsequent Conservative government the same strategy continued to be pursued, and was indeed radicalized. For example, in 1997 the provision of private schools was deregulated, and in 2000 the voucher system for the funding of private schools was changed and reinforced (Meadmore 2001). In 2000, the Commonwealth and the states agreed on a common national test to be implemented by 2008. In 2004, a Federal Act required school authorities to comply strictly with reporting and accountability requirements, and in 2005 the federal government asked all states to adopt new reporting standards from all parents. In 2006, plans were put in place for the creation of an Australian Curriculum, Assessment and Reporting Authority (ACARA), and this was actually established in 2009 by the then Labour government.

In 2008, under Rudd's Labour government, the Commonwealth and Australia's states signed the National Education Agreement (under the supervision of the Council of Australian Governments – COAG), according to which Australia's schools were to pursue a common set of performance targets. Between 2011 and 2012 the MCEETYA was abolished and replaced by two different standing councils within the COAG (the standing council on School Education and Early Childhood and the standing council on Tertiary Education, Skills and Employment).

Thereafter, the national curriculum project was launched and was fully implemented by 2012, together with the National Assessment Programme. Furthermore, the Labour government headed by Julia Gillard has since launched a renewed strategy of reform which capitalizes on the previous efforts made by the Commonwealth during the previous three decades, and on the practices implemented in certain Australian states (such as the abovementioned State of Victoria). The key objectives of this recent strategy include: a pay-per-performance scheme (with the best teachers in 2013 to be better paid in 2014); implementation of the Victoria state reform in a trial sample of 1,000 schools in 2012 and 2013; financial rewards for those schools that achieve the greatest improvements across a wide range of areas. This reform has received the endorsement of the OECD (OECD 2012a). Finally, through a National Agreement in Education, effective since July 2013, the Commonwealth has decided to increase the funding in education through specific contracts with the state under which a clear set of goals is stated.

Canada

Point of Departure and Critical Junctures

The Canadian case is somewhat unique in that there is no federal ministry or agency in charge of education, unlike in other federal countries. According to Section 93, the Canadian constitutional provision regarding education policy is of the standard type characteristic of segmented federalism: all powers regarding educational matters are allocated to the provinces (although the federal government is responsible for funding the aboriginals).

Governance arrangements were moderately centralized prior to reforms. In fact, the hierarchical coordination principle (provincial government being responsible for education) was a relatively soft one, with powers shared with the schools' boards (who had some power over the independent collection of revenues) and the schools themselves. This meant that schools enjoyed a certain degree of freedom to decide on teaching matters. It has been pointed out here that this moderate centralization was favoured by the country's constitutional provisions, since historically speaking the Canadian school system has always been locally based. However, the central provincial departments of education were in charge of directly managing the overall system within each province (Fleming 1997).

At the national level, the really important dates to remember in the field of education are 1967 (the establishment of the CMEC, Council of Ministers of Education, Canada), 1993 and 2008, representing respectively the signing of two joint ministerial declarations (the Victoria Declaration and the Learn Canada 2020 declaration), which revealed the common desire and will of the Provinces to cooperate in the pursuit of common goals and forms of governance in the educational field.

With regard to the all-important critical junctures, the only one of any real importance at the federal level seems to have been the period from the mid-1990s to 2000 when, owing to a financial crisis (1995), the Canadian federal government reduced funding to the provinces, thus leading provinces to redesign the governance of their educational systems in order to cope with this reduction in funding and to make them more efficient.

Things have been very different at the provincial level. Although there have been a series of interesting provincial shifts, these have failed to have any national impact. For example, the two reforms in Ontario, the first introduced by the Conservatives in 1995 under premier Harris, and the subsequent reform introduced by the Liberals under premier McGuinty in 2003. These were two critical junctures (the first one based on federal cuts and ideological pressure, the second based on widespread social dissatisfaction with the conflicting nature of the previous reforms) (Sattler 2012).

Another interesting case is that of the neo-liberal reforms in Alberta, introduced by Premier Klein as of 1994 (Levin and Young 2000; Taylor 2001). Ontario and Alberta represent the most important cases of reforms based on critical junctures, even though the 1990s as a whole witnessed reforms throughout Canada's provinces, involving the amalgamation of school boards, the introduction of standardized assessment procedures and the launching of programmes supporting parental choice of schools. From this point of view, it seems that, without being directly coordinated, there has nevertheless been a process of institutional isomorphism among provinces (with the possible exception of Manitoba, where reform has been slower and genuinely incremental) encouraged by financial restrictions but also by the incentive towards mutual learning resulting from increasing interprovincial cooperation.

Policy Developments

As mentioned above, in 1967 the CMEC was established in order to facilitate intergovernmental coordination and the relationship with pan-Canadian education organizations. It should be said that the CMEC has no representatives formally present in federal government: it is purely an instrument of horizontal interstate coordination. In 1993 the Victoria declaration strengthened the pan-Canadian convergence of education policy, and in particular of curriculum design and performance assessment. Furthermore, in 2007 the CMEC launched the Pan-Canadian Assessment Programme based on the voluntary participation of Canada's provinces, and designed to provide a uniform measure of students' proficiency.

This voluntary interprovincial attempt to construct a "national" education policy has clearly been inspired by the shared provincial need to respond to the challenge of economic competition, and by the intrinsic sensitivity of provinces to one another's actions, since they offer benchmarks for citizens' assessment of governmental performance (Harrison 2006).

From this point of view, provincial governments have found a way of legitimizing internal reforms (in the name of standardization and of the pursuit of educational excellence); at the same time, although there has not been any significant federal activity, there has been a clear strengthening of interstate cooperation in adopting common strategies.

In accordance with this approach, provincial and local administrations have been implementing new policies characterized by the following:

- some form of standardized, province-wide student achievement test;
- province-wide school and/or district measures aimed at educational improvement, commonly focused on students' achievements in mathematics and literacy;
- curricular policies designed to standardize learning outcomes;
- investment in the implementation of schemes to reduce class sizes;
- the creation of new multi-sector (i.e. educational, health and social services) early learning and development programmes;
- reforms aimed at improving high-school options and completion rates;
- the establishment of a variety of multi-sector programmes for children and young people vulnerable to less-than-optimal social, health and educational outcomes;
- and the introduction of new programmes designed to guarantee increased parent and community engagement in learning and in school-level decision-making (Cea 2009; Galway 2012).

Furthermore, the provincial governance of education has also begun to be regulated in a new way. The fundamental structural features of this paradigm change have been:

- a redesigned relationship between the three levels of governance. Greater powers have been bestowed upon provincial government – especially with regard to financial[8] and curricular matters – while the powers of the intermediate-level school boards have

been reduced, and schools themselves have been afforded a greater degree of autonomy and made more accountable for their actions (Galway 2012);
- parents have been given a greater degree of choice (through the offer of different forms of publicly subsidized education – charter schools, private schools, home schooling), and are involved to a greater degree in the governance of schools; schools have also opened up more to local communities (Levin 2005);
- a school rating system has been introduced (Lessard and Brassard 2006, 2009), although real institutional accountability has yet to be achieved in practice (Ungerleider and Levin 2007).

Due to the considerable powers of the provinces with regard to their education policy, there are clearly some, at times substantial, differences between the various provincial policy reforms, although the abovementioned trend has been followed by the most important provinces from the socioeconomic and demographic points of view (Lessard and Brassard 2009; Sattler 2012).

Germany

Point of Departure and Critical Junctures

The 1949 Basic Law endorsed the federalist tradition which had always assigned the majority of educational powers to the *Länder*, Germany's federal states.

The governance arrangements prior to the reforms were characterized by a highly centralized educational system controlled by the *Länder*. The specific organizational and structural functions and processes administered by the *Länder* included curriculum design, regulation on examinations and qualifications, financial management and the distribution of funds, the recruitment and hiring of personnel, the evaluation of school and staff standards.

Germany is a latecomer in terms of educational governance reforms, and all observers agree that the thing that really sparked education reform in Germany was the country's disappointing performance in the first Programme for International Student Assessment (PISA) exercise conducted in 2000; this can thus be considered the real critical juncture in the German case.

Policy Developments

Since the advent of the Federal Republic of Germany, and subsequent to reunification, there has been a continuous process of "nationalization" of this policy field. The key historical steps leading up to the current situation in German education are as follows (Erk 2003; Nieman 2010):

1. In 1949, the Standing Conference of Ministers of Culture (*Kultusministerkonferenz* – KMK) was established to coordinate national education policy.
2. The KMK's charter was amended in 1955 in order to reinforce the KMK's powers to deal with issues of supra-regional importance (and the reference to the jurisdictional divisions present in the 1949 text was eliminated). On that same occasion (the Dusseldorf Agreement, subsequently amended in 1964 and in 1971) the KMK agreed

to find common standards for educational assessment, the timing and duration of the academic year, curricula and recognition of academic qualifications.
3. In 1959, the *Länder* and the German federal government signed an agreement on scientific research which de facto permitted the federal government to give the *Länder* exclusive responsibility for education. Following this agreement, the Federal Ministry of Scientific Research was set up in 1962.
4. In 1964 and 1965, the publications of works by Georg Picht (*The German Education Catastrophe*) and by Ralph Dahrendorf (*Education is Citizenship*), denouncing the poor quality of education in Germany, caused a kind of collective shock legitimizing calls for the "nationalization" of educational policy.
5. In 1969, the Federal Ministry of Scientific Research was transformed into the Federal Ministry of Education and Science (that is, a ministry for a policy field in which the federal government should have no substantial constitutional powers. This decision reveals how the idea of a "national" system of education was substantial notwithstanding the constitutional provisions to the contrary).

These developments show that, from the early days, Germany (albeit in the then "limited version" represented by the Federal Republic) displayed an intrinsic tendency towards a nationalized education policy, which is clearly an expression of the fact that Germany is a decentralized state with a centralized society (Katzenstein 1987). However, this general governance framework did not change the substance of the organization and management of Germany's schools system, which remained firmly in the hands of the country's *Länder*. Furthermore, during the 1970s and 1980s, notwithstanding certain attempted reforms, the structure and organization of education, together with educational curricula, remained substantially the same (Wilde 2002). The cooperative style of German federalism produced deadlock and stalemate, and the nationalization of education never really went through. The traditional, centralized policy-making of the schools system (which had no institutional autonomy) characterized all *Länder* (including those within the former Democratic Republic) (Winter 2000).

The traditional nature of governance of the German education system only started to change at the beginning of the third millennium, following the poor performance of German students in the PISA conducted by the OECD in 2000. The results revealed not only the poor average performance of German pupils and students, but also considerable differences between the country's various *Länder*: an evident indicator of the failure and the merely rhetorical character of the collective emphasis on the need for a national education policy. It should be pointed out that the distribution of revenue (which is highly centralized in Germany) is based upon the principle of pure proportionality, meaning that there was no real opportunity to encourage change through financial leverage.

The PISA results represented a shock to Germany's education system, and the KMK, after having opposed the federal government's attempt to impose a general top-down plan, began to formulate a common strategy designed to change the way education worked in Germany (Kehm 2010).

As a result, all of the nation's *Länder* began modifying the traditional system of educational governance according to the common template adopted worldwide over the course of the previous 15 years (Niemann 2010). The supervisory authorities in charge of schools have had their powers reduced, to the benefit of the institutional autonomy of the schools themselves. Schools have been increasingly empowered with regard to organizational, financial and educational matters (Huber and GÖRDEL 2006; OECD 2012b). However, the bureaucratic logic persists regarding, for example, the role of school heads who up until now have always been conceived as bureaucrats rather than managers.

Evaluation, assessment and self-evaluation have been introduced in all of Germany's *Länder*. Between 2004 and 2007, the KMK agreed on developing national educational standards at grade 4 in primary schools, and at grade 9/10 in lower secondary schools, and at the last grade of upper secondary schools, in the following seven subjects: mathematics, German, French, English, biology, chemistry and physics. These standards are mandatory for all of Germany's 16 *Länder*, by common agreement among them, and are benchmarked against international standards. Furthermore, in 2006 the KMK agreed to develop a system of standard assessment by which to compare the performance of the 16 *Länder*, using a common national scale. Finally, each *Land* undertook to develop *Land*-wide testing systems based on the new standards. In many cases, Germany's *Länder* joined forces to develop such assessment systems (KMK 2011).

Furthermore, Germany's *Länder* have adopted a number of evaluation procedures: the development or further development of framework curricula, comparative tests across the *Länder* and schools in core subjects, the extension of external evaluation, the development of standards and their review, the development of quality management in schools, and centralized final examinations (lower and upper secondary education) (KMK 2013).

However, despite the prompt reaction to the results of the 2000 PISA exercise, and the adoption of many new policy instruments at both systemic and institutional levels, it has been observed that the process of change appears a rather slow one, and the cooperative style of German federalism acts as a genuine constraint upon the implementation of more radical reform (Kehm 2010).

Findings

The sequential reconstruction of policy developments in the three countries analysed here shows how the intrinsic dynamics of the different types of federalism have influenced the redesigning of governance arrangements in education at both levels of government. I have summarized the empirical findings by linking them to the three exploratory hypotheses formulated in section two, as follows.

Greater "National" Cooperation

The present reconstruction of the dynamics of educational governance reforms, in Australia, Canada and Germany, albeit rather brief and at times sketchy, nevertheless reveals certain extremely interesting aspects of the process. As expected (*H1*), "national" coordination, perceived in each case as a necessary response to external imperatives in education, has increased in accordance with the specific nature of federal dynamics. This process has not been based on any constitutional change, but has been driven by changes in intergovernmental relations.

This "nationalization" of education policy through changing governance arrangements has differed considerably, depending on the federal type in question (balanced, unitary, segmented), but is nevertheless clearly evident.

In Australia this process has been guided by the Commonwealth, through the exercise of continuous pressure on state governments. In this case, the role of federal government has clearly grown, as is clear from the considerable number of federal programmes, new federal funding schemes to encourage states' adoption of specific guidelines, and the establishment of a federal authority (ACARA). In this specific case, unlike in those of the other two countries, the role of the Ministry of Education's committees (MCEETYA/ Standing Council for Schools) is very different: this organization is an arena in which the federal government tries to encourage states, in part thanks to the financial leverage reinforcing the centripetal dynamics of federal relations, to converge with regard to the government's own proposals and policies (Jones 2008). In the Australian case, under both political parties the Commonwealth has pursued the cyclical re-launching of the same policy principles, which have increasingly become more specific and effective.

On the contrary, in the Canadian case the process of greater national coordination has been of a softer, voluntary nature, without any apparent pressure from the federal government. Here, where there is no Federal Minister of Education, the CMEC is a collective body where ministers share common strategies but have individual responsibilities for implementing them (Vergari 2010). This means that the strengthening of national trends is fundamentally conditioned by constitutional provisions. With its segmented form of federalism, Canada's national coordination can only be based on more shared projects (as in the case of curriculum design and performance assessment). However, since implementation is left up to the provinces, this kind of increased systemic coordination is a very soft instrument, and one that is very much left up to the will, and conditioned by the internal political situation, of Canada's provinces. Nevertheless, the increased degree of interprovincial cooperation reveals a shared perception of a common problem.

Germany, a nation characterized by a unitary form of federalism, has been characterized by increased activity at the national level, whereby the inherited cohesion of interstate relations has helped the nation respond to a critical situation. Here, the KMK (in which the federal Minister of Education plays no part) has had a pivotal role, and there has been centralized, albeit cooperative, supervision of the new policy strategy: the contents of governance reforms have been agreed at this level. Owing to the nature of German federalism, intrastate agreements in Germany are of a more binding nature than they are in the Canadian case, and thus common measures taken at the national level have been more effective, and more susceptible to institutionalization.

Governance Shifts in Subnational Education Governance

According to my second hypothesis (*H2*), the role of sub-national governments in steering their systems has not diminished, but has changed depending on the chosen design of governance. In Australia, where governance was strictly in the hands of the states' departments of education, there has been pressure, based on the "national policy", towards the reformulation of powers through their substantial devolution to schools. In Canada, on the other hand, there has been a strengthening of the role of provincial departments of education vis-à-vis local, intermediate bodies, with greater parental choice and stronger institutional autonomy at the school level. From this point of view, there has been a hierarchical shift in provincial governance. In Germany, although the *Länder* have loosened their hierarchical style of governance through the granting of increased powers to schools, and through the adoption of quality assessment procedures, they have maintained a centralized design with regard to governance arrangements. Reasoning in terms of general governance principles, it seems quite clear that the hierarchical principle has not been abandoned, but has been modified by the market principle (vouchers and parental choice). Generally speaking, there has been a trend towards the steering-at-a-distance model, whereby governments have granted schools greater autonomy (with regard to financial, managerial and curricular matters), but have implemented strong systems of monitoring and accountability.

The Choice of New Governance Modes

As regards the contents of the reforms, although they are apparently similar, the combination of policy instruments in reform policy strategies has led to certain substantial differences, as foreseen by my third hypothesis (*H3*). In fact, although the three countries are rather similar with regard to certain aspects of the reform process (the centralization of the curriculum at the state/provincial level, with certain clear tendencies towards a national curriculum, albeit less significant in Canada from an empirical point of view), there are obvious differences with regard to other aspects.

Firstly, owing to the different degrees of "nationalization" of such policy, greater use of testing and assessment has been made in Australia and Germany. Secondly, Canada makes more use of organizational tools (mergers and charters schools), which are not employed to any significant extent in the other two countries. Thirdly, the decentralization of management, with administrative powers being attributed to individual schools, is stronger in Canada than it is in Australia (which is working hard towards implementing such a policy, although to date it has only been fully implemented in the State of Victoria) or Germany. Fourthly, certain market-driven mechanisms are better developed in Australia than they are in Canada or Germany (where such policy instruments are not really on the political agenda).

It should be pointed out that, in the cases of Australia and Canada, the implementation of new policy instruments for the reform of the governance of primary and secondary education, had already begun in certain states and provinces prior to the "nationalization" of the issue. On the contrary, in Germany this process of "anticipation" has not been witnessed. This is very important, and merits further investigation, since it suggests how certain types of federalism (i.e. the balanced and segmented types owing to their disintegrated character) are more capable of producing a process of mutual, or systemic, learning precisely because of their federal dynamics.

Conclusion

To sum up then, this study reveals the nature of governance shifts in education policies in three different federal countries. According to the fundamental assumption underlying this special issue (i.e. that governance arrangements change, but they do so according to a government's need to adapt its behaviour and policy strategy in response to the new challenges arising), I have investigated how this trend has evolved where the problem of governance may be most complex, namely in federal countries. By adopting a specific typology of federalism, I have submitted that governments' reactions to changing governance arrangements in education have been affected by the features of their own federal dynamics, in terms of both the trajectory of the process and the nature of the choices made. Obviously, the macro-perspective adopted here not only gives this study an exploratory character, but it also leaves a number of unresolved questions regarding, in particular, the evolution of the instrument mix adopted when reforming existing governance arrangements, especially at the sub-national level. Further research is required in order to compare the trajectories and contents of governance reforms within sub-national units if we are to really understand if, and to what extent, the changes driven by federal dynamics have an impact at the state/provincial level.

Notes

1. The dimensions of the formal framework used to assess the degree of integration/disintegration are: the constitutional design (degree of intrastate-ness); the intergovernmental structure of decision and resources (degree of interdependence); the intergovernmental decision-making rules (degree of hierarchy). The diverse aspects of federal relations, through which their centripetal/centrifugal nature is evaluated, are as follows: interaction and joint-decisional styles (degree of collaboration/competition in interaction styles); the type of governmental actors' strategy (degree of solidarity orientation/assertiveness); lines of conflict and intergovernmental coalitions (degree of party orientation/territoriality) (Colino 2013).
2. The distinction between interstate and intrastate federalism represents a way of identifying the flow of power and of establishing how decisions are actually made in federal states. If the interstate dynamic prevails, it means that the political process is addressed by the relations among the component governments; if the intrastate dimension prevails, it means that the diverse interests of the federal polity are directly dealt with by national political institutions (Cairns 1979; Broschek 2010).
3. The accommodating type, as always happens in such classifications, seems to be less precise, focusing as it does on a transitional stage towards the other three types.
4. The interviews are part of a much broader comparison I am making, designed to reconstruct governance change from a micro-perspective. Owing to the macro-perspective adopted in this paper, they are not quoted but should be considered as a source of enlightenment for the sequential reconstruction provided for the three individual cases.
5. Section 96 provides that "During a period of ten years after the establishment of the Commonwealth and thereafter until the Parliament otherwise provides, the Parliament may grant financial assistance to any State on such terms and conditions as the Parliament thinks fit".
6. Unlike the other two federations, Australia has a large non-governmental sector in education. In 2010 around 40% of students were enrolled in non-governmental schools
7. Federal funding represents 12% of governmental schools' revenue, and 42% of that of private schools (Keating *et al.* 2011).
8. All the provinces, with the exception of Manitoba, have eliminated school boards' tax powers, and thus provincial governments now provide all education funding (Levin 2005; Garcea and Monroe 2011).

References

Bellamy, J. and Brown, A., 2008, *Federalism and Regionalism in Australia: New Approaches, New Institutions?* (Canberra: ANU Press).

Benz, A., 2004, Einleitung: Governance – Modebegriff oder nützliches sozialwissenschaftliches Konzept?, in: A. Benz (Ed) *Governance – Regieren in komplexen regelsystemen: Eine Einführun* (Wiesbaden: VS Verlag für Sozialwissenschaften), pp. 11–28.

Benz, A. and Colino, C., 2011, Constitutional change in federations. A framework for analysis. *Regional and Federal Studies*, **21**(4/5), pp. 381–406.

Bolleyer, N. and Thorlakson, L., 2012, Beyond decentralization. The comparative study of interdependence in federal systems. *Publius*, **42**(4), pp. 566–591.

Borzel, T., 2006, 'Coping with Accession – New Modes and EU Enlargement', in: G. F. Schuppert (Ed) *Europeanization of Governance – The Challenge of Accession* (Baden-Baden: Nomos), pp. 613–641.

Braun, D., 2011, How centralized federations avoid over-centralization. *Regional and Federal Studies*, **21**(1), pp. 35–54. doi:10.1080/13597566.2010.507401

Broschek, J., 2010, Federalism and political change: Canada and Germany in historical-institutionalist perspective. *Canadian Journal of Political Science*, **43**(01), pp. 1–24. doi:10.1017/S0008423909990023

Burgess, M., 2006, *Comparative Federalism: Theory and Practice*. (London: Routledge).
Cairns, A., 1979, *From Interstate to Intrastate Federalism in Canada*. (Kingston: Institute of Intergovernmental Relations).
Caldwell, B., 1998, *Self-Managing Schools and Improved Learning Outcomes*. (Canberra: DETYA).
Capano, G., 2011, Government continues to do its job. A comparative study of governance shifts in the higher education sector. *Public Administration*, **89**(4), pp. 1622–1642. doi:10.1111/j.1467-9299.2011.01936.x
Capano, G., Rayner, J. and Zito, A., 2012, Governance from the bottom up: Complexity and divergence in comparative perspective. *Public Administration*, **90**(1), pp. 56–73. doi:10.1111/j.1467-9299.2011.02001.x
CEA, 2009, *CEA'S 2009 Education Research Review*. (Toronto: Canadian Education Association).
Colino, C., 2010, Understanding Federal Change: Types of Federalism and Institutional Evolution in the Spanish and German Federal Systems, in: J. Erk and W. Swenden (Eds) *New Directions in Federalism Studies* (London: Routledge), pp. 16–33.
Colino, C., 2013, Varieties of federalism and propensities for change, in: J. Broschek and A. Benz (Eds) *Federal dynamics. Continuity, change, and Varieties of Federalism* (Oxford: Oxford University Press), pp. 48–69.
DEET, 1993, National Report on Australia's Higher Education Sector ('the blue book'), (prepared under the direction of Michael Gallagher, then first assistant secretary of DEET's higher education division), Canberra, AGPS.
Dudley, J. and Vidovich, L., 1995, *The Politics of Education*. (Melbourne: The Australian Council for Educational Research).
Elazar, D. S., 1987, *Exploring Federalism*. (Tuscaloosa: The University of Alabama Press).
Erk, J., 2003, Federal Germany and its Non-Federal Society: Emergence of an all-German Educational Policy in a System of Exclusive Provincial Jurisdiction. *Canadian Journal of Political Science*, **36**(2), pp. 295–317.
Erk, J., 2008, *Explaining Federalism*. (Routledge: London).
Erk, J. and Koning, E. A., 2010, New structuralism and institutional change: Federalism between centralization and decentralization. *Comparative Political Studies*, **43**(3), pp. 353–378. doi:10.1177/0010414009332143
Erk, J., and Swenden, W., (Eds.) 2010, *New Directions in Federalism Studies*. (London: Routledge).
Falleti, T., 2010, *Decentralization and Subnational Politics in Latin America*. (Cambridge: Cambridge University Press).
Fleming, T., 1997, Provincial initiatives to eestructure Canadian school governance in the 1990s. *Canadian Journal of Educational Administration and Policy*, (11). Available at http:/umanitoba.ca/publications/cjeap/articles/fleming.html (accessed 18 October 2013).
Friedrich, C. J., 1962, Federal constitutional theory and emergent proposals, in: A. W. Macmahon (Ed) *Federalism: Mature. And Emergent* (New York: Russell and Russell), pp. 510–533.
Gagnon, A. and Tully, J., 2001, *Multinational Democracies*. (Cambridge: Cambridge University Press).
Galway, G., 2012, Lessons in leadership: Insider perspectives on corporate managerialism and educational reform. *Canadian Journal of Educational Administration and Leadership*, (130). 5 March. Available at http://0-www.eric.ed.gov.opac.acc.msmc.edu/PDFS/EJ971060.pdf (accessed 6 October 2013).
Garcea, J. and Monroe, D., 2011, Reforms to education funding frameworks in Canadian provinces (1991–2011): A comparative analysis. Paper presented to the Canadian Political Science Association Annual Congress, May 2011.
Hannaway, J. and Woodroffe, N., 2003, Chapter 1: Policy instruments in education. *Review of Research in Education*, **27**(1), pp. 1–24. doi:10.3102/0091732X027001001
Harrison, K., 2006. Provincial Interdependence: Concepts and Theories, in: K. Harrison (Ed) *Racing from the Bottom? Provincial Interdependence in the Canadian Federation* (Vancouver: University of British Columbia Press), pp. 1–23.
Hinz, B., 2010, Australian federalism and school funding arrangements. Paper presented at the Annual Conference of the Canadian Political Science Association, Montreal, 1–3 June.
Huber, S. G. and Gördel, B., 2006, Quality assurance in the German school system. *European Educational Research Journal*, **5**(3), pp. 196–209. doi:10.2304/eerj.2006.5.3.196
Hudson, C., 2007, Governing the governance of education: The state strikes back? *European Educational Research Journal*, **6**(3), pp. 266–282. doi:10.2304/eerj.2007.6.3.266
Hueglin, T. and Fenna, A., 2006, *Comparative Federalism: A Systematic Inquiry*. (Peterborough, ON: Broadview Press).
Inman, R. P. and Rubinfeld, D., 2005, Federalism and the democratic transition: Lessons from South Africa. *American Economic Review*, **95**(2), pp. 39–43. doi:10.1257/000282805774670356

Jones, S., 2008, Cooperative federalism? The case of the ministerial council on education, employment, training and youth affairs. *Australian Journal of Public Administration*, **67**(2), pp. 161–172. doi:10.1111/j.1467-8500.2008.00579.x

Karmel, P., 1973, *Schools in Australia: Report of the Interim Committee for the Australian Schools Commission*. (Canberra: Australian Schools Commission).

Katzenstein, P. J., 1987, *Policy and Politics in West Germany: The Growth of a Semi-sovereign State*. (Philadelphia: Temple University Press).

Keating, J., Annett, P., Burke, G. and O'Hanlon, C., 2011, *Mapping funding and regulatory arrangements across the Commonwealth and States and Territories*. (Canberra: Ministerial Council for Education, Early Childhood Development and Youth Affairs).

Kehm, B., 2010, Germany: After reunification, in: I. Rotberg (Ed) *Balancing Change and Tradition in Global Education Reform* (New York: Rowman & Liettlefield), pp. 103–120.

Kickert, W. J. M., 1997, Public governance in the Netherlands: An alternative to Anglo-American managerialism. *Public Administration*, **75**(4), pp. 731–752. doi:10.1111/1467-9299.00084

KMK (Kultus Minister Konferenz), 2011, *The Education System in the Federal Republic of Germany 2010/11*. (Bonn: KMK).

KMK (Kultus Minister Konferenz), 2013, *The Education System in the Federal Republic of Germany 2010/11*. (Bonn: KMK).

Lessard, C. and Brassard, A., 2006, La "gouvernance" de l'éducation au Canada : tendances et significations. *Education et sociétés*, **18**(2), pp. 181–201. doi:10.3917/es.018.0181

Lessard, C. and Brassard, A., 2009, Education governance in Canada, 1990-2003: Trends and significance, in: C. Levine-Rasky (Ed) *Canadian Perspectives on the Sociology of Education* (Don Mills, ON: Oxford University Press), pp. 255–274.

Levin, B., 2005, *Governing Education*. (Toronto: University of Toronto Press).

Levin, B. and Young, J., 2000, The rhetoric of educational reform. *Journal of Comparative Policy Analysis*, **2**(2), pp. 189–209.

Lingard, B., Knight, J. and Porter, P., 1993, *Schooling Reforms in Hard Times*. (London: Falmer Press).

Maroy, C., 2009, Convergences and hybridization of educational policies around 'postbureaucratic' models of regulation. *Compare*, **39**(1), pp. 71–84.

Meadmore, P., 2001, Free, compulsory and secular? The re-invention of Australian public education. *Journal of Education Policy*, **16**(2), pp. 113–125. doi:10.1080/02680930010025329

Niemann, D., 2010, Turn of the tide. New horizons in German education policy through IO Influence, in: M. Kerstin, A. Nagel, M. Windzio and A. Weymann (Eds) *Transformation of Education Policy. The Impact of the Bologna Process and the PISA Study in Comparative Perspective* (Houndsmills: Palgrave Macmillan), pp. 77–104.

Oecd, 2012a, *Education at the Glance 2012*. (Paris: OECD).

Oecd, 2012b, *Reviews of Evaluation and Assessment in Education. Australia*. (Paris: OECD).

Rhodes, R. A. W., 1994, THE hollowing out of the state: The changing nature of the public service in Britain. *Political Quarterly*, **65**, pp. 138–151. doi:10.1111/j.1467-923X.1994.tb00441.x

Rhodes, R. A. W., 1997, *Understanding Governance*. (Milton Keynes: Open University Press).

Sala, G., 2014, Federalism without Adjectives in Spain. *Publius*, **44**(1), pp. 109–134.

Sattler, P., 2012, Education governance reform in Ontario: Neoliberalism in context. *Canadian Journal of Educational Administration and Policy*, (128). Available at http://www.umanitoba.ca/publications/cjeap/ (accessed 13 October 2013).

Sing, N. and Rao, G., 2006, *Political Economy of Federalism in India*. (Oxford: Oxford University Press).

Skelcher, C., 2000, Changing images of the State: Overloaded, hollowed-out, congested. *Public Policy and Administration*, **15**(3), pp. 3–19. doi:10.1177/095207670001500302

Taylor, A., 2001, *The Politics of Educational Reform in Alberta*. (Toronto: Toronto University Press).

Thorlakson, L., 2003, Comparing federal institutions: Power and representation in six federations. *West European Politics*, **26**(2), pp. 1–22. doi:10.1080/01402380512331341081

Ungerleider, C. and Levin, B., 2007, Accountability, funding and school improvement in Canada, in: T. Townsend (Ed) *International Handbook of School Effectiveness and Improvement* (Dordrecht: Springer), pp. 411–424.

Vergari, S., 2010, Safeguarding federalism in education policy in Canada and the United States. *Publius*, **40**(3), pp. 534–557.

Watts, R., 1996, *Comparing Federal Systems in the 1990s*. (Kingston: Institute of Intergovernmental Relations).

Whitty, G., Power, S. and Halpin, D., 1998, *Devolution and Choice in Education: The School, the State and the Market*. (Buckingham: Open University Press).

Wilde, S., 2002, Secondary education in Germany 1990-2000: One decade of non-reform in unified German education? *Oxford review of Education*, **28**(1), pp. 39–51. doi:10.1080/03054980120113625

Winter, K., 2000, School autonomy and the role of the state: Some reflections on the current school educational system in Germany. *European Journal of Teacher Education*, **23**(1), pp. 77–83. doi:10.1080/713667264

Importing Private Higher Education: International Branch Campuses

JASON E. LANE

ABSTRACT *International branch campuses (IBCs) evidence the increasing intention of some governments to use private higher education to fulfill public policy goals related to economic development and building capacity within the postsecondary sector. This study uses two exploratory case studies (Malaysia and Dubai) to investigate the relationship between the government, public policy, and IBCs. The IBCs imported by the governments investigated in this study tend to be from well-established institutions in countries that attract a large number of international students. The results from the study suggest that governments are actively recruiting institutions from other countries to aid in improving the host government's education-related reputation and signaling to the world that it is modernizing its economy and its desire to be a regional education hub. Thus, IBCs not only increase local capacity and provide a different type of education, but are intended to foster new regional interest in pursuing an education in the host country.*

Introduction

A quickly expanding aspect of private higher education, particularly in nations with developing economies, is the development of international branch campuses (IBCs). This expansion has been facilitated by changing regulation of private sectors in host nations, more aggressive expansion plans by institutions in developed nations, less expensive modes of travel and communication, and the increasing realization by developing nations that higher education should be a core component of economic development (Levy 2005; Verbik and Merkley 2006; McBurnie and Zyguris 2007; Guruz 2008; Becker 2009; Lane 2010b; Lane and Kinser, forthcoming). These factors have led several governments seeking to further develop their local economies to turn to established institutions in developed nations to build IBCs to assist with the achievement of governmental priorities.

While recent years have witnessed growth in the investigation of private higher education's development around the world (see Maldanado-Maldanado et al. 2004), very little field-based scholarship has focused on the development of IBCs, a form of cross-border education.[1] The warrant for this study is quite simple: limited information is known about the creation, operation, and regulation of IBCs. And, as regulation influences both creation and operation, this article focuses on institutional development as a means for exploring the outcome of local policy and regulatory environments. Indeed, what I propose here is not a new typology or framework with which to study educational organizations; rather I use a widely-recognized typology of private higher education institutions (Levy 1986) to analyze the roles of IBCs, thereby allowing for the identification of outputs from the policy environments in which they are operating.

Unlike the business management literature on multi-national corporations, multi-national operations of educational organizations remain relatively unexplored. Yet, they are a growing type of provider of educational opportunities globally. According to the Observatory for Borderless Higher Education (OBHE), the number of IBCs exceeded 160 in January of 2009; a tenfold increase in 15 years and double the number identified in 2006 (Verbik and Merkley 2006; Becker 2009). The purpose of this article is to analyze the policy environments of IBCs in two leading importing governments and concomitantly to assess how the institutions in these policy environments compare with previous development trends in private higher education. To broaden understanding of IBCs and the policy environment that helps shape them, this exploratory study applies the Levy (1986) typology of private higher education growth to two targeted case studies of IBC development by governments leading in the importation of IBCs (this typology is also used in Levy's (2011) article in this issue). Applying this foundational typology to IBCs helps identify the policy outputs of the selected policy arenas as well as assess how IBCs fit within the existing private higher education landscape.

The first part of this article provides an overview of IBCs, including what is currently known about their development and regulation. The second part summarizes the exploratory cases of the emergence of IBCs in Dubai and Malaysia. The cases are based on review of official documents, government and non-governmental organization (NGO) reports, scholarly and media articles, field work in both countries (including visiting more than 20 institutions in these two regions) and interviews with elite stakeholders. The article then discusses how IBCs, as policy instruments of the importing government, traverse and transcend the traditional categories of private higher education widely recognized in the scholarly literature. It concludes with suggestions for future research. The findings of the study should help further knowledge of IBCs and provide guidance for additional case studies of these entities.

The conclusions of this exploratory study are limited in two important ways. First, this is not a systematic investigation of IBCs nor is it a scientific sample thereof. As such, readers should be careful in how they apply the findings of this exploratory study to other IBC policy environments. For example, some nations do not engage in any regulation of IBCs; whereas both governments (or their agents) included here actively recruit and seek to regulate IBCs. Second, the study relies mostly on official policy documents and regulations, official statements, interviews with campus administrators and existing data collected by local and international non-government organizations. The limited available information about individual campuses (many of which are less than five years old) precludes a thorough investigation of the extent to which the government agenda is pursued by individual campuses, the differences between perfunctory and substantive reporting and oversight, and the variability of actual practice. However, such limitations need not overshadow the insights that this study provides in terms of government intentions toward IBCs, how the purposes of these entities compare with the purposes of other types of private higher education, and directions for future research.

Current Status of IBC Development and Regulation

Universities have operated campuses in other, mostly developed, nations since at least the mid-1950s for such purposes as providing study abroad opportunities, offering specialized graduate programs, or to provide options for foreign-based military personnel (Verbik and Merkley 2006). However, the growth in the number of these institutions was initially slow and largely idiosyncratic. Nevertheless, in the last 15 years, changes in the policy environments of many countries aimed at attracting IBCs has led to a relatively rapid increase in this type of venture.

Unlike most of their predecessors, many of the recently developing IBCs are designed to serve students in the host country and local region, operating alongside domestic providers.[2] No exhaustive list of these institutions exists; but, according to the OBHE, institutions in 22 countries are operating more than 160 IBCs in 51 countries (Becker 2009). They originated mostly from the exporting countries of Australia, United Kingdom, and the United States.

One aspect of the nature of cross-border higher education is that, regardless of whether a home campus is considered public or private, the IBC operates in the private sector of the host country (though it can fulfill some public purposes (Lane and Kinser 2011)). While there has yet to emerge one agreed upon definition of an IBC, there does seem to be agreement that an IBC must have a physical presence on foreign soil, the students at the IBC must be able to earn a degree from the home campus, and that it be fully or jointly owned by the institution from which the degree is awarded (Verbik and Merkley 2006; McBurnie and Zyguris 2007). As such, regardless of whether an IBC is regulated under the same provisions as apply to the public or private higher education sector, the academic enterprise is neither owned nor completely controlled by the host government. In some places, such as Qatar and Abu Dhabi the private–public distinction becomes blurred because of the amount of financial support the government is providing to some of the IBCS within their borders; however, from a legal perspective, the home campus retains the academic authority and ownership over the degree and curricular provisions (Lane and Kinser 2011). In both Malaysia and Dubai, the government considers IBCs part of the private sector.

Beyond these definitional assessments, the characteristics of IBCs can, in part, be explored through the relationship of these entities with the host government and comparison with other types of private higher education. First, the regulation of IBCs stems from a reversal in the relationship between developed and developing nations in these cases. For decades, students from developing nations, many supported by their home country, sought education abroad; leaving their home country to study at institutions in the developed world. Such study abroad initiatives did not always necessitate regulations by the students' home country; although some did impose rules on students who wanted to study abroad. The creation of IBCs fosters a small reversal of these flows. Instead of students travelling abroad, institutions based in developed countries send resources abroad to provide educational opportunities to foreign students in their home country. This reversal results in expanding educational capacity within the developing nation and allowing students to pursue a degree from a foreign provider without leaving their home country. The advent of IBCs has also brought foreign control to parts of the developing nation's education system, raising concerns about quality assurance. As Lane and Kinser (2008: 11) have noted, "[IBCs] can fall through the cracks of quality-assurance regulations, with both governments assuming the other (or some entity within the country) is providing oversight, but neither actively engaging in such a way". Studies such as those published by the International Institute for Educational Planning (Martin 2007) better illuminate quality assurance issues in cross-border higher education.

Existing work (Verbik and Jokivirta, 2005a, 2005b; McBurnie and Zyguris 2007; Guruz 2008; Lane and Kinser, forthcoming) suggests that regulation of IBCs by the importing nations has been limited and rapidly changing. As IBCs are relatively new enterprises, government regulations often change as the entities and government expectations for them evolve. Like the expansion of much of private higher education (see Levy 2006), the current expansion of IBCs started as more limited regulation made it, in some ways, easier for institutions to expand outside of their own nation than within it. Limited regulation and the ability of successful and prestigious universities to begin operating globally led some to fear that such developments would threaten existing local public systems and allow "the giants" to dominate the world education system (McBurnie and Zyguris 2007). However, like so many aspects of globalization the end game is not yet known. Some early expansion efforts were not as successful as many had hoped and resulted in a few causalities such as Royal Melbourne Institute of Technology (Australia) closing a campus in Malaysia due to their financial partner going bankrupt; Monash University (Australia) losing millions in its South Africa campus; Sylvan (United States) closing a campus in India after not receiving accreditation from the Indian government; George Mason University (United States) closing its campus in the United Arab Emirates over disagreements with its local partner; and the University of New South Wales closing its Singapore campus after only a few months due to a lack of student enrollments (Auditor General Victoria 2002, 2005; Verbik and Merkley 2006; Becker 2009; Lewin 2009; Lane 2010b).

The Cases

The two governments in these cases are prominent in the education and popular media; vary in economic conditions and policy regimes; and are among the largest importers of IBCs in the world. Malaysia and Dubai both have developing economies, extensive involvement in cross-border tertiary education, and foreign universities have been operating IBCs in these states since 1998 and 1993, respectively (Verbik and Merkley 2006; Guruz 2008; Lane 2010a, 2010b).[3] Further, Malaysia and Dubai have among the most IBCs in the world, have stated that the development of IBCs is part of their long-term education and economic development plans, and have declared a desire to become regional higher education hubs (Kinser and Lane 2010; Verbik and Lasanowski 2007).

Dubai

Dubai is one of seven emirates that comprise the United Arab Emirates (UAE), which is located in the Southeast region of the Arabian Peninsula and was founded in 1971. The Emirate of Dubai is a constitutional monarchy, governed by the Al Maktoum family since 1833 (Abdullah 1978). While it is part of a broader confederation, Dubai "has ensured that it retains a distinct national identity, controls its own natural resources, and maintains command of its largely independent development path" (Davidson 2008: 2) and the development of private higher education in each Emirate has developed separate from the others (Lane 2010b). Thus, its innovation in the development of IBCs warrants attention separate from the rest of the Emirates.

Over the past two decades, Dubai began moving toward building a post-petroleum economy. By investing its oil wealth from the 1970s and 1980s in such areas as finance, luxury tourism and commercial infrastructure, Dubai has overcome centuries of an underdeveloped economic infrastructure by developing an economy in which less than 6 per cent of its $37 billion (2006) economy is derived from petroleum (Kuran 2004; Sheik-Miller 2007; Davidson 2008). Now, the emirate has begun to invest in a knowledge-based economy, seeking to improve and expand research and development as well as educational opportunities. The latter coming, primarily, through the growth of IBCs with the desire of becoming a regional education hub.

Historically, access to post-secondary education throughout the UAE has been very limited and primarily the responsibility of the federal government. Further, public colleges and universities are accessible only to UAE nationals. The first public university in the UAE was created in 1976 (in the city of Al-Ain in the Abu Dhabi emirate), and access to higher education within Dubai was essentially non-existent until the late 1980s when the Islamic and Arabic Studies College (a private institution) began operating (Lane 2010b). In fact, most of the colleges and universities in Dubai opened after 2000.[4]

The innovations in private higher education witnessed in Dubai have been primarily facilitated by adaptations of the emirate's economic development policy. While Dubai has largely set its own developmental path, its participation in the UAE confederation requires it to be subject to regulations set forth by the federal government in Abu Dhabi. For example, the 1984 Commercial Companies Law requires all companies registered in the nation to be at least 51 per cent owned by a UAE firm (Davidson 2008). However, Dubai has found ways to work around such a requirement in order to attract more foreign investment. Dubai has created many "Free Zones" managed by special legal authorities. The Zones proved quite successful[5] as companies were attracted by "tax-free trading, minimal regulation, well-developed infrastructure, and the availability of reasonably priced skilled labour" (Wilkins 2001: 12). The success of the Free Zones spurred more specialized zones such as the Dubai Media City and Dubai Flower City. Further, the "free zones" also exempted institutions from existing federal quality assurance mechanisms in the UAE; instead the University Quality Assurance International Board (UQAIB) was created by the Dubai Knowledge and Human Development Authority to ensure that programs offered at the branch campus are comparable in quality to those provided on the home campus of the IBC.[6]

Although the first outpost of a foreign campus (University of Wollongong) opened in 1993, the number of IBCs did not grow rapidly until after free zones began to target them about a decade later. Now, half of the postsecondary educational institutions in Dubai are IBCs. As of January 2010, the education system in Dubai was comprised of three campuses of federal public institutions (Zayed University, Dubai Men's College and Dubai Women's College) and 47 private (i.e. non-federal) colleges or universities.[7] Thirty of the 47 private higher education campuses are located in four free zones and 25 of the free zone institutions are IBCs. The IBCs in Dubai include extensions of Rochester Institute of Technology (RIT) (United States), Herriot-Watt University (UK), and Manipal University (India).

The desire to bolster the private higher education sector is linked to the desire to improve economic development and recruit and retain highly skilled workers (Muysken and Nour 2006). Although data about non-nationals is not readily available; expatriates are reported to comprise approximately 90 per cent of the UAE workforce (*Economist* 2008b), with a large proportion supporting Dubai's economic expansion efforts.[8] And, this factor is playing a key role in the story of the development of private higher education. As one official at the Dubai Knowledge Village stated, "Our economy is being fueled by the work of non-nationals and we would like them to stay in our country. However, there have been limited opportunities for them or their children to receive a post-secondary education in a familiar environment. Thus, they have chosen to study outside of the country. Now, we bring those opportunities to them" (Personal interview, June 2007).[9] Development of IBCs provides prestige that would not be as readily available by investing in the domestic private higher education system and access that would not be available by feasible levels of investment in the public higher education system.

Malaysia

Malaysia is located in the South China Sea, is primarily divided between a peninsula below Thailand and part of the island of Borneo, and had approximately 25 million people according to the 2000 census. The country is governed by a federal government that includes a bicameral legislature and an elected monarchy. Since its creation in 1963, Malaysia has worked to develop its economy, transforming it from one based on agriculture and mining to manufacturing (Ang and McKibbon 2005). Over the course of the last decade, the government has begun to transition the nation to seek to be a leader in the knowledge economy (Evers 2003). Earlier this decade, the government adopted the *Knowledge-Based Economy Master Plan* (Malaysia Economic Planning Unit 2002), which included a multi-billion dollar higher education strategy to meet enrollment goals of decreasing the number of students studying abroad and increasing the number of foreign students studying in Malaysia The plan also targeted the further development of the private higher education sector, which has been deemed crucial for achieving Malaysia's enrollment and economic goals. Even if the physical capacity existed in the public sector (which it does not), foreign undergraduate enrollments in this sector are capped at 5 per cent (Morshidi 2008) and participation by ethnic minorities (or lack thereof) has been heavily influenced by government-mandated quotas designed to ensure access for indigenous groups (Lee 2001). (These quotas have since been eliminated, but their effect was still in place when most IBCs opened.) Still, the public sector does not have the capacity to meet the demand for higher education from its own citizens (Middlehurst and Woodfield 2004).[10]

The desire to be globally competitive in the knowledge economy and the goal of becoming a regional hub for higher education have led Malaysia to target the development of IBCs. Although Malaysia has been involved with various forms of transnational educational arrangements since the 1980s (McBurnie and Ziguris 2007), new laws implemented in the mid-1990s allowed foreign providers to open IBCs.[11] These institutions are subject to the same regulations as other institutions operating in the private sector, but the campus has to be run by an organization incorporated in Malaysia and is subject to various joint ownership requirements, one of which is that a local partner has to have a stake in the ownership (see Lane 2010b).[12] For example, University of Nottingham Malaysia Campus is an incorporated partnership of Boustead Holdings Berhad, YTL Corporation Berhad, and University of Nottingham UK (Mordishi 2005). Boustead and YTL are mostly held by Malaysian investors and focus on a wide range of interests including plantations, property, services (including education), and infrastructure building. These arrangements can restrict institutional autonomy, but also serve to protect the home campus from some financial risks, particularly if the endeavor proves unsuccessful (Lane 2010a). As of this writing, five IBCs operate in Malaysia; three are Australian based, while the other two are based in the United Kingdom. Unlike the situation in Dubai, these campuses comprise a relatively small portion of the private higher education system. However, like Dubai, these campuses seem to be a way for the country to signal its growing modernity to the outside world.

The government's interest in developing IBCs is very tightly linked with a variety of economic development factors. In the late 1990s, out of concern for the outflow of currency and talent, the government began working to diminish the number of students studying abroad. For example, Ziguras (2003) estimates that the 20 percent of Malaysian students studying abroad in 1995 resulted in a monetary outflow of approximately US$800 million and an untold loss of talent due to students not returning to Malaysia. Moreover, the loss of talent is believed to have partly contributed to a decline in the nation's global competitiveness.[13]

Government efforts to curtail these trends entailed building domestic capacity in information communication and technology (ICT), research and development, and the higher education system, including fostering partnerships with foreign providers to develop IBCs (Evers 2003; Morshidi 2005). All of the IBCs offer courses of study in high skill areas such as engineering and sciences, in addition to areas such as business and social sciences. In fact, some of the IBCs provide PhD level training and engage in research funded by the Malaysian government, which is meant to benefit the local region. Finally, these institutions provide a much desired product in the form of desired credentials from recognized universities in developed nations and expose students to English, which is increasingly recognized as the language of the global marketplace.

Discussion of Cases: How IBCs fit the Literature's Leading Categories of Private Higher Education Growth

IBCs represent an expansion of private higher education partly unlike that previously recorded in the scholarly literature. Understanding their current roles within the local private higher education contexts provides deeper understanding of the policy outcomes of the actions of host governments. Application of the Levy (1986) typology, which has been widely used to understand the growth of private higher education around the globe for more than 20 years, helps underscore how IBCs are similar to and different from previous expansions of private higher education. This framework suggests that private higher education institutions generally fill one of three purposes: provision of something superior, something different, or something more mass-based. These categories have remained remarkably consistent over time and even though some overlap occurs, most private higher education institutions "fit pretty clearly (even when not fully) into one category" (Levy 2008: 26). Before moving forward with the analysis, it is critical to note that the roles performed by IBCs fit these categories; however, this group of institutions does not seem to fit clearly into any one category and they "fit" in ways not usually defined in the academic literature. Furthermore, while the aggregate roles of these institutions do not easily fit within any one of these categories; it does not mean that all IBCs fit all categories. Indeed, the data suggests that a follow up study of sub-groups of IBCs is warranted in order to clarify the roles of particular IBCs or groups of them. Yet, an aggregate analysis such as this does provide important information about the intended and unintended outcomes of policy oriented toward IBCs.

Something Superior: Prestigious Nations and Semi-Elite Institutions

The categories used here have been molded to better fit the nature of IBCs, while still honoring the phenomenon originally being described by each in Levy's original typology. Both Malaysia and Dubai appear to be attracting semi-elite institutions from prestigious nations. With very limited exceptions, the universities opening IBCs are not considered elite institutions.[14] However, in this context, prestige extends beyond the ranking and includes the perceived prestige of the home country. For example, Michigan State University from the United States, which opened a campus in Dubai is an example of an above average university from a highly desirable nation opening an IBC. Similar is the University of Nottingham from the UK opening a campus in Malaysia. Both Dubai and Malaysia are primarily pursuing campuses which offer English-language instruction and are extensions of institutions in nations that are high-destination locations for students studying abroad.[15] Most of the IBCs are from the UK and United States, the two leading OECD study abroad destination countries, and Australia, which is one of the leading destinations for students from East Asia (OECD 2010). Further, as many of the campuses are extensions of public institutions in the home country, the association with a government may provide additional credence and prestige to the campus, even though they are legally private entities in the host nation.[16]

Traditionally, the category of "something superior" has been used to identify elite institutions that seek to provide an education superior to that which is already available to students. The problem with the traditional notion is that it is very narrow. As Levy (2008) notes, there exists only a very small number of private non-US institutions that can be classified as elite. He proposes, however, that there are a number of "semi-elite" institutions that have more than "average selectivity and status" and "on the upper end we can simply say that these institutions are good but not good enough to be considered elite"; however, these institutions often provide a quality of education relatively better than what is already available and, within the country they operate, tend to be at or near the top in terms of academic quality (Levy 2008: 27). The concept of the prestigious nation is one that is proposed here and which may be uniquely associated with cross-border higher education. The importing governments have been recruiting and admitting institutions primarily from nations with widely recognized, world-class higher education systems that attract the largest number of foreign students (e.g. Australia, United Kingdom, United States). Further, some students seem to attach a certain value to an "American education" or a "British education" or an "Australian" education, for example.

Some IBCs fit the "something superior" category in that the institutions are choosing to open in order to provide something superior to the mainstream options. Yet, we could also say that the governments are searching for increased prestige and recognition for the system, using IBCs to signal their desire to be an educational hub and/or their inclusion in the knowledge-based economy. Of course the two levels, system and institution, are interrelated but the system emphasis is striking in the IBC cases. Semi-elite institutions elsewhere appear to emerge to be above the bulk of the system. The IBCs are more to raise the reputation of the system. This distinction reflects the strong government (and, thus, system) concern when it comes to IBCs. Both governments have stated that they want to raise their global prestige level and become a regional higher education hub (Verbik and Lasanowski 2007). Their purpose is to both attract additional foreign students to study in their system and retain more of their own students to study domestically. One identified strategy for achieving this goal has been to attract known institutions from prestigious nations to provide educational opportunities as part of the higher education system of the developing nation. The argument is that students need not travel to America, the United Kingdom or Australia when they can receive a similar education locally from an American, British or Australian branch campus.

Something Different: Access and Pedagogy

The literature has used this category to describe the provision of a type of educational opportunity not provided by the government. Mostly, this category has been used to describe religious education – a common form of private higher education and something not typically offered by the government. The cases here suggest that IBCs provide something "different", but in two ways not commonly discussed in the literature: 1) providing access to those purposefully excluded in the past; and, 2) delivering different programs and/or pedagogy.

In both Dubai and Malaysia, government policy has excluded certain segments of the population from accessing the public higher education system.[17] IBCs provide an opportunity for these students to gain access to something that has historically not been provided. In Dubai, the public system is open only to nationals (with very few exceptions). The expats, which comprise a vast majority of the workforce, cannot take advantage of this system. In Malaysia, a large proportion of the minority groups in Malaysia have been historically excluded from the public sector by ethnic quotas and, though private higher education has not been bound by that restrictiveness, these institutions could not provide a university degree without partnering with a foreign institution (Lee 2001). In both cases, IBCs provided a new opportunity to those inhibited by government policies from obtaining a university degree from the public sector.

A second difference, particularly in the case of Dubai, is that the IBCs provide different types of academic programs and pedagogy than what is currently widely available. In fact, more than simply providing additional educational opportunities, Dubai has purposefully been recruiting IBCs from the different home nations (e.g. Australia, Belgium, India, United States, United Kingdom) of many expats as a way to provide the workers and/or their children with an educational opportunity familiar to them; as well as responding to the demand from students for a different type of education (e.g. an "American" education or an "British" education).[18]

Something More: Demand Absorption & Creation

IBCs present a possible solution to both the demand-side and supply-side dimensions of current public policy issues. IBCs fit the conventional definition of "something more" by absorbing some of the excess demand in the system; however, the IBC twist is that their presence may also create demand. The majority of all private higher education institutions can be classified as demand absorbing; that is they arose in order to absorb excess demand in the system. In these cases, both governments are seeking to meet the demand for higher education and also have indicated a desire to attract more foreign students. In terms of absorbing demand, IBCs provide a relatively inexpensive way for the governments included in this study to increase capacity; but the role of demand absorption is more dominant in Dubai than in Malaysia. In Dubai, IBCs account for half of the total number of colleges and university. In Malaysia, IBCs nationally account for a much smaller number of the overall institutions. Although, in the state of Sarawak, the Australian IBCs of Curtin University of Technology and Swinburne University of Technology are the only local access to private higher education at the university level.

Regarding demand creation, a phenomenon not seen elsewhere in the literature, IBCs are viewed by these governments as a development tool to create demand for the higher education system. Tied to the desire to import at least semi-elite institutions from countries with leading higher education systems, the governments want to use these campuses to spark interest in their higher education offerings and increase the number of foreign students attending local higher education institutions (and possibly retaining more domestic students). While the IBCs could compete with the domestic institutions, there could also be a coattail effect. The reputation of the IBCs may raise the overall reputation of the entire domestic system. This could create heightened demand from international students to study in that country, which may benefit both IBCs and non-IBCs.

Government Interaction: Public Policy and Private Higher Education

The recent iteration of IBCs both mimics and expands the type of growth of private higher education noted in earlier literature. IBCs, the semi-elite institutions from prestigious nations, provide "something superior" to most existing institutions; but the superiority is meant to raise the prestige of the system, not compete directly with domestic public institutions. They provide something different by offering a different pedagogical form or academic program, but also giving access to those historically excluded due to government policy. Moreover, these institutions may absorb local demand, but their presence may also create additional international demand for the system.

The findings in this study show the role of IBCs in the local education sector and policy domain. What is clear is that the two governments are using the IBCs to fulfill public policy initiatives. That the government is playing a role in the development of these campuses is not remarkable in their regions, though quite remarkable compared to the reality of private higher education emergence in most of the developing world; the extent and type of their engagement, however, is worth noting. While government involvement can range from nonexistent to quite active, Malaysia and Dubai come from regions known for having government actively involved in the planning and development of the private higher education sector (Levy 2006). In part, governments have recognized that it can be cheaper to utilize the private higher education sector to achieve public policy goals, rather than expanding and investing directly in the public higher education sector; particularly if the private sector can be shepherded to serve public purposes.

The engagement of Dubai in recruiting and stewarding of IBCs represents one of the most extensive examples of government involvement with private higher education. In Dubai, the government (or its agents) has been active in providing the infrastructure for IBC development, including deciding which institutions are allowed to open campuses and passing government policies that facilitate IBC growth. Malaysia adjusted its laws about private higher education to encourage the growth of cross-border educational activities, including international branch campuses and policy documents have targeted the development of IBCs as a strategy for advancing the nation's economy. Moreover, the Swinburne campus in Sarawak is a partnership of the Sarawak State government and Swinburne University in Australia (Morshidi 2005). In Dubai, free zones, governed by special authorities have been used to recruit IBCs, by providing campus facilities (at a cost to the IBC) and exempting them from federal regulations.

Conclusions and Directions for Future Research

IBCs are a new and relatively unexplored expansion of private higher education. And, indeed, they operate as private entities in the host countries, even though they may involve public institutions in home nations and, in these examples, the host governments clearly intend, for better or worse, for these institutions to serve the government's public policy needs. Dubai and Malaysia both regulate IBCs as part of their private higher education system. And, similar to what Pachuashvili (2011) found in several post-communist countries, government regulation of IBCs appears to be influenced by both political-economic and cultural-historical factors.

From applying the Levy (1986) framework for private higher education growth, two significant conclusions can be drawn. First, IBCs collectively transcend the framework categories, not fitting neatly into any one, but clearly serving, at some level, a function within each category. IBCs provide something superior to the existing higher education system by importing at least semi-elite institutions from leading developed countries. They provide something different by providing access to those students that are legally excluded from the public higher education system. They provide something more mass-based, by seeking to absorb excess demand. Second, the framework does not capture all characteristics of the IBCs. For example, the category of something different traditionally refers to the provision of religious-based education. In the case of IBCs, the government is actively recruiting an institutional type to, in part, provide secular education services to students who are or have been, by decree of the government, excluded from or underserved by the public sector. Moreover, IBCs have both demand-side and supply-side roles. While the literature has long recognized the role of private higher education in absorbing demand, this may be the first example of a type of private higher education institution that is also purposefully intended to create demand.

As this is an exploratory investigation, further study is needed to address an array of questions, including the extent to which the conclusions of this study apply to other nations' IBCs (where, for example, the regulatory environments, economies, or government relationships may be different). How will IBCs affect the future development of private higher education in the host nations? How will the involvement of the host government in the development of IBCs affect the growth of the nation's public academic sector? How will regulation of IBCs evolve? Will the regulatory evolution follow a similar trajectory to what has been chronicled previously in the literature on private higher education? What does it mean for a public institution in one country to be operating a campus in the private sector of another country? Is such an arrangement sustainable over a long period?

Relative to the total number of private higher education institutions worldwide, the number of IBCs is still minuscule; but, their potential to affect the evolution of higher education in developing nations is substantial. As such, much more research is needed about this type of institution and the public policy dynamics involved.

Notes

1. Cross-border supply of higher education encompasses a variety of forms including study abroad opportunities, faculty exchanges and the like. More recent developments include twinning programs (wherein a local institution partners with a foreign institution and local students take courses locally and then transfer to the foreign institution to complete their degree), onsite delivery of courses and programs, and operation of full branch campuses serving students in the host country.
2. Several IBCs were founded in Japan during the 1980s to serve Japanese students. Most of those campuses are no longer in operation (Chambers and Cummings 1999; Croom 2010).
3. The University of Wollongong in Dubai is the oldest branch campus in Dubai. It relocated to the Dubai Knowledge Village after the village opened; in 2008, it served approximately 3,300 students from more than 90 nationalities.

4. Data on the number of institutions comes from Dubai's Knowledge and Human Development Authority's online database as of January 15, 2010.
5. These Zones fall outside of the federal regulations and proved to be quite successful, with the first (started in 1985) having as many as 2000 companies, 40,000 employees, and $6 billion in investments (Davidson 2008).
6. At the time of this writing, the federal government is moving to exert control over the free zone institutions, but the issue had not yet been resolved and the growth of IBCs in Dubai took place during a period when the federal government exerted control over an IBC only if the IBC desired local accreditation. For more information, see Lane (2010b).
7. These numbers were calculated using the information provided by Dubai's Knowledge and Human Development Authority's database of licensed institutions.
8. To attract the labor it needs, Dubai has started expediting their immigration application process and increasing the number of foreigners allowed into the country (Mahroum 2002). They have also changed the groups targeted by their immigration policy. In the 1980s and early 1990s, all of UAE worked to import cheap labor from foreign nations (Zachariah et al. 2003). However, the focus is now on highly skilled labor, such as engineers (*Economist* 2008b).
9. The language in official publications supports this claim; the DIAC Corporate Brochure states that part of the reason for establishing the DIAC is to respond to the increasing demand for higher education in part due to the significant increase in expatriates working in Dubai. Also, Croom (2010) notes that only a "small proportion" of the students in DIAC institutions are from the emirate.
10. According to data from the Malaysian Ministry of Education (PROPHE 2009), the proportion of students enrolled in private higher education rose from 32 per cent in 1995 to 40 per cent of students in 2000. The private and public sectors continue to grow in the number of students being served. As of 2000, IBC enrollment was less than 1 per cent of the total private higher education enrollments.
11. The 1969 Essential (Higher Education Institution) Regulation legally prevented the domestic private institutions from granting degrees and barred foreign institutions from establishing campuses. Starting in the 1970s, private institutions were allowed to offer pre-university courses. Then, in the early 1980s, private institutions became involved with foreign providers via twinning and franchise arrangements to provide courses leading to a certificate, diploma, or professional credential. In 1996, a set of new parliamentary acts fostered the development of the private sector and made it possible for new institutional structures to operate, including IBCs (see Lee 2001 for an in depth discussion of the development of private higher education in Malaysia). The development of the IBCs was seen as a natural outgrowth of the existing twinning and franchise arrangements (Mazzarol et al. 2003).
12. Initially, the Malaysian government restricted the foreign institution from owning more than 49 per cent of the joint venture. Those requirements have been slowly reduced over time and it is expected that by 2012, the foreign institution will be able to retain 100 per cent ownership in the venture, if desired (Morshidi, personal communication, February 9, 2009).
13. Between 1994 and 2001, Malaysia's global competitiveness rank decreased from the nineteenth most competitive nation to the twenty-ninth (Knowledge-Based Economy Master Plan, 2002). Malaysia has regained some of its competitiveness, returning to nineteenth in 2008 (IMD 2008).
14. In both Malaysia and Dubai, the home campus of at least one IBC (University of Nottingham, England, [Malaysia] and Michigan State University (MSU) [Dubai]) was ranked as a top 100 research university in 2008 by Shanghai Jiao Tong Academic Ranking of Global Universities. Most, if not all, others were below this ranking. Regardless of whether such rankings measure or create prestige, they do serve as an indicator of the perception of prestige. It should also be noted that MSU closed most of its operations in July 2010, after less than two years of operations.
15. Anecdotal evidence suggests that students desire English-based education.
16. Malaysia's Ministry of Higher Education lists IBCs as private institutions and they are not considered part of the federal "public" higher education sector in Dubai.
17. Malaysia's ethnic quota policies no longer exist, but they were present when IBCs first appeared.
18. This demand was once addressed by the creation of institutions such as American University of Cairo or Beirut; however, IBCs meet this demand without an entirely new institution needing to be created and the home campus being located in the country of interest seems to provide a different level of quality assurance to the parent (regardless of whether such quality assurance actually exists).

References

Abdullah, M. M., 1978, *The United Arab Emirates: A Modern Histroy* (London: Croom Helm).

Ang, J. B. and McKibbon, W. J., 2005, Financial liberalization, financial sector development and growth: evidence from Malaysia. Brookings discussion papers in international economics. No. 168.

Auditor General of Victoria, 2002, Report on public sector agencies. Available at http://download.audit.vic.gov.au/files/PSA_report_2002.pdf (accessed 15 February 2005).

Auditor General of Victoria, 2005, Results of financial statement audits for agencies with other than 30 June 2004 balance dates, and other audits. Available at from http://download.audit.vic.gov.au/files/May05_fsa%20report.pdf (accessed 2 March 2006).

Becker, R., 2009, *International Branch Campuses: Markets and Strategies* (London: Observatory for Borderless Higher Education).

Chambers, G. and Cummings, W. K., 1999, Profiting from education: Japan–United States international education ventures in the 1980s. IIE Research Report 20. (New York: Institute for International Education).

Croom, P., 2010, Motivations and aspirations for international branch campuses, in: D. W. Chapman and R. Sakamoto (Eds) *Cross Border Partnerships in Higher Education: Strategies and Issues* (New York: Routledge), pp. 45–66.

Davidson, C. M., 2008, *Dubai: The Vulnerability of Success* (New York: Columbia University Press).

Economist, 2008a, The rise of the gulf, April 26, p. 15.

Economist, 2008b, How to spend it, April 26, pp. 37–40.

Evers, H.-D., 2003, Transition towards a knowledge economy: Malaysia and Indonesia in comparative perspective. *Comparative Sociology*, **2**(2), pp. 355–373.

Guruz, K., 2008, *Higher Education and International Student Mobility in the Global Knowledge Economy* (Albany, NY: State University of New York Press).

Kinser, K. and Lane, J. E., 2010, Deciphering "educational hubs" strategies: Rhetoric and reality. *International Higher Education*, (59), pp. 18–19. Available at http://www.bc.edu/research/cihe/ihe/issues/2010.html.

Kuran, T., 2004, Why the Middle East is economically underdeveloped: Historical mechanisms of institutional stagnation. *Journal of Economic Perspectives*, **18**(3), pp. 71–90.

IMD, 2010, *IMD World Competitiveness Yearbook 2010* (Switzerland: IMD).

Lane, J. E., 2010a, Joint ventures in cross-border higher education: International branch campuses in Malaysia, in: D. W. Chapman and R. Sakamoto (Eds) *Cross Border Partnerships in Higher Education: Strategies and Issues* (New York: Routledge), pp. 67–92.

Lane, J. E., 2010b, *Higher Education, Free Zones, and Quality Assurance in Dubai*. Policy Paper. Dubai School of Government.

Lane, J. E. and Kinser, K., 2008, The private nature of cross-border higher education. *International Higher Education*, (53), p. 11.

Lane, J. E. and Kinser, K., 2011, Reconsidering Privatization: The Sometime Public Nature of Private Activity. *Higher Education Policy*, **24**(2), 255–273.

Lane, J. E. and Kinser, K., (Eds), forthcoming, *The Multi National University: Leadership, Administration, and Governance of International Branch Campuses*, New Directions for Higher Education. (San Francisco: Jossey-Bass).

Lee, M. N. N., 2001, Private higher education in Malaysia: Expansion, diversification and consolidation. Paper presented at the *Second Regional Seminar on PHE: Its Role in Human Resource Development in a Globalised Knowledge Society*, organized by UNESCO PROAP and SEAMEO RIHED, 20–22 June, Bangkok, Thailand.

Levy, D. A., 1986, *Higher Education and the State in Latin America: Private Challenges to Public Dominance* (Chicago: The University of Chicago Press).

Levy, D. A., 2005, *To Export Progress: The Golden Age of University Assistance in the Americas* (Bloomington, IN: Indiana University Press).

Levy, D. A., 2006, The unanticipated explosion: Private higher education's global surge. *Comparative Education Review*, **50**(2), pp. 217–240.

Levy, D. A., 2008, The enlarged expanse of higher education. *Die Hochschule*, **2**, pp. 19–35.

Levy, D. C., 2011, Public Policy for Private Higher Education: A Global Analysis. *Journal of Comparative Policy Analysis: Research and Practice*, **13**(4).

Lewin, T., 2009, George Mason University, among first with an Emirates branch, is pulling out. *New York Times*, 1 March. Available at http://www.nytimes.com/2009/03/01/education/01campus.html (accessed 2 March 2009).

Mahroum, S., 2002, Europe and the migration of highly skilled labor. *International Migration*, **39**(5), pp. 27–43.

Malaysia Economic Planning Unit, 2002, *Knowledge Based Economy Master Plan* (Kuala Lumpur: Author). Available at http://www.epu.gov.my/knowledgebased (accessed 11 May 2010).

Maldonado-Maldonado, A., Cao, Y., Altbach, P., Levy, D. A. and Zhu, H., 2004, *Private Higher Education: An International Bibliography* (Boston: Center for International Higher Education).

Martin, M., 2007, *Cross-Border Higher Education: Regulation, Quality Assurance and Impact*, Vols. 1 & 2 (Paris: IIEP).

Mazzarol, T. W., Soutar, G. N., and Seng, M. S. Y., 2003, The third wave: Future trends in international education. *The International Journal of Education Management*, **17**(3), pp. 90–99.

McBurnie, G. and Zyguris, C., 2007, *Transnational Education: Issues and Trends in Offshore Higher Education* (London: Routledge).

Middlehurst, R. and Woodfield, M. S., 2004, The role of transnational, private, and for-profit provision in meeting global demand for tertiary education: Mapping, regulation and impact. Case study Malaysia. Summary report. Report commissioned by the Commonwealth of Learning and UNESCO.

Morshidi, S., 2005, Transnational higher education in Malaysia: Balancing benefits and concerns through regulations. National Higher Education Research Institute (Malaysia) working paper. Available at http://www.usm.my/ipptn/fileup/TNHE_Malaysia.pdf (accessed 15 September 2008).

Morshidi, S., 2008, The impact of September 11 on international student flow intro Malaysia: Lessons learned. *International Journal of Asian-Pacific Studies*, **4**(1), pp. 79–95.

Muysken, J. and Nour, S., 2006, Deficiencies in education and poor prospects for economic growth in Gulf countries: the case of the UAE. *Journal of Development Studies*, **42**(6), pp. 957–980.

OECD., 2010, Education at a Glance 2010: OECD Indicators (Paris: OECD).

Pachuashvili, P., 2011, Governmental Policies and Their Impact on Private Higher Education Development in Post-Communist Countries: Hungary, Latvia, Lithuania and Georgia, 1990–2005. *Journal of Comparative Policy Analysis: Research and Practice*, **13**(4).

PROPHE, 2009, National data on private higher education: Malaysia. Available at http://www.albany.edu/dept/eaps/prophe/data/national.html (accessed 14 March 2009).

Sheik-Miller, J., 2007, Oil share dips in Dubai GDP, AMEINFO, 9 June. Available at http://www.ameinfo.com/122863.html (accessed 25 June 2008).

Verbik, L. and Jokivirta, L., 2005a, *National Regulatory Frameworks for Transnational Higher Education: Models and Trends, Part 1*, Observatory on Borderless Higher Education. Available at http://www.obhe.ac.uk/documents/view_details?id=42 (accessed 2 October 2006).

Verbik, L. and Jokivirta, L., 2005b, *National Regulatory Frameworks for Transnational Higher Education: Models and Trends, Part 2*, Observatory on Borderless Higher Education. Available at http://www.obhe.ac.uk/documents/view_details?id=43 (accessed 2 October 2006).

Verbik, L, and Lasanowski, V., 2007, International student mobility: Patterns and trends. *The Observatory on Borderless Higher Education*, UK (September).

Verbik, L. and Merkley, C., 2006, *The International Branch Campus – Models and Trends* (London: Observatory for Higher Education).

Wilkins, S., 2001, Human resource development through vocational education in the United Arab Emirates: The case of Dubai Polytechnic. *Journal of Vocational Education & Training*, **54**(1), pp. 5–26.

Zachariah, K. C., Prakash, B. A. and Rajan, S. I., 2003, The impact of immigration policy on Indian contract migrants: The case of the United Arab Emirates. *International Migration*, **41**(4), pp. 161–172.

Ziguras, C., 2003, The impact of the GATS on transnational tertiary education: Comparing experiences of New Zealand, Australia, Singapore and Malaysia. *The Australian Educational Researcher*, **30**(3), pp. 89–109.

Introduction

Private Higher Education and Public Policy: A Global View

DANIEL C. LEVY and WILLIAM ZUMETA

Higher Education as a Privatizing Policy Arena

Although privatization is a powerful and multi-faceted global phenomenon in many policy fields, few have matched higher education for the scope and drama of privatization. As in some other fields, privatization in higher education occurs in two forms: one is increased privateness within the public sector and the other is growth of private sectors. It is the latter that this special issue treats.

Also, as often seen in other policy fields, higher education's privatization has been evident since roughly the last quarter of the twentieth century. In many cases, from banking to prisons to healthcare, this privatization has followed a long period of "publicization", a growth in the scope of the public sector, with increased state financing and control. The recent public to private reversal is particularly striking in fields like higher education where the belief was once dominant in much of the world that the subject matter in question was a natural public responsibility and that more than minimal private action was illegitimate; indeed that view remains wider and stronger than one might expect from the evident dimensions of higher education's privatization.

A half-century ago, and counting by legal designation, most of the world had small private sectors of higher education or none at all. The United States was the huge exception, indeed about half private in enrollment at the end of World War II, falling to below a quarter in ensuing decades, amid public growth, including that of community colleges. Today the United States is below the global average of 31.3 per cent private, though it still has the largest absolute private enrollment.[1] Asia, at 36.4 per cent private, has by far the largest raw private enrollment among the continents. This includes several countries with large majority private enrollment (Japan, Korea, Taiwan, Indonesia, and the Philippines), and Chinese private growth already makes its 20 per cent private share an enrollment giant, sure to boost the private global share still higher in the near future. But it is Latin America that has the highest private proportional share, 48.6 per cent. The private sector of higher education in both Latin America and Asia has historical roots – by 1965, 17 of 20 Latin American countries had some private higher education – but especially in Asia the absolute enrollment has exploded in recent decades.

Europe's 16.0 per cent private share is mostly the product of the post-communist private surge in the east and central part of the continent. Western Europe (outside Portugal) and developed countries of the British Commonwealth remain low in private share, even as they vigorously privatize within public institutions. But there is notable interest and private emergence in countries such as Germany and the UK. Newly independent Africa's emerging universities were almost all public. Today, almost all African countries have some private higher education, particularly in Anglophone Africa, and expectations are for further proportional growth. Other than Israel and a few "American" universities in a handful of countries, the Middle East and North Africa were without private higher education until the 1990s. Now almost every country in the region has launched private sectors, usually at the behest of government and often internationally linked.

The tremendous cross-regional coverage and growing size of private higher education, together with the variation in the extent and timing of its surge, underscores that public policy for private higher education is a matter of global importance. Indeed, public policies (or lack thereof) have played a key role in the emergence, growth, and nature of private higher education sectors. In many cases outside the United States, especially in recent decades, private enrollment growth has been mostly a response to *de facto* policies *not* to meet through public sector expansion social and economic demands for more higher education that are in turn driven by increased population and secondary school graduation and the perceived demands of contemporary economies. But, as private provision emerges and grows and touches more of the population and the interests of employers, as well as those of public higher education, governments are impelled to act. Regulations and other policy tools become more actively utilized. Although Levy has called this pattern *delayed regulation*, articles in this issue show that regulation is not the only policy tool employed.

Analysis of Public Policy and Private Higher Education

As in other areas of social policy – such as health care, social services, and primary and secondary education in many countries – higher education is a domain where, increasingly, government is readjusting its balance of control, supervision, steering, and apartness in regard to both public and private providers. This readjustment leads to dilemmas for policymakers, who may (or may not) seek to be evenhanded between the sectors, and to potentially tense and complex political dynamics as the sectors vie for influence over the policies that affect them. Public higher education interests may seek to ensure that competition from the private sector is restricted by pushing for strict controls over licensure or accreditation in the name of quality assurance. Private sector interests – although there are often variations in views among the various types and statuses of these institutions – tend to favor more "regulation by the market" and to argue that their students at least should have access to some state subsidies for higher education (e.g. grants, loans) because their enrollments reduce the burden on the state sector. Public institutions will in turn point to abuses by some lightly regulated private providers and will usually try to defend their monopoly of state subsidies. We see these dynamics illustrated in the higher education policy arena by the articles in this issue.

These articles also illustrate, to a greater or lesser degree, the use of various *policy tools* in governments' role in private higher education, and, by extension of tool impacts, of their entire higher education sectors. In the early stages of development of private higher education sectors, government policies may simply ignore them (the *laissez-faire* policy posture Zumeta refers to in this volume). Once they start formulating policies for private higher education, governments naturally turn first to basic legal authorization policies for private institutions (see Bernasconi, this volume), which in turn implies some standards for their operation, whether enforced strictly or not, and sometimes a categorization of types of institutions (as by level and scope of mission, size, etc.). Closely related then are often quality assurance policies, for a basic function of government is to protect consumers (here students) who suffer from what policy scientists call *information asymmetries* relative to providers with respect to knowledge about the quality and value of the services for which they are paying. Lane's contribution herein shows that this quality assurance function may be delegated to non-governmental bodies outside the country as when a developing country imports accredited higher education from abroad in the form of authorized branch campuses.

If private higher education output is thought to be important to a country's development strategy – or simply to access and equity considerations – the question may arise as to whether the state should subsidize the sector. As shown in this volume, direct subsidization of private institutions remains rare but indirect aid, as in student loans, is rising in practice and certainly in policy debate. Such subsidies may encourage enrollments at costs to the state well below those of supporting public sector expansion and can provide policymakers with leverage on quality, fields of emphasis, etc., within the private sector while also providing some competitive incentive to the publics. Policymakers increasingly see private higher education providers as part of their overall system of higher education and have at least some inclination to think about complementarity with the public system.

Scope and Content of the Special Issue

The special issue treats "higher education" inclusively as formal education beyond the secondary level. Thus, for example, it considers Chile's extensive private post-secondary training centers. Indeed the private sector generally has a proportionally greater presence in non-university than university institutions. Additionally, the treatment of "private" includes both nonprofit and for-profit. Many private higher education institutions are fundamentally for-profit under the cloak of nonprofit but even the subsector labeled for-profit is growing, as shown herein for the United States and cross-border cases. Brazil's 19 per cent for-profit/total higher education enrollment ratio probably gives it the world's largest for-profit sector in absolute terms after the United States.

The issue gives ample attention to the growth of private higher education and thus the shifting private–public balance. The policy focus is on public policy for private higher education, though this focus perforce carries the authors to considerations of public policy for public higher education.

In the first article Levy gives a global overview of private higher education and public policy. After first showing that the emergence and at least early growth of the private sector usually occurs outside of any government plan, Levy examines public policy towards each major sub-type of private institution. Setting the stage for much of what follows in this volume, his analysis highlights government funding and regulation. It identifies the key policy arguments for and against more funding and regulation by each of the sub-types. Despite inter-sectoral blurring, promoted in part by government involvement in the private sector, outside the US inter-sectoral distinctiveness is usually strong. At the same time, global trends show marked signs of pluralism and Americanization.

While Bernasconi's ensuing article highlights the policy and legal framework in Chile's remarkably market-oriented higher education system, it in fact provides comparative coverage within the Latin American context, focusing on the contrasting legal bases of private and public universities across seven countries (Argentina, Bolivia, Brazil, Chile, Costa Rica, Mexico, and Uruguay), and the implications for their ongoing treatment by governments. The analysis follows an institutionalist perspective, seeing the law as a source of coercive isomorphism as it concludes that the law assigns the same comprehensive mission and has similar expectations of both private and public sectors regardless of the degree of development of the private. Yet, the law permits greater autonomy for public institutions and provides separate oversight systems even where all of higher education is governed by the same law.

Intraregional policy variation across countries is then a major theme in Marie Pachuashvili's analysis of four post-communist European countries: Hungary, Georgia, Latvia, and Lithuania. She finds considerable similarities in these countries' tax and funding policies with regard to private higher education yet substantial variation in other policies, driven largely by ethnic–religious differences and interest group influences, including those of public universities. These policy differences are associated with marked differences in private sector paths of development and enrollment.

Drawing on her PhD dissertation, the most scholarly book-length treatment of private higher education in any single country, Prachayani Praphamontripong treats the Thai case within the East Asian context. She finds that private and public higher education institutions are fundamentally under different statutory frameworks and regulations yet are under the same important government policies regarding student loans and quality assurance. Compared to private counterparts, public universities have more institutional autonomy and tend to receive preferential treatment from the government. The private sector's demand-absorbing institutions are the most vulnerable to government policies because of their own limited capacity and resources.

Jason Lane's article then carries us into previously uncharted territory in the fast-expanding cross-country networks whereby some less developed countries seek to expand higher education rapidly within their borders by reaching beyond them to import sometimes "name brand" providers from the leading countries. His paper highlights and compares the strategies of Dubai and Malaysia along these lines. Lane concludes that these two nations wish to signal to the world that they are modernizing their economies and seeking to become regional education hubs, in addition to augmenting their capacity to educate domestic students. Lane calls next for finer grained studies of the implementation dynamics of the specific policies established to achieve these goals.

Finally, Zumeta addresses the US case, where much of nonprofit private higher education has been the envy of the world but, recently, the little studied for-profit sector has been the major growth engine. In the United States, states are the primary locus of higher education policy so Zumeta examines policy variation across the 50 American states, with an eye to implications of his approach for international comparisons. He develops a taxonomy of state higher education policy *postures* composed of approaches to the use of specific policy tools such as student aid policies, direct support of private institutions (including contracting), public sector tuition pricing, information and accountability policies, and others. The postures are shown to have a plausible association with several dimensions of policy outcomes. While the empirical analysis focuses on the nonprofit sector, he suggests implications for needed studies of the booming US private, for-profit sector.

Thus, the articles in this issue bring the important arena of private higher education further into the field of comparative policy studies. Even as scholarship on public policy for higher education grew, comparative work remained rare and the higher education treated was overwhelmingly public higher education. This special issue's pieces, each largely analyzing government policy, take us beyond such restrictiveness. The articles all deal with public policy comparatively, in a variety of geographic ways (global analysis, national case or cases in regional context, cross-national, and cross-state); four continents are strongly encompassed. All the articles also show how patterns of public policy, often by inaction, increasingly by explicit action, shape not just public but private higher education. Higher education clearly emerges as a policy field in which comparative study needs to take account of inter-sectoral dimensions.

Note

1. http://www.albany.edu/dept/eaps/prophe/data/international.html

Policy Analysis and Europeanization: An Analysis of EU Migrant Integration Policymaking

ANDREW GEDDES & PETER SCHOLTEN

ABSTRACT *This article analyses EU-level research–policy infrastructures and their role in the Europeanization of migrant integration policies at a time of perceived crisis and policy failure. Rather than focusing on either knowledge utilization or knowledge production, it focuses on what we call "knowledge infrastructures" or different ways of mobilizing research with specific purposes of knowledge utilization. Rather than finding one dominant configuration of research–policy relations, various infrastructures that co-exist and sometimes even overlap were found. Besides EU-sponsored infrastructures aimed primarily at horizontal exchange of knowledge and information between countries and between cities, there were also infrastructures that were more directly related to EU policy goals as well as an infrastructure that mobilized research as an informal tool to monitor policy compliance. This shows that the use of research in Europeanization does not always mean "going technical", but that precisely when the EU lacks formal competencies such as in the area of migrant integration policies, mobilizing specific types of research can form part of a political strategy designed to reinforce policy objectives.*

Introduction

This article analyses the role of an EU-level "research–policy infrastructure" and its contribution to the Europeanization of migrant integration policies. Whereas immigration policies have developed a strong EU component, the EU's involvement in the domain of migrant integration has remained relatively weak. Migrant integration policies have been dominated by a focus on "national models" in which "the mode of presenting problems and questions are politically constituted by the nation states for which migration becomes a problem or challenge" (Thranhardt and Bommes 2012, p. 202). In many European countries there has been a backlash against multicultural policies that have been denounced as a "failure", contributing to both a perception of crisis and to a revalorization of the content of "national models" in the form of, for example, language requirements and citizenship tests.

There are, however, very specific developments at the EU level that change these dynamics by introducing vertical as well as horizontal connections between the EU and nation states in the domain of migrant integration (Geddes 2005; Faist and Ette 2007; Goeman 2013). EU laws impinge directly on member states, but in areas of "high politics" that are more closely related to state sovereignty, such as migrant integration, the EU also uses "softer", non-binding governance modes. This includes forms of coordination within which policy-oriented research can play a key role. The development of institutional relations between research and policy appears to be a key element of this "soft governance" strategy. The European Commission in particular has mobilized significant funding through programmes such as the European Integration Fund and the European Refugee Fund to mobilize (mostly comparative) research in this area. Furthermore, an elaborate infrastructure of "boundary organizations" has emerged contributing to research–policy dialogues on the EU level. This includes a variety of organizations including think tanks such as the Migration Policy Group (MPG) and the Migration Policy Institute Europe (MPI), international organizations such as the International Organization for Migration (IOM) and the International Centre for Migration Policy Development (ICMPD), and state-led information gathering networks such as the European Migration Network (EMN).

To analyse the role of policy-oriented research in the Europeanization of migrant integration policies, we assess three hypotheses on the rationale for and role of policy-oriented research. These are grounded in the literatures on Europeanization and policy-oriented research. The first hypothesis draws from rationalist accounts of evidence-based policymaking to identify policy-oriented research as likely to occur in areas that are relatively technical and depoliticized. For highly politicized issues such as migrant integration this would seriously limit the role and impact of research because "intractable" policy controversies cannot be resolved by appeals to "the facts". The second hypothesis, based on a more critical and constructivist ontology, focuses on the role that research can play in the Europeanization of contested and politicized policy issues and the resultant emergence of a "politics of expertise". Research can feed conflicts and struggles over competencies and contestation between rival problem frames. A third hypothesis, with a more institutionalist background, points to a less instrumental or strategic way of mobilizing and utilizing research, arguing that European research will be mobilized with the purpose of legitimizing the policy role of EU institutions or substantiating EU policy competences for issues such as migrant integration that become defined as "problems of Europe". The analysis is based on 13 interviews with key informants in a range of organizations and institutions such as EU institutions and think tanks at EU level with responsibility for or involvement in these issues. These interviews were combined with desk research, including the analysis of policy and research documents (focusing on instruments and measures that have been developed at EU level in relation to migrant integration) as well as a review of the secondary literature. In addition, both authors have extensive experience of the European research networks and boundary organizations, such as think tanks, that are analysed in this paper. Both authors are also actors in the processes that they analyse.

Rather than focusing on either knowledge utilization or knowledge production, as other contributions in this special issue, our focus will be on what we call "knowledge infrastructures" (Hoppe 2011; Scholten 2011). Knowledge infrastructures involve a plethora of formal and informal connections linking research and policymaking. These infrastructures connect or "broker" knowledge from the research community to policy communities, leading to specific types of knowledge utilization. They also affect patterns of knowledge production within the research community. As such, they are ways of mobilizing knowledge production with the purpose of knowledge utilization. Our focus is on the research–policy infrastructure at EU level. We show this to involve EU institutions, particularly the Commission, European Council and European Parliament, boundary organizations such as think tanks that link research and policy, and academic researchers seeking funding and recognition for their work. It is also important to note that these EU institutions are not monoliths. Our analysis focuses on particular units within the Commission. In particular, we look at what was DG Justice and Home Affairs, which since 2009 has been split into two DGs with one dealing with Home Affairs and the other with Justice. DG Home Affairs has kept the migrant integration portfolio. In the remainder of this text, we disaggregate these EU institutions to exemplify our arguments. We also show that the research–policy infrastructure has a strong applied element, i.e. applied not only in the sense of having policy relevance, but also because of its focus on "problems of Europe". This involves attempts to frame migrant integration as a European issue requiring a stronger EU-level response.

Policy Research and Europeanization

This article focuses on the role of policy-oriented research in the Europeanization of migrant integration policies, as an example of what can be characterized as an "intractable policy controversy" (Rein and Schon 1994). We define "migrant integration" as referring to a range of policies and actions involving a wide variety of actors across levels of governance (sub-national, national and international) that focus on forms of adaptation (socially, culturally, politically, economically) by both migrants and host societies. Issues that are raised include thorny questions about the boundaries of national citizenship and also the scope for the accommodation of cultural diversity within multicultural societies.

Following the literature on the co-production of science and policymaking (Gieryn 1999; Jasanoff 2004; Scholten 2009), we do not consider knowledge production and utilization as separate processes. Although they may be analytically distinguishable, focusing on the infrastructures at the "boundaries" of research and policy reveals the entwined and iterative nature of processes of knowledge production and utilization. This means that the relation between knowledge production and utilization is far from linear, as the context in which knowledge is utilized also has an impact on the type of knowledge that is produced.

Our hypotheses focus on how research–policy infrastructures connect processes of knowledge production and knowledge utilization in specific ways. Research–policy infrastructures can involve formalized as well as informal structures that pass on expertise in the form of policy-oriented research to be used by policymakers (as so-called knowledge brokers), but can also play a role in the selection, mobilization or production of specific forms of expertise. Some scholars have described such infrastructures as "boundary configurations" (Hoppe 2011, Scholten 2011), or structural ways of demarcating research and policy as well as coordinating modes of exchange between research and policy. Such research–policy infrastructures can involve organizations or networks that operate on the boundaries of research and policy. This can involve advisory bodies or organizational networks designed to exchange knowledge and expertise, as well as more funding-oriented agencies involved in programming and coordinating research programmes. Such "boundary institutions" (Guston 2000) may not only coordinate the modes of exchange between research and policy, but they may also negotiate the boundaries between knowledge and expertise defined as relevant and its subsequent use.

When analysing Europeanization, it is important to distinguish between two very different conceptions of the role that the EU can play in specific policy areas. Though often confused under the term of "Europeanization" (Radaelli 2002), a distinction can be made between "horizontal" convergence between European countries and "vertical" processes of Europeanization that relate to the EU's role. The EU can be a *vertical point of convergence* through processes of Europeanization, i.e. when EU law induces change in member states' policies. It can also serve as a point of *horizontal convergence* by creating a new forum within which immigrant integration is discussed and understandings of policy develop. As an interview in a think tank put it:

> [W]e have many opportunities to meet with and talk with colleagues in the [EU] institutions. This isn't policy-making. I'm not sure what the right word for it would be, but we are there, we are present, we can contribute to the debate about policy. This is perhaps a "softer" side of things, but I think this side matter too, very much. (Interview, think tank employee, Brussels, December 2013)

This distinction between "softer" and "harder" governance is also highly relevant given that the EU does not possess formal competence in these areas. Both knowledge exchange and knowledge production are central components of this role.

Convergence and Europeanization are not the same thing. Convergence can refer to a more general process of policies becoming more alike. Europeanization attributes causal significance to European integration. The resultant analytical challenge is that policies within the EU might become more alike, but that the EU alone may not be the sole driver of convergence. For example, it is possible that EU states may adopt similar policies or approaches to immigrant integration to those adopted by non-EU states such as Australia, Canada or the USA. It would be hard to ascribe such a change to the effects of Europeanization. This suggests more general processes at play, which can be understood as indicative of diffusion (Börzel and Risse 2012). It has been shown that diffusion could have a more coercive aspect (linked for example to EU accession and the requirements of membership). Coercion would accord with an instrumental logic of institutional behaviour. In contract, social and communicative logics may be more evident as a result of the kinds of interaction that we analyse in this paper. This does not necessarily induce institutional isomorphism as the literature on Europeanization tends to emphasize "adaptation with national colours", but does suggest a breaking down of the barrier between the domestic and the international that has also been seen as a form of transgovernmentalism (Slaughter 2004).

Europeanization by "Going Technical"

The first hypothesis that this article explores is grounded in a rationalist perspective on policy analysis which claims that research–policy infrastructures play a direct role in the formulation of EU policies, particularly in depoliticized contexts. Schmidt (2005) argues that in some policy areas, the transfer of competencies to EU level has denuded national debate of content with the effect of creating "politics without policy" as a feature of domestic politics in member states. The counterpoint to this at EU level was a shift of substantive competencies but without a concomitant shift in the focus of debate to EU level, which is still plagued by a "democratic deficit". This leads to what Schmidt calls "policy without politics" as a feature of the EU system. This creates a conundrum for analyses of the EU and once which, in the past, could be resolved by making a distinction between low and high politics. By this is meant that some policy areas can be understood as being more technical in nature and predisposed to particular forms of regulatory politics that do not impinge too directly on the core content of democratic politics and rarely excite public debate. In such areas, there is more likely to be the deployment of technical expertise, such as scientific or academic research. The European Commission has been seen as particularly reliant on the deployment of outside expertise such as from academic researchers with the accusation that this led to technocratic rule (Schmidt 2005).

Scholars such as Radaelli (1999) and Majone (1989) have shown that EU institutions often derive their legitimacy for policy intervention from expertise. In fact, governance by technocratic consensus (Radaelli 1999, p. 5) has been seen as a legacy of the EU's origins with technocracy sustaining a functionalist approach to Europeanization that prevented politicization in the national arena. The Commission is interesting in the context of research-policy relations because the deployment of expertise has served to legitimate its role in the EU system. Across a wide range of policy areas, the Commission has co-opted experts into policy development processes. One reason that this has occurred is that many issues dealt with by the EU are of a technical nature and require specialist expertise. "Going technical" can, of course, also be a way of depoliticizing an issue. As Radaelli (1999, p. 1) has put it:

> At stake is the allegation of being a political system ruled by technocrats who ignore the basic thrust of democracy. Whilst democracy is based on legitimate consensus, free elections and participation, technocracy recognizes expertise as the sole basis of authority and power.

One reason for this advanced by Majone (1997, 2002) is that the EU is essentially a "regulatory state" devoted to the correction of market failure. This gives rise to technical tasks that in the member states would tend to be managed by regulatory agencies rather than be the subject of legislative scrutiny.

This view of the role played by expertise in "going technical" speaks particularly well to the rationalist perspective in policy analysis that stresses the cognitive function of expertise in policy processes by providing objective information and causal theories on problem developments as well as inputs into rational problem-solving strategies. From this perspective, policy scientists have conceptualized the role of policy-oriented research as "speaking truth to power" (Wildavsky 1979) that can lead to "knowledge creep" (Weiss 1977) whereby policymakers take knowledge and expertise as the foundation for policy choices. In recent literature, this rational perspective has been rephrased as "evidence-based policymaking".

Europeanization and the Politics of Expertise

In contrast to the instrumental role of knowledge specified above and its link to rationalist ontologies, we now focus on a more constructivist ontology of the role that expertise and knowledge can play in more politicized settings. As the EU moves into areas of "high politics" that impinge much more directly on national sovereignty then "expertise" may no longer be a sufficient basis for political action. One reason for this is that expert knowledge about social and political processes such as migrant integration cannot be value-free. Research in the late 1990s into the views of senior Commission officials suggests that these officials are themselves aware of the changed environment in which they operate and that the era of "benevolent technocracy in the tradition of Jean Monnet has come to a close" (Hooghe 2003). As such, a second hypothesis can be formulated which states that research–policy infrastructures play a symbolic rather than instrumental role as a form of political ammunition in the interplay between the EU and member states.

In more contested and politicized settings, scholars have identified processes of knowledge utilization that are of a more symbolic nature (Hilgartner 2000; Boswell 2008; Scholten and Timmermans 2010). Boswell distinguishes between a substantiating role of expertise where research supports decisions that have already been made and a legitimizing role where expertise helps boost the legitimacy of involved actors. Furthermore, Sabatier (1987) and Hall (1993) have shown that research will rarely have an instrumental role at the fundamental level of policy paradigms or "deep core policy beliefs". Fundamental premises about how policy problems are defined and interpreted appear more or less resistant to knowledge and information (Rein and Schön 1994). At this level, research utilization can be expected to be symbolic in order, for instance, to substantiate or legitimize specific policy discourses.

However, there is more to the role of expertise in policymaking than knowledge utilization. Patterns of knowledge utilization cannot be accounted for without looking at knowledge production as well. Just as there has been a process of "scientification" of policymaking in many areas, equally has there been a politicization of science (Beck 1992; Weingart 1999). Sociologists of science have shown that the knowledge claims that emerge (or are ignored or suppressed) should also be seen as a contextualized process. Policymakers often select and support specific knowledge claims, but researchers also tend to negotiate boundaries with policy to determine what knowledge claims are the best fit in specific settings (Jasanoff 1994; Gieryn 1999; Hoppe 2005).

The context in which knowledge is produced may promote different sorts of research. A differentiation can be made between research that provides information in the form of data or facts, and more conceptual types of research. Even for quantitative data, the choice for variables to measure and indicators to use is contextualized (Porter 1996). Similarly, Haas (2004) and Hajer (1995) have shown that conceptual research can form part of broader epistemic communities or discourse coalitions that compete for policy attention. Accepting that researchers can be part of specific discourse coalitions challenges the rationalist assumption that there is a clear boundary between research and policy. This means studying both knowledge production and utilization is order to understand whether the latter was instrumental or symbolic; otherwise there is no way of knowing where knowledge claims originated.

Fischer speaks in this respect of a politics of expertise, where the production of specific knowledge claims should also be seen in the broader political context (Fischer 1990). For instance, when focusing on the role of think thanks in US politics, Fischer shows how the provision of expertise itself is politicized and how research is not just used but also produced as forms of political ammunition. As such, knowledge claims lend authority to policy and political claims. Similarly, Scholten and Timmermans (2010) have shown that research does not always help to keep issues off the political agenda, but under specific circumstances can also put issues on the political agenda. This occurs in particular in settings where an authoritative venue like science or expertise can lend credibility to new policy ideas, or when there is simply a lack of alternative venues for agenda setting.

The Reconstitution of the Policy Field

Thus far we have distinguished between roles for expertise in the policy process that fulfil an instrumental role or, alternatively, play a role in strategic policy coordination. We now focus on the ways in which European integration has served to reconstitute the context within which expertise is deployed. While our focus is on migrant integration, the analysis can also connect with other trans-boundary issues where EU competencies have developed and where there have been analogous developments of research policy infrastructures. Of particular importance are two aspects of the EU's development as a political system. The first of these is the reconstitution of research through the creation of new funding opportunities at EU level. The EU now provides extensive funding for scientific research. This can take various forms, such as the funding for research from the EU's R&D DG for what has been known as "Framework" funding, Framework 7 being the most recent iteration. Within this has been funding for research in the Social Sciences and Humanities. The content of the calls for this funding will be influenced by EU policy priorities. In addition, the EU also makes more specific research funding available linked to the policy roles of its Directorate-Generals. A second key component of the reconstitution of the European field is the emergence of EU-level "boundary organizations" such as think tanks that mediate the relationship between scientific expertise (e.g. in academic institutions) and EU-level institutions. The development of such boundary organizations can be an indication of the institutionalization of research–policy relations at the European level and contribute to the construction of a European research and policy field beyond the national level. However, this contribution to "vertical Europeanization" of EU-level boundary organizations should not be assumed; it might equally be the case that these organizations are primarily instrumental in comparing national or local cases rather than sustaining an EU-level policy agenda.

Thus, a third hypothesis that we will explore emphasizes the role of policy research in substantiating and legitimizing a EU social and political field associated with migrant integration. The effect is to change the focus for the deployment of expertise towards what can be called "problems of Europe". The effect of funding and the specific requirements of the bidding process are to demonstrate the "added value" at the European level of research. A successful bid for funding must orient itself to problems of Europe and to the analysis of results in the context of European integration.

The remainder of the article is organized into two substantive sections. First, the following section provides empirical background on EU action in the area of migrant integration. This is followed by a section that explores our three hypotheses in relation to the development of a EU research–policy infrastructure in the area of migrant integration. We conclude by assessing the role of research–policy infrastructures in migrant integration policies, in Europeanization more generally, and speak to the broader literature on comparative policy analysis. The article is based on an in-depth qualitative analysis of the role of EU research–policy infrastructures in the area of migrant integration. As the European Commission is the key actor in the development of this policy domain, we have focused primarily on research–policy infrastructures around the Commission.

The Europeanization of Migrant Integration Policies

Between Europeanization and National Primacy

Formal EU competence for aspects of migration policy was established when the Amsterdam Treaty entered into force in 1999. This did not include specific competencies in the area of integration policy. In fact, the Lisbon Treaty (ratified in 2009) placed limitations on the EU's role. This does not mean that there is no EU action. There are both "harder" (legally binding) and "softer" (non-legally binding) forms of EU action on migrant integration. For example, two directives (agreed in 2000) take action against discrimination on grounds of racial and ethnic origin. There are also "integration measures" in the directives on family reunion and on the rights of long-term residents agreed in June and November 2003, respectively.

The Europeanization of migrant integration policies has been a hesitant process (see also Goeman 2013), with EU competencies much more limited than in the area of migration regulation. According to various scholars, the reluctance of member states to cede competencies to the EU level is related to the pertinence of historically rooted and nationally situated "models of integration", such as the French republican model (Bowen 2007), the British race relations model (Hansen 2000) or, for many years, the Dutch multicultural model (Entzinger 2003; Scholten 2011). These national "paradigms" were seen as closely bound to nation states,

> not just because of their context dependency and insufficient clarifications on the conditions of generalizability, they are national because the modes of presenting and questions are political constituted by the nation states for which migration becomes a problem or a challenge. (Thränhardt and Bommes 2010, p. 10)

The 2000s saw the first steps towards EU action on migrant integration. The conclusions of the meeting of the European Council held at Tampere, Finland in October 1999 outlined a policy plan for the period until 2004 dealing with key aspects of migration policies including both the internal ("fair treatment of third country nationals") and external dimensions ("root causes" approaches) of policy. Between 1999 and 2004, several directives were adopted that codified EU competencies in the area of migration regulation and had impacts on national migrant integration policies. Of particular importance are the Racial Equality Directive adopted in 2000 (2000/43/EC), the Employment Equality Directive (2000/78/EC), the family reunification directive (2003/86/EC) and the directive on the rights of long-term resident third-country nationals in 2003 (2003/109/EC). A distinction can be made between the two directives on anti-discrimination agreed in 2000 and the two directives agreed in 2003. The anti-discrimination directives drew from an equal treatment frame that was closely associated with development of the single market. In this sense, discrimination was presented as an impediment to attainment of the EU's core economic objectives. In contrast, the "integration" measures within the 2003 directives on family reunion and the rights of long-term residents contained "integration measures" that were closely linked to concerns in member states about the "failure" of migrant integration policies. The remedy that was being developed at national level – and was then reflected at EU level – was on a rebalancing of rights and responsibilities and a move away from multicultural policies. In particular, this was reflective of developments in Austria, Germany and the Netherlands, with all three of these countries active in the negotiation of the directive (and movement away from the more progressive ideas initially developed by the Commission in its proposals) (Geddes 2008).

Since 1999 there have also been efforts, especially by the European Commission, to become more involved in this policy area (Geddes 2005). This includes, in contrast to the "harder" legal mechanisms of directives a range of soft governance mechanisms (coordination, benchmarking, knowledge exchange, standards-setting) where the EU has developed itself as an arena within which ideas about immigrant integration can be shared and transmitted. These ideas will come from national, sub-national and local governments within member states, from EU institutions such as the Commission and European Parliament, as well as from think tanks, NGOs and academic researchers. This reflects a focus of the EU on promoting horizontal (coordination of networks) rather than vertical (EU legal competencies) convergence. The adoption by EU leaders of the Common Basic Principles on Integration (CBP) in 2004, under the Dutch EU presidency, signalled a new phase in attempts to Europeanize migrant integration. As Goeman (2012, p. 322) notes, academic experts played a key role in the development of the CBP under Greece's EU presidency in 2003, as a precursor to formal agreement by the member states on the CBP under the Dutch EU presidency at a meeting in Groningen in 2004. In 2003, a Washington-based think tank, the Migration Policy Institute, brought together a group of migration experts from various countries in the so-called "Athens Migration Policy Initiative" (AMPI). In fact, much of the drafting of what would become the CBP was delegated to the MPI think tank and to Dutch migration specialists. The broader international focus of the CBP, which involved developments during previous presidencies, such as that of the Greek government, also explains why not all the CBP reflected the Dutch government's policy preferences. The CBP played an important role in future development, including their adoption into the European Common Agenda for Integration in 2005. This can be seen as a defining moment when researchers helped to substantiate a "vertical" form of Europeanization, albeit primarily focused on "softer" measures given that this was not an area in which the EU possessed formal competencies. As a participant in the EMN from a member state put it:

> There is a huge amount of research out there. As a ... policy maker and financial practitioner, the difficulty is actually cutting through the research and to find something that is really relevant. But it's helped tremendously to inform the policies. Even if you go back to the Common Basic Principles. A huge amount of research done in the Netherlands that helped to formulate these Common Basic Principles. Even now we're looking at things like integration tests ... the stuff that migrants have to go through ... presentation during meeting from EPC on their research, and dialogue of how we could continue that. (Interview with National Contact Point in EMN, June 2013)

The CBP, although without legal force, provided a basis for a first European framework on migrant integration. They aim to assist member states in formulating integration policies, structure the relations between EU, national, regional and local governments and assist the Council to reflect on its role in supporting national and local level integration policy efforts. Besides very generic principles, such as that "integration is a dynamic and two-sided process" and that "integration means respect for the basic values of the EU", it also includes guidelines and some priority topics. For instance, it stipulates that it is important to "mainstream" integration policy measures into various relevant policy areas rather than in a separate policy area, as well as develop clear policy goals, indicators and evaluation mechanisms to render more effective the exchange of knowledge and information.

At the first Ministerial Integration Conference, held in Groningen in 2004, the CBP were elaborated into a first European Handbook on Integration. In 2005, the European Commission integrated the CBP into a "Common Agenda for Integration" (COM 2005, p. 389), signalling a key moment of interaction between national and EU-level institutions. Implementation of the CBP was embedded within "the Hague Programme" aimed at development of the EU's "area of freedom, security and justice". In 2011, the Commission adopted a renewed "European Agenda for the Integration of Third-Country Nationals". This agenda takes the EU's directive of November 2003 on the rights of long-term residents as the basis for EU action. It calls for more action in the socio-economic sphere of integration in particular ("participation"), as well as more focus on the local level and involvement of countries of origin (COM 2011, 455, p. 4).

EU-Level Research–Policy Infrastructures

Studying the role of policy-oriented research in the constitution of EU migrant integration policies requires analysis of research–policy infrastructures in this policy field. Our analysis suggests three types of research–policy infrastructures, each with different types of knowledge being mobilized as well as with research being utilized in the process of Europeanization in very different ways. We will first discuss each of these three forms separately, and then analyse them in terms of the three hypotheses on the role of research–policy infrastructures in Europeanization.

Infrastructures for Horizontal Knowledge Exchange

A first type of research–policy infrastructure arises primarily from horizontal forms of exchange of knowledge and information between member states and in some cases between cities or regions. Three very specific boundary organizations stand out in this respect. First, European Migration Network (EMN). The Laeken European Council meeting in October 2001 called for a system of information exchange on migration. In 2003 the EMN was launched as a pilot project and then as what is known as a "Preparatory Action" between 2004 and 2006 during which participation was voluntary. The Hague Programme for Justice and Home Affairs covering the period 2005–10 included a plan for a Green Paper on the future of the EMN. In August 2007, on the basis of the Green Paper the Commission proposed to the Council the creation of a legal basis for the EMN, which was agreed by Council Decision 2008/381/EC. The EMN's purposes are: "to meet the information needs of Union institutions and of Member States authorities and institutions on migration and asylum by providing up-to-date, objective, reliable and comparable information on migration and asylum with a view to supporting European policymaking in these areas". The EMN is coordinated by the Commission (DG Home Affairs), which is supported by two private sector contractors that assist with the exchange of information and with the development of the technology to support interchange. The work is supported by EMN NCPs in all member states (except Denmark, but including Norway) with at least three experts, one of whom is the national coordinator. These are mainly from ministries of the interior and justice but also involve research institutes, NGOs and international organizations (the International Organization for Migration is the NCP for three member states). The contact points liaise with a wide range of relevant "stakeholders", including academic researchers and think tanks, in their respective countries. Often, the exchange of knowledge and information has a strongly informal nature (Pratt, unpublished). Essentially, the EMN brings together "national" information on a wide range of migration and integration related issues and then, on the basis of national reports, develops a synthesis report. From more recently, the EMN also hosts a European Web Site on Integration for the European Commission, which further facilitates the exchange of knowledge on integration practices as well as on EU policy measures. In particular, the EMN is oriented at "the information needs of Union institutions and of Member States' authorities and institutions" (EMN website, 16 September 2012). However, originally at least, the horizontal function was dominant, also because of the strong embedding of the EMN in the national policy structures through the National Contact Points.

The EMN looks across a wide range of migration issues, including those related to integration and citizenship. For those close to the network, there is a recognition that it is a basis for exchange and learning.

> There is still a learning and exchange process that comes with that network. There is some kind of network effect to it, it's hard to put the finger on it, it's not a network that produces some groundbreaking new evidence that changes the course of policies, but that rather informs the policymakers and these people largely come from the institutions that also set policy course. (Representative of international organization, March 2013)

As an EMN National Contact Point put it:

> I am an avid reader of the country reports because ... I am interested in what works, so those country reports are extremely useful. There is a kind of hidden output of those. Are you aware of the informal networks? The integration contact points and the responsible authorities for the various funds that we manage have a number of informal networks ... so for example I was in Bratislava back in the spring talking very specifically about the funding issues ... that's a kind of offshoot of some of the work that's being done. You choose the networks you want to join on the basis of country reports ... so this particular network is Slovakia, Slovenia, Czech Republic, Poland, Netherlands, Austria and the UK ... looking at common factors around the funding of projects. You have the background information from the country reports ... so you can find out what are the similarities or what are the contrasts. We also have other informal bilateral relationships which are again informed by the country reports. I talk a lot to my opposite numbers in the Netherlands, in Germany, Italy, France on quite specific issues that come out of those reports ... things that we want to follow up on. (Interview with EMN National Contact Point, June 2013)

One key tool within the EMN is the ad hoc request, whereby a member state can request information from all other EMN participants. Some of these are then published on the EMN website. In total, around 500 such requests have been made since 2008. The importance of the ad hoc request was affirmed by a representative from an international organization:

> [M]y impression ... is that the EMN in particular has become important through its more kind of research gathering, the ad hoc queries. There is an enormous amount of queries that are circulated and that are requested on a state basis ... that really has become an important mechanism of policy learning .... Member States who have an interest to make or change a policy on a particular issue, sometimes on very specific issues ... even if it's just six or seven Member States replying to that, it's still something that you don't have, or something that individual Member States don't have the capacity to deliver in the same way. It's much more difficult for individual Member States to use their own contacts ... to get that kind of information in that timeframe. (Interview with Representative of international organization, March 2013)

Secondly, INTI (Preparatory Actions for the Integration of Third Country Nationals) represented a European funding scheme that served a similar horizontal function and ran from 2003 to 2006. INTI focused in particular on network formation and exchange of information and best practices, but also, more generally, on improving knowledge of integration issues, promoting information and dialogue and supporting innovative projects. An evaluation of the INTI programme revealed that the most important achievement of INTI concerned the "identification and exchange of good and best practice examples of measures to promote integration" (KANTOR 2006, p. 40). Some INTI projects involved not only national authorities but also local authorities, bringing together various cities in an exchange of best practices at this level. For instance, a large INTI project, "INTI-CITIES", contributed to the creating of a European network of cities ("Integrating Cities") that set benchmarks in integration governance. Furthermore, the evaluation states that the INTI programme contributed much less to the development of a scientific knowledge base on migrant integration, which reveals the policy-oriented nature of the INTI projects.

Thirdly, the Commission also played a key role in putting migrant integration on the agenda of the "framework" programmes for R&D. This contributed significantly to the development of comparative policy analysis and to the internationalization of the migrant research community. For instance, the pan-European network of excellence, IMISCOE (International Migration, Integration, Social Cohesion and Europe), was funded by the EU's 6th framework programme and now provides a major forum for research on migration, including migrant integration, with a strong comparative and international focus, including on the EU. It has played a key role in constituting a European research field on migrant integration and promoting a more comparative orientation in a research area that had long been characterized by a strong national orientation (Favell 2001; Thränhardt and Bommes 2010).

These infrastructures played a role primarily in what has been described above as the "soft governance" (i.e. non-binding measures) of migrant integration. In contrast to the third hypothesis on constituting a EU policy domain, or the second hypothesis on the selective mobilization of specific forms of expertise to specific political aims, these infrastructures reflect a more rationalist belief that if knowledge and experiences are exchanged freely this could lead organically to more horizontal convergence between EU member states. Interestingly, many well-known projects that have been developed in this context have focused on horizontal learning at the local or regional level rather than merely the national level. Taken together, these findings reflect our first hypothesis, i.e. "going technical" in areas where the EU may not have strong competencies itself and where nations in fact may be reluctant to concede such competencies to the EU. Precisely in the absence of formal competencies, promoting the exchange of knowledge and information may in fact be the only tool the European Commission has for promoting some form of, in this case, horizontal Europeanization.

EU Policy Agenda and the Mobilization of Expertise

In addition to horizontal infrastructures oriented towards knowledge exchange, a second type of infrastructure establishes a more direct relation between EU policy goals and the mobilization of specific types of research. These more "vertical" knowledge infrastructures emerged in the context of the adoption of the CBP. This created a EU-level framework to which knowledge infrastructures could be related, while also establishing a stronger impetus for EU institutions such as the European Commission to substantiate its position and its policies in the area of migrant integration.

First of all, in the mid-2000s, when migrant integration was highly politicized at national level in many EU member states, horizontal research infrastructures increasingly developed a more vertical dimension. Boswell (2009) shows that where initially the EMN concentrated on its instrumental function of exchanging knowledge and expertise, the European Commission gradually became more involved in its structure and work programme (Boswell 2009, p. 216). According to Boswell, this involved primarily a mobilization of expertise to substantiate the European Commission's policy agenda, but also a key effort to legitimize the involvement of the European Commission in this policy area by including many different stakeholders (experts, NGOs, national governments) in the EMN network. Furthermore, the evaluation (KANTOR 2006) of INTI projects showed that they played a key role in anticipating the components of the Hague Programme and the formulation of the CBP. As such, INTI and EMN played an important in a "softening-up" process by preparing the ground for later more vertical Europeanization in the form of the Common Agenda on Integration and the CBP.

This vertical dimension was further reinforced after the adoption of the Common Agenda on Integration and the CBP. An important programme through which this emerging EU framework on migrant integration was substantiated involved the establishment of a European Integration Fund (EIF, €825 million, 2007–13) as the successor of the INTI programme. The EIF's general objective was to "support member states efforts in enabling TCNs of different economic, social, cultural, religious, linguistic and ethnic backgrounds to meet the conditions of residence and to facilitate their integration into European societies". It was specifically designed to develop tools for the European Commission through the mobilization of research around clear EU policy objectives, derived directly from the Common Agenda on Integration. This became clear again with the adoption of the renewed "European Agenda for the Integration of Third Country Nationals" (2011). This agenda introduced a renewed focus on socio-economic participation in particular, and also signalled shifts in the allocation of EIF funding in that direction (COM 2011, p. 15). This shows that in contrast to the (at least originally) more horizontal or softening up function of the INTI programme, EIF was much more akin to a research programme that provided the European Commission with a tool to achieve its policy objectives in the absence of binding legal instruments.

A further clear example of vertical mobilization of expertise involved the commissioning from the Migration Policy Group think tank of three European Handbooks on Integration. MPG is a Brussels-based think tank delivering independent research, expert policy analysis, network building, advocacy, benchmarking and training. Besides an obvious horizontal function, in facilitating the exchange of knowledge and best practices, a vertical function was also evident in the translation of the CBP into practice. The first Handbook was presented at the Ministerial Integration Conference in Groningen in 2004, as a first step toward the implementation of the CBP. A second Handbook was presented in 2007 with the most recent version published in 2010.

Finally, there are clear indications of the institutionalization of boundary organizations at the EU level. For example, the MPG working with the British Council and a range of partners across the EU has developed comprehensive indicators of immigrant integration known as (Migrant Integration Policy Index) MIPEX (see below). Other Brussels-based migration policy think tanks such as the MPI and the Centre for European Policy Studies (CEPS) also seek to engage with EU policymakers and promote reflection on policy development. However, proximity does not always lead to easy relations and it should not be assumed that think tanks and EU institutions share a common agenda. A former European Commission official reflected certain unease when noting that: "some think tanks have been too much on the critical side" (Interview, former Commission official, November 2012).

A counterpoint to this apparent suspicion of think tanks is an observed tendency to cherry-pick research. For example, in relation to EMN ad hoc queries, but with relevance also to instruments such as MIPEX, the selective use of data

> allows them [member states] to then make the comparative claim themselves ... In the UK there was a green paper restricting family reunification, with many proposals ... and they were then using comparisons, you know, saying ... other countries do this ... and then they would give certain examples. Whereas they only chose very few countries in Europe that do this, not noting that all other countries do not do this. (Interviewee from Brussels think tank, March 2013)

The more vertical type of research infrastructure exemplified by MIPEX comes closest to the second hypothesis that argues that policy-oriented research can play an important role in politicized contexts. Rather than "going technical" to avoid politicization, this turns the selective mobilization of expertise into a key tool for promoting a more "vertical" process of Europeanization. The mobilization and utilization of research in this context supports not only EU policy goals but also boosts the Commission's institutional legitimacy as a key actor in migration and integration policies. Furthermore, indications of the institutionalization of EU-level boundary organizations to accompany this vertical Europeanization, points to the relevance of our third hypothesis on the effects of the constitution of a EU field. We can see that EU boundary organizations, such as the MPG, fulfil a clear role in substantiating EU policies, for instance through the integration Handbooks.

Infrastructures for Policy Monitoring

Finally, a third type of research–policy infrastructure seeks to mobilize expertise with the specific purpose of monitoring compliance with EU policies. This has occurred through the development of indicators of migrant integration, or, to be more precise, of national-level compliance with European normative standards that can include specific EU directives, but also Council of Europe measures (which do not have the legal effect of EU laws). A specific example of this is the MIPEX project led by the MPG working with the British Council. MIPEX measures and compares migration policies in EU member states plus non-EU countries such as Australia, Canada and the USA. The indicators use European benchmarks derived from both the EU and Council of Europe human rights standards as the basis for assessment. As a result, EU member states are compared with each other and evaluated in relation to their conformity with European standards and then to a group of non-EU countries such as Australia and Canada. Researchers that have been involved in establishing the MIPEX argue that the aim was neither to name and shame member states nor to provide the basis for referrals to the Court of Justice of the European Union (CJEU) in cases of non-compliance with EU laws (that are binding and have to be implemented) (interviews). MIPEX has, however, led to the production of league tables and rankings that allow for a fairly easy identification of better and worst performing member states and have led to increased debate with each iteration as MIPEX reached its third edition in 2011. An EMN National Contact Point highlighted a use of the MIPEX indicators:

> I like MIPEX because of how you can play with it. I don't know how many people play with it and factor in their possible policy changes to see how that may have an impact. I have done it myself ... it scares me sometimes ... policy changes around naturalization, for example. (Interview with EMN National Contact Point, June 2013)

It could be argued that the areas that are the focus of MIPEX might bear little relation to "on the ground" integration in communities and neighbourhoods. However, it provides an excellent illustration of why and how expertise is mobilized within the EU's institutional setting to help to frame the debate about immigrant integration at European level. More specifically, MIPEX used academic researchers as well as an extensive network of stakeholders from across the EU. For instance, the setting of comparative indicators along which to measure and compare migration policies has been a product of interplay between researchers and EU officials and is, as such, a clear example of boundary work). Furthermore, MIPEX outputs were designed to reinforce the mobilization and advocacy of stakeholders in member states. This was particularly relevant in newer immigration countries and in newer member states where these issues had not been long on government agendas. The expanded its focus to compare Europe on an international scale is important because these are countries that have been seen to "get it right" on these issues, or at least, do things better.

A key point is that MIPEX does not lead to the development of an EU migrant integration paradigm in the form of a "one size fits all" approach. Rather, it tests the ability of member states to implement in their national legal frameworks the various standards to which they have agreed either through directives or through other international standards. In this sense, MIPEX makes a contribution to the debate about a rights-based EU and to arguments for "more Europe".

Though this type of infrastructure seems to be relatively novel and is too weak to operate as a formal monitoring tool, it does form part of an evolving research–policy infrastructure and approximates to the third hypothesis that we identified, i.e. that the mobilization of research can contribute to the institutionalization of an EU migrant integration policy domain. Precisely in the absence of "hard" or legal instruments for assuring compliance, the mobilization of research to provide indicators on integration policies provides a welcome though softer instrument for monitoring compliance.

Conclusions

The aim of this article was to analyse EU-level research–policy infrastructures and their role in the Europeanization of migrant integration policies at a time of perceived crisis and policy failure. Rather than finding one dominant configuration of research–policy relations, we found various infrastructures that coexist and sometimes even overlap. Besides EU-sponsored infrastructures aimed primarily at horizontal exchange of knowledge and information between countries and between cities, we also found infrastructures that were more directly related to EU policy goals as well as an infrastructure that mobilized research as an informal tool to monitor policy compliance. In fact, there seems to be a succession in these infrastructures. Whereas originally the first type of infrastructure appears to have been dominant, the second and third types appear to have become more prominent over time. The gradual institutionalization of a EU policy area on migrant integration, associated with the shift from "horizontal" to more "vertical" Europeanization, is thus also reflected in a changing configuration of research–policy infrastructures.

On a theoretical level, our analysis shows that the use of research in Europeanization does not always accord to assumptions made by Majone and Schmidt about "going technical" with the effect of creating "policy without politics". In fact, precisely when the EU lacks formal competencies such as in the area of migrant integration policies, mobilizing specific types of research can form part of a political strategy designed to reinforce policy objectives. Our analysis of the European Commission's efforts to mobilize specific research through, amongst others, the European Integration Fund to support its claims and those of member states regarding the integration of TCNs with a greater focus on socio-economic adaptation by migrants, including language skills, provides a clear example of this. This was not an effort to "depoliticize" migrant integration policies, as the rationalist hypothesis predicts, but rather part of a broader political strategy from the European Commission and the member states. This insight can also be applied to the development and use of research for monitoring purposes, such as with the MIPEX indicators, as well as to research funded by the EIF. Of course, the European Commission does not control the outputs of this research and there are challenges to existing laws and frameworks that emerge. Rather, our argument is that there has been a reframing of these issues as "European challenges" that has influenced the focus of this work.

In the context of the broader literature on Europeanization, the analysis shows that as the EU moves into more politicized areas, the type of knowledge production and knowledge use changes. This is a significant finding as it serves as a corrective to ideas that the

EU is some kind of depoliticized "venue" to which member states seek to move in order to remove issues from the heat of domestic political debate. We argue that the institutionalization of responsibilities over time – for both harder and softer forms of action – changes both the dynamics and context of action. The issue of migrant integration has been reframed as an issue of Europe with a subsequent effect on how the issues are understood and how responses are developed. We do not argue that the EU drives this debate. Indeed, we have been careful to delineate its role in the context of multilevel politics where member states hold the upper hand. We have, however, shown that the social and political construction of a crisis of migrant integration has a European dimension that is linked to the constitution of a European policy field in this area within which the relationship between research and policy has been of great significance. This also serves to correct approaches that focus on "national models" with a tendency to retreat into these models in search of explanation rather than looking beyond them for sources of convergence at regional and international levels.

Finally, when speaking to the broader literature on comparative policy analysis, our analysis offers a perspective on the political relevance of comparative policy research itself. In the context of a policy domain for a long time dominated by a strong national focus, according to some even "methodological nationalism" (Favell 2001), comparative policy research can clearly open "national container views" and can pave the way for analysis of international policy learning and even policy convergence. This is what happened when in the 2000s migrant integration became increasingly politicized in national arenas while migration research became more internationalized, due in significant part to European funding schemes. In fact, our analysis shows that EU institutions mobilized policy research in this particular area with the purpose of first promoting horizontal convergence and, later, vertical convergence. As such, meta-policy analyses of comparative policy analyses can contribute significantly to our understanding of the "double hermeneutics" of how comparative research itself affects policy processes.

Acknowledgements

The research on which this paper is based was enabled by financial support from the Volkswagen Stiftung for the project 'Science-Society Dialogues on Migrant Integration in Europe'.

References

Beck, U., 1992, *Risk Society: Towards a New Modernity* (London: Sage).
Börzel, T. and Risse, T., 2012, From Europeanisation to diffusion: Introduction. *West European Politics*, **35**(1), pp. 1–19.
Boswell, C., 2008, The political functions of expert knowledge: Knowledge and legitimation in European Union immigration policy. *Journal of European Public Policy*, **15**(4), pp. 471–488.
Boswell, C., 2009, *The Political Uses of Expert Knowledge: Immigration Policy and Social Research*, (Cambridge: Cambridge University Press).
Bowen, J., 2007, A view from France on the internal complexity of national models. *Journal of Ethnic and Migration Studies*, **33**(6), pp. 1003–1016.
COM 2005, *A Common Agenda for Integration*, Brussels: Commission of the European Communities, COM (2005) 385 final.
COM 2011, *A European Agenda for the Integration of Third-Country Nationals*, COM(2011) 455 final.

Entzinger, H., 2003, The rise and fall of multiculturalism: The case of the Netherlands, in: C. Joppke and E. Morawska (Eds) *Toward Assimilation and Citizenship: Immigrants in Liberal Nation-States* (Houndmills: Palgrave MacMillan), pp. 59–86.

Faist, T. and Ette, A., 2007, *The Europeanization of National Immigration Policies. Between Autonomy and the European Union* (Houndsmill: Palgrave Macmillan).

Favell, A., 2001, Integration policy and integration research in Europe: A review and critique, in A. Aleinikoff and D. Klusmeyer (Eds.) *Citizenship Today: Global Perspectives and Practices* (Washington DC: Carnegie Endowment for International Peace).

Fischer, F., 1990, *Technocracy and the Politics of Expertise* (London: Sage).

Geddes, A., 2005, Migration research and European integration: The construction and institutionalization of problems of Europe, in: M. Bommes and E. T. Morawska (Eds) *International Migration Research: Constructions, Omissions and Interdisciplinarity* (Aldershot: Ashgate), pp. 265–280.

Geddes, A., 2008, *Immigration and European Integration: Beyond Fortress Europe?* (Manchester: Manchester University Press).

Gieryn, T., 1999, *Cultural Boundaries of Science: Credibility on the Line* (Chicago: University of Chicago Press).

Goeman, H., 2012, *Integrating Integration: the constitution of a EU policy domain on migrant integration* (PhD Dissertation, Vrije Universiteit Brussel).

Goeman, H., 2013, Integrating integration: the constitution of a EU policy domain on migrant integration, PhD Thesis, Free University of Brussels.

Guston, D.H., 2000, *Between Politics and Science. Assuring the Integrity and Productivity of Reseach* (New Jersey: Rutgers University).

Haas, P., 2004, When does power listen to truth? A constructivist approach to the policy process. *Journal of European Public Policy*, **11**(4), pp. 569–592.

Hajer, M., 1995, *The Politics of Environmental Discourse: Ecological Modernization and the Policy Process* (Oxford: Oxford University Press).

Hall, P., 1993, Policy paradigms, social learning, and the state: The case of economic policymaking in Britain. *Comparative Politics*, **25**(3), pp. 275–296.

Hansen, R., 2000, *Citizenship and Immigration in Post-War Britain: The Institutional Origins of a Multicultural Nation* (Oxford: Oxford University Press).

Hilgartner, S., 2000, *Science on Stage: Expert Advice as Public Drama* (Stanford: Stanford University Press).

Hooghe, L., 2003, *The European Commission and the Integration of Europe: Images of Governance* (Cambridge: Cambridge University Press).

Hoppe, R., 2005, Rethinking the science-policy nexus: from knowledge utilization and science technology studies to types of boundary arrangements. *Poiesis & Praxis: International Journal of Technology Assessment and Ethics of Science*, **3**(3), pp. 199–215.

Hoppe, R., 2011, *The Governance of Problems: Puzzling, Powering and Participation* (Bristol: Policy Press).

Jasanoff, S., 1994, *The Fifth Branch: Science Advisers as Policymakers* (Harvard: Harvard University Press).

Jasanoff, S., 2004, *States of Knowledge; the co-production of science and social order* (New York: Routledge).

KANTOR, 2006, *The Evaluation of the INTI Program* (Greece: KANTOR).

Majone, G., 1989, *Evidence, Argument, and Persuasion in the Policy Process* (New Haven, CT: Yale University Press).

Majone, G., 1997, From the positive to the regulatory state: Causes and consequences of changes in the mode of governance. *Journal of Public Policy*, **17**(2), pp. 139–167.

Majone, G., 2002, *Regulating Europe* (London: Routledge).

Porter, T., 1996, *Trust in Numbers: The Pursuit of Objectivity in Science and Public Life* (Princeton, NJ: Princeton University Press).

Radaelli, C., 1999, The public policy of the European Union: Whither politics of expertise? *Journal of European Public Policy*, **6**(5), pp. 757–774.

Radaelli, C., 2002, Whither Europeanization? Concept stretching and substantive change. *European Integration online Papers (EloP)*, **4**(8), http://eiop.or.at/eiop/texte/2000-008a.htm

Rein, M. and Schön, D., 1994, *Frame reflection: Toward the Resolution of Intractable Policy Controversies* (New York: Basic Books).

Sabatier, P., 1987, Knowledge, policy-oriented learning, and policy change an advocacy coalition framework. *Science Communication*, **8**(4), pp. 649–692.

Schmidt, V.A., 2005, Democracy in Europe: The impact of European integration. *Perspectives on Politics*, **3**(4), pp. 761–780.

Scholten, P., 2009, The coproduction of immigrant integration policy and research in the Netherlands: The case of the Scientific Council for Government Policy. *Science and Public Policy*, **36**(7), pp. 561–573.

Scholten, P., 2011, *Framing Immigrant Integration: Dutch Research-Policy Dialogues in Comparative Perspective* (Amsterdam: Amsterdam University Press).

Scholten, P. and Timmermans, A., 2010, Setting the immigrant policy agenda: Expertise and politics in France, the UK and the Netherlands. *Journal of Comparative Policy Analysis*, **12**, pp. 527–543

Slaughter, A. -M., 2004, *A New World Order: Government Networks and the Disaggregated State* (Princeton, NJ: Princeton University Press).

Thränhardt, D. and Bommes, M., 2010, *National Paradigms of Migration Research* (Osnabruck: V&r Unipress).

Weingart, P., 1999, Scientific expertise and political accountability: Paradoxes of science in politics. *Science and Public Policy*, **26**(3), pp. 151–161.

Weiss, C., 1977, Research for policy's sake: The enlightenment function of social research. *Policy Analysis*, **3**(4), pp. 531–545.

Wildavsky, A., 1979, *Speaking Truth to Power* (Boston, MA: Little Brown).

The Interplay of Knowledge Production and Policymaking: A Comparative Analysis of Research and Policymaking on Migrant Integration in Germany and the Netherlands

HAN ENTZINGER & PETER SCHOLTEN

ABSTRACT *This article speaks to the broader literature on how policy analysis does more than just "speaking truth to power". It focuses on the relation between policy setting and knowledge production, in particular on how the politicisation of migrant integration in Germany and the Netherlands has altered the interplay between knowledge production and policymaking. The analysis shows that the interaction between both worlds affects not just policymaking but also knowledge production. It nuances the hypothesis that in depoliticised settings the chances for the monopolisation of specific knowledge claims (or a "paradigm") are greater whereas in politicised settings a fragmentation of knowledge claims and knowledge conflicts is more likely to occur.*

Introduction

In many European countries research on migrant integration has evolved in close relation to the development of migration and migrant integration policies. The development of national policies spurred the demand for policy-relevant knowledge on how to promote migrant integration, which we define as a fuller participation of newcomers in the society of which they have become part. In various countries, like the Netherlands, Sweden and the United Kingdom, social researchers became involved in policymaking in this area at a rather early stage (Hammar 1985; Favell 2001; Scholten 2011). This specific development path also fed into the strongly policy-oriented and nationally situated character of migration research that prevailed in those countries (Favell 2001). In other countries, by contrast, the relationship between research and policymaking was much less intense. Politicians and policymakers often did not bother so much about immigrant integration; sometimes they did not even recognise the permanent nature of immigration and its potential for social tensions. Research was mainly an academic affair, not meant to influence policymaking. Germany, France and Austria provide good examples of this (Bommes and Thränhardt 2010).

In the past two decades, migrant integration has risen considerably on the political agenda all over Europe. In many countries there has been talk about an "immigration and integration crisis", and past policies were blamed for having contributed to this crisis rather than having prevented it from occurring. This politicisation has also had serious consequences for the relationship between research and policymaking, between knowledge producers and knowledge users (Boswell 2009; Scholten and Timmermans 2010). In some cases the role that migrant integration research had played in the development of these policies was put on the line as well. In other countries the opposite happened and awareness developed that a closer relationship between knowledge producers and the users of such knowledge might lead to more effective policies that would help play down on anti-immigrant sentiments, thus benefiting researchers and policymakers alike.

This article focuses on how knowledge production is affected by the policy setting, in particular on how the politicisation of migrant integration has altered the interplay between knowledge production and policymaking. This speaks to a broader debate in the policy sciences on the context of knowledge production. On the one hand, clearly working in Lasswell's (1970) tradition of knowledge *of* policy versus knowledge *for* policy, scholars such as Wildavsky have stressed the role of policy analysis in "speaking truth to power" (1979). On the other hand, scholars like Weingart (1999) and Hoppe (2005) have shown that besides a process of scientification of politics, to which policy analysis has contributed, there has been a politicisation of science as well. This reflects the transformation of society into a risk society, where not just the nature of social problems like migrant integration has changed due to uncertainty and risks, but the nature of knowledge as well (Beck 1992). In terms of the substantive or cultural dimension of knowledge production it means that knowledge has become more contested, with researchers and knowledge claims often seen as part of distinct "discourse coalitions" (Hajer 1995), rather than scientists "speaking truth to power". In terms of the structure of knowledge production this means, inter alia, that knowledge production has become more fragmented and that stable institutionalised relations between research and policy have become more difficult to maintain.

Policy-oriented research in the area of migrant integration provides an excellent case for studying the relation between politicisation and knowledge production. Studying knowledge production over a longer period, in terms of its structure as well as of substantive knowledge claims, allows us to analyse differences between the relatively depoliticised policy episodes (in this case up to the 1990s), and the last one or two decades that are characterised by a politicisation of migration and integration issues and the construction of an alleged "multicultural crisis". Focusing on two countries – the Netherlands and Germany – where this distinction between episodes of depoliticisation and politicisation applies rather sharply, but where the interplay of policymaking and research has taken very different forms, allows us to analyse the impact of policy changes on knowledge production in a comparative way.

Knowledge Production in an Institutional Policy Setting

The role of knowledge in the policy process is beyond doubt one of the classical themes in the policy sciences. In Wildavsky's (1979) approach research is the foundation of rational societal steering. Policy analysis and policy research more in general would play a key role in bridging the worlds of research and policymaking and facilitate the diffusion of knowledge to policy. Post-empiricist strands of policy literature (Fischer 1989) have questioned the rationalist idea of a linear and rational relationship between knowledge and policymaking, arguing amongst others that research is a specific source of power or ammunition in policy processes (Fischer 1993), or rather that research primarily plays a symbolic role in substantiating or legitimising policy choices that have already been made (Edelman 1988; Boswell 2009).

Some policy scientists have gone a step further by studying not just what roles research and knowledge can play in policy processes but also how and why knowledge may be selected or configured within specific institutional policy settings. Borrowing amongst others from the literature of science and technology studies, scholars like Ezrahi (1990), Jasanoff (2004) and Hoppe (2005) have shown that relations between research and policy affect the production of scientific knowledge claims and the organisation of knowledge production as well. They have drawn attention to what they describe as "boundary work" on the boundaries or nexus between research and policy. Studying boundary work appears particularly relevant when accounting for the role of policy research in problem areas that are as contested or "wicked" as migrant integration.

Boundary Work and Knowledge Production

The literature on knowledge production and boundary work draws attention to the co-production or co-evolution of research on the one hand and politics and policies on the other (Shapin and Schaffer 1985; Ezrahi 1990; Nowotny et al. 2001; Jasanoff 2004). Nowotny et al. (2001, p. 245) refer to the growing transgression of science–politics boundaries and the contextualisation of science, which means that science not only speaks to society but society also speaks back to science. According to Shapin and Shaffer (1985, p. 332), there is a "conditional relationship between the nature of the polity occupied by scientific intellectuals and the nature of the wider polity". Ezrahi (1990) has described the rise of modern science in relation to the rising demand by modern societies as an instrumental means to sustain administrative control. Science would have been an important political resource for depersonalising and depoliticising ideological state control, and thereby legitimising modern liberal democratic politics.

"Boundary work" refers to how actors, researchers as well as policymakers, in their actual social practices create a social boundary that defines research (its structural positions, its rules of the game, its species of capital) and differentiates it from non-research, policymaking, politics and other spheres. This notion allows for an empiricist study of the relationship between fields, studying actual boundary work practices instead of doing boundary work with ex ante models or "laws" of relations between fields such as research and policy. Shapin has drawn attention to the dual nature of boundary work: it not only demarcates research from non-research, but it also co-ordinates relations between research and other spheres, such as politics and policies (Shapin 1992, p. 335). Elaborating upon Shapin's definition, Halffman defines boundary work as follows:

> Boundary work defines a practice in contrast with other practices, protects it from unwanted participants and interference, while attempting to prescribe proper ways of behavior for participants and non-participants (demarcation); simultaneously,

boundary work defines proper ways for interaction between these practices and makes such interaction possible and conceivable (coordination). (Halffman 2003, p. 241)

For the study of knowledge production, the concept of boundary work captures how the definition of knowledge is related to the context in which these claims are validated. It recognises that the production and validation of knowledge claims is itself a stake in research–policy relations. It also recognises that such boundary work practices are driven not just by factual claims, but also by authority, interests and values. Especially in the production of knowledge that is to play a role in policymaking, the authority of knowledge producers, the interests of involved actors from the spheres of research as well as policy, and value preferences of what is considered proper research can make a significant difference.

Gieryn (1999) has distinguished four major types of boundary work practices. First, boundary work can be aimed at the *monopolisation* of a specific model of doing science or making policies by developing a specific relation with actors and capital in another field (Gieryn 1995, p. 394). For instance, with aid from other fields, actors can strengthen their position within their own field or alter the rules of the game in their favour. Secondly, boundary work can be aimed at the *expulsion* of specific actors, by redrawing the boundaries of a field so that specific actors are excluded (for example, depriving researchers of their scientific credibility) (Gieryn 1999, p. 16). Thirdly, boundary work can involve *expansion*, which occurs when actors that support a specific knowledge paradigm or specific values or ideas about proper science manage to expand that paradigm or those beliefs into other areas as well (ibid., p. 17). Finally, boundary work can be aimed at strengthening the *autonomy* of research versus other spheres like politics and policymaking. Autonomy does not mean that fields are not interrelated. Jasanoff has shown that "keeping politics near but out" (Jasanoff 1990) forms a very effective strategy for research institutes to strengthen their authority by being involved in policy to some degree.

The Role of Boundary Organisations

Policy analysis and policy research more generally are often carried out by organisations that have a niche on the boundaries of research and policy. Such "boundary organisations" (Guston 2000; Miller 2001) can come in many shapes and sizes, e.g. think tanks, foundations with combined social and scientific purposes, private consultancy firms or government contractors, government research bureaux, or advocacy think tanks. Although such organisations are often portrayed as "bridges" or "transmission belts" between research and policy, they generally have a more active role (and an interest) in boundary work. They are often hybrids of the structures of both fields, combining elements of both science and politics (Miller 2001). However, they derive much of their credibility from clearly demarcating science and politics, and from positioning themselves somewhere in between:

> Their credibility is grounded in the "two worlds" metaphor. … [I]t is in the interest of think-tanks in general to maintain the myth of the distinction between knowledge and scholarship on the one hand, and politics, policy and interests on the other. If policy research institutes are "above" politics they are not a threat to democracy. Portrayed

passively as a bridge or a transmission belt from the scholarly domain, the metaphor of two worlds gives them a safe distance from politics and protects their credibility and charitable status. (Stone 1998, p. 121)

The niche of these boundary organisations consists of their capacity to connect processes of knowledge production and knowledge utilisation. They often occupy positions within both fields and also have to find ways to blur the rules of the game within both fields in a way that allows for interaction between them. Internally, boundary work also involves a degree of balancing so as to maintain authority within both fields. Furthermore, in relation to the broader fields of research and policy, boundary organisations can form an important part of the institutionalisation of the research–policy nexus. Every boundary organisation will involve a particular way of demarcating and co-ordinating research and policy that tends to become institutionalised once the boundary organisation has been established.

This article focuses on how boundary work has affected knowledge production on migrant integration before and after the politicisation of this issue. It hypothesises that in politicised or depoliticised policy settings boundaries between research and policy will be drawn very differently and, consequently, that patterns of knowledge production will differ as well. Following Gieryn (1999), we expect that in depoliticised settings chances for monopolisation of specific knowledge claims (or a "paradigm") will be greater. The same holds for chances that contending knowledge claims will be expelled. We expect that in politicised settings a fragmentation of knowledge claims is more likely to occur, along with knowledge conflicts and potentially even contestation over the validity or credibility of knowledge claims and the involved researchers themselves. Finally, as both Gieryn (1983) and Jasanoff (1990) have argued, boundary work may also confirm or even strengthen the autonomy of researchers versus policymakers and enhance their mutual respect, even in times of greater politicisation.

In terms of methods, two case studies have been carried out in two countries that allow for a comparison between periods before and after politicisation of migrant integration: the Netherlands and Germany. In both countries we focus on the structure as well as on the knowledge cultures within migration research. For the former we will specifically look at the role of boundary organisations that are most involved with policy research. The latter will be interpreted in terms of the main schools of thought and major knowledge claims or paradigms in the field, sometimes associated with specific methodological preferences.

Our empirical data stem from the DIAMINT project, which assesses the interplay between research and policymaking on migrant integration at the EU level as well as in five European countries, including the two presented in this article. Here we have restricted ourselves to these two – leaving out Austria, Italy and the United Kingdom – because of the similarities between Germany and the Netherlands in their recent immigration histories and the dissimilarities in the interplay between producers and users of knowledge as it has developed over the years. In both countries – as in the other DIAMINT countries – this involved an in-depth qualitative analysis of research–policy relations, including an extensive review of literature on migration and integration, an analysis of key policy documents and policy advisory reports as well as qualitative interviews with key actors in research–policy relations, including academics, representatives from boundary organisations, policymakers and politicians.

Knowledge Production and Policymaking in the Netherlands

Research as well as policies on migrant integration was virtually non-existent in the Netherlands until the late 1970s, as the country did not consider itself a country of immigration. The settlement of growing numbers of post-colonial migrants since the 1950s and of Mediterranean "guest workers" since the 1960s was not recognised by the authorities as a permanent phenomenon and, for that matter, specific policy efforts to promote their integration were not deemed necessary. Only the Ministry of Social Work (CRM), which was the first to be faced with special needs among immigrants and also with growing tensions between immigrant communities and the native population, assumed a more proactive role. This Ministry, however, had virtually no experience in these matters, and therefore turned to the social sciences. In those days the belief was widespread that social scientists could provide the necessary tools for social planning and engineering and provide answers to the emerging challenges.

In this context the Social and Cultural Planning Office (SCP) – a think tank set up to provide data on social and cultural developments in society – began to collect information on the position of immigrants. Mobilising data would be a first step toward raising awareness that new policy measures would be required. Taking this approach a step further, the Ministry of Social Work installed the Advisory Commission on Minorities Research (ACOM) in 1978. ACOM was meant to advise the Ministry on the programming of research needed for the further development of policies in this area. This was a clear act of expansionary boundary work on behalf of the Ministry that attempted to raise awareness for the need for a migrant integration policy by mobilising research in that respect (Scholten 2011).

Another boundary organisation that played a pivotal role in the science–policy nexus was the Scientific Council for Government Policy (WRR), a high-level think tank, set up in 1972 to advise the Dutch government on new developments in society and their potential relevance for policymaking. The WRR is an independent body, free to decide its own agenda, but administratively part of the Ministry of the Prime Minister. The government is obliged by law to respond to its recommendations. Four times in the 40 years of its existence the WRR has produced a report on immigrant integration. The first report, called *Etnische minderheden* ("Ethnic Minorities"), was released in 1979 and became trendsetting for the initial multiculturalist approach of immigrant integration by the Dutch government. In fact, this report was taken as a direct basis for the first memorandum on migrant integration policies, the *Nota Minderhedenbeleid* ("Memorandum on Minorities Policy") of 1981, which was finalised in 1983.

This expansionary type of boundary work reflected the strong policy orientation of social scientists in this period, which was matched by a strong belief in rational societal steering amongst policymakers and politicians. There was little experience with migrant integration policies and the respondents in our fieldwork agree that a strong consensus prevailed that this should not be turned into a partisan issue. This created a context of depoliticisation, which enabled social science research to provide an authoritative venue for policy formulation.

This expansionary boundary work also affected the development of migration research itself. The construction of a direct nexus between migration research and policymaking in the late 1970s and early 1980s did not just lead to the formation of a(n Ethnic) Minorities Policy, but also facilitated the emergence of an ethnic minorities paradigm in migration research. Bovenkerk et al. (1991), for example, observes that "the development of political-economic theory on guest workers in the Netherlands was quite suddenly interrupted, precisely at the moment when the state incorporated researchers into its bureaucratic apparatus and initiated wide-scale funding for politically relevant research". Similarly, Penninx, one of the key architects of the WRR's *Ethnic Minorities* report, observes that significant criticism existed towards ACOM, which "in some circles of researchers ... was seen as a biased group of advisors that functioned as gatekeepers for ... research funding, and gave no or insufficient attention to certain topics or disciplines" (Penninx 1988, p. 37). Thus, the monopolising boundary work that supported the ethnic minorities paradigm led to the aversion of contending knowledge claims. This happened, for example, to those who were doubtful about the effects of mother tongue teaching for migrant children and also to adherents of the racism paradigm. The same happened to research initiatives that emerged, though agonisingly slowly, from among the ethnic communities themselves.

Until well into the 1990s, the ethnic minorities paradigm remained the dominant paradigm in the Netherlands, both in policymaking and in research. Research in the area expanded rapidly, mostly financed by a growing number of Ministries that felt the need for a sounder basis in order to legitimise their new policies. Only gradually the technocratic symbiosis (Rath 2001) began to yield. In an effort to strengthen the academic nature of immigration research, the Dutch Research Council (NWO), funded a special programme in which the need for more theory was emphasised. At several universities chairs in migration studies were established, while specialised research centres for migration and ethnic studies were set up at the Universities of Utrecht (ERCOMER, 1993) and Amsterdam (IMES, 1994). Gradually, other academic disciplines, less burdened with the minorities paradigm than sociology and anthropology, also took an interest in this research area, such as in particular economics and political sciences.

In another episode of boundary work a second report by the Scientific Council for Government Policy, *Allochtonenbeleid* (Immigrant Policy, 1989) punctuated the monopoly of the ethnic minorities paradigm. The Council's main argument for this was that its use had reinforced tendencies towards separation and increased the migrants' dependence on public services, rather than fostered their integration. As an alternative the Council proposed a policy of individual integration into mainstream institutions, such as labour and education, combined with facilities to improve the immigrants' knowledge of the Dutch language. Partly as an effect of the second WRR report, awareness grew among policymakers that the minorities paradigm would not hold. Immigration continued and diversified, while it was developing into a structural phenomenon, certainly after the collapse of the Iron Curtain. Besides, within the oldest migrant communities a second generation, born and raised in the Netherlands – and also more "Dutch" than expected – began to manifest itself. In 1994, Minorities Policy was officially relabelled as "Integration Policy", and the issue had begun to rise slowly on the political agenda. Policymaking had now reached a more mature stage, characterised by a growing number of policy instruments (e.g. the introduction of mandatory integration courses in 1998) and by stronger vested interests, also from civil society, including migrant organisations.

All these developments provoked a gradual alienation between the academic world and the policymakers. ACOM, a strong defender of the minorities paradigm had rejected the 1989 WRR report as "unscientific", thus trying to discredit the researchers involved; a typical example of expulsionary boundary work (see also Scholten 2011). However, the

WRR disposed of better and broader credits in both the academic and the political world than ACOM did, and that advisory commission ceased to exist in 1992. Migration research now became more fragmented, but also more pluriform. For the academic world this growing disconnection with policymaking did not mean that research funds became scarcer, as alternative funding sources gradually gained importance. The main change in those days was that the political agenda setting shifted from academia to policymakers, while the use of research outcomes became more selective and the type of research preferred by the latter became more instrumental.

The de-institutionalisation of the research–policy nexus of the 1980s and the first signs of politicisation in the early 1990s led to a demand for less conceptual and more instrumental and data-driven types of research. Policymakers needed more and more large-scale data, preferably based on surveys or derived from existing registration systems. Government-related institutions such as the Social and Cultural Planning Office and Netherlands Statistics (CBS) could provide these data much more readily than university research institutes could. Our interviews indicate that the mobilisation of instrumental data fulfilled a clear role in the interdepartmental co-ordination of migrant integration policies. The data produced by SCP and CBS allowed the co-ordinating Ministry of the Interior to organise its information position in relation to other ministries involved in migrant integration. This enabled it to monitor the implementation of policy measures by various departments, to identify potential deficiencies and to put issues on the agenda so that new policy measures could be developed. Also more evaluation studies were needed to assess the impact of earlier policies. Such studies were increasingly commissioned to research units within the respective ministries, like the Centre for Scientific Research and Documentation (WODC) of the Ministry of Justice, or to private consultancy firms. This made it easier to keep an eye on the work's progress and its outcomes.

In January 2000, Paul Scheffer, a Dutch public intellectual, published a much-debated essay called "Het multiculturele drama" (The Multicultural Tragedy), in which he criticised the minorities paradigm and advocated a more assimilationist approach (Scheffer 2000). It triggered a public debate of unprecedented vigour. Apparently, time was ripe for a more fundamental change in policy than just replacing "minorities" by "integration", as had happened in 1994. The actual policy change came two years later, greatly helped by the "9/11" events in the US. In the May 2002 parliamentary elections immigration and the fear of Islam were crucial themes, put on the agenda by politician Pim Fortuyn. Fortuyn was murdered a few days before the elections, but his newly established party came out second and became part of the new coalition government. That coalition embarked on a strongly assimilationist policy, characterised by ever-stricter immigration rules and a more and more compelling integration policy. Later, Pim Fortuyn's role was taken over by Geert Wilders and his Freedom Party, a dominant force in Dutch politics until the present day. Notwithstanding the enormous variety of coalition governments (six different coalitions in the space of ten years), immigration and integration policies have remained very strict since the days of Fortuyn. Only very recently they may have begun to lose some of their urgency, but none of their strictness.

In the context of this sharp politicisation of migrant integration the role of research declined even further. Some speak of the rise of "articulation politics", or a form of politics aimed at gaining legitimacy by responding to the voice from the street (Verwey-Jonker Instituut 2004). This became manifest soon after the dramatic 2002 elections when the new Dutch parliament adopted a motion asking for an investigation into *"why* immigrant integration had failed", without even asking *if* it had failed. The Parliamentary Committee set up for this purpose commissioned the Verwey-Jonker Institute, an independent institute for social research, to conduct a large study to assess the state of affairs, mainly based on existing research. Their final report was heavily contested in parliament as well as in the media as being biased and leaning too much to the left. In these debates the credibility of the social researchers involved in this institute was openly put on the line. Social researchers were blamed for having been too involved in policymaking and for reflecting a multiculturalist bias. At the same time, policymakers and politicians who had been involved in this area were blamed for lacking a clear political vision and for having delegated too much of the policymaking to researchers (Scholten 2009). This was another example of expulsionary boundary work, but this time driven primarily by politicians eager to discredit researchers who had been involved in the development of policies in preceding periods. The days of technocratic symbiosis were definitely over. Likewise, when the Parliamentary Committee itself came with its final report, it was also heavily criticised. The report stated that "immigrant integration had been relatively successful, *in spite of* all policies pursued, rather than *thanks to* these policies".

The gradual de-institutionalisation of the research-policy nexus since the 1990s has had significant effects on the academic world, though these effects have not necessarily been negative for the quality of their output. Research on immigration and particularly on integration is now being initiated in many more disciplines than before, including law, economics, psychology and medical sciences. It is also much less policy-oriented than in the early days and theoretically richer and broader. The growing availability of databases and their improved accessibility have led to a much larger number of quantitative studies, even though carrying out new large-scale surveys is not easy because of high costs and low response rates. Numerous PhD dissertations are being defended in this field, which in less than four decades has become one of the core specialisms, certainly in the social sciences. The growing availability of European research funds has led to a dramatic increase in comparative studies, thus making Dutch researchers less dependent on national funding sources, many of which have been drying up anyway. Moreover, as policymaking is becoming more decentralised, local authorities have been taking an interest in funding research, and often co-operate closely with the local university.

The Dutch case, in accordance with our hypothesis, indeed reveals a relationship between politicisation and knowledge production. Until the early 1990s, there was a strongly institutionalised research–policy nexus that prevented politicisation and promoted a monopolisation of the ethnic minorities paradigm. Politicisation in the 1990s, and even more so in the early 2000s, punctuated this symbiosis, allowed for more pluriformity in knowledge claims and also led to more open knowledge conflicts. The Dutch case does bring a specific nuance to this hypothesised relation, since the type of knowledge mobilised in politicised settings appears to differ from knowledge mobilised in depoliticised settings. In the former more conceptual types of policy research seem to dominate, whereas more instrumental forms of research prevail in the latter, since these generate data that can be used as tools for policy co-ordination.

Knowledge Production and Policymaking in Germany

The research–policy nexus in the field of migrant integration in Germany has followed a very different path. The recruitment of foreign workers in Germany had begun in the mid-

1950s, but it was not until ten years later that some scholarly discourse developed in the economic sciences on the advantages and disadvantages of foreign labour. From the early 1970s onwards the social sciences also began to take an interest in what soon became known as *Gastarbeiterforschung* (guest worker research). Research interests were mainly driven by social problems that the guest workers encountered, and by the need to develop modes of incorporation into the welfare and educational systems.

In fact, this stands for a more general trait of migration research in Germany, at least until well into the 1980s: much of it was characterised by a strong practical and also political-normative involvement and by a corresponding lack of scientific detachment. This holds for research carried out by universities as well as by public research institutes. However, unlike the situation in the Netherlands in those days, there was no outspoken paradigm shared by researchers and policymakers alike. In fact, contacts between researchers and policymakers were much less intense than in the Netherlands. This may have to do with the federal structure of Germany: the addressee is much less obvious than in less decentralised countries. Yet it is more likely that the fact that Germany did not consider itself a country of immigration made it difficult for researchers to table issues of immigrant integration with the authorities (Heckmann 1981). The non-immigration paradigm ("*Deutschland ist kein Einwanderungsland*") persisted in politics as a dominant mantra until the turn of the millennium.

Strong forms of institutionalised co-operation between academia and policymakers, as in the Netherlands, did not exist in Germany. Consequently academic research in this field developed more autonomously than in the Netherlands. This difference is indeed remarkable, particularly in the social sciences. After the initial period of problem-driven research, several "schools" began to develop in German academia from the mid-1980s onwards, which all had their own theoretical approach. This linked up German migration research with international research traditions at a relatively early stage (Bommes 2010). The three major "schools", which have continued to exist up to the present day, are: (1) methodological individualism and rational choice (with Hartmut Esser in Mannheim as its main exponent); (2) the socio-historical approach (Klaus Bade in Osnabrück); and (3) the ethnic minority approach (Friedrich Heckmann in Bamberg and Stephen Castles in Frankfurt). Thus, in contrast to the policy orientation of Dutch scholarship in that period, most German scholars positioned themselves at a greater distance from policymaking, while developing their own theoretical premises and thus safeguarding their scientific autonomy. In Gieryn's terms: boundary work was oriented at protecting autonomy and generating authority.

The institutionalisation of migration research in German academia continued to expand, in spite of the absence of a real policy interest. Apart from the ones already mentioned, many other universities set up chairs and research centres, and a considerable number of non-university research institutes of various disciplines (including law and economics) also engaged in this area. Many of these institutes were publicly funded, but an immediate link between their research agenda and policymaking remained rare. In contrast to the Netherlands, no institutionalised boundary organisations emerged in this period that would organise research–policy dialogues.

After the collapse of the Berlin Wall in 1989 and German reunification in 1990, the conceptual shortcomings of German immigration and integration policy became increasingly visible. Meanwhile, the federal as well as most regional governments had appointed so-called immigration councillors (*Ausländerbeauftragten*) who had links not only with migrant advocacy organisations but also with the research world. This fact, however, could not conceal the lacking ability of the authorities to deal with growing numbers of asylum seekers, refugees and ethnic Germans (*Spätaussiedler*) and with an increase in racist and xenophobic attacks against immigrants in the 1990s. All this provoked a strong politicisation of immigration and integration in Germany in that period.

Leading academics, followed by larger segments of the research community, took advantage of this situation by assuming a more active role in the public debate than before. They put forward numerous suggestions and recommendations for concrete and comprehensive migration policies, as well as for their institutional anchoring. As a general rule such initiatives were embraced much more readily by a variety of NGOs than by the public authorities, thus creating interesting alliances between civil society and academia. A major initiative that gained wide public attention was the 1994 "Manifest of the 60: Germany and Immigration", signed by 60 renowned researchers from various disciplines. They proposed a reform of legislation on citizenship as a precondition for improved integration, as well as a relaxation of strict immigration policies, also for demographic reasons (Bade 1994). As an effect of this initiative a first boundary organisation, the Council on Migration (*Rat für Migration*), was founded in 1998. This is a nationwide voluntary association of researchers, which still exists, and which has published a number of reports, based on academic research, that, according to some of our interviewees, have influenced policymaking. Much more recently, in 2008, another independent Expert Council for Migration and Integration (SVR) was created, this time with the financial support of several private foundations, which also publishes scientifically based reports, gives expert advice and participates in public debates. In many of these scientifically based advisory and advocacy activities the social-historian professor Klaus Bade has played a leading role. Though these councils may be qualified as boundary organisations, they have no formal ties with the public authorities and have always remained firmly rooted in the private sector.

At long last, in 2000, the Social Democratic–Green coalition government led by Gerhard Schröder conceded to the mounting pressure from politics, from civil society and from academia by formally acknowledging that Germany was a country of immigration. This provoked an almost immediate relaxation of the relationships between researchers and policymakers. The latter began to open up to external expertise. A major sign of this was the establishment, also in 2000, of a high-level Independent Commission on Migration, chaired by Rita Süssmuth, former President of the *Bundestag*. The aim of this Commission was to propose concrete recommendations for new immigration legislation. Its membership consisted of some senior politicians, representatives of NGOs, including the social partners, and also of academia. Opinions differ as to the effectiveness of the Commission's work (Unabhängige Kommission "Zuwanderung" 2001). Some claim that it was largely used to legitimise certain political positions and to increase their acceptance, while others argue that it had really encouraged a paradigm shift (Schneider 2010). Nevertheless, the Süssmuth Commission contributed to a substantial change in party-political discourse and helped to objectify heated debates on migration and integration, which was needed all the more in the aftermath of the "9/11" events in the USA. It also laid the foundations and provided input for the new Immigration Law that came into force in 2005 (Borkert and Bosswick 2007).

The new policy approach in Germany was also the sign for the federal government to step up its own research efforts on integration. Now that integration was no longer taboo, more knowledge was needed for the development of effective policies, even though most policy instruments that actually promote integration are in the hands of regional and local authorities, rather than of the federal government. To this purpose the Federal Institute for Migration and Refugees (BAMF) in Nürnberg has been equipped with a well-funded research department. Its task is to monitor integration processes and to evaluate policy measures in that field. It co-operates with other national and international research institutes and constitutes a major interface for information and knowledge transfer between science, policymakers, the administration, the economy and civil society. As such it can be qualified as a boundary organisation, even though Boswell (2009) has shown that BAMF, in a way very similar to SCP in the Netherlands, produces data and research that primarily help legitimise central government policies and monitor and identify areas for policy action.

After the major paradigm shift in German politics, some more new initiatives developed, aiming at bringing research and policymaking more closely together. In 2003 the Ministry of the Interior set up the Council of Experts for Immigration and Integration ("*Zuwanderungsrat*") to provide continuous consultancy for German migration and integration policy. This Council, however, was less effective than had been expected as it soon became torn apart by party-political controversies. In particular, its proposal for an annual immigration of up to 25,000 skilled foreigners into certain labour market segments did not fit into the political climate of the time. Schneider considers the establishment of this Council as a failed attempt of institutionalised external policy consultancy on migration and integration. The Council was dissolved a few years later (Schneider 2010).

The German case reveals a relationship between politicisation and knowledge production that is very different from the Dutch case. In fact, it shows a much more autonomous development of migrant integration research before immigration and integration became as politicised as they are now, and a proliferation of boundary organisations only after politicisation had gained momentum during the 1990s. The German case also shows that, in the absence of an institutional research–policy nexus, patterns of boundary work did not lead to the monopolisation of a single knowledge paradigm as in the early days of integration policymaking in the Netherlands.

Conclusions

This article speaks to the broader literature on how policy analysis does more than just "speaking truth to power". It focuses on the relation between policy setting and knowledge production, in particular on how the politicisation of migrant integration in Germany and the Netherlands has altered the interplay between knowledge production and policymaking. Indeed, the analysis shows that the "boundary work" in the interaction between both worlds affects not just policymaking (as also recognised in other articles in this Special Issue), but also knowledge production. However, it does nuance the original hypothesis that in depoliticised settings the chances for the monopolisation of specific knowledge claims (or a "paradigm") will be greater whereas in politicised settings a fragmentation of knowledge claims and knowledge conflicts is more likely to occur.

Leaving aside a few ad hoc efforts, research activities on immigrant integration began to get off the ground in both countries studied here in the early 1970s. It was also around that time that the authorities began to realise that existing policy instruments were inadequate to cope with integration issues. Subsequently, some form of co-operation developed between policymakers and researchers, but the nature of the relationship was very different. The Netherlands shows a strong institutionalisation of boundary activities dominated by a limited number of researchers who almost unanimously endorsed the ethnic minorities paradigm, which was subsequently taken over by the policymakers. In German politics the long-prevailing paradigm that Germany was not an immigration country blocked more intense forms of co-operation between policymakers and much of academia, which did not endorse that paradigm. The loose links between policymakers and researchers that resulted from this enabled the latter to develop their agenda much more autonomously. Consequently the German research landscape could become more differentiated than its Dutch counterpart, although to some extent differences in size between the two countries may also account for this.

In the Netherlands, knowledge production began to diversify after the minorities paradigm had been dropped in the 1990s. At the same time, the dominant boundary organisations gradually lost their influence and the policymaking process was less affected by research findings. In the early 2000s integration became much more politicised and the relationship between academia and policymaking cooled off even further. The Dutch landscape today shows a flourishing academic research world, increasingly oriented towards Europe, while policymaking is largely supported by data collection and evaluation studies carried out within the government bureaucratic system and by consultancy agencies.

In Germany, the research–policy nexus developed quite differently. Academia, together with civil society, played an active role in convincing the government of the erroneous nature of the non-immigration paradigm. Interestingly, this happened in a period when immigration became an increasingly politicised issue, largely as a result of growing numbers of migrants (and asylum seekers) and increased expressions of xenophobia. When the non-immigration paradigm was finally dropped in 2000, relations between researchers and policymakers relaxed. Since then several boundary organisations have been created that more or less effectively bridge the gap. However, none of these has ever become as closely involved with policymaking as in the case of the Netherlands during the days of the minorities paradigm. A careful protection of their autonomy may have helped to increase the researchers' authority.

We may conclude that knowledge production in a depoliticised setting is more likely to produce a single dominant paradigm. Boundary work in such policy settings may involve, as the Dutch case reveals, the monopolisation of one knowledge paradigm that is privileged in research–policy relations. The Dutch case does bring a specific nuance to the relation between depoliticisation and knowledge production since the type of knowledge mobilised in politicised settings appears to differ from knowledge mobilised in depoliticised settings. In the former more conceptual types of policy research appear to dominate, whereas more instrumental forms of research prevail in the latter, since these generate data that can be used as tools for policy co-ordination.

In politicised settings, where other considerations than academic ones also must be accounted for, research can still play a significant role. However, patterns of boundary activities in research–policy relations are very different here, as more distance is required between both worlds so as to keep up political primacy and academic authority alike. The German case, which reveals a proliferation of boundary organisations after politicisation had gained momentum during the 1990s, makes this very clear. The Dutch case, however, shows that such boundary activities are extremely difficult if there is a lack of mutual trust.

References

Bade, K. J., 1994, *Das Manifest Der 60. Deutschland Und Die Einwanderung* (München: Beck).
Beck, U., 1992, *Risk Society. Towards a New Modernity* (London: Sage).
Bommes, M., 2010, Migration research in Germany: The emergence of a generalized research field in a reluctant immigration country, in: M. Bommes and D. Thränhardt (Eds *National Paradigms of Migration Research* (Osnabrück: IMIS), pp. 127–185.
Bommes, M. and Thränhardt, D., 2010, Introduction: National paradigms of migration research, in: M. Bommes and D. Thränhardt (Eds) *National Paradigms of Migration Research* (Osnabrück: IMIS), pp. 9–38.
Borkert, M. and Bosswick, W., 2007, *Migration Policy-Making in Germany. Between National Reluctance and Local Pragmatism?* (Amsterdam: IMISCOE).
Boswell, C., 2009, *The Political Uses of Expert Knowledge: Immigration Policy and Social Research* (Cambridge: Cambridge University Press).
Bovenkerk, F., Miles, R. and Verbunt, G., 1991, Comparative studies of migration and exclusion on the grounds of race and ethnic background in Western Europe: A critical appraisal. *International Migration Review*, **25**, pp. 375–391.
Edelman, E., 1988, *Constructing the Political Spectacle* (Chicago: University of Chicago Press).
Ezrahi, Y., 1990, *The Descent of Icarus. Science and the Transformation of Contemporary Democracy* (London: Harvard University Press).
Favell, A., 2001, Integration policy and integration research in Europe: A review and critique, in: T. A. Aleinikoff and D. Klusmeyer (Eds) *Citizenship Today: Global Perspectives and Practices* (Washington, DC: Brookings Institute), pp. 349–399.
Fischer, F., 1989, *Technocracy and the Politics of Expertise* (London: Sage).
Fischer, F., 1993, Policy Discourse and the Politics of Washington Think Tanks, in: F. Fischer and J. Forester (Eds), *The Argumentative Turn in Policy Analysis and Planning* (Durham: Duke University Press).
Gieryn, T. F., 1983, Boundary-work and the demarcation of science from non-science: Strains and Interests in professional ideologies of scientists. *American Sociological Review*, **4**, pp. 781–795.
Gieryn, T. F., 1995, Boundaries of science, in: S. Jasanoff, G. E. Markle, J. C. Petersen and T. Pinch (Eds) *Handbook of Science and Technology Studies* (Thousand Oaks, CA: Pine Forge Press), pp. 393–443.
Gieryn, T. F., 1999, *Cultural Boundaries of Science; Credibility on the Line* (Chicago: University of Chicago Press).
Guston, D. H., 2000, *Between Politics and Science. Assuring the Integrity and Productivity of Research* (New Brunswick, NJ: Rutgers University).
Hajer, M. A., 1995, *The Politics of Environmental Discourse: Ecological Modernization and the Policy Process* (Oxford: Oxford University Press).
Halffman, W., 2003, *Boundaries of Regulatory Science: Eco/Toxicology and Aquatic Hazards of Chemicals in the US, England and the Netherlands* (Boechout: Albatros).
Hammar, T., 1985, *European Immigration Policy. a Comparative Study* (Cambridge: Cambridge University Press).
Heckmann, F., 1981, *Die Bundesrepublik, Ein Einwanderungsland? Zur Soziologie Der Gastarbeiterbevölkerung Als Einwandererminorität* (Stuttgart: Klett-Cotta).
Hoppe, R., 2005, Rethinking the science-policy nexus: From knowledge utilization and science technology studies to types of boundary arrangements. *Poiesis & Praxis: International Journal of Technology Assessment and Ethics of Science*, **3**, pp. 199–215.
Jasanoff, S., 1990, *The Fifth Branch: ScienceAadvisers as Policymakers* (London: Cambridge University Press).
Jasanoff, S., 2004, *States of Knowledge; the Co-Production of Science and Social Order* (New York: Routledge).
Lasswell, H. D., 1970, The emerging conception of the policy sciences. *Policy Sciences*, **1**, pp. 3–14.
Miller, C. A., 2001, Hybrid management: Boundary organizations, science policy and environmental governance in the climate regime. *Science, Technology and Human Values*, **26**, pp. 478–500.
Nowotny, H., Scott, P. and Gibbons, M., 2001, *Re-Thinking Science: Knowledge and the Public in an Age of Uncertainty* (London: Polity Press).
Pennix, R., 1988, *Minderheidsvorming En Emancipatie: Balans Van Kennisverwerving Ten Aanzien Van Immigranten En Woonwagenbewoners 1967–1987* (Alphen aan den Rijn: Samsom).
Rath, J., 2001, Research on immigrant ethnic minorities in the Netherlands, in: P. Ratcliffe (Ed) *The Politics of Social Science Research. Race, Ethnicity and Social Change* (New York: Palgrave).
Scheffer, P. 2000, Het multiculturele drama. *NRC Handelsblad*, January 27.

Schneider, J., 2010, *Modernes Regieren Und Konsens? Kommissionen Und Beratungsregime in Der Deutschen Migrationspolitik* (Wiesbaden: VS Verlag für Sozialwissenschaften).
Scholten, P., 2009, The co-production of immigrant integration policy and research in the Netherlands: The case of the Scientific Council for Government Policy. *Science & Public Policy*, **36**, pp. 561–573.
Scholten, P., 2011, *Framing Immigrant Integration: Dutch Research-Policy Dialogues in Comparative Perspective* (Amsterdam: Amsterdam University Press).
Scholten, P. and Timmermans, A., 2010, Setting the immigrant policy agenda: Expertise and politics in France, the UK and the Netherlands. *Journal of Comparative Policy Analysis*, **12**, pp. 527–543.
Shapin, S., 1992, Discipline and bounding: The history and sociology of science as seen through the externalism-internalism debate. *History of Science*, **30**, pp. 333–369.
Shapin, S., and Schaffer, S., 1985, *The Leviathan and the Air-Pump; Hobbes, Boyle and the Experimental Life* (Princeton, NJ: Princeton University Press).
Stone, D., 1998, *Capturing the Political Imagination: Think Tanks and the Policy Process* (London: Cass).
Unabhängige Kommision 'Zuwanderung, 2001, *Zuwanderung gestalten, Integration fördern* (Berlin).
Verwey-Jonker Instituut, 2004, *Bronnenonderzoek. Tijdelijke Commissie Onderzoek Integratiebeleid* (Den Haag: SDU).
Weingart, P., 1999, Scientific expertise and political accountability: Paradoxes of science in politics. *Science and Public Policy*, **26**, pp. 151–162.
Wildavsky, A., 1979, *Speaking Truth to Power; the Art and Craft of Policy Analysis* (Boston, MA: Little Brown).

Fiscal Federalism and the Politics of Immigration: Centralized and Decentralized Immigration Policies in Canada and the United States

GRAEME BOUSHEY and ADAM LUEDTKE

ABSTRACT *Why would immigration policy be centralized or decentralized in a federal system? What incentives do political actors at the central and sub-central levels of government possess vis-à-vis immigration policy? Taking account of the growing need to make sense of the unique features of immigration policy in a federal system (e.g. the mobility of labor, regional and national identities), and the unique challenges to federalism posed by immigration (e.g. public policy co-ordination, social cohesiveness), this paper advances a general theory of immigration politics in federations. It then illustrates this theory through discussion of two empirical cases: Canada and the United States.*

Introduction

In recent years political scientists have asked sophisticated questions about the economic and political benefits of federated systems of government (Weingast 1995, Rodden and Rose-Ackerman 1997, Oates 1999, Radin and Boase 2000, McKay 2001). Studies of federalism have been designed to explore two distinct claims about confederated power sharing: first, that federalism mediates costs of inter-state trade by reducing transaction costs on the flow of labor and goods across state lines; and, second, that federations permit national unity in ethnically diverse states by sharing the goods of national government at the federal level, while granting a degree of political autonomy to minority groups at the subnational level.

Given the increasing interest in the economic and political goods provided by federalism in recent years, it is surprising that no political scientists have developed models to integrate theories of immigration policy into a discussion of federalism. As government policy, immigration programs shape both the economic performance and ethnic make-up of the polity. Immigration policies recruit and distribute labor throughout federations, and in so doing they inevitably shift the demographic composition of the subnational units. Given this, we would expect immigration policy to be a source of institutional conflict between the central and subnational governments in federations.

This paper seeks to test these assertions by asking the following questions: why would immigration policy be centralized or decentralized in a federal system? What incentives do political actors at the central and subcentral levels of government possess vis-à-vis immigration policy? Taking account of the growing need to make sense of the unique features of immigration policy in a federal system (e.g. the mobility of labor, regional and national identities), and the unique challenges to federalism posed by immigration (e.g. public policy co-ordination, social cohesiveness), this paper hypothesizes an expected model of immigration politics in federations. It then tests this expected model against current and past reality through discussion of policy development in two empirical cases: Canada and the United States.

In the next section we draw from the literature on fiscal federalism to hypothesize an optimal, expected division of powers, whereby immigration *control* policy would be centralized, but immigrant *integration* policy would be decentralized. We then apply this model to the cases of Canada and the United States, assessing the actual degree of (de)centralization of these two aspects of policy, and explaining the reasons behind this (de)centralization. We analyze factors related to both economics and the preservation of "nations", including citizenship policy. We conclude by briefly speculating on the relevance of three other federal systems for our model: Switzerland, Australia, and the European Union. The EU is a fascinating test for our theory, as it represents an emerging federation that is experimenting with new policies for immigration control. We close by arguing that the EU's recent centralization of immigration policy holds important implications for our theory. As Europe's leaders attempt to create a common immigration policy, they are forced to balance the efficiency gains of a common policy against the high political costs that arise from turning over important features of national sovereignty to a supranational body.

Immigration Policy Devolution and Theories of Fiscal Federalism

Economic Implications of Immigration Policy

How can we explain the degree of decentralization of immigration policy in federal systems? That is, under what conditions would political actors in federal systems choose to decentralize immigration policy? Presumably, central and subcentral governments will face differing costs and benefits in controlling or not controlling various aspects of immigration policy. These costs and benefits might be economic, or they might manifest themselves in non-economic areas, such as cultural and linguistic preservation.

The literature on fiscal federalism (Tiebout 1956, Weingast 1995, Oates 1999) presents one line of reasoning on the likely costs and benefits of placing immigration policy jurisdiction at various levels of government, and thus the likely preferences of governments regarding whether or not to push for such jurisdiction. There are two features of the economics of immigration that hold relevance for federalism: a free-flowing labor market, and matching immigrants with the specific needs of a subnational market. We will deal with each of these in turn.

Take the public good of a free-flowing labor market.[1] Economic theory emphasizes the virtues of labor mobility. Because labor surpluses and shortages are variable over time and location, the faster that workers can shift to respond to relative changes, the more efficient the economy will be. Given discrepancies between labor markets, the market value of an individual is higher in one locale than in another, meaning that the gains from a move will normally outweigh the expected costs of a move, even given the existence of significant transaction costs. These gains are in theory reaped by both the immigrant and the employer, and are thus welfare gains for society as a whole, since such gains generally outweigh the costs that are imposed on social welfare services, and other externalities (Simon 1989). Any factor standing in the way of worker mobility becomes a hindrance to economic growth.

If we conceive of border controls as a transaction cost, then immigration control might be prohibitively expensive, since it could make an otherwise profitable move more costly than the expected gains. Visa checks, waiting periods, administrative fees, border patrols, customs agents, and immigration lawyers all cost money. Why is this especially relevant to federal polities? Because, *ceterus paribus*, one would expect that the crossing of *two* borders entails more transaction costs than the crossing of one border. Thus, despite the fact that a province may have an interest in keeping labor out (or in), federal polities will have an (overall) more efficient labor market if they permit the free flow of workers between subnational units, without the maintenance of subnational immigration controls. From an economic point of view, immigration *control* policy (monitoring immigrants at the frontier) should be centralized.

Further, the primary purpose of immigration controls is to keep out unwanted immigrants. Maintaining *subnational* immigration controls would not only impede the workings of labor market efficiency, but could also lead to another problem, commonly known in the fiscal federalism literature as a "spillover effect" or "externality" (Oates 1999). Imagine a federal polity (such as today's European Union) where 25 different territorial units all maintain their own immigration controls.[2] A given immigrant wants to gain entry to one of these 25 jurisdictions to look for work, and when he enters one jurisdiction (legally or illegally), that jurisdiction bears transaction costs in dealing with him. If the immigrant is denied legal access to that jurisdiction, and is unable to gain illegal entry due to the costly monitoring and border patrol by that jurisdiction, he faces incentives to immigrate into one of the other 24 polities that might need labor. So, he goes on to the second jurisdiction, which also faces transaction costs in monitoring his presence and keeping him out. In practice, immigrants who have been denied entry are often dumped onto neighboring polities, causing negative externalities (Geddes 2000). The problem here is that without co-operation or co-ordination between subnational units, one immigrant is free to attempt entry to all 25 units, forcing each jurisdiction to bear costs to keep him out. Despite the fact that they would be better off with a co-operative policy, all polities will scramble to be the least hospitable to unwanted immigrants, causing a "race to the bottom", whereby polities attempt to outdo each other by devising more costly and restrictive immigration control structures, and dumping more immigrants onto their neighbors. Here, the advantage of coordination is that it reduces all of these costs, including externalities, by centralizing the provision of the public good of immigration control. If there is a common administrative apparatus, which can identify immigrants when they arrive at any point on the market's external border, then instead of bearing the costs of multiple entry attempts, the combined polities must only bear the cost of one entry attempt. Thus, the nature of the public good itself militates towards centralized immigration *control* policies. From this discussion, we advance our first basic hypothesis regarding federal immigration policy.

H1a: Given the high costs and inefficiencies associated with maintaining immigration control policy at the sub-central level, immigration control policies in federal systems will be centralized.

Under what conditions might this hypothesis not hold? High negotiation costs and/or high political costs over giving up sovereignty would be the only situation in which a federal polity might maintain separate border controls for each sub-central unit. Thus, in the rare case that the political costs of negotiation/delegation exceed the political gains from economic growth, we might expect subcentral politicians to refrain from advocating federal control.

Immigration control policies are not the only aspects of immigration policy that have economic implications. Jeannette Money (1999) posits an important distinction between immigration *control* policy, and immigrant *integration* policy (also see Hammar 1985, 1990). Unlike immigration control policy, which deals with keeping out unwanted immigrants, immigrant integration policy deals with the recruitment, selection, welcoming and settlement of desired immigrants. We will here apply fiscal federalism logic to argue that immigrant integration entails public goods that are likely to be optimally provided at the subcentral level.

Assuming that immigrants and employers might not have perfect information about each other's preferences, it will be more efficient for this public good to be provided subnationally, as subnational governments can tailor the output of this good "to the particular preferences and circumstances of their constituencies" (Oates 1999: 1121–1122). Some labor markets might indicate that they do not need immigrants at all, while other constituencies might want only high-tech workers or unskilled workers, according to local variation in labor markets. The economic logic here is that "efficient level of output of a 'local' public good ... is likely to vary across jurisdictions as a result of both differences in preferences and cost differentials" (Oates 1999: 1122).

Efficiency for decentralized integration policy arises because subnational officials possess knowledge of "both local preferences and cost conditions that a central agency is unlikely to have" (Oates 1999: 1123). Also, "there are typically political pressures ... that limit the capacity of central governments to provide higher levels of public services in some jurisdictions than in others" (Oates 1999: 1123). Thus, even if one subnational unit could gain more from providing information to immigrants and employers than another unit, a centralized policy might not be flexible enough to respond to these varying potential gains in an optimal manner, perhaps due to political concerns over "equality" between subnational units.

Further, in line with the literature on "market-preserving federalism" (Weingast 1995), competition among jurisdictions in providing information and matching labor market needs with immigrants makes the provision of this public good more efficient. The logic is that mobile capital and immigrants will punish (through their exit) jurisdictions that do not efficiently provide the public goods of information and matching. If two jurisdictions need skilled high-tech workers but only one of them has an effective recruitment policy, with overseas promotional offices and suchlike, then both immigrants and capital will flock to the jurisdiction that is providing the more useful information and matching, thus providing gains to that jurisdiction, and incentives for other jurisdictions to improve their public goods to attract similar capital and workers, if they are needed.

In this situation, an additional argument for decentralization comes into play, which is the argument for "laboratory federalism" (Oates 1999). In this account, decentralized immigrant integration policies will provide an additional public good beyond their immediate uses to particular jurisdictions, that being the dissemination of knowledge about newer and better methods for recruiting and settling immigrants. That is, successful subnational immigrant integration policies will not only provide beneficial returns to their jurisdictions, but will also provide an exemplar and a model whereby the less successful jurisdictions can learn and benefit from the successful experiment of their counterpart.

Of course, the laboratory argument might also apply to immigration *control*. Why should immigration control not be decentralized so that subnational units can learn from the successes and failures of each other's immigration control strategies? The answer is that the efficiency losses from the aforementioned transaction costs and externalities/spillovers in the realm of control will most likely outweigh the potential gains from subnational experimentation and policy emulation. On the other hand, any efficiency losses from multiple immigrant *integration* policies would presumably be less than the benefits reaped from local differentiation in this policy area.

This discussion of immigrant integration policy in models of fiscal federalism serves as the basis for our second hypothesis regarding optimal immigration policy in federations.

H2a: Because subcentral governments are better suited to determine local needs and preferences, immigrant integration policy in federations will be determined through subcentral government policy.

Nation-Preserving Implications of Immigration Policy

Having covered the possible *economic* costs and benefits of (de)centralizing two aspects of immigration policy (control and integration), let us now turn to the most salient non-economic issues at stake. Immigration has a contentious political dimension that other economic issues lack, which is its connection with national identity, membership and belonging. This makes it a particularly acute challenge for all states, federal or not. Whether the "nation" is conceived as a subnational ethnic group, or all the people of a nation-state, immigration is much more than a technocratic issue of policy efficiency, because it can ultimately define who the nation is, and by doing so can challenge deeply held norms regarding the nature of belonging to the nation.

In federal polities, this question becomes even more complex, because subnational units often consider themselves as "nations" in their own right, or at least hold distinctive norms regarding language and culture. Thus, the particular needs of local jurisdictions take center stage, and become politically acute. Again, we can use the fiscal federalism literature to derive hypotheses about the costs and benefits of decentralization.

First, let us take immigrant integration policy. Regarding their unique "nation-preserving" needs, subcentral governments can tailor the output of immigrant integration policy "to the particular preferences and circumstances of their constituencies" (Oates 1999: 1121–1122). This would include language classes, "citizenship" classes on topics like local culture, and, most importantly, the recruitment of the "right" immigrants for matching distinct linguistic and cultural needs. Also, the "efficient level of output of a 'local' public good ... is likely to vary across jurisdictions as a result of both differences in preferences and cost differentials" (Oates 1999: 1122). In other words, some subnational units might stand to gain a great deal from a particular immigrant integration policy, while others might gain less. Also, subnational officials probably possess knowledge of "both local preferences and cost conditions that a central agency is likely to have" (Oates 1999: 1123). And, finally, "there are typically political pressures...that limit the capacity of central governments to provide higher levels of public services in some jurisdictions than in others" (Oates 1999: 1123). For example, Canadian taxpayers might balk at financing French classes for immigrants (and might punish central politicians that approved such a policy), but *Quebecois* voters would certainly be more willing to bear the costs of such a policy. A federal system as a whole might not have an interest in preserving a subnational culture or language, but a subcentral "nation" will have an interest in self-preservation, and thus will be more willing and able to design and finance a policy to ensure this survival.

When viewed from the lens of nation-preserving federalism, we might strengthen the rationale behind hypothesizing that immigrant integration policy would be devolved.

H2b: Given local preferences for specific linguistic and cultural preservation, immigrant integration policy is likely to be controlled by subcentral governments.

Of course, the strength of this proposition depends on the degree to which subcentral level politicians are under pressure to preserve regional identity. The less pressure subcentral politicians feel on this topic, the less the gains specified above become operative as motivators. Obviously, local identities must be under some degree of perceived "threat" before these gains become operative. One possible threat might be a dying language, where the rate of speaking it is reducing with each generation. Another possible threat might be a low birth rate (especially if it is below the replacement rate of 2.2 children).

If subcentral governments should be in charge of recruitment, settlement and the societal integration of immigrants, then why should the central government have any role in immigration *control*, especially in a multi-ethnic, multi-national or multi-lingual federal polity? Why should not passports, citizenship, visas, and so forth be made an all-provincial affair? Aside from the previously described economic and enforcement inefficiencies of multiple border controls, there are two "nation"-related reasons why immigration control, in theory, is likely to remain a central affair, even in a diverse polity. The first has to do with norms and traditions of national sovereignty, and the second has to do with the political goal of national cohesion in a federal polity.

Norms and traditions of national sovereignty arise out of the Westphalian system, and are important in determining why immigration control would theoretically remain centralized. Aside from the co-ordination problems and efficiency losses that would come from having multiple passports, visas, border controls, or rights of passage in a federal polity, there is also a strong tendency towards perceiving all the trappings of national "sovereignty" as a public good. This view is bound up with concepts like security and defense, and sees the protection of common borders as one of the powers that consistently lie at the centralized end of the federal spectrum. Riker (1964: 5) sees the advantage of federalism as allowing subnational units "to make use of the technological advantages in the size of treasuries and armies and thus to compete successfully with their neighbors". One of these technological implications is the ability to control a large border and patrol it with armies, police, airplanes, boats, radar, metal detectors, and so on. Pooling sovereignty to control a larger border allows subnational units to gain protection from any potential external threats, as well as to participate in the aggression of the polity and the expansion of these borders (Riker 1964). Again, our argument depends on gains/losses as perceived by subcentral politicians. If negotiation/sovereignty costs are perceived as high, then subcentral units may be reluctant to take advantage of the gains to be had in pooling resources.[3]

The second "nation"-related factor militating against devolution of immigration control is the goal of national cohesion. In addition to the traditional elements of territorial control inherent in statehood, the idea of *citizenship* is traditionally administered at the central level, even in multi-national polities. This is partly bound up with Westphalian norms and traditions, but is also employed as a practical political exercise in devising a baseline national identity. Indeed, if the "nation-preserving" aspects of immigration control policy (like passports and citizenship) were decentralized, then we might say that secession has already taken place – in other words, the federal polity would no longer be a polity!

Again, viewed from the perspective of nation-preserving federalism, we are again able to reinforce our hypothesis regarding centralized immigration control policy.

H1b: As both security and citizenship are traditional nation-preserving functions of the central government, immigration control is likely to be part of central government policy.

Thus, when viewed from either the perspective of market- or nation-preserving federalism, we hypothesize that immigration control policies will be centralized, and immigrant integration policies will be decentralized.

Late-Decentralizing Canada as a Ideal-Type Case of Federal Immigration Policy?

Based on the theories of fiscal federalism outlined above, we expect to find that immigration control policy in a federal polity will be centralized, while immigrant integration policy will be decentralized, since this arrangement would theoretically reap the largest political and economic gains. Let us now turn to the real world and measure these propositions against empirical fact. Oates (1999: 1124) calls on scholars of federalism to discover "the extent to which the potential gains from decentralization can explain the observed variation in actual governmental structure and policies".

Immigration is one of the few policy areas deemed a "concurrent power" in the Canadian constitution, meaning that jurisdiction is formally shared between Ottawa and the provinces. Federal legislation is given "paramountcy", but provincial legislatures possess the ability to make immigration laws, while the federal government is only given the ability "from time to time" to make immigration laws. As long as the provincial laws are not "repugnant" to the federal, they stand as official legislation. Furthermore, the provinces possess greater powers in the area of immigrant *integration* and settlement, because these tend to fall under the exclusively provincial jurisdictions of property and civil rights (Black and Hagen 1993). Thus, actual practice aside, Canada's constitution already leans toward the ideal-type model implied in the fiscal federalism literature, with immigrant integration being decentralized, and immigration control being centralized.

Despite this constitutional prerogative, the Canadian provinces went over 100 years without fully taking advantage of their constitutional powers in the area of immigration (Hawkins 1988). This section will show how provincial actors did this because there were few gains to be had in getting involved in immigration policy until recently, confirming Oates's theory regarding the explanatory power of the gains of decentralization.

How did the recent potential gains from decentralization manifest themselves politically? The 1991 Canadian devolution of immigrant integration policy was mainly caused by the efforts of politicians in Quebec, who sought to preserve its distinct French language and culture. But why were there no gains for Quebecois politicians to pursue immigration powers earlier? In fact, there were gains to be had in the much earlier period between confederation and 1874, when Quebec pursued an actively independent immigration policy, based upon "a blend of demographic, linguistic and economic considerations" (Black and Hagen 1993: 282), aimed at the preservation of its francophone character in the face of increasing anglophone immigration and settlement. This policy even included the establishment of provincial immigration offices overseas (a practice widely revived under the 1991 Accord). However, at a federal-provincial conference in 1874 it was decided that this arrangement should be scrapped as a needless exercise in duplication and overlap. Quebec complied in closing shop, since it had experienced little success with recruiting the francophone and Catholic immigrants it desired. As Quebec's birthrate was still quite high at that point in history, the demographic implications of such non-involvement were not nearly as severe as they would become under modern conditions. Thus, the Quebecois community willingly gave up the immigration game, preferring to isolate itself in rural, religious communities while non-francophone immigrants flocked into the province in substantial numbers.

This situation continued unabated for decades, until the Second World War and the subsequent boom in Canadian immigration. While this new influx was met largely by passive hostility from Quebecois, a small francophone elite began to spread an alternative discourse with four themes: the threat of growing immigration levels to French survival, the need for integration of new immigrants into the French community, the need for expanded French language education, and the need for the provincial government to take an active interest and involvement in meeting these challenges (Black and Hagen 1993: 285–286).

Along with the "Quiet Revolution" and growing French self-determination in the 1960s, the Quebecois government eventually asserted itself in immigration policy, using its constitutional mandate to take concerted action. Immigration was now newly conceived as a potential gain. Vineberg (1987: 307) argues that "in the past immigration had been perceived as a cultural invasion, destroying the linguistic balance of the province. From 1965, however, increasingly immigration came to be perceived as a tool to strengthen the francophone nature of Quebec society".

Along with linguistic motivations for provincial immigrant integration policy, demographic concerns played a large part in the reconceptualization of immigration as a gain. The massive drop in birthrate that followed the Quiet Revolution was seen as a critical threat to the survival of "the nation". This reinforced a perception that immigration policy, along with state-supported natalist policies, could counteract this demographic trend. Economic considerations also played a role, since Quebec's government took an active part in directing and stimulating the economy, especially intervening in labor markets. Such intervention matched with the "desire to maximize the economic benefits associated with the selection of skilled or capital-endowed candidates" (Black and Hagen 1993: 280), and meant that Quebec's government sought to take an increased role in selecting and integrating immigrants for economic purposes, while being willing to leave immigration control to the central government.

After a long period of constitutional turmoil and political contestation between Quebec and Canada, and in response to the new perceptions of potential economic, linguistic and demographic gains to be won, Quebec successfully negotiated the 1991 "Canada-Quebec Accord Relating to Immigration and Temporary Admission of Aliens", which decentralized aspects of immigrant integration policy (recruitment, selection, reception, settlement, and so forth) while leaving immigration control policy (border control, citizenship, passports, visas, and so on) as a federal power. This division of powers matches the ideal-type division proposed above, because it permitted Quebec to provide locally relevant, immigration-related public goods (integration) itself, while consuming nationally relevant, immigration-related public goods (control) provided by the government of Canada. Quebec now sets its own annual immigration targets, and has sole responsibility for selecting immigrants who wish to settle in the province (with the exception of refugees and family reunification). "The government of Quebec also assumes full responsibility for providing orientation and integration services to new permanent residents" (CIC 2003: 1). Quebec even has independent offices abroad, for recruitment, selection and screening purposes.[4]

Quebec's separatist movement clearly provided provincial decision makers with unique bargaining power in negotiating with Ottawa. But what of the other nine provinces? While identity-based arguments would see no gain for English-speaking provinces to pursue distinctive immigration policies, fiscal federalism theory would posit that even without the potential "nation-preserving" gains of recruiting and settling immigrants according to linguistic criteria, provinces should still want to take advantage of the *economic* benefits of decentralized immigrant integration policy (matching immigrants with the needs of the local labor market). Not surprisingly, leaders in other provinces were quick to assert powers in immigrant integration policy. Bilateral agreements have now been signed with all ten provinces (CIC 2003).

Some of these agreements fall under the "Provincial Nominee Program", which allows provinces to identify and nominate an agreed-upon number of potential immigrants who will "contribute to economic development by filling specific regional or local needs" (CIC 2003: 1). This matches well with the implied economic benefits of decentralization proposed by the fiscal federalism literature. "Many of the levers that make immigration work are the responsibility of the provinces... education, health, welfare, social housing... In general, provinces want... to influence immigration planning, policies and programs... to support their particular social, demographic and economic development" (Hall 2002: 3). For instance, in the province of Manitoba, small rural towns have used the program to bring in skilled workers. Under the Manitoba "Community Initiative", a number of stakeholders, such as the Chamber of Commerce, schools, churches and employers, provide guaranteed employment and social support for immigrants. Early indications show that "provincial nominees are staying in the rural areas, raising families, contributing to economic growth, integrating well into host communities" (Hall 2002: 9). Prince Edward Island, facing depopulation, uses its immigrant strategy for demographic purposes, whereas New Brunswick's strategy places a higher priority on immigrants who can be economically self-sufficient. British Columbia's strategy targets labor shortages in certain high-growth economic sectors, such as health, high-tech and management (Hall 2002).

From the diffusion of bilateral agreements across the provinces, it is clear that Quebec provided a policy laboratory that set an example for other provinces. While the impetus would perhaps have been absent without Canada's legacy of dual founding nations, we see that a distinct provincial "identity" is not a necessary condition for policy diffusion. Although the decentralization of immigrant integration policy in Canada is not complete (Ottawa still retains primary power over setting total *levels* of immigration, though this could be seen as a control issue), the Canadian case does seem to closely approximate the fiscal federalism theory outlined above. Some other factors might come to mind as possibly explaining the rapid policy diffusion across provinces, such as party politics or institutional factors that bias Canadian politics towards regional interests (McKay 2001, Rodden 2001). However, the above evidence shows that the economic, demographic and social costs and benefits of immigration offer a compelling explanation for the degree of policy devolution in Canada.

Early Centralization in the United States: Causes and Consequences

The Canadian experiment with immigrant integration policies differs drastically from the trend towards federal centralization of immigration policy in the United States. While Canada's policies have shifted to empower provincial governments to meet specific labor and cultural needs, authority over American immigration policy is almost exclusively located at the federal level of government. Congress legislates over both control and integration of immigrants in the US; first establishing criteria for selecting the number and type of immigrants granted legal residence in the US, and then specifying the guidelines for naturalization. State governments share some of the costs of immigrant integration programs – specifically in education, health care, and job training; however they have little formal authority in determining the flow of immigration into their jurisdictions. In this regard, the federal government oversees the significant market- *and* nation-preserving elements of American immigration policy.

This section briefly reviews the trend towards centralized immigration policy in the United States over the last 150 years. Importantly, it reviews the constitutional and political factors that led to federal control of immigration. We argue that nationally centralized immigration policies grew from congressional efforts to standardize state immigration policies following the Civil War. These federal efforts not only established a national immigration policy, but implemented specific controls over the ethnicity of immigrants, which reflected an emerging concern with national identity in the United States. Thus the incentives for centralization were rooted in market- and nation-preserving federal policies. The discussion concludes with an analysis of recent state-level efforts to address local costs from immigration. Although these policy experiments have yet to produce significant new powers for state governments, they suggest that a Canadian-style system of concurrent powers might prove politically popular in the United States.

The trend towards centralization of immigration policy in the United States is intriguing, as for much of early US history laws regulating immigration were determined at the state level. Historically, the United States can be said to have operated two distinct systems of immigration policy. The first system, from the founding until the late 1800s, evolved informally from concurrent policies enacted by both federal and state governments (Neuman 1993). The second system emerged well after the Civil War, when through judicial review and congressional legislation the national government asserted its constitutional authority to harmonize disparate immigration laws (Hutchinson 1981). In order to understand the centralization of immigration control policy in the United States, it is critical to understand both phases of immigration policy. The trend towards centralization emerged largely from an effort to reduce the significant transaction costs and spillover effects caused by state-level policies to *control* the flow of immigration.

The first system of US immigration policy stands as an historical example of the inefficiencies incurred by subnational controls on immigrant mobility. In an era when the federal government encouraged relatively free and unrestricted immigration, laws conferring rights of residence were largely enacted at the state level (Smith 1998). Border and port states from Massachusetts to Texas passed laws regulating the flow of "undesirable" immigrants. These laws specifically targeted those immigrants who would threaten or burden society – the poor, sick, criminals, slaves, and ethnically distinct populations (Neuman 1993). State legislatures adopted entry taxes or bonds to discourage the indigent from settling (Neuman 1993). In response to the justified concern that European states were exporting social deviants, laws were written that prohibited entry of criminals (Neuman 1993). Ethnic minorities were subject to some of the most restrictive regulation; in the North and

South, state policies regulated the mobility of free blacks across state borders (Neuman 1993). California passed a several laws severely restricting the intake of Chinese immigrants (Wey 1988). Although these state regulations stop short of an encompassing immigration policy per se, they demonstrate a pattern to mediate against the costs of the open immigration policy endorsed by the federal government (LeMay 1987).

Not surprisingly, state-level legislation in immigration control resulted in much policy variation across states, and caused friction between state and federal governments. Supreme Court hearings in the nineteenth century resolved many of these disputes.[5] Although the constitution did not explicitly confer immigration authority to the president or Congress, in 1875 the Court legitimized federal control of immigration policy, ruling that power over immigration control ultimately rested with congressional control over foreign trade and naturalization (Smith 1998).

Recognizing the problems and inefficiencies presented by the inconsistent immigration control laws at the state level, Congress enacted several successive laws to harmonize American immigration control policy (Hutchinson 1981). The Immigration Act of 1891 created a federal immigration service that oversaw entry into the nation. The Basic Naturalization Act of 1906 "proscribed standard naturalization forms, encouraged state and local courts to relinquish their naturalization jurisdiction to Federal courts, and expanded the Bureau of Immigration into the Bureau of Immigration and Naturalization" (Smith 1998: 1). Through the twentieth century, Congress enacted legislation that increasingly located the control of immigration at the federal level (LeMay 1987). In this sense, centralization of immigration control policy at the turn of the twentieth century follows the theoretical model of immigration in federations. By normalizing immigration control policies, the federal government lowered costs associated with state-level control of immigration policy.

The centralization of US recruitment/integration polices during the same period fits less neatly into our ideal-type model of immigration policy in federations. The rise of nativism across the states translated into national immigration policies that established race-based quotas for immigrant recruitment and integration. Indeed, policies governing the recruitment and naturalization of targeted ethnic populations of immigrants were among the first standardized policies authorized by Congress (LeMay 1987). After assuming control over immigration recruitment, Congress duplicated California's earlier efforts to limit Chinese immigration, enacting the Chinese Exclusion Act in 1882 (Wey 1988). This legislation only indicated the beginning of restrictive policies towards immigrant recruitment. The National Origins Act of 1924 established screening standards that gave priority to western and northern Europeans over other ethnic groups (Briggs 1991). US immigration policy continued through a system of racial quotas until the Immigration Act of 1965 effectively ended race-based admission standards in immigration (Briggs 1991). Today Congress continues to legislate over targeted populations – privileging certain immigrant groups (family members, refuges, skilled workers) over all others.

A major concern with modern US immigration policy is that it functions poorly in recruiting and distributing specialized labor (Briggs 1991). This is perhaps not surprising given the historical function of immigration policy in the US, to: a) encourage the flow of mass immigration for low-skilled industrial and agricultural labor; and b) exclude or target immigrant communities based on demographic and political factors. The United States does administer visiting worker visa programs to recruit immigrants with expertise in areas of need (technology; health care and so forth); however, these market-preserving immigration policies are determined by the central government. In practice, fairly perfunctory checks are done to ensure that specialized visas are granted according to local labor needs and shortages (Briggs 1991).

State governments have been left largely outside of immigration policy over the last 100 years. However they have nonetheless attempted to influence policy over the market-preserving elements of immigrant integration/recruitment programs. State representatives have petitioned for expansion of visa programs for specialized pools of labor that will meet the needs of their jurisdiction. For example, California representatives have advocated for the expansion of the H1B visa program to meet the growing demand for technical-oriented labor in Silicon Valley.[6] Yet these appeals are largely informal. State governments must communicate through congressional representatives, and have little say in the actual placement of new workers.

Some border states have also asserted limited powers over immigration control, and have taken steps to mediate against the high costs of both documented and undocumented immigration across their borders. While states have no authority in controlling the mobility of immigrants once they have entered the United States, they are responsible for providing basic social services (health care, education, welfare) to new immigrants. Those states with the highest rates of immigration have argued that this policy is unfair – as it demands that they shoulder much of the cost of mass immigration with limited support from the federal government (Borjas 1999). States have experimented with both federal lawsuits and local policies to address these concerns. In 1994 California and Texas together unsuccessfully sued the federal government for compensation for the costs of illegal immigration. California and Arizona have experimented with more dramatic strategies for deterring immigration. California voters passed the notorious Proposition 187 in 1994, designed to limit the social service spending on undocumented immigrants by restricting their access to publicly funded healthcare, education, and social welfare programs. Arizona voters approved a similar initiative (Proposition 200) in 2004. Both California and Arizona have also passed legislation requiring English language instruction in education.

These policies reflect state-level efforts to recover some authority in market- and nation-preserving aspects of immigration policy. Like the pauper laws at the founding of the Republic, California and Arizona have flirted with proposals to limit the influx of poor and unskilled laborers. Not surprisingly, it is difficult to separate these economic concerns with the rise of nativism in the southwest. Social policies in education are demonstrative of state-level identity-preserving policy.

Such experimentation with immigration policy at the state level suggests that local governments would welcome devolution of immigrant integration authority. The justification for this is both economic and cultural. Not only do state governments bear the economic costs of immigrant integration in the United States, but there is rising political and cultural friction over immigration in the southwest. States such as California, with a long tradition of nativism, are forced to balance policies to preserve their own "national identity" with the immigration programs of the national government.

The United States deviates from the hypothesized model of federal immigration policy in some significant ways. The centralization of immigration *control* policies solved the inefficiencies of early subnational control of immigration mobility. However, in this trend to centralization the federal government assumed control of virtually all aspects of immigration policy – from nation-preserving, race-based quota programs, to market-preserving labor recruitment programs. The result is that immigrant-heavy states are increasingly frustrated with their lack of voice in immigration policy. Where possible, state governments have experimented with immigrant recruitment and integration policies. However, these are weakened by a lack of formal concurrent powers with the center. This institutional arrangement has imposed costs on subnational governments in two key ways – first it has complicated the recruitment of specialized labor to meet local needs. Second, mass immigration remains a politically divisive issue in some of the nation's largest states.

Conclusion

Table 1 summarizes the findings of our two case studies for the ideal-type model proposed earlier. To recap, it was argued that based on the federalist theory of public goods provision and levels of government, immigration control policy will be

Table 1. Centralization of control and integration policies in Canada and the US

	Control – centralized?	Integration – decentralized?
Market-preserving federal immigration policy?	*Canada:* Yes. Free-flowing labor market, no externalities and no race to the bottom *US:* Yes. Free-flowing labor market, no externalities. (Note: some local experimentation with control – might lead to race the bottom)	*Canada:* Yes. Provinces that stand to gain can respond to local labor market needs, provide information to and match preferences for employers and immigrants *US:* No. National government controls recruitment of labor through visa programs. Number and type of immigrants are decided nationally. No state control over recruitment or placement of immigrant labor.
Nation-preserving federal immigration policy?	*Canada:* Yes. Despite separatist worries, they have preserved national cohesion, national security and Westphalian sovereignty. *US:* Yes. Strongly centralized border controls, security, etc. Early centralized immigration recruitment policy explicitly nation preserving.	*Canada:* Yes. Quebec's control over integration efficiently responds to local cultural and linguistic preferences while triggering relatively little political animosity. *US:* Partially. Significant central control over immigration recruitment and placement. State control over new immigrant education and social welfare.

centralized, while immigrant integration policy will be decentralized. Centralizing immigration control would preserve markets by allowing the free flow of labor, minimizing externalities and preventing a race to the bottom, and would preserve nations by upholding national cohesion, national security and Westphalian sovereignty. Decentralizing immigrant integration policy would preserve markets by allowing provinces that stand to gain to respond to local labor market needs, and to provide information and match preferences for prospective immigrants and employers, and would preserve nations by allowing provinces to efficiently respond to local cultural and linguistic preferences without triggering political animosity.

Generally, we see that both federations approximate the conditions of the model with regard to centralized immigration control policies. Both the United States and Canada operate centralized systems of border and port control, allowing provincial and state governments to share the costs of common security problems. As importantly, centrally standardized immigration policy allows for the free flow of immigrant labor across subnational units, reducing labor market inefficiencies, transaction costs and spillovers.

We see a good deal of divergence in immigrant integration policies between the two cases. Decentralized immigration recruitment and integration policies in Canada permit provincial governments to tailor specific immigration policies to meet specific labor needs of local economies.[7] Culturally, decentralized integration policy has permitted Quebec some leeway to recruit and educate immigrants in the province's distinct francophone culture without incurring higher costs on the remaining provincial governments. However, integration policies in the United States remain largely centralized, as the federal government controls economic and cultural policies in immigration recruitment, placement and naturalization. States are able to enact limited integration policies over education and acculturation, but these programs are secondary.

How does this stylized discussion of immigration policy help us understand the behavior of federations? Perhaps most importantly, the model allows us to advance new hypotheses about immigrant labor mobility, economic efficiency, and immigration policy in federal systems. It would be interesting to further test propositions about the increased economic efficiency of immigration policy, following the decentralization of immigrant integration policies in Canada. This comparison could look to shifts in provincial economic development over time, or make comparisons across nations, as this paper has done.

We might also anticipate further policy experimentation with local immigrant recruitment and integration policies in federal systems. The gains available from locally controlled recruitment of labor should encourage policy experimentation. As our historical discussion of the trend towards centralized immigration policy suggests, there is a place for state-level policy making in immigration in the United States. The Supreme Court has given constitutional authority over immigration to the federal government. However, this interpretation does not prohibit institutional innovations spurred by state/federal co-operation.

Finally, this model of immigration policy should prove instructive in evaluating the policies of other federations – significantly Australia, Switzerland, and the European Union. Each of these federations devolves immigrant integration powers to subcentral units, suggesting that US centralized control of integration policy stands as an outlier in federal policy. Switzerland, with distinct linguistic and cultural imperatives at the canton level, seems at first glance to match the Canadian case. Australia, however, has no territorially concentrated minority groups. Yet Australia also has decentralized immigrant integration policies, which would suggest that the *market-preserving* benefits are operative to a substantial degree (as they are in the nine English-speaking provinces of Canada).[8]

The European Union stands as a fascinating case because it is attempting to construct a single market with free-flowing labor across internal borders, coupled with harmonized control of external borders. However, some of the significant powers over immigration control policy remain vested in the hands of the member states (Papademetriou 1996, Geddes 2000, Givens and Luedtke 2004, Luedtke 2005). It will be interesting to see if the economic efficiency gained through standardizing immigration control policies can be balanced against the desire of nation-states to preserve unique cultural identities. Given that subcentral identities in Europe are well-entrenched "national" identities (in the Westphalian sense) with a centuries-old tradition of social cohesiveness, the ceding of immigration control powers to Brussels appears to trigger much higher political costs for leaders than it would in other federations (Luedtke 2005). For example, many analysts saw the recent Dutch "No" vote against the European constitution as being based on Dutch voters' fears about immigration. The EU constitution would have dramatically centralized immigration control in the European Union, giving new powers over immigration to the European institutions, while abolishing a national veto on immigration policy in the European Council, the legislative body that represents national governments (de Vreese and Boomgaarden 2005).

In general, we see that all the nations under investigation in this study have deviated from our ideal-type model to some degree. However, we have attempted to show that there are significant costs to be borne if nations do deviate from this model. In Europe, the lack of centralized control policy means that the labor market is not truly "free", and that approximately 20 million immigrant workers do not have the right to move to other countries to look for work, in express violation of the EU's principle of free movement of labor. The lack of centralized control policy also implies costs in the form of externalities, such as dumping unwanted immigrants onto neighboring countries.

However, if the political costs of negotiating an agreement and/or giving up sovereignty are prohibitively high, then federations might choose to continue shouldering the costs of inefficiency and externalities in deviating from our ideal-type model. Future studies should attempt to track and measure these political costs for leaders, so that we have a better understanding of the conditions under which political actors are able to (de)centralize immigration policy. Particularly in the European Union, it will be interesting to see if worries over national identity and sovereignty will trump the potential efficiency gains of centralizing immigration control policy.

Acknowledgements

The authors would like to thank Erik Wibbels, Johanne Poirier, Nathalie Jouant, Nadine Fabbi and Phil Shekleton for helpful comments and research support.

Prior versions of this paper were presented at conferences organized by COMFED, the Université Libre de Bruxelles and the Association for Canadian Studies in the United States. The authors would like to thank those organizations, as well as the Canadian Studies Center at the University of Washington, for providing a stimulating research forum.

Notes

1. A free-flowing labor market can be considered a public good, because its "consumption" is non-excludable and non-rival.
2. While most EU member states no longer have mutual border controls for short-term travel, they still maintain their own, individual immigration controls for longer-term entrants. The EU has made small steps towards a common immigration policy in recent years, but such a policy is still far from being centralized (see Givens and Luedtke 2004).
3. For instance, while the European Union has moved towards a common border guard in recent years, most aspects of border policing are still left up to national governments.
4. Though it should be noted that Quebec selects numbers of specific immigrants based on a national, overall numerical target set by the federal government (which we would argue is more of a control issue, of course).
5. For a discussion, see Neuman 1993.
6. In 2000, Senator Dianne Feinstein of CA co-sponsored legislation to increase the number of H1B visas available to skilled workers in order to meet industry needs. For information see: http://feinstein.senate.gov/releases00/competitiveness_act.html (accessed February 2, 2005).
7. Though the other provinces have obtained far less leeway than Quebec in selecting economic immigrants, under the aforementioned Provincial Nominee program.
8. For more discussion of the Australian case, including the relative weight of market-preserving and nation-preserving imperatives on policy outputs, see Baringhorst 2004.

References

Baringhorst, S., 2004, Policies of backlash: recent shifts in Australian migration policy. *Journal of Comparative Policy Analysis*, **6**, 131–157.
Black, J. and Hagen, D., 1993, Quebec immigration politics and policy: historical and comparative perspectives, in: Alain Gagnon (Ed) *Quebec State and Society*, 2nd ed (Scarborough: Nelson Canada), pp. 280–303.
Borjas, G. J., 1999, *Heaven's Door: Immigration Policy and the American Economy* (Princeton, NJ: Princeton University Press).
Briggs, V., 1991, Immigration policy: political or economic? *Challenge*, **34**, 12–19.
Citizenship and Immigration Canada (CIC), 2003, *Annual Report to Parliament on Immigration*, available at: http://www.cic.gc.ca/english/pub/immigration2003.html
De Vreese, C. H. and Boomgaarden, H. G., 2005, Projecting EU referendums: fear of immigration and support for European integration. *European Union Politics*, **6**, 59–82.
Geddes, A., 2000, *Immigration and European Integration: Towards Fortress Europe?* (Manchester: Manchester University Press).
Givens, T. and Luedtke, A., 2004, The politics of European Union immigration policy: institutions, salience, and harmonization. *Policy Studies Journal*, **32**, 145–165.
Hall, C., 2002, Canadian federal-provincial and territorial mechanisms to facilitate dispersion in immigration, Presentation delivered at Metropolis-APMRN Seminar, Wollongong, Australia, February 28.
Hammar, T., 1985, *European Immigration Policy: A Comparative Study* (Cambridge: Cambridge University Press).
Hammar, T., 1990, *Democracy and the Nation-State: Aliens, Denizens and Citizens in a World of International Migration* (Aldershot: Avebury).

Hawkins, F., 1988, *Canada and Immigration: Public Policy and Public Concern* (Kingston: McGill-Queen's University Press).

Hutchinson, E. P., 1981, *Legislative History of American Immigration Policy, 1798–1965* (Philadelphia: University of Pennsylvania Press).

LeMay, M. C., 1987, *From Open Door to Dutch Door: An Analysis of U.S. Immigration Policy Since 1820* (New York: Praeger).

Luedtke, A., 2005, European integration, public opinion and immigration policy: testing the impact of national identity. *European Union Politics*, **6**, 83–112.

McKay, D., 2001, *Designing Europe: Comparative Lessons from the Federal Experience* (Oxford: Oxford University Press).

Money, J., 1999, Defining immigration policy: inventory, quantitative referents, and empirical regularities, in: Proceedings of the annual meeting of the American Political Science Association, Atlanta, Georgia.

Neuman, G., 1993, The lost century of American immigration law (1776–1875). *Columbia Law Review*, **93**, 1833–1901.

Oates, W., 1999, An essay on fiscal federalism. *Journal of Economic Literature*, **37**, 1120–1149.

Papademetriou, D., 1996, *Coming Together or Pulling Apart? The European Union's Struggle with Immigration and Asylum* (Washington DC: Carnegie Endowment for International Peace).

Radin, B. A. and Boase, J. P., 2000, Federalism, political structure, and public policy in the United States and Canada. *Journal of Comparative Policy Analysis*, **2**, 65–89.

Riker, W., 1964, *Federalism: Origin, Operation, Significance* (Boston: Little, Brown and Company).

Rodden, J., 2001, Creating a more perfect union: electoral incentives and the reform of federal systems, Unpublished manuscript, MIT.

Rodden, J. and Rose-Ackerman, S., 1997, Does federalism preserve markets? *Virginia Law Review*, **83**, 1521–1572.

Simon, J., 1989, *The Economic Consequences of Immigration* (Oxford: Blackwell).

Smith, M. L., 1998, *A Historical Guide to the U.S. Government*, edited by George T. Kurian (New York: Oxford University Press).

Tiebout, C., 1956, A pure theory of local expenditures. *Journal of Political Economy*, **64**, 416–424.

Vineberg, R. A., 1987, Federal-provincial relations in Canadian immigration. *Canadian Public Administration*, **30**, 299–317.

Weingast, B., 1995, The economic role of political institutions: market-preserving federalism and economic growth. *Journal of Law, Economics and Organization*, **11**, 1–31.

Wey, N., 1988, Chinese Americans in California, in: *Five Views: An Ethnic Historic Site Survey for California* (California Department of Parks and Recreation Office of Historic Preservation).

Bureaucratic Control and Policy Change: A Comparative Venue Shopping Approach to Skilled Immigration Policies in Australia and Canada

ANNA BOUCHER

ABSTRACT *Governments increasingly seek to implement skilled migration programmes. Yet, the policies that ultimately result differ in important ways, particularly with regard to the human capital assets required of applicants. These differences in policy outputs can be attributed to important variations in the policy-making process, in particular in the extent of bureaucratic control over policy-making, and in the capacity for venue shopping on the part of internal and external actors. This article develops ideas around bureaucratic control and how it interacts with venue shopping in two Westminster-inspired systems of government in the skilled immigration area.*

1. Introduction

Globally nations are competing for "the best and the brightest" skilled immigrants (Shachar 2006: 151). Yet the capacity of receiving countries to "up-skill" their immigration policies is informed not only by policy goals but also, importantly, by opportunities and obstacles in the policy process. Raising language, educational and age requirements (key attributes of upskilling) creates clear winners and losers. The introduction of skilled immigration policies into settler societies where immigrant groups, lawyers, advocacy organisations and trade unions are often active will not always be an easy political process. In this article, I argue that the extent of bureaucratic control over the policy process shapes the skilled immigration policy outputs that result. "Bureaucratic control" refers to the degree to which the bureaucracy is protected from political challenge from outside interests that may seek to elevate conflict to more open political venues in order to realise their political goals. As discussed in this article, both policy-makers and external actors exploit institutional venues but often to different policy ends.

This article examines the realisation of more economically selective skilled immigration policies in Australia than in Canada over the 1990s and 2000s, with some reflection on the current period as well. The article adopts an institutional venue shopping perspective (Baumgartner and Jones 1993; Pralle 2003, 2006a,b,c) that compares four components of the Westminster systems that vary between the two jurisdictions: (i) a bureaucratic culture of insiders sympathetic to outside interests (here feminist and immigrant groups); (ii) the capacity for intervention by external actors within legislative committees; (iii) the existence of bicameral legislative chambers; and (iv) the presence of legal mechanisms that can be exploited to halt policy change. Opponents of an "upskilling" of immigration policy were partially successful in Canada in utilising these venues to thwart proposed policy changes, while in Australia policy-makers largely maintained the scope of political conflict within the bureaucracy. The second part of this article sets out the scholarship on venue shopping, particularly within Westminster-inspired systems. The third part of the article provides an overview of the Australian and Canadian case studies, and of the qualitative methodology adopted. Parts 4 and 5 display the case studies, while Part 6 provides a comparison of these two case studies and draws inferences for venue shopping more broadly.

2. Venue Shopping, Bureaucratic Control and Policy Outputs

Overview

Venue shopping refers to the strategy of policy actors to move between different institutional venues in order to achieve their policy goals. While the focus is generally on the activity of non-state actors, such venue shopping can also be undertaken by government bureaucrats who shift venues, or contain political debate in key venues, in order to limit the scope of political conflict, and to achieve quicker realisation of policies (i.e. Guiraudon 1997; Bulmer 2011). The institutional venue, or the "location where authoritative decisions are made concerning a given issue" (Baumgartner and Jones 1993, 31), is central to this conception of policy-making. According to Pralle (2006c: 26) institutional venues may be utilised by actors to shape policy-making in three main ways. First, the jurisdiction of an institution may be expanded or contracted in order to shape the decision-making power within that unit. Those who have traditionally been powerful within a particular venue may try to minimise the jurisdiction of another venue, to limit venue shopping by challengers. Second, groups may "shop" for a new institutional venue in order to bring about policy changes. For instance, groups may attempt to raise an issue from a regional to a national level, or from the bureaucratic to the legislative arena, in order to highlight its political salience and to broaden the scope of political conflict. Third, institutional venues may be used to alter rules of the game, meaning that certain policy options are opened or, alternatively, foreclosed.

The earlier venue shopping scholarship focused on the United States' presidential system, although in recognition of potential selection bias (Albaek et al. 2007: 3; Boothe and Harrison 2009: 292), has recently been extended cross-nationally (Baumgartner et al. 2006, 2011: 947). These comparative studies generally focus on singular venues, such as the legislature in coalitional parliamentary systems (i.e. Mortensen 2007; Bräuniger and Debus 2009; Breeman et al. 2009) or venue shopping within the European Union's intergovernmental system (i.e. Guiraudon 2000, 2003; Princen 2007; Menz 2010; Beyers and Kerremans 2011; Kaunert and Léonard 2012). Within this expanding comparative scholarship, the peculiarities of Westminster constitutional design have been largely overlooked. This is despite the fact that the broader political science scholarship identifies particular institutional implications of Westminster, in terms of the concentration of power within executive government (i.e. Lijphart 1999; Tsebelis 2000) and the subsequent withering effects upon external lobbying (Mezey 1979; Weaver and Rockman 1993; Timmermans 2001: 319; Pierson 2006).

Venue-shopping studies of Westminster do not bring sufficient attention to these central features (John and Margetts 2003; Daujberg and Studsgaard 2005; John 2006; Penner et al. 2006; Pralle 2006a,b; Boothe and Harrison 2009: 292). They also often focus on one venue and do not compare across systems, rendering comparative inferences impossible (see only Studlar 2007: 180). Further, venue shopping approaches have not been considered widely in the immigration and asylum policy domain (see only Guiraudon 2000, 2003; Hunt 2002; Timmermans and Scholten 2006; Maurer and Parks 2007; Bendel et al. 2011; Kaunert and Léonard 2012), and not at all in Australia and Canada, although both countries are leading selectors of immigrants.

Venue Shopping and Westminster-Inspired Systems: Challenging Bureaucratic Control

Analysing skilled immigration policy-making in Australia and Canada offers an important opportunity to consider the machinations of immigration policy-making and venue shopping in Westminster more broadly. In this article, I identify four factors that may impact upon the capacity of the bureaucracy to bring about changes within Westminster systems. First however, two caveats. The focus here is not on the extent of mobilisation by external actors or their resource capacity but rather on the institutional venues that enable, or disenable, both internal and external groups, in achieving policy change. As such, the supply-side dimension of the cases is not explored in detail, although it is addressed briefly in Part 6. Second, the argument presented here does not suggest that bureaucrats seek to circumvent the democratic rationale of delegated responsibility that underpins parliamentary sovereignty (Rhodes et al. 2009: 25–26). Rather, it proposes that the executive–legislative fusion that characterises Westminster-inspired systems heightens bureaucratic control over policy change (Beem 2009: 500–501).

The central question is therefore how particular institutional venues may affect the otherwise high level of control enjoyed by Westminster governments. Turning to this question, scholars in both Canada and Australia have emphasised that external actors in Westminster-inspired systems target the bureaucracy, rather than the legislature, in order to pursue policy change (Presthus 1973; Mezey 1979: 199–200; Thompson and Stanbury 1979; Matthews and Warhurst 1993: 89; Smith 2005: 109). Bureaucracies may also contain influential "insiders" who are supportive of the goals of "outsiders" (i.e. Guiraudon 2000: 263–264; Chappell 2002: Ch4).

Outside of allegiances with bureaucrats, external actors, especially those without pecuniary connections, may have limited capacity to appeal directly to the bureaucracy. The legislature, in particular legislative committees, will take on an elevated space as a relevant venue (Hunt 2002: 90–02, Tichenor 2002: 31–34). Such committees have been identified as key for interest group participation in

Westminster-inspired systems, although much will depend on their political composition, with bipartisan committees more influential (Matthews and Warhurst 1993: 89, Pross 1993: 69, Rhodes et al. 2009: 200–201).

Strong bicameralism is another potential factor that could ameliorate against the tendency towards bureaucratic control in Westminster systems (Lijphart 1999: 3). Senators of the upper house of the Australian federal parliament have played an increasing role in Australian politics since the adoption of proportional representational in the Senate in 1949 (Sharman 1999; Young 1999; Rhodes et al 2009: 205). Further, in Australia, if the government of the day does not retain power in the Senate, the most powerful parliamentary committees for legislative review will be found in that Chamber (Thomas 2009: 25). In contrast, in Canada, the Senate of Canada is an unelected body.

The legal system is often identified in the venue shopping scholarship as an important arena to halt or redirect policy change (Guiraudon 2000; Albaek et al. 2007; Pralle 2006a; Wood 2006; Flynn 2011: 383; Kaunert and Léonard 2012). The key issue is to *whom* legal protections extend. In Canada, the *Canadian Charter of Rights and Freedoms*, 1982, Art 15(1) provides constitutionally protected rights for discrete minorities, including immigrants (Carasco et al. 2007: 153). In contrast, in Australia, there are no express constitutional rights, and judicial review of administrative immigration decisions was significantly curtailed by statute in 1994 (Crock 1998: 46). Standing rules, or the rules governing the right to litigate, can also affect the level of bureaucratic control. If there is no standing in court, venue shifting to the judicial arena is barred.

3. Skilled Immigration Policy-Making in Australia and Canada: The Case Studies

This section of the article explores the role of venue shopping in skilled immigration policy-making in Australia and Canada over the 1990s and 2000s. Australia and Canada are appropriate cases for comparison, given their "most-similar" Westminster-inspired systems. Both countries share settler state immigration legacies (Freeman 1995: 887–889) and have similar institutional features including largely majoritarian, two-party-dominated electoral systems, with an increasing role played by minor parties (Lijphart 1999: 312–13). Broader macroeconomic factors such as liberal market economies and resource sector dominance of the labour market are controlled for (Richardson and Lester 2004: 2). The comparison therefore allows these factors to be held constant, while the relevance of the dimensions outlined above can be explored.

The particular case studies analysed in this article involve changes to points tests for skilled immigrants in Australia between 1997 and 1999 and Canada between 1995 and 2004. More recent changes are discussed briefly in Part 5. Points tests, or "quantitative assessments of human capital" (Papademetriou 2008) are a common feature of skilled immigration selection, initiated in Canada in 1967 and emulated in Australia from the early 1970s onwards (Hawkins 1989: 39). Policy-makers in both countries in the mid-1990s shared a similar vision of what an increase in human capital in immigration policy would mean – more economically active migrants, with higher earning potential, heightened native language skills and stronger educational credentials. However, policy-makers in

Australia were better able to realise these policy goals. In fact, Australia is generally identified as having more economically targeted skilled immigration policies than Canada (Richardson and Lester 2004; Hawthorne 2008). This article interrogates what influence differences in policy process may have had on these differing policy outcomes.

Methodologically, this article differs from other public agenda approaches that often focus on interchanges between various legislative houses and through counts or "mentions" of particular issues in congressional debates (i.e. Baumgartner and Jones 1993; Soroka 2002; Pralle 2006c: 64; Green-Pedersen 2007: 278). Quantitative approaches of this kind are less appropriate when analysing policy-making in Westminster-inspired systems, where policy change may occur within the executive and cannot therefore be easily coded quantitatively, given the unavailability of access to a full corpus of bureaucratic documents. Instead, a range of qualitative approaches were adopted. First, 90 elite interviews were conducted with senior bureaucrats, immigration lobbyists, academics, lawyers and parliamentarians in Australia and Canada between September 2008 and December 2009. Interviewees were selected purposively on the basis of their engagement in the policy process.[1] Triangulation is an important method to minimise validity concerns that can arise in reliance on elite interviews (Berry 2002: 680). As such, I triangulated this interview material with original archival research,[2] analysis of available legislative debates, legal analysis, close reading of government reports and qualitative media analysis, to create a rich picture of policy events. In the following section of the article, I outline the nature of the policy changes and policy processes in the two countries.

4. Australia

Changes to Skilled Immigration Policy in Australia, 1997–1999

Upon his appointment in 1996, the new Immigration Minister Philip Ruddock declared that he had "inherited a migration program that [was] out of balance and out of control" (Ruddock 1996: 8639). After achieving a rebalancing of the immigration programme to de-emphasise family immigration and focus upon skilled immigration, the minister and the Department of Immigration and Multicultural Affairs (DIMA) turned to the selection requirements for migrants undertaking the points test for skilled immigration. The first of these changes was to introduce mandatory English language testing for all forms of skilled immigration. An external review commissioned to analyse details of the points test in 1997 recommended more points for "the core employability factors of skill, age and English language ability" (DIMA 1999: 2). The review process, initiated in late 1998, culminated in a new points test introduced in mid-1999. The differences between the points test before and after the 1999 reforms are outlined in Table 1.

As is clear from this table, the pass mark was increased from 110 to 120 points. The amount allocated to work experience was also increased. While there was no change to the points allocated for English, mandatory language testing was introduced and the required level of language ability was raised across all International English Language Testing System (IELTS) bands. Points for arranged employment in Australia, and a small number of points for a spouse's education,

Table 1. The Australian points test for skilled immigration, before and after the 1999 reforms.

	Before reforms	After reforms
Points		
Occupation (based on general occupations list)	80	0
Occupational/training based factor – based on particular skill	0	60
Education	0	15
English ability	20	20
Australian work experience	0	10
Age	30 (age 18–65)	30 (age 18–45)
Demographic	0	0
Relative in Australia	15	15
Relative an Australian citizen for at least five years	10	0
Relative's employment situation	10	0
Arranged employment	0	15
Spouse's education	0	5
Bonus points	0	5
Total	165	150
Pass mark	**110**	**120**

Sources: Tabled compiled by author using Migration Regulations 1994, Schedule 6, consolidated on 1 July 1999; Migration Regulations 1994, Schedule 6A, consolidated on 10 December 1998. This table does not take into consideration changes made to the point tests after the 1999 reforms.

were also new additions from 1999. At the same time, points associated with familial links to those already in Australia were removed or reduced. The cut-off for maximum points for age was halved from pension age (65 for men and 60 for women) down to 30 years for both sexes, thereby strongly favouring the young. Those over 45 could no longer apply. There was also a move away from a general understanding of skill towards an occupationally targeted model and a Migrant on Demand List (MODL) was created to determine appropriate professions for selection. This explains the removal of 80 points for general occupational skill following the 1999 reforms.

The Policy-Making Process in Australia

In a short space of time, the Australian government achieved a substantial upskilling of the points test. While there was an external review of the new model, the consultation period only lasted a few months and did not result in any major departures from the model originally recommended by the bureaucracy. As one senior policy-maker remarked, the reforms were "driven by the bureaucracy. We had a list of things we wanted to achieve... and everything we put up government approved" (Interviews with policy officials, Canberra, 24 September 2009; see also 30 October 2009).

Most of the policy reforms that occurred were also consistent with academic advice to policy-makers regarding economically optimal selection criteria. This advice relied upon analysis of a new database, the Longitudinal Survey of Immigrants to Australia (LSIA), which DIMA had created from the mid-1990s. The external review presented reliance on the LSIA as "evidence-based policy-making" (DIMA 1999: 19). Experts were the most involved external interests in the process, an assessment consistent with Timmermans and Scholten's (2006) analysis of "low politics" in the integration field in Europe. There was no clear debate over the validity of the academic studies that relied upon the LSIA and DIMA and the minister was able to present a policy need for an economically selective skilled programme, quickly, and with limited opposition. For instance, the decisions to introduce mandatory English testing, to raise the overall standards for English and to make language a threshold requirement for all skilled applicants were based on research from the LSIA. This survey indicated that the most economically successful immigrants were those with the highest English language skills (Interviews with policy officials, Canberra, 24 September and 30 October 2009, see also Birrell et al. 1992: 27, 43; DIMA 1999: 3). A few migrant groups opposed mandatory English language testing, arguing that it would favour applicants from English-speaking countries. Yet these groups also found the economic arguments in favour of mandatory language testing difficult to rebut (FECCA 1998; interviews by author with ethnic organisations, Sydney, 2 October 2009 and Adelaide, 6 March 2010). Similarly, the decision to de-emphasise familial connections was based on economic factors (DIMA 1999a: 49). Policy officers argued that focusing on familial connections "did not produce very good migrants" as the focus was on the sponsor, rather than on the applicant (Interview with policy official, Canberra, 24 September 2009). The reduction in age was seen as necessary as applicants over 45 had reduced "employability" (DIMA 1999, 45–47). In short, the Minister for Immigration and the Department was able to achieve a radical "upskilling" to the points test for skilled immigration in a very short pace of time, and with limited pushback from external actors.

5. Canada

Changes to Skilled Immigration Policy in Canada, 1995–2004

In 1995, Immigration Minister Sergio Marchi released his *Immigration Report to Parliament* in which he emphasised the need for "education, official language ability, decision-making skills, motivation and initiative" among newly selected immigrants (CIC 1995: 9). The proceeding report, *Not Just Numbers*, reinforced a desire among government for heightened human capital endowment of selected skilled immigrants (ILRAG 1997: 6.1). Later departmental consultations provided additional evidence in favour of a "human capital" model that focused on general skills, such as education and language. These reports based their analysis on statistical models from the Immigration Data Base, which was a dataset of the labour market outcomes of newly arrived migrants, very similar in its design to the LSIA (CIC 1999a,b). Some of these policy initiatives – but crucially not all – culminated in the new points test, published in the regulations to the Immigration and Refugee Protection Act (2002) ('IRPA'). The path to realisation of this new points test was also significantly longer and more protracted than in Australia.

The key differences in the points test that emerged in 2002, compared with its predecessor, are outlined in Table 2. The IRPA points test saw a reduction of 18 points in the points allocated to occupational skill. This is understandable on the basis that the new selection grid, while also seeking to "upskill", marked an attempt to move towards an assessment of general human capital capabilities. There was an increase in points for education, language and work experience. However, unlike in Australia, language skills were not mandatory and, ultimately, education was not as tightly regulated as policy-makers originally envisaged because trade qualifications were also included. Finally, the pass mark for the new selection grid was set at 80. Yet, following legal action against the retroactive application of the points test and as a result of falling applications, it was reduced to 67, which was actually lower than its predecessor at 70. This legal action also meant that the new points test could not be applied retrospectively to an estimated 425,000 applicants (Van Rijn 2003).

The Policy-Making Process in Canada

The introduction of the new points test in Canada was a protracted and public process. It involved significant political compromises across a range of issues, in a variety of institutional venues. The policy process itself spanned almost a decade and was heavily entwined with legislative debate around the development of the new immigration act. There was considerable discussion over how 'skill' should be

Table 2. The Canadian points test for skilled immigration, before and after the 2002 reforms.

	Before reforms	**After reforms**
Points		
Occupation (based on general occupations list)	10	0
Occupational/training based factor – based on particular skill	18	0
Education	16	25
English ability (English and French	15	24
Work experience	8	21
Age	10 (ages 21–44)	10 (ages 21–49)
Demographic	10	0
Relative in Canada	5	5
Arranged employment	10	10
Spouse's work	0	5
Spouse's education	0	5
One year's work in Canada	0	5
Two year's work in Canada	0	5
Arranged employment	0	5
Relative in Canada	See above	5
Pass mark	**70**	**67**

Sources: Table compiled by author using *IRPR*, ss.78–83, consolidated on 11 June 2002; *Immigration Regulations* (1978) (Cth), Schedule 1, 2001 consolidation. Only the maximum points in each category are given. This table does not take into consideration changes made to the point tests after the 2002 reforms.

defined for the purposes of eligible occupations for the points test. Most of these debates took place within the Standing Committee on Citizenship and Immigration ("the Committee"), where opposition parliamentarians and external actors were successful in having the regulations to the new immigration act reviewed. This opened up analysis of the regulatory points test to the legislative venue, and influenced the final design of the new selection grid in a different way from that originally intended by the bureaucracy. It is important to note that subjecting the regulations to Committee review was itself a product of calls by minority parliamentarians. MP Madeleine Dalphond-Guiral (2001: 1150) of Quebec argued that: "I believe that it should be very clear that the regulations must be submitted to committee for consultation before their coming into force".

Some of the recommendations of the Committee were not in keeping with the original position of government. Activist critiques took on gender, race and class-based dimensions. For instance, feminist activists were concerned that the definition of "skill" encapsulated in the new points test reflected gendered labour market biases (CIC 2001; WCDWA 2002: 1). Following feminist lobbying, a Gender-Based Analysis (GBA) unit was established within CIC in 2001 to audit the gender sensitivity of the new laws (Boucher 2010). Backbenchers within the incumbent Liberal Party, members of the Standing Committee, trade union groups and the Canadian Bar Association also criticised the non-recognition of trade qualifications with the new points test (Thompson 2002a). Ultimately, this Committee activity led then Minister of Immigration, Denise Coderre to change the educational requirements to encompass trade certification, in addition to bachelor degrees (Coderre 2002).

Earlier statistical research by CIC using the IMDB found that higher age correlated with strong reductions in earnings at the "tail ends" of working life. It was for this reason that the age cut-off was initially retained at 45 (CIC 1998: 31–32; Interview with policy official, Ottawa, 19 August 2008). Yet after Committee debates, the cut-off for age was increased to 49. The change was the product of calls by the Committee to Minister Coderre. Employer groups were also identified by the department as important in influencing this increase in age (Interview with policy official, Ottawa, 19 August 2008).

The bureaucracy recommended mandatory language testing using certified international language examinations (CIC 1998: 20–28). The IMDB had found that English ability improved labour outcomes (CIC 1998: 52; Interview with policy official, Ottawa August 2008). Such testing was also proposed in 1997 by an external advisory report, *Not Just Numbers* (ILRAG 1997). However, following street protests by migrant groups in Vancouver and Toronto in early 1998, then Immigration Minister Lucienne Robillard quietly backed down from her government's position of introducing mandatory language testing. As put by one interviewee:

> They were the big force against mandatory language testing. . . . It was a strong lobby straight away. I think Minister Robillard announced the idea of mandatory language testing in Vancouver and she got a very strong, strong lobby the same day and she backed down. (Interview with policy maker, Ottawa, 27 August 2008)

In fact, as a result of this political contestation, it was only in early 2010 that compulsory language testing was introduced in Canada (Friesen 2010).

A final important development in Canada was the eventual lowering of the pass mark from 80 to 67. The setting of the pass mark is of crucial importance to those applicants who are borderline cases. Canadian policy-makers originally intended to increase the pass mark from 67 to 80. However, following complaints by external actors before the Committee that the pass mark was too high, it was reduced to 75 (Standing Committee 2002: 11–12; Coderre 2002). The Coalition for a Just Immigration and Refugee Policy, a Toronto-based immigration lobby group, for instance, argued that a pass mark of 80 would increase the "weight on education and language proficiency and... have an adverse impact on applicants from non-English and non-French speaking countries" (CJIRP 2002: 9). Similarly, the National Association of Women and the Law noted that raising the pass mark to 80 "only makes the gender bias of the existing points test worse" (NAWL 2002: 1). Even once the pass mark was lowered to 75, many were unhappy that it was to apply retroactively.

Lawyers within the Immigration Section of the Canadian Bar Association, in collaboration with immigrant litigants and immigrant organisations in Toronto, then elevated the conflict to the judicial venue. These groups brought a series of legal actions against the retroactive application of the points test, after they had sought, unsuccessfully, to reverse this in the Committee (Thompson 2002b). *Dragan v. Canada* ([2003] 4 FC 189) found that the retrospectivity of the new points test was illegal. Following this decision, a class action was brought using new class action laws that had recently been adopted in Canada. Counsel for the applicants filed an action for 104,000 individuals requesting a writ of mandamus – a form of public injunctive relief – that prevented the minister and his delegates from rejecting any applications that had been lodged before 1 January 2002 (*Borisova v. Canada* [2003] 4 FC 408). This case was successful and the pass mark was subsequently lowered to 67. As a result, around 425,000 applicants who would otherwise have had their applications rejected were processed under the old, easier pre-IRPA points test (Van Rijn 2003). *Borisova* was perceived as "significant litigation" by Citizenship Immigration Canada and contributed greatly to the backlog of applicants and to the final operation of an easier points test (Interview with policy official, Ottawa, 19 August 2008).

Recent Changes in Australia and Canada and Implications for Venue Shopping

Interestingly, since the mid-2000s, the trend towards "upskilling" outlined in this paper has increased in both countries. Changes in Australia in 2010 have narrowed the range of professions under which individuals can apply (DIAC 2010a). English language requirements were also increased for certain categories of skilled visas and a new system that requires immigrants to enter an expression of interest prior to formal application, has also been introduced (DIAC 2010b). All of these changes have the effect of increasing the skill requirements for application, and of distancing the applicant from judicial review rights, thereby further increasing bureaucratic control over the process. In Canada, changes are equally significant, with more emphasis placed on those applicants with Canadian experience. These changes were achieved through administrative reform in late 2008, following an amendment to the Immigration and Refugee Protection Act enacted through the Budget Implementation Act (2008) ('Bill C-50'). This change empowered the minister to issue instructions that establish orders and categories for the assessment of immigration applications (IRPA (2002) (Cdn)), s87(3), (6); CIC 2008). In pursuance of an instruction made on 29 November 2008, the minister dramatically restricted applications under the Federal Skilled Worker class to those with an offer of arranged employment in Canada, those who were previously international students or temporary workers in Canada, or those with work experience in a small number of professions. The significance of Bill C-50 was not lost on lobbyists, who pointed out that there were no legally guaranteed avenues for stakeholder input on future ministerial instructions, nor is there the possibility for legal challenges to administrative decisions made under a ministerial instrument (i.e. OCASI 2009). This decision had the effect of considerably narrowing the scope of political conflict over points test reform in Canada since 2009.

6. Comparison between Australian and Canadian Skilled Immigration Policies and Processes

These case studies not only describe skilled immigration policies in Australia and Canada during the 1990s and 2000s, but also outline the policy processes that led to their realisation. External actors utilised the legislative and judicial venues in Canada and the process was both protracted and contested. In Australia, the entire process was largely bureaucratically driven and completed within 18 months. While the new points test in Australia was viewed by its architects as a response to economic needs, in Canada the political compromises documented meant that economic factors could not be the only policy consideration for the bureaucracy. As a senior bureaucratic within Citizenship Immigration Canada summarised:

> When we started selecting immigrants for economic reasons, we did it for economic reasons and not for family or refugee reasons. But it is never completely black and white ..., so you know, we didn't completely move away ... from, non-economic, from adding other elements to it. (Interview, Ottawa, 19 August 2008)

Venue shopping by both internal and external actors was central in informing these differences. Table 3 sets out the shifts across venues that occurred across the two countries. In Australia, the bureaucracy was largely successful in containing conflict in the bureaucratic realm, through reliance on regulatory instruments and through the curtailment of legal review opportunities. In Canada, by contrast, activists and lawyers were successful first in bringing conflict to the legislative venue through a first-time demand to subject the regulations to the legislative committee. When not all Committee requests were adopted, this was followed by elevation of the dispute to the legal arena. Protest was also important in the Canadian case in halting the introduction of mandatory language testing until 2010.

It is useful to consider in detail the application of the theoretical arguments developed in Part 2. Looking first at the issue of sympathetic bureaucrats, the

Table 3. Venue shopping in Australian and Canadian skilled immigration policy

Policy issue – Australia	Venue – Australia	Policy issue – Canada	Venue – Canada
Design of new points test (1997–1999)	Bureaucracy	Design of new points test (1995–2001)	Bureaucracy
Review of new points test (1998)	Bureaucracy	Review of new points test (2002–2003)	Bureaucracy and legislative committee following activist intervention.
Introduction of compulsory languages testing (1999)	Through regulation	Introduction of compulsory languages testing (1998 attempt)	Attempted through bureaucracy; failed following street protests.
Challenges to new points test	N/a as legal avenues cut off through outsourcing of skills assessment and restrictions on judicial review.	Challenges to new points test (2002–2003)	Activists elevated regulatory reform to the legislative committee, and then challenging legally the retroactive application of the points test (2002–2004)
		Restrictions on future activism (2008)	Government centralises law-making powers through ministerial instruction to limit conflict scope in the future.

establishment of a Gender-Based Analysis unit within CIC can be seen as the institutionalisation of feminist actors within that department. The establishment of the unit was itself a product of feminist activist demands (see Boucher 2010). The GBA unit did appear to have influenced some thinking around the points test (Interview by author with policy officials, Ottawa, 19 July 2008, 8 August 2008). However, generally, such internal lobbying was not determinative in influencing the design of the points tests (see Boucher 2010).

Legislative committees adopted different functions in the two countries. In Canada, the Standing Committee on Citizenship and Immigration provided a vital venue for both migrant groups and other external actors to inform policy changes. The consideration of regulations in that committee offered a participatory space for the engagement of a broader range of actors in immigration regulation-making than had previously been the case in Canada. One former parliamentarian from the Committee argued: "By virtue of the fact that we did get the regulations sent to committee, we could have an effect. That was significant" (Interview with parliamentarian, Ottawa, 15 July 2008). Interviews with many of the key actors engaged in the Committee process clarify that they had different views as to its purpose. However, the focus on the migrant experience and migrant identity came through as central. For instance, another former committee member argued that "many members of parliament are elected by migrants... so you had to oppose [the points test] if you wanted to be elected" (Interview with parliamentarian, Montreal, 20 July 2008). By virtue of having the analysis of the points test elevated to the legislative space, lobbyists and opposition members of parliament were successful in opening the field of contestation in a way that was simply not the case in Australia. There, the Senate and its committees were not involved in the reforms over the points test, suggesting that the bicameralism hypothesis does not play out in this case.[3]

Legal venue also differed across the two countries. As noted, in Australia, this can be attributed to the reduction in judicial review opportunities in the immigration field broadly from the mid-1990s onwards (Crock and Berg 2011: 634). In addition, in Australia in 1999, the assessment of skills for the purpose of skilled immigration was outsourced, which had the effect of privatising this process and taking it outside of the realm of administrative law (see Boucher forthcoming). In Canada, overseas applicants have broader rights of standing for general administrative and judicial review, and private skills assessment has not yet been introduced. Class actions opportunities exist in the immigration field (IRPA, s72; Federal Courts Act (1985), s18.1(4)) and were used by immigrant applicants in the *Dragan* and *Borisova* cases, which both fell on administrative law grounds. At the same time as these developments occurred in Canada, class action possibilities were closed down in the immigration field in Australia (Crock and Berg 2011: Ch. 19). The capacity to elevate conflict to the judicial realm therefore appears important in these cases, particularly towards the end of the policy process.

One important point to note is that in both case studies, institutional factors alone may not have been determinative for venue shopping outcomes. Certainly, in Canada, there was greater use of venue shopping by external actors, and government was thereby less able to contain conflict. However, this poses the question of why Canadian civil society was more active in the area of skilled immigration policy in the first place. While not considered extensively here, research suggests that resources available to immigration lobbyists and the sources of funding vary in Australia and Canada (Boucher 2011). This resources-orientated argument resonates with recent work on venue shopping in the urban affairs arena, which indicates the centrality of group resources to the utilisation of venue shopping opportunities (Sapotichne and Smith 2012; 100–101).

It might also be argued that partisan politics was important. The election of a Conservative government in Australia in 1996, coupled with defunding of key immigration organisations and the dismantlement of the previously important Bureau of Immigration Research and the Office of Multicultural Affairs, contributed to weakened immigrant activism in Australia. Both bodies were important governmental advocates of immigrant issues and concerns (Fincher 2001; Jupp 2007: 72–75). As such, these changes to the social landscape could have shaped the extent of external actor engagement in Australia and the limited attempts at venue shopping by such actors documented in this case study.

Yet, in terms of the policy objectives of government, partisan politics does not appear central in the current case. While the election of a conservative government in

Australia in 1996 informed a preference for economically focused migration, it is clear that in both countries the government's clearly stated agenda was to increase the selectivity of economic selection policy, and to shift the relative mix of economic compared with family reunification migration. This was the case both in the left-of-centre Liberal Party in Canada and the more right-of-centre Liberal–National Coalition in Australia. In both countries, statistical databases pointed to the preferred selection model. However, in Canada, external actors utilised a range of institutional venues to delay the process of reform and to secure certain changes. This evidence suggests that while countervailing factors were important, and informed the policy context, institutional venues do appear to be crucial in offering opportunities for external actor venue shopping, or delimiting them.

7. Conclusion

In the global competition for highly skilled immigrants, states' capacities to compete will be informed not only by their policy preferences, or by the choices of incoming immigrants, but also by the extent of bureaucratic control over domestic policy processes. Institutional venues shape not only the politics of immigration, but also the eventual policies that emerge. Although "most-similar" Westminster-inspired systems, the Canadian policy context opened significant space for contestation over the new skilled immigrant points test, which was not available in Australia, where the process was bureaucratically determined and tightly controlled. In Australia, policy-makers were able to contain political debate by limiting debate to the fairly closed, bureaucratic venue and preventing venue shopping by external actors.

This comparison is instructive to the broader venue-shopping scholarship in a number of ways. First, it explores venue shopping across two Westminster-inspired systems, and across a variety of institutional venues within those systems. It shows that legislative committees and judicial systems, played an important role in the Canadian case. Second, this article highlights the value of a "venue systems" approach (Kaunert and Léonard 2012: 4) that considers the interactive role of a range of institutional venues, rather than focusing on only one venue. Finally, this paper emphasises the role of government actors, in addition to external actors, in venue shopping.

Much of the focus in the venue shopping scholarship is on issue expansion by lobbyists and external advocates of political causes. Yet conflict management by internal bureaucrats, whereby attempts are made to control the scope of conflict, is also a central part of venue shopping (see also Sapotichne and Smith 2012: 90). This will be the case particularly in Westminster bureaucracies when the fused nature of the legislative and executive function gives government heightened capacity to minimise the scope of political conflict. Importantly, such venue shopping may occur through altering the regulatory instruments that govern immigration decision-making, or privatising such decisions to remove the oversight of public law remedies, as was the case in Australia. As such, venue shopping in Westminster systems may involve a narrower terrain of conflict and more instances of venue-shopping restrictions than in the presidential system, with its multiple veto points. This does not mean that the dynamics at play do not constitute venue shopping, simply that such interaction may be less pronounced than in presidential systems, or take on different qualities. Future research should explore the importance of institutional venues for external actors in other Westminster-inspired systems, as well as in other policy domains. It will also need to weigh the importance of institutional venues against supply-side factors, such as the extent of external actor mobilisation, which have not been explored in detail in this article.

Acknowledgements

Thanks to anonymous reviewers and colleagues within the Public Policy Cluster at the University of Sydney, in particular Dr Betsi Beem, for comments on earlier versions of this paper. The research underpinning this paper was supported by the Commonwealth Scholarship Fund, the London School of Economics and Political Science, the Zeit Ebelin Bucerius Foundation, the University of London, the British Academy of Canadian Studies, the International Commission of Canadian Studies and the Australian National University.

Notes

1. Interviews were undertaken under the guarantee of confidentiality and therefore names cannot be revealed. All interviews were approved by the Ethics Committee of the London School of Economics and Political Science.
2. The archival research was original and, in the case of Canada, involved opening closed archival files in the National Archives in Ottawa.
3. A Freedom of Information Request identifies that in Canada in 1999, during the period when the points test was being designed, the Department of Citizenship and Immigration consulted with 250 groups and individuals, as well as receiving 850 submissions (CIC 2002). In Australia in contrast, 37 submissions were made to the External Reference Group (DIMA 1999, Attachment B). All submissions to both of these committees in both countries were analysed in detail.

References

Albaek, E., Green-Pedersen, C., *et al.*, 2007, Making tobacco consumption a political issue in the United States and Denmark: The dynamics of issue expansion in comparative perspective. *Journal of Comparative Policy Analysis: Research and Practice*, **9**(1), pp. 1–20.
Baumgartner, F. R. and Jones, B. D., 1993, *Agenda and Instability in American Politics* (Chicago: University of Chicago Press).
Baumgartner, F. R., Green-Pedersen, C., *et al.*, 2006, Comparative studies of policy agendas. *Journal of European Public Policy*, **13**(7), pp. 959–974.
Baumgartner, F. R., Jones, B. R., *et al.*, 2011, Comparative Studies of Policy Dynamics. *Comparative Political Science*, **44**(8), pp. 947–972.
Beem, B., 2009, Leaders in thinking, laggards in attention? Bureaucratic engagement in international arenas. *The Policy Studies Journal*, **37**(3), pp. 497–518.
Bendel, P., Ette, A., *et al.*, 2011, *The Europeanization of Control: Venues and Outcomes of EU Justice and Home Affairs Cooperation* (Berlin: Lit Verlag).
Berry, J., 2002, Validity and Reliability Issues in Elite Interviewing. *PS: Political Science and Politics*, **35**(4), pp. 679–682.
Beyers, J. and Kerremans, B., 2011, Domestic Embeddedness and the Dynamics of Multilevel Venue Shopping in Four EU Member States. *Governance: An International Journal of Policy, Administration, and Institutions*, **25**(2), pp. 263–290.
Birrell, R., Smith, T. F., *et al.*, 1992, *Migration Selection During the Recession* (Canberra: Department of the Parliamentary Library, Parliament House of Australia).

Boothe, K. and Harrison, K., 2009, The influence of institutions on issue definition: Children's environmental health policy in the United States and Canada. *Journal of Comparative Policy Analysis: Research and Practice*, **11**(3), pp. 287–307.

Boucher, A., 2010, Gender mainstreaming in skilled immigration policy: From Beijing 1995 to the Canadian Immigration and Refugee Protection Act (2002), in: A. Nevile (Ed.) *Human Rights and Social Policy: A Comparative Analysis of Values and Citizenship in OECD Countries* (Cheltenham, Edward Elgar), pp. 174–200.

Boucher, A., 2011, Venue-setting and diversity-seeking: Gender and immigration selection policy in Australia and Canada. Doctoral dissertation, London School of Economics and Political Science.

Boucher, A., forthcoming, Outsourcing skilled immigration assessment, in: G. Meagher and S. Goodwin (Eds) *Sold Off: Markets, Rights and Power in Australian Social Policy* (Sydney: Sydney University Press).

Bräuninger, T. and M. Debus. 2009, Legislative agenda-setting in parliamentary democracies. *European Consortium for Political Research*, **48**, pp. 804–839.

Breeman, G., Lowery, D., et al., 2009, Political attention in a coalition system: Analysing Queen's speeches in the Netherlands 1945–2007. *Acta Politica*, **44**(1), pp. 1–27.

Bulmer, S., 2011, Shop till you drop? The German executive as venue-shopper in Justice and Home Affairs, in: P. Bendel, A. Ette and P. Parkes (Eds) *The Europeanization of Control: Venues and Outcomes of EU Justice and Home Affairs Cooperation* (Berlin: Lit Verlag), pp. 41–76.

Carasco, E., Aiken, S., et al., 2007, *Immigration and Refugee Law: Cases, Material and Commentary* (Toronto: Edmond Montgomery).

Chappell, L., 2002, *Gendering Government: Feminist Engagement with the State in Australia and Canada* (Vancouver: University of British Columbia Press).

CIC, 1995, *A Broader Vision, 1996 Report to Parliament* (Ottawa, Citizenship Immigration Canada).

CIC, 1998, Towards a new selection model: Current selection criteria: Indicators of successful establishment? *Research Article* (Ottawa: Economic Policy and Programs Division, Selection Branch, Citizenship Immigration Canada).

CIC, 1999a, *Skilled Worker Selection Model, Federal–Provincial Working Group* (Ottawa, Canada: CIC).

CIC, 1999b, *The Economic Performance of Immigrants Education Perspective*, IMDB Profile Series (Ottawa, Canada: CIC).

CIC, 2001, *Draft Gender-Based Analysis of Bill C-31/C-11* (Ottawa: CIC).

CIC, 2002, Response to an information request for the Standing Committee on Citizenship and Immigration, 19 February 2002, filed in the National Archives of Canada, RG14 BAN 2007-0060-1, Box 17, Wallet 4 (Ottawa: Standing Committee on Citizenship and Immigration).

CIC, 2008, Ministerial instruction, 29 November 2008. *Government Notices*, 142(48) (Ottawa: Citizenship Immigration Canada).

CJIRP (Coalition for a Just Immigration and Refugee Policy), 2002, Submission to the Standing Committee on Citizenship and Immigration on the regulations to the Immigration and Refugee Protection Act, filed in the National Archives of Canada, RG14, BAN 2007-00060-1, Box 17, Wallet 4 (Ottawa: Standing Committee on Citizenship and Immigration, Parliament of Canada).

Coderre, D., 2002, Government response to the report of the Standing Committee on Citizenship and Immigration, Building a Nation: the Regulations under the Immigration and Refugee Protection Act, CIC.

Crock, M., 1998, *Immigration and Refugee Law in Australia* (Leichhardt and Sydney: The Federation Press).

Crock, M. and Berg, L., 2011, *Immigration Refugees and Forced Migration: Law, Policy and Practice in Australia* (Leichhardt: The Federation Press).

Daugbjerg, C. and Studsgaard, J., 2005, Issue redefinition, venue change and radical agricultural policy reforms in Sweden and New Zealand. *Scandinavian Political Studies*, **28**(2), pp. 103–124.

Dalphond-Guiral, M. 2001, Amendments to Bill C-11 Standing Committee on Citizenship and Immigration, Parliament of Canada, 15–17 May.

DIAC (Department of Immigration and Citizenship), 2010a, *New List of Skilled Occupation Intended to Replace the Current Skilled Occupation List* (Canberra: DIAC).

DIAC (Department of Immigration and Citizenship), 2010b, *Tighter English language requirements for GSM visas from 1 January 2010* (Canberra: DIAC).

DIMA (Department of Immigration and Multicultural Affairs), 1999, *Review of the Independent and Skilled-Australian Linked Categories* (Canberra: DIMA).

FECCA (Federation of Ethnic Communities Council of Australia), 1998, Mr Randolph Alwis, Chairperson, Federation of Ethnic Communities Councils of Australia, Submissions to the External Reference Group on the Skilled and Australian-Linked Categories, 1998, DIMIA, Canberra.

Fincher, R., 2001, Immigration research in the politics of an anxious nation. *Environment and Planning D: Society and Space*, **19**(1), pp. 25–42.

Flynn, G., 2011, Court decisions: NIMBY claims, and the siting of unwanted facilities: Policy fames and the impact of judicialization in locating a landfill for Toronto's solid waste. *Canadian Public Policy*, **XXXVII**(3), pp. 381–393.

Freeman, G., 1995, Modes of immigration policies in liberal democratic states. *International Migration Review*, **29**(4), pp. 881–902.

Friesen, J., 2010, English profs not amused over immigration quiz. *The Globe and Mail*, 29 July, p. A4.

Green-Pedersen, C., 2007, The conflict of conflicts in comparative perspective: euthanasia as a political issue in Denmark, Belgium and the Netherlands. *Comparative Politics*, **39**(3), pp. 959–974.

Guiraudon, V., 1997, Policy change behind gilded doors: Explaining the evolution of aliens' rights in contemporary Western Europe. Doctoral dissertation, Harvard University.

Guiraudon, V., 2000, European integration and migration policy: Vertical policy-making as venue shopping. *Journal of Common Market Studies*, **38**(2), pp. 251–271.

Guiraudon, V., 2003, The constitution of a European immigration policy domain: A political sociology approach. *Journal of European Public Policy*, **10**(2), pp. 263–282.

Hawkins, F., 1989, *Critical Years in Immigration: Australia and Canada Compared* (Ontario: McGill Queen's University Press).

Hawthorne, L., 2008, *The Race for Talent – Comparing Canada, US and Australia's Approach to Skilled Worker Migration* (Toronto: Maytree Foundation/Institute for Research on Public Policy, University of Toronto, 26 September).

Hunt, V., 2002, The multiple and changing goals of immigration reform: A comparison of House and Senate activity, 1947–1993, in: F. R. Baumgartner and B. Jones (Eds) *Policy Dynamics* (Chicago and London: University of Chicago Press), pp. 73–95.

ILRAG (Immigration Legislative Review Advisory Group), 1997, *Not Just Numbers: A Canadian Framework for Future Immigration* (Ottawa: Minister of Public Works and Government Services Canada).

Lijphart, A., 1999, *Patterns of Democracy: Government Forms and Performance in Thirty-Six Countries* (New Haven, CT: Yale University Press).

John, P., 2006, Explaining policy change: The impact of the media, public opinion and political violence on urban budgets in England. *Journal of European Public Policy*, **13**(7), pp. 1053–1068.

John, P. and Margetts, H., 2003, Policy punctuations in the UK: Fluctuations and equilibria in central government expenditure since 1951. *Public Administration Review*, **81**(3), pp. 411–432.

Jupp, J., 2007, *From White Australia to Woomera: The Story of Australian Immigration* (Cambridge: Cambridge University Press).

Kaunert, C. and Léonard, S., 2012, The development of the EU asylum policy: Venue shopping in perspective. *Journal of European Public Policy*, **16**(23), pp. 1–18.

Matthews, T. and Warhurst, J., 1993, Australia: Interest groups in the shadow of strong political parties, in: C. S. Thomas (Ed.) *First World Interest Groups: A Comparative Perspective* (Westport, CT: Greenwood Press), pp. 81–95.

Maurer, A. and Parkes, R., 2007, The prospects for policy-change in EU asylum policy: Venue and image at the European level. *European Journal of Migration and Law*, **9**(2), pp. 173–205.

Menz, G., 2010, Stopping, shaping and moulding Europe: Two-level games, non-state actors and the Europeanization of migration policies. *Journal of Common Market Studies*, **49**(2), pp. 437–462.

Mezey, M. L., 1979, *Comparative Legislatures* (Durham, NC: Duke University Press).

Mortensen, P. B., 2007, Stability and change in public policy: A longitudinal study of comparative subsystem dynamics. *Policy Studies Journal*, **35**(3), pp. 373–394.

NAWL (National Association of Women and the Law), 2002, Submission to the regulations to the Immigration and Refugee Protection Act before the Standing Committee on Citizenship and Immigration, by C. Tie, S. Aiken and A. Cote (Ottawa: Standing Committee on Citizenship and Immigration, Parliament of Canada).

OCASI (Ontario Council of Agencies Serving Immigrants), 2009, OCASI deputation on changes to IRPA under Bill C-50, Toronto. Available at http://www.ocasi.org/index.php?qid=967 (accessed 16 April 2009).

Papademetriou, D., 2008, Selecting economic stream immigrants through points systems. *Migration Information Source*. Available at http://www.migrationinformation.org/Feature/print.cfm?ID=602 (accessed 27 November 2012).

Penner, E., Blidook, K., et al., 2006, Legislative priorities and public opinion: representation of partisan agendas in the Canadian House of Commons. *Journal of European Public Policy*, 13(7), pp. 1006–1020.

Pierson, P., 2006, The new politics of the welfare state, in: H. J. Wiarda (Ed.) *Comparative Politics: Critical Concepts in Political Science*, Vol. II: *Western Europe and the United States: The Foundations of Comparative Politics* (London and New York: Routledge), pp. 107–140.

Pralle, S. B., 2003, Venue shopping, political strategy and policy change: The internalization of Canadian forest advocacy. *Journal of Public Policy*, 23(3), pp. 233–260.

Pralle, S. B., 2006a, Timing and sequence in agenda-setting and policy change: A comparative study of lawn care pesticide politics in Canada and the US. *Journal of European Politics*, 13(7), pp. 987–1005.

Pralle, S. B., 2006b, The "Mouse that roared": Agenda setting in Canadian pesticides politics. *Policy Studies Journal*, 34(2), 171–194.

Pralle, S. B., 2006c, *Branching Out, Digging In: Environmental Advocacy and Agenda Setting* (Washington, DC: Georgetown University Press).

Presthus, R. V., 1973, *Elite Accommodation in Canadian Politics* (Toronto: Macmillan of Canada).

Princen, S., 2007, Agenda-setting in the European Union: A theoretical exploration and agenda for research. *Journal of European Public Policy*, 14(1), pp. 21–38.

Pross, A. P., 1993, The mirror of the state: Canada's interest group system, in: C. S. Thomas (Ed.) *First World Interest Groups: A Comparative Perspective* (Westport, CT: Greenwood Press), pp. 67–79.

Rhodes, R. A. W., Wanna, J., et al., 2009, *Comparing Westminster* (Oxford: Oxford University Press).

Richardson, J. and Lester, L., 2004, *A Comparison of Australian and Canadian Immigration Policies and Labour Market Outcomes* (Adelaide: The National Institute of Labour Studies, Flinders University).

Ruddock, P., 1996, Minister for Immigration and Multicultural Affairs, Ministerial Statement, Management of the Migration Program, House of Representatives, 13 December.

Sapotichne, J. and Smith, J. M., 2012, Venue shopping and the politics of urban development: Lessons from Chicago and Seattle. *Urban Affairs Review*, 48(1), pp. 86–110.

Shachar, A., 2006, The race for talent: Skilled migrants and competitive immigration regimes. *NYU Law Review*, 81, pp. 148–206.

Sharman, C., 1999, The representation of small parties and independents in the Senate. *Australian Journal of Political Science*, 34(3), pp. 353–361.

Smith, M., 2005, *A Civil Society? Collective Actors in Canadian Political Life* (Peterborough: Broadview Press).

Soroka, S., 2002, *Agenda-setting Dynamics in Canada* (Vancouver: UBC Press).

Standing Committee on Citizenship and Immigration, 2002, *Building a Nation: The Regulations under the Immigration and Refugee Protection Act* (Ottawa, Standing Committee on Citizenship and Immigration, March 2002, third report, Ottawa: House of Commons).

Studlar, D. T., 2007, Ideas, institutions, and diffusion: What explains tobacco control policy in Australia, Canada, and New Zealand. *Commonwealth and Comparative Politics*, 45(2), pp. 164–184.

Thomas, P., 2009, Parliamentary scrutiny of government performance in Australia. *Australian Journal of Public Administration*, 68(3), pp. 373–398.

Thompson, A., 2002a, MPs plan to revolt over entry proposals. *Toronto Star*, 29 January, p. 17.

Thompson, A., 2002b, Minister set to soften immigration proposals. *Toronto Star*, 30 January, p. A01.

Thompson, F. and Stanbury, W. T., 1979, *The Political Economy of Interest Groups in the Legislative Process in Canada* (Montreal: Institute for Research on Public Policy).

Tichenor, D., 2002, *Dividing Lines: The Politics of Immigration Control in America* (Princeton, NJ: Princeton University Press)

Timmermans, A., 2001, Arenas as Institutional Sites for Policymaking: Patterns and Effects in Comparative Perspective. *Journal of Comparative Policy Analysis*, 3, 311–337.

Timmermans, A. and Scholten, P., 2006, The political flow of wisdom: Science institutions as policy venues in the Netherlands. *Journal of European Public Policy*, 13(7), pp. 1104–1118.

Tsebelis, G., 2000, Veto players and institutional analysis. *Governance: An International Journal of Policy and Administration*, 14(4), pp. 441–474.

Van Rijn, N., 2003, Court rejects change in entry rules. *Toronto Star*, 22 February, p. A04.

WCDWA (West Coast Domestic Workers Association), 2002, Submission to the Regulations to the Immigration and Refugee Protection Act, filed in National Archives of Canada, Ottawa, RG14, BAN 2007-00060-1, FA 14-59, Box 18, Wallet 5 (Ottawa, Standing Committee on Citizenship and Immigration, Parliament of Canada).

Weaver, R. and Rockman, B., 1993, *Do Institutions Matter?* (Washington, DC: Brookings Institution).

Wood, R., 2006, The dynamics of incrementalism: Subsystems, politics and public lands. *Policy Studies Journal*, **34**(2), pp. 1–16.

Young, L., 1999, Minor parties and the legislative process in the Australian Senate: A study of the 1993 Budget. *Australian Journal of Political Science*, **34**(1), pp. 7–27.

Setting the Immigrant Policy Agenda: Expertise and Politics in the Netherlands, France and the United Kingdom

PETER SCHOLTEN and ARCO TIMMERMANS

ABSTRACT *Policy making and agenda setting often are analyzed either in terms of how policy problems are defined, or in terms of the structural setting producing stability or opportunities for change. Building on different fields of scholarly work, this paper aims at an integration of structural and substantive elements in studying agenda setting. We analyze how particular frames of immigrant issues emerge in the interaction between policy makers and experts within this immigrant policy domain. By comparing this key element of agenda setting in the Netherlands, France and the United Kingdom, we show how different types of interaction produce different substantive policy frames. If immigrant integration is shaped primarily as a policy issue in broader political arenas and the media, a different frame emerges than when venues such as advisory bodies, think tanks and bureaucracies with limited access and less public exposure are involved.*

Introduction

Immigrant integration has become a major policy theme across European countries. Controversies over labour market access, civil rights and obligations, and cultural and religious issues indicate that immigrant policy problems have become nearly intractable. The policy responses of governments were and still are different.

Accounting for policy differences requires a systematic analysis of the dynamics of attention to immigrant integration. Immigrant policy is driven by "high politics" involving public and political debate, as well as "low politics", involving less visible venues such as administrative agencies and bodies for scientific expertise and policy advice. Immigrant policies have been effectively depoliticized, but became a subject of heated public and political debate in the past decade. These two modes of policy making involve quite different venues and participants. As earlier studies of agenda setting and policy making on immigrants have shown, the scope of debate, the degree of openness and the level of politicization determine policies (Schattschneider 1960,

Downs 1972, Rochefort and Cobb 1994, Guiraudon 1997). Existing work on immigrant policy making, however, rarely connects the different spheres of high and low politics, showing how venues play a part in setting the immigrant policy agenda.

This paper focuses on the role of expert venues in immigrant policy making. Most research on the relationship between expertise and policy deals with issues of technology and economics (Nelkin 1979, Fischer 1990). Interactions between experts and policy makers in social policy areas such as immigrant integration have been much less analyzed. But throughout Europe, expert venues have been involved in immigrant policy making in various ways. These venues varied between countries and within countries over time. While science has long been a venue for low politics, limiting the scope of debate to groups of insiders and policy specialists, beliefs in the contribution of social scientific research to resolving policy problems eroded and science became politicized (Weingart 1999). However, even in the high politics of current immigrant integration policies in many countries, scientific expertise continues to play an important role, though perhaps in ways that are more symbolic in legitimizing policy discourse rather than instrumental in more substantive terms (Boswell 2009). Studying the role of expert venues may provide a better understanding of the ways in which low and high politics alternate in agenda setting and, as a consequence, how policy responses vary.

We compare the role of venues of expertise in the policy process in three countries: France, the United Kingdom and the Netherlands. In these countries, policy responses also varied over time. Generally, policy venues at the levels of high and low politics are seen to produce different frames and images of problems (Baumgartner and Jones 1993, Guiraudon 2000, Pralle 2003). Using existing and differently oriented studies of immigrant policy in the three countries, we consider how for immigrant issues, policy venues and problem frames are related. We begin this study by presenting the theoretical perspective in which policy venues and problem frames are related, and more specifically the possible ways of interaction between venues of expertise for immigrant issues and policy makers. Then we analyze empirical patterns of this interaction in the Netherlands, France and the United Kingdom. We conclude with a discussion of similarities and differences and the theoretical relevance of this analysis.

Relating Venues and Frames in Policy Dynamics

Policy dynamics over time may involve different change patterns (Sabatier 1987, Baumgartner and Jones 1993, Hall 1993, Pierson 1994). Many authors followed in Lindblom's footsteps, arguing that small incremental change is the typical mode in policy making, constrained by sticky beliefs and institutional thresholds. Agenda theorists focus on political processes of agenda setting and argue that long episodes of stability are interrupted by opening windows of opportunity followed by attention and policy shifts (Cobb and Elder 1983, Kingdon 1995). Most explicit is the punctuated equilibrium model of Baumgartner and Jones (1993), which states that cognitive and institutional friction can long uphold a "policy monopoly", but eventually change occurs (Jones and Baumgartner 2005).

The strength of the punctuated equilibrium theory used by Baumgartner and Jones is that it integrates problem content and institutional context for analyzing how long-term policy dynamics involves both stability and change. They show how processes of feedback operate in sustaining or dismantling prevailing views and arrangements in a policy subsystem. Negative feedback neutralizes countersignals, positive feedback is the build-up of pressure originating from one or more venues where rival views are expressed, cascading into macropolitical arenas where policy shifts are formally decided.

This approach connects well to the work on problem framing by Rein and Schön (1994). Frames provide ways of selecting and organizing views of problems and their appropriate solutions; they involve discourses in which social groups and target populations are named (Schneider and Ingram 1993), they also include causal theories used for explaining the problem, and normative arguments why the problem needs attention in the first place. Frames usually are tacit. Even if actors may want to promote simple images, problems are ambiguous and their framing becomes contested. Framing always happens in a structural setting. Such a setting involves its own "criteria by which judgments are made about the legitimacy of participants and their standing as participants in the policy conversation" (Rein 1986: 13). As such, the institutional structure of problem framing can reinforce the mobilization of bias in a policy domain.

Both policy change and stability can be explained by the interaction between institutional structures and frames. Change will occur when the mutual sustainment of a problem frame and policy-making structures is interrupted, and such a change process begins in venues of agenda setting where attention is directed. Baumgartner and Jones (1993, 2002) not only made this interaction between venues and policy images explicit in their theoretical work, they also showed how it can produce both stability and change. This interaction between frames and institutional venues has become visible in several studies of policy making. In analyzing car accidents in the United States, Gusfield (1980) showed the relationship between the dominant position of the National Safety Council, several insurance companies and car industries, and the culture and image of this problem, with an emphasis on unsafe drivers ("the drinking driver") rather than on unsafe cars and roads. Likewise, Baumgartner and Jones (1993) and Rochefort and Cobb (1994) showed how for different issues such as smoking, nuclear power, urban renewal and child abuse, the portrayal of problems was sustained by favourable properties of policy venues within the policy field.

Such institutionally-induced equilibria have been referred to as subsystems (Lauman and Knoke 1987), iron triangles (Heclo 1978), systems of limited participation (Cobb and Elder 1983) and policy monopolies (Baumgartner and Jones 1993). A policy monopoly may be upheld for a long time and the scope of debate may be limited, but no policy subsystem is immune to contending views. Opposition pressure can build up and erupt after what Baumgartner and Jones (1993) call a process of positive feedback. Mobilization of support by contenders and events uncontrollable by existing policy goals and tools may make decision makers more receptive to alternatives. As issues move from venues of "low politics" involving policy specialists to broader arena of "high politics", the conditions are set for policy change.

Problem Frames and Venues of Expertise for Immigrant Issues

Frames of Immigrant Policy

In many countries, immigrant integration involves multiple frames. The frames used in immigrant policy making have been reconstructed by several authors (Castles and

Miller 2003, Koopmans et al. 2005), which has resulted in a distinction between four types of frames. First, *assimilationism* frames and portrays integration in terms of national social cohesion and identity, which is seen to be eroded by migration and cultural diversity. Hence the solution is a policy of national identity preservation by stressing socio-cultural adaptation. Thus, assimilationism attributes a strongly national symbolic importance to immigrant integration and suggests paths of action that are mainly located at this national level – they require central government control. Second, *multiculturalism* frames integration as an issue of socio-cultural emancipation of specific groups, whereby it is acknowledged and accepted that society is multicultural. This frame is void of references to a "national community", which it considers to be fiction and a harmful concept. Third, *universalism* frames integration of immigrants as a color-blind and individualized process. It stresses the socio-economic participation of immigrants as new citizens but does not pursue this through strongly centralized policies. In this frame, the target population is seen as a category in need of developing individual autonomy. Finally, *differentialism* (also referred to as *segregationism*) stresses that cultural and ethnic differences are obstacles to immigrant integration, and therefore this frame includes a model of "living apart together", much alike the Dutch traditional structure of pillarization (Lijphart 1968) and Apartheid in South Africa until the 1990s.

Varying Venues of Expertise for Immigrant Policy

Venues of expertise and policy advice may involve expert committees, advisory bodies, research councils, think tanks and other experts that may be more or less institutionalized. Sometimes, expert advice is formally required before a policy can be presented, in other cases such advice happens at the discretion of political decision makers. In these varying ways, venues of expertise play a role in agenda setting. Such venues can provide venues for getting new topics or new views on the agenda; they can provide routes for agenda setting, for instance in situations where scientific authority can support the credibility of specific knowledge claims. They also may have a negative agenda function by suspending attention and keeping issues off the political agenda, producing frames that are technical rather than dramatic (Nisbet and Huge 2006). Despite an expanding body of empirical and normative work on expert advice in policy making (Wildavsky 1979, Jasanoff 1990, Rich 2004, Maasen and Weingart 2005), the mobilization of expertise in agenda setting has received little scholarly attention (Rich 2004, Timmermans and Scholten 2006).

We focus specifically on the relationship between venues of scientific expertise and substantive policy frames. The literature on immigrant policy suggests that organizations of expertise and policy advice are prominent in immigrant policy making (Guiraudon 1997, Favell 1998, Ratcliffe 2001, Rath 2001, Amiraux and Simon 2006, Boswell 2009, Scholten 2010). A dominant notion about the role of scientific knowledge in the policy process is that of "speaking truth to power" (Wildavsky 1979), but more variation is possible – including rather mundane functions of scientific expertise for depoliticization and limiting the scope of conflict. To capture this empirical variation, we use a model developed by Wittrock (1991) distinguishing between four types of interaction between expert organizations and policy makers. Each type involves different institutional positions and relationships between them, attributing primacy to experts or to policy makers, and demarcating the extent to which the two domains are set apart by different roles and modus operandi, or are close or overlapping.

First, the *enlightenment model* stays closest to the standard model of scientific institutions belonging to an autonomous sphere involved only in the pursuit of scientific truth. Science is considered to be "exceptional" and clearly demarcated from the domain of politics, but has influence on it through a process of enlightenment or gradual "knowledge creep" (Weiss 1977). In the *technocratic model*, science also enjoys primacy but is more directly involved in policy making, leaving its ivory tower position more characteristic of the enlightenment model. In the technocratic model, science not only speaks truth per se, but also "speaks truth to power" (Wildavsky 1979). Indeed, politicians frequently invoke scientific experts to legitimate decisions, depoliticize issues, and avoid political blame. By contrast, in the *bureaucratic model*, political primacy renders scientific institutions in a position of knowledge delivery on demand. Science thus has a role clearly demarcated from the domain of politics. Science provides data and "facts", politics values. This model is thus based on a Weberian fact-value dichotomy between administration and politics. Finally, in the *engineering model*, politics is on "top" and science on "tap", but the division of labor is demarcated less than in the bureaucratic model. Scientists and experts are not only data producers but are also drawn into the political, social and ethical values that underlie their advice. This model is closest to the idea of "mandated science" (Salter and Levy 1988).

With these models (see overview in Figure 1) of research-policy relations we aim to capture the diverse ways in which expertise can be involved in policy-making. Beyond the standard model of "speaking truth to power", these models can capture situations in which venues of scientific expertise play a primary role in setting new frames on the policy agenda, and situations in which scientific expertise provides legitimacy or instrumental data for sustaining specific policy frames and policy monopolies. Below, we present country analyses of France, the United Kingdom and the Netherlands in which we deal with the following three questions: 1) What changes took place in policy framing over time? 2) How was the interaction between expert organizations and policy-making institutions structured when these changes occurred? And 3) to what extent can this interaction explain the prevalence of particular frames in different time periods in the three countries? Our focus is on "immigrant policy", or policies aimed at the incorporation of migrants into society, as distinguished from "immigration policy", or policies on the regulation of entry and exit from these societies

Figure 1. Models of interaction between expert institutions and policy institutions

		Coordination of relations	
		Scientific primacy	Political primacy
Demarcation of roles	Sharp	**Enlightenment model**	**Bureaucratic model**
	Diffuse	**Technocratic model**	**Engineering model**

Source: Wittrock (1991).

(see Hammar 1985). Furthermore, in our definition of "immigrant" we follow the dominant policy definition in the three examined countries, which includes first generation migrants as well as their second generation descendants.

The choice for the Netherlands, France and the United Kingdom is based on the existence of a developed policy subsystem dealing with immigrant issues for several decades, producing policies that diverged between the countries and also changed within them. Furthermore, recent work on the long term development of policy agendas in these countries shows that attention to immigrant integration has risen, and that the attention cycle includes both "low" politics and "high politics" (Breeman et al. 2009, Jennings and John 2009, Brouard et al. 2009). We do not intend to generalize beyond these three countries, but our findings may enable us to shed more theoretical light on framing effects of types of interaction between venues of policy expertise and political venues on immigrant policy issues, or even beyond this specific policy domain to broader sets of issues.

The Netherlands

The "No Policy" Monopoly

In the late 1970s, immigrant integration emerged on the policy agenda in the Netherlands. Immigration was framed as a temporary phenomenon, expressed in the use of terminology such as "guest workers" and "international commuters". In this frame, there was no need for immigrant integration policy. This differentialist framing had distinct structural roots. Specific government departments used economic and demographic arguments why the Netherlands was not and should not be an immigration country. Most politicians also feared social tensions as a consequence of immigration. Further, welfare organizations advocated a differentialist approach because it would make migrant groups more autonomous. Until the 1970s, these conditions upheld a structural equilibrium preventing the development of immigrant integration policy. This was also reflected in the absence of research interest in minorities: only few studies were done, focusing on the position of minorities within Dutch society (Penninx 2005). Thus, in this period there was a mutually reinforcing logic between the policy idea of not being an immigration country and the absence of research attention.

The Technocracy of Minorities Policy

This equilibrium was destabilized in the late 1970s. A series of terrorist attacks by Moluccan immigrants led to increasing attention to immigrant integration on the public and political agenda. Following these events, an "ethnic minorities policy" was developed aimed at integrating diverse minority groups. Migrants were framed as permanent "cultural" or "ethnic minorities" in Dutch society. The goal was to "achieve an open multi-ethnic society in which ethnic minorities, individuals as well as groups, enjoy an equal position and full opportunities for their development" (Minorities Memorandum 1983: 107). This policy had multiculturalist elements, focusing on cultural emancipation of minority groups. The underlying causal story was that emancipation of minorities would help socio-economic participation.

This ethnic minorities policy was formulated through a centralized policy structure, involving co-optation of experts and ethnic elites (Guiraudon 1997). Government departments and political actors attributed primacy to experts in policy development. The Department of Welfare stimulated research on ethnic minorities to convince other departments of the need for a minorities policy (Entzinger 1981). It founded an Advisory Committee on Minorities Research (ACOM) that was to provide a crucial stimulus to the development of migration research in the Netherlands. Also, political actors delegated policy formulation to experts because no party wanted to politicize this issue. Researchers became increasingly involved in policy making. Many researchers had a commitment to the position of minorities and advocated a policy-oriented role for experts. Research was seen to serve societal transformation. Next to the ACOM, the Scientific Council for Government Policy (WRR) began to claim a role on immigrant issues. An advisory report on ethnic minorities (WRR 1979) directly informed the formulation of the minorities policy. One of the main contributors to this report also became an author of the Minorities Memorandum issued by the government (Penninx 2005).

This pattern of interaction between experts and policy makers had technocratic elements, with a primary role for research and close relations with policy makers. It has been described as a "technocratic symbiosis" (Rath 2001), narrowing the scope of political debate to a limited number of experts and policy makers who shared a specific focus on minorities issues (Scholten 2010). Thus, the "technocratic symbiosis" provided the venue for a multiculturalist framing of the minorities policy emphasizing what was specific to ethnic and cultural minorities. At the same time, this multiculturalist frame insulated the emerging policy subsystem from broader themes such as economic status and national identity.

The Short Age of Enlightenment and Universalism

Immigrant integration returned to the political agenda in the late 1980s and early 1990s. Disappointing results of the minorities policy and broader concerns about the viability of the welfare state put pressure on the minorities policy monopoly. Increasingly, immigrant integration was linked to other policy topics, in particular welfare state retrenchment and urban renewal. This led to policy change in 1994, when a new government coalition took office. A more universalist perspective emerged, focusing less on what was specific to migrants and more on citizenship. Migrants were defined as citizens from outside the Netherlands (*allochtonen*), rather than as cultural groups. The new integration policy stressed socio-economic participation of migrants, claiming that participation would benefit emancipation.

Expert organizations again played a central role in this policy frame shift. A second report from the WRR (1989), triggered broad public and political debate about the need for policy change. The WRR developed a new policy approach that focused on migrant citizenship and socio-economic participation. This reflected a broader agenda of the WRR and specific political parties in this period on welfare state reform. Several years later, this report played a central role in a broad national debate on minorities, triggered by a prominent opposition party leader (Frits Bolkestein), who advocated a stricter approach towards immigrants. In this debate, powerful taboos were at stake, such as not treating migrants as "dependants" but as citizens with rights and obligations. This change in tone provoked fierce criticism from researchers, as it rejected the dominant minorities paradigm. None the less, a shift in the dominant frame and the development of the integration policy containing new policy ideas mentioned in the 1989 WRR report had passed the point of no return.

The frame also involved a change in structural relations between experts and policy makers. Experts had less direct effect on policy, but their work became more indirectly relevant by stirring public and political debate. Also, experts again were attributed a primary role in policy change but more as a consequence of the strategy of specific actors (WRR, politicians) to utilize expert venues for challenging the established policy monopoly. The type of interaction between experts and policy makers now accorded to the model of enlightenment, in which authoritative expert bodies were prominent. Thus, in this episode scientific venues contributed to dismantling the existing policy monopoly, and contributed to a process of positive feedback in which a new frame emerged, emphasizing what immigrants and other citizens had in common, not what separated them. This implied a replacement of multiculturalism with universalism.

Assimilationism as Political Engineering

The universalist integration policy of the 1990s could not prevent growing controversies over social and cultural attributes of immigrants. Another national debate driven by a number of public intellectuals (among them Ayaan Hirsi-Ali) and the rise of the populist politician Pim Fortuyn in the "long year of 2002" in Dutch politics, triggered attention to an alleged "clash of civilizations" in Dutch society. Immigrant integration was now linked to national identity and social cohesion. It was framed not just in terms of socio-economic participation but also as a matter of language proficiency, acceptance of national norms and values and residential dispersion. A "new style" integration policy was developed, aimed at common citizenship and emphasizing the commonalities of minorities and natives as "citizens of one society".

This assimilationist policy frame emerged primarily from the public and political debate which had expanded in scale rapidly. Immigrant integration had become a major agenda item for populist politicians in search of the increasing group of floating voters in parliamentary elections. The alleged failure of earlier integration policies became symbolic of a larger popular outcry against "elitist" and "old" politics and the neglect of the *vox populi*. This coincided with a growing scepticism about scientific expertise. The involvement of experts still adhering to the now contested views on immigrant policy was debated openly. Even a parliamentary enquiry committee investigating immigrant integration policy came in the firing line when it adopted the conclusions of a research institute previously involved in immigrant policy making (Scholten and Van Nispen 2008). A new report by the Scientific Council for Government Policy (WRR 2001) was also ignored because of an alleged multiculturalist bias. Politicians promoting an assimilationist frame engaged in scientific venue shopping and embraced the Social and Cultural Planning Agency (SCP) which openly advocated an assimilationist approach. The assimilationist approach thus resulted more clearly from political agenda setting in which policy entrepreneurs punctuated the institutionalized nexus between policy makers and organizations for policy advice. This structural reshuffle can be characterized with the engineering model of interaction, in which expertise is used selectively to endorse views articulated in political arenas.

France

Technocracy and "the Right to be Different"

As in most European countries, in France until the 1970s there was a widespread belief that immigration was temporary. The issue of immigrant integration did not reach the agenda, in spite of large scale immigration in the 1960s, especially from (former) French colonies. When it became evident in the mid-1970s that most migrants where there to stay, France gradually developed a policy aimed at immigrant integration or at "insertion" (*politique d'insertion*) (Favell 1998). It focused on ethno-cultural accommodation, or the establishment of conditions for equality for immigrant communities in several domains. This policy had distinct multiculturalist traits, proclaiming the right to be different (*le droit à la différence*) as one of the cornerstones of the French approach (Feldblum 1999: 33).

The development of this insertion politics was, however, not a consequence of political agenda setting. The scale of political debate remained constrained (Guiraudon 2000). Policy making was mainly an administrative and legal activity, involving "a maze of decrees, circulars, departmental memos or even telexes" (Wihtol de Wenden 1988) and a strong involvement of the French Council of State and the Constitutional Court. These administrative and legal bodies forced the French government to adopt a policy for immigrant integration. The issue was depoliticized, restricting the scale of debate to "internal state discussions and revisions ... defined as technical issues" (Feldblum 1999: 59). Researchers paid little attention to minorities issues, except a few studies sustaining the multiculturalist approach to integration.

Hence, the development of the French insertion policy was described as a project of "technocratic elite management" (Favell 1998). This technocratic structure enabled politicians to keep this topic away from the deep political cleavages characteristic of French politics. It established a focus on basic welfare and social needs of migrants, and did not deal with symbolic questions related to immigrant integration (Favell 1998: 47). Technocracy provided the institutional conditions for a multiculturalist framing of immigrant integration, focusing on the specific needs of immigrants and keeping it away from broader concerns about national identity.

Political Engineering and the French Republican Model

Republicanism was an important part of the founding myth of the French Republic and still is a powerful cultural idiom. In the late 1980s, republicanism provided the basis of a more assimilationist approach to immigrant integration. This involved a strongly inclusive approach to immigrant integration, opening access to French citizenship to all those born on French territory (Brubaker 1992). This involved a colour-blind approach, in which ethnic categorization of migrants was taboo (Schain 1999). This sensitivity around ethnic categorization was rooted in the Vichy period in French politics (Wihtol de Wenden 2009). Instead of a right to be different, it contained a right to be indifferent (*droit à l'indifférence*), or the right of equal treatment. This implied a rejection of policies seeking accommodation of cultural differences. However, French republicanism also has assimilationist elements: it focused more on cultural adaptation of immigrants to the central values and norms in French society, such as to the powerful norm of *laïcité*, the separation between religion and the public sphere.

The republicanist model of integration occurred as a consequence of political and public agenda setting in the early 1980s. Within the competitive structure of French political elites, immigrant integration became a central issue of polarization between the political Left and Right (Schain 1988, Guiraudon 1997, Bleich 2003). The political Right revived the republican model for immigrant integration as part of a broader agenda to restore national solidarity. Jean-Marie le Pen radicalized the emerging universalist model of political discourse and advocated assimilation. One of the effects of the radical frame of Le Pen was a reinforcement of the consensus between the Left and Right about the republican model.

This wave of public and political attention was strongly mediatized, focused on the national level and involved public intellectuals such as Todd, Taguieff, Schnapper and Kriegel. France has a tradition of involvement of intellectuals in public and political life, and the involvement of these opinion leaders in the immigrant policy debate contributed to a "public reflection of a highly philosophical nature, extraordinary in its abstract and theoretical content, and peculiar to the French political scene" (Favell 1998: 40). Policy venues for these intellectuals were several think tanks and government-related bodies such as the High Council for Integration, and various ad hoc committees such as the Commission des Sages and more recently the Stasi Committee.

In the 1990s, these public intellectuals continued to play a central role in sustaining French republicanism in often strongly mediatized debates. Focus events such as the headscarf or "foulard" affairs in the late 1980s were taken as opportunities for defending republicanism. In his study of the French response to headscarves, Bowen (2007) shows how various intellectuals played a role in framing headscarves as an issue of laïcité and public space rather than a social problem of participation and emancipation. The intellectuals were also well represented in the so-called Stasi Commission (Independent Commission of Reflection on the Application of the Principle of Laïcité in the Republic), that recommended a legal ban on headscarf wearing in French public schools because of their ostentatious nature. The involvement of academics and intellectuals in policy making in France was much less institutionalized than in the Netherlands, and few structural arrangements existed in the research-policy nexus.

Yet French intellectuals played a prominent part in upholding a republicanist frame of integration: they sustained the "normative, historical and political grounding for the new republican philosophy" (Favell 2005). According to the enlightenment model, they did this by ad hoc participation in public and political debate. At the same time, French governments restructured the research-policy nexus towards the engineering model in order to legitimize the emerging assimilationist policy discourse. This involved a selective use of scientific research in policy making. The High Council for Integration, advising the government but also engaged in research programming, played a central role in this. According to Favell (2001: 379), the High Council "set in motion a machine of empirical evidence gathering, explicitly constructed to find the data that the public theory had set out to prove". Still, expertise contradicting the colour blind French approach was ignored or prevented, "race based statistics" were banned almost completely, because of the taboo on categorizing minorities in a way that interfered with their citizenship status (Bleich 2003). Also among researchers, the use of race or ethnicity based statistics was controversial (Amiraux and Simon 2006, Sabbagh and Peer 2008). The engineering of French republicanism thus involved a specific use of research.

The French Model in Disarray?

Since the late 1990s, the French republican model is contested, though it remains the model informing French immigrant policies (even more so after Nicolas Sarkozy was elected as president). First of all, several researchers have indicated a growing decoupling (*décalage*) of national policy rhetoric and local policy practices, or, as Favell put it, a "décalage between the highbrow republican rhetoric of the centre ... and the void of appropriate and consistent discourse and methods at the local level" (Favell 1998: 184). At the local level, often for more pragmatic reasons, policy measures have been adopted that conflicted with the republican model. In particular, local governments adopt a more pragmatic approach to categorizing ethnic differences, a requisite for defining target groups and policy implementation. Riots in the French *banlieues* drew more attention to the problems of the colour blind French approach in addressing social problems manifest in urban areas with a large migrant population.

Second, the republican model with its taboo on ethnic categorization became contested in research (Amiraux and Simon 2006, Sabbagh and Peer 2008). Researchers with a background in empirical social sciences tried to break the taboo on ethnic categorization. This led to a heated scientific debate in 1998 around an attempt to include ethnic categories in survey research by Tribalat (1996). Also due to the internationalization of migration research, the French "exceptionalism" in the impossibility of recognizing minorities became contested (Favell 2001, Amiraux and Simon 2006). Still, there remains support for French republicanism by public intellectuals and social scientists, leading to a neglect of more empirical research work (Bowen 2007). This was illustrated by the proceedings of the so-called Stasi commission, or commission on Laïcité, installed in 2003. This commission narrowly focused on the Islamic veil as an issue of symbolic importance to laïcité, and ignored claims based on empirical research to social problems behind the veil, such as socioeconomic participation. Thus, a "décalage" seems to emerge between the involvement of public intellectuals in debates that sustain French republicanism, and research-policy relations that are more technocratic and sustain pragmatic multiculturalist policies at the local level.

The United Kingdom

The Technocratic Conception of British Multiculturalism

The British approach to immigrant integration differs from the French and Dutch approaches in several ways. An important condition for British immigrant integration policy was that most migrants from (former) British colonies already enjoyed British citizenship. Citizenship was not a defining characteristic for immigrant policy development. Instead, colour and race were central to policy framing. The main policy goal was to improve race relations (Joppke 1999, Garbaye 2005). This approach differs strongly from the French colour blind approach, and resembles more the American approach (Bleich 2003). This multiculturalist frame was combined with universalist elements. Improving race relations was placed in the perspective of preserving public order. Furthermore, a welfare state approach was adopted by ensuring equal opportunities for racial minorities on socio-economic matters, and by elaborating extensive anti-discrimination programs (Joppke 1999).

Immigrant integration emerged on the political agenda relatively early in Great Britain. In the late 1950s a series of race riots took place in Nottingham and Notting Hill. Also, immigrant integration was briefly politicized by a political speech by the conservative Enoch Powell on "rivers of blood" that would flow if race relations matters were not addressed well. However, this brief politicization was followed by a policy equilibrium sustained by depoliticization. The events of the 1950s and 1960s had sparked fears that emphasizing race could undermine public order. An informal political agreement emerged to refrain from politicizing this issue (Geddes 2003, Garbaye 2005), described as "conspiracies of silence" (Messina 1989). Consequently, the development of British immigrant policy was mainly an elite project (Favell 1998). Bleich (2003) shows how the focus on race relations entered the problem frame through a series of informal and formal contacts between British and American policy makers.

This elite-technocratic process of policy making also involved a more institutionalized involvement of British social researchers. Through institutes such as the Policy Science Institute and the Centre for Research on Ethnic Relations, experts had a strong influence on agenda setting on race relations in the UK. At an early stage, a convergence occurred between social scientists (often anthropologists and sociologists) and policy makers focusing on issues of colour and race. An early report by the researcher Rose from the Institute for Race Relations ("Colour and citizenship" 1969) was an important moment in this convergence. In the 1970s, the British Social Science Research Council provided funding to the Centre for Research in Ethnic Relations, which would exert great influence on the development of British research in this field (Ratcliffe 2001). The central position of this institute contributed to a dominant position of the sociology of race (Small and Solomos 2006), at the cost of for instance more critical Marxist approaches (Favell 2001). Furthermore, similar to the Dutch case, these researchers were policy-oriented, maintaining close relationships with state agencies and attuned to the political-ideological environment (Martins 1993, Ratcliffe 2001). For instance, John Rex, a former director of the Centre for Research in Ethnic Relations, strongly believed that the "is" and "ought" in sociological research should not be divided (Turner 2006). At the same time, the British government relied on these experts for policy making in its attempts to avoid politicization. This institutional relationship is described somewhat critically as the British "race relations industry".

The framing of the British approach to immigrant integration thus had a distinct technocratic-elitist character. Again, we can observe a clear relationship between the dynamics of agenda setting and problem framing. The race relations industry with empirical social scientists and pragmatic policy makers created a structural setting for problem framing emphasizing the practical rather than the a priori deontological aspects of immigrant integration. In contrast to France, where such a priori deontological thinking was common from the 1980s, a more or less overt preference existed for "calculated, piecemeal, evolutionary, anti-philosophical pragmatism" (Favell 1998: 96).

Evidence-based Policy Making and the Reinvention of a British Model

Immigrant integration spiralled back onto the political agenda at the beginning of the twenty-first century, as it did in the Netherlands, France and other European countries. Whereas the "new" Labour governments of the end of the 1990s had held on to the multiculturalist model, a frame shift emerged in the aftermath of 9/11 (Small and Solomos 2006). International developments but also urban unrest in the UK in the summer of 2001 drew attention to alleged pathologies of the British approach (Favell 1998, Geddes 2003). Also, the growing visibility of Muslim immigrants as a category that defies the racial definition of minorities (Modood 2005) put pressure on the technocratic status quo that long upheld multiculturalism. Following the government-commissioned Cantle Report (2001), in 2002 the British Home Office announced it would stress civic integration (Joppke 2003). Attention had risen on redefining the British imagined community by seeking a standard of what it means to be British – a search for commonalities instead of compatibilities. This led to attempts to move beyond multiculturalism, and to thicken the British citizenship concept to a stronger sense of belonging and identity (Singh 2004).

This gradual reframing of the immigrant policy agenda was associated with a change in the research-policy nexus. The technocratic policy monopoly in which the "race relations research industry" played such a central part was now gradually dismantled. Political actors and the national government in particular acquired a more prominent role in keeping immigrant integration on the policy agenda. This change however did not push expertise to the margins but involved a change in orientation on more "evidence-based policy" (Boswell 2009). The government established a research agency within the Home Affairs Department: the Immigration Research and Statistics Office (IRSS) in 2000. However, as Boswell (2009) shows, the role that this in-house research agency played was mainly one of legitimizing British policy discourse.

Beyond the technocratic model that had prevailed thus far, politics after the turn of the century thus acquired a stronger primacy while immigrant research remained policy-oriented. This development carries, again, a clear resemblance to the Dutch case, where an engineering type of research-policy nexus emerged in recent years to support the more assimilationist new style integration policy.

Discussion and Conclusion

In this paper we have focused on the relationship between expert venues in political agenda setting and frames of immigrant policy in the Netherlands, France and the United Kingdom. Our theoretical argument was that relating policy venues and problem frames enables a better understanding of policy dynamics over time. We found that in all three countries, immigrant policy "monopolies" were temporal –

endorsed for some time, but not immune to events and alternative views. While policy variation was a criterion for case selection, our analysis shows the more specific patterns of change in agenda setting and policy frames over time. We focused on how venues of expertise influence the political agenda, either as venues for getting issues on the agenda ("high politics") or as venues to keep issues off the agenda and generate "low politics". To this end, we used a typology of four different modes of interaction between experts and policy makers. We found that these developments involving shifts between "low" politics and "high" politics followed their own institutional rhythms in the three countries.

Considering the patterns of interaction between experts and policy makers and the ways of framing immigrant problems, we found that the two types of interaction most visible in this policy domain were the technocratic model and the engineering model, with some sign of the enlightenment model in France and the Netherlands. In all three countries, the nexus between experts and policy makers showed an initial primacy for knowledge organizations or individual experts, where political actors remained relatively low key and relied on social scientific expertise for setting the immigrant policy agenda. Our analysis suggests that a relationship exists between this technocratic structure where expert organizations are central to limiting the scope of debate, and the emergence and endorsement of a multiculturalist frame of immigrants as distinct groups supported by the government. Such a frame was institutionalized in France and lasted until the early 1980s, in the United Kingdom it emerged in the 1960s, and in the Netherlands in the mid-1980s. This multiculturalism thus was sustained by elite policy making to which venues of expertise functioned to depoliticize issues, keeping them away from arenas of high politics in which problems may be dramatized. The growing "minorities industries" involved scientific expertise and professional knowledge at the local level, where the immigrant policy frame institutionalized in systems of policy delivery.

Once the initial immigrant policy agenda was set, interrelationships between experts and policy makers began to shift from the technocratic type towards enlightenment. Politicians obtained more primacy, but they remained receptive to input from scientific experts. This shift was visible mostly in France in the mid 1980s and in the Netherlands in the early 1990s, and it suggests that politicians obtained political control over immigrant issues. This changing interaction also involved a shift in these two countries towards a universalist problem frame and a policy image of general citizenship. In the United Kingdom, universalism was less visible because of the general dispersion of citizenship among British immigrants and because British citizenship has a relatively thin cultural meaning. In France and the Netherlands, immigrant integration policy became increasingly connected to broader issues of the welfare state.

This enlightenment was however a short intermezzo. The other relationship we found is between the engineering model and an assimilationist policy frame. While engineering in itself does not imply politicization of issues, immigrant policy appeared particularly sensitive to social and political polarization. In France this already happened in the 1980s, when the idiom of republicanism was applied in political debate over immigrant issues. In the United Kingdom and the Netherlands, immigrant issues became a subject of social and political controversy more recently. Focus events related to Muslim immigrants provoked a drastic expansion of the scope of debate, with immigrants becoming less a "dependent", and more a "deviant" target group (Schneider and Ingram 1993). Multiculturalist and universalist frames were considered too weak and new policy entrepreneurs mobilized support for an assimilationist frame in which national identity and cultural adaptation of immigrants were central. Expansion of political debate and skepticism about vested expert organizations for policy advice were part of this strategy to produce a frame shift.

These findings correspond to observations in earlier studies that a limited scope of debate on immigrant policy facilitates extension of rights, whereas debate expansion leads to curtailing or reducing immigrant rights (Freeman 1995, Guiraudon 1997). Our analysis adds a structural element by showing how different modes of interaction between experts and policy makers are conducive to the emergence and endorsement of particular problem frames. We have shown that expert organizations are significant to building problem frames on immigrant issues, even though experts mostly are formally located outside the political arenas of agenda setting. Expert organizations can be venues in agenda setting by inspiring politicians, by providing ammunition in political debates, or they can function as vehicles for depoliticization. They are more or less visible in the definition of problems and are a part of agenda setting via the route of low politics by narrowing the scope of debate, or a high politics route involving drama, mass mobilization and conflict expansion. Thus expert organizations are not somewhere "out there" in what Schneider and Ingram (1993) call "scientific exceptionalism". They are endogenous to agenda setting. Science sometimes may speak truth to power from a position of autonomy, but our analysis provides evidence for three countries that power also speaks back. The talk of expertise and politics mostly happens in interaction, with substantive consequences for the immigrant policy agenda, and for the way this agenda is sustained in a policy monopoly.

References

Amiraux, Valérie and Simon, Patrick, 2006, There are no minorities here: cultures of scholarship and public debate on immigrants and integration in France. *International Journal of Comparative Sociology*, **47**, 191–215.

Baumgartner, Frank and Jones, Bryan, 1993, *Agendas and Instability in American Politics* (London: University of Chicago Press).

Bleich, Erik, 2003, *Race Politics in Britain and France: Ideas and Policymaking since the 1960s* (Cambridge: Cambridge University Press).

Boswell, Christina, 2009, *The Political Uses of Expert Knowledge. Immigration Policy and Social Research* (Cambridge: Cambridge University Press).

Bowen, John, 2007, *Why the French Don't Like Headscarves. Islam, State and Public Space* (Princeton, NJ: Princeton University Press).

Breeman, G., Lowery, D., Poppelaars, C., Resodihardjo, S., Timmermans, A. and De Vries, J., 2009, Political attention in a coalition system: analyzing Queen's Speeches in the Netherlands 1945–2007. *Acta Politica*, **44**, 1–27.

Brouard, Sylvain et al., 2009, les productions legislatives: enjeux et methodes, *Revue Internationale de Politique Comparée*, special issue (16), 381–404.

Brubaker, Rogers, 1992, *Citizenship and Nationhood in France and Germany* (Cambridge, MA: Harvard University Press).

Cantle, A. O., 2001, *Community Cohesion* (London: Home Office).

Castles and Miller, 2003, *The Age of Migration. International Population Movements in the Modern World* (New York: Palgrave Macmillan).

Cobb, R. W. and Elder, C. D., 1983, *Participation in American Politics: The Dynamics of Agenda-building* (Baltimore, MD: John Hopkins University Press).

Department of Home Affairs, 1983, *Minderhedennota* (SDU: The Hague).

Downs, A., 1972, Up and down with ecology: the issue attention cycle. *Public Interest*, **28**, 38–50.

Entzinger, Han, 1981, De ACOM als voorbeeld van onderzoeksprogrammering; maar wat levert het nu op aan kwaliteitsverhoging?, in: B. W. Frijling and C. Rottländer-Meyer (Eds.) *Sociaal beleidsonderzoek; luxe of noodzaak?* (Zoetermeer: Actaboek), pp. 105–136.

Favell, Adrian, 1998, *Philosophies of Integration. Immigration and the Idea of Citizenship in France and Britain* (Basingstoke: Palgrave).

Favell, Adrian, 2001, Integration policy and integration research in Europe: a review and critique, in: T. A. Aleinikoff and D. B. Klusmeyer (Eds.) *Citizenship Today: Global Perspectives and Practices* (Washington, DC: Brookings Institute).

Favell, Adrian, 2005, Integration Nations: The Nation-State and Research on Immigrants in Western Europe, in: M. Bommes and E. T. Morawska (Eds.) *International Migration Research: Constructions, Omissions and the Promises of Interdisciplinarity* (Aldershot: Ashgate).

Feldblum, M., 1999, *Reconstructing Citizenship. The Politics of Nationality Reform and Immigration in Contemporary France* (New York: State University of New York Press).

Fischer, F., 1990, *The Technocracy of Expertise* (London: Sage).

Freeman, G. P., 1995, Modes of immigration politics in liberal democratic states. *International Migration Review*, **29**, 881–902.

Garbaye, R., 2005, *Getting Into Local Power* (Oxford: Blackwell Publishing).

Geddes, Andrew, 2003, *The Politics of Migration and Immigration in Europe* (London: Sage).

Guiraudon, Virginie, 1997, Policy change behind gilded doors: explaining the evolution of aliens' rights in France, Germany and the Netherlands, 1974–94. Doctoral dissertation, Harvard University).

Guiraudon, Virginie, 2000, European integration and migration policy: vertical policy-making as venue shopping. *Journal of Common Market Studies*, **38**, 251–271.

Hall, Peter, 1993, Policy paradigms, social learning, and the state. The case of economic policymaking in Britain. *Comparative Politics*, **25**, 275–296.

Hammar, Thomas, 1985, *European Immigration Policy. A Comparative Study* (Cambridge: Cambridge University Press).

Heclo, H., 1978, Issue Networks and the Executive Establishment. American Political System, in: A. King (Ed.) *The New American Political System* (Washington, DC: American Enterprise Institute for Public Policy Research), pp. 87–124.

Jasanoff, Sheila, 1990, *The Fifth Branch: Science Advisers as Policymakers* (London: Cambridge University Press).

Jennings, Will and John, Peter, 2010, Punctuations and turning points in British politics. The policy agenda of the Queen's Speech 1940–2005. *British Journal of Political Science*, **40**(3), 561–586.

Jones, Bryan and Baumgartner, Frank, 2005, *The Politics of Attention. How Government Prioritizes Problems* (Chicago: University of Chicago Press).

Joppke, Christian, 1999, *Immigration and the Nation-State. The United States, Germany and Great Britain* (Oxford: Oxford University Press).

Joppke, Christian, 2003, *The Retreat of Multiculturalism from the Liberal State* (New York: Russell Sage Foundation).

Kingdon, John, 1995, *Agendas, Alternative, and Public Policies* (Amsterdam: Addison Wesley).

Koopmans, R., Statham, P., Giugni, M., and Passy, F., 2005, *Contested Citizenship. Immigration and Cultural Diversity in Europe* (Minneapolis: University of Minnesota Press).

Lauman, E. O. and Knoke, D., 1987, *The Organizational State. Social Choice in National Policy Domains* (London: University of Wisconsin Press).

Lijphart, Arend, 1968, *The Politics of Accommodation: Pluralism and Democracy in the Netherlands* (Berkeley: University of California Press).

Maasen, S. and Weingart, P., 2005, *Democratization of Expertise? Exploring Novel Forms of Scientific Advice in Political Decision-Making* (Dordrecht: Springer).

Martins, H. (Ed.), 1993, *Knowledge and Passion: Essays in Honour of John Rex* (London: Tauris).

Messina, A., 1989, *Race and Party Competition* (Oxford: Oxford University Press).

Modood, Tariq, 2005, *Multicultural Politics: Racism, Ethnicity and Muslims in Britain* (Minneapolis: University of Minneapolis Press).

Nelkin, D., 1979, *Controversy: Politics of Technical Decisions* (Beverly Hills: Sage).
Nisbet, M. C. and Huge, M., 2006, Attention cycles and frames in the plant biotechnology debate: managing power and participation through the press/Policy Connection. *Harvard International Journal of Press/Politics*, **11**(2), 3–40.
Penninx, Rinus, 2005, Bridges between research and policy? The case of post-war immigration and integration policies in the Netherlands. *International Journal on Multicultural Studies*, **7**, 33–48.
Pierson, Paul, 1994, *Dismantling the Welfare State? Reagan, Thatcher and the Politics of Retrenchment* (Cambridge: Cambridge University Press).
Pralle, Sarah, 2003, Venue shopping, political strategy, and policy change: the internationalization of Canadian forest advocacy. *Journal for Public Policy*, **23**, 233–260.
Ratcliffe, P., 2001, Race and ethnicity research in Britain: key ethical and political considerations, in: P. Ratcliffe (Ed.) *The Politics of Social Science Research. Race, Ethnicity and Social Change* (Basingstoke: Palgrave), pp. 108–133.
Rath, Jan, 2001, Research on immigrant ethnic minorities in the Netherlands. The politics of social science research, in: P. Ratcliffe (Ed.) *The Politics of Social Science Research. Race, Ethnicity and Social Change* (Basingstoke: Palgrave), pp. 137–159.
Rein, M., 1986, *Frame-Reflective Policy Discourse* (Leiden: Leiden University).
Rein, Martin and Schön, Donald, 1994, *Frame Reflection: Toward the Resolution of Intractable Policy Controversies* (New York: Basic Books).
Rich, A., 2004, *Think Tanks, Public Policy, and the Politics of Expertise* (Cambridge: Cambridge University Press).
Rochefort, D. A. and Cobb, W., 1994, *The Politics of Problem Definition. Shaping the Policy Agenda* (Kansas: University of Kansas Press).
Rose, E. J. B., 1979, *Colour and Citizenship* (Oxford: Oxford University Press).
Sabatier, P. A., 1987, Knowledge, policy-oriented learning and policy change. *Knowledge: Creation, Diffusion, Utilisation*, **8**, 649–692.
Sabbagh, P. and Peer, S., 2008, French color-blindness in perspective: the controversy over statistiques ethniques. *French Politics, Culture and Society*, **26**(1), 1–6.
Salter, L. and Levy, E., 1988, *Mandated Science: Science and Scientists in the Making of Standards* (Dordrecht: Kluwer Academic Publishers).
Schain, Martin, 1988, Immigration and Changes in the French Party System. *European Journal of Political Research*, **16**, 597–621.
Schain, Martin, 1999, Minorities and immigrant incorporation in France: the state and the dynamics of multiculturalism, in: Joppke and Lukes (Eds.) *Multicultural Questions* (Oxford: Oxford University Press).
Schattschneider, E. E., 1960, *The Semisovereign People* (New York: Holt, Rinehart & Winston).
Schneider, A. L. and Ingram, H., 1993, Social construction of target populations: implications for politics and policy. *The American Political Science Review*, **87**, 334–347.
Scholten, Peter, 2010, *Framing Immigrant Integration. Dutch Research-Policy Dialogues in Comparative Perspective* (Amsterdam: Amsterdam University Press).
Scholten, Peter and Van Nispen, Frans, 2008, Building bridges across frames? A meta-evaluation of Dutch immigrant integration policy. *Journal of Public Policy*, **13**, 181–205.
Singh, G., 2004, Multiculturalism in contemporary Britain: community cohesion, urban riots and the "Leicester model", in: Rex and Singh (Eds.) *Governance in Multicultural Societies* (Aldershot: Ashgate).
Small, S. and Solomos, J., 2006, Race, immigration and politics in Britain: Changing policy agendas and conceptual paradigms 1940s–2000s. *International Journal of Comparative Sociology*, **8**, 235–257.
Timmermans, Arco and Scholten, Peter, 2006, The political flow of wisdom. Science institutions as policy venues. *Journal of European Public Policy*, **13**, 1104–1118.
Tribalat, M., 1996, *De l'immigration a l'assimilation: une enquête sur la population étrangère en France* (Paris: INED).
Turner, B., 2006, British sociology and public intellectuals: consumer society and imperial decline. *The British Journal of Sociology*, **57**(2), 169–188.
Weingart, Peter, 1999, Scientific expertise and political accountability: paradoxes of science in politics. *Science and Public Policy*, **26**, 151–161.
Weiss, Carol, 1977, Research for policy's sake: the enlightenment function of social science research. *Policy Analysis*, **3**, 531–545.

Wihtol de Wenden, C., 1988, *Les immigrés et la politique. Cent-cinquante ans d'évolution* (Paris: Presses de la FNSP).
Wildavsky, Aron, 1979, *The Art and Craft of Policy Analysis: Speaking Truth to Power* (London: Macmillan).
Wihtol de Wenden, C., 2009, The Evolution of French Immigration Policy after May 1981. *International Migration*, **22**(3), 199–213.
Wittrock, Björn, 1991, Social knowledge and public policy: eight models of interaction, in: Wagner et al. (Eds.) *Social Sciences and Modern States: National Experiences and Theoretical Crossroads* (Cambridge: Cambridge University Press).
WRR, Scientific Council for Government Policy, 1979, *Etnische Minderheden* (The Hague: SDU).
WRR, Scientific Council for Government Policy, 1989, *Allochtonenbeleid* (The Hague: SDU).

Democracy, Colonial Legacy, and the Openness of Cabinet-Level Websites in Developing Countries

IVAN KATCHANOVSKI and TODD LA PORTE

ABSTRACT *This article examines the effects of political, cultural, economic, and technical factors on openness of cabinet-level websites in developing countries. The question is whether these factors affect openness of electronic governments. This paper uses regression analysis of a comparative database of national-level public agency websites that is produced by the Cyberspace Policy Research Group (CyPRG). Regression analysis shows that the level of democracy, colonial legacy, and the level of economic development affect openness of cabinet-level websites in the developing countries. Implications of these findings are discussed in the conclusion.*

E-government Openness: Hypotheses

The Internet and the World Wide Web represent a new class of information technologies that offers governments an unprecedented capacity both to connect citizens to government and to improve the internal administrative structures and processes that are necessary for effective governance. Increasingly, the World Wide Web is an important element of the functioning of government agencies in many developed, post-communist, and developing countries. The adoption of information technology and a move toward electronic governance represent new areas of international development. Widespread use of the Web enables the comparison of websites of the governments of many countries around the world (see, for example, Fountain 2001, La Porte *et al.* 2002, Bimber 2003, Chadwick and May 2003, Jaeger 2003, Wong and Welch 2004, Rose 2005, West 2005).

Academic and policy studies have found significant cross-national differences in various aspects of e-government. However, only a few of the studies examined the factors associated with these differences in developing countries (see Holliday 2002, United Nations and American Society for Public Administration 2002, Basu 2004, Pons 2004, Chen *et al.* 2006). Research has focused on analysis of government websites in advanced Western countries (see, for example, Chadwick and May 2003, Katchanovski and La Porte 2005, West 2005). Few studies have examined e-government in developing countries from a comparative or cross-national perspective. Some previous studies included certain developing countries along with advanced Western and post-communist countries in global comparisons (see La Porte *et al.* 2001, Prattipati 2003, Wei 2004, Wong and Welch 2004, Gascó 2005, Rose 2005, Siau and Long 2006). However, the number of developing countries in many of these statistical analyses was relatively small compared to the overall number, and it was not always representative from the point of view of geographic diversity.

This paper seeks explanations for government website openness in cabinet-level websites in developing countries. Previous research has established the validity of openness as a measurable attribute of administrative behavior that has direct consequences for governance and for government performance. The openness index has been used to measure the development of electronic government in different countries. It was applied to cabinet-level websites and to local government websites. Data from countries around the world suggests that openness in e-government leads to improvement in administrative effectiveness, and that even agencies that are otherwise badly managed benefit from the deployment of public networked information technologies such as the Internet and the World Wide Web[1] (see Demchak *et al.* 1999, La Porte *et al.* 2001, La Porte *et al.* 2002, Wong and Welch 2004).

Previous studies identified a number of political, economic, cultural, and technical factors that affect the development of e-government in different countries. Many studies indicated that the level of economic development was a major factor related to e-government development. (La Porte *et al.* 2001, La Porte *et al.* 2002, Prattipati 2003, West, 2005, Siau and Long 2006). Some studies linked openness of government websites to government performance (Demchak *et al.* 1999, Wong and Welch 2004). The level of democracy and Western Christianity had a positive effect on the level of openness in OECD and post-communist countries, while a Western historical legacy was negatively associated with openness when other factors, such as the levels of economic development and internet use, were held constant (Katchanovski and La Porte 2005).

The question is which of these factors are associated with the openness of government websites in developing countries. We focus our analysis on cabinet-level websites. Websites of government ministries, parliaments, and supreme courts are the most advanced and the most comparable. Our first hypothesis is that the level of democracy is positively associated with the openness of cabinet-level websites. It is logical to expect a positive association between the level of democracy and the openness of government websites in developing countries. Democratic governments are likely to be more open than authoritarian governments in making information available and accessible on cabinet-level websites.

E-government and e-democracy are often regarded as conceptually related. For example, such international organizations as the World Bank and the United Nations link e-government development with promotion e-democracy in developing countries (Wade 2002, Amoretti 2007). Electronic democracy or cyberdemocracy is still in early stages of its development. Many theoretical and practical issues concerning cyberdemocracy have remained unsettled (see, for example, Vedel 2006). Such factors as the poor quality of participation and the digital divide between countries and between ethnic groups, socio-economic classes, age categories, and gender categories of populations limit the reach and effectiveness of electronic democracy, in particular, in developing countries (Norris 2001, Wade 2002). However, e-democracy creates new opportunities for interactions between citizens and governments, and it represents an extension of democracy in the age of information technology (see, for instance, Hacker and Dijk 2001, Bimber 2003). Because the spread of the Net and the World Wide Web in many developing countries is a recent occurrence, and because only a fraction of the population in these countries has access to these technologies, it is not very likely that the openness of government websites will affect the level of democracy in developing countries.

Our second hypothesis is that cultural legacies affect the openness of electronic governments in developing countries. Previous studies linked historical legacies to various aspects of political and economic development in developed countries (see, for example, Lipset 1990, North 1990, Putnam 1993). Similarly, historical legacies affect economic and political development in post-communist countries (see, for instance, Katchanovski 2000).

A growing number of studies reveal the persistent impact of the colonial legacy in developing countries. British colonial rule implanted stronger traditions of the rule of law in its colonies. In contrast, Spain and Portugal in their Latin American colonies established institutions that fostered authoritarianism and clientelism (North 1990). The legacy of British colonial rule has a positive effect on the level of democracy in developing countries, while the former colonies of other countries, such as Spain, Portugal, and France, are much less likely to be democratic than their British counterparts (Lipset et al. 1993, Clague et al. 1991). Similarly, the former British colonies in Africa have higher levels of primary school enrolment compared to the former French colonies when other factors, such as the level of economic development, are held constant (Brown 2000).

Such differences are typically attributed to the indirect rule and to the influence of legal-administrative institutions used by Great Britain in most of its colonies, compared to the more direct and assimilationist rule employed by other colonial powers (see Bollen and Jackman 1985, Brown 2000, Bernhard et al. 2004, Lange 2004). The reliance on indirect rule resulted in a small and relatively weak central government bureaucracy (Lange 2004). British rule in many of its colonial possessions also fostered a stronger civil society compared to more state-centered approaches adopted by other European countries in their colonies (see Rueschemeyer et al. 1992).

Spain and Portugal transferred to their colonies a centralized and authoritarian form of governance, compared to the more decentralized and democratic form of governance that was transplanted by the British in their colonies. For example, former Spanish and Portuguese colonies in Southern America formally adopted constitutions that were inspired by the US Constitution, which reflected a British tradition of the rule of law and its colonial policies of decentralized and indirect rule. However, these seemingly liberal, democratic, federalist constitutions represented a facade which disguised statist, authoritarian, centralized institutions in Latin America (North, 1990: 101–117, Lipset and Lakin 2004: 282–310).

We expect that the legacy of colonial rule would be a major factor affecting openness in developing countries. The rule of the British Empire, France, the Netherlands, Spain, Portugal, and other colonial powers shaped political culture in almost all developing countries, and this legacy affected organizational culture in the governments of the respective developing countries. The history of colonial rule represents an important legacy, because in most cases this rule lasted for generations. Colonial rule was in place at a crucial period, from the eighteenth century through the first half of the twentieth century. This rule by Western colonial powers coincided with the formation of modern educational systems and the bureaucracy in many developing countries, almost all of which had gained independence by the end of the twentieth century. Socialization in educational and governmental institutions helped to transfer many elements of the political and organizational culture of the colonial period to post-colonial generations.

In contrast to democracy, the legacy of British colonial rule is likely to have a negative effect on openness of cabinet-level websites in developing countries, while Spanish and Portuguese colonial legacies are likely to be positively associated with openness. In particular, such a pattern of a relationship between the colonial legacies and the openness of cabinet-level websites is expected because, as noted, Spain and Portugal transferred to their colonies a centralized form of governance with a large central bureaucracy, in comparison to a decentralized form of governance and a small central government bureaucracy that was transplanted by the UK in British colonies. Therefore, national-level government websites are likely to be more developed and elaborate in former Spanish and Portuguese colonies than in former British colonies. This pattern of relationship can also be attributed to the phenomenon of "Potemkin e-villages", wherein cabinet-level websites are used as elaborate facades designed to create a false impression of great government openness.[2] In this sense, the Web is similar to colonial architecture. The Spanish and Portuguese design of government buildings, in these countries and in their colonies, often focused on elaborate facades, while the British tradition of architecture in government buildings, in the center of the empire and in its colonies, focused on internal openness and access.

Religion, another possible determinant of openness, represents both religious beliefs and religious tradition, an element of cultural legacy. Previous studies linked religion to various political phenomena, including quality of government and democracy. The Protestant ethic was a major factor in the development of capitalism in the West (Weber 1958). Because of changes in the Catholic religion, differences between Catholic and Protestant cultures had diminished significantly by the end of the twentieth century (see Novak 1993). By this time, not only Protestant but also most predominantly Catholic countries, especially in Latin America, became democratic, in contrast to Muslim countries (see Huntington 1991).

The influence of religious traditions is likely to result in a positive relationship between Protestant or Catholic religion, on the one hand, and the openness of cabinet-level websites in developing countries, on the other. Protestant and Catholic religions are positively associated with government performance (La Porta et al. 1999). However, religion in many developing countries was also significantly influenced by colonial rule. Western colonial powers helped to establish Catholic, and to a lesser extent Protestant, religions in their colonies. Therefore, the religious tradition might also reflect the effect of the historical legacy.

The following hypotheses are based on common-sense theoretical expectations and factors identified in previous empirical studies. The fourth hypothesis is that the level of economic development is positively associated with the openness of government websites in developing countries. A higher level of economic development means more economic resources are available to be used for the establishment and expansion of cabinet-level websites.

The fifth hypothesis is that the level of internet use has a positive effect on openness in developing countries. The greater level of internet development not only creates a better technological base, which allows the development of more open cabinet-level websites, but it also creates a greater demand from citizens for e-government services.

The sixth hypothesis is that government performance affects the openness of cabinet-level websites. It is logical to expect that a better level of government performance leads to a greater level of openness in government websites. In other words, we expect to find a positive relationship between government performance and openness in developing countries.

Data and Methodology

This study uses regression analysis of data from a global database of public agency websites from the Cyberspace Policy Research Group (CyPRG). From 1997 to 2001, the CyPRG conducted surveys of government websites in most countries of the world. In essence, every available cabinet-level website in every country of the world was targeted for examination by a team of multilingual researchers with knowledge of local languages during the same time frame, in 2001. Comparable data for later years are not available because the collection of such data for all cabinet-level websites in every country of the world would have required significantly expanded resources, as both the number of such websites – which by 2001 had reached several thousand – and their complexity have rapidly increased (see Cyberspace Policy Research Group 2005).

The score in the openness index of cabinet-level websites in developing countries in 2001 is the dependent variable in our study. This time period represents a crucial stage in the development of government websites in developing countries. By 2001, the absolute majority of developing countries had cabinet-level websites, but the numbers and levels of openness of those websites varied significantly.

The openness index is based on transparency and interactivity scores and on the availability of cabinet-level websites. The same set of indicators was used to code the transparency and interactivity of government websites in different countries. The Website Attribute Evaluation System enabled CyPRG researchers to evaluate each available cabinet-level website in each country for the presence of specific attributes (see Appendix A). Cabinet-level websites included websites of ministries of national governments, prime ministers, presidents, parliaments, central banks, and Constitutional and Supreme courts.[3]

The terms "transparency," and "interactivity" characterize elements of both information technology deployment and government reform. Transparency measures the extent of efforts that a cabinet-level agency makes to provide information through its website. Transparency includes 23 criteria, such as agency involvement with the website; and whether the website provides phone numbers, postal addresses, organizational structure, publications, a searchable index, the ability to download or print publications free of charge, and in-depth explanations of requirements imposed on citizens. Interactivity measures the ease with which visitors can use information provided on a cabinet-level website. Interactivity includes 22 criteria, such as website privacy, security, listings of email addresses of senior officials, employees, and webmasters; whether the website provides links to sub-elements within the agency, to other government and non-government websites, to an automatic update announcement or newsletters, submission forms; and the extent to which the website is accessible to disabled people (see Appendix A, Cyberspace Policy Research Group 2005, Katchanovski and La Porte 2005, La Porte et al. 2005).

Although the world of the web is changing, it is also the case that the CyPRG data capture a characteristic of governments that does not change very fast. The 2001 openness index is very strongly and positively correlated with the openness indexes for earlier years even though items included in the index in various years differed somewhat (Cyberspace Policy Research Group 2005). The correlation coefficients between the 2001 openness indexes in developing countries and similar indexes in 2000 and 1999 are, respectively, 0.83 and 0.77. These correlations are statistically significant at the .001 level. We assume that a radical alteration of cross-national patterns of the openness index is unlikely even though the openness scores might have changed more since 2001 than they changed from 1999 to 2001. Reform of government organizations is undoubtedly possible, but it is unlikely to happen very quickly in most cases. In addition, there is a positive relationship between implementing open websites and subsequent government effectiveness improvements (see La Porte et al. 2002, La Porte et al. 2005).

The openness index is related to other measures of e-government, such as the global e-government assessment developed by Brown University researchers (see West 2002). However, these two measures are not identical. The openness index in 2001 is positively correlated with the 2001 global e-government assessment measure. The correlation coefficient is 0.52 in all countries examined by the CyPRG, and it is 0.34 in the developing countries. The correlations are significant at the 0.01 level in both cases.

There is significant variation in the openness of cabinet-level websites in developing countries. Many East Asian countries, such as Malaysia (1.24), Singapore (1.15), South Korea (1.09), Indonesia (1.07), Taiwan (0.97), and Thailand (0.91) have top scores on the openness index. A significant number of Latin American countries, such as Mexico (1.17), Peru (1.05), Colombia (0.92), Brazil (0.88), Panama (0.73), and Argentina (0.71), are also in the top ranks on the openness index. Turkey (0.88) and Lebanon (0.65) represent a few Middle Eastern countries which have high levels on the openness index. African countries with high levels of openness of cabinet-level websites include Mauritius (0.75), Uganda (0.72), South Africa (0.68), and Burkina Faso (0.60). Cayman Islands (0.69) and the Dominican Republic (0.57) are the highest-scoring Caribbean countries. Micronesia, the highest-scoring Pacific country in terms of openness (0.35), lags significantly behind top countries from other regions.

Many African countries have the lowest scores on the openness index of cabinet-level websites. For example, Burundi (0.01), Liberia (0.02), Cote d'Ivoire (0.02), Djibouti (0.03), Zaire (0.03), and Nigeria (0.04) are at the very bottom of the openness index. North Korea (0.01), Bangladesh (0.08), Nepal (0.09), Sri Lanka (0.09), and Syria (0.09) have the least open government websites among Asian countries. Such Caribbean and Latin American countries as Dominica (0.01), Antigua and Barbuda (0.03), Bahamas (0.03), Grenada (0.03), and Costa Rica (0.05) also score at the very bottom of the openness index. Pacific Ocean countries with the lowest openness scores are Vanuatu (0.05), Fiji (0.08), and Papua New Guinea (0.08) (see Table 1).

Political, cultural, economic, and technical factors are quantified using different measures of democracy, political culture, level of economic development, level of internet use, and government performance. The independent variables include the level of democracy, colonial legacy, religion, government performance index, GDP per capita, and number of internet users per 1,000 people (see Table 2, Barraclough 1998, La Porta *et al.* 1999, CIA 2002, UNDP 2003, Kaufmann *et al.* 2003, Political Regime 2003). Correlation analysis shows that multicollinearity among the independent variables is not a problem for regression analysis (see Appendix B).

The Polity index of democracy, which evaluates the degree to which states are democratic or autocratic, is used to measure the level of democracy in developing countries. Higher scores mean stronger democracy, while lower scores mean stronger autocracy in the political area (Political Regime 2003). The British colonial legacy, the French colonial legacy, and the Spanish and Portuguese legacy are measured by dummy variables. These variables represent countries that were ruled, respectively, by Great Britain, France, Spain, and Portugal either as full-fledged colonies or protectorates for significant periods of time. The "other legacy" variable includes developing countries which were either ruled by other colonial powers or remained independent. In case a country was a colony of two or more powers, the most recent longest rule defines its colonial legacy.

We employ multivariate regression analysis of determinants of openness of cabinet-level websites in developing countries. This type of statistical analysis has been widely used in cross-national studies in the social sciences and policy studies. We use two similar regression models to analyze the openness. The first model includes political, cultural, economic, and technical variables. The second model adds government performance to these factors. The government performance index is an aggregate measure derived by World Bank researchers from expert evaluations of government effectiveness, regulatory quality, accountability, rule of law, control of corruption, and political stability in different countries. Higher scores mean better performance. (see Kaufmann *et al.* 2003). The aggregate government performance index is positively correlated with the openness index.

Table 1. Openness of cabinet-level websites in developing countries

Country	Openness	Country	Openness
Malaysia	1.24	Algeria	0.19
Mexico	1.17	Kuwait	0.19
Singapore	1.15	Swaziland	0.18
South Korea	1.09	Tunisia	0.18
Indonesia	1.07	Cyprus	0.17
Peru	1.05	Honduras	0.17
Taiwan	0.97	Pakistan	0.17
Colombia	0.92	Cameroon	0.16
Thailand	0.91	Malawi	0.16
Brazil	0.88	Angola	0.15
Turkey	0.88	Niger	0.15
Mauritius	0.75	Zimbabwe	0.15
Panama	0.73	Madagascar	0.14
Uganda	0.72	Saudi Arabia	0.14
Argentina	0.71	Trinidad & Tobago	0.14
Brunei	0.71	Mozambique	0.13
Cayman Islands	0.69	Philippines	0.13
Venezuela	0.69	Belize	0.11
South Africa	0.68	Cape Verde	0.11
Malta	0.66	Guinea	0.11
Lebanon	0.65	Rwanda	0.11
Uruguay	0.64	Ghana	0.10
Chile	0.62	Mali	0.10
Bolivia	0.61	Sierra Leone	0.10
Burkina Faso	0.60	Barbados	0.09
El Salvador	0.59	Ethiopia	0.09
India	0.59	Lesotho	0.09
Yemen	0.59	Nepal	0.09
Dominican Republic	0.57	Sri Lanka	0.09
Nicaragua	0.54	Syria	0.09
Gaza and Jericho	0.52	Togo	0.09
China	0.51	Bangladesh	0.08
Botswana	0.46	Fiji	0.08
Jamaica	0.45	Papua New Guinea	0.08
Namibia	0.44	Sudan	0.08
Morocco	0.42	Tanzania	0.08
Guatemala	0.41	Anguilla	0.07
Micronesia	0.35	Gabon	0.07
UAE	0.35	Soloman Islands	0.07
Ecuador	0.33	Gambia	0.06
Iran	0.33	Costa Rica	0.05
Senegal	0.31	Kenya	0.05
Vietnam	0.31	Mauritania	0.05
Bahrain	0.30	San Tome & Principe	0.05
Guyana	0.29	Vanuatu	0.05
Paraguay	0.28	Zambia	0.05
Cambodia	0.26	Nigeria	0.04
Egypt	0.26	Antigua & Barbuda	0.03
Maldives	0.25	Bahamas	0.03
Myanmar	0.25	Djibouti	0.03
Saint Lucia	0.25	Grenada	0.03
Benin	0.24	Zaire	0.03
Jordan	0.23	Cote d'Ivoire	0.02
Iraq	0.22	Liberia	0.02
St Kitts & Nevis	0.21	Burundi	0.01
Mongolia	0.20	Dominica	0.01
Oman	0.20	North Korea	0.01
Qatar	0.20		

Table 2. Political, cultural, economic, and technical variables in developing countries

Country	Democracy score[1]	Protestants, %[2]	Catholics, %[2]	Muslims, %[2]	British colony[3]	French colony[3]	Spanish or Portugese colony[3]	Other colony or non-colony[3]	Government performance[4]	GDP per capita[5]	Internet users per 1,000 people[6]
Algeria	−3	0	0.5	99.1	0	1	0	0	−4.87	5388	1.95
Angola	−3	15	38	0	0	0	1	0	−8.16	974	4.44
Argentina	8	2.7	91.6	0.2	0	0	1	0	−3.45	12732	88.03
Bahrain	−8	0.9	0.8	95	1	0	0	0	3.18	15650	215.36
Bangladesh	6	0.2	0.2	85.9	1	0	0	0	−4.65	1546	1.87
Benin	6	2.8	18.5	15.2	0	1	0	0	−1.54	1001	3.88
Bolivia	9	2.3	92.5	0	0	0	1	0	−2.25	2518	17.62
Botswana	9	26.8	9.4	0	1	0	0	0	4.65	6557	29.5
Brazil	8	4	87.8	0.1	0	0	1	0	0.14	6477	46.41
Burkina Faso	0	1.6	9	43	0	1	0	0	−1.85	978	1.64
Burundi	0	4.9	78.3	0.9	0	0	0	1	−8.37	707	0.86
Cambodia	2	0.1	0.1	2.4	0	1	0	0	−3.56	1289	0.82
Cameroon	−4	18.1	35	22	0	1	0	0	−5.48	1645	2.96
Chile	9	1.9	82.1	0	0	0	1	0	7.7	9988	201.42
China	−7	0	0	2.4	0	0	0	0	−2.01	3535	26.5
Colombia	7	0.9	96.6	0.2	0	0	1	0	−3.98	6196	26.82
Costa Rica	10	5.8	90.5	0	0	0	1	0	4.89	6626	99.15
Cote d'Ivoire	5	4.7	18.5	24	0	1	0	0	−6.61	1598	4.27
Cyprus	10	0.6	1.3	18.5	1	0	0	0	5.26	13803	197.2
Djibouti	2	0.2	6.7	90.6	0	1	0	0	−4.25	1246	5.12
Dominican Republic	8	1.4	96.6	0	0	0	1	0	−1.03	5628	21.87
Ecuador	6	1.9	96.4	0	0	0	1	0	−3.94	2822	25.45
Egypt	−6	0.2	0.2	81.8	1	0	0	0	−2.2	3552	9.21
El Salvador	7	2.4	96.2	0	0	0	1	0	−1.07	3848	
Ethiopia	1	3.8	0.7	31.4	0	0	0	1	−5.01	595	0.38
Fiji	5	39.1	9	7.8	1	0	0	0	−0.19	6988	18.36
Gabon	−4	18.8	65.2	0.8	0	1	0	0	−1.69	6305	13.48
Gambia	−5	0.4	1.9	84.8	1	0	0	0	−3.17	1063	13.43

(*continued*)

Table 2. (Continued).

Country	Democracy score[1]	Protestants, %[2]	Catholics, %[2]	Muslims, %[2]	British colony[3]	French colony[3]	Spanish or Portugese colony[3]	Other colony or non-colony[3]	Government performance[4]	GDP per capita[5]	Internet users per 1,000 people[6]
Ghana	2	25.8	18.7	15.7	1	0	0	0	−0.93	1880	2.06
Guatemala	8	4.9	94	0	0	0	1	0	−3.16	3561	17.12
Guinea	−1	0.1	1.1	69	0	1	0	0	−5.91	1313	1.98
Guyana	6	18	18	9	1	0	0	0	−1.48	4877	123.98
Honduras	7	2.6	95.8	0.1	0	0	1	0	−2.95	2654	
India	9	1.1	1.3	11.6	1	0	0	0	−1.11	2136	6.78
Indonesia	7	4.8	2.7	43.4	0	0	0	1	−5.07	2863	19.14
Iran	3	0	0.1	97.9	0	0	0	1	−4.35	6245	15.57
Iraq	−9	0	1.8	95.8	1	0	0	0	−10.95	2443	
Jamaica	9	55.5	9.6	0.1	1	0	0	0	−0.17	3639	38.61
Jordan	−2	0.3	1.7	93	1	0	0	0	−0.07	3357	42.14
Kenya	−2	19.3	26.4	6	1	0	0	0	−4.88	1482	16.27
Korea, North	−9	0	0	0	0	0	0	1	−7.39	1001	
Korea, South	8	12.2	3.9	0	0	0	0	1	4.03	15961	514.97
Kuwait	−7	0.1	2.1	95.1	1	0	0	0	2.18	14349	97.83
Liberia	0	18.6	1.9	21.2	0	0	0	1	−9.16	1038	0.31
Madagascar	7	22	26	1.7	0	1	0	0	−0.43	770	4.38
Malawi	5	31.5	27.6	16.2	1	0	0	0	−2.53	891	3.33
Malaysia	3	1.4	2.8	49.4	1	0	0	0	2.68	10063	273.1
Mali	6	0.2	0.7	80	0	1	0	0	−2.11	827	2.9
Mauritania	−6	0	0.3	99.4	0	1	0	0	−0.48	1966	2.7
Mauritius	10	0.9	31.2	16.4	1	0	0	0	4.2	10338	131.6
Mexico	8	1.2	94.7	0	0	0	1	0	0.79	8981	36.2
Mongolia	10	0	0	1.4	0	0	0	1	1.25	1770	16.52
Morocco	−6	0	0.2	99.4	0	1	0	0	−0.27	3426	13.71
Mozambique	6	6.8	31.4	13	0	0	1	0	−2.41	986	0.83
Myanmar (Burma)	−7	3.2	0.9	3.6	1	0	0	0	−9.55	1517	0.21
Namibia	6	64.2	19.1	0	0	0	0	1	1.89	4228	25.11

(continued)

Table 2. (Continued).

Country	Democracy score[1]	Protestants, %[2]	Catholics, %[2]	Muslims, %[2]	British colony[3]	French colony[3]	Spanish or Portugese colony[3]	Other colony or non-colony[3]	Government performance[4]	GDP per capita[5]	Internet users per 1,000 people[6]
Nepal	6	0	0	3	1	0	0	0	−3.95	1333	2.6
Nicaragua	8	4.4	94.7	0	0	0	1	0	−2.12	2663	14.4
Niger	4	0	0.2	87.9	0	1	0	0	−3.85	966	1.1
Nigeria	4	15.8	12.1	45	1	0	0	0	−7.18	924	1.0
Oman	−9	0.1	0.1	98.9	0	0	0	1	3.6	7475	45.7
Pakistan	−6	0.8	0.5	96.8	1	0	0	0	−5.06	1950	
Panama	9	5.2	85	4.5	0	0	1	0	−3.85	5833	41.4
Papua New Guinea	10	58.4	32.8	0	0	0	0	1	−6.03	2416	9.4
Paraguay	7	1.9	96	0	0	0	1	0	−1.32	4569	10.6
Peru	9	2.7	95.1	0	0	0	1	0	−1.31	4475	76.6
Philippines	8	3.8	84.1	4.3	0	0	0	1	4.15	3742	31.92
Qatar	−10	0.9	1.2	92.4	1	0	0	0	2.9	19632	
Rwanda	−4	11.6	55.6	8.6	0	0	0	1	−6.12	875	37.82
Saudi Arabia	−10	0.1	0.1	98.8	0	0	0	1	−0.31	10195	
Senegal	8	0.1	5.6	91	0	1	0	0	−0.97	1556	10.24
Singapore	−2	2.6	4.7	17.4	1	0	0	0	10	25532	363.11
South Africa	9	39	10.4	1.3	1	0	0	0	2.3	8466	70.95
Sri Lanka	6	0.4	6.8	7.2	1	0	0	0	−0.72	3231	8.01
Sudan	−7	0.1	4.4	73	1	0	0	0	−8.38	989	1.77
Swaziland	−9	33.9	10.8	0.1	1	0	0	0	−2.55	3984	13.11
Syria	−7	0.2	1.3	89.6	0	1	0	0	−3.94	3043	3.62
Taiwan	9	3	1.5	0.5	0	0	0	1	5.42	17255	
Tanzania	2	11.2	28.2	32.5	1	0	0	0	−3.21	693	8.71
Thailand	9	0.2	0.4	3.9	0	0	0	1	1.51	6683	57.79
Togo	−2	6.1	29.3	17	0	1	0	0	−4.35	1417	32.23
Trinidad and Tobago	10	13.2	35.8	6.5	1	0	0	0	2.01	9575	91.63

(continued)

Table 2. (Continued).

Country	Democracy score[1]	Protestants, %[2]	Catholics, %[2]	Muslims, %[2]	British colony[3]	French colony[3]	Spanish or Portugese colony[3]	Other colony or non-colony[3]	Government performance[4]	GDP per capita[5]	Internet users per 1,000 people[6]
Tunisia	−3	0	0.1	99.4	0	1	0	0	0.66	6471	41.35
Turkey	7	0	0.1	99.2	0	0	0	1	−1.57	6677	36.48
Uganda	−4	1.9	49.6	6.6	1	0	0	0	−4.4	1092	2.63
United Arab Emirates	−8	0.3	0.4	94.9	1	0	0	0	4.41	22430	327.93
Uruguay	10	1.9	59.5	0	0	0	1	0	4.2	9226	119.01
Venezuela	7	1	94.8	0	0	0	1	0	−5.27	1931	51.34
Vietnam	−7	0.2	3.9	1	0	1	0	0	−2.9	1483	12.69
Yemen	−2	0.1	0	99.5	1	0	0	0	−5.65	797	0.94
Zaire	0	29	48.4	1.4	0	0	0	1	−10.89	578	0.11
Zambia	1	31.9	26.2	0.3	1	0	0	0	−3.43	870	2.43
Zimbabwe	−6	21.4	14.4	0.9	1	0	0	0	−8.02	2481	7.8

Notes:
[1] Democracy scores for 2001 are derived from the Polity database. See Political Regime (2003).
[2] La Porta et al. (1999).
[3] Barraclough (1998).
[4] Aggregate government performance scores are calculated from Kaufmann et al. (2003).
[5] Purchasing power parity GDP per capita data for 2001 are from *World Factbook* (2002).
[6] Data for 2001 are from *Human Development Report* (2003).

The correlation coefficient is 0.55 in all countries examined by the CyPRG and 0.30 in developing countries. These correlations are statistically significant at the 0.01 level in both cases.

Regression Analysis

Ordinary least squares regression analysis shows that the level of democracy has a positive effect on the openness of cabinet-level websites in developing countries. This variable is statistically significant at the 0.05 level in both regression models. British and French colonial legacies have negative scores on the openness index, and scores are statistically significant at the 0.01 level in both models. Standardized regression coefficients show that the magnitude of the effect of the British colonial legacy on openness exceeds the effects of all other variables, with the exception of GDP per capita. Regression analysis indicates that Spanish and Portuguese colonial legacies, which are the omitted dummy variables in the regression model, are positively associated with the openness index. Colonial legacies of the other countries have a negative association with openness, but this effect is statistically insignificant. These findings support our hypothesis that the openness of government websites in developing countries is linked to both the greater level of democracy and to "Potemkin e-villages" (see Table 3).

The proportion of Catholics and Protestants in the country's population has a statistically insignificant effect on the openness index of cabinet-level websites in developing countries. The proportion of Muslims in the country's population also has a statistically insignificant effect on openness in both regression models (see

Table 3. Determinants of openness of cabinet-level websites in developing countries, OLS regression

	Model I		Model II	
	Unstandardized coefficient	Standardized coefficient	Unstandardized coefficient	Standardized coefficient
Democracy	.013* (.005)	.243	.013* (.006)	.249
British colony	−.298** (.099)	−.451	−.297** (.100)	−.449
French colony	−.351** (.117)	−.433	−.349** (.119)	−.431
Other colony	−.185 (.105)	−.217	−.185 (.106)	−.218
Proportion of Protestants and Catholics	−.002 (.001)	−.236	−.002 (.001)	−.237
Proportion of Muslims	−.001 (.001)	−.093	−.001 (.001)	−.094
Internet users per 1,000 people	−.001 (.000)	−.195	−.001 (.000)	−.195
GDP per capita ($1000)	.036** (.007)	.525	.037** (.010)	.540
Government performance			−.002 (.011)	−.020
Constant	.516** (.130)		.507** (.143)	
Adjusted R-squared	.37		.36	
N	85		85	

Notes: *Significant at .05; **significant at .01. Standard errors are in the parentheses.

Table 3). These results contradict the hypothesis concerning the relationship between religion and e-government.

The level of economic development, measured by GDP per capita, has a positive effect on the openness index of cabinet-level websites in developing countries. This variable is statistically significant at the 0.01 level. In contrast, the effect of the level of internet use on openness is statistically insignificant.

Keeping other variables constant, the government performance index has a statistically insignificant effect on the openness of cabinet-level websites in developing countries. The introduction of this factor in the regression model does not increase the proportion of the variance explained (adjusted R squared) (see Table 3).

Conclusion

Data produced by the Cyberspace Policy Research Group (CyPRG) show that developing countries differ significantly in the openness of their cabinet-level websites. This study demonstrates that many factors are associated with the openness of government websites in this group of countries. In regression analysis, democracy, colonial legacy, and the level of economic development show significant effects on the openness index.

As expected, the levels of democracy and economic development are positively associated with openness. In contrast, the British and French colonial legacies are negatively associated with the level of openness in the government websites of developing countries. Regression analysis does not support the hypotheses concerning the effects of religious tradition, level of internet use, and government performance on the openness of cabinet-level websites in developing countries.

This paper shows a need for including cultural factors, such as historical legacy, in analyses of e-government adoption and use in different countries. Limitations, which are inherent in coding websites and in using multivariate statistical analyses, call for in-depth studies which provide thick description of a relationship between culture and information technology.

These findings are helpful in understanding the reasons behind the wide variation in the implementation of the Web in government websites and improving service delivery through the Internet in developing countries. The study shows that the adoption of information technology by governments in developing countries depends not only on the level of economic development in these countries but also on the level of democracy and on differing cultural legacies. These results imply that e-government promotion policies, which are focused on technological factors, need to take into account political and cultural institutions in developing countries.

Notes

1. By putting information the Web government agencies can achieve greater openness. However, openness is not confined to mere quantity of information provided by governments on their websites (see, for example, Demchak et al. 1999). Since computer technology, software, and expertise needed to create websites became widely available and within reach of national governments, including in almost all developing countries, governments can also put information that is useless or simply not accessible to a significant proportion of citizens because of lack of Internet access or other reasons. In addition,

national security considerations can lead government agencies to restrict availability of certain information, which they deem as sensitive, on their websites.
2. The concept of "Potemkin e-villages" denotes the practice of creating elaborate websites by government agencies for "window dressing" purposes. This term is derived from "Potemkin villages" that originally referred to fake villages, which were, allegedly, built by Governor Potemkin in the Russian Empire (Katchanovski and La Porte 2005).
3. Additional detailed information concerning the openness index methodology is available on the CyPRG website (see Cyberspace Policy Research Group 2005).

References

Amoretti, Francesco, 2007, International organizations ICTs policies: E-democracy and e-government for political development. *Review of Policy Research*, **24**(4), 331–344.
Barraclough, Geoffrey (Ed.), 1998, *HarperCollins Atlas of World History* (Ann Arbor, MI: Borders Press).
Basu, Subhajit, 2004, E-government and developing countries: an overview. *International Review of Law, Computers & Technology*, **18**(1), 109–132.
Bernhard, Michael, Reenock, Christopher and Nordstrom, Timothy, 2004, The legacy of Western overseas colonialism on democratic survival. *International Studies Quarterly*, **48**(1), 225–250.
Bimber, Bruce, 2003, *Information and American Democracy: Technology in the Evolution of Political Power* (Cambridge: Cambridge University Press).
Bollen, Kenneth A. and Jackman, Robert, 1985, The economic and noneconomic determinants of political democracy in the 1960s, in: Richard G. Braungart and Margaret M. Braungart (Eds) *Research in Political Sociology*, Vol.1 (Greenwich, CT: JAI Press), pp. 27–48.
Brown, David S., 2000, Democracy, colonization, and human capital in Sub-Saharan Africa. *Studies in Comparative International Development*, **35**(1), 20–40.
Chadwick, Andrew and May, Christopher, 2003, Interaction between states and citizens in the age of the internet: "e-Government" in the United States, Britain, and the European Union. *Governance*, **16**(2), 271–300.
Chen Y. N., Chen, H. M., Huang, W. and Ching, R. K. H., 2006, E-government strategies in developed and developing countries: an implementation framework and case study. *Journal of Global Information Management*, **14**(1), 23–46.
CIA, 2002, *World Factbook 2002*, available at http://www.cia.gov/cia/publications/factbook/ (accessed 12 July 2003).
Clague, Christopher, Gleason, Suzanne and Knack, Stephen, 2001, Determinants of lasting democracy in poor countries: culture, development, and institutions. *Annals of the American Academy of Political and Social Science*, **573**, 16–41.
Cyberspace Policy Research Group, 2005, available at http://www.cyprg.arizona.edu/ (accessed 9 September 2007).
Demchak, Chris C., La Porte, Todd M. and Friis, Christian, 1999, Webbing governance: national differences in constructing the public face, in: G. D. Garson (Ed.) *Handbook of Public Information Systems* (New York: Marcel Dekker), pp. 179–196.
Fountain, Jane E, 2001, *Building the Virtual State: Information Technology and Institutional Change* (Washington: Brookings Institution Press).
Gascó, Mila, 2005, Exploring the e-government gap in South America. *International Journal of Public Administration*, **28**(7–8), 683–701.
Jaeger, Paul T., 2003, The endless wire: e-government as global phenomenon. *Government Information Quarterly*, **20**(4), 323–331.
Hacker, Kenneth L. and Van Dijk, Jan (Eds), 2001, *Digital Democracy: Issues of Theory and Practice* (Thousand Oaks, CA: Sage).
Holliday, Ian, 2002, Building e-government in East and Southeast Asia: regional rhetoric and national (in)action. *Public Administration & Development*, **22**(4), 323–335.
Huntington, Samuel, 1991, *Third Wave: Democratization in the Late Twentieth Century* (Norman: University of Oklahoma Press).
Katchanovski, Ivan, 2000, Divergence in growth in post-communist countries. *Journal of Public Policy*, **20**(1), 55–81.
Katchanovski, Ivan and La Porte, Todd, 2005, Cyberdemocracy or Potemkin e-villages: e-government in OECD and post-communist countries. *International Journal of Public Administration*, **28**(7–8), 665–681.

Kaufmann, D., Kraay, A. and Mastruzzi, M., 2003, Governance matters III: governance indicators for 1996–2002. Working paper, World Bank.

La Porta, Rafael, Lopez-de-Silanes, Florencio, Shleifer, Andrei and Robert, Vishny, 1999, The quality of government. *Journal of Law, Economics and Organization*, **15**(1), 222–279.

La Porte, Todd, Demchak, Chris C. and Friis, Christian, 2001, Webbing governance: global trends across national level public agencies. *Communications of the ACM*, **44**(1), 63–67.

La Porte, Todd M., Demchak, Chris C. and de Jong, Martin, 2002, Democracy and bureaucracy in the age of the web: empirical findings and theoretical speculations. *Administration & Society*, **34**(4), 411–446.

La Porte, Todd M., Demchak, Chris C. and Weare, Christopher, 2005, Governance in the era of the World Wide Web: an assessment of organizational openness and government effectiveness, in: D. G. Garson (Ed.) *Handbook of Public Informational Systems* (New York: CRC Press), pp. 155–170.

Lange, Matthew K., 2004, British colonial legacies and political development. *World Development*, **32**(6), 905–922.

Lipset, Seymour Martin, 1990, *Continental Divide: The Values and Institutions of the United States and Canada* (New York: Routledge).

Lipset, Seymour Martin and Lakin, Jason, 2004, *The Democratic Century* (Norman: University of Oklahoma Press).

Lipset, Seymour Martin, Seong, Kyoung-Ryung and Torres, John Charles, 1993, A comparative analysis of the social requisites of democracy. *International Social Science Journal*, **45**(2), 155–175.

Norris, Pippa, 2001, *Digital Divide: Civic Engagement, Information Poverty and the Internet in Democratic Societies* (Cambridge: Cambridge University Press).

North, Douglass C., 1990, *Institutions, Institutional Change and Economic Performance* (Cambridge: Cambridge University Press).

Novak, Michael, 1993, *The Catholic Ethic and the Spirit of Capitalism* (New York: Free Press).

Political regime characteristics and transitions, 1800–2001; Polity IV project, 2003, available at http://www.bsos.umd.edu/cidcm/inscr/polity/index.htm (accessed 29 October 2004).

Pons, Alexander, 2004, E-government for Arab countries. *Journal of Global Information Technology Management*, **7**(1), 30–46.

Prattipati, Satya, N., 2003, Adoption of e-governance: differences between countries in the use of online government services. *Journal of American Academy of Business*, **3**(1–2), 386–401.

Putnam, Robert, 1993, *Making Democracy Work: Civic Traditions in Modern Italy* (Princeton, NJ: Princeton University Press).

Rose, Richard, 2005, A global diffusion model of e-governance. *Journal of Public Policy*, **25**(1), 5–27.

Rueschemeyer, Dietrich, Stephens, John D., and Huber, Evelyne, 1992, *Capitalist Development and Democracy* (Chicago: University of Chicago Press).

Siau, Keng and Long, Yuan, 2006, Using social development lenses to understand e-government development. *Journal of Global Information Management*, **14**(1), 47–62.

United Nations and American Society for Public Administration, 2002, *Benchmarking E-government: A Global Perspective – Assessing the Progress of the UN Member States* (New York: United Nations and American Society for Public Administration).

UNDP, 2003, *Human Development Report 2003* (New York: UNDP).

Vedel, Thierry, 2006, The idea of electronic democracy: origins, visions and questions. *Parliamentary Affairs*, **59**(2), 226–235.

Wade, Robert Hunter, 2002, Bridging the digital divide: new route to development or new form of dependency? *Global Governance*, **8**(4), 443–466.

Weber, Max, 1958, *Protestant Ethic and Spirit of Capitalism* (New York: Charles Scribner's).

Wei, June, 2004, Global comparisons of e-government environments. *Electronic Government*, **1**(3), 229–252.

West, Darrell M., 2002, Global e-government, 2002, Center for Public Policy, Brown University, http://www.insidepolitics.org/egovt02int.html (accessed 18 December 2007).

West, Darrell M., 2005, *Digital Government: Technology and Public Sector Performance* (Princeton, NJ: Princeton University Press).

Wong, Wilson and Welch, Eric, 2004, Does e-government promote accountability? A comparative analysis of website openness and government accountability. *Governance*, **17**(2), 275–297.

Appendix A. Coding criteria used in the openness index

	Scoring (0 = No, 1 = Yes)
Transparency	
Ownership	
T1a: agency involvement with site	0 or 1
T1b: webmaster appears to be different from the one running the main government page, if one exists	0 or 1
T1c: provides obvious tailoring indicating agency itself has ownership of site content	0 or 1
T1d: provides published date (e.g. "2/15/01" or "February 15, 2001") on main page or, if none, a key subordinate page, within the last year	Date listed or 0 if no date listed
Contacts/Contactability	
T2a: provides central agency non-email addresses	0 or 1
T2b: provides phone numbers or postal addresses for employees within agency beyond most senior officials	0 or 1
T2c: provides e-mail address to person responsible for both content of the site and technical support for the site	0 or 1
T2d: provides e-mail address to someone solely responsible for technical support for the site	0 or 1
T2e: provides e-mail address to someone solely responsible for content of the site	0 or 1
T2f: person responsible for technical support for the site appears NOT to be a commercial firm	0 or 1
Organizational Information	
T3a: provides details on senior official's experiences or vision of future for organization	0 or 1
T3b: provides mission statement and various activities of agency	0 or 1
T3c: provides organizational structure in graphic form	1 for having an organization chart, and 0.1 for each level shown in graphic
Issue Information	
T4a: provides issue-related addresses for other government agencies	0 or 1
T4b: provides non-issue-related addresses for other government agencies	0 or 1
T4c: provides issue-related addresses for other non-governmental information sources	0 or 1
T4d: provides reports, research, laws, and regulations in easily readable format on screen	0 or 1
T4e: provides a searchable index for archived newsletters, laws, regulations, and requirements	0 or 1
T4f: provides all downloaded or printed publications for free	0 or 1
T4g: provides link to or text of public information law or regulation	0 or 1
Citizen Consequences/Responses	0 or 1
T5a: provides in depth explanations of requirements imposed on citizens resulting from agency activities	0 or 1
T5b: provides instructions on how to complete these actions	0 or 1

(continued)

Appendix A. (*Continued*).

	Scoring (0 = No, 1 = Yes)
T5c: provides instructions for appeal process for decisions or address of an ombudsman inside agency	0 or 1
Interactivity	
Security and Privacy	
I1a: does NOT use information gathering techniques such as cookies to gather information about site visitors	0 or 1
I1b: does NOT require personal information (beyond return e-mail address) to communicate with agency	0 or 1
I1c: site entails use of security access method, such as a password, or secure server (https://...)	0 or 1
I1d: security access method, such as password or secure server use, is associated with transaction with agency or access to personal information	+1 if site IS associated with financial transaction or access to personal information; 0 if don't know or none found; −1 if site IS NOT associated with financial transaction or access to personal information
Contacts/Contactability	
I2a: provides e-mail link to webmaster	0 or 1
I2b: provides e-mail link to senior agency official	0 or 1
I2c: provides e-mail link to a number of agency employees	0 or 1
I2d: agency avoids dictating format or content of citizen communication, e.g., no preset subject or manual insertion of contact information.	0 or 1
I2e: provides an online issue-related forum for outsider participation such as chat lines, and listserves.	0 or 1
Organizational Information	
I3a: provides link to listed sub-elements within agency	1 for having org chart, 0.1 for each link provided
I3b: provides link to sublevels noted in agency's organizational structure graphic	1 for having org chart, 0.1 for every level
I3c: provides automatic update announcement or newsletter via subscription	0 or 1
Issue Information	
I4a: provides link to outside issue-related government addresses	0 or 1
I4b: provides link to outside non-issue-related government addresses	0 or 1
I4c: provides link to outside issue-related non-governmental information sources	0 or 1
Citizen Consequences/Responses	
I5a: provides any required submission forms onscreen for download	0.1 for each form available for download
I5b: provides online form completion and submission	0.1 for every form available for online completion and submission

(*continued*)

Appendix A. (*Continued*).

	Scoring (0 = No, 1 = Yes)
I5c: provides an automatic response limit for response to online submissions	0 or 1
I5d: provides link to appeal process for decisions and/or an ombudsman	0 or 1
I5e: provides other language access to site for visitors unable to speak or read the language of the host country	0 or 1
I5f: provides iconographic access to site for visitors unable to speak or read the language of the host country	0 or 1
I5g: provides audio access to site	0 or 1
I5h: disability access score: "Priority 1 Accessibility" and "User Checks" using evaluation criteria of the Center for Applied Special Technology, http://www.cast.org/bobby by Bobby	Basic accessibility measure (Priority 1 Accessibility) to left of decimal, and number of "user checks" for first level of accessibility to right of decimal

Source: See Cyberspace Policy Research Group (2005).

Appendix B. Correlation matrix

	Openness index	Democracy	British colony	French colony	Spanish or Portuguese colony	Other colony	Proportion of Protestants and Catholics	Proportion of Muslims	Internet users per 1,000 people	GDP per capita	Government performance index
Openness index	1										
Democracy	.379**	1									
British colony	−.152	−.179	1								
French colony	−.187*	−.170	−.424**	1							
Spanish or Portuguese colony	.296**	.419**	−.424**	−.214*	1						
Other colony	.061	−.004	−.434**	−.220*	−.220*	1					
Proportion of Protestants and Catholics	.075	.456**	−.089	−.225**	.510**	−.145	1				
Proportion of Muslims	−.106	−.450**	−.004	.247**	−.309**	.079	−.700**	1			
Internet users per 1,000 people	.189	.163	.040	−.222*	.049	.142	.049	−.075	1		
GDP per capita	.418**	.033	.209*	−.227**	−.021	−.021	−.012	.025	.533**	1	
Government performance index	.298**	.313**	.280**	−.221**	.001	−.140	.156	−.174*	.382**	.699**	1

Note: *Significant at .05; **significant at .01.

Federalism and the Regulation of Agricultural Biotechnology in the United States and European Union

ADAM D. SHEINGATE

ABSTRACT *The United States and European Union have pursued markedly different paths in the development of policies toward genetically modified foods and crops. In considering the sources of these policy differences, this article explores the influence of federal arrangements on agricultural biotechnology policy. Two dimensions of federalism shape policy: an administrative component that shapes the distribution of regulatory authority across multiple levels of government, and a representative component that influences the degree to which constituent units have a formal voice in policy decisions taken at the federal level. This representative component most clearly distinguishes policymaking in the United States and European Union, and contributed to the distinct styles of decision-making in biotechnology on either side of the Atlantic.*

For scholars of comparative public policy, the issue of agricultural biotechnology poses an intriguing set of questions. What explains the divergent approaches to regulation on either side of the Atlantic? Whereas the United States has adopted a promotional approach to the commercialization of agricultural biotechnology, the European Union has embraced a precautionary approach to the risks of genetic modification (Pollack and Shaffer 2009). Second, what explains the varying degrees of public attention to this new technology? Although some in the United States are skeptical about GM foods, levels of public concern about the health or environmental effects of genetic modification are much higher in Europe where the issue has been a matter of national and supranational importance (Ansell and Vogel 2006). Finally, what accounts for the distinct styles of decision-making in US and EU biotechnology policy? Whereas in the United States, regulatory decisions take place in narrowly technocratic terms largely outside the public eye, European decisions are often visibly contentious with member states divided over broad policy issues related to biotechnology (Skogstad 2006).

Scholarly attention to the GM food debate suggests a number of explanations for the differences that separate public attitudes and policies toward biotechnology in the United States and Europe. Recent studies, for example, contrast a skeptical European public, their faith in regulatory agencies shaken by recent food scares, with the high levels of trust displayed by American consumers toward the regulatory authorities responsible for GM foods and crops (Lofstedt and Vogel 2001, Vogel and Lynch 2001, Gaskell *et al.* 2002). Others contrast a robust coalition of environmentalists, consumer organizations, and farm groups in Europe opposed to GM foods with a fragmented green lobby in the United States and a policy process dominated by biotechnology industry concerns (Bernauer 2003). Finally, studies of comparative public policy contrast European regulatory agencies focused on the uncertain risks of genetic modification with a US regulatory system that evaluates the products of biotechnology the same as those produced by conventional means (Jasanoff 2005). Together, these studies provide valuable insights about the public's understanding, images, and acceptance of biotechnology, the scope and character of interest groups aligned for and against, and many of the salient characteristics of the policy process in the United States and Europe.

This article hopes to contribute further to this understanding of transatlantic differences by focusing on the way federal institutional arrangements have contributed to the distinct styles of decision-making, the levels of public attention, and ultimately the promotional and precautionary approaches to agricultural biotechnology on either side of the Atlantic. As Schattschneider noted long ago, institutions determine the scope of conflict over policy priorities, the character of interests involved, and the alternatives admitted to policy debates. As a result, the rules that determine the location of decision-making authority will have far-reaching consequences for public policy outcomes (Schattschneider 1960). Institutional features critically shape which concerns, opinions, interests, or values come to enjoy privileged positions in policy decisions.

In exploring the effects of institutional differences on biotechnology policies in the United States and European Union, this article focuses on two dimensions of federal arrangements. The first is the distribution of administrative authority between the constituent units (states or member states, in this case) and the national or supranational governments in regulatory matters. In both the United States and European Union the supremacy of national or supranational authority in some areas is balanced by the preservation of powers for states and member states in others. This distribution of regulatory authority across multiple levels of government is a characteristic feature of federal systems. However, the precise character of multi-level governing arrangements in a particular policy domain also depends on historical legacies such as court decisions that define jurisdictions or the development of administrative capacities at different levels of government to implement regulatory policy (Montpetit 2002). Similarly, in the case of biotechnology, jurisdictional conflicts and administrative capacities shape federal arrangements in the United States and Europe. In the United States, where separate statutes govern the regulation of different biotechnology products, federal and state authority varies considerably from product to product and many states lack the scientific and technical resources to play a meaningful role in policy, leaving much of the regulatory authority for biotechnology in the United States at the federal level. In the European Union, the scope of member state authority in biotechnology remains much broader and the implementation of EU regulations depends heavily on national capacities, despite recent policy changes designed to centralize regulatory functions at the EU level.

The second dimension of comparison that highlights the differences between federalism in the United States and European Union is the representation of constituent units in national or supranational policy decisions. In the United States, individual states do not play a formal role in federal policymaking, but instead seek influence through informal and ad hoc channels such as lobbying, consultations, or public hearings. In the European Union, however, member states are formally represented in the biotechnology policy process, most directly through the Council of Ministers, but also through the regulatory committees comprised of scientists appointed by each member state that ratify Commission proposals for the approval of individual biotechnology products (the comitology procedure). It is this representative feature of EU federalism that distinguishes the European biotechnology policy process most clearly from the United States and, more important, contributed directly to the political stalemate over genetic modification in the European Union. By contrast, the skeptics of genetic modification in the United States enjoyed few points of access to the policy process or opportunities to challenge policies that promoted the commercial development of agricultural biotechnology.

The Administrative Dimension: Regulatory Federalism in the United States and EU

As EU scholars routinely note, it is in the area of regulation that the institutions of the European Union most closely resemble a supranational federal state (Majone 1999). Like the United States, where the US Constitution asserts the supremacy of federal law yet also reserves certain powers for the states, the supremacy of EU authority in some areas is balanced by the preservation of powers for the member states in others. And in both the US and EU, high courts play a critical role in adjudicating jurisdictional conflicts that inevitably arise. These dynamics of multi-level administrative authority are clearly evident in the area of biotechnology policy. However, whereas authority for US biotechnology policy resides mostly at the federal level, EU member states retain significant roles in policy, particularly at the implementation stage and despite recent reforms intended to centralize biotechnology policymaking. These contrasts reveal the importance of administrative capacities in federal systems and the critical role of courts in addressing the uncertain boundary between state and federal levels of authority (Kelemen 2004).

Regulatory Federalism in US Biotechnology Policy

In the United States, regulatory authority for biotechnology rests on a number of broad statutes that govern environmental protection, food safety, and agricultural practices more generally. This distinctive feature of US policy is the result of a political decision to incorporate biotechnology under existing law rather than develop separate regulatory standards for genetically modified organisms. Put differently, it is the *product* of biotechnology, rather than the *process* of genetic modification that is the trigger for regulatory review (Jasanoff 1995). Specifically, the Coordinated Framework for the Regulation of Biotechnology, an administrative decision issued by the Reagan White House in 1986, divided regulatory jurisdiction for biotechnology among three federal agencies. The US Department of Agriculture (USDA) oversees open-air field tests and the approval of genetically modified crops for commercial sale under the Plant Pest Act (PPA). The Food and Drug Administration (FDA) is responsible for foods containing genetically modified organisms under the Federal Food Drug and Cosmetic Act (FFDCA). Finally, the Environmental Protection Agency (EPA) regulates crops genetically engineered to have characteristics of a pesticide under the Federal Insecticide Fungicide and Rodenticide Act (FIFRA). These administrative jurisdictions reflect the product-based inspiration behind US regulatory policy: pesticides for the EPA, foods for the FDA, and plants for the USDA (Sheingate 2006).

Because regulatory responsibility is divided in this manner, the involvement of individual states in biotechnology policy depends on the specific provisions of the different statutes authorizing federal action. Article VI of the US Constitution, the Supremacy Clause, states that the laws of the United States are "the supreme Law of the Land" when state and federal laws conflict.[1] In theory, this means that the federal government may preempt duplicative state action in a particular area or policy domain. In practice, however, such matters are far from clear, leaving the courts to decide the scope of federal and state authority. Because most statutes are rarely explicit on these matters, the courts try to ascertain congressional intent in the legislative histories of particular statutes, and decide whether federal preemption of state law was express or implied, plenary or partial.[2] The result is a patchwork of regulatory authority in American federalism.

In biotechnology, for example, FIFRA expressly preempts states from imposing labeling requirements for agricultural chemicals beyond those approved by the EPA.[3] However, FIFRA also leaves room for state action, specifically regulations on "the sale or use of any federally registered pesticide or device".[4] The FIFRA preemption provision has been the subject of several court cases that have attempted to define the boundaries of federal and state authority in pesticide regulation.[5] A 1992 court decision, for example, noted that, "FIFRA expressly authorizes state pesticide regulation ... Consequently, a state could prohibit the sale of a pesticide within its borders."[6] Whether a state could similarly prohibit the sale of a genetically modified organism remains to be seen, and would almost certainly hinge on judicial interpretation of FIFRA preemption.

However, the product distinctions of the Coordinated Framework limit state regulatory authority under FIFRA to plants genetically modified for insect resistance. To date, the widest application of this kind of biotechnology are *Bt* varieties of corn and cotton, crops genetically engineered to produce a bacterium (*Bacillus thuringiesis*) toxic to certain insects.[7] As of 2008, more than half of all corn and cotton planted in the United States was modified for insect resistance and therefore fell under the regulatory purview of FIFRA.[8]

More common are herbicide tolerant (HT) crops, such as Roundup Ready soybeans modified to withstand the effects of Roundup herbicide. In 2008, three quarters of all soy, corn, and cotton planted in the United States was genetically engineered for herbicide tolerance.[9] However, field testing and commercialization of these biotechnology varieties fall entirely under the jurisdiction of the USDA. Moreover, the Plant Pest Act, which provides the statutory authority for USDA oversight in biotechnology, has a very different preemption provision than the one found in FIFRA. Specifically, whereas FIFRA establishes a regulatory floor, the Plant Pest Act establishes a regulatory ceiling. In the case of FIFRA, Congress intended "to leave the states the authority to impose stricter regulation on pesticides uses than that required under the Act".[10] By contrast, the preemption language in PPA stipulates that, "A State ... may impose prohibitions or restrictions ... that are consistent with and *do not exceed* the regulations or orders issued by the Secretary [of Agriculture]."[11] This may limit the authority of individual states once the USDA renders a regulatory decision on the use of a genetically modified crop, although no court cases to date have tested the limits of PPA preemption in biotechnology. Nevertheless, this illustrates how the limits of state and federal authority depend on the particular preemption provisions of different statutes and, critically, judicial interpretations of the scope of preemption in a particular context.

Another feature limiting the role of individual states in US biotechnology policy is their limited administrative capacity for regulatory implementation and oversight. Most states do not posses the scientific expertise or the financial resources to participate actively in biotechnology policy. As the authors of a recent study of state biotechnology policies note:

> At the state level, the resources available for regulatory oversight of biotech crops for plant health purposes are very limited. The organizational units responsible for plant health in general are typically very small, and many states rely on the part-time efforts of one or a few individuals within these units to carry out or coordinate the state's biotech oversight activities. (Taylor *et al.* 2004: 42)

Furthermore, states do not receive federal financial support and "rely solely on their own resources for any biotech oversight" (Taylor *et al.* 2004: 43). By contrast, biotechnology expertise and resources are concentrated at the federal level. In 2002, for example, the USDA created a Biotechnology Regulatory Services (BRS) unit within the Animal and Plant Health Inspection Service (APHIS) to coordinate regulatory responsibilities for field trials and approvals for commercial use of genetically engineered crops. The BRS currently employs more than 80 people with an annual budget of $12 million, an amount that has more than doubled since 2003.[12]

Second, since publication of the Coordinated Framework in 1986, federal agency rulemaking has left individual states uncertain about their role in regulatory oversight. Under a 2001 rule that addressed the status of plants genetically engineered for pest resistance under FIFRA, or plant-incorporated protectants as the EPA refers to them, EPA authority only covers the pesticidal substance itself, but not the plant or seed that produces it.[13] In other words, the EPA regulates the *Bt* toxin like other pesticides, but not the seed or plant that produces the toxin. This has left states uncertain about precisely what role they would play in regulatory oversight of these crops since, in effect, the EPA leaves them nothing to regulate. Together, the lack of state administrative resources and federal rulemaking guidance limit the scope of state involvement in biotechnology policy, even though states play a large role in the implementation and enforcement of federal pesticide policy more generally.[14]

However, individual states are involved in other areas of biotechnology policy. For example, the BRS does consult with state officials during federal review of field trial applications for genetically engineered crops. This consultation typically includes a forwarded copy of the application, a preliminary safety assessment by the BRS, and a form for the individual state to indicate its opinion on the proposed field test permit. Although state opinions are only advisory and have no legal force, BRS has never issued a field trial permit over state objections (Taylor *et al.* 2004: 47).

In addition, some states have taken a more direct role in biotechnology regulation. For example, Minnesota law requires state permits for the field test and use of certain genetically modified crops. Vermont law requires state permits or copies of federal paperwork submitted to the relevant state agency before the environmental release of genetically modified crops and genetically modified seeds must carry labels specifying safe handling instructions. Finally, California has been at the center of debates over the approval of genetically modified rice that produced a pharmaceutical for human consumption. In 2004, Ventria Life Sciences applied for an APHIS permit to commercially plant a rice variety genetically modified to produce an antibiotic useful for treating diarrhea. Because of the commercial implications of cross-contamination for conventional rice, Ventria also needed the approval of the California Rice Commission, a state advisory body authorized under the California Rice Certification Act to "maintain the integrity and prevent the contamination of rice" that may "adversely affect the marketability of rice in the event of commingling". Although a closely divided Rice Commission approved the application, the California secretary of agriculture denied a request for an expedited decision, effectively barring the rice until the 2005 growing season. Since then, Ventria has suspended its activities in California, although continues to test crops in North Carolina (Taylor *et al.* 2004: 91–99).

As these examples illustrate, there is pronounced variability among states and among products in the regulation of biotechnology. This variability partly reflects the complexity of biotechnology policy and its reliance on multiple statutes, each with its own language and legal precedents guiding state–federal relations. This variability also illustrates the complexity of federalism itself and the range of possibilities for divisions of regulatory authority within the same policy domain. However, with the exception of a few states, the regulation of biotechnology in the United States has largely been a federal affair.

Regulatory Federalism in EU Biotechnology Policy

In contrast to the relatively narrow role played by individual states in the American context, the member states of the European Union continue to play a central part in the administration of EU policies for biotechnology. Although recent changes in EU law have centralized some regulatory functions, the strict labeling and traceability requirements recently established for genetically modified foods and crops increased the implementation responsibilities that ultimately fall on individual member states. Most important, the safeguard provisions included in European biotechnology directives and regulations permit individual member states to impose national bans on the use of a particular biotechnology product.[15]

Currently, much of the EU regulatory process for biotechnology still begins with the competent authorities (food safety or other agencies) of individual member states. Directive 2001/18/EC (which replaced 90/220/EC) governs the deliberate release of genetically modified organisms into the environment for either experimental purposes (field tests) or commercial use. In the case of the former, an applicant need only secure the approval of the member state in which the field test is to take place. According to the Commission, "the decision to authorize – or reject – the [experimental] release of a GMO is exclusively incumbent on the competent national authority which has received the notification. Hence the authorization procedure is a purely national one" (European Commission 2003). This stands in rather sharp contrast with the United States where notifications and permits for field tests fall under the authority of the USDA, which conducts informal consultations with individual states as a matter of courtesy but is not required to by law. Consequently, there is wide variation in the conduct of field tests across EU member states: Spain has authorized 207 field tests of genetically engineered plants since 2002, whereas no field tests have occurred in Austria or Luxembourg, countries vocally opposed to genetic modification.[16]

Decisions on the deliberate release for commercial use, or marketing, of a genetically modified crop also typically begin with the national competent authorities, although other member states may raise objections before EU-wide approval is given. In such cases, a conciliation procedure among the member states and Commission takes place. If objections persist, the decision moves to the EU level where the newly created European Food Safety Authority (EFSA) issues an opinion. Based on the risk assessment of EFSA, the Commission formulates a draft decision and forwards it to a regulatory committee composed of member state representatives for approval. If the regulatory committee approves the draft, the Commission adopts the decision. However, if the committee is unable to reach a decision, the Commission forwards the draft to the Council of Ministers, which may adopt or reject it by qualified majority. If the Council is unable to reach a decision after three months, the Commission may approve the GMO for EU-wide use (European Commission 2003: 6–7).

In the case of genetically modified crops used for food or animal feed, applicants seeking approval for commercial use may pursue a newly centralized "one door, one key" procedure. Under Regulation (EC) No. 1829/2003, EFSA conducts a single risk assessment procedure that includes both environmental release and food/feed use. As under Directive 2001/18/EC, the Commission incorporates the EFSA opinion into a draft decision and, if neither a regulatory committee nor the Council is able to reach a decision by qualified majority, the Commission is authorized to adopt the decision and approve the product for food and feed use (European Commission 2003: 10–11).

The new centralized procedure and the prominent role EFSA plays in the regulatory process reflect Commission efforts to enhance its own regulatory capacity and (re)build public confidence in EU institutions following various national food safety scandals and widespread concerns among European consumers about the safety of genetic modification. In addition, the Commission has issued detailed rules and guidance documents that specify, for example, how national competent authorities should conduct environmental risk assessments or stipulate precisely the form and content of reports and documents regarding applications.[17] Such detailed implementation requirements are increasingly characteristic of EU regulatory federalism, as are judicial actions before the European Court of Justice to enforce member state compliance with EU law (Kelemen 2004). Article 226 (ex Article 169) of the Treaty permits the Commission to bring infringement proceedings against a member state that does not fulfill its obligations under EU law; since 1994, the Commission has brought 12 such infringement proceedings against seven countries for failure to transpose EU biotechnology directives into national legislation. In all but one case, the ECJ found in favor of the Commission.[18]

Despite efforts to centralize the approval process and harmonize procedures for handling genetically modified foods and crops, tensions between member states and the Commission over the implementation of biotechnology regulations are likely to persist for two reasons. First, member states retain a central role in the new labeling and traceability requirements that came into force in 2004. Regulation (EC) No. 1830/2003 mandates that downstream users and consumers of food and feed be informed when genetically modified organisms are present. In large measure, this can be accomplished only through strict labeling and reporting procedures that detail the content and origin of food products. Because of the nature of shipping and storage of bulk commodities, coupled with the risks of cross-contamination of conventional crops, some "adventitious" or technically unavoidable traces of a genetically modified organism can be present. EU law establishes a threshold for such traces, below which labeling and traceability is not required. However, the designation of such a threshold requires that a testing regime be put in place to detect the presence of genetically modified organisms, a responsibility that falls entirely on the member states. A report by the European Commission on the implementation of Regulation 1830/2003 noted that although member states viewed the goals of labeling and traceability in a positive light, concerns about the technical feasibility and administrative burdens associated with testing for traces of genetically modified varieties were common (European Commission 2006a).

Second, and more important, the power to temporarily ban the national sale or use of genetically modified organisms continues to be a source of conflict between member states and the Commission. Questions about the scope of member state authority to invoke safeguard provisions have been at the heart of European disputes over genetic modification and continue to plague Commission efforts to move forward with a new and improved regulatory regime for biotechnology. As mentioned previously, these member state prerogatives are protected by the Treaty: Article 30 (ex article 36) authorizes temporary restrictions on imports for "the protection of health and life of humans, animals or plants" and Article 174 (ex article 130r) requires all EU environmental measures to include a safeguard clause that permits member states to enact national prohibitions provided they rest on a scientific basis.[19]

Disputes over the scope and legality of the safeguard provisions in EU biotechnology policy have been at the heart of disputes over genetically modified crops since the 1990s. In 1997, Austria invoked the safeguard provision to prohibit the marketing of a genetically modified corn approved by the Commission despite member state opposition in the Council and a deadlocked regulatory committee. Two years later, in February 1999, the Commission ordered Austria to remove its ban on the GM corn after a scientific committee reviewed the Austrian claim and found no evidence of environmental or health risks that justified the ban.[20] By this time, however, five other countries (France, Luxembourg, Greece, Germany, and the

United Kingdom) had also invoked the safeguard clause for various biotechnology products. Although the merits of these claims were also rejected by scientific committees, concerns about genetic modification had become so widespread that the Commission called a halt to its approval procedures and the bans remained in place pending a wholesale revision of EU biotechnology policy.[21]

Although a new system for the approval of genetically modified organisms is now in place, conflicts over the status of safeguard provisions persist. In December 2003, the Commission asked member states with active safeguard measures to reconsider and, if necessary, resubmit their claims under the new biotechnology directive (2001/18/EC). France, Luxembourg, Austria, and Greece decided to maintain their safeguard measures under the new directive. However, in April 2004 an EFSA panel reported that it had not found evidence of any additional risks that would justify the bans. Accordingly, the Commission submitted a draft decision to a regulatory committee requesting that the four countries lift their national safeguard measures. However, the regulatory committee deadlocked, sending the decision to the Council. In a visible setback for the Commission, a June 2005 vote of the Environment Council rejected by a qualified majority the Commission proposal to lift the national bans. In issuing its decision, the Council noted that "there is still a degree of uncertainty in relation to the safeguard measures" and called on the Commission "to gather further scientific evidence". Consequently, the Commission turned again to EFSA, which in March 2006 issued an opinion that "there is no reason to believe that the continued placing of the market ... [of the genetically modified organisms currently banned] is likely to cause any adverse effects for human and animal health or the environment". Meanwhile, an October 2005 decision by the Court of First Instance ruled in favor of the Commission in a case concerning a regional ban on genetically modified organisms issued by the province of Upper Austria and was upheld on appeal by the European Court of Justice in September 2007. Although the decision calls into question efforts by a number of regional governments to designate "GM-free zones", the Commission and the Council remain deadlocked about what to do about the national bans by Austria and other member states still in effect.[22]

As the conflicts over safeguard provisions illustrate, member states retain significant powers over the regulation of biotechnology in the European Union. The European Commission still depends on member state resources for important regulatory functions. Disputes between the member states and the Commission over their respective spheres of regulatory authority continue to be a characteristic feature of European biotechnology debates. This stands in sharp contrast to the United States, where most states lack the resources to effectively participate in the administration of biotechnology policy. Although the American states retain important powers under the Constitution and in some of the specific statutes governing biotechnology policy, for the most part it is the federal government that oversees the testing and approval of genetically modified organisms.

Further differences emerge when the representative dimension of federalism is examined. As described in the next section, there is no parallel in the United States to the role played by individual member states in EU policy decisions. The representative feature not only distinguishes EU federalism most clearly from its American counterpart, but also explains why disputes over the distribution of regulatory authority between the EU and the individual member states continue to hobble European biotechnology policy.

Representative Federalism in the United States and European Union

As students of comparative federalism point out, the institutions of the European Union afford the constituent member states corporate or territorial representation in EU affairs (Weiler 2001). Consequently, many of the institutions of the European Union preserve and protect this corporate or territorial character through the formal representation of member states in EU policy decisions. The most direct form of member state representation is the Council of Ministers made up of national ministers and the European Council comprised of heads of state and government. As Halberstam emphasizes:

> Ministers meeting in the Council represent their governments: they are members of their respective State governments, subject to recall by their government, and required to cast an undivided vote on behalf of their State. Member states thus have a voice in the decision making process of the EU. (Halberstam 2001: 234)

In this regard, the Council of Ministers resembles the *Bundesrat* in German federalism comprised of members of the *Länder* governments.

To put it differently, "the Councils represent territorial governments rather than territorial electorates" (Moravcsik 2001: 175). This contrasts quite clearly with US federalism where members of the Senate represent various state constituencies, rather than individual states themselves. This was the case even before the 17th Amendment ratified in 1917 that required the direct election of senators (rather than selection by state legislatures). However, the difference is even more pronounced in the contemporary era of candidate-centered campaigns and entrepreneurial politicians that characterize the Senate and American politics more generally (Sinclair 1989).

Another important instrument of member state representation is the comitology procedure that requires the Commission to submit draft measures to a committee made of scientific experts appointed by each member state. In some cases, these committees only perform an advisory role. In other cases, known as the regulatory procedure, the Commission can only act with the approval of a committee; that is, a qualified majority in favor of the Commission proposal. Such is the case in biotechnology policy under Directive 18/2001/EC on the deliberate release of genetically modified organisms into the environment and Regulation 1829/2003 on the marketing of genetically modified food and feed. Both stipulate the more stringent regulatory procedure requiring a regulatory committee of member state representatives to approve by qualified majority all Commission proposals for the marketing of agricultural biotechnology products.[23] EU scholars have debated whether regulatory committees and other elements of the comitology procedure are instruments of member state control over the Commission or represent a deliberative forum for a transnational network of experts that transcends national interests (Joerges and Neyer 1997, Pollack 2003). Although the truth likely resides somewhere in the middle, regulatory committee decisions on biotechnology have reflected distinct member state concerns and often reproduced the pattern of member state preferences evident in the Council and elsewhere. Put simply, scientific experts from countries that adopt a more precautionary approach to biotechnology are more likely to reject applications for GM products within the regulatory committees. In a February 2004 committee decision on genetically modified corn, for example, Denmark, Italy, Austria, Luxembourg and Greece – countries consistently opposed to agricultural biotechnology – voted against the proposal.[24]

Moreover, the formal representation of member states in the regulatory process through comitology procedures and the Council (which must vote on Commission proposals if a regulatory committee cannot reach a qualified majority for or against approval) has no parallel in the United States. Instead, individual American states seek influence over national regulatory decisions in informal or ad hoc ways. For example, states may lobby Congress or federal agencies individually or through intergovernmental organizations such as the National Governors Association. States may also present their views through the rulemaking process governed by the Administrative Procedures Act, which requires a period for public comment before federal rules can take effect. However, such comments are nonbinding on agency decisions. Similarly, recent presidential administrations have operated under executive orders that require agencies to assess the effect of proposed federal rules on states and conduct intergovernmental consultations. However, research suggests these executive orders are routinely ignored in federal rulemaking (Mendelson 2004). In some policy areas, such as the environment, more formalized intergovernmental partnerships have evolved to facilitate consultation between the federal government and the states. However, these partnerships are frequently voluntary and generally address questions of how to implement complex regulations rather than give states a voice in regulatory decisions. Finally, states may sue the federal government over specific regulations as a coalition of nine northeastern states did in 2003, successfully blocking the EPA from implementing a regulation that would have relaxed federal pollution controls on coal-fired power plants (Scheberle 2005). As these examples show, there is no formal representation of state interests in the federal regulatory process.

Differences in the representative dimension of federalism have important consequences for agricultural biotechnology. Unlike the ad hoc mechanisms of state influence in the United States, the European Union displays characteristics of what Fritz Scharpf calls a joint-decision system in which central government action requires the agreement of the constituent units. Moreover, as Scharpf (1988) notes, such joint-decision systems often require that agreement be unanimous or nearly so, a decision rule that strongly biases the status quo and makes adaptation difficult in the face of divergent interests.

The drawbacks of such joint-decision systems are evident in EU biotechnology policy where the representation of member states in regulatory decisions produced deadlock in the 1990s. As mentioned previously, EU biotechnology policies unraveled when several member states invoked the safeguard clause to ban a genetically modified corn approved for EU-wide use by the Commission. The decision by Austria and others reflected a dissatisfaction with the EU regulatory process, specifically, the approval of GM corn over the opposition of several member states. However, the events leading up to the Austrian ban illustrate the drawbacks of a system in which regulatory decisions require the assent of constituent units. Although the Commission drafted a proposal for approval of GM corn, a regulatory committee was unable to reach a qualified majority either for or against it. With the regulatory committee deadlocked, the Commission forwarded the application to the Council, which also failed to either approve or reject the proposal despite opposition from several member states. With neither the Council nor the regulatory committee of member states able to act, the Commission authorized marketing of the genetically modified corn, citing three additional reports from scientific advisory committees on its safety.[25] Austria then invoked the safeguard clause of Directive 90/220/EC, the legality of which remains a matter of dispute with the Commission. In sum, the absence of member state consensus over the safety of GM corn left the Council and the regulatory committees unable to act, pushing the decision to the Commission which was forced to act over the objection of some member states. Ironically, the same procedures designed to preserve member state representation in regulatory decisions ultimately weakened the legitimacy of EU institutions in matters of biotechnology.

These problems continue under the new rules for biotechnology adopted in the early 2000s because the representative components of EU federalism give voice to the persistent divisions among member states over genetic modification. Moreover, decision rules within EU institutions, namely the use of population-weighted qualified majority voting (QMV), make it especially difficult to break the deadlock over biotechnology that has existed since the late 1990s.

Votes on the approval of genetically modified crops illustrate how institutional features contributed to the political stalemate over biotechnology in the European Union. Figure 1 ranks the EU-15 member states using a GMO support score calculated from 19 votes on agricultural biotechnology taken by either a regulatory

Figure 1. Member state support for GMOs

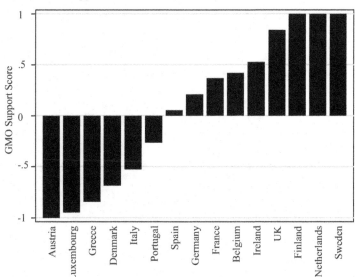

committee or the Council between December 2003 and October 2005. The support score ranges from 1 (support for GMOs) to –1 (opposition to GMOs).[26] As indicated by Figure 1, member states fall into roughly three groups. On the left side of Figure 1 are member states that consistently voted against the approval of genetically modified foods and crops: these are Austria, Luxembourg, Greece, Denmark, and to a lesser extent Italy. On the right of Figure 1 are member states that consistently voted in favor of the approval of genetically modified foods and crops: Sweden, the Netherlands, Finland, the UK, and to a lesser extent Ireland. In the middle of Figure 1 are countries that weakly support or are moderately opposed to biotechnology: Belgium, France, Germany, Spain, and Portugal.

Figure 2 offers a clearer picture of these divisions and reveals a peculiar feature of member state voting: the high rate of abstentions among some countries. Again, Austria, Luxembourg, Greece, and Denmark make up the core of the anti-GMO bloc, with Sweden, the Netherlands, Finland, and the UK the core supporters of GMO proposals since 2003. However, Germany and Spain abstained on 79 per cent and 84 per cent of GMO votes, respectively, and abstentions made up almost half of all Irish votes and about a quarter of Belgian votes on GMOs.

These abstentions have hampered the ability of member states to decide collectively on matters of agricultural biotechnology by denying the Council or regulatory committee a majority either for or against the approval of GMOs. Figure 3 provides the results of each of the 19 votes and reveals the effect of QMV procedures used in Council and regulatory committee decisions.[27] As indicated, the tendency for member states to abstain means that the percentage of weighted votes either for or against the approval of GMOs falls far short of the supermajorities

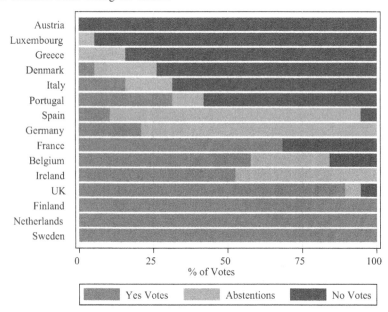

Figure 2. Member state voting on GMOs

Figure 3. Qualified majority voting on GMOs

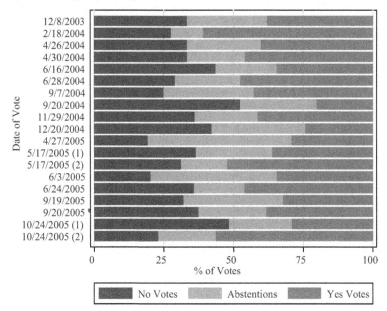

required under QMV (see Appendix), much less approach a simple majority in most cases.[28]

As indicated in Table 1, the high voting thresholds under QMV have made decisions on GMOs exceedingly difficult. For example, a regulatory committee vote on whether to authorize the import and processing of genetically modified corn in February 2004 secured a majority of weighted votes and more than half of the member states, representing a majority of the EU population. Because the vote failed to reach the required supermajorities, however, the proposal was sent to the Council (which also failed to reach a decision).[29] However, even this degree of agreement was unusual. As the shaded entries in Table 1 indicate, a majority of votes were cast either for or against a GMO proposal in only four out of the 19 votes taken between 2003 and 2005, a majority of member states voted for or against a proposal only five times during this period, and only five votes represented more than half of the EU population. Although a majority of member states have on occasion opposed GMOs, these countries do not represent a majority of the EU population. Conversely, support for GMOs among the more populous member states at times has reached a majority of weighted votes and of population, but nevertheless constituted a minority of member states. In sum, EU rules have translated member state divisions over GMOs into a policy stalemate that continues to this day.[30]

It is this representative dimension of federalism that most clearly distinguishes the European Union from the United States. Whereas individual states under American federalism have only informal and ad hoc channels through which to influence national policy decisions, EU member states enjoy formal representation in regulatory decisions taken in Brussels. This distinction has had important implications for biotechnology policy, particularly in the European context. Ironically, the same rules that guarantee

Table 1. Opposition and support for GMOs (%)

	NO votes			YES votes		
Date of vote	Weighted votes	Member states	EU population	Weighted votes	Member states	EU population
12/8/2003	33	40	26	38	40	37
2/18/2004	28	33	22	61	60	59
4/26/2004	33	40	26	40	40	41
4/30/2004	33	40	26	46	47	44
6/16/2004	44	44	43	35	36	28
6/28/2004	29	36	21	48	44	47
9/7/2004	25	32	19	43	40	41
9/20/2004	52	56	46	20	20	20
11/29/2004	36	44	29	41	32	54
12/20/2004	42	52	33	24	24	23
4/27/2005	19	20	18	29	32	26
5/17/2005 (1)	36	36	31	36	32	38
5/17/2005 (2)	31	32	29	52	36	64
6/3/2005	20	32	10	35	32	36
6/24/2005	36	52	26	46	32	60
9/19/2005	32	48	23	32	28	35
9/20/2005	37	40	31	38	36	39
10/24/2005 (1)	48	52	45	29	32	25
10/24/2005 (2)	23	44	11	56	44	69

Note: Shaded entries indicate majority vote. See Appendix for voting weights and member state populations.

member state representation in the regulatory process have left representative institutions such as the Council and regulatory committees unable (or unwilling) to act. A lack of member state consensus coupled with supermajoritian decision rules has pushed responsibility for a biotechnology away from national governments, forcing controversial decisions upon a European Commission frequently criticized for its lack of democratic legitimacy (Skogstad 2003).

Conclusion: Institutions and the Politics of Agricultural Biotechnology

A number of important factors have contributed to transatlantic differences over agricultural biotechnology. In contrast to a skeptical European public shaken by a number of food scares and national scandals over lax food safety standards, most Americans hold the federal regulatory authorities responsible for food safety in fairly high regard, and even today US consumers remain relatively nonplussed by the prospect of mad cows (Strauss 2004). Second, in contrast to the rather robust anti-GMO coalition of environmentalists, consumer groups, and small farmers found in Europe, American groups opposed to genetically modified foods and crops appear fragmented and weak, particularly when compared to the focused lobbying efforts of the US biotechnology industry (Bernauer and Meins 2003). Finally, European concerns about the risks of genetic modification occurred within a historical context of rising green activism and government intervention, a time when the European tortoise overtook the American hare in a variety of environmental policy areas (Vogel 2003).

These broader historical and social contexts are important, but they also reflect the way distinct institutional mechanisms transmit and translate political forces into policy outcomes. As explored here, federalism is one such mechanism: multi-level governing arrangements shape the location of policy authority as well as the avenues through which various actors and interests may pursue political goals. In the case of agricultural biotechnology, two dimensions of federalism – one administrative, the other representative – are particularly important for understanding the politics and policies surrounding genetically modified foods and crops.

Examining the administrative dimension of regulatory federalism reveals that the distribution of authority across multiple levels of government depends on more than just the broad constitutional structure of federal arrangements. In addition, the specific legal and statutory context as interpreted through court decisions, as well as the historical resource capacities for different levels of government to engage in regulatory implementation and oversight also matter (Montpetit 2002). In this regard, the case of agricultural biotechnology confirms recent research on the important role that courts play in federal systems, particularly in adjudicating jurisdictional conflicts and securing compliance with centrally imposed regulatory standards among potentially wayward constituent states (Kagan 2001). However, the case of agricultural biotechnology also illustrates that these relationships can vary considerably. In the United States, the constitutional limits on state action through federal preemption depend on such particulars as whether a crop has been modified to be tolerant to herbicides or resistant to insects. The uncertainty that accompanies this variability, coupled with a general lack of state-level capacities in the area of biotechnology, have left many states unwilling or unable to participate in regulatory implementation and oversight, leaving most of these functions to the federal government.

Examining the representative dimension of federalism illustrates how institutions shape the articulation of interests within the policy process. In the case of agricultural biotechnology, this can lead to outcomes contrary to the purpose for which the institutions were originally designed. In the European Union, where member states enjoy a formal voice in regulatory decisions, voting rules and a lack of member state consensus has frequently produced deadlock over genetic modification. This confirms previous work on the "joint-decision trap" characteristic of certain kinds of federal arrangements (Scharpf 1988). In addition, however, the case of agricultural biotechnology suggests that efforts to enhance the democratic legitimacy of European regulations through the formal representation of member states in policy decisions also creates opportunities to shift the blame for unpopular or difficult decisions on to the European Commission and in a way that lowers public trust in EU institutions (Gaskell et al. 2003).[31]

Moreover, European experiences illustrate that representative institutions not only transmit interests, they also transform them. Put differently, the mobilization of interests partly depends on the institutional context of policy contestation (Ansell et al. 2006). Were it possible to transport EU procedures to the United States, approval of a controversial product like genetically modified wheat or rice would require the assent of 50 state secretaries of agriculture under population-weighted voting. Under such circumstances, one could imagine a coalition of states – perhaps California, Wisconsin, Minnesota, Vermont, North and South Dakota – voting against approval. More important, placing responsibility for regulatory decisions in the hands of state officials might galvanize opponents of genetic modification, forcing state governments to take a stand for or against agricultural biotechnology and catching the attention of a generally uninformed public.[32] In some states, a more attentive public might raise the political costs of supporting agricultural biotechnology, perhaps leading government officials to oppose or abstain from decisions on the approval of genetically modified foods and crops, resulting in regulatory uncertainty at the federal level.

Although an unlikely counterfactual, as a thought experiment it raises an important point when drawing transatlantic comparisons about the politics of agricultural biotechnology. In the European Union, the rules of federalism, its administrative and representative dimensions, give voice to national concerns about genetic modification and provide the opponents of biotechnology with an opportunity to build coalitions around related issues such as the legitimacy of EU institutions, concerns about globalization, the transformation of agriculture, and environmental degradation (Ansell *et al.* 2006). In the United States, on the other hand, the regulation of genetically modified foods and crops remains almost entirely in the hands of federal agencies that examine risks and benefits in narrowly technocratic terms (Jasanoff 2005). Consequently, critics of genetic modification have had limited opportunities to raise issues that might engage a wider public about the merits of agricultural biotechnology. Although divergent historical, social, and cultural contexts may separate Americans and Europeans, transatlantic differences over agricultural biotechnology also reflect the important role institutions play in the definition of issues and the constitution of interests.

Notes

1. U.S. Constitution, Article VI.
2. There is a vast literature on preemption (see for example, Gardbaum 1994).
3. 7 USCS § 136v(b) (see Weiland 2000).
4. 7 USCS § 136v(a).
5. Whereas the Supreme Court has defended state and local regulations on pesticide use, it has struck down tort claims for injuries caused by pesticides that hinge on the supposed inadequacy of EPA labels (see Carrier 1996).
6. *Chemical Specialties Manufacturers Association, Inc. v. Allenby*, 958 F.2d 941, 944 (9th Cir. 1992). The D.C. Circuit drew a similar conclusion in *Ferebee v. Chevron Chem. Co.*, 736 F.2d 1529, at 1541 (D.C. Cir. 1984) (see Carrier 1996).
7. Because of concern about the development of background resistance, EPA requires that licensed dealers of Bt seeds enter into contracts with growers in which the latter agree to limit the percentage of acreage planted in Bt varieties and include non-Bt refuges in their fields (see Taylor *et al.* 2004: 51).
8. Calculated by author using data from http://www.nass.usda.gov/QuickStats/Create_Federal_All.jsp (acreage) and http://www.ers.usda.gov/Data/BiotechCrops/alltables.xls (biotechnology adoption) (accessed July 10, 2008).
9. It is common for farmers to plant "stacked" varieties of corn and cotton that are both insect resistant and herbicide tolerant. There is no commercially available Bt soy. In 2008, 92% of all soy was planted in HT varieties (for data, see note 8).
10. *Federal Environmental Pesticide Control Act*, Senate Report 92-270, 92d Congress, 2d Session (1972), p. 9 cited in *Ferebee*, 736 F.2d at 1541.
11. 7 USCS § 136v; 7 USCS § 7756 (emphasis added).
12. United States Department of Agriculture, *FY 2009 Budget Summary and Annual Performance Plan*, available at http://www.obpa.usda.gov/budsum/fy09budsum.pdf (accessed July 11, 2008). For information on BRS staff and structure, see http://www.aphis.usda.gov/biotechnology/organization/about_brsorgchart.shtml (accessed July 11, 2008).
13. EPA, "Regulations Under the Federal Insecticide Fungicide and Rodenticide Act for Plant-Incorporated Protectants", *Federal Register* 66 (139) 37772.

14. An exception is Minnesota, which passed a biotechnology-specific statute in 2003 that authorizes its agriculture commissioner to accept, deny, or impose conditions on the experimental use (e.g. field tests) of certain genetically engineered crops (Minnesota Statute 18B.285 "Experimental genetically engineered pesticide product regulation") (see Taylor et al. 2004: 55).
15. The authority for these safeguard provisions comes from Article 30 (ex article 36) of the Treaty, which stipulates that member states may enact national provisions that erect prohibitions or restrictions on imports in contravention of the common market in the name of "public morality ... the protection of health and life of humans, animals or plants; the protection of national treasures ... or the protection of industrial and commercial property" (Treaty of Rome, Article 30).
16. Field test data available from European Commission, Biotechnology and GMOs Information Website, http://gmoinfo.jrc.ec.europa.eu/gmp_browse.aspx (accessed July 11, 2008). It is interesting to note changes over time in field tests. Prior to 2000, France had authorized 459 field tests, more than any other country. Since then, the number of French field tests has declined dramatically and since 2002 only 73 tests have been authorized.
17. See for example Commission Decision 2002/623/EC on guidance notes of environmental risk assessments and Commission Decision 2003/701/EC on formats for presenting the results of deliberate release into the environment. Both available at http://eur-lex.europa.eu/RECH_naturel.do.
18. The seven countries were Luxembourg (3), Belgium (3) France (2), Portugal, United Kingdom, Greece, and Spain. Author search of Celex Database using search term "genetically modified", available through Lexis-Nexis.
19. Treaty of Rome, Article 30 (ex article 36); Article 174 (ex article 130r); see also Article 95 (ex article 100a), §4 and 5. Article 23 of Directive 2001/18/EC on the Deliberate Release of GMOs into the environment allows member states to suspend the marketing of a previously approved food or feed, subject to scrutiny of its scientific merit by the Commission and its regulatory committees (for a discussion, see Poli 2003).
20. "Austria Seeks Euro-Wide Ban on Transgenic Maize", *European Report*, Number 2211 (March 28, 1997); "Vienna and Luxembourg Ordered to Repeal National Provisions", *European Report*, Number 2385 (February 24, 1999).
21. "Commission Suspends Licensing Procedures", *European Report*, Number 2409 (May 22, 1999) (see also, European Commission 2006b).
22. See European Food Standards Agency 2006; "EFSA Rejects GM-Crop Bans in Austria and Greece", *European Report*, Number 2889 (July 28, 2004); "Commission Faces Stinging About-Turn in Council on GMO Bans", *European Report*, Number 2974 (June 29, 2005); "EU Court Rules Against Upper Austria's GM Ban", *European Report*, Number 2995 (October 8, 2005); "Commission Tries to Force Vienna's Hand Again on GE Maize", *European Report*, Number 3390 (October 11, 2007); "Commission is Thrown Back Against the Ropes", *European Report*, Number 3404 (October 31, 2007). For text of the ECJ decision on Austria, see 2007 ECJ Eur-Lex Lexis 1834.
23. Committee procedures are detailed in articles 30 and 35, respectively.
24. "Member States Split over Imports of Monsanto's NK603 Transgenic Maize", *European Report*, Number 2845 (February 21, 2004).
25. "Member States Reject Ciba-Geigy's Genetically-Modified Maize", *European Report*, Number 2144 (June 29, 1996); "Transgenic Maize Gets Commission Marketing Authorisation", *European Report*, Number 2185 (December 21, 1996).
26. The support score is calculated by assigning a 1 for yes votes, a –1 for no votes and a 0 for abstentions. For each member state, this score is summed across all 19 votes and then divided by 19 to produce a support score that ranges between –1 and 1. The source for these votes is Friends of the Earth Europe, an anti-GM advocacy group (http://www.foeeurope.org/GMOs/pending/votes_results.htm). Because votes by regulatory committees and the Council are not routinely published, the accuracy of these figures must be approached with some caution. However, as the following figures indicate, the results are consistent with general member state views on biotechnology. For a discussion of broader patterns of voting within the Council of Ministers, see Hayes-Renshaw et al. 2006.
27. Under qualified majority voting (QMV), each member state is accorded a number of votes roughly in proportion to the size of its population. For votes taken prior to May 1, 2004, a proposal required 62 out of 87 total votes to be ratified. With the addition of 10 new countries to the European Union on May 1, 2004, the requisite threshold for approval under QMV increased to 88 out of 124 total votes. As of November 1, 2004, voting weights and rules for QMV changed again. Under the revised system, a

proposal needed 232 out 321 total votes, the assent of a majority of member states (13), and at least 62% of the total European population. With the addition of Romania and Bulgaria on January 1, 2007, a proposal must receive 255 out of 345 votes. For voting weights, see Council of the European Union 2002 and for a general discussion see Wood and Yesilada 2002: 111–113.
28. For votes taken after May 1, 2004, Figure 3 includes 10 new countries of Central and Eastern Europe that joined the European Union. As indicated, EU expansion has not fundamentally altered the voting alignment on GMOs.
29. "Member States Split Over Imports of Monsanto's NK603 Transgenic Maize", *European Report*, Number 2845 (February 21, 2004). Germany was the only country to abstain.
30. "No Majority on New GMOs", *European Report*, Number 3474 (February 20, 2008).
31. In a 2002 survey, about half of Europeans thought the Commission was "doing a good job for society" in biotechnology, with 46% holding similar views about national governments. Consumer and environmental groups both rated higher (70% and 59%, respectively).
32. According to the authors of a recent study, "the American public is generally unaware of GM food. Most Americans have heard or read little about it, are not aware of its prevalence in their lives, and are confused as to which type of GM products are available" (Hallman et al. 2004: i)

References

Ansell, Christopher and Vogel, David, 2006, The contested governance of European Food Safety Regulation, in: Christopher Ansell and David Vogel (Eds) *What's the Beef? The Contested Governance of European Food Safety* (Cambridge, MA: MIT Press), pp. 3–32

Ansell, Chistopher, Maxwell, Rahsaan and Sicurelli, Daniela, 2006, Protesting food: NGOs and political mobilization in Europe, in: Christopher Ansell and David Vogel (Eds) *What's the Beef? The Contested Governance of European Food Safety* (Cambridge, MA: MIT Press), pp. 97–122.

Bernauer, Thomas, 2003, *Genes, Trade, and Regulation: The Seeds of Conflict in Food Biotechnology* (Princeton, NJ: Princeton University Press).

Bernauer, Thomas and Meins, Erika, 2003, Technology revolution meets policy and the market: explaining cross-national differences in agricultural biotechnology regulation. *European Journal of Political Research*, **42**, 643–683.

Carrier, Michael K., 1996, Federal preemption of common law tort awards by the Federal Food, Drug, and Cosmetic Act. *Food and Drug Law Journal*, **51**, 509–611.

Council of the European Union, 2002, Report on Enlargement, December 10 (Document 15524/1/02), pp. 130–137, available at http://register.consilium.europa.eu/pdf/en/02/st15/15524-r1en2.pdf.

European Commission, 2003, *Questions and Answers on the Regulation of GMOs in the European Union*, available at http://ec.europa.eu/food/food/biotechnology/gmfood/qanda_en.pdf (accessed June 8, 2006).

European Commission, 2006a, *Report from the Commission to the Council and the European Parliament on the Implementation of Regulation (EC) 1830/2003*, (COM 197 Final), available at http://eur-lex.europa.eu/LexUriServ/site/en/com/2006/com2006_0197en01.pdf.

European Commission, 2006b, Environment DG, *EU Policy on Biotechnology*, available at http://ec.europa.eu/environment/biotechnology/pdf/eu_policy_biotechnology.pdf.

European Food Standards Agency, 2006, Opinion of the Scientific Panel on Genetically Modified Organisms on a request by the Commission related to genetically modified crops. *The EFSA Journal*, **338**, 1–15, available at http://www.efsa.eu.int/science/gmo/gmo_opinions/1439_en.html (accessed May 25, 2006).

Gardbaum, Stephen A., 1994, The nature of preemption. *Cornell Law Review*, **79**, 767–815.

Gaskell, George, Allum, Nick and Stares, Sally, 2003, Europeans and biotechnology in 2002. *Eurobarometer 58.0* (March 2003), available at http://europa.eu.int/comm/public_opinion/archives/ebs/ebs_177_en.pdf (accessed September 27, 2003).

Gaskell, George, Thompson, Paul and Allum, Nick, 2002, Worlds apart? Public opinion in Europe and the USA, in: Martin W. Bauer and George Gaskell (Eds) *Biotechnology: The Making of a Global Controversy* (Cambridge: Cambridge University Press), pp. 351–378.

Halberstam, Daniel, 2001, Comparative federalism and the issue of commandeering, in: Kalypso Nicolaidis and Robert Howse (Eds) *The Federal Vision: Legitimacy and Levels of Governance in the United Sates and the European Union* (Oxford: Oxford University Press), pp. 213–215.

Hallman, W. K., Hebden, W. C., Cuite, C. L., Aquino, H. L. and Lang, J. T., 2004, Americans and GM food: knowledge, opinion and interest in 2004. (Publication number RR-1104-007). New Brunswick, NJ: Food Policy Institute, Cook College, Rutgers – The State University of New Jersey, available at http://www.foodprocessing.com/Media/MediaManager/RutgersGMFoodStudy.pdf (accessed May 12, 2006).

Hayes-Renshaw, Fiona, Van Aken, Wim and Wallace, Helen, 2006, When and why the EU Council of Ministers votes explicitly. *Journal of Common Market Studies*, **44**, 161–194.

Jasanoff, Sheila, 1995, Product, process, or programme: three cultures and the regulation of biotechnology, in: Martin Bauer (Ed) *Resistance to New Technology: Nuclear Power, Information Technology, and Biotechnology* (Cambridge: Cambridge University Press), pp. 311–334.

Jasanoff, Sheila, 2005, *Designs on Nature: Science and Democracy in Europe and the United States* (Princeton, NJ: Princeton University Press).

Joerges, Christian and Neyer, Jurgen, 1997, Transforming strategic interaction into deliberative problem-solving: European comitology in the foodstuffs sector. *Journal of European Public Policy*, **4**, 609–625.

Kagan, Robert A., 2001, *Adversarial Legalism: The American Way of Law* (Cambridge, MA: Harvard University Press).

Kelemen, Daniel R., 2004, *The Rules of Federalism: Institutions and Regulatory Politics in the EU and Beyond* (Cambridge, MA: Harvard University Press).

Lofstedt, Ragnar E. and Vogel, David, 2001, The changing character of regulation: a comparison of Europe and the United States. *Risk Analysis*, **21**, 399–405.

Majone, Giandomenico, 1999, The regulatory state and its legitimacy problems. *West European Politics*, **22**, 1–24.

Mendelson, Nina, 2004, Chevron and pre-emption. *Michigan Law Review*, **102**(March), 773–800.

Montpetit, Eric, 2002, Policy networks, federal arrangements, and the development of environmental regulations: a comparison of the Canadian and American agricultural sectors. *Governance*, **15**, 1–20.

Moravcsik, Andrew, 2001, Federalism in the European Union: rhetoric and reality, in: Kalypso Nicolaidis and Robert Howse (Eds) *The Federal Vision: Legitimacy and Levels of Governance in the United Sates and the European Union* (Oxford: Oxford University Press), pp. 161–190.

Poli, Sara, 2003, The emerging EU regulatory framework on genetically modified organisms: dilemmas and challenges, in: Giandomenico Majone (Ed) *Risk Regulation in the European Union: Between Enlargement and Internationalization* (Florence: Robert Shuman Centre for Advanced Studies European Union Institute), pp. 79–124.

Pollack, Mark A., 2003, Control mechanism or deliberative democracy? Two images of comitology. *Comparative Political Studies*, **36**, 125–155.

Pollack, Mark and Shaffer, Gregory C., 2009, *When Cooperation Fails: The International Law and Politics of Genetically Modified Foods* (Oxford: Oxford University Press).

Scharpf, Fritz, 1988, The joint-decision trap: lessons from German federalism and European integration. *Public Administration*, **66**, 239–278.

Schattschneider, E. E., 1960, *The Semisovereign People: A Realist's View of Democracy* (New York: Holt, Rinehart, and Winston).

Scheberle, Denise, 2005, The evolving matrix of environmental federalism and intergovernmental relationships. *Publius*, **35**(Winter), 68–86.

Sheingate, Adam D., 2006, Promotion versus precaution: the evolution of biotechnology policy in the United States. *British Journal of Political Science*, **36**, 243–268.

Sinclair, Barbara, 1989, *The Transformation of the U.S. Senate* (Baltimore: Johns Hopkins University Press).

Skogstad, Grace, 2003, Legitimacy and/or policy effectiveness? Network governance and GMO regulation in the European Union. *Journal of European Public Policy*, **10**, 321–328.

Skogstad, Grace, 2006, Regulating food safety risks in the European Union: a comparative perspective, in: Christopher Ansell and David Vogel (Eds) *What's the Beef: The Contested Governance of European Food Safety* (Cambridge, MA: MIT Press), pp. 213–236.

Strauss, Robert, 2004, The cows may be mad but the people aren't fazed. *The New York Times*, February 8, Section 14NJ, p. 3.

Taylor, Michael R., Tick, Jody S. and Sherman, Diane M., 2004, *Tending the Fields: State and Federal Roles in the Oversight of Genetically Modified Crops* (Washington, DC: Resources for the Future).

Vogel, David, 2003, The hare and the tortoise revisited: the new politics of consumer and environmental regulation in Europe. *British Journal of Political Science*, **33**, 557–580.

Vogel, David and Lynch, Diahanna, 2001, The regulation of GMOs in Europe and the United States: a case-study of contemporary European regulatory politics. Occasional Paper, Council on Foreign Relations.

Weiland, Paul S., 2000, Federal and state preemption of environmental law: a critical analysis. *Harvard Environmental Law Review*, **24**, 237–286.

Weiler, J. H. H., 2001, Federalism without constitutionalism: Europe's *Sonderweg*, in: Kalypso Nicolaidis and Robert Howse (Eds) *The Federal Vision: Legitimacy and Levels of Governance in the United States and the European Union* (Oxford: Oxford University Press), pp. 54–117.

Wood, David M. and Yesilada, Birol A., 2002, *The Emerging European Union*, 2nd edition (New York: Longman).

Appendix

Table A1. Member state populations and vote allocations under QMV

	Population	Council votes		
		Before May 1, 2004	May 1- Oct. 31, 2004	Nov. 1, 2004- Dec. 31, 2006
Germany	82.5	10	10	29
France	59.9	10	10	29
United Kingdom	59.7	10	10	29
Italy	57.9	10	10	29
Spain	42.3	8	8	27
Netherlands	16.3	5	5	13
Greece	11.0	5	5	12
Portugal	10.5	5	5	12
Belgium	10.4	5	5	12
Sweden	9.0	4	4	10
Austria	8.1	4	4	10
Denmark	5.4	3	3	7
Finland	5.2	3	3	7
Ireland	4.0	3	3	7
Luxembourg	0.5	2	2	4
Poland	38.2		8	27
Czech Republic	10.2		5	12
Hungary	10.1		5	12
Slovakia	5.4		3	7
Lithuania	3.4		3	7
Latvia	2.3		3	4
Slovenia	2.0		3	4
Estonia	1.4		3	4
Cyprus	0.7		2	4
Malta	0.4		2	3
Total Votes		87	124	321
Qualified Majority		62	88	232

Source: Council of the European Union, "Report on Enlargement", December 10, 2002 (Document 15524/1/02), pp. 130–137. Population figures: Eurostat.

Note: Entries in bottom row refer to minimum number of votes required for a qualified majority.

Direct Legislation in North America and Europe: Promoting or Restricting Biotechnology?

CHRISTINE ROTHMAYR ALLISON and FRÉDÉRIC VARONE

ABSTRACT *This article analyzes the impact of direct legislation, such as initiatives and referenda, on policies for agro-food and medical biotechnologies. Between 1980 and 2007, citizens around the world voted on biotechnology policies on 25 occasions. The analysis of these referenda and initiatives has shown that the mobilization of the popular initiative has proven to be an institution for successfully promoting more state intervention, in particular for agro-food biotechnology. Direct democracy contributed to opening up the policy-making process for interests critical towards biotechnology and thus helped to produce a more inclusive policy-making process and provided a counterweight to the influence of physicians and research interests on public policies. However, direct legislation also allowed proponents of biotechnology to promote medical research and applications.*

The development of biotechnology has been characterized as revolutionary, with the perceived potential to transform the human condition (Fukuyama 2002). Indeed, the controversy over the risks and benefits associated with biotechnology has sparked debates around the globe (Bauer and Gaskell 2002), mobilizing local, national and transnational actors in a quest to influence the resulting laws and regulations. Given the highly technical character of biotechnologies, the initial debates about regulatory activities were largely driven by governmental and non-governmental experts (e.g. Jasanoff 2005: 43–67). In some countries, policy-making remained within a rather closed network of specialized actors, primarily from industry and research. In other countries, a wider spectrum of actors were mobilized, thus opening up the debate to a broader set of issues, which produced greater competition for influence on the future governance of biotechnology and often resulted in stricter regulatory frameworks (Varone *et al.* 2007: 10–13, 2007: 274ff). Although the current literature has not identified one single institutional or partisan feature to explain why policy-making sometimes takes the form of a larger, open network with more public debate and stricter regulatory frameworks, various characteristics such as national institutional features, partisan constellations, legal and institutional traditions regarding science, cultural traditions regarding the attitudes towards science and scientific progress have all been invoked in order to explain regulatory activities or the lack thereof (see e.g. Bernauer and Meins 2003, Vogel 2004, Jasanoff 2005, Green-Pedersen 2007, Fink 2008). In this article, we focus on the role of direct legislation,[1] i.e. initiatives and referenda, as it is the one particular institution that has a propensity to radically enlarge the scope of conflict and engage a larger public (Schattschneider 1960, Baumgartner and Jones 1993: 57–125).

Direct democracy has been at the center of much normative debate in political science. Proponents of direct democracy argue that instruments of direct legislation – such as popular initiatives and referenda – enhance responsiveness, accountability and give neglected or less well-organized interests the opportunity to influence the political agenda (Cronin 1989). Critics of direct democratic procedures argue that they are too costly, that citizens are ill-informed and have no serious interest in public affairs, and are not sufficiently qualified to participate directly in political decisions, with the risk that their direct participation will lead to bad policy choices or pose a threat to minority rights (for overview see Cronin 1989: 60–124, Budge 1996: 59–83). Furthermore, direct legislation provides an opportunity for undue influence by special interest groups, thus subverting the notion of being a tool for empowering and educating regular citizens. In light of this debate, we raise three questions that have so far remained unanswered for the case of biotechnology policies: What interest groups pursue policy change in the field of biotechnology through direct legislation? How do policies change as a result thereof? By taking into account the policies resulting from direct legislation, does direct democracy give an advantage to a specific set of interests over biotechnology policies?

These research questions will be addressed through an empirical analysis of all cases worldwide of popular votes that have touched upon biotechnology issues between 1980 and the end of 2007, which produced a total of 25 cases.

There is an inherent tension in the case of biotechnology between a highly expert-driven, technical field, which is not readily accessible or understandable to non-experts, and the nature of direct legislation, whereby the right to vote is the sole requirement to select from various policy solutions. As the history of innovation shows, the emergence of new technologies is often confronted with a resistance from the general public and technological progress is no longer perceived to be only beneficial and benign (Jasanoff 2005: 13). Without an adequate regulatory framework, critics of biotechnologies will draw a picture that emphasizes the risks and potentially negative outcomes for the environment and health – or raise moral concerns in the case of biomedical applications. They may present their opposition as giving a voice to citizens who have so far been excluded from any public debate, which has been limited to a closed elite. We might therefore suppose that the mobilization of direct legislation attributes more influence to interests critical towards biotechnology. Yet these critical interests are confronted with economically powerful interests from industry and research that are likely to invest in campaigning – if direct legislation is mobilized by opponents to biotechnology – in order to promote biotechnology and limit state intervention by emphasizing the multiple benefits of the new technology. The basic question of who comes out ahead when direct legislation is mobilized in a highly technical, yet also ethically contentious policy issue, underpins our research interest.

Theoretical Framework: Mobilization and Impact of Direct Legislation

In order to formulate working hypotheses about the mobilization and impact of direct democracy we need first to define what we understand by direct democratic procedures and their relevant features. Researchers on direct democracy have proposed a variety of classifications of direct democratic instruments (Cronin 1989, Möckli 1994, Budge 1996, Gallagher and Uleri 1996, Auer and Bützer 2001). The most important criteria for classification include: who initiates a popular vote, whether it is mandatory or optional, who has control over the content of the proposal, whether it addresses statutory or constitutional law, or whether the result is binding or not (Uleri 1996). For the purpose of our research, we are interested in two criteria for classifying *binding* direct legislation: the *source* of the proposition to be voted on, i.e. who is responsible for the content of the proposition; and the *origin*, i.e. who has the power to initiate the procedure of direct legislation (Kriesi 2005: 20–21). These two criteria allow us to distinguish between three basic direct democratic procedures: the popular initiative, the optional referendum and the mandatory referendum (see Table 1).

Depending on the type of instrument, the content of the proposition might be formulated either by the government and the legislature or by the citizens. In the case of a *referendum*, the legislature and the government have formulated the law or constitutional change to be voted upon. In the case of an *initiative*, organized interests from within the citizenry sponsor the initiative and thus formulate the policy proposition.[2] In terms of who requires a popular vote, we also distinguish between two possibilities. A popular vote might be legally required, e.g. by the constitution, and is thus *mandatory*. If citizens or other political actors, such as opposition MPs or federated units, have the right to initiate a popular vote, it would be characterized as *optional*.

Table 1. Binding direct democratic procedures

Origin	Source of the content of the proposition	
	Government/Legislature	Citizens
Required by constitution or law	Mandatory referendum	–
Citizens, opposition, federated units	Optional referendum	Popular initiative

Source: Adapted from Kriesi 2005: 21.

With popular initiatives, the policy content to be voted on will be produced, whereas the optional and mandatory referenda only offer the possibility of a veto in reaction to a decision by the legislature without specifying precisely what the desired policies ought to look like. Initiatives and optional referenda require that citizens and organized interests mobilize, which requires in turn that there is sufficient interest and resources available to try to influence policies. In contrast, the mandatory referendum takes place even if there is no, or very little, interest and mobilization by social actors and its timing is entirely defined by the government. Given our stated research interest, we are mainly interested in the impact of popular initiatives and optional referenda.

In most political systems, the government also has the prerogative to consult with the public on certain questions. We label such non-binding popular votes not as a referendum but as a consultation. In many political systems, citizens also have the right to petition the government. Again, we distinguish this type of non-binding procedure from the case of a popular initiative. Both types of procedures, consultation and petition, are not covered in the discussion of mobilization and impact, as their non-binding character makes it difficult to formulate hypotheses about their use and impact on public policies.

The Mobilization of Direct Democracy

In democratic political systems, organized interests seeking to influence policy-making can make use of a broad range of possible actions, e.g. street mobilization, lobbying, or even litigation (Hilson 2002, Bouwen and McCown 2007). Different strategies are combined or employed sequentially. Institutional rules influence and define actors' strategies and affect their timing. We can therefore reasonably assume that organized interests choose a variety of strategies, and that the choice of direct legislation is influenced by a number of factors, some pertaining to the interests themselves, such as available resources, and others to the institutional rules in place, such as the conditions for successfully launching an initiative and referendum (e.g. number of signatures, the required form of the proposition, and deadlines to respect). Given the costs implied in mobilizing direct legislation, we can assume that organized interests strategically choose when and on what issue to use direct legislation and when to turn to other means.

A number of different actors have a stake in how biotechnology is governed. Industry and research interests, such as pharmaceutical and agricultural companies, biotech companies and university researchers have a high stake in research and the commercialization of biotechnologies and generally advocate for both minimal regulatory intervention and strong governmental promotion. Actors pushing for the regulation of various applications and research in biotechnologies have included environmental interest groups, consumer interest groups, groups representing the disabled, patient lobbying groups, animal protection groups as well as pro-life advocates, "alter-globalization" interests and groups engaged in developmental issues depending on the type of research and application at hand. Governments have an interest in minimizing risks while maximizing economic benefits and potential future benefits, such as cures for common diseases. To simplify the range of potential actors, we distinguish between opponents and proponents of biotechnology.

Opponents of biotechnology seek a strict regulation of biotechnology research and applications on the basis of ethical, religious, environmental and social grounds. Proponents of biotechnology have an interest in limiting state intervention, given that they are also the target groups of potential regulation.

In the 1980s, when the issue of biotechnology stated to emerge, potential target groups formed closed policy communities with the administrative agencies in charge in order to keep the issue off the political agenda and to avoid potentially stricter regulations. Another strategy for pre-empting strict regulation is to self-regulate (Rothmayr 2003, Bleiklie *et al.* 2004, Varone *et al.* 2007). Based on our earlier research, we suppose that biotechnology applications in various fields will develop without considerable state regulation as long as the opponents to biotechnologies do not mobilize in order to obtain more restrictive policies. We might, therefore, expect that *popular initiatives*, if any are launched, are used by opponents of biotechnologies in order to put the issue on the political agenda and to promote stricter regulation by the state. In the case of biotechnology policies, we suppose that initiatives would typically address and emphasize potential risks and ethical concerns of scientific research and the subsequent commercial applications of the technology.

Which interests might launch an *optional referendum* depends, in contrast to the case of the popular initiative, on the preceding policy-making processes,[3] namely which interests dominated the policy-making process and were thus able to influence policy content in their preferred direction. In the case of policies that impose unwanted restrictions on industry and research, proponents of biotechnology might turn to the optional referendum. This scenario would be likely if opponents of biotechnologies have previously succeeded in influencing policy-making through strong public mobilization or through existing networks that gave them privileged access to administrative agencies in charge. For example, we could imagine a close collaboration between pro-life groups and a Ministry of Justice, if the latter is in charge of elaborating policies in regulating Assisted Reproductive Technologies (ART) and stem cell research. The opposite scenario is also possible. In case of policies considered to be too permissive, opponents of biotechnology might get mobilized, for example, which could be the case if legislation explicitly allowed for controversial techniques, such as therapeutic cloning. Of course, the use of the referendum also depends on whether the popular initiative as an instrument is available in a political system or only the optional referendum, and what the likelihood is to successfully mobilize one or the other instrument.

These theoretical considerations lead to the formulation of a first hypothesis:

Hypothesis 1: Opponents are more likely to launch popular initiatives, while proponents are more likely to rely on self-regulation and lobbying in order to prevent state intervention. However, opponents and proponents are both likely to mobilize for optional referenda, depending on which side failed to achieve their main policy objectives in the prior policy-making process.

Policy Impact of Direct Democracy

Whether direct democracy makes a difference or not comes down to the question of whether the policy outcome would be different with or without direct legislation.

Answering this seemingly straightforward question poses several theoretical and methodological challenges. The first issue is whether direct democracy only has an impact on public policy when popular initiatives and referenda are successfully launched, or whether the fact that direct democratic institutions exist and are used on a regular basis itself has an impact on policy outcomes. Recent research on state policies in the United States from a rational choice perspective has argued that in states with direct legislation, legislatures are more responsive to voter preferences (Gerber and Hug 2001: 106). From a more institutionalist point of view, democratic legislation does not just influence governmental decision-making, but also the configuration of organized interests and their presence in the media (Höglinger 2008). Boehmke, for example, argues that direct legislation has an effect on the structure of interest representation by showing that US states with direct democracy have a larger interest group population and that direct legislation strengthens underrepresented citizen groups compared to traditional economic interests (Boehmke 2002).

In order to capture this spectrum of possible effects, the distinction of direct and indirect effects is useful. *Direct* effects flow from the actual ballot result, that is whether as a consequence of the popular vote a specific policy is or is not adopted. If a popular initiative is accepted, the direct effects consist of policies that would otherwise not have been adopted by the government. Popular initiatives that do not directly contain a proposed ballot measure, but rather just require that the government take action on a specific issue, leave considerable leverage to decision-makers, and research has also demonstrated that the supposed effects of an accepted ballot might change during the policy-implementation process (Lupia and Matsusaka 2004: 467).

In the case of an optional referendum the result is the rejection or acceptance of policies previously adopted by the legislature. The optional referendum constitutes a veto point at the end of the policy-making process. If the policy is rejected, alternative solutions might be adopted in subsequent policy-making cycles or the issue might be off the political agenda for some time.

The concept of *indirect* effects supposes that there is an impact on policy outcomes even if direct legislation has not been successfully used in a specific policy field. The literature suggests a number of such indirect effects. Linder has argued that direct democracy in the Swiss context has been important to less well-organized interests, such as women and environmentalists, by enabling them to influence the political agenda through the instrument of the popular initiative (Linder 1994). The credible threat of an optional referendum is also seen as a means of influencing ongoing political debates, encouraging the search for viable compromises before and during the parliamentary stage in order to preempt an optional referendum. If an interest group can credibly threaten to use referendum mechanisms and has successfully done so in the past, the mere possibility of the successful use of a referendum could have an impact on the adopted policies (Neidhardt 1970, Linder 1994, Kriesi 2005, Papadoupoulos 1997, 2001). Direct legislation can therefore "open doors" to the policy-making process independently of the final ballot result. Furthermore, direct legislation can also have an important function for the organizations that launch them, in terms of internal mobilization within a social movement, or in order to profile a political party in view of upcoming elections (Linder 1994). For our analysis we distinguish two categories of impacts: "substantial effects" on the content of the policy output (direct effects) and "procedural effects" (indirect effects) on the policy-making process through agenda-setting, problem-framing, opening up the public debate and influencing ongoing debates and negotiations.

If we compare initiatives and referenda as "institutional venues" (Baumgartner and Jones 1993: 25ff) for influencing policy-making processes, initiatives – at least in their direct version – are more powerful in terms of directly influencing the content of policies into the preferred direction, because they allow for the precise definition of the policy solution to be adopted. The agenda-setting effects are also more important, and initiatives can be launched at any point in the policy process. The credible threat of a referendum, early in the policy-making process, might have some anticipatory effects on the decision-making process, but it could always be ignored, given that signatures have yet to be collected. Thus, our second hypothesis is based on the assumption that initiatives, if successfully launched, have a greater impact on the policy-making process and the outcome. By impact we mean *direct substantial* as well as *indirect procedural* influence on public policy-making.

Hypothesis 2: If opponents of biotechnology successfully launch an initiative, they are more successful in influencing public policies according to their preferences of regulating biotechnologies than if they – or the proponents – launch an optional referendum.

Case Selection and Empirical Analysis

An obvious strategy for analyzing the impact of direct democracy on biotechnology policies would be to compare regulation of biotechnologies in countries with direct democracy against those without (Gerber and Hug 2001: 95ff), while taking into account other relevant factors such as voter preferences, the size of the biotechnology industry, the composition of the government, or characteristics of key interest groups. For the case of policy fields where regulation is mainly decided on the national level, which is normally the case for biotechnology, this is not feasible, due to the limited number of countries where direct democracy is used on a regular basis on the *national* level, without being restricted to a few constitutional issues or questions related to European integration (Switzerland, Italy). In this article, therefore, we have chosen another strategy, namely to identify all instances of direct legislation from around the world in order to analyze the direct substantial effects of the vote and, where possible, the indirect procedural effects. In order to determine the impact of direct democracy, i.e. whether the policy outcome would be different with or without direct legislation, we will rely on counterfactual reasoning (Gerber and Hug 2001: 95–98, Fontana *et al.* 2008).

In order to test our two hypotheses, we have conducted extensive research to identify all instances of popular votes on biotechnology issues from around the world. This research included systematic keyword research in two databases[4] combined with an extensive search across internet resources and a thorough review of the relevant literature. Our research identified 25 instances of *popular votes* related to biotechnology issues.[5] We found a total of 16 popular initiatives, six of which were from Switzerland[6] and 10 from the United States. Three of the cases were optional referenda from Switzerland, Italy and Slovenia. From the remaining six cases, five were mandatory referenda in the USA. The last case is a referendum in Switzerland that was not mandatory, but does not meet our criteria for an optional referendum, as it was initiated by the government. These six cases will not be the object of detailed analysis from the aforementioned reasons (see section on theoretical framework).

Breaking down the 25 cases in terms of policy issues, we found 11 cases dealt with red biotechnologies, five addressed stem cell research and five concerned more general issues within assisted reproductive technologies, and one dealt with genetic engineering. Nine cases were focused on agricultural biotechnologies and the remaining five cases dealt with research issues and applications of biotechnology in general.

Not surprisingly, three of the four countries are from those in which direct democratic instruments are used on a regular basis, i.e. Switzerland, the United States and Italy. As a result, we are comparing policy-making processes in four countries: with 15 cases of popular votes from the United States, seven from Switzerland, and one each from Italy and Slovenia. All four countries have very different political systems. Having to adopt a most different system design for our empirical studies is not in itself a problem as previous comparisons of biotechnology policies have shown that conventional classifications of countries according to institutional features (e.g. unitary versus federal state, majoritarian versus consensus democracies, etc.) are of little help in explaining variation in policies across countries (e.g. Rothmayr et al. 2005; Varone et al. 2006, 2007). The values, beliefs and interests of policy actors, the policy networks that they build up, as well as the decision-making arenas that they mobilize appeared to be more important than the formal institutional framework.

Comparing the Effects of Direct Democracy

Switzerland: Adopting Restrictive Regulation through Direct Legislation

In *Switzerland* the constitution provides for three categories of direct democratic instruments on the federal level. First of all, the popular initiative allows for a total or partial revision of the constitution and can either present a *formulated draft* of the policy – which has so far always been the case – or a *general suggestion* for the direction of the policy. Launching an initiative requires 100,000 signatures; a successful initiative requires a double majority of both the people and the cantons to pass.[7] In the case of a formulated draft, parliament can submit a counter-proposal on which the citizens vote at the same time as the initiative, if the initiative has not been withdrawn.[8] There are also two types of referendum: the mandatory and the optional. A mandatory referendum is required in cases of revision of the constitution, entry into international organizations and urgent laws under certain conditions; a simple majority is required to pass. For federal statutes, urgent statutes exceeding one year of validity and international treaties under certain conditions, 50,000 citizens or eight cantons may launch an optional referendum, also requiring a simple majority to pass. These direct democratic instruments exist on the federal, cantonal and local levels.

In both the ART and GMO sectors, Switzerland has adopted very restrictive policies (Rothmayr and Serdült 2004; Rothmayr 2008). Federal ART policies (Federal Constitution: Article 119, Federal Law on Assisted Reproduction, FmedG: SR: 814.90) prohibit a number of techniques such as egg and embryo donation, pre-implantation diagnostics, cryopreservation of embryos,[9] surrogate motherhood, genetic engineering on gametes, germ cells and embryos, therapeutic and reproductive cloning. Producing an embryo solely for research purposes is prohibited and stem cells used for research can only be derived under specific conditions from leftover embryos (Federal Law on Stem Cell Research, StFG, SR 810.31).

The Swiss design for *GMOs in the agro-food* sector (Federal Constitution: Article 120, Federal Law on Gene Technology, SR 814.91) is strongly based on the precautionary principle. The contained use, deliberate release, and production and distribution of GMOs and products containing GMOs are submitted to strict procedures of authorization, labeling (1% threshold)[10] and traceability, in order to guarantee freedom of choice and transparent information to consumers. Furthermore, since November 2005, there is in place a five-year moratorium on GMOs in Swiss agriculture.

On the federal level, Swiss citizens voted five times on legislative projects related to biotechnology (see Table 2) – four initiatives and one popular (in Swiss terminology, an optional) referendum. One of the initiatives passed and the counter-proposal to another initiative was accepted. The two other initiatives and the referendum failed. All four initiatives and the one optional referendum were launched by interests critical to ART and GMO and were aimed at rendering policies more restrictive. We begin with an analysis of the two successful initiatives, which both had direct substantial effects on biotechnology policies, and then turn to the failed initiatives and the referendum in order to discuss whether they had some more indirect, procedural effects.

Consumer protection and citizen advocate groups launched the *Beobachterinitiative* in the mid 1980s, which was the first initiative to push the issue of biotechnology and ART onto the federal agenda. The goal of the initiative was to amend the federal constitution in order to protect humans and their environment from the potential negative effects of biotechnologies. The interests sponsoring the initiative perceived biotechnology as a potentially dangerous new technology, and in their proposition for a constitutional amendment they emphasized the risks and not the potential benefits of red and green biotechnologies. Parliament formulated a counter-proposal to the initiative that also emphasized the potential risks and the need for protection from potential negative consequences. This view of biotechnology translated into a number of prohibitions of red biotechnology applications, namely cloning of human embryos, but also egg and embryo donation. The counter-proposal satisfied the sponsors, who withdrew the initiative. The counter-proposal was accepted in a popular vote in 1992. All Swiss legislation on biotechnology adopted since is based on this constitutional article and basically restates the idea that biotechnology is a potentially dangerous technology and needs to be restrictively regulated. The initial negative framing of biotechnology, written into the constitution by the *Beobachterinitiative*, persists today for medical as well as agro-food biotechnology. The substantial impact of the initiative on policy content, hence, exceeds the initial phase of policy-making.

Table 2. Initiatives and referenda for ART and GMO in Switzerland

Year of vote	Title	Form[1]	Sponsors (H1)	Impact (H2)
1992	Constitutional article resulting from 'Beobachterinitiative'	Initiative[1]	Opponents	Accepted: direct substantial effects towards restrictive policies
1998	'Gene-Protection Initiative'	Initiative	Opponents	Rejected: indirect procedural effects towards restrictive policies
2000	'Initiative for Procreation respecting Human Dignity'	Initiative	Opponents	Rejected: indirect procedural effects towards restrictive policies
2002	Referendum against Federal Law on Stem Cell Research	Optional referendum	Opponents	Rejected: no substantial or procedural effects
2005	'Initiative for foods from gene-technology-free agriculture'	Initiative	Opponents	Accepted: direct substantial effects towards restrictive policies
1993	Basel-Stadt: Law on assisted reproduction	Referendum[2]	Government	Law accepted, but no direct substantial effect as the core provisions of the law were later invalidated by Swiss Federal Supreme Court
1988	Glarus: assisted reproduction	Initiative (citizen assembly)	Opponents	Accepted: direct substantial effects toward restrictive policies nullified through Supreme Court decision
1993	Thurgau: Initiative to prohibit genetic engineering on humans	Initiative	Opponents	Law adopted by parliament: indirect procedural effects towards restrictive policies

Notes: [1]The Swiss people voted on the counter-proposal to the initiative, which had been adopted by the legislature after the initiative was withdrawn. [2]The referendum was decided by the government, but was not mandatory.

The second successful initiative, 'Initiative for foods from gene-technology-free agriculture', also had direct substantial effects on Swiss policies on GMOs in the agro-food sector. It instituted a five-year moratorium for GMOs in Swiss agriculture, rendering Swiss policies more restrictive than those of its EU neighbors. The effective impact on Swiss agriculture remained limited. So far, no genetically modified crops have been planted in Switzerland and only a few small-scale experimental scientific releases have been approved since 1990. In addition, the two major food distributors had already banned all GM food from their shelves by the end of the 1990s. The moratorium merely codified existing practices.

It would be mistaken to think that the two initiatives that were rejected did not have an impact on the policy-making processes. The 'Gene Protection Initiative' sought to prohibit genetically modified animals, the deliberate release of GMOs, and the patenting of genetically modified animals and plants. The 'Initiative for Procreation respecting Human Dignity' in turn wanted to prohibit in-vitro fertilization (IVF) and insemination by donor in the constitution. In fact, the two initiatives were a "pledge" in negotiating policy solutions in the pre-parliamentary and parliamentary stages (Linder 1994, Papadopoulos 1997, 2001) for ART and GMOs alike. This was possible, because the governmental parties were divided over some of the issues, and majorities were not clear-cut. In the case of ART, the Federal Council[11] proposed a restrictive federal law on ART in order to counteract the second popular initiative, the 'Initiative for Procreation respecting Human Dignity' that asked for total prohibitions of IVF and gamete donation in the federal constitution. In the case of the 'Gene Protection Initiative', the use of the popular initiative also influenced ongoing legislative processes such as the revision of the Federal Environmental Protection Law (SR 814.01) in 1995 and the subsequent adoption of various ordinances, as well as the elaboration of the Federal Law on Gene Technology (SR 817.91). It forced the government to rapidly address existing legal gaps and sustained pressure for strictly regulating biotechnology. The impact of these two initiatives was indirect by lending support to interests in favor of restrictive policies. At the same time, they did not succeed in changing the constitution in an even more restrictive direction. This is important to note, as the adoption of the two initiatives would have had long-lasting effects on future legislation, by prohibiting fundamental research in crucial areas such as embryonic stem cell research and pharmaceutical biotechnology research using animals.

The optional referendum has been mobilized on only one occasion. Religious and anti-abortion groups launched an optional referendum in order to veto the embryonic stem cell research law, which allowed the use of leftover embryos for deriving stem cells. The referendum did not pass. We did not find any indication that this referendum had any substantial or procedural effects. The threat of a referendum can influence deliberations under the condition that the referendum has a good chance to pass. The odds were not in favor of the referendum for three reasons. First of all, the law was broadly supported by the main political parties. As prior research has demonstrated, clear support by the major parties is a crucial explanatory factor for rejecting a referendum (Sciarini 2007: 465–499). In addition, the law was supported by several economically powerful actors, such as the pharmaceutical industry, which had just won the battle around the Gene Protection Initiative, while the anti-abortion groups had just recently lost the referendum on abortion. Under these circumstances, the threat of a referendum did not weigh into the adoption of the stem cell research law by the legislature.

Our first hypothesis stipulates that popular initiatives are launched by opponents, whereas referenda are launched by proponents and opponents alike. In the Swiss case, all four initiatives and the one optional referendum were launched by interests critical towards ART and GMO, which supports our first hypothesis. The analysis on the federal level also revealed that anti-biotechnology interest groups successfully used popular initiatives to influence the policy design in the direction of restrictive policies. For the one occasion where they mobilized the optional referendum we could not find any effect on the policy-making process. Our second hypothesis is thus also supported by our findings.

The cases on the cantonal level equally support hypotheses 1 and 2. In Switzerland, policy-making for biotechnology started out in the 1980s on the cantonal level. All the laws adopted on the cantonal level were later replaced by federal legislation and in some cases invalidated by the Swiss Federal Supreme Court. On the cantonal level, citizens were called to vote on biotechnology issues on three occasions. In the canton of Basel City citizens voted in 1991 on a very restrictive law on ART, which had been elaborated by the cantonal parliament and which was submitted to an extraordinary mandatory referendum. It was accepted with a clear majority but declared largely unconstitutional by the Swiss Federal Supreme Court two years later (BGE 119 Ia 460). In the canton of Thurgau, a popular initiative sought to prohibit genetic engineering on embryos and gametes. On the basis of the initiative, the cantonal parliament adopted a law prohibiting genetic modifications on embryos and gametes in 1993. The third canton with a popular vote is the canton of Glarus. In the late 1980s, this very small Swiss canton still decided on cantonal laws through a yearly citizen's assembly (Landsgemeinde). Following a proposition by the Christian Democrats, the citizen assembly, in 1988, prohibited any type of assisted reproductive technology except for inseminations (without donor). This law became unconstitutional after a decisions of the Swiss Federal Supreme Court in 1989 that declared a similar law of the canton of St. Gallen to be largely unconstitutional (BGE 115 1a 234). The cases of St. Gallen and Basel-Stadt must be seen as precursors to the restrictive direction that federal legislation would adopt in the future. These cantonal policies together with the Supreme Court decisions influenced policy-making at the federal level. On the one hand, they reinforced the sense of urgency for the adoption of federal policies. On the other hand, the decisions of the Federal Supreme Court had to a certain degree a moderating effect on the federal debates (Rothmayr 1999). Thus, legal action counteracted the effects of direct legislation to a large degree.

The United States: Promoting Biomedical Applications

Direct democratic institutions in the US are limited to the state and local levels. A significant number of US states have direct democratic institutions similar to those in Switzerland. Popular initiatives, present in 24 states, can take a direct or indirect form, i.e. legislators have the possibility of amending or changing a proposition before the ballot in the indirect case, and they can be used to adopt statutory or constitutional law or both. The time spans, from around 60 days to no limits, and the number of required signatures, 2–15 per cent of the electorate in a previous election, vary greatly between states, but majority rule applies with a few exceptions. The optional referendum is present in 24 states, requiring signatures of 2–15 per cent of the electorate to be collected within a typical time span of 90 days after a law has been passed. In most states, constitutional changes are subject to a mandatory referendum.

In the case of assisted reproductive technology and stem cell research (Goggin and Orth 2004, Garon and Montpetit 2007) the policies on the federal level are limited to restricting public funding for stem cell research and reporting requirements for Fertility Clinics (Fertility Clinic Success Rate and Certification Act). In 2001, the Bush administration limited federal public funding of embryonic stem cell research to stem cells derived from leftover embryos before August 2001, created for procreation and donated with informed consent that did not imply any financial compensation. Attempts to prohibit reproductive or therapeutic cloning on the federal level have up to now all failed. In contrast, on the state level, some states have introduced bans on cloning.[12] Therapeutic and reproductive cloning is prohibited in Arkansas, Indiana, Iowa, Michigan, North Dakota, South Dakota, and Virginia.[13] Reproductive cloning is also prohibited in Rhode Island, Massachusetts, Connecticut, California, New Jersey and Missouri. In addition, with respect to the practice of ART, a few states have addressed questions such as informed consent, donation and parentage issues, i.e. California, Colorado, Florida, Louisiana, North Dakota, Oklahoma, Texas, Utah, Virginia, Washington and Wyoming.

The overall picture is not that different when it comes to GMOs in the agro-food sector, where federal and state policies have so far remained rather permissive (Sheingate 2004, Taylor *et al.* 2004, Garon and Montpetit 2007). Policy programs adopted before biotechnology became a salient issue continue to regulate GMOs in the agro-food sector on the federal and state levels, including programs for plant protection, pesticides and food safety. For almost all GM plants, the only restriction is a notification procedure whereby developers must inform the US Department of Agriculture about any releases. Government permits are only required for products listed as a plant pest (Environmental Protection Agency and Animal and Plant Health Inspection Service). With respect to GM food, the Food and Drug Administration implements a voluntary notification procedure for GM food prior to commercialization. Policies on the state level have also remained permissive.[14] Vermont's new policy, which shifts liability in cases of contamination from the farmers to manufacturers, constitutes a modest policy change in a more restrictive direction. With respect to food safety, two states have adopted regulation on labeling food. In Maine, GMO-free foods (1% threshold) can be labeled as such, if desired. Alaska has passed a bill for the mandatory labeling of genetically engineered fish, a novelty for the US.

In the US, popular initiatives have only recently, since 2002, become an instrument for opponents and proponents of biotechnology (see Table 3). Three initiatives on the state level address embryo and stem cell research, and seven initiatives, one on the state level and six on the county level, deal with agro-food biotechnology. The remaining five cases were mandatory referenda on issuing bonds for biotechnology research and applications. As in the Swiss case, popular initiatives

Table 3. Initiatives and optional referendums in the USA since 1980

Year of vote	Title	Form	Sponsors (H1)	Impact (H2)
1998	Maine: General Fund Bond Issue for Development and Research	Mandatory referendum	–	Accepted: direct substantial effects by providing funding for biotechnology research and development
2002	Oregon: Labeling GM Food	Initiative	Opponents	Failed: no direct substantial or indirect procedural effects
2002	Oregon: Bonds for OHSU medical research and biotechnology opportunities	Mandatory referendum	–	Accepted: direct substantial effects by providing funding for biotechnology research and development
2004	California: Stem cell research	Initiative	Proponents	Accepted: direct substantial effects towards permissive policies
2004	Rhode Island: Bonds for University of Rhode Island Center for Biotechnology and Life Sciences	Mandatory referendum	–	Accepted: direct substantial effects by providing funding for biotechnology research and development
2006	Missouri: Stem cell research	Initiative	Proponents	Accepted: direct substantial effects towards permissive policies
2007	Maine: Bond Issue: Economic Development and Job Creation	Mandatory referendum	–	Accepted: direct substantial effects by providing funding for biotechnology research and development
2007	New Jersey: Stem Cell Research Bond Issue	Mandatory referendum	–	Failed: no direct substantial or indirect procedural effects
2008	Michigan: Permitting Human Embryo and Embryonic Stem Cell Research	Initiative	Proponents	Accepted: direct substantial effects towards permissive policies
2004	California, Mendocino County GE-free agriculture	Initiative	Opponents	Accepted: direct substantial effects towards restrictive policies and emulation effects
2004	California, Marin County GE-free agriculture	Initiative	Opponents	Accepted: direct substantial effects towards restrictive policies and emulation effects
2004	California, Humboldt County GE-free agriculture	Initiative	Opponents	Failed: no direct substantial or indirect procedural effects, but emulation effects
2004	California, Butte county GE-free agriculture	Initiative	Opponents	Failed: no direct substantial or indirect procedural effects, but emulation effects
2004	California, San Louis Obispo County GE-free agriculture	Initiative	Opponents	Failed: no direct substantial or indirect procedural effects, but emulation effects
2005	California, Sonoma county GE-free agriculture	Initiative	Opponents	Failed: no direct substantial or indirect procedural effects, but emulation effects

addressing agro-food biotechnology sought to establish more restrictive regulations and were sponsored by interests opposing biotechnology. The initiative in Oregon sought to introduce mandatory labeling for GM food. In six California counties popular initiatives sought to establish a Genetic Engineering-free agriculture. In Switzerland, the direct and indirect effects of popular initiatives have contributed to adopting both policies. To the contrary, in the US context, popular initiatives on agro-food biotechnology had very limited success. Only two of the local initiatives passed and we can say that the direct effects on regulating agro-food biotechnology were very modest, geographically limited, and only local. Popular initiatives are, however, not the only instrument for banning GM crop and animals on the county level. One county (Trinity) and two cities (Arcata, Point Arena) have adopted bans through regular legislative processes. As a reaction to the local GE-free movement, several US states have prohibited the local level from regulating biotechnology.[15] In California, however, such an attempt to pass a bill pre-empting counties and cities from banning GMOs died on the order paper.

Three popular initiatives on the state level concerned embryonic stem cell research (California, Missouri, Michigan). The stem cell research initiatives were sponsored by proponents of stem cell research in order to formally permit this type of research and to provide for state funding. All three initiatives passed. The three stem cell initiatives had direct substantial effects on state policies. In the case of Missouri, the initiative led to a prohibition of cloning in the state constitution, but otherwise "legalized" stem cell research in accordance with federal law. The new California policies on stem cell research aim at promoting research through special funding for this type of research. The successful Michigan initiative amended the state constitution in order to allow for stem cell research and regulate it, by limiting to 14 days the period during which stem cells can be derived from embryos that have been created for fertility treatment, are not suitable for implantation or were left over from treatment and have been donated by patients for this purpose. In particular, the California initiative, and more recently the Michigan case, have been widely reported in the media. It is, however, difficult to isolate possible indirect effects of these initiatives, in terms of agenda-setting in other states, from other relevant agenda-setting factors. Since the Bush government's decision to ban federal funding, the issue of stem cell research has become a highly publicized election issue. Popular initiatives contribute to the mediatization of the issue, but are only one among other media events. Policies promoting stem cell research have been adopted without direct legislation in other states, such as New Jersey (2004) or Ohio (2005).

The issuing of bonds for financing research on biotechnology has been subject to a mandatory referendum in five states (Maine, Oregon, Rhode Island, and New Jersey). Some of these bonds were directed specifically towards stem cell research, whereas others proposed financing research activities in general, with biotechnology being just one among other types of research. The proposition was rejected in only one of the five cases (New Jersey).

The findings only partially support our first hypothesis. The popular initiative is the instrument of opponents to green biotechnology and for proponents of red biotechnology. Successful initiatives have contributed to push state and local policies in the opposite direction of national policies. In the case of agro-food biotechnology initiatives have established much more restrictive policies, however, only in two

California counties. As for stem cell research a number of states chose to actively promote stem cell research through direct legislation. Regarding our second hypothesis, we have not found any optional referenda and thus cannot compare the impact of the two instruments.

Italy and Slovenia: Challenging Existing Policies on Assisted Reproductive Technologies

The options for using direct democracy in Italy and Slovenia are more modest compared to states in the US and to Switzerland. In Italy, an optional referendum can be held for the total or partial repeal of a law, whenever it is requested by 500,000 voters (=1% of the electorate) or by five regional councils (article 75 of the Italian Constitution). The result of a referendum is legally binding only if it receives a majority of the votes cast and a participation quorum of 50 per cent.

Until 2004, the Italian policy on assisted reproduction was among the most permissive in the world (Ramjoué and Klöti 2004). This situation was frequently labeled as the lawless "Far West" of fertility treatments or as a "free bioethical marketplace". However, after decades of failed legislative attempts, the center-right dominated legislature that was elected in May 2001 eventually adopted a law entitled "Norms regarding medically assisted reproduction".[16] In February 2004, the law was passed by a slim majority (277 MPs in favor, 222 against), with part of the opposition (mostly Catholics) siding with the center-right government. This new ART policy is one of the most restrictive in Europe. It bans research on stem cells from leftover embryos, pre-implantation diagnosis for preventing genetic diseases, artificial insemination with an outside donor, and it denies single women or same-sex couples access to ART.

The left libertarian Radical Party launched an abrogative referendum (according to Article 75 of the Constitution) against this law, with the support of various women's groups and lawmakers. This anti-establishment and anti-Catholic party has promoted a large number of referenda, taking on the characteristics of a "referendum party", attempting "to win, through referendum campaigns, the potential for coalition or blackmail potential that it was unsuccessful in gaining through elections" (Uleri 2002: 878). The Radical Party easily collected approximately 4 million signatures by the end of September 2004, far more than the 500,000 required.

In January 2005, the Italian Constitutional Court rejected the referendum on the entire law, as proposed by the Radical Party, but decided that voters had the right to decide by referendum the following four issues: (a) the rights given to a human embryo; (b) the limits placed on research involving embryos; (c) the fertilization of a maximum of three embryos during each IVF, as well as the requirement for the woman to have all three embryos implanted; and, finally, (d) the ban on IVF for couples who use sperm or egg donors.

The governmental parties could have pre-empted the referendum by passing a different version of the law in Parliament. But this did not take place as many political parties and party coalitions were internally divided. Both Prime Minister Silvio Berlusconi and Romano Prodi, the leader of the opposition, supported the NO campaign (i.e. to maintain the law unmodified). Gianfranco Fini, deputy prime minister, foreign affairs minister and president of the right-wing party Alleanza Nazionale, campaigned in support of the referendum, while Francesco Rutelli, former center-left prime minister, opted for abstention. Furthermore, as Uleri notes in the conclusion of his empirical analysis of referendum practices in Italy until 2000, the influence of political parties in referendum campaigns is generally limited when dealing with ethical issues (e.g. previous referenda on divorce and abortion).

In contrast, the Roman Catholic Church invested considerable resources in campaigning, urging Italians to abstain or to vote NO. In his first intervention in Italian politics, on 31 May 2005, Pope Benedetto XVI endorsed the efforts of Cardinal Camillo Ruini, head of Italy's Bishops' conference, who argued that staying away from the polls could be an act of defending human life. On the opposite side, more than 100 scientists and fertility physicians, including Nobel Laureates, wrote a statement in which they urged citizens to vote "YES" to the rights of women, the freedom of research and a secular Italian state. However, researchers were split over the referendum question related to embryo research.

According to the constitutional referendum rules, at least 50 per cent of voters must participate in order for the results to be considered legitimate. The popular vote was organized on June 12 and 13, 2005: the turnout was only 26 per cent with participation being higher in the northern regions and in big cities such as Rome and Milan. More than 80 per cent of the voters supported the abrogation of the articles of the law submitted to the referendum. However, the results of the referendum were declared void failing electorate turnout of more than 50 per cent. Thus, the Radical Party and the proponents of a more liberal ART policy failed to overturn the restrictive 2004 law. This result is mostly interpreted as a success for the Catholic Church (Fenton 2006), in comparison to its two previous crushing defeats, when it lost in referenda allowing divorce (1974, turnout: 88%, YES: 60%) and de-criminalizing abortion (1981, turnout: 80%, YES: 88%).

This brief empirical analysis of the Italian referendum supports the first and second hypotheses (see Table 4). The proponents of a more permissive ART policy (than the restrictive law enacted in 2004) successfully launched an abrogative referendum, but they eventually lost as the participation quorum of 50 per cent was not reached.

In the case of Slovenia, direct legislation is not a regularly used instrument as is the case for Italy. Article 90 of the Slovenian Constitution states that an optional referendum shall be held to repeal a law whenever it is requested either by one-third of the MPs of the National Council or by 40,000 voters. The first time that Slovenes were ever called upon to vote in an optional referendum, they opted for more restrictive policies governing assisted reproduction.

In July 1977, the former Yugoslavia adopted a permissive law on health measures for implementing the right of free choice concerning the birth of a child.[17] Articles 31, 32 and 34 of this law granted the right to medical assistance for infertility treatment and to artificial insemination to all women, regardless of the medical indication of fertility or infertility. In 1982, the Constitutional Court ruled in a case that this right is an individual right rather than a right of spouses or of couples.[18]

After gaining its political independence (i.e. advisory referendum in December 1990), the Republic of Slovenia enacted its own law on infertility treatment and ART procedures. This policy change represented a step backward, as its article 5 states

Table 4. Referenda for ART in Italy and Slovenia

Country/ Year of vote	Title	Form	Sponsors (H1)	Impacts (H2)
Italy 2005	Referendum against the "law regulating medically assisted reproduction"	Optional referendum	Proponents	Rejected (vote not valid): no direct substantial or indirect procedural effects
Slovenia 2001	Referendum against the "law on infertility treatment and ART procedures"	Optional referendum	Opponents	Accepted (law rejected): direct substantial effects towards restrictive policies

that only a man and a woman living in wedlock or in a marriage-like relationship have access to ART. However, this more restrictive rule was then challenged by the parliamentary Committee on Health, Labor, Family, Social Affairs and the Disabled. Despite the opposition of the National Committee for Medical Ethics, this Committee proposed, in June 2000, that the National Assembly support an amendment, according to which single women are also eligible for ART treatments. In March 2001, the Faculty of Moral Theology in Ljubljana openly expressed its disapproval of the amendment. Such a legislative modification would open the door to irresponsible parenting of single or even same-sex couples. In the same vein, the Family Initiative Association wrote in an open letter to MPs that the amendment would reduce the child to a woman's right. The National Organization of Physicians also came out against the proposal.

In April 2001, the National Assembly discussed the legislative proposal, which was seen as morally objectionable by MPs from the Slovenian National Party (SNP), the Social Democratic Party (SDS), the New Slovenian Party (NSi) and the Slovenian People's Party (SLS) and Slovenian Christian Democrats (SKD). All four parties rejected the amendment taking the view that it destroyed the traditional family, subordinated the child's rights to the wishes of a single woman, and did not consider the opposing views of the medical profession. On April 19, 2001, the parliament eventually passed changes to the Slovenian law on infertility treatment and ART procedures (43 MPs in favor, 2 against, and 45 abstaining). The two major governmental parties, Liberal Democracy of Slovenia (LDS) and United List of Social Democrats (ZLSD), strongly supported the legislative change, which was an integral part of the coalition agreement negotiated after the election of November 2000 by then-Prime Minister Janez Drnovsek (LDS).

The parliamentary opposition managed, however, to force a legislative referendum by gaining the backing of 34 MPS in the 90-seat parliament. The popular vote was set to take place in June 2001. Several interest groups and politicians were campaigning against or in favor of the amended law. The National Organization of

Physicians and an extended Professional College for Gynecology and the Slovene Bishop Conference, the Conference of Religious Orders and the Council of Catholic Laymen of Slovenia appealed to citizens to vote against the law. On the opposing side, a Committee for Freedom of Choice, several women's organizations, the Human Rights Ombudsman and, last but not least, the Prime Minister and Health Minister pointed out that the amendment would restore the rights of women that had previously existed (under the law of 1977); its rejection by popular vote would thus mean nothing less than a degradation of the democratic values and rights established in Slovenia.

The referendum was held on June 17, 2001. It was the first time that Slovenian citizens were called on to decide on a law already adopted by the country's legislative body. The turnout was a low 35.7 per cent; however, the Slovenian constitution does not require a participation quorum of 50 per cent (as is the case in Italy) so the referendum was valid. Seventy-three per cent of voters said NO, overturning the two-month-old law that had expanded access to ART from only married women to single women as well.

In summary, the first hypothesis is clearly supported by these empirical findings. Opponents to a broader access to ART launched the legislative referendum at a low cost (as it only requires 34 out 90 MPS) and knowing that the Catholic Church as well as the medical profession would support them during the campaign. The second hypothesis is not supported as the opponents eventually won the referendum.

Comparison and Conclusion

The empirical data reveals that the mobilization of the popular initiative has proven to be an institution for successfully promoting more state intervention, in particular for agro-food biotechnology. Direct democracy contributed to opening up the policy-making process for interests critical to biotechnology and thus contributed to a more inclusive policy-making process and provided a counterweight to the influence of physicians and research interests on public policies. At the same time, it also allowed interests in favor of biotechnology to promote medical research and applications, thus policy change also went in the direction of promoting research in and the application of biotechnology.

Our *first hypothesis* stipulated that popular initiatives would mainly be mobilized by interests critical to biotechnology, while optional referenda are used by both proponents and opponents depending on the result of the previous policy-making process. This hypothesis has been supported by our data for the majority of the cases. In 13 out of 16 *popular initiatives*, the sponsors were opponents to biotechnology. Except for one initiative, all addressed issues related to agro-food biotechnology. One initiative dealt with green and red biotechnology issues at the same time. In Switzerland, popular initiatives and direct legislation were exclusively mobilized by organized interests critical of green and red biotechnology. In contrast, in the United States, popular initiatives were also used by proponents of biotechnology, more precisely interests seeking to adopt policies promoting stem cell research. Optional referenda (three cases) were mobilized by opponents (one case in Slovenia and one in Switzerland) and proponents (one case in Italy) alike, as predicted by our first hypothesis. In the case of Switzerland and Slovenia, the optional referendum sought to change legislation adopted by parliament regarding assisted reproduction and stem-cell research that opponents judged too permissive or liberal. In the case of Italy, the very restrictive law on assisted reproduction was challenged by interests favoring a more moderate state intervention. Overall, the findings support our first hypothesis. The comparative analysis confirms that the popular initiative is primarily the instrument of opponents to biotechnology. However, as the US cases of stem cell research indicate, proponents also turn to direct legislation and accordingly initiatives can also seek policies promoting and supporting research and application.

The *second* hypothesis stated that the popular initiative, if successfully mobilized, is a more powerful tool for opponents compared to the optional referendum in order to influence orientation of public policies. The results neither support nor disconfirm the hypotheses clearly. Referenda and initiatives are unequally distributed across the four countries. There were no optional referenda related to biotechnology in the United States while there were only optional referenda in Slovenia and Italy. In Switzerland, there were six initiatives and only one optional referendum. This unequal distribution can be explained by the institutional characteristics, as well as the specificities, of the policy-making process. Slovenia and Italy do not provide for popular initiatives on the national level. In the United States, policies on the state level have remained modest in scope and regulatory intervention compared to Europe, hence creating limited opportunity to turn to the optional referendum.

Popular initiatives and optional referenda are also unevenly distributed across the policy issues. All optional referenda dealt with assisted reproduction and stem cell research in the three European countries. Again institutional and policy process-specific variables help an understanding of this pattern. European Union directives govern GMOs in Slovenia and Italy. The non-conforming transposition of EU law into national law would rather be challenged in court or by the EU Commission itself than through direct democratic procedures. To the contrary, assisted reproduction has remained a national issue, and a great number of European states have legislated in this area, many, however, considerably less restrictive than Italy, Switzerland and Slovenia.

Other factors might contribute to the patterns of many popular initiatives versus few referenda and the unequal distribution across policy issues. There were, however, limits to what we could investigate in this research. For example, we did not include any analysis of the resources (e.g. expertise, finances, coalition building, etc.), and overall political strategies of proponents and opponents of biotechnology, which would allow us to better understand when and why organized interests turn to direct legislation. Furthermore, biotechnology has only recently emerged as a domain of policy-making. As research on the number of applications evolves, so do political debates and actor networks. The use of initiatives might be more typical for these initial decades of policy-making and it remains to be seen whether the patterns of mobilization and the use of initiatives versus referenda found in our study will remain the same over the coming decades.

Even though we cannot satisfactorily compare the effects of the two types of direct legislation, the popular initiative and the referendum, we can assess the overall impact of direct legislation on biotechnology policies. In two out of three cases the *optional referendum* did not have any direct impact on the content of the adopted policies, because they failed (in Switzerland and Italy). In the third case of Slovenia, however, the referendum was accepted and led to more restrictive ART policies. The question discussed in Slovenia was whether single women and consequently lesbian couples should be allowed to use assisted reproduction to start a family. The issue at stake in Slovenia is what we might label a morality policy. Such policies concern political conflicts over personal values of a moral nature, regarding life, personal identity and religious beliefs (Mooney 2001, Smith and Tatalovich 2003). Research on direct legislation for social issues in the US has demonstrated a conservative bias of direct democracy (Matsusaka 2007). The case of Slovenia supports these findings, while the successful initiatives on stem cell research in the US that succeeded in establishing liberal policies, disconfirm them. From a comparative perspective, we know that there are a number of countries that have adopted very restrictive assisted reproduction or embryonic stem cell research policies without direct democracy, for example in Germany, Austria, Norway and Ireland (Montpetit et al. 2007, Griessler and Hadolt 2006; Gottweis 2002; Banchoff 2005; Fink 2008). One recurrent factor in explaining this outcome is the presence of Christian Democratic parties. The role of Christian Democratic parties appears to be crucial here as they transpose issues of morality along the cleavage between secular and non-secular parties (Green-Pedersen 2007). Focusing on the laws regulating stem cell research in 21 countries, Fink (2008) has postulated that the strength of Christian Democratic parties and a high proportion of Catholics in a country are positively correlated with the strictness of embryo research policies.

The fact that direct democracy is neither a sufficient nor a necessary institution for achieving restrictive policies for the fields of assisted reproduction and stem cell research, is also valid for agro-food biotechnology. Moratoriums or total bans of GMOs in agriculture have been achieved through direct democracy in some California counties and in Switzerland. However, the EU adopted similar policies in the 1990s under a very different institutional context, and there are also a number of cities, counties and regions that declared themselves GE-free zones without resorting to direct legislation, when it was available at all. Alaska has adopted mandatory labeling for salmon through representative institutions. In contrast to biomedical applications, however, direct legislation in the agro-food sector aimed exclusively at rendering policies more restrictive. In the US, the overall impact remains modest as policy change is local and limited to California. For the Swiss case, there are important direct and indirect impacts of popular initiatives towards a strict regulatory framework, and this took place before the EU moved in the same direction.

In conclusion, no clear-cut picture emerges from the data of who comes out ahead in direct legislation. While in the three European countries forces critical towards assisted reproduction and stem cell research were successful in initiating and influencing policy change towards more restrictive solutions and once such policies were adopted also to defend them, the picture for the United States is very different. Research interests and the biotechnology industry seem to mobilize direct legislation successfully when it comes to stem cell research. They are also particularly successful when it comes to mandatory referenda on financing research, where four out of five cases that sought to issue bonds for biotechnology research and development won a popular majority. In the case of agro-food biotechnology the picture is also mixed.

Opponents were successful in initiating policy change in some instances, on a very modest scale in the USA, and more importantly in Switzerland.

A last remark concerns the impact of other institutions. Policy change achieved through direct democracy might also be reversed or slowed down through decisions by other actors, such as courts in the Swiss case. Inversely, court decisions can also support policies adopted through direct legislation, as is the case for California, where opponents to stem cell research unsuccessfully tried to challenge the policies adopted on the ground of Proposition 71, the California Stem Cell Research and Cures Initiative. Implementation of public policies might further have an impact on the effectively achieved changes.

Given the fact that the number of countries where direct legislation on a variety of policy issues takes place on a regular basis is limited, which in turn hinders the systematic comparison of the impact of direct democratic institutions, future research could enlarge the empirical basis by including other policy domains, related or close to the policy issues addressed by direct legislation in the case of biotechnology. On the one hand, research could include other highly specialized technical sectors, such as nuclear power, or nanotechnology. On the other hand, the "morality" aspect of biotechnology policies could be enlarged by including other issues such as abortion or genetic testing. This kind of comparison would enable us to better understand whether the combination of scientific complexity with ethical concerns in the case of biotechnology leads to a pattern of use and impact of direct legislation distinct from other policy issues.

Acknowledgements

We would like to thank Uwe Serdült and his team from the Centre for Research on Direct Democracy (c2d) in Aarau, Switzerland for the research in their database on direct democracy; Audrey L'Espérance for her assistance in researching the US cases, and Sara Rozman, for her research on the case of Slovenia. We would also like to thank the four anonymous reviewers for their useful comments and suggestions.

Notes

1. By using the term of direct legislation, we do not exclude popular initiatives that allow amending or revising the constitution, as is for example the case in Switzerland.
2. Depending on the procedure for scrutinizing the content of an initiative, the government and the courts may, however, have a say in whether a proposition is admissible, i.e. constitutional, or not.
3. If the policy-making process results in no state intervention or the adoption of self-regulatory mechanism organized interests might turn to the popular initiative.
4. Database: Database of the C2D, Center for direct democracy http://www.c2d.ch/ and National Conference of State Legislators, Ballot Measure Database, http://www.ncsl.org/programs/legman/elect/dbintro.htm: search for years 1980 to 2005 by October 2005, Keywords: biotechnology, biomedicine, stem cell, in vitro fertilization, eggs, sperm, donation, surrogacy, surrogate motherhood, cloning, genetic, genetically modified, genetically engineered, genes, DNA.
5. We are not taking into account cases where initiatives or referenda failed to collect the necessary signatures, where they did not reach the ballot stage for legal reasons such as the conformity of initiatives to basic constitutional principles. Ballots voted on and the policies later declared unconstitutional by a court have been taken into account.

6. In the canton of Glarus, the yearly citizen assembly voted on the issue of assisted reproductive technology. The initiative for the proposal came from the citizens; we have thus classified this case with the initiatives, even though it was legally speaking not a popular initiative.
7. With the exception of total revisions of the constitution and initiatives taking the form of general suggestions.
8. In the case of an initiative and counter-proposal a third question is added asking the citizen which of the two they prefer.
9. The cryopreservation of impregnated eggs is permitted.
10. Swiss norms also allow for 'negative' labeling, i.e. using the fact that a food product does not contain GMO for marketing purposes.
11. The Federal Council is the government.
12. National Conference of State Legislation: http://www.ncsl.org/programs/health/genetics/charts.htm, http://www.ncsl.org/programs/health/genetics/geneticsDB.cfm (last consulted December 2008).
13. In the case of Virginia, it is not clear whether therapeutic cloning is prohibited, or only reproductive cloning. Louisiana prohibits research on IVF embryos: further investigations are needed to interpret this prohibition.
14. A number of states also adopted bills imposing more severe penalties for activists destroying GM crop fields. A few states issue their own authorizations for field trials (Minnesota, Oklahoma, and Vermont), taking into account, however, prior decisions of the APHIS (US Department of Agriculture). In the case of pesticides, with some exceptions, states base their decisions and also the registration on the EPA's decision and registration. California runs its own authorization and registering program with respect to pesticides (see Taylor *et al.* 2004).
15. Arizona, Florida, Georgia, Idaho, Indiana, Iowa, Kansas, Michigan, North Dakota, Ohio, Oklahoma, Pennsylvania, South Dakota, Texas, Virginia, West Virginia, source: http://environmentalcommons.org/gmo-tracker.html.
16. Norme in materia di procreazione medicalmente assistita; Law No. 40/2004 of 19 February 2004, published in the Official Journal on February 24, 2004.
17. *Official Gazette*, No. 11 (1977), p. 572.
18. Handbook of Committee for Freedom of Choice 2001: 4.

References

Auer, Andreas and Bützer, Michael, 2001, *Direct Democracy: the Eastern and Central European Experience* (Aldershot: Ashgate).
Banchoff, Thomas, 2005, Path dependence and value-driven issues. The comparative politics of stem cell research. *World Politics*, **57**, 200–230.
Bauer, Martin W. and Gaskell, George, 2002, *Biotechnology: The Making of a Global Controversy* (Cambridge: Cambridge University Press).
Baumgartner, Frank and Jones, Brian, 1993, *Agendas and Instability in American Politics* (Chicago: University of Chicago Press).
Bernauer, Thomas and Meins, Erika, 2003, Technological revolution meets policy and the market: explaining cross-national differences in agricultural biotechnology regulation. *European Journal of Political Research*, **42**, 643–683.
Bleiklie, Ivar, Goggin, Malcolm and Rothmayr, Christine, 2004, *Comparative Biomedical Policy: Governing Assisted Reproductive Technologies* (London: Routledge).
Boehmke, Frederick, 2002, The effect of direct democracy on the size and diversity of state interest group populations. *The Journal of Politics*, **64**, 827–844.
Bouwen, Pieter and McCown, Margaret, 2007, Lobbying versus litigation. *Journal of European Public Policy*, **14**, 422–443.
Budge, Ian, 1996, *The New Challenge of Direct Democracy* (Cambridge: Polity Press).
Cronin, Thomas E., 1989, *Direct Democracy. The Politics of Initiative, Referendum, and Recall* (Cambridge, MA: Harvard University Press).
Fenton, Rachel A., 2006, Catholic doctrine versus women's rights: the new Italian law on assisted reproduction. *Medical Law Review*, **14**, 73–107.

Fink, Simon, 2008, Politics as usual or bringing religion back in? The influence of parties, institutions, economic interests, and religion on embryo research laws. *Comparative Political Studies*, **41**, 1631–1656.

Fontana, Marie-Christine, Afonso, Alexandre and Papadopoulos, Yannis, 2008, Putting the special case in its place: Switzerland and small-n comparison in policy research. *Swiss Political Science Review*, **14**, 521–550.

Fukuyama, Francis, 2002, *Our Posthuman Future: Consequences of the Biotechnology Revolution* (New York: Picador).

Gallagher, Michael and Uleri, Pier V., 1996, *The Referendum Experience in Europe* (London: McMillan).

Garon, Francis and Montpetit, Eric, 2007, Different paths to the same result: explaining permissive policies in the USA, the politics of biotechnology, in: E. Montpetit, C. Rothmayr and F. Varone (Eds) *The Politics of Biotechnology in North America and Europe: Policy Networks, Institutions and Internationalization* (Lanham, MD: Lexington), pp. 61–82.

Gerber, Elisabeth and Hug, Simon, 2001, Legislative response to direct legislation, in: M. Mendelson and A. Parkin (Eds) *Referendum Democracy: Citizen, Elites and Deliberation in Referendum Campaigns* (London: MacMillan), pp. 88–108.

Griessler, Erich and Hadolt, Bernhard, 2006, Policy learning in policy domains with value conflicts: the Austrian cases of abortion and assisted reproductive technologies. *German Policy Studies*, **3**, 698–746.

Goggin, Malcolm L. and Orth, Deborah, 2004, The United States. National talk and state action in governing ART, in: I. Bleiklie, M. L. Goggin and C. Rothmayr (Eds) *Comparative Biomedical Policy: Governing Assisted Reproductive Technologies* (London: Routledge), pp. 82–102.

Gottweis, Herbert, 2002, Stem cell policies in the United States and Germany: between bioethics and regulation. *Policy Studies Journal*, **30**, 444–469.

Green-Pedersen, Christopher, 2007, The conflict of conflicts in comparative perspective: euthanasia as a political issue in Denmark, Belgium and the Netherlands. *Comparative Politics*, **39**, 273–291.

Hilson, Chris, 2002, New social movements: the role of legal opportunity. *Journal of European Public Policy*, **9**, 238–255.

Höglinger, Dominic, 2008, Verschafft die direkte Demokratie den Benacheiligten mehr Gehör? Der Einfluss institutioneller Rahmenbedingungen auf die mediale Präsenz politischer Akteure. *Swiss Political Science Review*, **12**, 207–243.

Jasanoff, Sheila, 2005, *Designs on Nature. Science and Democracy in Europe and the United States* (Princeton, NJ: Princeton University Press).

Kriesi, Hanspeter, 2005, *Direct Democratic Choice. The Swiss Experience* (Lanham, MD: Lexington).

Linder, Wolf, 1994, *Swiss Democracy. Possible Solutions to Conflict in Multicultural Societies* (Houndmills: Macmillan).

Lupia, Arthur and Matsusaka, John G., 2004, Direct democracy: new approaches to old questions. *Annual Review of Political Science*, **7**, 463–482.

Matsusaka, John G., 2007, *Direct Democracy and Social Issues*, http://ssrn.com/abstract=989682 (version March 2009).

Möckli, Silvano, 1994, *Direkte Demokratie: Ein internationaler Vergleich* (Bern: Haupt).

Montpetit, Eric, Varone, Frédéric and Rothmayr, Christine, 2007, Regulating ART and GMOs in Europe and North America: a qualitative comparative analysis, in: E. Montpetit, C. Rothmayr and F. Varone (Eds) *The Politics of Biotechnology in North America and Europe: Policy Networks, Institutions and Internationalization* (Lanham, MD: Lexington), pp. 263–283.

Mooney, Christopher, 2001, *The Public Clash of Private Values: The Politics of Morality Policy* (New York: Chatham House).

Neidhardt, Leonhard, 1970, *Plebiszit und pluralitäre Demokratie. Eine Analyse der Funktion des schweizerischen Gesetzesreferendums* (Bern: Francke).

Papadopoulos, Yannis, 1997, *Les processus de décision fédéraux en Suisse* (Paris: L'Harmattan).

Papadopoulos, Yannis, 2001, How does direct democracy matter? The impact of referendum votes on politics and policy-making. *West European Politics*, **24**, 35–58.

Ramjoué, Celina and Klöti, Ulrich, 2004, Art policy in Italy: Explaining the lack of comprehensive regulation, in: I. Bleiklie, M. L. Goggin and C. Rothmayr (Eds) *Comparative Biomedical Policy*, (London: Routledge), pp. 21–41.

Rothmayr, Christine, 1999, *Politik vor Gericht* (Bern: Haupt).

Rothmayr, Christine, 2003, Regulatory approaches to biomedicine: the impact of self-regulation on the public policies for assisted reproductive technology, in: U. Serdült and T. Widmer (Eds) *Politik im Fokus, Festschrift für Ulrich Klöti* (Zürich: NZZ Verlag), pp. 425–445.

Rothmayr, Christine, 2007, Switzerland: direct democracy and non-EU-membership – different institutions, similar policies, in: E. Montpetit, C. Rothmayr and F. Varone (Eds) *The Politics of Biotechnology in North America and Europe: Policy Networks, Institutions and Internationalization* (Lanham, MD: Lexington), pp. 237–262.

Rothmayr, Christine and Serdült, Uwe, 2004, Switzerland: policy design and direct democracy, in: I. Bleiklie, M. L. Goggin and C. Rothmayr (Eds) *Comparative Biomedical Policy* (London: Routledge), pp. 191–208.

Rothmayr, Christine, Varone, Frédéric, Serdült, Uwe, Timmermans, Arco and Bleiklie, Ivar, 2004, Comparing policy design across countries: what accounts for variation in ART policy? in: I. Bleiklie, M. L. Goggin and C. Rothmayr (Eds) *Comparative Biomedical Policy* (London: Routledge), pp. 425–445.

Schattschneider, Elmer E., 1960, *The Semisovereign People: a Realist's View of Democracy in America* (New York: Holt, Rinehart and Winston).

Sciarini, Pascal, 2007, The Decision-Making Process, in: U. Klöti, P. Knoepfel, H. Kriesi, W. Linder, Y. Papadopoulos and P. Sciarini (Eds) *Handbook of Swiss Politics,* 2nd edition (Zurich: NZZ Verlag), pp. 491–525.

Sheingate, Adam, 2004, The politics of biotechnology in the United States: medical and agricultural applications compared. *Annual Meeting of the American Political Science Association*, Chicago, September 2–5, 2004.

Smith, Alexander T. and Tatalovich, Raymond, 2003, *Cultures as War. Moral Conflict in Western Democracies* (Petersborough: Broadview Press).

Taylor, Michael, Tick, Jody S. and Sherman, Diane M., 2004, Tending the fields: state and federal roles in the oversight of genetically modified crops. A report commissioned by the Pew Initiative on Food and Biotechnology and prepared by Resources for the Future, http://www.rff.org/RFF/Documents/RFF-RPT-TendingtheFields.pdf (March 2009).

Uleri, Pier V., 1996, Introduction, in: M. Gallagher and P. V. Uleri (Eds) *The Referendum Experience in Europe* (Houndmills: McMillan), pp. 1–19.

Uleri, Pier V., 2002, On referendum voting in Italy: YES, NO or non-vote? How Italian parties learned to control referendums. *European Journal of Political Research*, **41**, 863–883.

Varone, Frédéric, Rothmayr, Christine and Montpetit, Eric, 2006, Regulating biomedicine in Europe and North America: a qualitative comparative analysis. *European Journal of Political Research*, **45**, 317–343.

Varone, Frédéric, Rothmayr, Christine and Montpetit, Eric, 2007, Comparing biotechnology policy in Europe and North America: a theoretical framework, in: E. Montpetit, C. Rothmayr and F. Varone (Eds) *The Politics of Biotechnology in North America and Europe: Policy Networks, Institutions and Internationalization* (Lanham, MD: Lexington), pp. 1–33.

Vogel, David, 2004, The hare and the tortoise revisited. The new politics of risk regulation in Europe and the United States, in: M. Levin and M. Shapiro (Eds) *Transatlantic Policymaking in an Age of Austerity: Diversity and Drift* (Washington: Georgetown University Press), pp. 177–202.

Index

Note: **Bold** page numbers refer to tables; *italic* page numbers refer to figures and page numbers followed by "n" denote endnotes.

accommodating federalism 299
Adachi, Yukio 3
Administrative Procedures Act 454
agricultural biotechnology: GM foods 444–445; GMO support score 455, *455*, *456*, **457**; institutional differences, effects of 445; institutions and politics 458–460; joint-decision systems 454–455; member state populations and vote allocations 453–458; multi-level governing arrangements 459; QMV 453–458, **455**; regulatory federalism 446–453, 459; in United States and EU 453–458
Alber, Jens 32, 36
Alesina, A. 181
Allegretto, S. 152
American federalism 447, 457
Ansell, C. 16
Antonovsky, Aaron 105
Asian tigers 86
Assisted Reproductive Technologies (ART) 469
Australia 301–303; Australian Curriculum, Assessment and Reporting Authority (ACARA) 303; changes to skilled immigration policy, 1997–1999 391–392; childcare standards 192; Childcare Tax Rebate program 192; choice of new governance modes 310; Commonwealth in education 301; corporate federalism 302; Department of Immigration and Multicultural Affairs (DIMA) 391, 393; educational measures 302; education policy 301–302; federalism in 54; for-profit and community-based childcare 190–191; full-time preschool services 192–193; governance shifts in subnational education governance 309; greater "national" cooperation 308–309; liberal welfare states, ECEC quality 190–191; Longitudinal Survey of Immigrants to Australia (LSIA) 393; Migrant on Demand List (MODL) 392; Ministerial Council of Education, Employment, Training, and Youth (MCEETYA) 302–303; National Assessment Programme 303; non-profit provision model 191; point of departures and critical junctures 301–302; policy developments 302–303; policy-making process 392–393; private childcare 191; recent changes and implications for venue shopping 396–397; "School of the Future" programme 303; skilled immigration policies and processes 397–400; skilled immigration policy-making in 387, 390–391; smart regulation 17; test for skilled immigration 391, **392**
Australian Curriculum, Assessment and Reporting Authority (ACARA) 303
Austrian health care system 41
Austrian SHI system 35

Bache, Ian 56
Baehler, K.J. 5
Baker, M. 197
balanced federalism 298, 300
Ball, S.J., 193
Banting, K. 180
Baumgartner 407, 408
Bay, A.-H. 181
Bell, L. 249
Bernasconi 332, 333
Bernstein, J. 152
Bjørklund, T. 168
Blank, R. 152
Blondel, Jean 47
Boase, A., 7
Boehmke, Frederick 470
Bolderson, Helen 57
Boswell, C. 340, 347, 365, 418
Boushey, G. 7
Bovenkerk, F. 360

492 INDEX

Brandsma, G.J. 278
Brennan, D. 192
British "internal market" 42
British model, evidence-based policy making and reinvention of 416–418
British multiculturalism, technocratic conception of 416–418
British NHS system 28, 34, 41, 42, 64, 135, 142
bureaucratic control and policy change: Australia 391–393, 397–400; Canada 393–400; and policy outputs 388–390; skilled immigration policy-making 390–391; venue shopping 388–390; Westminster-inspired systems 388, 389–390
Burkhardt, C. 170

cabinet-level websites in developing countries: coding criteria used in openness index 440–442; correlation matrix 443; Cyberspace Policy Research Group (CyPRG) 428–429, 437; data and methodology 428–430, 436; determinants of openness, OLS regression **436**; e-government openness: hypotheses 425–428; independent variables 430; multivariate regression analysis 430; openness index 428–430, **431**; political, cultural, economic, and technical variables in developing countries **432–435**; polity index of democracy 430; regression analysis 436–437; transparency and interactivity scores 428–429
Canada: alternate funding plans (AFPs) 124–125; archival research 401n2; Canada Health Act 134, 138, 146; Canadian health policy 127–128; Canadian Medicare 120; centralization of control and integration policies 382, **382**; changes to skilled immigration policy, 1995–2004 393–394; choice of new governance modes 310; cost control 115–116, 121–122; decentralized immigration recruitment 383; Family Health Teams (FHTs) 125; financial crisis 304; fundamental structural features 305–306; Gender-Based Analysis (GBA) unit 395; governance arrangements 304; governance shifts in subnational education governance 309; greater "national" cooperation 309; health policy 120; health policy contexts 118–120; health policy directions 115–116; "human capital" model 393; Immigration and Refugee Protection Act (2002) ('IRPA') 393–394; and medical care arrangements 145–147; Medicare program 132, 135, 146; at national level 304; national values 133; neo-liberal reforms 304; payment mechanisms 124; point of departure and critical junctures 304–305; points test for skilled immigration 394, **394**; policy developments 305–306;
policy-making process 394–396; primary health care reform 124–125; Primary Health Transition Fund 124; provincial and local administrations 305; provincial economic development 383; recent changes and implications for venue shopping 396–397; skilled immigration policies and processes 397–400; skilled immigration policy-making in 390–391; versatile governance in health policy 118
Canada Health Act of 1984 (CHA) 89
Canadian constitution 376
Canadian Health Care: abandonment of Canadian values 147; Canadian Institute for Health Information (CIHI) report 136–137; command and control monopolistic system 139; context and convictions 136–139; crisis mentality, origin of 136, 147; Medicare's basic funding 136, 138; national values 137; principles of quality and accountability 137–138; public administration feature 138; public healthcare system 137
Capano, G. 7, 282
Caramani, D. 236
Carley, M. 254n12
case-based payment 88
cash limits, introduction of 28
Castles, F.G. 47, 235
Chile: Banmedica 67; CONSALUD 67; expansion of private insurance 86, 87; FONASA 67; health care reform in 65–67; Institución de Salud Previsional (ISAPRE) 66, 67; "integrated forms of managed care" 67; policy and legal framework 333; population, improvement of health 66; primary care and case-based payments 67; public pensions and health insurance 65; public/private mix of health insurance 62; Servicio Médico Nacional de Empleados (SERMENA) 65–66; size, population, income and economic growth in 96, **97**; social health insurance 65
Chinitz, D. 91n4
choice strategy 206–207
Clasen, J. 226
Classics of Comparative Policy Analysis Studies 4–5, 8
Classics of Policy Analysis Studies 8
Clegg, D. 226
Cobb, W. 408
Colino, C. 298, 300
Collier, David 49
Colombia: abbreviations and acronyms 282, **283**; accreditation of high quality 283–284; categorization scheme 286; discourse of higher education quality assurance in 284–288; and Ecuador, comparing 280; HEIs 287; HEQA policy 288; higher

education system 282; legal and institutional frameworks for quality assurance in 282–284; message of transparency, stability, and collaboration 288; narrative and institutionalized legitimacy 290; notion of "stories" or narratives 289; Plan Nacional de Buen Vivir (PNBV) 288; stories 285, 287–288; system of QA 283; targeted audiences and purposes 287
comparative policy analysis (CPA) 3, 5
competitive individualism 135
consociational corporatism 144
contracting model 141
corporatist-governed health care system 26
cost control and primary health care reform: in Canada and New Zealand 118–120; cost control 121–123; health decision-making 117; hierarchical governance 117; modes of governance 123–124, 126–127; primary health care reform 124–127; steering mechanisms (modes of governance) 116–117; versatility and modes of governance 117–118
country-level variables 172; ethnic diversity of immigrants 174; inequality 173, 180; selectivity 173; share of non-western immigrants 174; strictness of employment protection 173–174; unemployment 173
Crepaz, M.M.L. 181n1
culture theory 168
Cyberspace Policy Research Group (CyPRG) 428–429, 437, 438n3

Damron, R. 181n1
Deber, R.B. 188
Deleon, P. 3, 46
Denmark: empirical research 112n1; Health Market 104, 105; Healthy Cities movement 104–105; policy of Ringkjøbing county 105–106; provision of healthcare services 102–103; public health nurses 111; public health policies, integration of policy transfer within local 99, 104–106, **108**; public health program co-ordinators 109, **109**; SDOH 109; two-tier welfare system 181
diagnosis related groups (DRG) 88
direct democracy: actors' strategies 468; direct and indirect effects 470–471; effects of 466, 472–483; institutional venues 471; mobilization of 468–469; optional referendum 469, 470; policy impact of 469–471, 483
disarray, French model in 416
Douglas, C. 64, 135
Dubai: access and pedagogy 323–324; demand absorption & creation 324; economic expansion efforts 320; "free zones" 319; immigration application p 327n8; international branch campuses 315, 319–320; prestigious nations and semi-elite institutions 322; public policy and private higher education 325
Dutch health insurance of 2006 88

early childhood education and care (ECEC): "educational" childcare 199; multiple issues 185–186; in OECD countries 186; public finance and private delivery 187–188; quality and investment choices (*see* liberal welfare states, ECEC); Swedish approach 188–190
earner-carer strategy 207, 221
earnings: effect of motherhood 214, **215**, *216*; motherhood penalty 217, 233n11; reconciliation policies and effects of motherhood 214–217; of women 214, **214**
Ecuador: Colombia and, comparing 280; discourse of higher education quality assurance in 284–288; HEIs 290; HEQA policy 288; legal and institutional frameworks for quality assurance in 282–284; notion of "stories" or narratives 289; policy- and sense-making levels 290–291; stories 285–288; targeted audiences and purposes 287
e-democracy 426
education: Australia 301–303; Canada 304–306; choice of new governance modes 310; empirical evidence 301; exploratory hypotheses 300; Germany 306–308; governance shifts, defining content of change 296–297; governance shifts in subnational education governance 309–310; governments as agents of change in federal countries 297–301; greater "national" cooperation 308–309; issue of governance reform 296; primary and secondary education 295; socioeconomic growth 295–296; universalization of 295
e-government openness: authoritarianism and clientelism 426; cabinet-level websites 428; comparative or cross-national perspective 425; cultural legacies 426; electronic democracy or cyberdemocracy 426; influence of religious traditions 428; Internet and the World Wide Web 424; legacy of colonial rule 427; legal-administrative institutions 426; phenomenon of "Potemkin e-villages" 427, **436**, 438n2
Elazar, D.S. 298
employment rates: effect of motherhood 210, *211*, 212; full-time employment 212, **212**, 221; reconciliation policies and effects of motherhood 205–207, 210–214; Women's 210, **210**
Esping-Andersen, G. 47, 167, 170, 173, 179, 205, 226, 235, 258
EU-level research–policy infrastructures: European Integration Fund 347; European Migration Network (EMN) 344–346; framework programmes 346; infrastructures

for horizontal knowledge exchange 344–347; infrastructures for policy monitoring 349–350; INTI 346; knowledge infrastructures 336–337; methodological nationalism 351; Migrant Integration Policy Index (MIPEX) 348, 349; policy agenda and the mobilization of expertise 347–348; policy-oriented research 336, 348; softening-up process 347; soft governance strategy 336, 346–347; variety of organizations 336

Europe: annual paid vacation entitlement and public holidays 245, **246**; comparative institutional analysis of aid policies for young people 261–273; declining full-timers' hours 241; economic and social citizenship 259; establishment of public holidays 246; Eurostat 257; family allowances 263–264, **264**; family policy 261–265; feminist critiques 258–259; housing benefits 268, **269–270**, 270; institutional framework 242, **243**; maintenance obligations **262**, 263, 272; method 261; "new social risk groups" or "outsiders" 258; proportion of undergraduate students 266, *266*; social assistance 270–272, *271*; social security cover, young people's 272, *273*; student support 265–268; theorizing young people's social citizenship in 258–259; two figures of young people's social citizenship 259–261; unemployment benefits and social assistance 258; weekly working hours 243, **244–245**; work-family reconciliation policies 204; "work/family reconciliation policies" 162n2; working time policies 242–247; working time reductions 241; working time reform 252; young people and social welfare 258–259

Europeanization: "Athens Migration Policy Initiative" (AMPI) 343; "boundary institutions" 337; British race relations model 342; Common Basic Principles on Integration (CBP) 343–344; and convergence 338; "Framework" funding 341; French republican model 342; by "Going Technical" 338–339; "harder" legal mechanisms 343; "integration measures" 342; knowledge production and utilization 337; "migrant integration" 337; of migrant integration policies 342–344; and national primacy 342–344; policy-oriented research 339; policy research and 337–341; and politics of expertise 339–341; "politics without policy" 338–339; process of "scientification" of policymaking 340; reconstitution of the policy field 341; science and policymaking 337; "softer" and "harder" governance 338; "vertical Europeanization" 341

European Social Survey (ESS) 172

European Union: approval of genetically modified organisms 452; approval process and harmonize procedures 451; biotechnology policy, regulatory federalism in 449–453; comitology procedure 453–454; European Food Safety Authority (EFSA) 450; "one door, one key" procedure 450; representative dimension of federalism 452–453; representative federalism in 453–458; safeguard provisions 451–452

European values: funding and provision of health care in OECD 141–143, **142**; interest bargaining 145; and medical care: similar values, divergent arrangements 139–145; public attitudes towards government's role in health care 139–141, **140**; styles of policymaking 143–144

Eurydice 258, 274n2

evidence-based policymaking 6, 16

Ezrahi, Y. 356

Fagnani, J. 251
Fair Labor Standards Act (FLSA) 245
Falleti, T. 300
"family wage" strategy 205
federalism: accommodating federalism 299; balanced federalism 298, 300; segmented federalism 298–299, 300; unitary federalism 298, 300; varieties of **298**
Figart, D.M. 252
Fink, Simon 485
Finland: health service providers 36
fiscal federalism and politics of immigration: centralization of control and integration policies 382, *382*; citizenship policy 370; early centralization in the United States 378–382; immigration policy 370; immigration policy devolution and theories 370–375; late-decentralizing Canada 375–378; reducing transaction costs 369
Flinders, Matthew 56
France: experts and policy makers 419; French model in disarray 416; healthcare and public health policies 103; political engineering and the French republican model 414–416; public health physician inspectors 103, 110; public health policies 99, 106–108, **108**; reception of policy transfer 111; regional health programs 106–107; republicanist model of integration 415; research-policy nexus 415–416; for Revenu de Solidarité Active (RSA) 257; role of venues of expertise 407; SDOH 106, 107; Stasi Commission 415; technocracy and "the right to be different" 414
Fraser, Nancy 206
Freeman, Gary 8, 29, 48, 54, 56, 152, 249

French republican model 414–416
Friedrich, C.J. 298

Gash, A. 16
Gelman, A. 178
German SHI system 42
Germany 306–308; for the Arbeitslosengeld II (ALG II) 257; "Bismarckian" model of employment-related health insurance 142; choice of new governance modes 310; compulsory health insurance 142; corporatism 51; development of effective policies 365; expansion of social insurance in 55; governance shifts in subnational education governance 309–310; greater "national" cooperation 309; health policies in 35; home and community based health care, funding for 55; immigration councillors 363–364; increase of total health expenditures 32, *32*; knowledge production and policymaking 362–365; *Länder* 308; long-term care insurance 143; market mechanisms 27, 29; migration research 363; "neo-corporatist" style of governance 64; new Immigration Law 364; point of departure and critical junctures 306; policy developments 306–308; politicisation and knowledge production 365; Programme for International Student Assessment (PISA) 306, 307; provided model of employment-based social insurance 65; researchers and policymakers 363; research–policy nexus 362–363, 366; risk-adjustment mechanism 29–30; SHI scheme 32; sickness funds and doctors' associations 29; weekly working hours 243, **244–245**
Geva-May, I. 4
Gevers, J. 139
Giaimo, Susan 26
Gieryn, T.F. 357–358
Glaeser, E.L. 181
Gornick, J.C. 7
Grabosky, P. 17
Greece: private out-of-pocket payments 40
Green-Pedersen, C. 5, 227
Grubb, D. 249
Gunningham, N. 17
Gusfield 407
Guy, Peters B. 3, 4

Haas, P. 340
Hajer, M.A. 340
Halberstam, Daniel 453
Halffman, W. 356
Hall, P. 340
Ham, C. 49
Harrop, Martin 50

health care governance 49
health care providers: and health expenditure 37, **38**, 39, **40**; indicators of **37**
health care provision: health expenditure and health care financing 31–35; health service provision 35–41; "index of health care providers" 36, 41–42; modes of public policy in health care arena 28–31; "production process" 28, *28*, 41
health care reform: in Chile 65–67; comparative methodology and empirical findings 62; country categorizations 90; debates, reforms and policy adjustments 86–90; distribution of financial risk 61; governance 91n2; institutions matter 89; in Israel 68–70; market competition, introduction of 63; in Netherlands 81–86; policy making 92n15; qualitative research 91n4; reforming health care systems 89–90; shifts in decision-making 61; in Singapore 70–74; social values (or dominant cultural orientations) 62; in Switzerland 74–79; in Taiwan 79–81; values matter 89; "windows of opportunity" 88
health care states: across nine countries 51, **52**; command and control 50, 53; corporatist funding 50; cultural embeddedness 56; formal and informal care 55, 56; gender arrangements, concept of 56; governance of provision, definition 55; health and social care 55; home and community based 54–55, 56; institutional embeddedness 54; and institutional embeddedness 50–54; non-medical based health care, emergence of 55; and non-medical health policies 54–56; OECD Health Project 55; providers, role of 50–51; real, approximation of 53–54
health care systems: categorizing countries and 64–65; competitive individualism 64; contracting model 64; funding, contracting and ownership 64; hierarchical collectivism 64; integrated model 64; private insurance 64; sectarianism 64; social policy, welfare principles 65
Health Maintenance Organizations (HMOs) 30–31
health policy, comparing: health care states 50–56; typologies of health systems (*see* health systems, typologies of)
health service provision: health policy 35–36; quality of health care 36
health systems, typologies of: assessment of 46–58; in comparative health policy 47–50; comparative health policy analyses 57; comparative renaissance 46; comparative study of health policy 49–50; definition 47;

democratic and state regimes 47; families of nations, notion of 47; institutional context of health policy 57; medical health policies 57; national health service (or Beveridge) model 48; organizing framework 50, 56; in perspective 57–58; private insurance (or consumer sovereignty model) 48; single broad-brush categorizations, deconstruction of 57–58; social insurance (or Bismarck) model 48; types of, by provision and funding 47, *48*; welfare state regimes 47

Heron, Alexandra 7

hierarchical collectivism 135

higher education: cross-regional coverage and growing size 331; development strategy 332; intraregional policy variation 333; *laissez-faire* policy 332; private sectors of 330; privatization and publicization 330; as privatizing policy arena 330–331; and public policy; scholarship 334; scope and content of special issue 332–334; social policy 331

higher education quality assurance (HEQA) 278; accountability, quality assurance and accreditation 278; in Colombia and Ecuador (*see* individual entries); discourse of 284–288, 289, 291; examining policy change through discourse analysis 280–282; higher education QA in Latin America 278–280; interpreting the findings 288–291; legal and institutional frameworks 282–284

Hill, J. 178

Hook, Jennifer 208

Hoppe, R. 355, 356

Hospital Trusts 28, 29

Howlett, Michael 282

Ignatieff, Michael 134

immigrant policy agenda: assimilationism frames 409; bureaucratic model 410; differentialism 409; engineering model 410; enlightenment model 410; France 414–416; multiculturalism frames 409; multiculturalist and universalist frames 420; Netherlands 411–414; policy differences 406; policy monopolies 408; policy subsystem 411; problem frames of immigrant policy 408–409; relating venues and frames in policy dynamics 407–408; research-policy relations 410, *410*; role of expert venues 407; scientific expertise and substantive policy frames, venues of 409; technocratic model 410; United Kingdom 416–418; universalism frames 409; varying venues of expertise for immigrant policy 409–411

immigration policy devolution and theories: economic implications of immigration policy 370–373; evolution of immigration control 375; free-flowing labor market 371, 384, 385n1; illegal immigration 381; immigrant integration policy 374; immigration control policies 372; laboratory federalism 373; market-preserving federalism 373; national sovereignty 375; nation-preserving federalism 374, 375; nation-preserving implications of immigration policy 373–375; New Brunswick's strategy 378; political costs of negotiation/delegation 372; Provincial Nominee Program 378; Quiet Revolution 377; spillover effect or externality 371; state governments 381

"independent practice associations" (IPA) 76

Indian Health system, 135

individual-level variables 172, 174–175

Ingram, H. 420

institutional theory of welfare chauvinism *172*; control criterion 171, 172; identity criterion 170, 172; labor-market trajectory 169, 171–172, 179; need criterion 171, 172; selectivity and inequality dimensions 169–171, 172

"internal markets," establishment of 28

international branch campuses (IBCs): advent of 318; development and regulation 317–318; development of 315–316, 317–318; in Dubai and Malaysia 316; expansion of 316; non-government organizations. 316; policy environments 316; something superior category 323; systematic investigation 316

Israel: basic sick fund model 62, 68, 69; Bismarckian model of employment-based insurance 87; Chalit 68; funding sources for health care 68; health care providers 69–70; health care reform in 68–70; health expenditure/care professionals/profile of 96–97, **98**; health policy-making 70; larger choice of health plans in 86; MoH and sick funds 69; National Health Insurance Law (NHI) 68, 70; neo-corporatist policy traditions 88; private health insurance 69; private insurers 70; size, population, income and economic growth in 96, **97**

Italy: abrogative referendum 480–481; assisted reproduction 480; challenging existing policies on assisted reproductive technologies 480–483; constitutional referendum rules 481; optional referendum 480, 484; Referenda for ART **482**, 485

Japan: annual work hours 241; expansion of social insurance in 55; Gold Plan 55; institutional framework 242, **243**; international branch campuses (IBCs) 326n2; long-term care insurance 143; National Health Insurance 51; unitary political system in 51; working time policies 242–247

Japel, C. 196–197

Jasanoff, S. 356, 358
JCPA and ICPA-Forum Award for Best Comparative Paper: case study and method 102–103; community health 113n3; gray literature (health programs) 103; integration of policy transfer within local public health policies 103–108; mapping the circulation of policy transfer through actors' backgrounds 108–111; reception of policy transfer 100–102; social determinants of health (SDOH) 100; WHO and public health academics 111
Jones, Bryan 407, 408
Jones, Gill 259
Journal of Comparative Policy Analysis (JCPA) 3–4, 5

Kangas, O. 36
Kersbergen, K. van 274, 236
Kinser, K. 318
knowledge production and policymaking: boundary work and 356–357, 365; DIAMINT project 358; in Germany 362–365; "immigration and integration crisis" 354–355; in institutional policy setting 355–358; multicultural crisis 355; in Netherlands 359–362; process of scientification of politics 355; role of boundary organisations 357–358
Korpi, Martin 189, 226, 228
Koster, Ferry 182n6
Kymlicka, W. 180

Lally, Ron 192
Lane, Jason 318, 333
Larsen, Christian Albrekt 168, 169, 173, 175
Lasswell, H.D. 355
Latin America: "dominant neopositivist/ empiricist approach" 280–281; higher education institutions (HEIs) 279; higher education policies 281; higher education QA in 278–280; methodology of discourse analysis 279; neoliberalism or "Washington Consensus" 279–280; "pink tide" 280; public and private universities 279; quality assurance and accreditation systems 278–279; systematic comparisons or region-wide comparisons 279
Lebeaux, C.N. 227
Letablier, M.-T. 251
Levin, H.M. 187
Levitsky, Steven 49
Levy, D.A. 322, 323, 326, 333
Lewis, J. 139
liberal welfare states, ECEC: Australia 190–193; New Zealand 197–199; Quebec 196–197; summary of trends 199; The United Kingdom 193–196
Lijphart, A. 47
Lima, L. 259

Linder, Y. 15, 470–471
Luedtke, A. 7
Luxembourg: health service providers 36; Luxembourg Income Study (LIS) 205, 222n6
Lynn, Laurence E. 3

Mabbett, Deborah 57
McRae, Duncan 3
Majone, G. 339, 350
Malaysia: access and pedagogy 323–324; demand absorption & creation 324; information communication and technology (ICT) 321; international branch campuses 320–321; Knowledge-Based Economy Master Plan 320–321; prestigious nations and semi-elite institutions 322; public policy and private higher education 325
"male breadwinner/female caregiver" 205
Manow, P. 26
"marketdriven" health care system 26
Marmor, T.R. 57
Marshall, T.-H., 167, 168, 169, 259
maternity leave 152
Mathers, S. 195
Mau, S. 170
Maxwell, C. 139
Medicaid 30, 135
Medicare 30, 135
Mishel, L. 152
Mitchell, L. 186, 198
Money, Jeannette 372
Moran, E. 29, 47, 49, 50, 54, 55
Mutari, E. 252

National Health Service (NHS) 28, 34
national values: Canadian Health Care 136–139; Canadian values and medical care arrangements 145–147; European values and medical care 139–145; presumptions of inquiry 133–136; public opinion 134–135; social institutions 135
Naumann, I. 189
neo-corporatism 143
Netherlands: Advisory Commission on Minorities Research (ACOM) 359, 360, 412; Algemene Wet Bijzondere Ziektekosten (AWBZ) 82, 85; ambiguous welfare regime 182n3; articulation politics 361–362; assimilationism as political engineering 413–414; basic health insurance 82–83; "Beveridgean" 262; de-institutionalisation of research–policy nexus 361–362; Dutch welfare policies 82; employment-based contract 83; ethnic minorities paradigm 360; expansionary type of boundary work 359–360; expansion of private insurance 86; experts and policy makers 419; health care reform in 81–86; health expenditure/care

professionals/profile of 96–97, **98**; health insurers 83; health professionals 84; income support 271; knowledge production and policymaking 359–362, 366; larger choice of health plans in 86; legacy of societal pillars 54; long-term care insurance 143; marketing and advertising 84; minorities paradigm 361; national competition authority (NMa) 84; neo-corporatist policy making 81, 88; "neo-corporatist" style of governance 64; no-claim restitution 85–86; "No Policy" Monopoly 411; number of uninsured 83; private funding 40; public control of health care costs 51; regulated private insurance 62; role of venues of expertise 407; Short Age of Enlightenment and Universalism 412–413; size, population, income and economic growth in 96, **97**; Social and Cultural Planning Agency (SCP) 359, 413; social policy process 144; technocracy of minorities policy 411–412; technocratic symbiosis 412; WRR report 412–413

"new politics theory" 168

New Zealand: community-based and for-profit centers 198; cost control 115–116, 122–123; Crown Health Enterprises (CHEs) 122–123; District Health Boards (DHBs) 123; Early Childhood Development Unit (ECDU) 197; early childhood training program 197; ECEC quality and investment choices in liberal welfare states 197–199; expansion of corporate providers 199; governance versatility 127, 128; government funding 198; health policy contexts 118–120; health policy directions 115–116; hospital spending 120; market-type mechanisms 123; new institutional economics (NIE) 122; primary health care reform 125–126; Primary Health Care Strategy (PHCS) 125, 126–127; Primary Health Organizations (PHOs) 125, 126; processes of policy development and implementation 125–126; QPECE group proposals 198; Regional Health Authorities (RHAs) 122; Ten-Year Strategic Plan 197–198; use of market and quasi-market mechanisms 116–117; versatile governance in health policy 118

Nickell, Stephen 152

Nispen, Frans Van 3

North America and Europe: binding direct democratic procedures 467, **467**; case selection and empirical analysis 471–472; direct democracy, effects of (*see* direct democracy); direct legislation, role of 466; Italy and Slovenia 480–483; nuclear power or nanotechnology 486; political systems 468; stem cell research 483–484; Switzerland 472–476; United States 476–477, 479–480

Okma, Kieke G.H. 57
Organisation for Economic Co-operation and Development (OECD) 64, 186
Orloff, A.S. 205
out-of-pocket expenditure 141

Pachuashvili, P. 325
paid leave: for adult family members' health 155, 157; analyses 155, **156**; for children's health 155; comparative work/family literature 151; data sources 153, **154**, 155; description of sources reviewed 153, **154**; for employees' health 157; for family illness 150–151; macroeconomic indicators and sources 155, **156**; OECD countries 151; relationship to macro-economic criteria 157–158, *158, 159, 160*; rise in globalization 151; work/family policies 152–153, 158; working caregivers' ability 160–161; in working families 151
paid maternity leave 151
paid parental leave 152
paid paternity leave 151
paid sick/vacation leave 151
Pal, L.A. 5
Palme, J. 226, 228
Part-Time Directive 247
Penn, H. 195
Perry Preschool Project 186
Peter, Lindert 152
Peters, B. 15
Pettit, Becky 208
Pfau-Effinger, Birgit 56
Pierson, P. 234
point-of-service (POS) plans 31
policy analysis and Europeanization: EU-level research–policy infrastructures 344–350; Europeanization of migrant integration policies 342–344; policy research and Europeanization 337–341
policy design studies: defining and studying effectiveness 13; study of policy effectiveness 14–17; study of policy formulation 13–14
policy effectiveness, study of: defining and studying effectiveness 13; design environments 15–16; "evidence-based" policy process 16; instrument mixes 16–17; of specific policy tools 14–15
policy formulation, study of 13–14
policy transfer: and convergence 112; embeddedness of public health policies 111–112; within local public health policies 103–108; reception of 100–102; through actors' backgrounds, mapping circulation of 108–111
policy transfer, reception of: ideas and practices 100, 101–102; importance of proximity 101; role of actors 101

Portugal: private out-of-pocket payments 40
poverty: logistic regressions 218, **219**; marital and motherhood status 217, **218**; primary caregiver model 218–219; reconciliation policies and effects of motherhood 217–221, *220*
"power resource theory" 168
Pralle, S.B. 388
preferred provider organizations (PPOs) 31, 76
Prescott, E.C. 249
primary caregiver/secondary earner strategy 206, 221
Primary Care Trusts (PCTs) 28–29
primary earner/secondary carer strategy 206, 221
primary health care reform (PHCR) 119; Canada 124–125; modes of governance 126–127; New Zealand 125–126
primary health care strategy (PHCS) 125, 126–127
primary health organizations (PHOs) 125, 126
private health insurance 141
private higher education: cases 318–321; Dubai 319–320; international branch campuses 317–318; Malaysia 320–321; something superior category 322–323
private insurance 30
private out-of-pocket financing 30
public contracting model 141
public financing 37; health care package 38–39; health service providers 39
public funding sources 141
public health expenditure (PHE) 33, **33**
public health financing 33, 43n4
public health policies: Denmark 104–106, **108**; France 106–108, **108**
Public holiday laws 253n6
public policies: control of health care financing and service provision 26, 27; in health care arena 28–31; market mechanisms 26, 27; and method of financing 27; self-regulation by non-governmental actors 26, 27
public/private delivery system 187; in early childhood 187–188; not-for-profit (NFP) or for-profit (FP) 188; public funding 188; Swedish model 187; in twenty-first century welfare states 187–188

qualified majority voting (QMV) 455, 461n27
Quebec: childcare quality 196–197; ECEC quality and investment choices in liberal welfare states 196–197; efforts of politicians 376; part-day to full-day kindergarten 196; $5-per-day childcare program 197; separatist movement 377

Radaelli, C. 339
Radin, Beryl 3, 6
Ragin, C.C. 4

Rauch, D. 233
receiving system 42
reconciliation policies and effects of motherhood: earnings 214–217; employment rates 210–214; measuring equality 209–210; poverty 217–221; theoretical expectations 207–208; welfare state regimes, employment, and caregiving 205–207
Regional Health Authorities (RHAs) 122
regulatory federalism: in United States and EU 446–453
reimbursement model 141
Rein, M. 407
Resnick-Terry, Phyllis 46
Revised Health Insurance Law 91n6
Rico, Ana 26
Rochefort, D.A. 408
Ruskin, Michael 56

Saarinen, T. 281, 289
Sabatier, P.A. 340
Sainsbury, Diane 207
Scharpf, Fritz 454
Schattschneider, E.E. 445
Schillemans, T. 278
Schmidt, V.A. 338, 350
Schmitter, Phillippe 116
Schneider, A.L. 420
Scholten, Peter 340
Schön, Donald 407
Schwartz, H.L. 187
Scott, Claudia 48
Scruggs, L. 173
sectarianism 135
segmented federalism 298–299, 300
Shapin, S. 356
Sheingate, A.D. 7
short-term leave 151, 158
sick funds 142
sick leave 151; for employees 160–161; policies 153; rights 153
Sinclair, Barbara 17
Singapore: basic medical services 87; Central Provident Fund (CPF) 71; choice of providers 73; country-specific institutional contexts 51, 53; Eldercare Fund 72; funding sources 70–71; government revenues 71; health care planners 74; health care reform in 70–74; Health Corporation of Singapore (HCS) Private Limited 72–73; health expenditure/care professionals/profile of 96–97, **98**; hospital restructuring process 72; individual self-reliance in 54; Joint Commission International (JCI) accreditation 73; market orientation and individualism 73–74; Medisave, Medishield and Medifund 71–72, 89; Medisave system 48, 53; National Healthcare Group 73; public control of health

care costs 51; quasi-privatized schemes in 62; Singapore Health Services 73; Singapore's Companies Act 72; size, population, income and economic growth in 96, **97**
Slovenia: challenging existing policies on assisted reproductive technologies 480–483; law on health measures 481; Referenda for ART **482**
social citizenship: Bismarckian welfare state and Beveridgean 260; categorization of countries 274; familialization and individualization 273; familialization of 259, **260**, 274n1; family policy 266; grants and loans 266–267; independent individuals 260; individualization of 259, **260**; "rudimentary assistance regime" 272; tax relief for families 264, **265**; tripartition of life course 259–260
Social Citizenship Indicator Program (SCIP) 182n4
social citizenship of young people, Europe: comparative institutional analysis, young people 261–273; theorizing young people's social citizenship 258–261
social determinants of health (SDOH) 100, 102, 111
Social Health Insurance (SHI) systems 29–30
social spending: legislative changes 234; reliability of secondary spending data 234; social rights 235; welfare effort 225–226, 233–235
social unit 4
Soler-Castillo 281
state-led health care system 26
Stone, D. 289
Streeck, W. 116
Swedish approach: to ECEC 188–190; employer-provided programs 189; grants and loans 267; preschool services 189–190; public/private delivery system 187; for Socialtjänstlagen, no age limit 257
Switzerland: adopting restrictive regulation through direct legislation 472–476; ART and GMO sectors 473, **474**; *Beobachterinitiative* 473; decentralized decision-making and cost control 78–79; decentralized health system 62; direct democracy and federalism 74–75; expansion of private insurance 86; Federal Health Insurance Law 78; formulated draft 472; 'Gene Protection Initiative' 475; GMOs in the agro-food sector 473; government regulation 76; health care provision 77–78; health care reform in 74–79; health expenditure/care professionals/profile of 96–97, **98**; health insurance 75–76; issue of biotechnology 473; larger choice of health plans in 86; managed care and consumer choice 76–77; managed competition, notion of 76; new insurance, introduction of 76–77; optional referendum 472, 475–476; policy-making for biotechnology 476; private funding 35, 40; Revised Health Insurance Law 75; size, population, income and economic growth in 96, **97**; Swiss Constitution 75–76; Swiss health insurance law 75
Sylva, K. 195

Taiwan: health care reform in 79–81; health expenditure/care professionals/profile of 96–97, **98**; health insurance 79–81; Medicare program 80; National Health Insurance (NHI) 79, 80, 81; size, population, income and economic growth in 96, **97**; uniform nationwide social health insurance 62, 87
Timmermans, A. 340
Titmuss, R.M. 167, 168, 169
total health expenditure (THE) 33, **33**, *33*, **34**, 37, *38*, *39*
Tribalat, M. 416
Tuohy, Carolyn 26, 117, 146
twenty-first century welfare states: public finance and private delivery 187–188

unitary federalism 298, 300
United Kingdom (UK): Childcare Tax Credit (CTC) 194; ECEC quality and investment choices in liberal welfare states 193–196; elite-technocratic process of policy making 417; evidence-based policy 418; evidence-based policy making 416–418; health policies in 35; immigrant integration 417–418; Jobseeker's Allowance (JSA) 257, 271; National Childcare Strategy 193, 194; national health service (or Beveridge) model 48; private early education services 195; private non-profit and for-profit providers 194–195; role of venues of expertise 407; state hierarchy 27; technocratic conception of British multiculturalism 416–418; UK's childcare market, growing corporate dominance 195–196; Working Tax Credit (WTC) 194
United States: American immigration control policy 380; bans on cloning 477; biotechnology policy, regulatory federalism in 446–449; Busy Bees 196; centralization of control and integration policies 382, **382**; centralization of immigration control policy 379; centralized and decentralized immigration policies; early centralization, causes and consequences 378–382; embryonic stem cell research 479, 480; federal agency rulemaking 448; Federal Food Drug and Cosmetic Act (FFDCA) 447; federal immigration policy 382; Federal Insecticide Fungicide and Rodenticide Act (FIFRA)

447–448; Food and Drug Administration (FDA) 447; genetically modified foods 460; Genetic Engineering-free agriculture 479; health care system 30; health maintenance organizations (HMO) 76; Health Maintenance Organizations (HMOs) 64; herbicide tolerant (HT) crops 447–448; immigration policy 380–381; initiatives and optional referendums in 477, **478**; institutional framework 242, **243**; "managed care" plans 30; mandatory referendum 477, 479; market-oriented 41; Medicare or Veterans' health Services 91n8; Plant Pest Act (PPA) 447, 448; presidential system 388; private funding 40; "private market model' 27, 30; recruitment/integration polices 380; representative federalism in 453–458; role of individual states 448; state-level legislation 380; total health expenditure in 35; US Department of Agriculture (USDA) 447, 448; workers' average annual hours in paid work 241, *242*; working time policies 242–247

Van de Velde, C. 258, 259
venue shopping approach: in Australian and Canadian skilled immigration policy 397, **398**; bureaucratic control and policy outputs 388–390; decision-making power 388; institutional venues 388; legal system 390; scholarship 388, 400; strong bicameralism 390; Westminster-inspired systems 401; and Westminster-inspired systems 389–390
Veterans Administration health program 135
Vincent, C. 193

Walther, A. 258
Weimer, David 3
Weingart, P. 355
welfare chauvinism, three worlds of: country-level variables 172, 173–174; dependent variable 180; ethnic competition theory 180; individual-level variables 172, 174–175; institutional theory of 169–172; ordered-logit multilevel analyses 175, **176–177**; research format, data and operationalization 172–175; selectivity and inequality 179
welfare effort: basic security model 228; budget allocations 229; budget size 228; capitalism approach, 227; cross-national variations 230–233, **233**, 236; education statistics 229, **231**, 231–232; health care statistics 229, **230**, 230–231; large-N-based welfare state literature 225; in literature 227–228; old-age pensions, sickness insurance and unemployment 228–229, 233, 235; size of budget 233–235; social spending data 225–226, 233–235; unemployment protection statistics **232**, 232–233; welfare programs 228–229
welfare state regimes: choice strategy 206–208; earner-carer strategy 207, 208; male breadwinner/female caregiver or family wage strategy 205; modes of caregiving and employment 205; mothers and non-mothers earnings 208; poverty rates 208; primary caregiver/secondary earner strategy 206; primary earner/secondary carer strategy 206; reconciliation policies and effects of motherhood 205–207
Wells, W. 249
White, L.A. 40
Wildavsky, A. 64, 135, 355
Wilensky, H.L. 226, 227, 235
Wittrock, B. 409
Wolf, A. 5
Work, Family, and Equity Index (WFEI) 153, 155
work-family reconciliation policies 204, 221–222; annualized hours (AH) schemes 250–251; cross-national rankings 248, *248*; cross-national variation in hours 247–250; demands of parenthood and employment 240; in Europe, Japan, and the US 242–247; gender equality perspective 251–252; part-time and fulltime workers 246–247; part-time legislation, effects of 249–250; policy conundrums 250–252; policy variation 242–247; protective mechanisms for workers 251; reduced-hour work 251–252; regulation of working time 240–241; shorter-hours options 252; work family conflict 239; work-family or work-life balance 241; work hours and days 246–247; working time regulation 239–242; work-life advocates 240
World Health Organization (WHO) 100
Wright, Deil 7

"youth guarantee" approach 272

Ziguras, C. 321
Zumeta, W. 334